Transition Planning for Secondary Students with Disabilities

Second Edition

Transition Planning for Secondary Students with Disabilities

Second Edition

Robert W. Flexer
Kent State University

Thomas J. Simmons
University of Louisville

Pamela Luft
Kent State University

Robert M. Baer
Kent State University

PEARSON
Merrill Prentice Hall

Upper Saddle River New Jersey
Columbus, Ohio

Library of Congress Cataloging-in-Publication Data
Transition planning for secondary students with disabilities / Robert W. Flexer . . . [et al.].
p. cm.
Includes bibliographical references and index.
ISBN 0-13-112377-7
1. Youth with disabilities—Education (Secondary)—United States. 2. Youth with disabilities—Vocational education—United States. 3. Students with disabilities—Services for—United States. 4. School-to-work transition—United States. I. Flexer, Robert W.

LC4031.T733 2005
371.9'0473—dc22

2003068642

Vice President and Executive Publisher: Jeffery W. Johnston
Acquisitions Editor: Allyson P. Sharp
Editorial Assistant: Kathleen S. Burk
Production Editor: Sheryl Glicker Langner
Production Coordination: Jolynn Feller
Design Coordinator: Diane C. Lorenzo
Cover Designer: Bryan Huber
Production Manager: Laura Messerly
Director of Marketing: Ann Castel Davis
Marketing Manager: Autumn Purdy
Marketing Coordinator: Tyra Poole

This book was set in Novarese Book by Carlisle Communications, Ltd. It was printed and bound by R. R. Donnelley & Sons Company. The cover was printed by The Lehigh Press, Inc.

Photo Credits: Center for Innovation in Transition and Employment, p. 2, 20, 42, 53, 56, 76, 83, 92, 110, 121, 138, 141, 142, 151, 164, 178, 191, 201, 211, 215, 221, 224, 246, 260, 276, 305, 309, 317, 336, 346, 360, 370, 378, 405, 424, 447, 460, 465; Gary Harwood/Kent State University, p. 388.

Pearson Education Ltd.
Pearson Education Singapore Pte. Ltd.
Pearson Education Canada, Ltd.
Pearson Education—Japan
Pearson Education Australia Pty. Limited
Pearson Education North Asia Ltd.
Pearson Educación de Mexico, S.A. de C.V.
Pearson Education Malaysia Pte. Ltd.

PEARSON
Merrill
Prentice Hall

10 9 8 7 6 5 4 3 2
ISBN: 0-13-112377-7

Educator Learning Center: An Invaluable Online Resource

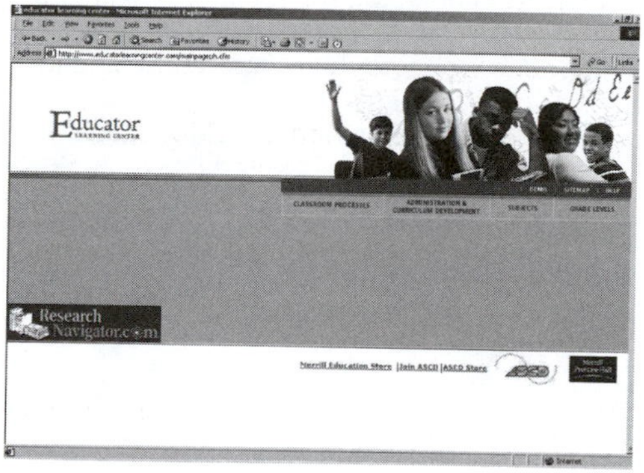

Merrill Education and the Association for Supervision and Curriculum Development (ASCD) invite you to take advantage of a new online resource, one that provides access to the top research and proven strategies associated with ASCD and Merrill—the Educator Learning Center. At **www.EducatorLearning-Center.com** you will find resources that will enhance your students understanding of course topics and of current educational issues, in addition to being invaluable for further research.

How the Educator Learning Center will help your students become better teachers

With the combined resources of Merrill Education and ASCD, you and your students will find a wealth of tools and materials to better prepare them for the classroom.

Research

- More than 600 articles from the ASCD journal *Educational Leadership* discuss everyday issues faced by practicing teachers.
- A direct link on the site to Research Navigator™ gives students access to many of the leading education journals, as well as extensive content detailing the research process.
- Excerpts from Merrill Education texts give your students insights on important topics of instructional methods, diverse populations, assessment, classroom management, technology, and refining classroom practice.

Classroom Practice

- Hundreds of lesson plans and teaching strategies are categorized by content area and age range.
- Case studies and classroom video footage provide virtual field experience for student reflection.
- Computer simulations and other electronic tools keep your students abreast of today's classrooms and current technologies.

Look into the value of Educator Learning Center yourself

A four-month subscription to Educator Learning Center is $25 but is **FREE** when used in conjunction with this text. To obtain free passcodes for your students, simply contact your Merrill/Prentice Hall sales representative, and your representative will give you a special ISBN to give your bookstore when ordering your textbooks. To preview the value of this website to you and your students, please go to **www.EducatorLearningCenter.com** and click on "Demo."

Contributors

Robert Baer, Ph.D.
Kent State University
Kent, OH

Debra Bauder, Ph.D.
University of Louisville
Louisville, KY

Greg Clary, Ph.D.
Clarion University
Clarion, PA

Randall L. De Pry, Ph.D.
University of Colorado at
Colorado Springs
Colorado Springs, CO

Robert Flexer, Ph.D.
Kent State University
Kent, OH

Penny Griffith, Ph.D.
Kent State University
Kent, OH

James Knoll, Ph.D.
Morehead State University
Morehead, KY

Lynn Koch, Ph.D.
Kent State University
Kent, OH

Janice Kreiner, Ph.D.
Baldwin-Wallace College
Berea, OH

Pamela Luft, Ph.D.
Kent State University
Kent, OH

Laura Huber Marshall, M.A.
University of Colorado at
Colorado Springs
Colorado Springs, CO

James Martin, Ph.D.
University of Oklahoma
Norman, OK

Rachel McMahan, M.Ed.
Kent State University
Kent, OH

Thomas Simmons, Ph.D.
University of Louisville
Louisville, KY

Joyce Strand, Ph.D.
University of Minnesota
Duluth, MN

Deborah Durham Webster, Ph.D.
Cleveland State University
Cleveland, OH

Carolyn Bardwell Wheeler, Ph.D.
Interdisciplinary Human
Development Institute
Lexington, KY

Preface

Beyond the meaning of everyday learning and living, all students, on varying timetables and with individual urgency, take on a future orientation during the high school years. Looming in the background is the question, "What am I going to do after high school?" The importance of high school programs and transition activities directly relates to the degree to which they provide learning and experiences that will move students toward or clarify their transition goals. For the student to have an investment in their education, meaningful participation in the "right" programs is essential. For students with disabilities, access is necessary to realize the benefits of participation in regular education, vocational education, and school-to-work programs as well as transition and special education programs. *Transition Planning for Secondary Students with Disabilities* (Second Edition) describes the varied transition needs of students with disabilities and the myriad options and career paths potentially available.

The purpose of education and transition is to move students towards selected postschool outcomes. Quality of life is the major benchmark of the Individuals with Disabilities Education Act (IDEA) as assessed through the careers and lifestyles achieved by students. Make no mistake about it. As logical and principled as these assumptions are, there are many competing forces on the national educational agenda. For one, standardized test scores are viewed by some stakeholder groups as the major focus of educational efforts. From a transition perspective, academic achievement is considered very important, but academic achievement alone is insufficient for successful postschool outcomes. Moreover, contextualized and authentic learning in which academics are embedded shows better learner outcomes than academic subjects taught in the abstract.

Since education is a cultural process, new educators need to identify their values and determine which actions are consistent with them. Do we care whether our students enjoy successful careers, meaningful relationships, and community membership? Do we care whether students obtain the best possible foundation to launch them into their young lives? If you answered yes to these two questions, then you will be motivated to learn how transition needs can be met in an academic achievement environment and you will read this book with interest.

The Second Edition

Transition Planning for Secondary Students with Disabilities (Second Edition) provides broad coverage of transition content, ranging from the legislative–policy base to specific transition activities. A framework of four essential elements of transition provides themes to organize each chapter, connecting content across chapters and topics. The resulting integration of policy and practice systematically builds the reader's understanding and provides guidelines for daily transition activities.

The redesign of this text focused on how to support the inservice and preservice teacher or professional in developing and implementing transition activities that meet a dual criteria. Foremost, the outcomes of special education and achieving a quality of life must remain the broad educational framework from which to judge the merits of transition efforts. Just as important, the process of transition provides the means to these goals. Students achieving quality of life outcomes for themselves is partly dependent on a service system with integrity—basing services on students' needs, interests, and preferences, providing an outcome orientation and planning processes, and effectively coordinating all the services required. When these activities result in movement toward student goals, they are on the right track. The four essential elements are a quality check on whether things are being done right.

These two broad goals of transition outcomes and process were embedded in the major reorganization of the content of this text. On the surface, redundancies and the number of chapters were reduced. Also, chapters and concepts are presented in a more logical sequence. Finally, organization of the content reflects, more than the first edition, transition issues confronted at the high school level and problem-solving strategies.

Section I, Transition Contexts: Implementing Transition Systems, provides the broad background that is required to understand the complex developmental and education process that takes place from early adolescence through young adulthood. A new Chapter 1, Life Satisfaction and Productive Futures, provides an evolution of issues of adolescence, a quality-of-life framework, and the four essential elements. The field of transition is traced within a framework of the maturing disability rights movement and government initiatives. The chapter shows that requirements and the need for transition services are no longer debatable. The legislation, models, and exemplary practices that have been developed over the roughly 50 years of the modern era are described in Chapters 2 and 3, as before, but in a streamlined fashion. A more accessible format is used for the theoretical base of career development presented in Chapter 4, as well. A career development framework remains central to enabling the transition team to view the student as evolving and maturing, and to providing a general approach for fitting the student's transition goals within high school programs and preparation options.

As in the first edition, Section II, Transition Programs: Creating a Transition Perspective of Education, moves from the foundations of transition addressed in Section I to its programmatic implementation at the high school level. The four chapters in this section provide the application of career theory to career and technical education, curriculum options and course of study, and the implementation of these programs through valid assessment and effective instruction. Assessment practices show how to monitor and evaluate programs to ensure success, and instruction and the use of technology guarantee access to these programs as well as a full range of optimizing life and career opportunities.

In order to fill in the practices implied in a broad framework, Section II is completely reconceptualized and features three new chapters. As in the prior edition, the section starts with transition assessment, which is important in identifying future environments and the students' needs, interests, and preferences. Transition is unique in that the process always starts with the students' goals and their related postschool outcomes.

The three remaining chapters in succession describe and illustrate: a) a model for general education curriculum that incorporates transition, b) instructional strategies that work, and c) transition services as prescribed in IDEA. The information presented will allow transition teams to guide students toward a high school course of study consistent with their transition goals. The further application of the methods and strategies described fully informs team members to support student movement toward their goals. At times, students with disabilities will be educated and supported in completing high school courses and requirements much like other students but with necessary accommodations and transition services. However, if necessary, the transition team and teachers must make choices that implement career and technical preparation, in conjunction with academic content and life skill areas, that prepare the student for his or her individually chosen transition outcomes. When these choices are integrated and assembled across the student's profile of educational and transition strengths and needs they become an individualized curriculum.

Integrated throughout all chapters are descriptions of several of the technologies available that allow students to access the full range of curricular and postschool options that lead to a quality adult life. Team members are provided with the processes needed for investigating and making decisions about technology and transition services that will lead to long-term satisfaction with careers and chosen life styles.

Section III, Transition Planning: Planning for Transition to Adulthood, moves from a discussion of programs in rehabilitation and special, general, and career and technical education to a discussion of how these programs can be integrated into transition planning and program development for youth with disabilities. These four chapters can be viewed as a technical manual that describes how to weave policy, promising practices, and a myriad of programs and services into transition activities that promote student self-determination, effective transition planning, service coordination, and family involvement.

Chapter 9 presents an in-depth look at how students move from passive spectators to involved decision makers, and a step-by-step process for supporting students in this process. Chapter 10 describes working with families from a multicultural perspective so that professionals can best guide and support families in working with their children toward postschool goals.

With the student and family at the center of the process, Chapter 11 moves the reader through the process of developing a transition planning process, preplanning for the IEP meeting, conducting that meeting, and evaluating progress. Still included in Chapter 11 is a question and answer section that can be helpful to parents and professionals in dealing with the jargon of transition. The section concludes with Chapter 12, which talks about transition service coordination from both an individual and systemic perspective. Overall, Section III describes a planning process that places the family and the student in a central position so that exemplary practices can be supportive of their hopes for adult life in the community.

Section IV, Transition Outcomes: Achieving Quality Outcomes, makes concrete the issue of employment, postsecondary education, recreation and leisure, and independent living with four updated chapters. These four domains of postsecondary experience are discussed at length in the prior sections regarding the execution of planning and the formulation of future goals, educational preparation, collaborative enterprises, and joint programmatic efforts. This section is filled with information that will expand understanding of transition issues after students leave school and explore issues that most educators don't think about. The authors believe that these future environments have a very important role, and they often require a special effort by transition teams. Communication and interaction among team members in future environments enhance the goal setting process and assists students to "keep their eye on the ball."

The purpose of *Transition Planning for Secondary Students with Disabilities* (Second Edition) is to provide a comprehensive, yet practical, text for advanced students at the undergraduate level and for students at the graduate level from the diverse fields that contribute to the transition process. School-based teachers from regular, vocational, and special education and other professionals, including psychologists, related services professionals, and guidance counselors, also would benefit from reading this text, especially if they are in the process of establishing or improving interdisciplinary and collaborative transition services. Families and a variety of postschool service providers (e.g., rehabilitation counseling, case managers, etc.) would also benefit from the broad framework and specific examples that illustrate the varied educational, career, and personal issues that arise in students' transition to postschool life.

In this text, the reader is continuously brought back to the four basic questions raised by the *essential elements*:

1. Is there meaningful student involvement?
2. Are student goals directed toward postschool outcomes shared by the student and his or her family and team?
3. Are all team members working in a coordinated fashion in relation to the student's goals?
4. Are the education and transition services promoting movement toward the student's accomplishing his or her goals?

The application of the essential elements provides a test of transition services both for individual students and across all school and postschool services. Transition is treated in a generalized way by cross-categorical, practical, and real transition examples.

Acknowledgments

For 20 years, the Center for Innovation in Transition and Employment at Kent State University has had as its mission supporting the efforts of people with disabilities in realizing quality in their lives. In developing programs to prepare transition professionals and in reaching out to schools and communities, innumerable individuals have had an impact on our programs. We hope that they gained insight and useful skills for supporting students. The first author, there from the start, will be indebted forever to his three friends, coauthors, and colleagues for all they have taught him. All the authors thank all of the students with disabilities who contributed so much to us personally and professionally. Likewise, all the Kent State University students and professionals trained in transition at the Center, families of students with disabilities, and Center collaborators who have contributed to our efforts need to be acknowledged for the important lessons they have taught us. All of these individuals with whom we have interacted provided the data and stories upon which this book is based. These relationships brought much joy and will endure into the future. Our profession is about caring, commitment, and trust. The authors hope that this book will serve you, the reader, in the same way that all our associations have enhanced us as people. We would like to thank our spouses, Carol, Debbie, Drew, and Judy, whose love and appreciation of us provided much of the "staying power" on this journey. We would like to thank Sherrie Blalock, especially, who kept us organized and provided timely assistance in preparation of the first edition. The team at the Transition Center were truly remarkable in the giving of their time: George Ackerman, Al Daviso, Stephen Denney, Valerie Gilbert, Thomas Hoza, Rachel McMahan, and Mary Toepfer.

Large projects like a book always involve innumerable individuals who give their time to make the book the best possible product it can be. We are very thankful and indebted to individuals at Merrill and Carlisle Publishers Services who have supported us in a thoughtful, kind way—Allyson Sharp, Sheryl Langner, and Jolynn Feller. The individuals who provided reviews of the book provided an invaluable service to us by providing useful suggestions for improvement. We would like to thank these individuals:

Kathleen McCoy, Arizona State University; Judith Presley, Tennessee State University; and Kathleen Chinn, New Mexico State University.

Discover the Companion Website Accompanying This Book

The Prentice Hall Companion Website: A Virtual Learning Environment

Technology is a constantly growing and changing aspect of our field that is creating a need for content and resources. To address this emerging need, Prentice Hall has developed an online learning environment for students and professors alike—Companion Websites—to support our textbooks.

In creating a Companion Website, our goal is to build on and enhance what the textbook already offers. For this reason, the content for each user-friendly website is organized by topic and provides the professor and student with a variety of meaningful resources. Common features of a Companion Website include:

For the Professor—

Every Companion Website integrates **Syllabus Manager™**, an online syllabus creation and management utility.

- **Syllabus Manager™** provides you, the instructor, with an easy, step-by-step process to create and revise syllabi, with direct links into Companion Website and other online content without having to learn HTML.
- Students may logon to your syllabus during any study session. All they need to know is the web address for the Companion Website and the password you've assigned to your syllabus.
- After you have created a syllabus using **Syllabus Manager™**, students may enter the syllabus for their course section from any point in the Companion Website.
- Clicking on a date, the student is shown the list of activities for the assignment. The activities for each assignment are linked directly to actual content, saving time for students.
- Adding assignments consists of clicking on the desired due date, then filling in the details of the assignment—name of the assignment, instructions, and whether or not it is a one-time or repeating assignment.
- In addition, links to other activities can be created easily. If the activity is online, a URL can be entered in the space provided, and it will be linked automatically in the final syllabus.
- Your completed syllabus is hosted on our servers, allowing convenient updates from any computer on the Internet. Changes you make to your syllabus are immediately available to your students at their next logon.

For the Student—

- **Overview** and **General Information**—General information about the topic and how it will be covered in the website.
- **Web Links**—A variety of websites related to topic areas.
- **Content Methods and Strategies**—Resources that help to put theories into practice in the special education classroom.
- **Reflective Questions** and **Case-Based Activities**—Put concepts into action, participate in activities, examine strategies, and more.
- **National and State Laws**—An online guide to how federal and state laws affect your special education classroom.
- **Behavior Management**—An online guide to help you manage behaviors in the special education classroom.
- **Message Board**—Virtual bulletin board to post and respond to questions and comments from a national audience.

To take advantage of these and other resources, please visit the *Transition Planning for Secondary Students with Disabilities*, Second Edition, Companion Website at

www.prenhall.com/flexer

Brief Contents

Contents

Note: Every effort has been made to provide accurate and current Internet information in this book. However, the Internet and information posted on it are constantly changing, and it is inevitable that some of the Internet addresses listed in this textbook will change.

Section I

Transition Context: Implementing Transition Systems

1

Life Satisfaction and Productive Futures

Robert Flexer

Robert Baer

LEARNING OBJECTIVES

The objectives of this chapter are:

1. Understand how cultural concepts of disability influence services.
2. Explain the interrelationships among concepts of adolescence and transition planning.
3. Describe the importance of transition planning.
4. Describe the various influences on transition planning.
5. Explain the essential elements of transition and how they reflect best practice.
6. Describe transition milestones across the school years.

Introduction

The concept of "disability" has been undergoing a radical change in the modern world. Only three generations ago, it was widely believed that individuals with disabilities were a menace to the health of society, and many were sterilized or even euthanized with the full sanction of the law. This did not simply happen in Germany, but also in the United States. For example, a popular American sex education book stated:

> While everyone will agree there are large sections of our population which are composed of very undesirable individuals, it is hard to get agreement on methods of eliminating them. No one denies the staggering cost to the State of our institutions for the feeble-minded, the insane, and the criminals; if we add to this the costs of courts and legal procedures, of charitable and relief measures, to say nothing of clinic and hospital service which is largely supported by the responsible members of society for the benefit of the irresponsible. (Richmond, 1934, p. 275)

Following World War II, eugenics fell into disfavor, but the concept of disability as a burden to society remained. A new medical model of disability emerged that promised to wipe out disabilities by providing cures and treatments (Shapiro, 1993). This medical model provided some successes, but persons with disabilities continued to be devalued and excluded from social participation. They were often viewed as "sick" and as "objects of pity" and their participation in society was contingent on them first getting "well" (Shapiro). Later behavioral–developmental models shifted the focus of disability programs to training rather than medical treatment, but the premise remained the same—persons with disabilities could not fully participate in society until they were cured or rehabilitated.

Despite large investments in medical and behavioral treatment, habilitation, and rehabilitation programs, few persons with disabilities moved into more independent settings and the number of adults in these programs increased dramatically (Bellamy, Rhodes, Bourbeau, & Mank, 1986). Additionally, advances in medicine sharply reduced mortality rates associated with many disabilities. By 2000, persons with disabilities made up one of the largest minority groups in the United States, with more than 49.7 million persons (or nearly 20% of Americans) reporting significant disabilities. Of this number, 30.6 million were of working age with 43% of them unemployed (U.S. Census, 2000). The number of persons with disabilities in Social Security programs showed a similar trend with more than 10 million persons with disabilities under age 65 receiving Supplemental Security Income (SSI), Social Security (SSDI), or both (Social Security Administration, 2003).

In the 1980s, new community support strategies showed considerable promise in regard to providing integrated employment, residential living, and community participation options for persons with disabilities. The supported employment programs developed in this decade indicated that with individualized supports, virtually any individual with a disability could be employed for pay (Wehman, 1996). Supported living programs showed similar promise by keeping individuals with even the severest disabilities in their own homes with family and community supports (Knoll, 1992). These programs showed long-term benefits not only in the quality of life for persons with disabilities, but also in their ability to become productive and contributing members of society (Baer, Simmons, Flexer, & Smith, 1994). The transition initiative discussed in this book grew out of this new support paradigm and the need to include and go beyond the general curriculum in promoting quality-of-life outcomes.

Critical Point There have been dramatic changes in the U.S. approach to disability from models focused on treatment to models based on support.

Adolescence and the Transition to Adulthood

To understand the problems facing youth with disabilities, it becomes necessary to understand the challenges faced by all youth in this critical period. The transition to adulthood has been a concern of societies from the dawn of humanity when this process was first codified in tribal "rites of passage" (Ferguson, 2001). These rites involved a variety of socially sanctioned activities where youth practiced the roles of adults and participated in important social customs. As societies moved to agrarian economies, adult roles became more specialized and youth were apprenticed to experienced adults who were responsible for seeing that they learned both work skills and appropriate social behavior (Scheerenberger, 1983). This model served well until the industrial revolution caused such rapid economic change and social complexity that youth could no longer expect to enter the occupations of their parents, or even jobs in their community. Increasingly, the transition to adult roles became the responsibility of professional educators who provided much longer periods of preparation.

Until recently, youth had the option of moving into occupations without secondary education, with 90% of them exiting school at the middle school level in 1900. Typically these young adults entered occupations (e.g., farm or factory work) where skills were taught on the job (Lichtenstein, 1998). During this period, only students who were expected to enter "elite" positions as managers or professionals continued through high school. However, mechanization and computerization of nearly all economic sectors caused shrinkage in the unskilled occupations from 90% to less than 15% (Levesque, Lauen, Teitelbaum, Martha, & Librera, 2000). For all youth, this meant that the path to adult work roles required relatively long periods of education (Hamburg, 1993). In modern societies, the average age of full transition to adult roles moved from around age 13 in 1900 to the mid-20s in 2000 (Levesque et al., 2000). Additionally, the transition to adulthood now required performance in several spheres, including education, the family, the economy, and the political/legal system (Pallas, 1993).

Critical Point The transition to adulthood has become more complex and extended for all adolescents.

The period of adolescence has become so extended in modern society that it has been defined as three periods—early adolescence, middle adolescence, and late adolescence. Early adolescence has been defined as the period when youth are aged 10 to 14 years and when they begin drawing away from their parents to begin exploring adult roles and to become more oriented to their peers (Lichtenstein, 1998). This period has been conceptualized by Piaget as the period when youth depend heavily on problem solving through trial and error, but begin to think in terms of abstract thought and deductive reasoning (Piaget, 1966). Erikson conceptualized early adolescence as a period when youth begin the task of reconciling their beliefs, abilities, and desires with adult norms and expectations (Erikson, 1963). During this period, parents usually serve as a secure base from which adolescents can explore new roles and environments and become more focused on peer relations (Erikson). Transitional objectives for early adolescence must therefore focus on developing youths' self-knowledge and knowledge of a range of possible adult roles that are compatible with their unique needs, interests, and preferences.

Middle adolescence has been defined as the period when youth are 15 to 17 years of age. It has been characterized as a period when they experience mounting pressure to conform, engage in risk-taking behaviors, and when the discrepancy between the actual self and the ideal self is most pronounced (Lichtenstein, 1998). Greenberger and Steinberg (1986) argued that too much pressure to conform during this period could result in an "identity foreclosure" where adolescents conform to the roles handed to them by adults, leading to passivity and an inability to accept responsibility. Some risk-taking behavior characterizes normal adolescence during this period as adolescents experiment with adult roles, but dangerous risk taking may lead to problems with the legal system (Erikson, 1963). Additionally, the discrepancy between ideal and actual self-perceptions may lead many students, especially students with disabilities, to drop out of school to avoid frustration and embarrassment. Transitional objectives for this period should therefore focus on giving youth the chance to take risks and to experience successful work, education, independent living, leisure, and extracurricular experiences that are designed to develop self-confidence and to reduce the incidence of dropping out.

Late adolescence typically occurs from age 18 to the mid-20s. This period has been characterized as ideally involving closure in resolving problems of personal identity and intimacy. This requires the ability to make sensible decisions, engage in problem solving, and participate in adult roles. For a growing number of students, this period has been extended by their participation in postsecondary education where they can continue to explore adult roles and careers. However, for youth entering employment after graduation this period may be much shorter, resulting in problems of identity foreclosure or identity incoherency (Erikson, 1963). Transitional objectives for this period therefore must focus on helping youth *secure* long-term postsecondary education, work, leisure activities, and residential options by helping them link with postsecondary environments. For students with disabilities linkages may also include adult service programs that can continue to provide support to them as adults.

Critical Point Adolescents need to achieve key developmental milestones as they move through adolescence in order to avoid long-term problems as adults.

An Ecological View of Adolescence

An ecological assessment identifies all of the important environments that influence an individual or organization. An ecological view of adolescence has been nicely conceptualized by Lichtenstein and is included in Figure 1–1.

The first ecological domain in Lichtenstein's model is *relationships with peers*. Like all individuals, students with disabilities become increasingly focused on the acceptance of peers as they progress through adolescence. This ecological domain has been identified as important in developing interpersonal skills and in validating self-concepts (Lichtenstein, 1998). Students with disabilities may lack experiences in this domain, if they have significant disabilities and/or are in classes or schools that provide little opportunity for interactions with peers. Research indicated that successful peer relationships ranged from 91% of youth with learning disability, to only 56% of students with multiple handicaps, to 35% of students who were deaf and blind (Wagner, D'amico, Marder, Newman, & Blackorby 1992). Additionally, research has indicated that these peer relationships tended to decline after students left high school (Chadsey-Rusch & Shelden, 1998). Transitional implications of this domain are related to the need to provide students with opportunities to establish social

FIGURE 1–1
Ecological Influences in Adolescence

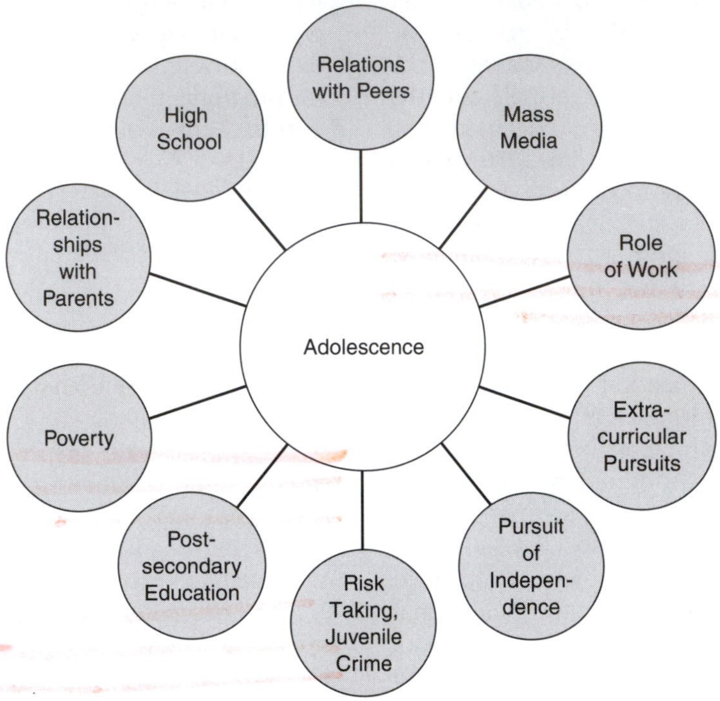

Source: From Lichtenstein, S. (1998). Characteristics of youth and young adults. In F. R. Rusch and J. G. Chadsey, (Eds.) *Beyond high school: Transition from school to work.* Wadsworth Publishing, Boston. Reprinted with permission of Wadsworth Publishing, a division of Thompson Learning.

connections in high school and to plan for community participation following high school (Chadsey-Rusch & Shelden).

At the 1:00 position on Lichtenstein's model is *mass media*. All youth tend to emulate behaviors of the actors and performers portrayed in the mass media. This becomes problematic when they imitate the antisocial behaviors portrayed by many media icons. Additionally, youth with disabilities may be confused by the media's ambiguous and often negative presentations of disability as something that should be feared, pitied, overcome, or hidden. The media's use of one-dimensional terminology such as "the disabled" or "the crippled" has continued to create the impression that persons with disabilities are not like other persons. This terminology has persisted despite more than 20 years of effort by self-advocacy groups to use person-first language such as "persons with disabilities" or "persons with mobility impairments." The transitional implications of the mass media domain include the need to expose students with disabilities to positive role models and to help them develop a realistic and positive understanding of their own disability.

The next ecological domain going clockwise is the *role of work*. In America, youth work while going to school at a higher rate than any other country in the Western world (Lichtenstein,

1998). The role of work in adolescence has been debated by experts with some arguing that work detracts from schooling and has little value for them as adults (Cole & Cole, 1993; Greenberger & Steinberg, 1986; Stern, McMillion, Hopkins, & Stone, 1990). Another group of experts has argued that work while in high school promotes vocational development and provides "real life" experiences that students could not obtain in school (Phillips & Sandstrom, 1990; Steele, 1991), and that longitudinal outcome and follow-up studies indicate a strong relationship between high school employment and employment after graduation (Blackorby & Wagner, 1996; Baer et al., 2003). Halpern (1993) found that employment in high school was beneficial to the extent that it related to student career paths. The transition implications of this domain suggest that work experience programs have clear objectives and should be related to students' postsecondary goals.

Extracurricular activities are a fourth ecological domain of adolescence identified by Lichtenstein (1998). These activities have been identified as an important way to promote student attachment to their school and as a way to develop teamwork, loyalty, leisure skills, and peer relationships (U.S. Department of Education, 1995). For students with disabilities extracurricular activities become particularly important as a means of developing self-esteem, confidence, and peer relationships (Mahoney & Cairns, 1997; Newman, 1991; Sarkees & Scott, 1985). The transition implication of this domain suggests that youth with disabilities need to be encouraged and supported in selecting and obtaining extracurricular activities as part of the IEP (Individualized Education Program, described later) planning process.

The *pursuit of independence* is a fifth ecological domain and has been identified as critical for establishing a sense of responsibility and control (Lichtenstein, 1998). For all students, obtaining a driver's license, getting a job, and spending time with peers is important. Independence also means the opportunity to make important choices. For students with disabilities, the ability to make choices and pursue goals has been called self-determination, which has been positively related to both school performance and postschool outcomes (Wehmeyer & Schwartz, 1997). Transition implications for the ecological domain of independence include the need to help students develop travel, independent living, and self-determination skills and opportunities.

Risk taking is an ecological domain of particular concern for adolescents. Social psychologists have argued that risk taking allows youth to experiment with adult roles and individual choices (Erikson, 1963). However, students with disabilities have often been sheltered from taking risks to the point that they did not participate in experiences that would promote normal development. Perske (1973) identified this concern and developed a concept known as "the dignity of risk," which stated that persons with disabilities should have the opportunity to take reasonable risks in the pursuit of independence and happiness. On the other hand, risk-taking behavior can be a problem when risks are taken needlessly. Students with learning and emotional disabilities may develop risk behaviors of alcohol and drug abuse, unsafe sex, or other dangerous behaviors. Transition implications for the ecological domain of risk taking include activities designed to acquaint students with their rights and responsibilities and the development of activities that are designed to teach them safety precautions, wise choice-making, and emergency procedures.

Postsecondary education has been an ecological domain of growing concern for all students, including students with disabilities. As discussed earlier, education requirements have steadily grown over the past century. This trend accelerated in the 1990s, with 68% of all students and 28% of students with disabilities attending two- and four-year postsecondary education programs. College enrollment for students with disabilities has shown particularly steep increases, rising from 2.6% in 1978 to 9.2% in 1994 (Henderson, 1995). In fact, the completion of a postsecondary education program may have become as critical as completion of high school was just 40 years ago (Fairweather & Shaver, 1991). Additionally, for students with disabilities, postsecondary education provides the opportunity to postpone the transition to adulthood for several years, resulting in considerable advantages in terms of long-term earning ability and career satisfaction. The transition implications for the postsecondary education domain include activities designed to assist students with disabilities in decisions related to postsecondary education, taking of college entrance examinations, applications for financial aid, and choosing colleges with adequate support services.

Poverty has been an ecological concern for adolescents because it exposes them to problems, including lack of opportunity, crime, low expectations, health risks, and high-risk behaviors (Lichtenstein, 1998). Students in poverty often do poorly at school because they may lack parental support, may be required to care for siblings, or may be forced to work to support the family (Kozol, 1996). Poverty is a particular concern for students with disabilities because high proportions of these students come from low-income families (Kozol). Additionally, poverty can worsen the effect of a disability by limiting transportation, employment, social, and educational options. Transition implications for this ecological domain include the need to provide social services, support personal hygiene, and develop financial and community supports.

Parents continue to be one of the most influential ecological domains for adolescents. They serve as role models, provide supports, and serve as important resources in connecting youth with employment, educational, and community resources (Blackorby & Wagner, 1996; Hasazi, Gordon, & Roe, 1985). For students with disabilities, parents typically provide a place to live well into adulthood and can strongly influence decisions about employment, postsecondary education, independent living, and community participation (Blackorby & Wagner; McNair & Rusch, 1991). Additionally, parents of students with disabilities often take over the role of service coordinators when students with disabilities exit secondary education. Transition implications for the parental domain include the need to educate and involve parents in transition planning, to use them as resources in finding and maintaining employment, and to plan for their role in the transition process after school services have been terminated.

The final ecological domain in Lichtenstein's model is that of the *high school*. As students move from elementary to middle and secondary programs they encounter increasingly impersonal relationships with teachers, new challenges in navigating between classes, and greater pressures to compete and perform (Lichtenstein, 1998). During this period students choose or are placed in classes that can have a profound effect on postschool opportunities. For students with disabilities the transition to secondary education settings often results in less consideration of their unique needs, increased stress, and increasing segregation from nondisabled peers (Lichtenstein). Transition implications for this ecological domain include the need to support students in choosing a course of study, in getting into desired courses, in organizing schedules, and in mastering an increasingly difficult curriculum. As students with disabilities approach graduation, their need for linkages to adult services and postsecondary settings also becomes critical.

Critical Point Many environments have an impact on adolescents as they move toward adulthood and each of these environments may present unique challenges to students with disabilities.

A Rationale for Transition Planning

For students, whether they have a disability or not, high school is a critical juncture where each year forms a foundation for the next, culminating in the student's graduation and move to postschool environments. This process of moving from one status to the next is called *transition* and during this period all students must ask the question, "What am I going to do after high school?" High school programs should address this question and provide steppingstones to the future through a process known as *transition planning*. For students with disabilities transition planning is particularly important because, in addition to the normal upheaval in the transition to adulthood, students with disabilities exchange the security of a single contact point—special education—for the complexity of multiple systems serving adults with disabilities (Baer, McMahan, & Flexer, 1999).

Transition planning helps secondary students with disabilities find meaning in their educational activities. Since the 1950s, high school programs in the United States have become primarily focused on college preparation for four-year programs, leaving many other students wondering whether their high school programs have deserted them in favor of the more "promising" students (Rusch & Chadsey, 1998). This has had a particularly hard impact on students with disabilities who have responded by dropping out of school at higher rates than their peers (Blackorby & Wagner, 1996; Grayson, 1998). For these students to invest in their education, participation in the "right" programs is essential. If they cannot say to themselves, "I'm going somewhere and this is the way or path to my goals," their disengagement is inevitable. Supporting students in setting postschool goals and in choosing educational programs is therefore one of the most effective practices in assuring their participation in high school programs, and this requires that they have access to the full range of high school programs and the opportunity to participate in individualized and varied work experiences. Access, participation, and movement toward individualized postschool goals therefore constitute the primary criteria for judging the effectiveness of high schools.

Traditionally, educators and professionals have ignored the aspirations of students with disabilities by placing them in segregated or remedial classes that had little or no relevance to achieving their postschool goals (Wehmeyer, 1998). Until the seminal book *Normalization* by Wolf Wolfensberger, persons with disabilities were viewed as inevitably moving to devalued roles as adults (Wolfensberger, 1972). However, groups of persons with disabilities and their families began to demand that their voices be heard, and new planning approaches emerged that focused on the individual's dreams, strengths, and preferences. This "person-centered" planning became popular among advocacy groups and showed considerable promise in regard to improving the individual's choices, quality of life, family support, and community participation.

Critical Point Transition and person-centered planning approaches can improve outcomes by making education more relevant, by giving students more control over their lives, and by focusing on goals important to them.

Transition planning drew heavily on the concept of person-centered planning to employ an array of educational experiences and strategies (or *transition services*) designed to promote students' movement to the postsecondary environments of *their* choosing. Educators supported students and families in transition planning by conveying positive future expectations (Conley 2002; Pearlman, 2002), by helping them understand the transition process, and by providing them with strategies designed to remove many of the inevitable obstacles encountered on the road to responsibility and independence. Transition planning could be assessed according to the number and quality of learning experiences that promoted movement toward the student's postschool goals (Gray, 2002) and by the students' postschool outcomes as evidenced by their everyday lives, careers, and community participation (Blackorby & Wagner, 1996). To understand transition planning, three basic questions must therefore be answered:

1. What are the transition outcomes for former high school special education students?
2. Which transition frameworks provide the best means to plan for quality outcomes?
3. How can educators use these frameworks to make students' time in high school productive and enhance their quality of life?

Research on the Postschool Outcomes

The Education of the Handicapped Act (EHA) in 1975 established the right to a free and appropriate education for all students with disabilities and created a combined federal, state, and local system for the delivery of special education. Several years after implementation of this landmark legislation, researchers began asking how it was impacting postschool outcomes for students with disabilities. They began conducting follow-up studies of the sort that were used in the 1950s and 1960s to evaluate work–study and vocational programs. These early post-EHA follow-up studies were designed simply to provide a picture of the status of graduates of special education. They generally found that, although some students with disabilities benefited from special education, a disproportionate number continued to experience unemployment, low wages, low-level jobs, lack of postsecondary education, and lack of community participation and independent living (Hasazi, Gordon, & Roe, 1985; Wehman, Kregel, & Barcus, 1985).

Since these seminal outcome studies, several outcome investigations have been implemented at local, state, and national levels. All of these studies have provided "snapshots" of postschool outcomes, but their purposes varied on several dimensions. Some studies told how former students were faring—where they fell on a continuum of "success" in adult life—while others addressed more difficult questions related to determining: (a) how helpful the students' high school programs were, (b) what help former students still needed, and (c) how educators could improve on services and the education provided. An example of the latter kind of outcome research was the National Longitudinal Transition Study (NLTS), which Congress funded to assess postschool outcomes and related transition services of special education students who were three and five years postgraduation. This study used a random national sample of more than 8,000 special education students from all geographic regions, socioeconomic groups, school settings, and disability categories (Blackorby & Wagner, 1996). From these data, NLTS was able to measure the relationship between high school programs and postschool outcomes.

Blackorby and Wagner (1996) reported that the initial NLTS study showed that 10 years after the implementation of EHA, postsecondary education attendance, wages, employment, and independence for students with disabilities still lagged far behind their peers. The NLTS found that positive employment outcomes were related to certain high school programs (i.e., work-based training and vocational education), but Halpern, Doren, and Benz (1993) reported that these outcomes were still not driving education for students with disabilities. They concluded that special education was still deficient in what was taught, how it was taught, and where it was taught. Initial reports from a second NLTS study (which is at the time of this writing in the early phases) have shown some increases in work study jobs and employment outcomes (Wagner, Cameto, & Newman, 2003), but taken as a whole, the NLTS studies and other outcome research from the 1980s and 1990s have suggested that secondary special education needs to continue to move from a focus on special education process to a focus on postschool outcomes.

Critical Point Research on the outcomes of special education programs established the need to support students with disabilities in their transition to adulthood.

Quality-of-Life Considerations

As special education moved from a focus on following correct procedure to promoting meaningful postschool outcomes, defining these outcomes became a critical philosophical concern (West, 1991). Consequently, policy makers and advocates began to focus on answering the question, "What quality-of-life perspectives underlie special education's professional philosophy, American cultural values, and the values of the individuals and the families we are serving?" This led to early efforts to define quality of life by asking individuals with disabilities what they valued. Goode (1990) conducted research with focus groups consisting of individuals with disabilities and concluded:

> When an individual, with or without disabilities, is able to meet important needs in major life settings (work, school, home, community) while also satisfying the normative expectations that others hold for him or her in those settings, he or she is more likely to experience a high quality of life. (p. 46)

Halpern (1993) assessed special education quality-of-life frameworks by analyzing 41 outcome studies for students with disabilities. He found that these studies had a primary focus on education and employment, a minor focus on social networks and relationships, and none on personal fulfillment. Halpern's analysis led him to call for an expansion of the notion of quality of life to include three quality-of-life domains: (a) physical and material well-being, (b) performance of adult roles, and (c) personal fulfillment. These quality-of-life and related concepts are presented in Table 1–1.

Halpern's (1993) model suggested that employment outcomes could not be isolated from other facets of a person's life and that problems in one area (e.g., physical and personal well-being and personal fulfillment) would have a

TABLE 1–1

Quality-of-Life Domains and Desired Postschool Outcomes

Physical and material well-being:

- Physical and mental health
- Food, clothing, and lodging
- Financial security
- Safety from harm

Performance of adult roles:

- Mobility and community access
- Vocation, career, employment
- Leisure and recreation
- Personal relationships and social networks
- Educational attainment
- Spiritual fulfillment
- Citizenship (e.g., voting)
- Social responsibility (e.g., does not break laws)

Personal fulfillment:

- Happiness
- Satisfaction
- Sense of general well-being

Source: From Quality of life as a conceptual framework for evaluating transition outcomes, by A. S. Halpern, *Exceptional Children, 59*(6), 1993, p. 491. Copyright (1993) by the Council for Exceptional Children. Reprinted with permission.

corresponding impact on the others (e.g., performance of adult roles or employment). He asserted that transition programs for students with disabilities should address *physical and material well-being* because food, shelter, rehabilitation services, and health care were not an entitlement in the United States, even for persons with disabilities. *Performance of adult roles* was considered prerequisite to achieving physical well-being and personal fulfillment, so Halpern suggested that transition professionals must also develop strategies for students to learn the necessary skills and obtain the necessary supports to participate in these roles. The outcome of *personal fulfillment* was closely connected to Halpern's outcomes of physical well-being and adult competency, but clearly distinguished from them in that personal fulfillment was to be measured subjectively.

Halpern (1993) stated that ultimately, quality-of-life models must consider the experience of individuals, because only the individuals themselves could assess how well their physical well-being and performance of adult roles met their personal and emotional needs. This, in turn, implied that persons with disabilities had to achieve some degree of self-determination and control over the choices that were made in their lives for this life domain to be fully realized. Halpern noted that although a happy fulfilled life in a caring community was what all persons wanted, the specific desired lifestyle and related personal fulfillment were different for every person.

Critical Point Postschool outcomes should be measured according to how well they address personal and material well-being, performance of adult roles, and personal fulfillment.

IDEA-Mandated Transition Services

Follow-up studies of special education students generated widespread concern over quality-of-life outcomes and resulted in a legal mandate for transition planning and service provision in the Individuals with Disabilities Education Act (IDEA) of 1990. This legislation mandated that public schools develop a "statement of needed transition services" for students with individualized education programs (IEPs) age 16 or older, or younger if appropriate (IDEA Amendments of 1990, Pub L. 101-476, 20 U.S.C. § 1401). The IDEA was amended in 1997 to include an additional "statement of transition service needs" that was designed to support a student's high school course of study (e.g., career and technical education or advanced academics) (IDEA Amendments of 1997, Pub. L. 105-17 20 U.S.C. § 1414). The Individuals with Disabilities Education Act (IDEA) of 1997 definition of transition services read:

> The term "transition services" means a coordinated set of activities for a student, with a disability, that: (A) is designed within an outcome-oriented process, that promotes movement from school to post-school activities, including postsecondary education, vocational training, integrated employment (including supported employment), continuing and adult education, adult services, independent living, or community participation; (B) is based on the student's needs, taking into account the student's preferences and interests; (C) includes instruction, *related services*, community experiences, the development of employment and other post-school objectives, and, when appropriate, acquisition of daily living skills and functional vocational evaluation. ([20 U.S.C. § 1401 (30)])

According to this IDEA definition, transition services must: (a) be based on student needs, taking into account the students' preferences and interests, (b) be designed within an outcome-oriented process, (c) include a coordinated set of activities, and (d) promote movement from school to postschool activities. It is the authors' contention that the design and implementation of transition services will foster positive postschool outcomes when they address these four essential elements contained in the IDEA definition of transition. All of the transition strategies and programs discussed in this book will be evaluated relative to these four transition criteria, and the degree to which they address them will serve as a basis for discussing their relative merits. Additionally, these four essential elements from IDEA encompass a range of best practices in transition including student self-determination (i.e., based on students' needs, taking into account students' preferences and interests), person-centered planning (i.e., outcome-oriented process), interagency collaboration (i.e., a coordinated set of activities), and follow-up and follow-along services (i.e., activities that promote movement from school to postschool activities).

The authors view the *Individualized Education Program* (IEP) as the cornerstone for addressing these four essential elements of transition because it takes into account the needs of the student and holds educators responsible for the delivery of appropriate education services. However, secondary IEPs must be substantially different than elementary level IEPs. Whereas the elementary-age student's IEP typically relates instructional activities to achieving in-school outcomes, the secondary student's IEP must relate instructional activities to achieving quality-of-life outcomes beyond the classroom. This is reflected in the IDEA of 1990's requirement that the IEP include linkages to postschool activities for students by no later than age 16 ([20 U.S.C. § 1414 (d)(1)(A)(vii)(III)]), and the IDEA of 1997's requirement that the IEP include middle school linkages to a high school "course of study" by no later than age 14 ([20 U.S.C. § 1414 (d)(1)(A)(vii)(I)]). Secondary transition planning is therefore concerned with appropriate and effective IEPs for youth in both middle and high school.

Critical Point The four essential elements of transition are drawn from the IDEA definition and these elements form the essential criteria for evaluating whether a school or adult service program or activity is indeed a quality "transition service."

In summary, the rationale for provision of transition services is based on research of postschool outcomes, quality-of-life research, and the IDEA mandates. In this book, the *outcomes* of transition services (across various middle school, secondary, and postsecondary programs) will be viewed from the perspective of postschool outcomes and quality of life, while the transition *process* will be viewed in the context of the four essential elements as contained in the IDEA. This combined process and outcome analysis will help the reader determine whether transition programs are doing *things right*, and if they are doing the *right things*.

Promising Practices and the IDEA Transition Mandates

In addition to the transition criteria established by the IDEA, the authors will consider "promising practice" concepts of transition as established by learned societies. The Division of Career Development and Transition (DCDT) of the Council for Exceptional Children (CEC) (as the primary professional group of transition service providers within special education) has provided a definition of transition that reflects professional consensus, and that includes references to promising practices in transition. The DCDT definition of transition specifies that the IDEA's *outcome-oriented process* should specifically focus on the change in status from behaving primarily as a student to assuming emergent adult roles in the community, including employment, postsecondary education, independent living, community participation, and satisfactory relationships. It more broadly defines transition IDEA *coordinated set of activities* as including elementary and middle school years. DCDT elaborates on IDEA's activities designed to *promote movement from school to postschool activities* as embracing the broader concept of career development and education. Interpreting IDEA's transition definition in relation to DCDT's suggests that transition is an integral part of the student's education process, beginning with primary school and not ending until well into early adulthood.

It is possible to incorporate other "promising practice" definitions of transition services into the four essential elements of transition services as defined by IDEA, and these and other best practices in transition will be discussed in the ensuing chapters. IDEA's first essential element of transition services (i.e., based on student needs, interests, and preferences) encompasses several promising practices, including *family involvement* (Kohler, 1993), *promoting student self-determination* (Field, Martin, Miller, Ward, & Wehmeyer, 1998), and *person-centered planning* (Mount & Zwernick, 1988; O'Brien, 1987). Family involvement and student self-determination provide two of the most important perspectives in determining students' needs, interests, and preferences and have been shown to provide richer descriptions than professional assessments (Wehmeyer). Person-centered planning strategies have been shown to elicit considerably more input from students with disabilities and their families, and therefore also promote better identification of student needs, interests, and preferences (Menchetti & Piland, 1998).

The second IDEA element of transition services (i.e., an outcome-oriented process) includes two transition promising practices known as *person-centered planning* (Mount & Zwernick; O'Brien) and *backward planning* (Steere, Wood, Pancsofar, & Butterworth, 1990). In the context of this IDEA element, person-centered planning focuses on development of meaningful postschool outcomes in the areas of community presence, choice, respect, competence, and community participation (O'Brien). Backward planning starts with the outcome in mind and focuses all secondary education activities on the achievement of a few quality outcomes, thereby creating a "transition perspective of education" (Kohler, 1998).

The third element (i.e., a coordinated set of activities) includes the best practices of *interagency collaboration* and *career education*. Interagency collaboration requires looking at the classroom as only one part of education, with vocational education, extracurricular activities, adult services, family activities, and community experiences all working in concert to support the student with a disability. Career education approaches suggest that these activities must take the career maturity, life experiences, and personal and social characteristics of the individual into consideration in shaping the student's school program (Luft, Koch, Headman, & O'Connor, 2001).

All the other elements would be for naught if transition services did not address the fourth essential element (i.e., promoting movement to postschool outcomes). This includes transition promising practices that have been shown to promote positive postschool outcomes, including *community- and work-based training, career and technical education, inclusion*, and *preparation for postsecondary education*. Community- and work-based approaches and career and technical education both have a strong theoretical and research bases and have been shown to be related to positive postschool outcomes (Blackorby & Wagner, 1996). Inclusion has been supported by research indicating that students with disabilities benefited from postsecondary education and were entering it in steadily increasing numbers (Henderson, 1995).

Critical Point The four essential elements of transition from the IDEA definition encompass a range of exemplary transition practices often referred to as "promising practices."

Timelines for Transition

The application of transition strategies must vary according to student maturity, personal characteristics, and cultural preferences from the elementary level on. Comprehensive longitudinal transition needs are shown in Figure 1–2, which suggests that transition foci and needs range from fairly broad to more specific as one views transition from the elementary to secondary levels. For example, the needs of elementary students revolve around understanding the nature of careers, whereas high school students' needs relate to preparation for specific career outcomes. At the middle school and early high school levels, exploration of needs and preferences is important, in contrast to the later high school level when students are testing specific goals through experiences and activities. Transition activities therefore become increasingly critical as students with disabilities approach graduation, because at this stage transition goals become more specific and there is less time to develop linkages with postschool service providers.

The transition focus by level as listed in Figure 1–2 is pertinent regardless of the type of disability. At the primary school level, the transition focus on developing work ethic and knowledge of the world of work is relevant to all students. The focus may begin to diverge at the middle school level, with students with mild to moderate disabilities typically examining vocational, college preparatory, and school-to-work, and students with severe disabilities typically exploring experiences across a variety of community environments as the focus for their high school program. At the high school level, goals, supports, and linkages will vary by the student's unique needs and preferences. Students with disabilities may be looking toward postsecondary education, and/or they may be planning and preparing for a community job. The following section provides an overview of how this book will address the topics that have been summarized thus far.

Overview of This Book

Section I – Transition Context

Section I of this book examines the "why?" of transition and is designed to provide a background on how the transition initiative came into being, how it has been regulated, its evolving models, and its relation to career development. In Chapter 2, *History and Transition Legislation*, the evolution of transition law and policy is traced within a framework of the maturing disability rights movement and other transition initiatives. This chapter is designed to provide the reader with an understanding of the complex interlocking systems of rehabilitation, special education, career education, and developmental disability programs.

Chapter 3, *Transition Models and Promising Practices*, describes major transition models and best practices that have been developed over the last 50 years, delineates the major components of transition as related to IDEA's essential elements, and provides a description of best practices that have emerged from the literature. This chapter goes beyond the legislative mandates of the second chapter to include an overview of state-of-the art transition models and practices. This chapter also examines the research supporting transition practices and problems in defining best practices for all students with disabilities.

Chapter 4, *Career Development: Theories for Transition Planning*, is designed to provide a description of career theories and how they relate to the unique needs of students with disabilities and suggests the use of this approach for aligning

FIGURE 1–2
Essential Elements: Focus and Needs

Primary Level: Grades 1–4

Focus
Employability and independent living skills and attitudes.

Needs
1. Develop positive work habits.
2. Appreciate all types of work.
3. Develop an understanding of how to cope with disability.

Middle School: Grades 5–8

Focus
Career exploration and transition planning relative to course of study.

Needs
1. Understand relationship of school to work.
2. Understand interests, preferences, aptitudes.
3. Understand work, education, independent living, and community options.
4. Determine a general course of secondary study.
5. Identify needed accommodations and supports for secondary education.
6. Specify transition services needed to participate in desired course of study by no later than age 14.

Four Essential Elements
1. **Student needs and preferences:** Transition planning and activities should involve the student in a meaningful way.
2. **Outcome oriented:** Transition services should result in development of postschool goals.
3. **Coordinated set of activities:** Transition services should involve teamwork and communication among school and postschool professionals and the student and family.
4. **Promote movement to postsecondary environments:** Transition services should result in progress toward postschool goals.

High School: Grades 9–10

Focus
Career exploration and transition.

Needs
1. Develop meaningful and realistic postsecondary goals.
2. Develop work, education, residential, and community participation skills and supports relevant to goals.
3. Learn to manage disability technology and request accommodations.

High School: Grades 11 and up

Focus
Transition and overlap into postsecondary environments desired by the student.

Needs
1. Test goals through experiences and activities.
2. Secure options for postsecondary education and/or employment.
3. Develop residential and community participation supports and contacts.
4. Develop linkages with adult services.
5. Empower families to function in adult service environments.

transition programs with general education programs. This chapter is designed to prepare the reader to develop inclusionary transition practices using mainstream career education programs and models. This chapter also includes a discussion of the problems of using these mainstream approaches for students with disabilities who may lack the life experiences, career maturity, and support systems of their nondisabled peers. A career development framework enables the transition team to view the student as evolving and maturing.

Section II – Transition Programs

The five chapters in Section II are designed to identify the key players in transition programs and how they can be brought together to develop school transition programs.

Chapter 5, *Transition Assessment and Postschool Outcomes*, describes common assessment practices and how they can be used in determining special education eligibility, in developing a course of study focused on postschool outcomes, and in the monitoring of students' progress. This chapter is designed to provide the reader with a knowledge of the major assessment approaches (e.g., informal, formal, situational, and curriculum-based) and how they can be used to support students' postschool outcomes. It also includes a discussion of common concerns of using assessments for persons with disabilities that have been normed on nondisabled populations.

Chapter 6, *A Curriculum Framework for Transition*, examines educational approaches and how students' transition needs can be addressed by aligning these educational programs to create a transition perspective of education. As with the legislation chapter, this chapter examines the sometimes-contradictory goals of these educational systems and how these contradictions can be resolved by developing broad and inclusive curricula.

Chapter 7, *Instructional Strategies and Transition Settings*, provides strategies for adapting curricula to the needs of students with disabilities using a variety of support, accommodation, and assistive technology approaches. This chapter provides an overview of strategies that allow students with disabilities access to the general curriculum and to community participation. It also touches on issues of using technology and curricular adaptations across classrooms and environments.

Chapter 8, *Transition Services*, examines the roles of educational and adult service professionals and describes several interdisciplinary planning approaches commonly used by these professionals. This chapter is designed to provide the reader with an overview of common transition service providers and describe how these professionals can collectively support the vision of the student with a disability.

Section III–Transition Planning

Section III moves from a discussion of "why?" and "who?" of transition to "how?" transition planning occurs at the individual level. These four chapters can be viewed as a technical manual that describes how to weave policy, best practices, and a myriad of programs and services into transition activities that promote student self-determination, effective transition planning, service coordination, and family involvement. Chapter 9, *Participatory Decision-Making: Increasing Student Self-Determination*, provides an overview of how students can be involved in developing their own education goals through self-determination training and discusses one self-determination curriculum in detail. This chapter discusses the importance of choice and participation by students with disabilities and their families and provides some practical examples of how individuals with disabilities can take greater control of their lives.

In Chapter 10, *Multicultural Competence for Working with Families*, describes how the transition process is viewed by various cultural groups and provides strategies for engaging students and families from other cultures in the transition process. This chapter discusses the values underlying various transition models and how these values may conflict with other cultures.

Chapter 11, *Transition Planning*, describes various individual planning strategies and how to prepare for, conduct, and evaluate progress for the IEP meeting in which transition is discussed. This chapter discusses the importance of eliciting student and family input through the use of person-centered, self-determination, and/or career planning models as a base for the IEP and provides practical examples of meeting agendas, transition plans, IEPs, and portfolio assessment.

Chapter 12, *Coordinating Transition Services*, discusses transition service coordination from a combined individual and systemic perspective and examines state-of-the-art case management and service coordination models and barriers in applying these models in a highly bureaucratic and fragmented transition system. This chapter discusses the important role that the transition coordinator plays in developing interagency collaboration and provides examples of interagency agreements.

Section IV–Transition Outcomes

Section IV of this book examines the demands and supports available in the postsecondary environments of employment, postsecondary education, community participation, and independent living. Chapter 13, *Transition to Employment*, discusses various employment situations available to graduates with disabilities, including competitive employment, individual supported employment, enclaves, mobile work crews, and sheltered work and the general demands and supports of these settings. This chapter is designed to provide the reader with an understanding of the pros and cons of these employment situations, the students who are likely to be eligible for services of this kind, and agencies that typically provide one or more of these services.

Chapter 14, *Postsecondary Education and Career Paths*, discusses various postsecondary education options for students with disabilities, including two- and four-year colleges, technical schools, and other continuing education options, and the general demands and supports characteristic of these settings. It includes a discussion of the role of student disability services and the importance of students understanding their disability needs, of researching supports offered by postsecondary programs, and of advocating for themselves in postsecondary education settings.

Chapter 15, *My Home and Community: Developing Supports for Adult Living*, provides an overview of adult residential options for individuals with disabilities, including independent living, group homes, and supported living. Chapter 15 provides a brief history of residential services and restates the value that people with disabilities should be able to live and recreate in their own homes and communities. Finally, recreation and leisure activities (Chapter 16) are critical for a complete life in the community. This final chapter describes recreation needs and preferences and how to link the student to the community.

Study Questions

1. How has the social response to disability changed in the last 60 years and how has that influenced the provision of disability services?
2. What are some of the characteristics of early adolescence and what transition goals should be typically pursued during this period?
3. What are some of the characteristics of middle adolescence and what transition goals should be typically pursued during this period?

4. What are some of the characteristics of late adolescence and what transition goals should be typically pursued during this period?
5. Identify one of the ecological domains in the Lichtenstein model and the transition implications for that domain.
6. What was found in researching postschool outcomes for students with disabilities and what did this imply for secondary education?
7. What quality-of-life concerns were addressed in Halpern's model?
8. When did the IDEA mandate the provision of transition services and how has this mandate evolved in later amendments to this legislation?
9. What are the four essential elements of transition?
10. Choose one essential element of transition and identify at least one related best practice in transition.
11. What national organization developed its own definition of transition services and how did it differ from the IDEA definition?
12. Discuss the life-span approach to transition and how activities in the primary level can support transition programs at the middle and secondary levels.

Websites

The IDEA and Transition
http://www.ldonline.org/ld_indepth/transition/law_of_transition.html

Quality of Life—Bibliography
http://www.utoronto.ca/qol/biblioqol4.htm

The Real Facts About Disability and "Quality of Life"
Compiled by Not Dead Yet *in consultation with* Carol J. Gill, Ph.D., April 1999

http://www.independentliving.org/docs3/gill99.html

Quality of Life indicators
*http://www.ont-autism.uoguelph.ca/*STRATEGIES4*.shtml*

Quality of Life for Minorities with Disabilities
http://www.hawaii.edu/hivandaids/Improving%20the%20Quality%20of%20Life%20for%20Minorities%20with%20Disabilities.pdf

Handbook on Quality of Life for Human Service Practitioners
*http://www.aamr.org/*Bookstore/QUAL*/handbook.shtml*

Erik Erikson's 8 Stages of Psychosocial Development
http://www.childdevelopmentinfo.com/development/erickson.shtml

Effects of Disability on Psychosocial Development
http://www.ssta.sk.ca/research/students/91–05a.htm#eff

Adolescent Stages of Development
http://www.childdevelopmentinfo.com/development/teens_stages.shtml

Ecological Issues in Adolescence
http://admin.vmi.edu/ir/dev/devseven.htm

Family Ecology Issues
http://www.ncoff.gse.upenn.edu/litrev/fpmlr.htm

National Longitudinal Transition Study—1
http://www.sri.com/policy/cehs/nlts/nltssum.html

National Longitudinal Transition Study—2
http://www.nlts2.org/

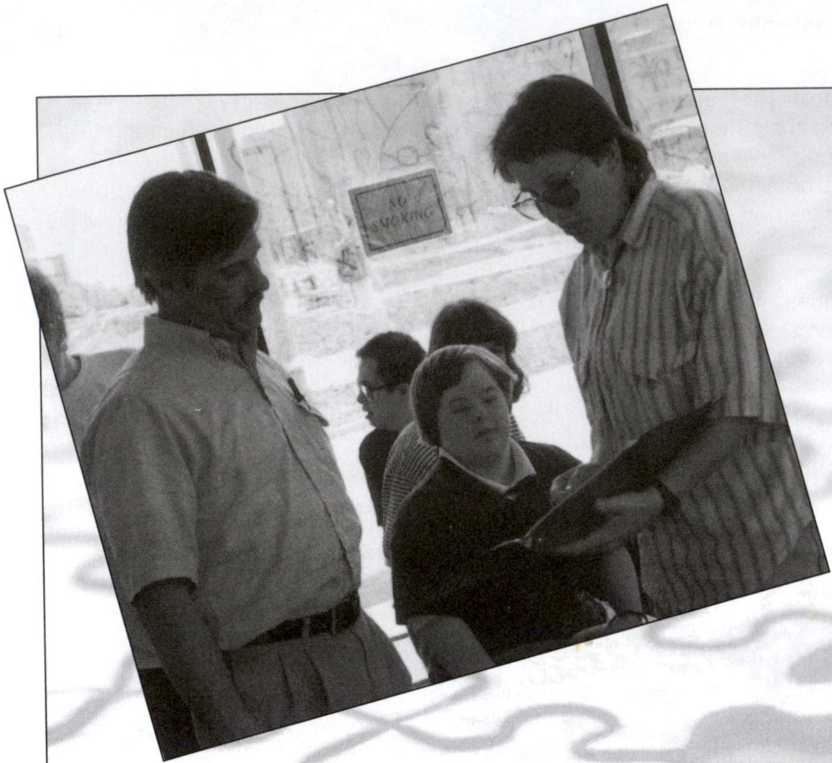

2 History and Transition Legislation

Robert W. Flexer

LEARNING OBJECTIVES

The objectives of this chapter are:

1. Explain the disability policy background for each period of legislation.
2. Describe the basic principles and provisions of transition and related legislation for each period.
3. Explain how legislation in different areas is coordinated and what this means.
4. Describe changes in transition focus across the periods of legislation.

Introduction

The purpose of this chapter is to provide the social and policy context from which the transition requirements of the IDEA developed. It will describe five periods of policy and legislation—programs prior to the 1960s, the 1960s and the 1970s, the 1980s, the 1990s, and the early 2000s. For each period, the author will provide background information and specific information on how each policy period was affected and contributed to general developments in the disability field. Throughout this book, the term "essential elements" will be used to organize commonalities in transition services or programs and to provide a common ground between the legal requirements for transition and scientifically based practices. Through a discussion of each area of legislation, the author hopes to provide an integrated view of transition across various middle school, secondary, and postsecondary programs. Through this analysis, the reader should begin to have an understanding of the transition disciplines of rehabilitation, special education, and career and technical education. By analyzing special education, career and technical, and rehabilitation legislation, it is possible to implement transition services throughout the curriculum that foster positive postschool outcomes, individualization, and interdisciplinary service delivery.

Transition services for youth with disabilities became official policy in secondary special education with the passage of the Individuals with Disabilities Education Act (IDEA) of 1990. A specific component of IDEA related to the incorporation of transition services into the Individualized Education Program (IEP). These requirements directly addressed the fundamental purpose of secondary education as preparation for life. Moreover, this mandated planning process also emphasized student, family, and professional attention to the challenges, uncertainties, and promises of making the transition to adulthood. Quality transition programs that can engage youth during the adolescent period were the added focus of the IDEA amendments [20 U.S.C. § 1400(c)(5)(E)] in 1997. Embedded in these requirements is the need to have the availability of a full range of preparation programs and experiences and access to all the academic and career possibilities within the high school curriculum. Turnbull, Liehmeyer, and Park (2003) argued that this stated intent of IDEA required that administrators adopt the goals of work and independent living as special education outcomes and that student performance in this regard *must* be measured. The latest IDEA amendments further emphasize the importance of results in the context of access to and continuous improvement in general education.

In addition to this longstanding focus on postschool outcomes, the IDEA of 1997 also required that students with disabilities have access to, and make progress in, the general curriculum [20 U.S.C. § 1414(d)]. This requirement was added to enhance rather than replace IDEA's focus on postschool outcomes (Turnbull et al., 2003). The IDEA's focus on the general curriculum was echoed in other education legislation. The Goals 2000: Educate America Act of 1994 (P.L. 103-227) required standards-based, quality education for all students and stipulated that qualified youths with disabilities should have the opportunity for meaningful participation in programs of their choice in general education. The Carl D. Perkins Act of 1998 (P.L. 105-800), stated that vocational education should bring out special talents and provide challenges to all students in order to motivate them toward high skill careers and jobs. The School to Work Opportunity Act (STWOA) of 1994 (P.L. 103-239) was designed to provide transition support and work-based learning for all students as a means that they may discover previously unknown career paths. The IDEA and its related legislation therefore provided guidance to transition teams to get students into the "right" programs in all areas of the school curriculum, including academics. This broad view of transition further implied the need to develop a "transition perspective" of education (Kohler, 1998).

The results and quality-of-life outcomes described in legislation require access to programs for career enhancement and personal growth from the elementary through the postsecondary levels for students with all types of disabilities. Because students with disabilities are very individual, and, as a group, represent a full range in their needs, preferences, and abilities, it is necessary that opportunities within all school programs be accessible to qualified youth. The laws and policy framework for transition provide guidance to transition teams to get students into the right programs in all areas of the school curriculum.

The Four Essential Elements of Transition

The essential elements of transition services in the IDEA addressed how to educate and support individual students working toward their future using services based on educators, youth and families, and communities working in partnership. These partnerships must be guided by legislation as applied across professions and programs and at all levels of government. The discussion of the legislation shows that transition services should be

1. Student oriented and directed (i.e., based on students' needs, taking into account students' preferences and interests).
2. Focused on the future (i.e., designed within an outcome-oriented process).
3. Delivered consistently by both transition and school staff (i.e., use a coordinated set of activities).
4. Tracked and monitored in relation to student goals (i.e., promote movement from school to postschool activities).

Throughout this book the four essential elements of transition as defined in the IDEA have been adopted to identify commonalities in transition services and programs and to provide a common ground between the legal requirements for transition and empirically supported practices. Through systematic discussion of each area of legislation, the authors will provide an integrated view of transition services based on the essential elements—services using student-focused goals for a future life in the community and coordinated activities directed toward their accomplishment. Diverse laws describe transition services across various middle school, secondary, and postsecondary programs providing a longitudinal and holistic view that includes the domains of community life and employment. By following the mandates in special education, career and technical, and rehabilitation legislation, the design and implementation of transition services foster positive postschool outcomes and individualization and interdisciplinary service delivery.

Critical Point The essential elements spell out a framework to meet transition requirements. They serve as the policy framework to determine effective transition services.

Because transition is a concept that is both holistic (across life domains) and longitudinal (across age levels), a framework for transition legislation spans a variety of programs, services and needs. Laws are enacted for a variety of purposes. In most transition related legislation, two major issues that were addressed were:

1. Who are people with disabilities?
2. What are the needs of various categories of people with disabilities?

Under each legislative authority (e.g., special education, rehabilitation, vocational education) there appeared a definition of what constitutes a disability. This is important because it identified which specific persons with disabilities are covered under the act in question. Most of the acts are either categorical (IDEA), list specific disabilities, or refer to substantial functional limitations in major life activities (e.g., mobility) due to physical or mental impairments. Yet other acts refer to an existing law's definition (e.g., the Perkins Act refers to the definition in IDEA). Needs identified by studies, professional and advocacy groups, or government agencies provided the major framework for defining the major provisions of the acts. These needs assessments described services corresponding to limitations in major life activities either for people with disabilities in general or specific categories (e.g., learning disabilities).

The myriad transition activities derive their authority from the laws on special education, rehabilitation, vocational education, ongoing lifelong supports, higher education, employment and training, and general education among others. Legislation within each area has provisions to protect the rights of persons with disabilities. Understanding the unique provisions of legislation and how they are related to transition requirements is part of what transition teams need to know in their role in service coordination.

Critical Point The essential elements of needs and preferences and postschool goals may require programs outside the purview of special education requiring coordination among special education, career/technical education, regular education, and postschool service providers.

In the following sections, groups of laws are broken into five time periods. Through the 1960s, national interest in disability issues developed. During the 1970s, a foundation for a delivery system was laid down, whereas the 1980s dealt with refinements of transition systems and expansion of services to all youth regardless of disability. With the 1990s and 2000s, consolidation and cooperative models were outlined in laws to provide mandated transition services and a coordinated system of services.

Policy and Social Foundations Through the 1960s

Modern concepts of disability can be traced back to the Elizabethan Poor Laws in seventeenth-century England, which differentiated between the deserving and undeserving poor. The undeserving poor were seen as living in poverty as a result of poor moral character and, therefore, were expected to work and "pull themselves up by the bootstraps." In contrast, the deserving poor, primarily the "crippled," the blind, and orphans were responded to with charity and were usually not expected to work (Macklesprang & Salsgiver, 1996). Throughout history, persons with disabilities were seen as both the deserving and undeserving poor, depending on the type of disability and depending on prevailing cultural values. This notion of charity had its drawbacks, both for persons considered as deserving and those who were not. When seen as deserving, persons with disabilities were patronized and not expected to work or contribute. When seen as undeserving, they faced unemployment and servitude, or a life of crime and imprisonment. This concept can be viewed as underlying much of Western society's response to disability to the present day. For example, "deserving" persons with blindness receive much higher benefits than persons with emotional disturbances who are considered less deserving in social security income programs.

Wolfensberger in 1972 provided one of the seminal works on cultural or historical models of disability. The thesis behind historical models of disability was the concept and value assigned to disability (perception) subsequently plays out in how people with disabilities are treated by society and social institutions. The

TABLE 2–1
Sociohistorical Deviancy Role Perceptions and Resultant Service and Staffing Models

Role Perception	Service Model	Staff Model
Subhuman: Animal Vegetable Insensate object	Neglect, custody, destruction	Catcher, attendant, caretaker, keeper, gardener, exterminator
Menace, or object of dread	Punitive or detentive segregation, or destruction	Guard, attendant, exterminator
Object of ridicule	Exhibition	Entertainer
Object of pity	Protection from demands	Member of religious bodies, charitable individual
Burden of charity	Industrial habilitation	Trainer, disciplinarian, work master
Holy innocent	Protection from evil	Member of religious bodies, charitable individual
Eternal child	Nurturant shelter	Parent
Sick person	Medical	Physician, nurse, therapist

Source: From Overview of normalization, by W. Wolfensberger in *Normalization, social integration, and community services,* Flynn, R. J. & Nitsch, K. E. (Eds.), 1980, Table 2, p. 10, Chap. 1. Reprinted with permission.

models described how, at various times in history, people with disabilities were treated as less than human "at worst, or charitable cases, at best." (See Table 2–1.)

The power in models is that they filter the perception of individuals through disability and place individuality in the background. Several examples that extended to the more modern period in the history of human services were:

- Institutional exposés like Willowbrook, portrayed in *Christmas in Purgatory* (Blatt, 1966) and reported by Geraldo Rivera, demonstrated that in the 1970s people with severe and profound mental retardation were still abused and lived in horrific conditions.
- Children with more severe disabilities were excluded from public school until 1975.
- Day activity centers served people with mental retardation but provided little meaningful activity and people were separated from the community in the 1970s.

Early Rehabilitation Influences

Early in the 1900s, the evolution of the concept of disability was influenced by the emergence of rehabilitation services. This was an outgrowth of medical and technical progress in World War I. In 1917, the Smith–Hughes Act (P.L 64-347) provided government support for this notion of disability by providing rehabilitation services for World War I veterans with disabilities. The Smith–Sears Act (P.L. 65-178) in 1918 embodied both a notion of charity and rehabilitation by caring for veterans as deserving and by rehabilitating them to meet employer needs through vocational education and early forms of disability technology. Two years later, in 1920, the Smith–Fess Act (P.L. 66-236) offered vocational training (e.g., in the form of guidance, occupational adjustment, and placement) for civilians who had become disabled while engaged in civil employment. This early rehabilitation legislation focused on the correction of individual deficits, not on social change. These early twentieth-century roots of American concepts of disability can still be seen in the philosophy and strategies of many current disability professions, including rehabilitation, vocational education, and special education (DeStefano & Snauwaert, 1989).

Critical Point Early professional concepts and service models of disability were influenced greatly by cultural meanings. These societal influences are still in evidence today.

Legislation from 1917 to 1943, the period between the "two great" wars (World War I and World War II), dealt with fairly limited populations and a more limited service delivery system. Legislation during this period dealt primarily with the support and training of veterans and civil service (government) employees with disabilities. In 1943, the Barden–LaFollete Act (P.L. 77-113) was passed to provide vocational training and retraining to civilians other than those who were government workers. Besides retraining or training for employment within limits set by the individual's disability, needed medical services such as examinations, surgery, and prosthetic and orthotic devices that were essential to becoming employed were included as rehabilitation services under the program. In principle, rehabilitation services were expanded to include people with mental retardation and those with mental illness, although no funded services were provided. It was not until 1954 (with the Vocational Rehabilitation Amendments P.L. 83-565) that funding for expansion of vocational and rehabilitation programs and research and professional training became available. These monies did not make work-study, sheltered workshops, and job placement services generally available to all people with disabilities in all states. They were "seed" monies for the establishment of pilot programs and the building of capacity of states and local programs to make the services part of an overall system.

Development of Advocacy Organizations

Rehabilitation services were gradually extended to more persons as technologies improved; however, persons with severe disabilities continued to be seen as charity cases with nothing to contribute to society. In 1950, a challenge to this concept came from the National Association for Retarded Citizens (now known as the ARC), an organization formed by parents. Initially, the ARC and other parent organizations (such as United Cerebral Palsy) set out to fund and create skill development programs and activities for children and adults with severe disabilities (e.g., moderate to severe mental retardation, cerebral palsy, autism, and other developmental disabilities). Early childhood programs and special schools were established for children who were excluded from school, and sheltered employment and day activity centers were established for adults. Parent information and support were a cornerstone for these organizations that supported countless families in facing a challenge few professionals understood or had resources to deal with (Turnbull & Turnbull, 1990).

Critical Point The first national attention to disability issues stemmed from efforts by family-based advocacy organizations.

Numerous advocacy organizations were the early stimulus for community and societal awareness of the need for special education and rehabilitation services. The 1960s were a period of emerging visibility of disability issues and the first national commitment of the government to persons with disabilities and their needs, hopes, and desires. The Kennedy administration stressed a new program of public welfare, service, and training, rather than prolonged dependence resulting from the absence of community and educational programs. This national commitment, attention, and awareness are embodied in the recommendation of the first President's Panel on

TABLE 2–2

President's Panel on Mental Retardation: 1962 Recommendations

- The establishment of research centers for the study of retardation, its causes, and especially its prevention
- The improvement of welfare, health, and general social conditions of all the people, particularly those in the greatest need
- Improved educational programs and availability of appropriate education for all; the extension of the definition of education beyond the academics
- The training of professional and service personnel to work in all aspects of retardation, particularly at the leadership level
- The development of comprehensive, community-centered services on a continuum to meet all types of needs

Source: From President's panel on mental retardation (1962). A proposed program for national action to combat mental retardation. Washington, DC: U.S. Government Printing Office.

Mental Retardation (see Table 2–2). These recommendations have stood the test of time and are as relevant today as they were over 40 years ago. The language may be somewhat different but the values and concepts underlying the recommendations remain central to the current efforts to improve the quality of services and outcomes for persons with disabilities.

Legislation of the 1960s

Following the Kennedy administration's panel, legislation in the 1960s was also directed at meeting the educational and developmental needs of children with disabilities. In 1965 and 1966, legislation was passed that provided support for the education of children with disabilities in state-operated schools, hospitals, and in the local schools. These acts also set up the Bureau for Education of Handicapped Children, whose function was to administer all federal authorities for the education of children with disabilities. The first legislation specifically addressing the needs of children with disabilities was the Handicapped Children Early Education Assistance Act, in 1968 (P.L. 90-583). This act established experimental demonstration centers for the education of preschool children with disabilities.

Other legislative authorities were created and had specific provisions for meeting the needs of children and adults with disabilities. The Vocational Education Act of 1963 (P.L. 88-210) developed vocational programs for disadvantaged populations and students with disabilities. Funding was not specifically provided for students with disabilities until 1968 when the Vocational Education Act amendments authorized and set aside up to 10% of funding for education and services to students with disabilities. The Rehabilitation amendments of 1967 created new programs for recruitment and training of rehabilitation service providers and funded rehabilitation services and research at much higher levels. An example of this expansion was the development of work–study programs, which provided work experiences and functional academics and life skills for persons with mild mental retardation. In 1969, 37 directors of vocational rehabilitation services reported a total of 1,344 cooperative agreements with special education nationwide. A total of 96,604 secondary students with mental retardation were served in these programs (State Agency Exchange, 1969).

Critical Point The beginnings of federal laws in the 1960s laid a foundation to meet the national need in disability services. This was the governmental response to meet the needs of unserved persons with disabilities.

Developmental disabilities and mental health legislation also expanded during this era. The legislation sharpened the definitions, eligibility, and scope of services for these two populations. For example, the Mental Retardation and Facilities and Construction Act of 1963 (P.L. 88-164) established, for the first time, a federal priority to meet the needs of persons with mental retardation on a national level. A framework was set up to define the need and subsequently to develop a national framework for service delivery. Monies became available to states and community agencies to establish community-based services with government support. This legislation (P.L. 88-164) was an important beginning in defining functional needs in major life activities and a comprehensive system (across life domains) for individuals who may need assistance and ongoing support throughout their lifetime. At that time, people with moderate to profound mental retardation or other significant disabilities of childhood, who lived in the community, were virtually unserved or identified as in need of services and supports. Special education, vocational education, rehabilitation, developmental disability, and mental health legislation outlined some basic service needs and funded the beginning of what is now a federal–state–local service delivery system.

Critical Point The period from 1915 to 1945 focused on support and training for veterans with disabilities and marked the beginning of a federal government role. The period from 1945 to 1968 saw expansion of training and rehabilitation for the whole population of persons with disabilities and the emergence of a disability policy and a larger government role.

Summary of Policy Through the 1960s

From 1917 to 1945, the primary federal role was rehabilitation for veterans with disabilities and the development of vocational education alternatives in public schools. Beginning in the late 1950s and continuing into the 1960s, legislation was passed for special education, special needs vocational education, statewide rehabilitation programs, and a developmental disability and mental health service system. This was the beginning of disability policy development and a federal government role in the education and rehabilitation of people with disabilities. Table 2–3 compares and contrasts the federal role in disability services through the 1960s.

Policy Foundation and Legislation of the 1970s

PARC v. Commonwealth of Pennsylvania, 1972

While continuing to provide community services, the ARC expanded its advocacy role into the political arena in the 1970s. Students with severe disabilities, particularly those with more severe mental retardation, were excluded from public school in most states prompting the Pennsylvania ARC (PARC) to file a class action law suit. This suit demanded public education for all children regardless of disability under the argument that their rights to education could not be taken away without due process of law (PARC *v. Commonwealth of Pennsylvania*, 1972). The case was won by PARC (the plaintiff) and this class action suit was instrumental in creating the structure of the Education of All Handicapped Children Act (P.L. 94-142) in 1975. In the consent decree were provisions for a right to an appropriate education and due process of law.

Critical Point Legislation mandating education for students with disabilities and establishing an appropriate education as a right was accomplished as a result of parental efforts. Parents and families knew all too well the impact of children and youth being excluded from education or inappropriately served.

Independent Living Movements

While parents and families were advocating for children and some adults with disabilities, adults with physical and sensory disabilities began advocating for themselves. In Berkeley, California, a small group of young adults challenged the

TABLE 2–3

Legislation Prior to and During the 1960s

1917–1945

Focus on support and training for disabled veterans
Beginnings of a federal government role:

- 1917 Smith-Hughes Act (P.L. 64-347): Provided for vocational rehabilitation and employment for veterans with disabilities and vocational education
- 1918 Smith-Sears Act (P.L. 65-178): Provided additional support for veterans with disabilities
- 1920 Smith-Fess Act (P.L. 66-236): Provided funding for vocational training for civilians with disabilities who worked in federal civil service jobs
- 1943 Barden-LaFollette Act (P.L. 77-113): Provided for vocational rehabilitation for all civilians with physical disabilities and mental retardation

1945–1968

Expansion of training and rehabilitation for the whole population of persons with disabilities
Emergence of disability policy and federal government role:

- 1954 Vocational Rehabilitation amendments (P.L. 83-565): Provided funding for research and training of professionals and for expanding and improving rehabilitation
- 1963 Vocational Education Act (P.L. 88-210): Provided for expansion of vocational programs and services for person with disabilities
- 1966 Elementary and Secondary Education Act amendments (P.L. 89-750): Provided for support of state programs of special education and created federal Bureau of Education of the Handicapped
- 1968 Vocational Education amendments (P.L. 90-576): Established set-aside of basic state funding for special populations (10% for students with disabilities and 15% for students with academic and economic disadvantages)
- 1967 Vocational Rehabilitation amendments (P.L. 90-99): Provided increased funding for rehabilitation, research, demonstration, and training projects
- 1968 Vocational Rehabilitation amendments (P.L. 90-391): Provided increased funding for rehabilitation, research, demonstration, and training projects
- 1963 Mental Retardation and Facilities and Construction Act (P.L. 88-164): Provided funding for creation of community-based programs for people with mental retardation

Source: Adapted from School-to-work transition: Overview of disability legislation by R. A. Stodden in *Beyond high school: Transition from school to work,* Rusch, F. R. & Chadsey, J. G. (Eds.), 1998, Wadsworth Publishing Company.

University of California to make its programs and education accessible to persons with physical disabilities. This resulted in the "independent living movement," which emphasized that community participation and access to social institutions were the right of all citizens, including persons with disabilities.

With leadership from a variety of advocacy groups, the Rehabilitation Act of 1973 (P.L. 93-112) was passed, which was considered a major victory. Passage of the Rehabilitation Act of 1973 mandated equal access for persons with disabilities to all federally funded programs. However, the implementation of this law was hindered because the government did not write regulations. Five years later, in 1978, advocates and persons with disabilities had to stage a sit-in at the office of the cabinet secretary and in regional offices of the U.S. Department of Health, Education, and Welfare to spur the government into promulgating the needed regulations. This bureaucratic stonewalling was typical of the battles that disability movements faced in affirming the rights of people with disabilities.

Critical Point Legislation mandating access to employment, postsecondary education, and the community was achieved by coalitions, including persons with disabilities.

People First

The 1970s were also a period for the self-advocacy of other disability groups. The origins of People First, the self-advocacy organization of people with mental retardation, was a case in point and a poignant story. Because of cognitive limitations, persons with mental retardation were not being heard, except through their parents. A group of these individuals came together in Oregon to tell professionals what they wanted from their programs. Accounts of the meeting describe a young woman standing up and saying, "We want to be people first!" This sparked a movement in the disability community that persons with disabilities should be referred to and treated as "persons first." People First challenged society and professionals to attach primary attention to "personhood" and to view disability as only a part of a whole person, not the defining characteristic (Perske, 1988).

The "people first movement" led to a change in thinking and talking about persons with disabilities. Professional and social discourse about persons with disabilities began to discard terms such as "retardate," "cripple," and "the disabled." Person-first language and disability etiquette has been characterized as political correctness, but respect was seen as very important in increasing the presence and participation of people with disabilities. Person-first language conveys respect for the person with a disability by:

1. Recognizing a person's right to self-esteem.
2. Recognizing a person's right to be thought of as a person first and foremost in word and in thought (in other words, the person is "first a person" and "second a person with a disability").
3. Accurately describing a person without being judgmental (i.e., just as it is not always necessary to convey the color of a person's hair, it is also not always necessary to mention that a person has a disability).

Table 2–4 provides both an overview of some issues that are important in interacting with people with disabilities and some useful guidelines to personal and professional behavior. Person-first language should generally be used in talking about persons with disabilities unless they request otherwise. It may also be necessary to educate others (e.g., send guidelines to the media) so that they can support social behaviors that show respect for persons with disabilities.

Critical Point People with mental retardation directly experience the rejection and fear resulting from others who define them only through the label of their disability.

During the period of the 1970s, legislation was expanded in education (e.g., special education, career education, and vocational education) and in adult services and postschool supports. Cross-references to requirements in special education were made in vocational education legislation. Interagency cooperation was more clearly outlined within rehabilitation and developmental disability and mental health legislation and between education and rehabilitation. Interagency cooperation

TABLE 2–4
Person-First Language Suggestions

- Refer to people first and disability second.
- Avoid the use of terms which equate a person with his or her disability (i.e., the "quadriplegic" or "epileptic"; instead, use the person with a seizure disorder or the person with quadriplegia).
- Use adjectives that do not have negative connotations (i.e., "stricken," "afflicted," "victim," or "crippled").
- Use the words "typical" and "normal" appropriately (i.e., in comparison to people without disabilities, people with disabilities are "atypical," but the term "abnormal" conveys inaccurate, negative meanings).
- Focus on what a person with disabilities can do rather than what they cannot do.
- Avoid describing persons as having disabilities when it is not pertinent to the conversation.
- Avoid sensationalizing or implying that superhuman qualities are possessed by persons with disabilities (persons with disabilities have the same range of talents and successes as others; to sensationalize their accomplishments implies that they must overcompensate to succeed—most need only a regular effort when they have equal access and reasonable accommodations with which to accomplish their work).
- Avoid using words associated with disability in a manner that has negative connotations (i.e., terms such as "deaf and dumb," "retarded," or "spastic" evoke negative images and are easily replaced by accurate descriptions).
- Avoid the use of terms such as "wheelchair bound" or "confined to a wheelchair" (persons who *use wheelchairs* view them as most people view cars, as tools which enable freedom and independence, not traps! It is inappropriate to associate wheelchairs with helplessness and dependence and to treat wheelchairs as an extension of personal space; to lean or hang on it is like leaning or hanging on the person using the wheelchair).

Source: Adapted from class materials "Disability Policy," developed by Deborah Durhan Webster, Kent State University, 1999.

was a requirement in all the legislation with the goal that services would be coordinated among the systems and that professional training and interaction would reflect common philosophies, goals, and commitments within a teamwork and interdisciplinary framework.

School-Based Legislation of 1970s

During the 1970s, special education and vocational education legislation was closely coordinated through cross-references in the specific acts. The Education for All Handicapped Children Act (EHA) of 1975 (P.L. 95-142) mandated multifactored evaluations (MFE) every 3 years, parental right to due process, free appropriate public education (FAPE), least restrictive environment (LRE), and the Individualized Education Program (IEP), which were the cornerstones of special education. Provisions for the IEP included career and vocational objectives for youth with disabilities under the EHA. The Education Amendments of 1976 (P.L. 94-482) required coordination of the state plans of special education and vocational education and established priority for access to regular vocational education as opposed to specialized vocational education. Assurances that the full range of program options were accessible was an important requirement in state plans for vocational education. IEPs and the need for vocational teacher participation were highlighted in this legislation. The teaming of vocational and special education instructional staff was expected for participation in regular vocational education. Consequently, many states developed a continuum of vocational education services and options for students with disabilities. These continuums were like alternatives based on least restrictive environment concepts (i.e., regular vocational education, with support, or specialized).

In 1977, the concept of career education was put into legislation and introduced as "the totality of experiences through which one learns about and prepares to engage in work as part of his or her way of living" (Hoyt, 1977). States were to implement programs on:

1. Encompassing the total curriculum of the school and providing a unified approach to education for life.
2. Encouraging all members of the community to share responsibility for learning within classrooms, homes, private and public agencies, and the employment community.
3. Providing for career awareness, exploration, and preparation at all levels and ages.
4. Encouraging all teachers to review their subject matter for its career implications.

Special educators increased their career education emphasis because of its functional and skill orientation and as a method to link academic and vocational preparation (Clark, 1979). Career education, although legislated, was passed with a sunset provision; when the act expired in 1982 so too did funding to states for career education efforts. Nonetheless, the concept and structure to bring career education into the overall school curriculum was implemented in various ways and has left some structures that still exist in schools today. These changes most notably can be seen in counseling and guidance, special education, and career and technical education. In fact, the School to Work Opportunity Act of 1994 is a belated federal initiative and successor to the Career Education Implementation Incentive Act of 1977.

Critical Point The common underpinnings of special education, vocational education, and career education were established through legislation. Preparation beyond academic subjects and career and personal development became important goals of public education.

Rehabilitation Act of 1973

Historically, the Rehabilitation Act of 1973 is of great importance for several reasons. First, the act was completely rewritten and was a "new" law (rehabilitation legislation prior to 1973 consisted of amendments to the Barden–LaFollete Act of 1943). Second, the 1973 act was also a reflection of comprehensive and functional service delivery as was other legislation (e.g., developmental disability legislation). Third, most importantly, with passage of the Rehabilitation Act of 1973, Congress for the first time officially enacted a law on disability rights.

The Rehabilitation Act of 1973 had three important provisions. First, rehabilitation programs in the states were to give priority to persons with the most severe disabilities. Because many of these people did not receive services, Congress stated that people with severe disabilities should have the opportunity to receive services in order to become employed. This was the beginning of an ongoing trend in service delivery, which highlights insufficient resources to meet the need.

The second area address by the Rehabilitation Act was independent living services. These were included as a Title—a section of the law to cover those kinds of services. Independent living programs emphasized two major points: (1) Living in the community and getting help with activities of daily living was as important as working, and (2) Independent living made it necessary that the client or consumer of services should have considerable input and control over what services are provided and how they are delivered. The underlying principle was that the act should deal with the whole person and all the domains of living in the community.

The third area of the Rehabilitation Act described the rights of persons with disabilities as they pertain to employment and participation in the community. Of particular importance was Section 504, the nondiscrimination requirements pertaining to people with disabilities. Section 504 reads:

> No otherwise qualified person with a disability in the United States . . . shall, solely on the basis of disability, be denied access to, or the benefits of, or be subjected to discrimination under any program or activity provided by any institution receiving federal financial assistance or under any program or activity conducted by any Executive Agency or by the U.S. Postal Service (29 U.S.C. § 794).

Critical Point Independent living services and priority for persons with severe disabilities provided through the Rehabilitation Act of 1973 broadened the concept of rehabilitation beyond simple employment processes and addressed the role of environments and societal attitudes as handicapping factors.

Use of the terms "otherwise qualified persons with disabilities" in Section 504 of the Rehabilitation Act of 1973 required that the person with a disability be defined as a person first. A "person with a disability" was defined as anyone with a physical or mental impairment that interferes with at least one major life activity (e.g., employment, independent living, etc.). "Otherwise qualified" means that the person meets the requirements for skills, abilities, degrees, and training for gaining entrance into, for example, school or a job (DuBow, Geer, & Strauss, 1992). This indicates that people with disabilities must be evaluated on their qualifications and not on their disability. When a person has a disability, it is important that he or she know and meet the qualifications for gaining entrance into the program of choice.

"Solely by reason . . . disabilities, be excluded . . . denied or subjected" means just what it says. Disability in and of itself cannot be a determinant in decisions by schools, employers, and others. More often, when a disability presents a barrier in a given environment, like a classroom, there are ways to alter the environment so that the person can perform or participate. Besides banning discrimination, this part of the definition affirms that participation must be meaningful and that the person with a disability has some opportunity to benefit from the activity or program. Persons with disabilities need to have access to activities that are important to functioning within a particular environment so that they can perform and compete on the same level as others.

Critical Point The Rehabilitation Act established both basic rights of persons with disabilities and the importance of community integration and inclusion in employment, housing, and postsecondary education.

"Any program or activity . . . receiving federal financial assistance" includes all aspects of programs and institutions, including education, employment, housing, transportation, and so on. For postsecondary education, this includes almost all types of schools, public and private, because most students receive money from the federal government. Colleges and universities and other postsecondary programs must not discriminate in the recruitment, admission, or treatment of students, under Section 504 of the Rehabilitation Act. Under subpart E of Section 504, qualified students with documented disabilities may request modifications, accommodations, or auxiliary aids that will enable them to participate in and benefit from programs and activities (see Table 2–5).

A major theme throughout rehabilitation and special education legislation during the 1970s is that the person with a disability has a central role in the accommodation process.

TABLE 2–5
Subpart E of Section 504

104.41 Applies to recipients of federal funds
104.42 Admissions and recruitment
- May not limit the number of persons admitted
- Nondiscriminatory criteria and test
- May not make preadmission inquiry

104.43 Treatment of students; general
- Covers overall and general discrimination
- Operates programs in most integrated settings

104.44 Academic adjustment
- Modification to requirements to include qualified persons
- Does not apply to essential requirements
- Course examinations should reflect achievement, not disability
- Auxiliary aids must be provided to ensure access (i.e., for students with impaired sensory, manual, or speaking skills)

104.45, .46, .47
- Also covered are housing, financial and employment assistance, and nonacademic services

Source: Adapted from Section 504 of Rehabilitation Act of 1973, 29 U.S.C. § 794 *et seq.*, subpart E.

That is, there are many responsibilities that go along with exercising one's right. Moreover, without participation, the development of workable accommodations is unlikely. Therefore, the student needs to understand the educational implications of disability and educate and inform others. All these skills then are applied in transition and career planning in the student's educational program in high school and beyond.

Critical Point Teachers and transition staff need to know policies like Section 504 because this information is important for students to know for self-advocacy.

Developmental Disability and Mental Health Legislation

The field of developmental disabilities is perhaps unique in that its origins can be traced to an act of Congress. As the mental retardation legislation of the 1960s was expiring, leaders and advocacy groups grasped the opportunity to expand the previous laws to benefit not only individuals who were mentally retarded but also disability groups whose impairments were developmental in nature and who had similar service needs. Consequently, P.L. 91–517, the Developmental Disabilities Services Facilities Construction Act of 1970, was enacted and included persons who were mentally retarded and also persons who were affected by cerebral palsy, epilepsy, and other neurological conditions found to be closely related to mental retardation or to require comprehensive services similar to those required by individuals with mental retardation.

Two important background factors were related to these changes. One was the desire to focus on the developmental aspects of these conditions. Developmental disabilities result in impairment to a broader range of functions, which in turn affect the acquisition of basic life skills, while the word "developmental" also reduces the stigmatizing effect of the mental retardation label. The second factor concerned the lifelong nature of the disability and the need for extended services. Clearly, the intent of the earlier laws was to serve those who have substantial unmet needs (Lubin, Jacobson, & Kiely, 1982; Summers, 1981).

Critical Point The developmental disability legislation established that some disabilities will require services and support throughout the person's lifetime. Substantial impairments were tied to the concept of major life activities such as employment, independent living, and so on.

Since many persons with severe disabilities still were not receiving services after the passage of the 1970 act, P.L. 95-602, in 1978, dropped the specification of categories of disability in favor of reference only to substantial impairment. Public Law 95-602, Rehabilitation, Comprehensive Services, and Developmental Disability (DD) amendments of 1978, defined developmental disability as a severe, chronic disability of a person which:

A. Is attributable to mental or physical impairment, or combination of mental and physical impairments.
B. Is manifested before the person attains age 22.
C. Is likely to continue indefinitely.
D. Results in substantial functional limitations in three or more of the following areas of major life activity:
   1. self-care
   2. receptive and expressive language
   3. learning
   4. mobility
   5. self-direction
   6. capacity for independent living
   7. economic self-sufficiency
E. Reflects the person's need for a combination and sequence of special, interdisciplinary, or generic care, treatment, or other services that are individually planned and coordinated.

The major implications of the definition are that comprehensive, coordinated lifelong management of services will be required to meet the needs of the person with a developmental disability.

Critical Point The rights of school-age children with disabilities were protected as well as the right to access for persons with disabilities in the general population. In the 1970s, legislation established the main parts that are needed for a coordinated service system to meet the needs of transition students and adults.

Similar legislation to that in the DD amendment was passed in the area of mental health in the 1960s and 1970s. This legislation also focused on community-based services and support over extended periods of time. Individuals had pervasive needs and were referred to as having psychiatric disabilities. These individuals may have substantial functional limitations, but due to psychiatric problems, and not mental retardation.

Summary Policy Foundation and Legislation of the 1970s

Table 2–6 shows the legislative progression through the 1970s. The focus during this period was on appropriate education for special education youth and access and accommodation for all persons with disabilities, including adults. On the special education side, all students were to be provided with a free appropriate public education (FAPE) at no expense to parents and a program that meets unique needs (i.e., IEP). This was to include vocational education for secondary-age students. The focus on career education brought special and regular education closer together after years of separation. The career development and outcome orientation of the 1970s addressed education beyond pure academics

TABLE 2–6

Legislation During the 1970s

Ensured rights to appropriate education and access for persons with disabilities in general; Established service system supported by federal government:
• 1970 Developmental Disabilities and Bill of Rights Act of 1970: Provided support to states' creation of a developmental disabilities service system—emphasized long-term support
• 1973 Rehabilitation Act (sections 503 and 504) (P.L. 93-112): Funded independent living centers, prioritized rehabilitation of persons with the most severe disabilities, provided protection from discrimination
• 1973 Comprehensive Employment and Training Act (P.L. 93-203): Provided manpower services to raise employment levels of unemployed, unskilled youth and adults
• 1975 Education of Handicapped Children Act (P.L. 94-142): Partially funded a free appropriate public education (FAPE) in the least restrictive environment; included vocational education
• 1976 Vocational Education amendments (P.L. 94-482): Emphasized access to regular vocational education and development of new vocational programs; funded vocational assessment and support services for students with special needs

Source: Adapted from School-to-work transition: Overview of disability legislation, by R. A. Stodden in *Beyond high school: Transition from school to work,* Rusch, F. R. & Chadsey, J. G. (Eds.), 1998, Wadsworth Publishing Company.

needed by all students. Rehabilitation and developmental disability and mental health legislation provided guidelines for definitions and service systems for children and adults with the most severe disabilities, those historically underserved. Further, integration and participation in the mainstream of schools and communities and society was central to all the disability legislation while, for the first time, rights for people with disabilities were spelled out, for both school-age children and youth and adults.

Legislation of the 1980s

Whereas legislation of the 1970s laid a foundation for special education and a service system for adults with disabilities, the 1980s were a period of consolidation and further coordination among legislative acts. Further clarification was provided on the appropriate education to be provided within vocational education by the Carl D. Perkins Vocational Education and Technology Act of 1984 (P.L. 98-210). Within the rehabilitation system, the Rehabilitation Act amendments of 1986 (P.L. 99-506) provided a specific program and service structure (i.e., supported employment) to serve individuals with the most severe disabilities. This period, known for the legislative activity of the 99th Congress, was particularly active regarding issues surrounding employment rates of persons with disabilities (e.g., disincentives to employment such as the loss of Social Security benefits).

Special Education Legislation

As a result of concern generated by outcome studies, the 1983 amendments to the Education of Handicapped Children Act (P.L. 98-199) included Section 626 on secondary education and transition and a federal initiative was launched. Substantial discretionary programs were implemented for the purpose of researching the transition process and providing demonstration and capacity-building activities to improve transition services in state and local education agencies. Through these projects, secondary education improvements were addressed through projects on direct transition services, community-based education and services, cooperative models, job training, self-determination, and local education agency capacity to deliver transition services among others. Moreover, research and demonstration activities in the postschool arena were also funded for follow-up/follow-along systems, special populations, and postsecondary supports and education (Rusch & Millar, 1998). The amendments also strongly recommended that individual transition plans be developed for high school youth and provided focused activity on teams, teamwork, and interagency activity.

Critical Point In the 1980s, the federal initiative on transition brought national attention to the needs of secondary youth with disabilities.

Vocational Education Legislation

The strengthening of transition services for youth with disabilities was also an important component of the Carl D. Perkins Vocational Education Act of 1984 (P.L. 98-524). The emphasis in this act was to assure access to quality vocational education programs and the expansion of programs that were to be developed from the 10% of funds set aside for students with disabilties. In 1984, the Carl D. Perkins Vocational and Technical Education Act was passed with the following intent:

> . . . assure that individuals who are inadequately served under vocational education programs are assured access to quality vocational education programs, especially individuals who are disadvantaged, who are disabled, men and women who are entering non-traditional occupations, adults who are in need of training and retraining, individuals with limited English proficiency, and individuals who are incarcerated in correctional institutions. (P.L. 98-524, 98, Stat. 2435)

Access to vocational education was viewed as critical to youth preparing for the transition from secondary education to work environments in their local communities. Youth who were identified as disabled and disadvantaged were now required to receive vocational assessment, counseling, support, and transition services; IEPs were to include vocational goals; vocational education in the least restrictive environment was reemphasized; and state and local education agencies were to coordinate vocational education programs with requirements under P.L. 94-142 and amendments. Underlying all these legal requirements and assurances is the question of students enrolling in and completing vocational education. The test of effectiveness of vocational education mandates was determined through the national assessment of vocational education. By and large, vocational education was serving students with special needs, except (1) students with disabilities were still underserved and (2) access to regular vocational education was still an issue (Boesel & McFarland, 1994).

Critical Point The development of transition models and practices and the expansion of transition services resulted in greater numbers of students receiving a broader array of secondary options.

Employment and Training Programs

Within the U.S. Department of Labor, programs were also developing in a way that required more coordination with education legislation. From the programs of the 1970s (e.g., Comprehensive Employment and Training Act [CETA]) in which federal employment and training programs were consolidated, the Job Training and Partnership Act (JTPA) (P.L. 97-300) emerged in 1982, providing significant funding for job training and placement programs directly benefiting youth with disabilities. With CETA and JTPA, the needs and unemployment of both youth and adults were addressed, providing occupational skills to those who were not able to contribute to the nation's economy.

Rehabilitation and Developmental Disability Legislation

The rehabilitation legislation of the 1980s again took on the rehabilitation service needs of persons with the most severe disabilities. "Supported employment" was defined as paid employment in integrated real-work situations in which one must work at least 20 hours a week (P.L. 99-506). The significance of these amendments was that supported employment was to be a regular case service like other services and that interagency cooperation was required between rehabilitation services and adult service agencies that were to provide extended services and the long-term support implicit in service need definitions of persons with severe disabilities. There were corresponding changes in developmental disabilities legislation and mental health legislation to be consistent with delivery of employment and other services.

Critical Point Supported employment was a major postschool rehabilitation and adult service that was legislated and that benefited students with severe disabilities.

Social Security: Section 1619a & b

Supplemental Security Income (SSI) is an income support program run by the Social Security Administration. Monthly benefits can be paid to youth or adults with disabilities if their individual or family income falls below a certain level, and if their disability is severe and expected to last at least 12 months. SSI can be helpful in supplementing student income while in postsecondary education or entry-level work.

People who meet the eligibility requirements for SSI are usually eligible for Medicaid benefits as well. Medicaid benefits are administered by each state and applied for at the local departments of human services. A person may be eligible for Medicaid and not receiving SSI, if they are working and need Medicaid to maintain health benefits.

SSI programs encourage recipients to work through a number of allowances and work incentives. Generally, SSI recipients lose only one dollar for every two they earn, over the allowed threshold, and are able to exclude $85 of earned and unearned income. SSI has work incentives that include deductions for: (1) impairment-related work expenses (IRWEs), (2) student earned income exclusion, (3) blind work expenses, (4) Plans for Achieving Self-Sufficiency (PASS), (5) property essential to self-support, and (6) continued payment under vocational rehabilitation programs.

Technology-Related Assistance for Individuals with Disabilities Act

The Tech Act (P. L. 100-407) was passed in 1988. This was the first time specific legislation addressed the need for a statewide system focusing on technology supports for individuals with disabilities. Assistive technology was first defined in this legislation, thus providing the framework to which all other legislative acts refer. The act was a state-grants program similar to much previous legislation in disability. Grants were provided to develop a consumer responsive, comprehensive, statewide program of technology-related assistance for individuals of all ages. The Rehabilitation Engineering Society of North America (RESNA) provided technical assistance to states funded under this act. The Tech Act was important because the assistive technology and services enumerated within the act provided great promise for increasing, maintaining, and improving functioning in natural environments that are part of students' transition goals.

Summary of Legislation of the 1980s

The 1980s were a period of legislation that focused on coordination among the various legislative authorities. As already noted, the 99th Congress attempted to update and revise legislation in rehabilitation, developmental disabilities, income maintenance and health programs, as well as employer incentives in order to improve the employment prospects of persons with disabilities. As shown in Table 2–7, major amendments or new bills were passed across every disability-specific and transition-related area. The 1980s could be considered the period of federal initiative. As you will see, federal initiatives do not equate with quality transition programs in every community. Nonetheless, during the 1980s, a general framework tying together all the relevant legislation was established, issues of capacity were identified, and programs were put into place.

Transition-Related Legislation of the 1990s

The 1990s have come to an end and we are embarking on the "new millennium." The 1990s, therefore, defined how far transition has come in the twentieth century. Like all previous decades, the 1990s had its ups and downs. The decade started with the Americans with Disabilities Act (ADA) and new special education legislation (i.e., the IDEA). The rights of people with disabilities in all segments of society were affirmed and given protection by federal law; in other words, constitutional rights were reaffirmed. Also, in 1990, the IDEA mandated transition services as part of the IEP. Full participation and equal opportunity marked the beginning of the decade. These two pieces of legislation represented a pivotal point in the disability rights

TABLE 2–7

Legislation During the 1980s

Authorized funds to develop transition models and practices
Provided further clarifications of rights, reinforced coordination of legislation across transition and related areas, and expanded service eligibility

- 1982 Job Training Partnership Act (P.L. 97-300): Provided significant funding for job placement and training programs directly benefiting youth with disabilities
- 1983 Individuals with Disabilities Education Act (P.L. 98-199): Provided funds for grants to demonstrate support and coordination among educators and adult service programs to foster transition to postschool settings
- 1984 Carl D. Perkins Vocational Education Act (P.L. 88-210): Set aside funds to facilitate equal access to full range of vocational education activities through supplemental services; includes vocational education in IEPs
- 1986 Rehabilitation Act amendments of 1986 (P.L. 99-506): Provided definition and funding for supported employment
- 1984 Developmental Disabilities amendments of 1984 (P.L. 98-527): Defined supported employment and emphasized productivity and participation in the community

Source: Adapted from School-to-work transition: Overview of disability policy, by R.A. Stodden in *Beyond high school: Transition from school to work,* Rusch, F.R., & Chadsey, J.G., 1998, Wadsworth Publishing Company.

movement and the transition movement. Advocacy and professional groups truly became part of a national movement, which no longer viewed disability and the service system as charity.

Americans with Disabilities Act

In 1990, the ADA was passed into law and signed by President George Bush. The ADA was designed to be comprehensive and to cover all aspects of rights within all areas of citizen participation. It was overarching; that is, it provided organizing principles from previous laws and a standard for measuring policies on how to implement the law (West, 1991). The ADA dealt more with breadth than with new concepts. Before the ADA, only federal contractors and recipients of federal funds were required not to discriminate against people with disabilities. Now, the private sector must comply with a comprehensive disability antidiscrimination mandate.

The ADA sends "a message about what society's attitude should be toward persons with disabilities: respect, inclusion, and support" (West, 1991, p. xviii). Of course, attitudes cannot be mandated. A corollary to this principle is that legislation about rights is based on values, not on knowledge. This can be tricky, however, because values are very broad statements about beliefs and have importance in both the group and individual context. Respect, in part, means that people without disabilities view disability as a unique characteristic without devaluing the person. The disability is part of the identity and self-concept of the person. Disability is a natural way in which persons differ from each other. Inclusion and support mean that society values the contributions and participation of people with disabilities. The goal of inclusion is to create an experience that is a meaningful, equal opportunity for the person with a disability. Because the social and physical environment can create barriers and prohibit meaningful involvement, accommodations are required in order to provide a means of participation for people with disabilities. The value is that society should make that extra effort to include everyone. The "accommodation" imperative means that a fair society would make experiences accessible while the inclusion ethic deals with the value that society wants to give everyone an equal opportunity (West).

Critical Point Respect, inclusion, and support are the philosophical and value base of the ADA. Interaction and communication on equal ground are necessary to create positive attitudes.

The ADA is organized into five sections called "Titles." As pointed out, the ADA covers aspects of living and participating in community life that have not already been covered by other laws, reinforces standards in applying the law, and generalizes rights protections to the private (as opposed to only public or publicly supported) activities. In the ADA law, the major entities covered are (1) private employers who do not receive federal money; (2) state and local government agencies; (3) public accommodations (e.g., restaurants, hotels, and theaters); and (4) telephone companies (for "functionally" equivalent relay services: TTY). The fifth title covers miscellaneous areas. These titles of the ADA require that reasonable accommodations (employment) be made and that other entities, activities, and programs be made accessible (e.g., government agencies and public accommodations).

Critical Point An important precept of the ADA is "qualified person with a disability." The definition of "qualified" includes accommodation: an alternative manner to accomplish tasks or activities.

Title I of the ADA prohibits an employer from discriminating against a qualified individual with a disability in the following areas: (1) job application procedures; (2) hiring; (3) discharge; (4) compensation; (5) advancement; and (6) any other terms, conditions, and privileges of employment. Under the ADA, a qualified individual is one who, with or without reasonable accommodations, is able to perform the essential functions of the job. "Essential functions" are those duties of a job that are basic—not marginal—to the position (DuBow et al. 1992). For example, in many jobs, answering the telephone is listed as a qualification when, in fact, it is not essential to the job. This requirement would tend to screen out, unnecessarily, persons with hearing impairments who could not answer the telephone. Reasonable accommodations can be a variety of strategies to enable the hard-of-hearing person to perform the essential functions of a job (i.e., modifications, adjustments, or technology). The employer is exempt from providing accommodations if they are too expensive or difficult (undue hardship).

Title II of the ADA requires all state and local government agencies to make all their services accessible to individuals with disabilities. It also requires public transportation agencies to be accessible. State and local governments must ensure effective communication with individuals with disabilities. For persons with vision, hearing, or speech impairments, appropriate auxiliary aids or services are often needed for effective communication. Agencies and services should publicize how to request special services. Auxiliary aids include qualified interpreters, assistive listening devices, real-time recorders, television captioning and decoders, TTYs, videotext displays, readers, taped texts, and large print materials. The important point is that the activity, service, or program must be made accessible so that persons with disabilities can use and benefit from the activity and achieve meaningful participation. The person's expressed choice of auxiliary aids or services should be given primary consideration. Nonetheless, the public entity has the final decision on how accommodations are provided.

Title III of the ADA provides people with disabilities with rights to equal access to public accommodations. Title III covers many places, such as hotels, theaters, restaurants, doctors' and lawyers' offices, retail stores, banks, museums, parks, libraries, day-care centers, and private schools. Again, auxiliary aids and services must be provided to ensure meaningful access. Title IV requires telephone companies to provide both local and long-distance telecommunications relay services across the nation.

Critical Point Accommodations require a two-way communication and problem-solving process.

Rehabilitation Act Amendments of 1992

Whereas the ADA established a new paradigm for disability and the rightful place of persons in society, the Rehabilitation Act of 1992 further reinforced the ADA precepts and addressed, specifically, accessibility and responsiveness to the needs and goals of the customers of vocational rehabilitation. Several parts of the Rehabilitation Act of 1992 illustrated connections to IDEA and the ADA. The following were some highlights of the Rehabilitation Act amendments of 1992:

1. The statement of purpose of the bill notes that "disability is a natural part of the human experience and in no way diminishes the right of individuals to live independently; enjoy self-determination; make choices; contribute to society; pursue meaningful careers. . . ." This bill further embraces principles of "equality of opportunity, full inclusion and integration in society, employment, independent living and economic and social self-sufficiency."
2. Presumption of employability: "Individuals with disabilities, including the most severe disabilities, are generally presumed to be capable of engaging in gainful employment."
3. Use of appropriate existing data and information provided by other agencies and individuals and their families is required "to the maximum extent appropriate" as "a primary source" to determine eligibility and "for choosing rehabilitation goals, objectives and services."

4. Individualized written rehabilitation plan (IWRP): New language requires the "IWRP to complete an assessment for determining . . . vocational rehabilitation needs. . . ." Changes to the IWRP also ensure personal choice in the development of the plan, including "a statement by the individual, in the words of the individual. . . " on how he or she was involved in the process.
5. Title I services: Services available under Title I include personal assistance services, transition services, and supported employment services.
6. Use of natural supports: Families and natural supports can play an important role in the success of a vocational rehabilitation program, if the individual with a disability requests, desires, or needs such supports.

It should also be noted that Rehabilitation Act Amendments of 1992 (P.L. 102-569), addressed rehabilitation technology. Rehabilitation technology is defined as "the systematic application of technologies, engineering methodologies, or scientific principles by individuals with disabilities in areas including education, rehabilitation, employment, transportation, independent living, and recreation" (P.L. 102-569). It should be noted that the term rehabilitation technology includes rehabilitation engineering, assistive technology devices, and assistive technology services. (P.L. 102-569). Devices are actual items or equipment, while a service is any service that directly assists the individual in selection, acquisition, or use of assistive technology devices.

Workforce Investment Act and Rehabilitation Act Amendments of 1998

The rehabilitation amendments were part of the Work Force Investment Act (WIA) of 1998 (P.L. 105-220). The inclusion of rehabilitation legislation within workforce development reflected an attempt to integrate employment and training programs on a federal, state, and local level. WIA was a comprehensive job-training bill that consolidates over 45 previous federally funded programs. The intent of the bill was to simplify the worker–training system. More emphasis on meeting skill shortages in the labor market and career individualization were prominent features. Therefore, local needs of business and individual needs and preferences of those served were the major factors to determine what education and services were provided and how the delivery system was set up.

Three block grants to states are used as the major funding mechanism in the WIA: adult employment and training, disadvantaged youth employment and training, adult education and family literacy. Under Title I, workforce investment systems with state and local boards are established, along with a "one-stop" delivery system. Youth councils are set up as a subgroup of local boards. Accountability systems and standards are part of the requirements of local boards to ensure that consumer needs are met.

Title IV of WIA contained the 1998 amendments to the Rehabilitation Act of 1973, as amended. The amendments were a bipartisan consensus with emphasis on increasing opportunities to prepare for, secure, maintain, and regain employment. Informed choice and a "fair shot" at rehabilitation to employment were hallmarks of the new amendments. A "fair shot" included provisions for presumptive eligibility in cases that historically were determined ineligible because of the severity of the disability (IWRP is now designated as the Individual Program of Employment). At the other end of the continuum, other individuals with rehabilitation needs, who were not served because of the order of selection (services provided to the most severely disabled), were now to have available a referral and information system designed to assist them in obtaining an appropriate service within the workforce investment system or other community service.

Critical Point The Rehabilitation Act amendments reflect a customer focus. Programs and service design must reflect a partnership and joint decision making.

Goals 2000: Educate America Act of 1994 (P.L. 103-227)

Reform of the public education system has been a "hot topic" of discussion, on and off, since the early 1980s. Regular and vocational education are important because many students with disabilities receive their education within these two systems. Access to the education and curriculum in these systems in many instances constitutes an appropriate education for students and reflects transition services that students need to make movement toward their postschool goals. IDEA is now more aligned with the curricula provided in general education. The generic systems, in coordination with special education transition, meets the requirement for a coordinated set of activities. There are numerous ways to identify how provisions of vocational education, general education, and school-to-work programs line up with what is meant by the statement of needed transition services as provided within the IEP with the IDEA legislation.

This legislation provided a framework for restructuring education based on national goals—in essence, the act was about educational reform. Reform is concerned with the outcomes of education and how these outcomes are affected by education, curriculum, and school structure. Numerous benefits for the transition arena can be drawn from the implications of national goals. Since students with disabilities have higher dropout rates than the general student population, the goal of high school completion (goal 2) could have tremendous benefit to transition students if accomplished. This is especially so for students with behavior disorders who drop out at a 40% rate (Blackorby & Wagner, 1996). High academic achievement, lifelong learning, and productive employment will enhance transition goals for students that reflect high expectations, meaningful career goals, and participation in the economy in high skill, high-paying jobs (goals 3 and 6). Partnering with parents (goal 8) has been a keystone of transition services since the very earliest efforts to work with high school youth in order to achieve adult success. Even the teacher education and professional development (goal 4) goal has transition implications, that is, preparing students for the future. This requires working with youth so that they can define and envision their own and their community's future.

School to Work Opportunity Act of 1994 (P.L. 103-239)

Transition was the underlying and defining principle in the School to Work Opportunity Act (STWOA) of 1994 (P.L. 103-239). (P.L. 103-239 had a sunset provision and expired in 1998.) This act called on states to plan and implement transition systems that enabled all youth to make the transition from school to postschool environments. The components and expected

Career programs often are an appropriate eduaction.

outcomes of statewide school-to-work systems included provisions (1) to enable all youth to acquire the skills and knowledge necessary to make the transition smoothly from school to work or further education and training, (2) to impact the preparation of all youth for a first job toward a career and to increase opportunities for further education, (3) to expand ways through which school- and work-based learning can be integrated, and (4) to link occupational and academic learning and to strengthen the linkage between secondary and postsecondary education (Norman & Bourexis, 1995). All these provisions were consistent with and reinforce special education transition requirements. Again, there is emphasis on outcomes, career development and education, and education and training beyond high school. The point is that preparation for life and career after school must begin when the student is still in high school. This preparation must and can be integrated with academic core subject learning necessary for further education in postsecondary programs.

Indeed, two of the purposes of STWOA were (1) "to build on promising school-to-work activities, such as tech-prep education, career academies, school-to-apprenticeship programs, cooperative education, youth apprenticeship, school-sponsored enterprises" and (2) "to improve the knowledge and skills of youths by integrating academic and occupational learning, and building effective linkages between secondary and postsecondary education" (p. 5). As with prior education-for-work legislation, STWOA addressed the need for all students to have access to programs and specifically mentions individuals with disabilities, low-achieving youth, school dropouts, and those from disadvantaged or diverse racial, ethnic, or cultural backgrounds (Kochhar & West, 1995). It is interesting to note that some of the practices used in vocational special education for the past 20 years, such as career awareness and exploration activities, exposing students to broad career opportunities, and matching students' interests, goals, strengths, and abilities with program options were highlighted in STWOA.

The Perkins Acts of 1990 and 1998

The 1990 Carl D. Perkins amendments had two major themes:

1. To improve the quality of vocational education programs
2. To provide supplemental services to special populations

The 1990 amendments moved away from traditional job skills orientation to integrating vocational and academic skills training; focused more on poor districts and reform issues; and restructured the state–local administration structure, with local schools getting involved in reform and states developing standards. Apprenticeships were emphasized and tech-prep came into existence. Special funding set-asides for special populations were eliminated. Nonetheless, as shown in Table 2–8, the Perkins Act of 1990 had numerous provisions that addressed transition issues for students with disabilities.

The 1998 Carl D. Perkins Act amendments represented many consistencies with the 1990 act but also included provisions that presented challenges to the vocational education system. As Kimberly Green, the executive director of the National Association of State Directors of Vocational Education, said: "Legislators want vocational education graduates on the same level as someone who goes through regular academics so that students are just as prepared and have as many options as a person who is college bound." There were no longer any set-asides for special populations, giving schools more control over how they spend funds but now schools have to set and meet performance standards. The bill did not include school-to-work requirements but that does not

TABLE 2–8

Carl D. Perkins Vocational and Applied Technology Education Act of 1990

Criteria for services and activities for individuals who are members of special populations—required assurances:

- Equal access to *recruitment*, *enrollment*, and *placement activities*
- Equal access to the full range of vocational education programs available
- Provision of vocational education in the *least restrictive* environment
- Vocational planning for individuals with disabilities coordinated by representatives of *vocational education*, *special education*, and *state vocational rehabilitation agencies*
- Vocational education monitored for students with disabilities to ensure consistency with their IEP
- Notification to members of special populations and their parents at *least one year prior to eligibility, including information about specific courses, services, employment opportunities, and job placement*
- Assistance with transitional service requirements for individuals with disabilities
- Provision of supplementary services, including such things as curriculum modification, equipment modification, classroom modification, supportive personnel, and instructional aids and devices
- Provision of guidance, counseling, and career development activities by professionally trained counselors and teachers
- Provision of counseling and instructional services designed to *facilitate the transition from school to postschool employment and career opportunities.*

Source: From Carl D. Perkins Vocational and Applied Technology Education Act. (1990) Pub. L. No. 101–392, 104, Stat. 756.

mean that existing school-to-work systems will not be coordinated with vocational education systems. Tech-prep came out strong in the bill. There are longer reauthorization periods, and separate funding streams have been set up for tech-prep.

Critical Point In the 1990s, one of the goals of federal initiatives in transition was to reinforce special education's fit within the general education system.

The IDEA of 1990

IDEA 1990 provided the basic definition of transition services used in special education today. Under P.L. 101-476, the term "transition services" meant a coordinated set of activities for a student with a disability that is designed within an outcome-oriented process. The activities were to promote movement from school to postschool activities, including postsecondary education, vocational training, integrated employment (including supported employment), continuing and adult education, adult services, independent living, or community participation. Based on the individual student's needs, taking into account the student's preferences and interests, transition services included instruction, community experiences, the development of employment and other postschool adult living objectives at a minimum, and, when appropriate, acquisition of daily living skills and functional vocational evaluation. The definition of transition services and its essential elements from IDEA provided the framework for this book.

The essential elements start with needs and preferences and the outcome orientation to highlight the importance of involving the student and looking to the future and transition goals as the distinctive features of the high school transition. As the DCDT definition emphasizes, the high school transition is a status change, which is of extreme significance as a life stage—moving from school and being a student to becoming an adult with rights and responsibilities and the need to find one's place in the community and society. Transition also has unique coordination features with major linkages during the middle, high school, and post–high-school periods. Moreover, the essential elements and IDEA demand that the high school curriculum and transition services directly connect to the students' postschool transition goals, bringing the process back to the beginning.

Of great significance to IEP development is that, with high school students, the required outcome-oriented process is based on the student's expressed goals for postschool activities. IEPs for high school students are not bound anymore to a single schoolyear framework. Also, the coordinated activities and process for transition planning must address movement from school to postschool, specifically referencing the discussion to what students want in employment, college, services from community agencies, vocational training, continuing and adult education, independent living, and community participation. Movement toward postschool activities implies that the students' goals are addressed in a systematic way from year to year during the final years of formal secondary education.

In addressing the requirement of an outcome-oriented process, there are several general types of activities in developing and implementing IEPs that meet these requirements. In conducting transition planning in an outcome-oriented process directed by meaningful postsecondary goals, students should include such activities as career exploration and job shadowing that relate to their goals. As students progress toward completion of high school, postschool goals should become more clearly stated in the IEP. In promoting movement to postschool activities, IEPs should include referrals to adult service agencies 2 or more years before graduation while providing exposure to desired postschool settings (e.g., colleges, businesses, and other community settings).

In basing the coordinated activities on individual students' needs, preferences, and interests, personal future planning, student surveys, career inventories, and counseling, IEPs can have some positive impact on student empowerment in goal setting and involvement in the planning process. The coordinated set of activities intends to be inclusive of all available and possible activities that will address the students' goals. Instruction is based on classroom or community curriculum that is designed to teach skills relative to work, postsecondary education, independent living, and community participation. Community experiences should be provided to allow the student to try out or become established in work, education, independent living, and community participation roles. The development of employment and other postschool adult living objectives include activities and experiences to help the student develop or refine postschool goals. Activities within transition services can also include the acquisition of daily living skills and functional vocational evaluation.

Critical Point Transition, as defined by IDEA 1990, mandated the incorporation of transition services into the IEP. The focus, then, must be on students' postschool goals, with all activities in the IEP supporting the acquisition of those goals.

The IDEA of 1997

The IDEA of 1997 incorporated several broad policy shifts reflecting major changes in the way that persons with disabilities would receive an education (Stodden, 1998). One change from earlier special education legislation and IDEA of 1990 was that special education was to emphasize educational and transition results rather than the process, steps, and procedures to implement programs. This shift represented an increasing focus on what happens to students when they exit the educational system and their quality of life and success in postschool environments. Specifically, a quality-of-life approach was to be the framework in the design of individual transition services and to be the ultimate outcome educationally. It was hoped that IDEA 1997 would address the generally unfavorable outcomes for students documented in follow-up studies. The inclusion of related services indicated that they may be necessary to implement transition services and activities (e.g., transportation to a work experience; speech language and audiology, physical and occupational therapy, psychological and counseling services).

Another change from earlier legislation and the IDEA of 1997 was the emphasis on the general educational curriculum framework in assessment processes, planning, and instructional activities when compared to the past. With these amendments, special education needed to make larger efforts in ensuring participation of children with disabilities in statewide performance tests and accountability systems. Within the IEP, annual instructional goals were to be referenced to the general education curriculum. With a greater mixing of general and special education instruction, participation in inclusive programs and the variety of curricula available in regular education required participation of general and vocational education teachers in the IEP process. Finally, changes reflected more emphasis on how assessment and planning have an impact on the results of instruction. The improvement in results from adaptations and supports in the general education curriculum were to take precedence over past practices focusing on disability categories and remediation models.

With IDEA 1997, related services were also available so that students could participate in and benefit from education and what takes place in the classroom and community settings. Impairments or lack of technology to enhance learning environments could not be used as a reason for excluding students from the classes and curricula of their choice. Disability rights have to do with contributing to, participating in, and benefiting from activities in all aspects of community living, citizenship, and the pursuit of personal and career goals. Education is a basic right under the U.S. Constitution because without education one can neither fully exercise other rights nor realize the benefits of citizenship.

With IDEA 1997, there were a variety of wording changes to several major sections. Noteworthy in the purposes section (601) was the addition of "prepare them for employment and independence," an outcome orientation, to the assurance of FAPE. The limitations of FAPE for incarcerated youth with disabilities was spelled out for the first time. Participation in assessments (section 612), composition of state advisory panels, local funding for service coordination and interagency cooperation and personnel training, and transfer of rights to students at the age of majority represented some broad changes that were new to IDEA 1997. See Table 2–9 for a comparison of IDEA 1990 and 1997. Additionally, it was now stipulated that each child receiving specially designed instruction, assistive technology (device and/or service) would need to be considered.

Critical Point Legislative changes in IDEA 1997 changed the focus of special education from process and procedures to accountability in educational and transition postschool outcomes. Additionally, there is greater focus on the general education curriculum assessment processes and planning and instructional activities within the IEP.

TABLE 2–9
Comparison of the Transition Requirements of the IDEA of 1990 and 1997

Transition and the IDEA of 1990	Transition and the IDEA of 1997
Definition of Transition The term "transition services" means a coordinated set of activities for a student, designed within an outcome-oriented process, that promotes movement from school to post-school activities, including postsecondary education, vocational training, integrated employment (including supported employment), continuing an adult education, adult services, independent living, or community participation. The coordinated set of activities described in paragraph (a) of this section must be based on the student's needs, taking into account the student's preferences and interests, and shall include (i) instruction, (ii) community experiences, (iii) the development of employment and other post-school objectives, and (iv) when appropriate, acquistion of daily living skills and functional vocational evaluation (20 U.S.C. 1401 (19)).	**Definition of Transition** The term "transition services" means a coordinated set of activities for a student with a disability that (A) is designed within an outcome-oriented process, that promotes movement from school to post-school activities, including postsecondary education, vocational training, integrated employment (including supported employment), continuing and adult education, adult services, independent living, or community participation; (B) is based on the student's needs, taking into account the student's preferences and interests; (C) includes instruction, related services, community experiences, the development of employment and other post-school objectives, and, when appropriate, acquisition of daily living skills and functional vocational evaluation (Section 602).
Transition Statement and the IEP The term "individualized education program" means a written statement for each child with a disability . . . which statement shall include: (C) a statement of needed transition services for students beginning no later than age 16 and annually thereafter (and, when determined appropriate including, when appropriate, a statement of the interagency responsibilities or linkages (or both) before the student leaves the school setting (20 U.S.C. 1401 (2)).	**Transition Statement and the IEP** (vii)(I) beginning at age 14, and updated annually, a statement of the transition service needs of the child . . . that focuses on the child's courses of study (such as participation in advanced-placement courses or a vocational education program); (II) beginning at age 16 (or younger, if determined appropriate by the IEP Team), a statement of needed transition services for the child, including, when appropriate, a statement of the interagency responsibilities or any needed linkages; (III) beginning at least one year before the child reaches the age of majority under State law, a statement that the child has been informed of his or her rights under this title that will transfer to the child . . . on reaching the age of majority under 615 (m) Section 614(d).
Individualized Education Program a. Definition: (1) IEP is a written statement developed by a representative of LEA or IEU who is qualified to provide or supervise specialized instruction to meet the unique needs of children with disabilities, teacher, parents, and when appropriate the child;	**Individualized Education Programs** a. Contents of the IEP-current law with the following additional statements: (1) Present level of educational performance, including (a) how the child's disability affects involvement and progress in general curriculum; or,

(continued)

TABLE 2–9 *(continued)*

Transition and the IDEA of 1990	Transition and the IDEA of 1997
(2) IEP shall include statements of . . . (a) present levels of educational performance; (b) annual goals, including short-term objectives; (c) specific educational services to be provided and extent to which child will participate in regular educational programs; (d) needed transition services for students, beginning no later than age 16, including as appropriate interagency responsibilities or linkages; (e) projected "start" date and duration of service; and, (f) objective criteria and evaluation procedures, and schedule for determining at least annually whether objectives are being met. b. LEA or IEU must provide assurance that will establish or revise an IEP for each eligible child at the beginning of each school year, and will review and revise, if necessary, at least annually. (Section 602 (a)(20); 614 (a)(5)).	(b) for preschoolers, how disability affects participation in appropriate activities; (2) Special education & related services and supplementary aids & service to be provided and program modifications or supports provided for personnel . . . to advance appropriately toward attaining annual goals; (b) to be involved and progress in general curriculum and to participate in extracurricular and other nonacademic activities; explanation of extent to which child will not participate in regular class; (2) Any individual modifications needed for student to participate in State and district-wide assessments; and if child will not participate in general assessments, why assessment is not appropriate and how child will be assessed; (3) Frequency and location of services and modifications; (4) Beginning at age 14, transition service needs focusing on child's course of study; (5) Beginning at least one year before child reaches age of majority; information regarding rights transferred on reaching age of majority; and, (6) How child's progress toward annual goals will be measured, and how parents will be regularly informed of progress. b. IEP Team—current law with following additions: (1) At least one regular education teacher if child is or might be participating in regular education environment; (2) At least one special education teacher; (3) LEA representative knowledgeable about general curriculum and about availability of LEA resources; (4) Individual who can interpret evaluation results; and, (5) At parents' or LEA's discretion, other individuals with knowledge/expertise about the child, including related services personnel. (Section 614 (d)).

Transition and the IDEA of 1990	Transition and the IDEA of 1997
Participation in Assessments Not addressed in the IDEA of 1990	**Participation in Assessments** (A) IN GENERAL—Children with disabilities are in cluded in general State and district-wide assess ment programs, with appropriate accommodations where necessary. As appropriate the State or local education agency— (I) develops guidelines for the participation of chil dren with disabilities in alternate assessments for those children who cannot participate in State and district-wide assessment programs; and (ii) develops and, beginning not later than July 1, 2000, conducts those assessments (Section 612) (a) (17).
Transfer of Rights at the Age of Majority Not addressed in the IDEA of 1990	**Transfer of Rights at the Age of Majority** . . . when a child with a disability reaches the age of majority under State law (except for a child with a disability who has been determined to be in competent under State law)— (A) the public agency shall provide any notice required by this section to both the individual and the parents; (B) all other rights accorded to parents under this part transfer to the child; (C) the agency shall notify the individual and the parents of the transfer of rights . . . (2) . . . a child who has not been determined to be incompetent, but who is determined not to have the ability to provide informed consent with respect to the educational program of the child, the State shall establish procedures for appointing the parent of the child, or if the parent is not available, another appropriate individual, to represent the education interests of the child throughout the period of eligibility of the child under this part (Section 615).

Summary of Transition-Related Legislation of the 1990s

The 1990s were a period when transition was introduced to the general field of special education through legislation. National policy debates, federal initiatives, and intense interdisciplinary activity took place for the few years leading up to IDEA. At the same time, more attention was paid to the lack of participation in the economy and career satisfaction by adults with disabilities. Legislation emphasized employment, needs of the labor market, and efficiency issues in the delivery of services.

The 1990s also represented an era in which transition was defined and mandated in special education legislation. It was also a period of intense debate on disability policy. The IDEA of 1990 required a statement of needed transitions no later than age 16 and at 14 if appropriate. The basic requirements and definition of transition were set out in IDEA of 1990. Coordinated activities necessitated interdisciplinary services reflecting regular, vocational, and special education while closer connections between secondary and postschool education and services were needed. This coordination pointed toward more communication and cooperation among all segments of transition, disability, and general education systems up through college and other postsecondary education. An outcome-oriented process must be set up in which students set goals, and progress and movement toward those goals are monitored. IDEA of 1997 required looking at the entire period of education from middle school through postsecondary education and employment in order to establish a career path that is based on the student's needs, preferences, and interests. (see Table 2–10).

The Twenty-First Century

The IDEA of 1997 was the result of numerous factors requiring compromise by several different stakeholder groups. The issues needing to be negotiated ranged across a diverse set of topics as well. The primary changes in policy from 1990 were:

TABLE 2–10
Legislation of the 1990s

Legislation during the 1990s

- Established a policy framework for the rights movement;
- Refined and extended access, community participation, and quality-of-life perspectives;
- Established standards-based education and accountability for results for *all* students.

IDEA 1990: required that a transition plan be incorporated into the IEP by age 16.

ADA 1990: provided for equality and integration in all aspects of community life.

1990 Carl D. Perkins Amendments: focused on integrating vocational and academic skills training and eliminated special funding set-asides.

Rehabilitation Act Amendments of 1992: increased requirements and provisions for accessibilty to rehabilitation services and self-determination.

Educate America Act of 1994: Goals 2000: mandated education based on goals related to achieving student outcomes through reform of education.

School to Work Opportunity Act of 1994: provided for state laws for education for transition systems and schoolwide programs for preparation for a career.

Technology-Related Assistance Act of 1994: provided for statewide systems of assistive technology.

IDEA 1997: required a transition course of study by age 14 and access to general curriculum.

Rehabilitation Act Amendments of 1998: increased provision for employment and required coordination with one-stop employment and training center.

Workforce Investment Act of 1998: comprehensive job training that consolidates 45 previous federally funded programs.

1998 Carl D. Perkins Amendments: provided for tech-prep to be centerpiece of careeer/tech system—2 + 2 programs in technical fields bridging secondary and postsecondary programs.

1. Access, participation, and progress in the general curriculum so that special education would be in alignment with standards-based curriculum reform.
2. The corresponding requirement of the standards movement of participation in state- and district-wide proficiency tests.
3. Functional behavior analysis, manifest, and behavior management plans for special education student misconduct. If the behavior in question is considered part of the disability, then removal and placement into an alternative program (i.e., in-school suspension) would be considered a change in placement requiring an IEP team decision.
4. The requirement of transition service needs statement at age 14. This would provide identification of high school courses of study (e.g., career and technical education, or advanced academics) leading to postsecondary goals, which adds a middle school transition.

These policies have been in effect for some time, as of the writing of this book. The reauthorization of the Elementary and Secondary Education Act (ESEA—the federal law guiding general education and other compensatory programs) was issued as the No Child Left Behind Act (NCLB) of 2002. Because special education is considered part of general education (or at least must be consistent in its policies and procedures), changes in the ESEA have had a profound effect on the IDEA reauthorization, which is currently in progress.

Prior to the reauthorization of IDEA, President George W. Bush appointed a commission to collect information, hear testimony, and create a report on improving educational achievement for special education students. The Commission's final report contained three major recommendations. One, the report recommended a focus on results, not on process. This is very consistent with the NCLB Act, but is not clear what results are the important ones and what processes are essential (such as right to due process). The second recommendation calls for a model of prevention and not a model of failure. Exactly what resources can be garnered and at what levels to make the shift and still meet the needs of students needing special education services is unknown. Lastly, considering children with disabilities as general education, children first was the final recommendation. The precise meaning of this is not clear, but could mean that equality of education means getting an education the same as children without disabilities; or, if education is to move "forward," all children should be moving forward.

The President's Commission on Special Education (2002) made several recommendations within the transition area:

1. The commission transition recommendations appear to support the principles of an *outcome-oriented, coordinated services approach* to achieve postsecondary education and employement goals. There is an emphasis on *full participation* by parents and students and student self-advocacy and the need for a broad array of transition services (e.g., work experience, career exploration, etc).
2. The report called for improving cooperation and collaboration among agencies serving students during the transition period. Several specific recommendations on *interagency collaboration* dealt with more effective implementation of existing legislation for transition services and study and reporting of barriers to transition coordination (i.e., IDEA, Rehabilitation Act, Higher Education Act, Ticket to Work Act, and Workforce Investment Act).
3. The report argued for a uniform age for transition planning (not having different requirements for ages 14 and 16) at a point that makes sense educationally. *Transition*

planning should always be done with the student in which the student identifies (understands) the link between transition goals and IEP goals, objectives, and activities. Graduated diplomas were recommended that "more accurately represent levels of skill and ability."

With both the NCLB Act and IDEA, there continues to be an emphasis on outcomes (Turnbull, et. al., 2003). Content standards for academic areas and performance standards defining levels of proficiency accompany this outcomes focus. State and district assessments measure student performance in meeting the students' standards—student performance being the outcome (Thurlow, 2002). Interpretation and uses of student performance can have important consequences, including: (1) qualifications of the students who get promoted or graduate; (2) the teachers and principals who are promoted, receive raises, and keep their jobs; and, (3) the schools and districts that get funding and are accredited under NCLB Act.

Study Questions

1. What are the differences between disability services as an entitlement versus based on eligibility?
2. Why is disability considered a rights issue?
3. Why are disability and disability policy generally misunderstood by the general public?
4. Why are access and accommodation important in vocational and regular education and postsecondary education?
5. How would you characterize disability policy and services in the 1960s?
6. How would you characterize disability policy and services in the 1970s and 1980s?
7. How would you characterize disability policy and services in the 1990s?
8. What were the changes in emphasis in legislation among the 1960s and 1970s and 1980s?
9. What were the changes in emphasis in legislation between the 1970s, the 1980s, and the 1990s?
10. Why is general education and disability legislation other than special education (SPED) important to transition and IDEA requirements?
11. What were changes in transition with IDEA of 1990?
12. What were changes in transition from IDEA of 1990 to IDEA of 1997?

Websites

Facts about School-to-Work Transition
http://TheArc.org/faqs/transit.html

National Information Center for Children and Youth with Disabilities
http://www.nichy.org

National School-to-Work Office
http://www.stw.ed.gov/

National Transition Alliance for Youth with Disabilities
http://www.dssc.org/nta/html/index_2.htm

Office of Special Education Programs Outcome Data
http://www.ed.gov/pubs/OSEP95AnlRpt/ch3a.html

School-to-Work Site Devoted to Students with Disabilities
http://www.ici.coled.umn.edu/schooltowork/default.html

3

Transition Models and Promising Practices

Robert Baer

Robert W. Flexer

Rachel K. McMahan

LEARNING OBJECTIVES

The objectives of this chapter are:

1. Know the history of practices to help youth with disabilities in the transition to adulthood.
2. Understand how transition history shaped transition policy.
3. Identify problems in defining the "promising practice" in transition for youth with disabilities.
4. Know the nine promising practices in transition.

Introduction

Halpern reviewed the 25-year history of the transition initiative and concluded that transition programs were essentially "old wine in new bottles," although he noted that new transition models have matured over time (Halpern, 1992). Halpern also reported that the new transition approaches were variations of the "tried and true" approaches of the past and warned transition advocates to avoid the danger of discarding past research in favor of new and untried approaches marketed as a "silver bullet." This chapter will provide the reader with the history and social context of school-to-work interventions that have come to be regarded as promising practice in transition. The reader will note many parallels between these promising practices and the history of transition legislation presented in Chapter 2, which outlined the four essential elements of transition services as defined in the Individuals with Disabilities Education Acts (IDEA) of 1990 and 1997. To review, these essential elements required transition services to be: (a) based on students needs, taking into account their interests and preferences, (b) developed within an outcome-oriented process, (c) a coordinated set of activities, and (d) designed to promote movement from school to postschool settings. In this chapter, these four essential elements of transition will be used to organize and evaluate nine practices that have been considered the promising practices by transition policy makers, advocates, and researchers.

Early Transition Models

Precursors to transition models date back to the 1930s when educators began to realize that a strictly academic curriculum was not sufficient to meet the needs of students with mild mental retardation. During this period, educators (in urban areas in particular) advocated for a curriculum change, and some states developed functional curricula that reflected a life skills and a vocational approach to special education for secondary youth (Clark & Kolstoe, 1995; Neubert, 1997). Similarly, a functionally based job skills approach was implemented in the early workstudy programs in the late 1950s (e.g., Frey & Kolstoe, 1965). Studies spanning a 20-year period documented the effectiveness of this functional life skills approach for students with mild mental retardation (see Cobb, 1972). The success of these early functional life skills programs raised the possibility of serving greater numbers of students with mental retardation; and various models, approaches, and perspectives were proposed and implemented. These included general models that had applicability across disability groups and targeted models that focused on persons with specific disabilities. These early transition models focused heavily on promoting movement to postschool settings, but only lightly addressed the three other essential elements of transition in the IDEA.

Work–Study Programs

As vocational rehabilitation (VR) became a federal–state partnership (i.e., federal money being matched by state money), various populations of people with disabilities were identified as "in need" of rehabilitation and employment-related services, including students with mild mental retardation in high school. Consequently, the *work-study* model emerged in the late 1950s as a collaboration between public schools and local offices of state rehabilitation agencies (Halpern, 1992). These programs provided integrated academic, social, and vocational curriculum coupled with community work experiences to prepare youth with mild disabilities for productive community adjustment. Work-study was the first example of formal interagency cooperation between education and rehabilitation agencies. Halpern

(1992) observed that work-study programs had many elements in common with transition programs, including:

1. Community employment was legitimized as part of the curriculum and recognized for its educational value, and part-time work experiences were combined with part-time school, with school credits given for work experience.
2. Work-adjustment classes and functional academics supported these work experiences by helping students obtain work-related reading, writing, and mathematics skills.
3. The classroom teacher and the rehabilitation counselor worked as an interdisciplinary team with students being eligible for all services of vocational rehabilitation.
4. Local and state interagency agreements were used to combine school and vocational rehabilitation resources, and local VR offices sometimes had counselors who were assigned exclusively to serving schools.

Through work-study programs, thousands of students with mild mental retardation became clients of the state rehabilitation agency to help them make the transition to successful employment. Although it held great promise, the work-study cooperative arrangement with rehabilitation services lasted little more than a decade. Halpern (1992) suggested that the collaboration between schools and state rehabilitation programs was undermined by both funding mechanisms and the "similar benefits" requirement of the 1973 amendments to the Vocational Rehabilitation Act. The funding mechanism used to support work-study programs included the use of teachers' salaries as an "in-kind" match required to obtain federal dollars. Using teachers in this way, however, required that certified rehabilitation personnel supervise them, an arrangement that was not agreeable to many school principals. But the ultimate demise of rehabilitation-funded work-study programs was due in large part to the passage of Education of All Handicapped Children Act (P.L. 94-142) in 1975. This legislation was interpreted as passing the responsibility for work-study to schools as part of the requirement that they provide "free appropriate public education" (FAPE). This made it difficult for rehabilitation agencies to justify purchasing work-study services from schools since these services were now considered the schools' responsibility (Halpern, 1992).

After 1975, many schools continued to operate work-study programs by hiring specific staff persons to develop programs that were typically designed for students with learning disabilities, behavior disorders, and mild mental retardation. The survival of the work-study model may be attributed to the fact that research continued to find a relationship between work experiences in high school and better employment outcomes (Hasazi, Gordon, & Roe, 1985; Blackorby & Wagner, 1996). Researchers found that work-study programs helped students to learn the basic skills required in all work settings and to make contacts that led to employment after graduation (Blackorby & Wagner). They also found that these programs provided students with real-life experiences that made their education more relevant and contributed to their staying in school (Blackorby & Wagner). Work-study programs, therefore, strongly addressed the essential elements of promoting movement to postschool settings and creating a coordinated set of activities between rehabilitation and education, but focused less on the other two essential elements of transition.

Critical Point Work-study programs emerged during the 1960s to serve students with mild mental retardation in the high schools. State rehabilitation programs and the high schools worked collaboratively to provide employment-training experiences. Although these cooperative agreements no longer exist, most states have work-study programs to serve high school students with learning disabilities, emotional and behavioral disorders, and mild mental retardation.

Career Education Models

The career education initiative was designed to address all four of the essential elements of transition. Career education, a second precursor to transition, emerged in the 1970s and was established in 1977 with passage of the Career Education Implementation Incentive Act (P.L. 95-207). The career education model addresses all four of the essential elements of transition services. Halpern (1992) said this initiative could be seen as an extension of the earlier work-study movement, but noted that unlike work-study programs, career education programs included all ages and types of students and also focused on broader goals. In career education, added emphasis was placed on the elementary and middle schools as the foundations for the development of career maturity and life skills. Programs were developed to increase students' self-understanding, occupational awareness, and skills in the interpersonal, domestic, and community curricular domains. Although the Career Education Implementation Incentive Act expired in 1982, career education in special education continued to be an integral approach to transition.

Career education models tended to be: (a) systematic, (b) developmental, (c) focused on self-awareness, and (d) oriented to a wide range of occupations. In developing Life-Centered Career Education (LCCE), Brolin and Schatzman (1989) used career education approaches and applied them to students with disabilities. The LCCE delineated 22 major competencies that could be infused into primary, middle, and secondary curricula to address the major life domains of work, home, and academics (Brolin & Gysbers, 1979). Another career education model for students with disabilities was the School-Based Career Development and Transition Education Model, which focused on student skill and support needs in the areas of: (a) employment, (b) further education, (c) daily living, (d) leisure activities, (e) community participation, (f) health, (g) self-determination, (h) communication, and (i) interpersonal relationships (Clark, 1979).

Work experience is vital to career education programs.

For students with severe disabilities, career education approaches developed in the form of community-based instructional programs. These approaches were developed within the framework of the *criterion of ultimate function* (Brown et al., 1979). Under this approach, education and supports addressed the skills students needed to function as independently as possible in their future, as well as their present environments. Research indicated that students with severe disabilities who were instructed in community environments were much more likely to function in these environments as adults (Blackorby & Wagner, 1996).

Critical Point The career education programs differed from work-study programs in that they included students of all ages (with and without disabilities). The goals of this movement were broader than work-study because elementary and middle school students were targeted for career awareness and exploration.

Models of Transition in the 1980s

Will's Bridges Model

Follow-up studies through the 1970s documented that many students were experiencing poor outcomes after high school (Hasazi, et al., 1985). This, coupled with the expiration of the Career Education Act (P.L. 95-207), underscored the need for more effective approaches to direct youth with disabilities to meaningful postschool outcomes. In 1984, Madeleine Will, a conservative parent advocate and assistant secretary of the Office of Special Education and Rehabilitation Services (OSERS) within the U.S. Department of Education, proposed a model for transition from school to work that emphasized "bridges" or linkages between school and postschool environments (Will, 1983). With Will's position statement, transition services became a set of school activities that were recognized by the federal government.

Will's model focused on employment and conceptualized transition as three bridges to employment: (a) transition without special services (e.g., postsecondary education), (b) transition with time-limited services (e.g., vocational rehabilitation), and (c) transition with ongoing services (e.g., supported employment). This "bridges" concept of transition was narrower in focus than either the work-study or career education movements (Halpern, 1992). The basic concept behind this model was that secondary and postsecondary environments for youth with disabilities needed to be connected by services and supports that overlapped. Will's model addressed the fact that special educators and adult service providers often labored under differing assumptions about who was to be served, what types of services should be available, and who was responsible (DeStefano & Snauwaert, 1989) (see Figure 3–1). Edgar (1987) conducted research on postschool services and supports and found that they were lacking for the majority of students with disabilities after graduation. He argued that school systems would have to change to create the variety of services prescribed in Will's bridges model.

FIGURE 3–1
OSERS Transition Model, 1984

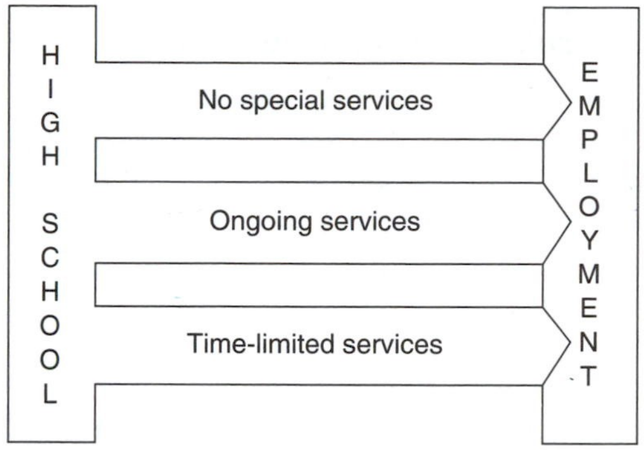

Source: From OSERS programming for the transition of youth with disabilities: Bridges from school to working life, by M. Will, 1984, U.S. Office of Education.

Will's model addressed two of transition's essential elements in focusing on coordinated activities and promoting movement to postschool settings. However, it was designed to promote movement only to employment settings, providing little guidance in terms of determining student needs, interests, and preferences and in terms of using an outcome-oriented process in planning.

Critical Point The "bridges" model emerged in a time when transition did not exist in special education. Will believed that in order for students to be successful upon graduation, they must be directly linked to adult service employment and training opportunities.

Halpern's Community Adjustment Model

Halpern's model challenged Will's total focus on employment. His research showed that employment was not the sole factor in quality of life, and that the residential and interpersonal domains must also be considered (Halpern, 1985). Halpern proposed that community adjustment should be the broader outcome toward which transition services should be directed. He developed a model that focused on three "pillars" of community adjustment: employment, residential environments, and social and interpersonal networks. According to Halpern (1985), transition programs were needed to build each of these pillars in order to affect the overall quality of life and community adjustment for students with disabilities (see Figure 3–2).

Like Will, Halpern addressed the bridges aspect of transition, relabeling what Will referred to as "no services" as "generic services." He noted that generic services (such as postsecondary education and employment training programs that are available to persons without disabilities) were also important to students with disabilities, and that a variety of specific social welfare and community programs were also available to

FIGURE 3–2
Halpern's Revised Transition Model, 1985

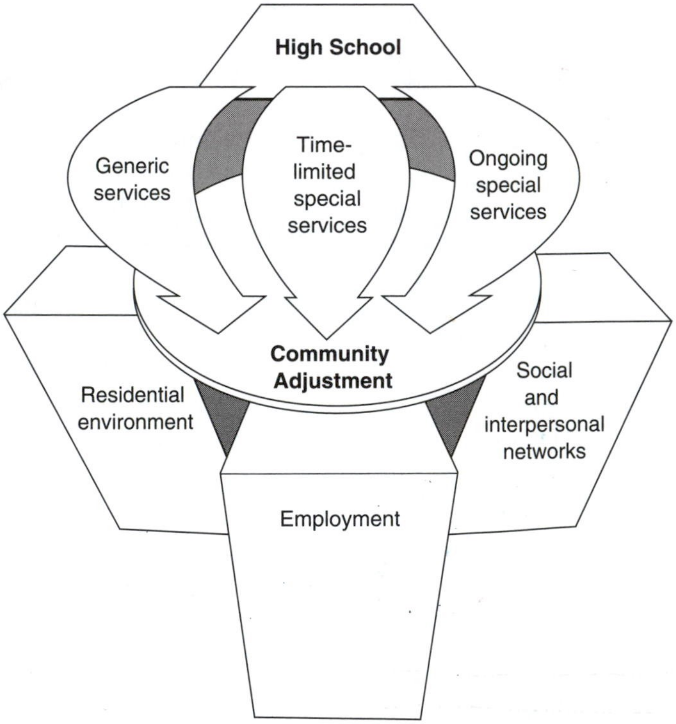

Source: From Transition: A look at the foundations, by A. S. Halpern, *Exceptional Children, 51*(6), 1985, p. 481. Copyright (1985) by the Council for Exceptional Children. Reprinted with permission.

them. Halpern (1985) suggested that although these generic services did not provide disability-specific services, they were often necessary to help students achieve quality of life after graduation. Halpern's model emphasized that transition was more than simply the process of the school's "handing off" the student. He argued that it was closer to a career education model that prepared and linked students to postsecondary environments (Halpern, 1992). Halpern's model essentially established the four essential elements of transition and served as the basis for defining transition services in the IDEA (Johnson & Rusch, 1993).

Critical Point Whereas the "bridges" model focused on employment, Halpern looked at the broader issue of "quality of life." He expanded Will's model to include residential environments and social and interpersonal networks, in addition to employment. Halpern believed that all three "pillars" must be addressed to enhance the student's overall community adjustment.

Work Preparation Models

Two specific transition approaches emerged during the "bridges" period, including (a) special needs vocational education and (b) community-based vocational training. Special needs vocational education grew out of the legislation that set aside funds to serve special populations (such as students with disabilities) and to serve primarily students with mild to moderate disabilities. Community-based vocational training and supported employment programs resulted from rehabilitation and ongoing support legislation to assist students with severe disabilities. Special needs vocational education was designed to provide adapted and modified occupational specific programs with supplemental services to serve students with mental retardation, learning disabilities, behavioral disorders, and sensory and physical impairments. Community-based vocational training (e.g., supported employment, on-the-job training services, and community-based instruction) was initiated while students were still in high school. Before graduation, students were placed in a permanent job with the plan that community agencies would take over support and case management services after the student graduated (Wehman, Kregel, & Barcus, 1985).

The special needs vocational model required that students with disabilities gain access to all forms of vocational education that were critical to their career path. Figure 3–3 shows one model for providing access to vocational and career education developed by the Ohio Department of Vocational Education. The first level of vocational access applied to students who needed no special accommodations. At the second level, students could be served in any regular vocational program with a standard curriculum with supports or tutoring. On the third level, access was obtained through a combination of supports and curriculum adaptation. Finally, the fourth level recognized that some students needed not only supports and curriculum adaptations, but also training in alternative or community-based sites, such as supported employment. In Ohio, two positions were created to support this continuum of vocational services. The Vocational Special Needs Coordinators were special educators who focused on curriculum adaptations and supports. The Job Training Coordinators (also known as Option 4 Coordinators) were special and vocational educators who developed and conducted training in community sites.

Wehman's community-based vocational training model (Wehman et al., 1985) focused on students that typically would have been served in Ohio under the Option 4 model. Wehman's model was an example of a work preparation model where special education, vocational education, and rehabilitation were linked to support transition for students with severe disabilities (see Figure 3–4). The principles of Wehman's model were:

1. Members of the multiple disciplines and service delivery systems must participate.
2. Parent involvement is essential.

FIGURE 3–3
A Continuum of Vocational Placement Options for Students with Disabilities

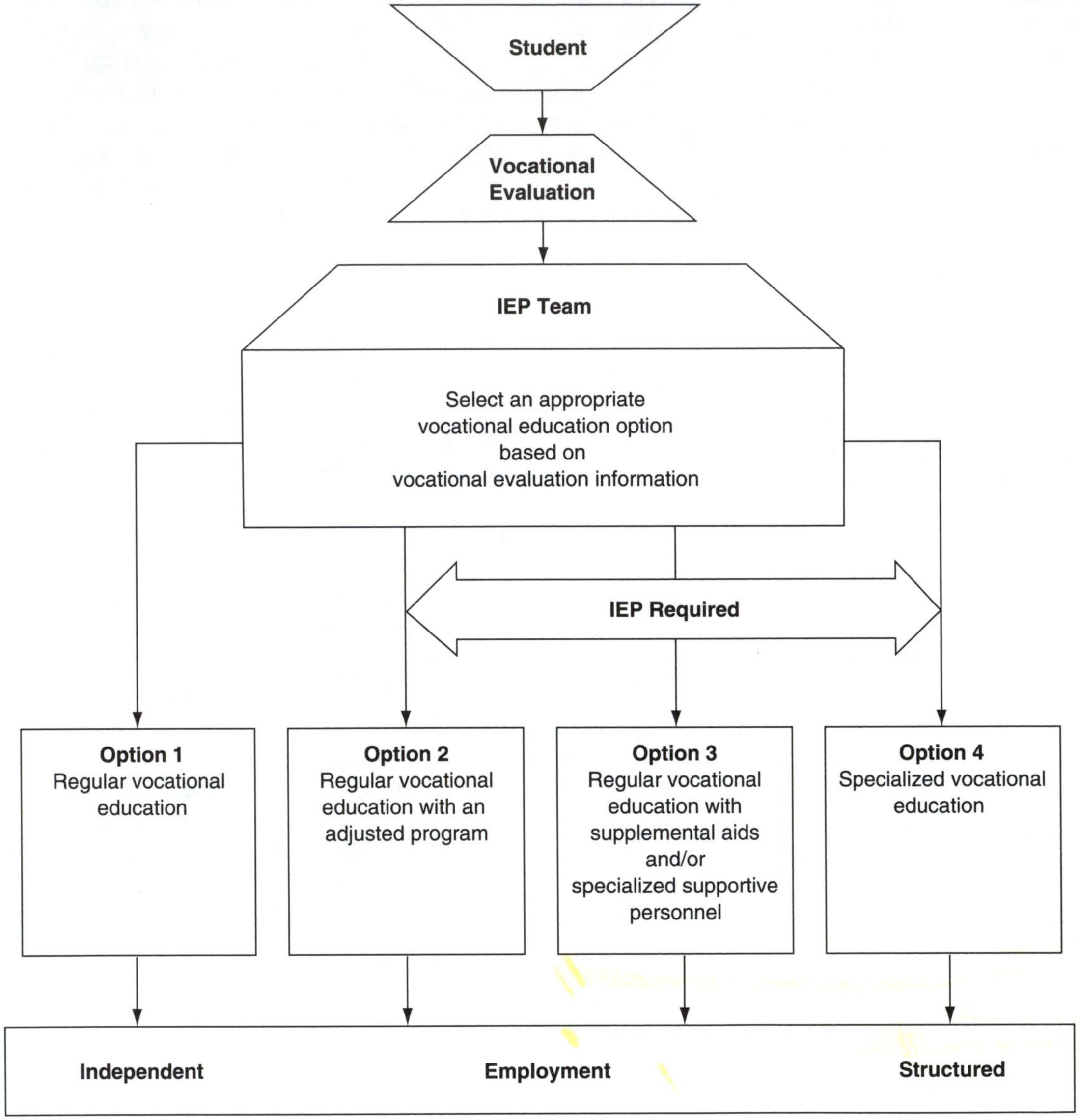

Source: From *Vocational Education for Ohio's Handicapped Children,* by Ohio Division of Career and Vocational Education, N.D.

FIGURE 3–4
Three-Stage Vocational Transition Model for Youth with Disabilities

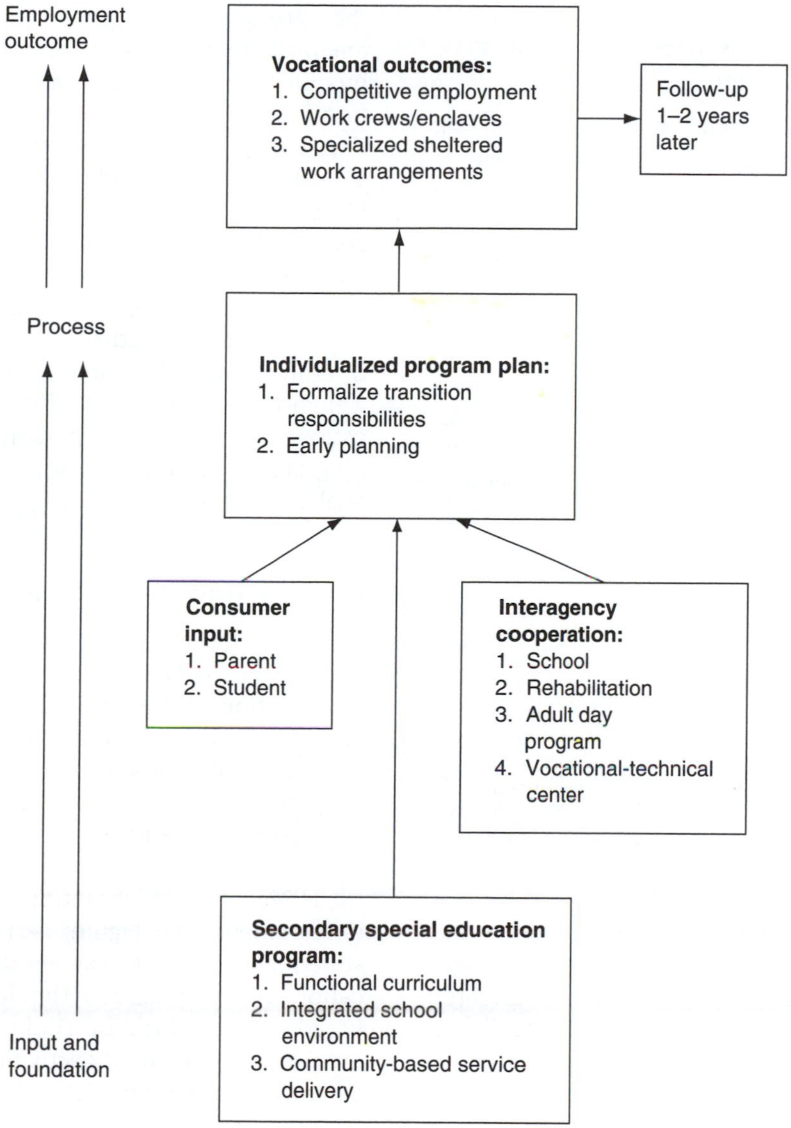

Source: From School to work: A vocational transition model, by P. Wehman, J. Kregel, & J. M. Barcus, *Exceptional Children, 52* (1), 1985, 28. Copyright (1985) by the Council for Exceptional Children. Reprinted with permission.

3. Vocational transition planning must occur well before 21 years of age.
4. The process must be planned and systematic.
5. The vocational service provided must be [of] a quality nature. (p. 26)

Wehman's model required movement through the three stages of school: (a) instruction, (b) planning for the transition process, and (c) placement into meaningful employment. The first stage was important because instruction in the public school should support the postschool goals of students with disabilities by including functional curriculum, integrated school environments, and community-based training. The second stage of Wehman's model focused on the planning process, where he argued that students and their families must be core members because they often take over the role of transition coordinators after graduation. Wehman also recognized that adult service providers must also be involved in the planning process to establish linkages and ensure that no interruption in critical services occurs. The final stage of Wehman's model was the vocational outcome of competitive employment, supported employment, or specialized sheltered work. Wehman and his colleagues stated that students should be placed before leaving the school environment in order to make a smooth transition to adulthood (Wehman et al., 1985).

The work preparation models, therefore, addressed transition's essential elements of promoting movement to postschool settings, need for coordinated activities, and outcome-oriented planning. For students with severe disabilities, these models also provided considerable power in addressing individual student needs.

Critical Point Transition work preparation models included the special needs vocational preparation model and community-based vocational training models. Wehman's model focused on students with severe disabilities who were in need of community-based vocational training.

Emerging Models in the 1990s

Johnson and Rusch (1993) noted that during the 1980s, several other transition models emerged that focused on transition more broadly than the bridges or even work preparation models. These included the career education models such as the life-centered career education model (Clark & Kolstoe, 1995), the life-planning program model (Schumaker, Hazel, & Deshler, 1985), the independent living and community adjustment model (Halpern, 1985), and person-centered planning models such as personal futures planning (Mount & Zwernick, 1988). The career education models were a natural extension of earlier career education movements, and person-centered planning models drew heavily on approaches from ecological psychology.

Kohler's Transition Education Model

Kohler (1998) offered an infusion-based career education model called a "transition perspective of education." Kohler's model emphasized the importance of a broad view of what education was, or should be, and delineated a taxonomy (or categories) of transition services, namely: (a) student-focused planning, (b) family involvement, (c) program structure and attributes, (d) interagency collaboration, and (e) student development (see Figure 3–5). This approach stated that transition was another facet of education and emphasized the importance of a broad view of education (Kohler, 1998). Kohler emphasized three major activities that provided a framework for her model:

- Postschool goals were identified based on student abilities, needs, interests, and preferences.
- Instructional activities and educational experiences were developed to prepare students for their postschool goals.

FIGURE 3–5
Emerging Model of Transition Practices

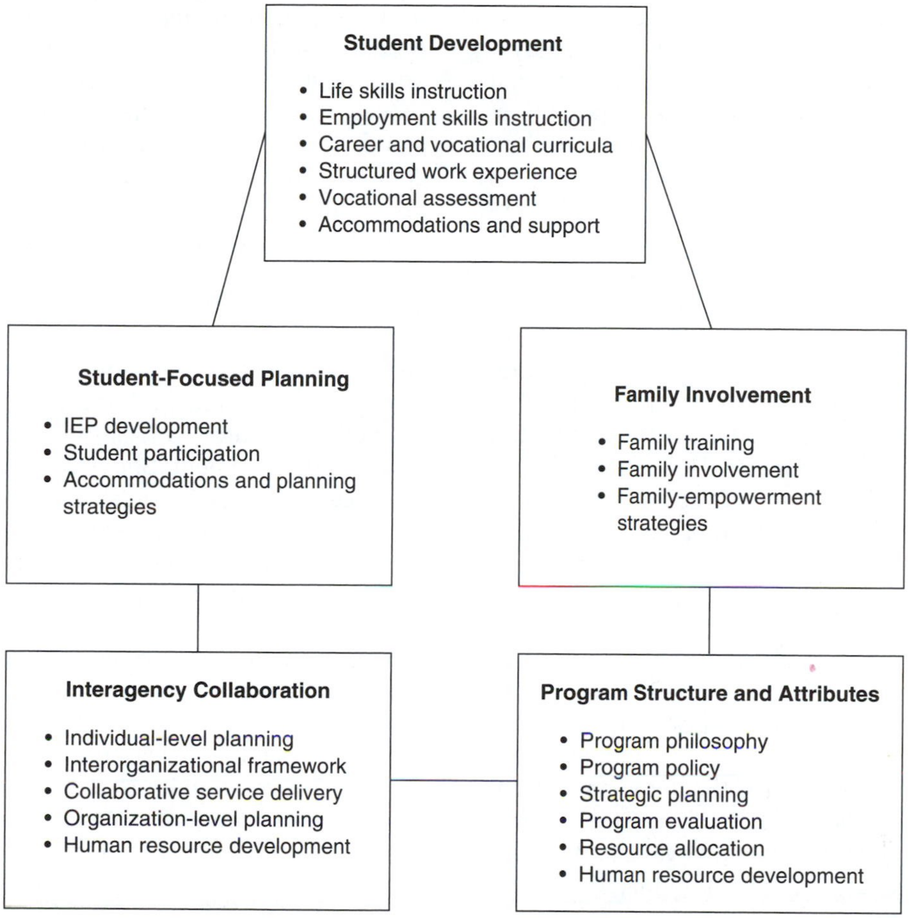

Source: From Implementing a transition perspective, by P. D. Kohler in *Beyond high school: Transition from school to work,* Rusch, F. R. & Chadsey, J. G. (Eds.), p. 208. Copyright 1998. Reprinted with permission of Wadsworth Publishing, a division of Thomson Learning. FAX 800-730-2215.

- A variety of individuals, including the student, worked together to identify and develop the goals and activities.

An outcome-oriented planning process and the related need to individualize curricula were at the core of Kohler's transition planning model that addressed all four essential elements of transition. The five categories of Kohler's model defined the transition perspective as tasks that must be performed in order to promote a transition-focused education. The first category, student-focused planning, included: (a) IEP development, (b) student participation, and (c) planning strategies. Student participation was inherently important in individualized planning because the IEP was seen as the main vehicle for determining appropriate goals, objectives, and services.

The second category, student development, included: (a) life skills instruction, (b) employability skills instruction, (c) career and vocational curricula, (d) structured work experiences, (e) assessment, and (f) support services. Kohler (1998) argued that schools must provide options in which students could learn the skills necessary to become successful participants of society. These options must also be provided in a number of different settings to enhance the generalization of skill acquisition. Kohler (1998) emphasized that schools should: (1) provide academic and vocational instruction through a number of curricular options, (2) identify and provide supports to facilitate learning by all students, (3) conduct and utilize assessment related to instructional planning, and (4) provide structured work experiences where needed.

Kohler's third category, interagency and interdisciplinary collaboration, encompassed the collaborative framework as well as collaborative service delivery. She noted that the lack of collaboration and cooperation often created barriers to programming for students with disabilities and suggested that interagency transition teams that included key stakeholders (e.g., parents, students, employers, and service providers) could often (1) eliminate service gaps, (2) avoid service duplication, (3) increase efficient use of resources, (4) reduce territorial issues, and (5) create holistic planning and service delivery. Kohler suggested that participants of interagency transition teams could increase their personal knowledge about other delivery systems, create contacts within those systems, and work collaboratively to work out resource problems through cooperative agreement. She stated that "establishing methods of communication among providers is a key practice in developing [a] collaborative framework" (Kohler, 1998, p. 186).

Kohler's fourth category (family involvement) included participation, empowerment, and training. She noted that students and their families were participating more in the planning process, but they continued to feel uncomfortable about becoming active participants in the process for several reasons: (a) problems understanding the assessments, (b) ambiguity and confusion of requirements and practices of professionals, (c) lack of familiarity with all professionals, (d) jargon, and (e) domination of meetings by professionals.

The final category of Kohler's taxonomy, program structures and attributes, looked at the service system and the corresponding philosophy, policies, planning procedures, evaluation methods, resource allocations, and human resource development. She noted that, in many instances, the way in which school and adult service delivery systems were managed was not conducive to implementing transition and suggested that educational programs must look at postschool goals and provide a variety of curricular options. Kohler recommended that school systems dedicated to improving transition services must have: (a) systematic community involvement in the development of educational options, (b) community-based learning opportunities, (c) systematic inclusion of students in the social life of the school, and (d) increased expectations related to skills, values, and outcomes for all students.

Critical Point Kohler's transition perspective of education described transition planning in a broad context and emphasized the need for outcome-oriented planning and individualization.

Career Pathways Models

Career pathways models strongly addressed the essential elements of promoting movement to postschool settings and of coordinated school and postschool activities. The essential element of outcome-oriented planning was addressed primarily by developing general courses of study (or career paths), while the determination of student needs, interests, and preferences was focused on determining the students postschool goals and the most effective path for reaching them.

Siegel (1998) proposed an infusion career pathways model of transition with a heavy emphasis on integrating transition with school-to-work programs. This approach was also designed to address all four of the essential elements of transition. Siegel suggested that the collective educational experiences of students should answer three basic questions:

1. Who am I?
2. What is my community?
3. How do I engage in a meaningful way?

In Siegel's multiple-option school-to-work system, students had the flexibility to adjust their individualized program as their interests and needs changed over time. Career pathways consisted of coursework clustered in five or six career areas (e.g., communication and arts, marketing and business, health occupations, and human services). A career application context for an entire curriculum allowed students to shape their course of study in a way that was meaningful to them. Siegel suggested that pathways serving all levels of students must be broadly defined (e.g., an introduction to health occupations course may serve future surgeons, students interested in obtaining a nursing license, or students who may be projecting career interests in volunteer or entry-level work in a hospital). Table 3–1 shows Siegel's intensity level model of transition. Students may use combinations of levels, going back and forth between levels depending on need.

Siegel's model of multiple options in a school-to-work system consisted of five levels of transition services. These levels differed by the intensity of student need and were not determined by the student's disability label but rather by his or her individualized need to participate with other students and to become independent after graduation. Siegel's levels were not to be used as a tracking system; rather, they were multiple options that students could utilize depending on their individual needs at a given time.

Gary Greene (2003) proposed a career pathways model based on the postschool outcomes being pursued by students. This model included four major pathways: (a) four-year college, (b) community college or technical school, (c) paid competitive employment, and (d) supported employment. For each pathway Greene suggested that the student's desired postschool environments should help determine the type of assessments used, the type of curriculum employed, the most effective instructional settings, and transition planning and related services concerns. Greene also emphasized that the provision of career pathways should not result in career tracking (Greene, 2003).

Promising Practices in Transition

In the 1980s, research on the promising practices in transition yielded approximately 12 criteria for model transition programs. However, Kohler (1993) found that only four promising practices were well supported by empirical research. These were parent involvement, vocational training, paid work, and social skills training. Research on demonstration projects also suggested areas of promising practice in transition. These included interagency cooperation, effective placement techniques, systems change strategies, coordinated needs assessment, outreach, and barrier resolution (Johnson & Rusch, 1993). Research on transition projects funded by OSERS suggested that vocational assessment, prevocational and vocational classes, on-campus work experience, placement, and orientation to adult agencies were typical approaches used by model transition programs (Heal, Copher, & Rusch, 1990). A meta-analysis of transition

TABLE 3–1
Siegel's Five Intensity Levels of Transition

Youth	Service Needs	STW System Should Provide . . .
Level 5: Low-achieving or with significant disabilities and/or at high risk of chronic unemployment/illegitimate career paths	Early intervention; immersion programs; intensive follow-along services	Middle school-initiated programs; job corps; conservation corps; supported employment; model community programs; new and experimental models under the Americorps and other initiatives
Level 4: Low to average achievers; at risk of dropping out, school failure, illegitimate career paths; need all of level 3, but with more intensity	Early interventions; supervised work-experience internships; paced training options; assistance with college education; intensive follow-along services	Intensified community-based agencies and programs; new and innovative school programs; new and innovative vocational rehabilitation and other state/regional programs
Level 3: Low to average achievers; some college-bound; lower socioeconomic status; need reasonable opportunities and career counseling; advocacy and some monitoring	Early interventions; monitored work-experience internships; paced training options; assistance with college education	Vocational/special education cooperatives, tech-prep; existing community-based agency programs; school district; Private Industry Council; adult education; community and technical colleges
Level 2: Average to high achievers; some college-bound; more from a low socioeconomic status; lack only reasonable job opportunities	Job and job-training opportunities; unsupervised work-experience internships; targeted college scholarships and options	Tech-prep, private sector; school district; academies; adult education, community college, college and university
Level 1: Average to high achievers; many college-bound; average to high SES; have social and professional connections	Existing college and employment options	Tech-prep, existing education and employment institutions

Source: From Foundations for a school-to-work system that serves all students by S. Siegel in *Beyond high school: Transition from school-to-work* by Rusch, F. R. and Chadsey, J. G., 1998, p. 154. Copyright 1998. Reprinted with permission of Wadsworth Publishing, a division of Thomson Learning. Fax 800-730-2215.

practices by Phelps and Hanley-Maxwell (1997) found two transition practices as universally supported by research: (a) functional curriculum and (b) school-supervised work experiences. In their study, vocational education was strongly, but not universally supported (Phelps & Hanley-Maxwell).

Baer, Simmons, and Flexer (1996) surveyed Ohio's special education supervisors and administrators, work-study coordinators, vocational special education coordinators, and school psychologists to determine statewide implementation of IDEA transition mandates and four other promising practices in transition. The promising practices were identified and recommended by the Ohio Futures Forum: Goal 4 Committee on Transition (Ohio Department of Education, 1990). These practices included:

(a) follow-up studies on students who have exited special education, (b) interagency transition teams, (c) parent/student involvement, and (d) employer involvement. The committee found that reported compliance with IDEA transition mandates was the highest in areas related to procedural issues. In addition, it was determined that policy compliance scores were higher for those respondents who reported the use of interagency transition teams.

Halloran (1993) and Wehman (1996) identified several issues that needed to be addressed to define the promising practices in transition. Browning (1997) summarized the identified issues in the form of the following questions:

1. To what extent is the field truly ready to shift from teacher/service provider control to that of student recipient control?
2. Should the type and range of opportunities for choice-making be contingent on the student's cognitive level?
3. Should all students be subjected to the same curriculum?
4. How much curriculum will need to be devoted to functional life skills?
5. Does career education aid or hinder mainstreaming or inclusive education efforts?
6. How can the system devote students' teen years helping them to prepare for successful postschool outcomes when, in fact, continued needed services are not readily available to them once they exit school?
7. Should all students be required to meet minimum competency standards to qualify for a high school diploma?
8. Are the current trends and issues in educational reform increasing the dropout rate?
9. How aligned are public policies truly when:
   a. Students cannot become employed after graduation without fear of losing important benefits?
   b. So many disincentives to work exist in federal programs?
   c. Disagreement exists between regular and special educators on the meaning of inclusion, "all means all," and benefits and costs to disabled and nondisabled students for either a separate system or a merged system?

Problems in Defining "Promising Practices" in Transition

As Paula Kohler noted, "transition planning means different things to different people" (Kohler, 1998, p. 180). Some saw transition narrowly as a process of linking traditional education, rehabilitation, and vocational services to promote postsecondary outcomes, whereas others saw it as fundamentally restructuring the core of education (Kohler; Stodden & Leake, 1994). Distilling principles of the promising practice from transition research can, therefore, be hampered by differing definitions of transition.

As Stodden and Leake (1994) noted, the process of importing and adapting the promising practices in transition may be more exportable than the practice itself. This is because unique cultural, community, policy, and individual characteristics define transition promising practice. Consequently, the transition promising practice must be adapted to (1) the policies governing education and rehabilitation, (2) the community and postsecondary environments that the student will be entering, and (3) the needs of the individual and the family.

In addition to problems of transition definition and local context, the definition of transition promising practices has been hampered by rapid changes in postsecondary environments, which have created new economic, independent living, and community involvement demands on individuals with disabilities and their families. For example, the growth in technology jobs created a greater demand for postsecondary education. As more students with disabilities entered postsecondary education, transition practices were needed to address the needs of increasing numbers of students with significant disabilities entering 2- and 4-year postsecondary education programs.

Education and rehabilitation policy impacted the definition of transition promising practice from another side. Special education, regular education, vocational education, and rehabilitation policy defined how transition was characterized and how it was to be researched. As IDEA required greater alignment with the general education curriculum, transition programs based on specialized curriculum were less likely considered as the promising practice. Stodden (1998) has characterized educational reform practices of the late 1990s and early 2000s as focused on downsizing, cost reduction, consolidation, use of generic services, and use of cost benefit analysis. Research and practice in transition will undoubtedly be impacted by these policy trends by: (a) becoming increasingly consolidated with regular, vocational, and classroom special education programs; (b) becoming more focused on outcomes rather than on processes; and (c) being less specialized to disability populations.

Policy related to transition can be seen as both a support and a barrier to student and family access to promising practices in transition (Stowitschek & Kelso, 1989). For example, IDEA's requirement that transition curriculum be aligned with the general education curriculum may have created problems for students needing access to life skills training and functional vocational education. Another policy barrier that has been perceived as limiting access to transition was the requirement for high-stakes graduation tests in many states. These tests were seen as forcing many secondary educators back toward remedial academics to such an extent that they had curtailed other transition activities.

The authors cannot fully answer these questions. As Kauffman (1999) noted, when selecting rules for any type of practice, professionals must consider: (a) the need for different rules for different purposes, since no single set of rules is a fully satisfactory guide to all aspects of living; (b) all rules are grounded in values and we must specify the values of our rules; (c) the origins and appropriate application of particular rules are often misunderstood; (d) personal experience and popularity of ideas are often unreliable guides to rule making; and (e) all truths are tentative. . . (p. 266).

Critical Point Defining promising practices in transition has been hampered by lack of consensus on the purpose of education and the definition of "transition services."

Although the authors are reluctant to endorse any transition practice as being good for all students all of the time, it is possible to establish some general principles that should be considered in the adoption of any transition practice. Wehman (1996) listed nine guiding principles for transition implementation:

1. Self-determination
2. Support focus
3. Family and student attitudes
4. Person-centered planning
5. Secondary curriculum reform
6. Inclusion
7. Career development
8. Longitudinal curriculum
9. Business connections and alliances

Kohler (1993) conducted a review of literature to determine what transition promising practices were well-supported by research. She determined that vocational training, parent involvement, interagency collaboration, and service delivery were strongly supported. She also found support for (a) social skills training, (b) paid work experience, (c) individualized transition planning, (d) transition and career planning within the IEP, (e) focus on integrated employment, and (f) functional community-referenced curricula.

Policy makers have also defined the transition promising practice in establishing goals for transition grant competitions. Rusch & Millar (1998) reported that since 1983, these goals have included:

1. Community-based training
2. Postsecondary education
3. Career placement
4. Vocational training
5. Job placement
6. Cooperative planning
7. Self-determination
8. Follow-up of graduates
9. Use of formal and informal supports
10. Student involvement
11. Assistive technology

A review of transition policy and research shows some areas of disagreement about promising practices in transition for youth with disabilities (Kohler, 1993; Phelps & Hanley-Maxwell, 1997). However, the following list provides some common themes and related concepts that have been identified by advocates, researchers, and policymakers as principles of the promising practice in transition:

1. Student self-determination (social skills training)
2. Ecological approaches (use of formal and informal supports)
3. Individualized backward planning
4. Service coordination (interagency collaboration)
5. Community experiences (paid work experiences)
6. Access and accommodation technologies (assistive technology)
7. Supports for postsecondary education (postsecondary education)
8. Systems change strategies (vocational career education, secondary curricular reform, and inclusion)
9. Family involvement (parent involvement)

Self-Determination

With the arrival of self-advocacy movements such as People First and the "independent living center movement" in the 1970s and 1980s, the discussion of disability began to focus on self-determination and individual fulfillment. This expanded the notion of quality of life that stressed individual decision making and control of programs that provided services to persons with disabilities. Starting with the nondiscrimination provisions of the Rehabilitation Act of 1973 (P.L. 93-112) and culminating in the Americans with Disabilities Act of 1990 (P.L. 101-336), advocates defined self-determination as a right rather than as something earned through rehabilitation. This movement was, in part, a response to the fact that social programs were not delivering on their promises to make persons with disabilities "ready" to assume valued adult roles and employment (e.g., segregated schools and sheltered workshops).

Student self-determination further emerged in the 1990s as a principle for effective transition programs. Studies showed that disability self-awareness was a characteristic of students who succeeded in college and who made good employees (Dalke, 1993). Studies also showed that students with disabilities and their family–friend networks played major roles in finding employment and achieving independence (Halpern, Doren, & Benz, 1993; Haring, Lovette, & Smith, 1990; Hasazi et al., 1985, Scuccimarra & Speece, 1990; SRI International, 1992). Across all these studies, less than 25% of the jobs that were found for students resulted from school/agency contacts or efforts.

While Nirje (1972) addressed self-determination in the context of normalization (as discussed in Chapter 1), "this seed did not blossom" (Browning, 1997, p. 44) until 1992 with the federal initiative on self-determination. The Office of Special Education and Rehabilitation Services (OSERS) funded projects across the country to develop self-determination assessments and curricula for students with disabilities. Some efforts dealt with the fundamental psychological and emotional development of students, whereas other curricula focused on specific programs for student involvement in setting goals and participating in their own IEPs. As Wehmeyer (1993) concluded, "students with disabilities must be allowed to assume greater control over and responsibility for educational and transition planning and to be involved in selecting and prioritizing goals and objectives" (p. 144). The self-determination movement required a tremendous shift in the way transition planning and services were delivered and was reflected in the IDEA of the 1997 requirement that students with disabilities should be informed that IDEA rights transfer to them upon reaching the age of majority.

Self-determination was defined from several perspectives, including empowerment, self-advocacy training, and sensitivity to values. Knowlton, Turnbull, Backus, and Turnbull (1988) asserted that "a fundamental aspect of the transition into adulthood involved increasing the exercise of direct consent in making decisions about one's own life within one's inherent capacities and means and consistent with one's values and preferences" (p. 61). Ward (1988) suggested that self-determination needed to address both individual attitudes and abilities. Woolcock, Stodden, and Bisconer (1992) noted that: "transition is a highly value-driven process in which the values of educational personnel are coordinated with the values of the student's family and, most importantly, the values of the student who is about to enter adulthood" (p. 236).

Wehmeyer, Agran, & Hughes (1998) provided a synthesized definition of "self-determination" as a combination of skills, knowledge, and beliefs that enabled a person to engage in goal-directed, self-regulated, autonomous behavior. An understanding of one's strengths and limitations, together with a belief in one's self as capable and effective, was seen as essential to self-determination. Wehmeyer (1998) suggested that acting from these skills and attitudes, individuals were able to take control of their lives and to assume the role of successful adults. Wehmeyer et al. (1998) further developed this concept by developing a secondary curriculum that considered student needs in the areas of (1) self-awareness, (2) decision making, (3) self-advocacy, and (4) goal expression and exploration.

Critical Point Wehmeyer defined self-determination as a combination of skills, knowledge, and beliefs that enable a person to engage in goal-directed, self-regulated, autonomous behavior. For people to be self-determined, they must understand their strengths and limitations and view themselves as individuals with the ability to take control of their lives and to assume adult roles. (Wehmeyer et al., 1998)

Practical Implications

Self-determination approaches represent promising practice in addressing two essential elements of transition. First, research indicates that these approaches are one of the promising ways of identifying students' needs, interests, and preferences because traditional approaches such as career interest inventories often lack validity for students' with disabilities (Menchetti & Piland, 1998). Additionally, self-determination approaches involve students in the outcome-oriented process of planning by helping them to become active participants in defining their goals and aspirations.

Whether students desire employment or postsecondary programs, high school programs should provide the knowledge, attitudes, and skills to perform, grow, and learn how to learn. Work and education beyond high school provide paths to the realization of personal goals relating to both starting out in life and changing the course in life. The purpose of transition planning is to help students get into postschool environments that are "right" for them and prepare them for success in their chosen endeavors. Students need to take control of their lives and the critical planning and preparation processes. Involvement in planning and preparation activities is time well spent because students enter life with those tools needed to get the best start possible.

In addition to self-determination approaches, students need information specific to their disability. To do this, they need related services providers (e.g., audiologists, physical therapists, psychologists) who can explain the impact of their disability. They also need to know about technology and strategies that provide both access to their strengths and a compensation for barriers presented by their disability. Some students may require psychology services to promote emotional growth and to help them come to terms with a psychiatric disability. Transition specialists therefore need to be sure that students understand their disability and needed accommodations by providing training and opportunities for self-determination and by involving related service providers in helping them understand their disability.

Ecological Approaches

Ecological approaches were designed to provide opportunities to learn and perform in a variety of environments. By assessing and training in settings with varying demands and requirements, students learned about their abilities, talents, and interests in real-life contexts. Ecological approaches placed student goals in relation to specific present and future environments. An ecological framework was found as crucial to: (a) focusing transition curriculum, (b) developing a variety of formal and informal (natural) supports, (c) providing experience in a variety of environments, and (d) instilling consistency in performance across varied environments (Syzmanski, 1994).

Lou Brown's model of curriculum development had a strong ecological focus and was the first model to make a significant departure from more clinically oriented developmental approaches (Snell, 1983). In his model, Brown defined four ecological domains: domestic, leisure-recreation, community, and vocational (Brown et al., 1979). He recommended that all four domains be assessed for individual students for both current and future natural environments. These four domains or environments could then be broken into subenvironments for each student through the development of an ecological inventory of where the student went each day and where he or she could go in the future. Each of these environments was then surveyed for relevant activities performed there. Activities were then broken down into teachable units and instructional programs were developed to teach the identified skills.

Ecological approaches to transition were supported by Halpern's model of transition. The initial "bridges to employment" model of transition, although defining it as concerned only with the ecological domain of employment, redefined the purpose of special education as an outcome rather than as an activity. In the intervening years since the bridges model of transition, the transition initiative became ecologically broader, both in scope and duration. The IDEA of 1990 (P.L. 101-476) identified adult living and community participation as transition outcomes, and the IDEA of 1997 (P.L. 105-17) extended transition to the student's course of study. Increasingly, ecological life-span approaches were being discussed as the most effective way to conceptualize transition (Syzmanski, 1994). The age at which transition services were initiated extended downward from age 16 and younger in 1990, to age 14 and younger in 1997. Repetto and Correa (1996) even proposed integrating the concepts of early childhood transition, middle school transition, secondary transition, and adult transition.

Critical Point An ecological approach to transition provided opportunities for students to learn in a variety of environments. By assessing and training in different environments, students were able to develop their abilities, talents, and interests in a real-life context.

Practical Implications

Ecological approaches represent a promising practice in developing a coordinated set of activities that promote movement to postschool environments. As Halpern (1985) noted, the three pillars of transition (i.e. residential, social/interpersonal, and employment) all contribute to quality-of-life and community adjustment. Indeed, residential, social/interpersonal, and employment issues impact on one another and often cannot be effectively dealt with in isolation.

An ecological perspective of transition services requires schools to become more involved with the current and future environments of students with disabilities. In this process, teachers and students learn (a) what is expected of them, (b) what goals they hope to achieve, (c) how they will negotiate their disability in the context of expectations, and (d) the process of planning. For many students with disabilities, this will require teachers to become much more involved with the student's communities and families. Teachers, parents, adult service providers, employers, and friends need to be enlisted to provide transition activities that support and assist students in learning skills, cultivating supports, and developing transition goals. Through ecological approaches, transition planning becomes more relevant and culturally sensitive and provides more individualized and focused options. This, in turn, enhances individual opportunities and the capacity of educators to help bring about meaningful outcomes.

Person-Centered and Backward Planning

Even for students with transition plans as part of their IEP, research showed very little orientation to postsecondary outcomes. Lombard, Hazelkorn, and Neubert (1992) examined IEP transition plans for students with disabilities and found that only 18% of students with learning disabilities, 17% of students with emotional disturbances, and 21% of students with mild mental retardation had any postschool transition goals. This research validated concerns expressed by Stowitschek and Kelso (1989), who warned that transition planners may fall into the same traps as IEP planners. These traps included irrelevant activities, low-quality goals, and infeasible strategies (Gallivan-Fenlon, 1994; Grigal, Test, Beattie, & Wood, 1997). In response to these problems, user-friendly planning approaches began to be put forward in the late 1980s. Although organized in many formats, these approaches would generally be referred to as person-centered planning (Pumpian, Fisher, Certo, & Smalley, 1992). Steere, Wood, Panscofar, and Butterworth (1990) described a model using "backward planning," where personal goals drove the development of the transition plan, which in turn drove annual goals in the IEP (see Figure 3–6).

Planning approaches emphasizing *person-centered planning* have been used primarily for individuals who have difficulty developing career goals due to the extent of their disability or due to a difficulty in expressing preferences (Menchetti & Piland, 1998). While typically used with students with severe disabilities, they may also benefit students with milder disabilities who have no postsecondary goals or direction to their IEPs (Rojewski, 1993). Person-centered

FIGURE 3–6
Relationship of Outcomes to Individualized Transition Plan and Individualized Education Program

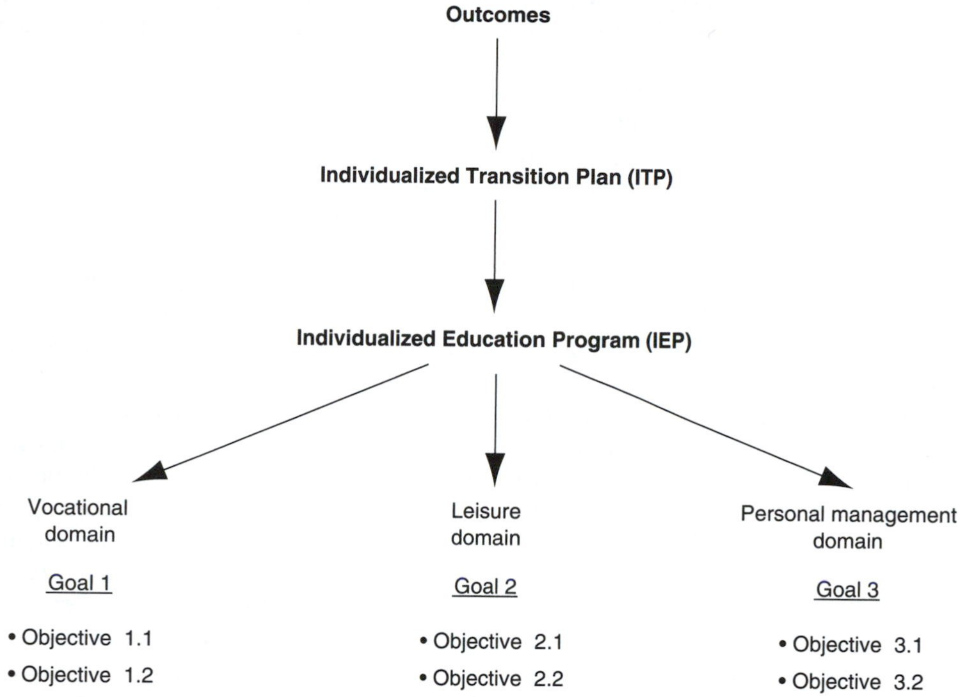

Source: From Outcome-based school-to-work transition planning for students with disabilities, by D. Steere, R. Wood, E. Panscofar, & J. Butterworth. *Career Development for Exceptional Individuals, 13* (1), 1990, p. 67. Copyright (1990) by The Council for Exceptional Children. Reprinted with permission.

planning approaches typically involve a facilitator, a recorder, the student, and various family, friends, classmates, and coworkers who work together to answer questions regarding the student's: (a) history, (b) dreams, (c) nightmares, (d) relationships, (e) abilities, and (f) plan of action.

Critical Point It is important that transition planning be postschool oriented because the students' individualized programming must reflect their preferences for adult life. The process of person-centered planning and backward planning involves helping students to focus on their future and working backward to ensure that their years of transition programming reflect their desires for adult life.

Practical Implications

Person-centered and backward planning approaches focused on postschool outcomes, therefore, represent promising practices in developing an outcome-oriented process, especially for students with more significant disabilities. These approaches also contribute to the development of a coordinated set of activities by involving both professional and natural supporters in the planning process. This is a difficult process since many students and families have only been able to focus on current issues and stressors. They often ask, "How will we get through the next year?" or "What seems to be the best available program in the high school program?" For professionals, this creates a strong incentive to deal with current issues. Consequently, extra effort and new ways of relating to education are required to carry out this planning successfully. Person-centered planning provides the greatest promise in this area.

Transition planning requires that the student and the transition team consider what the student wants to do after high school. The transition planning process must be very open, nonjudgmental, and student focused. Person-centered planning promotes this by addressing not only what outcomes the student desires (going to college or employment) but also why the student desires these outcomes. It helps the student to focus on the future and to delineate his or her strengths, talents, and interests. Person-centered planning also helps students to visualize themselves doing something meaningful and fulfilling. The principles of person-centered planning suggest that a plan about a person's future ecologies (e.g., work, education, living, and community environments) must begin with the person's understanding of him or herself and what the plan is to accomplish.

Brainstorming is a key beginning to help students describe themselves and their future. An outcome orientation requires communication and consensus. Team members must come to their own understanding of the students' goals and engage in collaboration and sharing, in order to achieve consensus. Because the team plan outlines how the students will pursue their goals, team members must be in communication about how (in what context) they know the students. These diverse and varied viewpoints are necessary to get a complete picture of the individuals. The brainstorming process should be positive; that is, it should focus on the students' desired future and capabilities. In subsequent steps and stages in the process, reality testing should take place as the students and team members gain greater understanding of the students' goals.

Service Coordination

The problem of integrating services in a transition system (that was really a nonsystem) was discussed by a number of authors. Ward and Halloran (1989) suggested that there was a serious discrepancy between the entitlement philosophy of school programs and the availability of adult services. Szymanski, Hanley-Maxwell, and Asselin (1990) noted that differences between state and local special education programs and state and local vocational rehabilitation programs were rooted in history, definitions of disability, funding differences, and differences in evaluation standards. Kochhar and Deschamps (1992) maintained that vocational and special education policies were often at odds in assuring services for learners with special needs, while Kortering and Edgar (1988) emphasized the need for more cooperation between special education and vocational rehabilitation. To address these needs, various individuals have recommended the development of school-interagency transition teams to develop channels of communication and to "iron out" policy differences (Everson, 1990; Heal, Gonzalez, Rusch, Copher, & DeStefano, 1990; Phelps & Maddy-Bernstein, 1992; Wehman, 1990; Wehman, Moon, Everson, Wood, & Barcus, 1988).

Many authors also saw the involvement of employers and other community members as an important function of transition teams. Wehman (1990) stated that a school–business linkage was a critical element of a successful transition program. Rhodes, Sandow, Mank, Buckley, and Albin (1991) indicated that activities involving employers would be the major source of growth for training in a future in which special education and adult service budgets were expected to show little or no growth. Rhodes et al. (1991) noted that employer resources were greater than those that were available through special education and rehabilitation. Phelps and Maddy-Bernstein (1992) found that the benefits of business–education partnerships included additional resources, employment opportunities, increased personal attention, improved facilities, and better teacher morale.

Critical Point Interagency transition teams should include students, parents, educators, adult service professionals, employers, and community service agencies. These teams can provide a point of reference for information sharing and problem solving among transition service providers.

Practical Implications

Effective service coordination represents a promising practice in developing a coordinated set of activities that promote movement to postschool environments. It is critical that person-centered and backward plans be followed up with effective service coordination. Otherwise, the best person-centered plans quickly fall apart (Holburn & Vietze, 2002). The practical implications of this research suggest that the student, family, and team members must understand generic and special services in the transition plan. Transition services provide direction and motivation for completion of goals on the IEP and heighten efforts and performance both in and out of the classroom. The focus in coordinating services is on identifying specific needs and finding the "right" service to meet the need. Students have the right to all available resources and must be knowledgeable and willing to work with team members in accessing needed services.

Once there is agreement on the student's future goals, professionals and the family must work in a united manner to support the student in taking action in reference to those goals. Coordination speaks to all parts of the transition plan to be consistent with each other. Regular and special education staff need to work in concert to help the student achieve his or her programs of choice. The regular education teacher has to be clear about what the student must achieve in the program, whereas the special educator must obtain necessary adaptations and accommodations and work with the regular teacher to use them. Educators must also communicate with representatives of postschool environments and adult service professionals to convey the direction of the students' transition plan and how the high school program connects to the students' desired postschool environments.

Community Experiences

Community experiences have been found to be critical for youth with disabilities in transition to postschool activities. Research showed a strong correlation between community experiences and postsecondary employment. SRI International (1990) determined that students who had work experience as part of a vocational education program experienced 13.9% better employment outcomes. Wehman (1990) also noted that community work experiences provided students with exposure to social situations and natural contingencies that are unavailable in the school setting. Unfortunately, researchers found that many special educators remained committed to training in classroom settings (Lynch & Beare, 1990; Stowitschek & Kelso, 1989). The IDEA mandate, therefore, was necessary to move many special educators away from an excessive focus on remedial programs and academics in the classroom to community-based approaches.

Community experiences were also seen as critical to the development of career maturity. Rojewski (1993) determined that students with disabilities were less able than typical students to identify career options due to limited experiences and opportunities. Additionally, Lombard et al.

Students learn about career interests through community experiences.

(1992) found that less than one-fifth of the transition-age students they surveyed had any postsecondary transition goals on the IEP. Having community experiences (e.g., career exploration, job shadowing, and community work experiences) was significantly related to career maturity and postschool outcomes for youth with disabilities (Gill & Edgar, 1990; Halpern et al., 1993; SRI International, 1990; Storey & Mank, 1989; Wehman, Kregel, & Seyfarth, 1985a). Community experiences were also identified as critical to the acquisition of daily living and social skills (Halpern, 1985; Johnson & Rusch, 1993).

Community experiences were generally supported as the promising practice in functional vocational assessment. Research indicates that standardized assessment procedures often lack validity for students with disabilities because they do not consider the effects of supports, technology, and training on student performance (Menchetti & Piland, 1998). Hagner and Dileo (1993) point out that standardized assessment procedures may have little use for students with severe disabilities since they lack the pressures, clues, sights, and sounds of the environments where students will have to perform. These researchers advocate strongly for the use of situational assessments, or authentic assessments that are conducted in the actual environments in which the student is expected to perform.

Critical Point Community experiences are important for students with disabilities because exposure to social situations and natural settings enhances the transition to postschool activities. Community experiences are critical to the acquisition of work skills and daily living and social skills.

Practical Implications

Community work experiences, therefore, represent a promising practice in promoting movement to postschool environments. They can also be used to determine student needs, interests, and preferences. It is critical, however, that community experiences be tied to the outcome-oriented process and to the course of study being pursued by the secondary student with a disability.

Students with disabilities need help in exploring work, living, and community participation opportunities in the community. This can include school-supervised work experiences. Vocational rehabilitation or the school can provide job coaches for students with intense support needs while they are still in high school. School districts may choose to hire their own job coaches or to use vocational rehabilitation services for eligible students. It is important to establish eligibility and to involve adult service providers in transition planning, if they are providing or paying for job coaches.

Community experiences should not be limited to work. Research indicates that students with disabilities may become more isolated as they grow older. Due to lack of mobility, income, and social networks, students with disabilities may have difficulty in making safe choices regarding friends and in meeting appropriate people to assure a good adult quality of life. Membership in religious/cultural affiliations (e.g., church or synagogue), clubs, and recreational programs provide natural and ongoing support networks that can assist persons with disabilities in maintaining friendships throughout their life.

Access and Accommodation Technologies and Related Services

Access and accommodation for youth with disabilities imply a particularly broad range of specialized assessment perspectives and related services (e.g., assistive technology, audiology, ophthalmology, orientation and mobility training, speech-language pathology, physical therapy, rehabilitation engineering, ergonometrics, and job carving) that may require interdisciplinary collaboration (Cavalier & Brown, 1998). For many students, access and accommodation technologies (including assistive technologies) will be inherent to students' basic ability to function, especially in terms of having basic receptive and expressive communication or access to school and natural environments and environmental control. Students with mild disabilities may depend on technology for performance in both school and transition activities. For example, Behrmann (1994) identified seven areas of assistive technology applications that may be essential in achieving positive educational, employment, and independent living outcomes. These include:

1. Organizational technologies (e.g., computers and electronic organizers)
2. Note-taking technologies (e.g., optical character recognition, microcassette recorders, videotapes and CDs, and voice synthesizers)
3. Writing assistance (e.g., grammar/spell-checkers, and macros)
4. Productivity (e.g., personal digital assistants, calculators, and software)
5. Access to reference materials (e.g., telecommunication networks and multimedia)
6. Cognitive assistance (e.g., computer tutorials and multimedia)
7. Materials modification (e.g., instructional software)

Access and accommodation also imply the ability to integrate individual assistive technologies with the many technologies used in employment, educational, and independent living environments. In the year 2000, it was estimated that 75% of jobs would involve the use of computers (Bender, Richmond, & Pinson-Millburn, 1985, cited in Sowers & Powers, 1995). These technologies include telephone technologies, environmental controls, robotics, constructed devices, and other adaptive strategies (Sowers & Powers, 1995).

Technology is also an important consideration in educational, independent living options, and community activities of persons with disabilities. There are many types of assistive technology devices that may be used in all or specific settings. However, it should be understood, when determining appropriate assistive technology (AT), that each situation is individualized and all relevant information must be obtained in order to decide what device or service will best meet an individual's needs (Esposito & Campbell, 1993; Inge & Shepherd, 1995). Some *common* examples of AT include electric page turners, books on tape, computers, switches, adapted keyboards, orthotics, FM systems, prosthetic devices, and augmentative communication devices. Independent living technology (commonly known as daily living aids, DLA) includes remote control units, talking alarm clocks, adapted silverware, and gripping cuffs for brooms and mops. Community participation and recreation technology includes adapted easels, beeper balls, adapted sport wheelchairs, bowling chutes and audio description services for theatrical events or museum tours (Bauder & Lewis, 2000).

Critical Point Access to services requires appropriate assessment and a selection of technologies to enhance the individual's participation in education, employment, and living environments.

Practical Implications

Technologies that accommodate student disabilities or that provide them access to education therefore represent a promising practice in promoting their movement to postsecondary environments. However, it is important that technology interventions be tied to students' needs, interests, and preferences so that they are used rather than discarded. It is also important for technologies to be developed as part of an outcome-oriented process and maintained as part of a coordinated set of activities.

Access and accommodation technology is a concept based on some basic principles and values that span the major legislation pertaining to transition in regular, vocational, and special education, and in rehabilitation. All the education-related acts emphasize the need to evaluate the individual's qualifications aside from disability in relation to the important performance requirements or outcomes for a given program. Access concerns meaningful participation in activities and programs. It is the central idea embedded in the requirements of the Americans with Disabilities Act (ADA) and section 504 of the Rehabilitation Act of 1973 and its amendments.

Determining student accommodations in career programs involves a process that requires communication among team members, who need to understand a student's future goals and the current year's transition activities. Interdisciplinary communication is needed whereby team members have gained knowledge of and respect for the expertise of one another. In the case of access to the general curriculum, the regular education teacher needs to articulate and make clear the curriculum and the classroom philosophy and environment. The special education teacher needs to provide a framework and rationale for individualization and curriculum adaptation within the framework of the regular classroom. The student in question must be able to explain his or her disability and how accommodations are designed to provide an opportunity to participate and complete requirements within the class. Thereby, the student gains an ability to play this role in the process because the process has provided the problem-solving experiences, framework, and practice in being adept at requesting. Requesting accommodations and explaining the reasons they are necessary in the context of one's disability is a lifelong skill that a student will use and is fundamental to education across the life span in the domain of self-understanding and communication.

Supports for Postsecondary Education

Postsecondary education has been a rapidly growing outcome of transition programs for youth with disabilities. There are four major types of postsecondary education: (1) vocational/technical schools, (2) community colleges (2-year), (3) liberal arts colleges, and (4) state universities. Students with disabilities have been attending postsecondary education programs and their numbers steadily grew through the 1990s. SRI International (1992) found that 4.2% of special education graduates enrolled in 4-year colleges 3 to 5 years after graduation, 15.9% enrolled in vocational schools, and 15.9% enrolled in 2-year colleges. In 1998, federal statistics indicated that 10.5% of all postsecondary students had disabilities, which represented a significant increase from 1988 (Gajar, 1998).

The research on the promising practice in helping youth with disabilities in the transition to postsecondary education has been limited to date. However, Dalke & Schmitt (1987) have laid down several principles for transition programs serving youth who are planning to enter postsecondary education (cited in Gajar, A. H., 1998). These included:

1. Provide educational experiences similar to those in postsecondary education.
2. Identify of strengths and needs relative to higher education settings.
3. Provide experiences where students with disabilities are outside their familiar support system of family, friends, and teachers.
4. Provide students the opportunity to practice self-advocacy.
5. Familiarize students with the physical environments of postsecondary education.
6. Familiarize students with campus and community supports available to student.
7. Provide [students] instruction related to study skills, time management, test taking, and library use.
8. Provide [students] direct instruction in academic areas such as reading, writing, and mathematics.
9. Provide staff with formal and informal performance data.

Critical Point Access to postsecondary environments requires careful coordination of transition services early in the student's secondary program.

Practical Implications

Supports for postsecondary education represents a growing promising practice for students with disabilities who are entering these postschool environments at unprecedented levels. These supports should be developed as part of an outcome-oriented process and should be coordinated with academic activities pursued by the student while in secondary education. Postsecondary options should be explored early in high school to select the proper coursework and to choose a postsecondary program that provides the services and supports that the student will need after graduation. Every postsecondary program has academic requirements that must be met, although state universities and community colleges often have remedial programs for students who have had difficulty in general areas of course work such as mathematics and English. The student should receive training in requesting the necessary accommodations and supports and should visit and/or audit classes from desired schools (Turner, 1996).

Family Involvement

McNair and Rusch (1991) noted that 63% of the parents they interviewed had a plan for what their child should be doing once school was completed. SRI International (1990) found that parents and guardians had definite expectations about postschool activities of youth with disabilities, with 84% expecting their children to be working in a paying job and 78% expecting them to live independently. SRI International (1992) determined that 55% of the youth with disabilities whom they surveyed continued to live with their parents 3 to 5 years after graduation and that parents found jobs for 11.3% of them 3 to 5 years after graduation. Scuccimarra and Speece (1990) and Halpern et al. (1993) found that parents located jobs for 25 to 30% of the graduating youth they surveyed. Students with disabilities reported that parents and families were their most important supporters (Morningstar, Turnbull, & Turnbull, 1996). Outcome studies showed that after graduation from high school, the family was often the only consistent source of support for students with disabilities (Hanley-Maxwell, Pogloff, & Whitney-Thomas, 1998).

Despite the important role parents played in shaping student career goals and outcomes, they continued to be largely under-involved in transition planning. McNair and Rusch (1991) found in a study involving 200 parents of transition-age students that nearly 70% desired involvement in transition programs, while only 30% experienced involvement. McNair and Rusch also found that parents wanted to be involved in finding job placements and community-living arrangements more often than they were afforded the opportunity to do so.

Parental lack of information was another concern in regard to student and parent self-determination. McDonnell, Wilcox, Boles, and Bellamy (1985) determined that only 32% of parents they surveyed reported receiving any information about adult services from school personnel. Carney and Orelove (1988) noted that parental influence toward community integration depended on parents' beliefs about both their children's needs and capabilities and the availability and appropriateness of community services. They found that parental ability to make informed decisions related to six factors:

1. Knowledge of the range of options
2. Ability to evaluate options
3. Knowledge of the child's skill
4. Knowledge of the child's preferences
5. Knowledge of how to get services
6. Knowledge of how to advocate for services that are not available

Critical Point Parents continue to be largely underinvolved in transition planning. Following graduation from high school, large numbers of students with disabilities continue to live with their parents, and parents are the ones who often find them jobs.

Practical Implications

Family involvement therefore represents promising practice in the area of determining student needs, interests, and preferences and in promoting movement to postschool settings, especially when families take over the role of transition coordination after the student exits school. Family involvement should be a major focus of the outcome-oriented process used in transition planning, and family activities may play an important part in developing a coordinated set of activities to support the student's postschool transition.

The promising practices relative to family involvement must address these issues. Hanley-Maxwell, Pogoloff, and Whitney-Thomas (1998) outline the four promising practices in family involvement relative to transition planning. These are:

1. Reciprocal family education
2. Cultural sensitivity
3. Personal futures planning
4. Longitudinal involvement in transition planning

Systems Change Strategies

Researchers, advocates, and policymakers have recognized systems change as an essential strategy for capacity building in transition (Halpern, Benz, & Lindstrom, 1992). It can take place from either the "bottom-up" or the "top down." Major systems change efforts in transition were funded by the federal government and OSERS, who awarded grants to states in order to create structural changes in the statewide system of transition services. Two basic objectives had to be met by states in order to receive these grants:

1. To increase the availability, access, and quality of transition assistance through the development and improvement of policies, procedures, systems, and other mechanisms for youth with disabilities and their families as those youth prepare for and enter adult life.

2. To create incentives for the implementation of lasting statewide system changes in the transition of students with disabilities to

postsecondary training, education, and employment. (Sec 626([e]) of IDEA)

The program was initiated in 1991; all states have received grants; and most have concluded their 5-year projects. The results of these projects highlighted what became the central themes of policy debates leading up to IDEA of 1997. Issues relating to how to serve all students in one overall system and at the same time to design individual programs are the challenges that emerged from system change efforts and found expression in IDEA of 1997.

During the same time period that state system issues were being addressed, local transition issues were also a focus of systems change efforts. Based on approaches developed through the discretionary programs funded by section 626 of the Education for All Handicapped Children EHCA Act amendments in 1983, community transition teams were developed as a mechanism to meet transition needs comprehensively on the local level. Members of core transition teams (Wehman et al., 1988) consisted of a full array of people who had a stake in outcomes for secondary students with disabilities. Local or community transition teams pooled their efforts in identifying and meeting needs at the local level. Inherent in the continued functioning and success of such teams were skills related to teamwork and group processes.

Practical Implications

Often, educational and adult services systems present transition barriers that cannot be addressed at the individual level. To deal with these issues, the transition services coordinator must be aware of exemplary transition practices and be able to mobilize transition stakeholders toward incorporating these practices in the school. The school-level interagency transition team can be an effective way of accomplishing this. Transition system issues that may be addressed by the schoolwide transition team include:

1. Development of accommodations and procedures for proficiency testing of students with disabilities
2. Adoption of person-centered IEP planning approaches
3. Definition of graduation requirements for students with severe disabilities
4. Cross-training for students, parents, and professionals
5. Strategies to empower youth with disabilities and their families
6. Development of linkages with providers of career opportunities for students with disabilities

The membership of the school-level interagency transition team should include all transition stakeholders, consisting of families, adult service providers, administrators, educators, employers, and transition specialists. The makeup of the team may vary from meeting to meeting depending on the students or on the issues to be discussed.

Conclusion

Transition policy and practice is a dynamic concept that has changed along with beliefs about promising practice in education. Its early roots can be traced to work-study and career education programs. It has evolved from the narrowly focused bridges model of Madeline Will (1983) to the broadly defined transition education models of Kohler (1998). Defining the best models and practice for transition remains difficult because of the interaction of local variables, including divergent concepts of education, different needs of individuals with disabilities, and the changing environments that youth with disabilities are likely to be entering in the future. The authors present factors where these transition practices are contingent upon postsecondary environments, transition and education policy, and individual needs, interests, and preferences. In the remainder of this book, the authors will provide the readers with a basic understanding of the aforementioned transition promising practices from these three perspectives. While transition concepts continue to evolve, some general principles of the transition promising practice are widely held by educators, advocates, and policymakers. The authors present nine practices for transition that have wide support from advocates, policymakers, and researchers.

Study Questions

1. What were the main models through the 1980s that form today's concept of transition?
2. What are the major differences between Will's and Halpern's models of transition?
3. Why did the work-study movement start and what services were added to improve transition?
4. Name two promising practices in transition and discuss how they are related to postsecondary outcomes, transition policy, and individual/family needs.
5. How is self-determination addressed in the IDEA of 1990 and 1997?
6. How is service coordination addressed in the IDEA of 1990 and 1997?
7. How is family involvement addressed in the IDEA of 1990 and 1997?
8. How does the IDEA of 1990 and 1997 support ecological approaches?
9. How has alignment of transition curriculum and regular education curriculum helped and hampered the implementation of career education approaches to transition?
10. How is the School to Work Opportunity Act similar to transition?

Websites

California School-to-Work Interagency Transition Partnership:
http://www.everhart.leon.k12.fl.us/bestprac.htm

Models of Transition for At-Risk Students:
http://www.ericfacility.net/ericdigests/ed321158.html

National Center to Improve Practice:
http://www.ncip.org

National Transition Alliance Model Programs:
http://www.dssc.org/

The Transition Center Project:
http://tac.elps.vt.edu/

4

Career Development: Theories for Transition Planning

Pamela Luft

Lynn C. Koch

LEARNING OBJECTIVES

The objectives of this chapter are:

1. Describe how using a broad definition of career development can lead to enhanced and consistent transition planning.
2. Describe at least two ways in which a disability can negatively impact each of the following: (a) school, (b) employment, and (c) career development outcomes.
3. Describe how each of these four theoretical categories define (a) the worker, (b) the work environment, and (c) career success: structural, developmental, work-adjustment, and learning theories.
4. Choose one of the four theories and use it to describe your own career development path.
5. Explain why one must be careful in applying any career theory and its related instruments and materials to persons with disabilities.
6. Describe the difference between constructs and processes in the ecological model, and then apply these to how this model can be

used across more than one career development theory.

7. Describe how to use the linking framework's questions for making intervention and strategy choices, and how these choices may utilize multiple theories.

Introduction: Why Is Career Development Theory Important?

As a member of a transition planning team, faced with turning everyday teenagers into successful adults, teachers and other professionals face a rather daunting task. So how does knowing about theories of career development truly help to accomplish this? The answer lies in using the theories in understanding and sorting through a range of programs and assessments and identifying those that are more likely to help this transitioning teenager/student. This chapter provides a general background by describing a number of the commonly used theories and their related materials. It ends by showing two models that try to integrate several career development theories so the team can be more effective in the decision-making processes. In addition, references to these theories will continue in Chapters 5, 6, and 7 via their application to assessments, curriculum planning programs, intervention strategies, and transition planning processes. Thus, these theories are providing introductory information for these later chapters, as well.

Why is career development important? In Chapter 3, several different models of transition, and how careers and work fit into these models were described. Some models have placed work in a central position (such as Will, 1983 and Wehman & Kregel, 1985). Many others view work as one aspect of a fulfilled adult life. There are similarities in how career development theories define work: some focus on it almost entirely, and others view it as one important role across a lifetime.

When a room full of successful people are asked how many of them had been fired from their first job (usually as teenagers), often a surprising number of hands are raised. So is this career development gone wrong? Are these people unusual because although they failed, they later become successful? And what about students with disabilities—what if they "fail" at an initial job? What if it's a job the team identified and tried to support? What is the team's responsibility in this case?

One important concept regarding success and failure experiences is a widespread belief that career development is a lifetime process of growth and experiences, both positive and negative, which results in some type of work—and this specific type of work may also change over the person's life (Beveridge, Craddock, Liesener, Stapleton, & Hershenson, 2002; Sitlington, Clark, & Kolstoe, 2000; Super, 1990). This perspective has some implications for the individualized education program and transition team, for although the team is responsible for school-based career and transition planning, the broader aspects of career development go far beyond *school-based learning*. The initial roots of career learning start back in infancy with the child's first attempts at understanding the world, and the process continues even into retirement (Brown & Brooks, 1984; Hershenson & Szymanski, 1992; Super, 1990). How career development fits with transition services provides a big piece of the puzzle in understanding a lifelong process of experiences and learning.

In terms of element #1 (of the essential elements from IDEA), essentially no career decision should be made that is not based on *the student's needs, interests, and preferences*. If the student isn't committed to a particular career path, the rest of the team is pretty much wasting its efforts. Fortunately, the past decade has seen dramatic improvements in devices offering increased accessibility options (i.e., greatly improved speech synthesis and voice recognition, real-time captioning, motorized and computerized wheelchairs, assistive communication devices, and so on). And the ADA insists that work positions (and also leisure and recreation opportunities) are made accessible and available to persons with disabilities. This means there are far more work and career options available, and are continuing to be so, making it more likely that a team can identify a realistic career within the student's interests and preferences. And although no one can guarantee that a certain career will be motivating and engaging for many years into adulthood, choosing a career that *does not* fit the student's preferences is almost a guarantee of failure.

The student's family and their support is also critical to building a career path that will be successful. *Family involvement* in career decision making and planning is critical; families are important sources of support as the student moves into the world of work and their support of career opportunities often is a critical factor to the success of the plan or program (Heal, Gonzalez, et al., 1990; Schalock, Wolzen, Ross, Elliot, Werbel, & Peterson, 1986; Siegel et al., 1993).

Element #2, an *outcome-oriented process*, aligns well with career development whose endpoint is lifelong work. Although only a few decades ago, most individuals with disabilities were not considered able to work (and you may find fellow team members of even parents who have similar beliefs), work is now a typical outcome of transition. This is important because work is an important adult activity in American society (Szymanski & Hershenson, 1998) and contributes to an improved *quality of life* (Halpern, Doren, & Benz, 1993). The IEP team will need to be flexible in addressing individually defined outcomes that may not include full-time paid work; however, some type of work, including part-time or volunteer, is a key goal of career development.

Because work and career often impact other aspects of transition planning, incorporating career development into a *coordinated set of activities*, element #3, makes sense. These activities may go well beyond the school grounds, especially as the student nears graduation. Therefore, developing linkages and cooperative agreements between the school and community agencies can provide important opportunities for additional career preparation options that may better fit with a student's preferences. For example, a student may have a strong interest in working with animals. If no specific school-based training is available in this field, the team will need to develop some training and work experiences with local pet groomers or pet stores in the area that extend school and classroom-based skill training into the community. This also means that *collaboration* among team members is critical to achieving maximal transition planning outcomes (Gajar, Goodman, & McAfee, 1993; Sitlington et al., 1997).

Transition element #4, to *promote movement to postsecondary environments*, is central to career development. In fact, as stated earlier, many researchers define career development as extending well beyond the team's focus on postschool planning and addressing long-term adult career and life roles (Beveridge et al., 2002; Sitlington, Clark, & Kolstoe, 2000; Super, 1990). Preparing for the student's postgraduation activities, then, becomes one phase of his or her lifelong plan.

In summary, career development is a core aspect of transition that contributes to the successful functioning of the four essential elements of exemplary planning practices. The theoretical framework that a team chooses to guide its career assessments and interventions will influence how each of these four transition elements and concepts is implemented.

In the Beginning: Setting the Stage for Theory Choice

At age 14, transition legislation mandates that the IEP team and student begin making career-based curricular decisions. In order to begin this decision-making process, it is important to develop a profile of the student's interests, needs, and preferences across academic, life skills, and career activities. From this, the team can then better choose a theoretical perspective that is likely to be both appropriate and useful. Only a few career theories have been developed in consideration of individuals with disabilities, so a few caveats are in order (Conte, 1983; Curnow, 1989; Szymanski, Hershenson, et al., 1996; Wolffe, 1997). When reviewing theories and their related instruments, the team members should always keep in mind that they may need to make modifications or accommodations.

Many researchers and practitioners believe that an individual's career development is a lifetime process that encompasses the growth and change process of childhood, the formal career education in school, and the maturational processes that continue throughout a person's working adulthood and into retirement (Brolin, 1997; Brown & Brooks, 1984; Clark & Kolstoe, 1995; Hoyt, 1977; Sitlington, Clark, & Kolstoe, 2000; Super, 1990). However, not all career development theories define career in this way. Some focus narrowly on a single career choice that occurs during young adulthood with individuals remaining in that career field throughout their work-life (Brown, 1996; Hershenson & Szymanski, 1992). Other theories take a broader perspective that include opportunities for many decisions that impact a career, such as marriage, children, community and leisure activities, and so on. These broader models tend to view choices as occurring throughout a lifetime, being made according to changing development and needs, and responding to influences from other life roles and responsibilities. These place career development within the fuller quality-of-life issues, with both as a lifelong process that grows and changes with one's life needs. Thus, initially, the choice of career perspective by the transition team will impact how they define quality of life and work when working with the student.

This book supports the lifelong career perspective because this allows students with disabilities the time, opportunities, and experiences they may need in order to fully develop, express, and refine their career and life interests (Clark & Kolstoe, 1995; Hershenson & Szymanski, 1992; Szymanski & Hershenson, 1998). In certain cases these students may not have had access to information or experiences to help them make choices and to learn about their needs, preferences, and abilities. A precept of this lifelong perspective is that a person's pursuit of a particular career path is the result of multiple life experiences and influences that begin in childhood, and continue throughout his or her working years and beyond (Hershenson & Szymanski, 1992; Super, 1990). These factors influence the choices made by students with disabilities and their families, in terms of how competent and capable they view themselves to be, what goals and options seem the most realistic, and what barriers or needs must be overcome in order to implement these choices and goals. The student's, the family's, and society's beliefs about these goals and their implementation will be important factors that impact the student's career development and adult roles (Garcia, 2002; Hershenson & Szymanski, 1992; Wolfe, Boone, & Barrera, 1997).

The lifelong perspective considers the growth and change of these multiple key people. For example, the family's beliefs about work and working, as well as the neighborhood's and the community's perceptions, all influence the child's later ideas regarding possible careers (Garcia, 2002; Wolfe, Boone, & Barrera, 1997). The school also transmits values about working and evaluates the child's successes and failures in comparison to other children (cf. Erikson's Stage IV: Industry vs. Inferiority and Stage V: Identify vs. Role Diffusion; Erikson, 1968). All of these fundamental experiences with values, attitudes, habits, human relationships, and learning about caring for oneself and one's belongings occur long before the initiation of formal programs that address work and possible career choices (Clark & Kolstoe, 1995).

Sometimes there is confusion between career development (and its related programs of career education) and vocational education. The latter is fairly narrowly focused on job preparation (Sitlington, Clark, & Kolstoe, 2000). These programs generally lead to certificates or licenses to perform some type of skilled work. High school programs often begin such training with completion occurring in postsecondary vocational or technical training facilities (2 + 2 programs; Sitlington et al., 2000). Again, these are narrowly defined programs leading to a specific type of job.

Critical Point Viewing career development from a life-span perspective allows students with disabilities multiple opportunities and extended time lines to move into fulfilling life and employment roles.

Once the team chooses a likely career theory to follow, the type of information collected about the student, and the timing and manner in which career decisions are made will vary. The types of curricular choices (scheduled to begin at age 14) and assessments that are used by the team can become highly prescribed, depending upon the theory. Each theory tends to focus on specific aspects of the career development process with tests, curricula, and career instruments reflecting this focus. Depending on the needs and preferences of the student, a particular theory may not match well and as a result, the related instruments and interventions will not always be successful or helpful (Savickas, 1996).

Critical Point Career development theory is an important element in the team's successful compliance with fulfilling transition planning requirements.

Career Experiences for Individuals with Disabilities

As we stated earlier, work is a highly valued activity in the American society. Not only does it provide economic support, but it also has a major impact on one's social status and self-image (Szymanski & Hershenson, 1998). Unfortunately, people with disabilities often encounter obstacles to participation in the workforce. Hagner Fesko, Cadigan, Kiernan, and Butterworth, (1996) point to several interrelated factors that contribute to the high unemployment rate among people with disabilities:

1. Discrimination in employment and other aspects of life
2. Practical difficulties (e.g., transportation, nontraditional means of communication) that make it difficult to seek employment
3. Limited access to the "hidden job market" and those jobs not advertised by formal means
4. Employer presumptions about the characteristics and abilities of qualified job applicants

As one can see, the barriers listed above have no relation to demonstrating important job skills and abilities. In fact, individuals with disabilities face a number of deterrents to their continued employment. Factors include physical and attitudinal barriers within the work site, health insurance issues (because of existing disabilities and possible medical conditions), and work disincentives inherent in the social security system (which provides important medical insurance coverage when one is *not* working, in addition to basic subsistence support). When these negatively impact the worker, they function as deterrents to career maintenance (strategies to keep and improve one's position) and to the person's motivation to stay in the current job choice.

Often transition teams do not adequately identify these less obvious employment problems and, therefore, do not fully address the multiple aspects transitioning students face in moving successfully into the world of work. Clearly, career development does not end with acquiring job skills. Teams who actively develop agency and employer linkages can use these relationships to address these frequent barriers to the student. Other sets of career obstacles are frequently encountered when individuals with disabilities attempt to maintain a certain position or even advance in their employment. In fact, employed people with disabilities often experience career patterns that consist primarily of movement from one entry-level job to another, with extended periods of unemployment in between jobs (Roessler & Bolton, 1985).

Critical Point Individuals with disabilities have high rates of unemployment and underemployment. The use of a career development theory that helps the team to identify and address important career issues will help to improve these employment statistics.

Teams are likely to face a number of challenges in terms of the students' own school and work outcomes, many of which are less positive than those of their peers. In a review of research on postschool outcomes, Hanley-Maxwell, Szymanski, and Owens-Johnson (1998) found that students with disabilities have the following difficulties:

1. Are at least twice as likely as their nondisabled peers to drop out of school
2. Experience difficulties in other areas of their lives such as independent living and relationship building
3. Are less likely than their nondisabled peers to participate in postsecondary educational programs
4. Receive low wages when they do obtain employment
5. Experience high rates of unemployment regardless of whether or not they graduate from high school

Many of the unique life experiences of people with disabilities are not taken into account in existing career theories. However, the team may be able to adapt a particular theory to a student if appropriate considerations and modifications are made. These things include the role of reasonable accommodations and newly developed technology, in addition to augmenting what may have been the student's prior limited work-related learning experiences. Adapting and modifying these kinds of factors can greatly expand a student's possible career options as well as the usefulness of many career theories (Szymanski & Hershenson, 1998). One caveat, however: If the team is using normed and standardized assessment instruments, then changes to any of the procedures (such as allowing more time or providing certain prompts) or to instrument items (such as providing alternative and more familiar choices that are within the student's experience) will, of course, impact their interpretation.

Clearly, the poor school outcomes and employment patterns are major career development concerns for students with disabilities and their teams (Conyers, Koch, & Szymanski, 1998; Luft & Koch, 1998). How aggressively and successfully a team intervenes for students who are at risk for or considering dropping out of high school or postsecondary training, who are facing non–performance-based job barriers, who are experiencing relationship or independent living problems, or who are encountering other barriers to their career and transition success, is critical to their escaping from these lifelong patterns.

Many issues are too complex to solve within the team or through school-based resources only. Again, linkages with other agencies are essential for supporting students—in creating a series of supports to ensure program completion or that independent living issues are resolved. For example, a student living in a group home may have significant limitations placed upon available working hours and transportation (because of the group home's schedules). Frequently, staff are not available (i.e., paid to be "on duty") during daytime hours to supervise or monitor residents or to provide support services. Other students, including those in urban settings, may begin living independently at age 16 or 17 but be too young to sign a lease, and their Supplemental Security Income (SSI) is insufficient to afford good housing. Resolving these types of situations will require all of the resources of the team and the linkages they are able to make.

These unduly negative employment and schooling outcomes underscore the team's need to incorporate career planning activities into the curricula of students with disabilities. This supports the Individuals with Disabilities Education Act's (IDEA) requirement that career planning begin at age 14. These career planning decisions should be based on a theory that aligns closely with the needs, interests, and preferences of the student. Because of the potential vastness of career development factors, each theory provides a unique description of the experiences, attitudes, values, and competencies that individuals need in order to choose and maintain a satisfying and optimal career path. This next section describes important career planning stages and an overview of major theory categories to help with theory choice.

Getting Started: Ensuring Appropriate Choices

From the earlier descriptions, the reader can see that students with disabilities are likely to experience highly unique career development paths. This may be due to their disabilities, the reaction of others to their disabilities, and the presence of physical or societal barriers that reduce their access and experiences with work-related activities (Clark & Kolstoe, 1995; Hershenson & Szymanski, 1992; Szymanski & Hershenson, 1998). The way that these affect the students' perceptions of their work abilities and limitations can have a dramatic impact on their vision of adulthood and life goals. Ultimately, this will influence all other aspects of transition planning.

Successful career development requires involvement of key individuals across all the student's school, work, training, and living environments. As the student moves into greater community participation and work, including and welcoming employers, supervisors, and coworkers into the team process can greatly contribute to his or her career success. The addition of these individuals and other community members who may form part of the family's informal support network can greatly increase information and developmental opportunities for the student, leading to more realistic outcome planning. The information that these individuals gain from attending team meetings will, in turn, assist the team in working better with the student. Including these individuals during school-based transition planning can greatly help the student and his or her family when it is time to leave school; they will still have a network of nonschool supports. These people can help with potential adult-based career development decisions and issues that arise and can help adult agency personnel to provide continuous, high-quality services. This collaborative network is the key to ensuring maximum success (Gajar, Goodman, & McAfee, 1993; Sitlington, Neubert, & Leconte, 1997).

Stages of Career Development

An important precept of career decision making is that individuals need opportunities to try various types of work in order to make a meaningful decision about their preferences. As stated earlier, the transition team may need to provide experiences the student did not have during his or her earlier development: through work exploration, work-study, or through summer and after-school work experiences. Some students may have had little or no exposure to work environments, typical work expectations, and "work culture"—sometimes as a result of physical or also attitudinal barriers related to their disability (Clark & Kolstoe, 1995; Hershenson & Szymanski, 1992). So, even before a team can help a student make curriculum and career development choices at age 14, they will need to ensure that students are exposed to a variety of work environments, work settings, and typical tasks within each.

How and when should a team begin building and scheduling these work experiences? The Life Centered Career Education (Brolin, 1995) suggests dividing career development into four stages:

1. Career awareness—beginning in elementary levels through an awareness of work and how the student will fit into a work-oriented society
2. Career exploration—an emphasis in middle school to help students explore their interests and abilities in relation to lifestyle and occupations, including hands-on and community experiences
3. Career preparation—emphasized in high school to provide career decision making and skill acquisition by identifying specific interests and aptitudes
4. Career assimilation—postschool movement into training and community settings in which students participate in satisfying avocational, family, and civic as well as paid employment activities

Because many students are 14 in the eighth grade and should begin focusing on specific career preparation by high school (ninth grade), the team will need to ensure that sufficient awareness or exploration activities occur early enough. This will help to ensure that valid career information is obtained and that tentative curriculum choices made at age 14 have some basis in the student's experience. Therefore, the student should have had some hands-on and community experiences prior to age 14, from which tentative career-based curriculum decisions can then be identified. These choices should move the student logically from exploration of interests and abilities into more specific ideas about career preparation by the end of high school.

During the student's career exploration and early training experiences, the team should gather data on the student's needs, interests, and preferences. However, many of the interest, aptitude, and readiness tools are based on theoretical frameworks (from theories of career development) that view the individual, the environment, and his or her interaction in specific ways (Savickas, 1996). The team may want to investigate assessments across several theoretical frameworks, particularly if the student hasn't yet demonstrated strong interests or abilities that can later help identify an appropriate theoretical approach. These data-gathering and assessment tools need to be individually determined—what may have worked well with one particular student may not be successful or yield particularly helpful information with another student (Savickas, 1996). In addition, because these assessment tools can sample only limited portions of work-related behaviors, the team must be aware that some results may be inaccurate representations of the student's true abilities in a *real* work environment. The team should always check each instrument's assumptions about prior experiences with work and work settings—questions that ask preferences between several work conditions or tasks *assume* that the person has experienced these or something similar.

Several of the newer assessment protocols may be helpful in collecting these data. For example, an ecological perspective may be helpful in initial information-gathering stages—this approach examines information across settings to identify patterns across many existing personality, work, and environment variables. This is helpful when no strong preferences have yet been identified (but also helpful to confirm existing preferences or to explore related career areas to a current preference). Regardless, the team needs to examine for accuracy the instruments and the student's results in order to develop an accurate transition profile (see Chapter 5 for more information). Situational assessments also are useful for observing the student in work or community environments in order to identify those settings in which he or she is most likely to be successful and satisfied (Sitlington, 1996). Career portfolios and other types of authentic assessments can be used with paper/pencil and interview assessments to confirm potential career and lifestyle preferences.

A typical combination of these assessments could include observational measures of the student's performance in various work sites, at home performing chores and self-care tasks, and in the community or at school interacting with friends and engaging in hobbies. Videotapes also are a powerful tool for documenting skills over a period of several years and across several settings and can be convincing evidence of ability when developed into a career portfolio for potential employers (cf. Sarkees-Wircenski & Wircenski, 1994). These authentic and ecological assessments respond also to needs and circumstances that change over time—as society becomes more accessible and supportive, as technologies open up new work positions, and as the student becomes more mature and self-aware. These assessments can also provide important data to support results from specific theoretically based assessments.

To summarize: The transition team faces choosing among an array of popular and well-recognized assessments and strategies, only some of which will best help any particular student. Identifying a reasonable "match" between the student's career needs and preferences and a particular theory's primary focus is important. But assessing a student's needs and preferences often presumes that he or she has had some initial career and work exposure and experience. Therefore, the team needs to ensure that these activities have occurred (and can use the four stages from Brolin, 1995, as a guideline). Broad ecological and situational assessments can help collect data to identify initial preferences. From here, team members will be better prepared to select from among the theories and, as a result, develop a career and transition plan more likely to be successful. This next section summarizes some of the major types of career theories.

Examining Types of Career Theory

A variety of career development theories have been generated in the past 70 years and, as a result, there is no universal, or all-encompassing perspective for teams to use. Career development has alternately been described as the "lifelong process of getting ready to choose, choosing, and typically continuing to make choices from occupations available in our society" (Brown & Brooks, 1984, p. ix) and, more broadly, as "the total constellation of psychological, sociological, educational, physical, economic, and chance factors that combine to shape the career of any given individual over the life span" (Herr & Cramer, 1992, p. 27). As stated earlier, we believe that a broad and lifelong definition is most supportive and inclusive of potentially unique life paths of individuals with disabilities.

This broad definition allows the transition team to examine all possible adult roles that a student may wish to undertake, and to use these multiple aspects as the basis for *comprehensive* transition plan development. The rationale is that life roles intersect and interact: What one does on the job, including time schedule and constraints, physical and mental energies expended, impacts how and when one assumes family roles, engages in recreation and leisure, and so on. The transition team should view career development as the combination of all life roles (e.g., child, student, volunteer, worker, person of leisure, parent, teacher, and mentor) that the student will assume at various stages of his or her life (Wolffe, 1997). Many of the career theories in this chapter have been adopted from career and vocational research done with people *without* disabilities. These theories bring insights about careers in general, but also can lead to difficulties, particularly in their lack of attention to the unique experiences and abilities of people with disabilities (Hershenson & Szymanski, 1992).

One reason for the lack of universality of career theories is a result of the variety of their originating disciplines: counseling, organizational psychology, sociology, and business, to name a few (Szymanski, Fernandez, Koch, & Merz, 1996). Several decades ago, theories were designed according to one of three perspectives: occupational choice, work adjustment, or career development. Hershenson and Szymanski define these three concepts as follows:

1. *Occupational choice*: the process of choosing a specific job at one point in time through examination of personal and situational factors that lead to a satisfactory job choice
2. *Work adjustment*: an examination of conditions within both the worker and the work environment that support a good "match" and including adjustment to the work process itself, independent of the occupation in which it is performed
3. *Career development*: an examination of lifelong work patterns and change, often examining the impact and interrelationships of multiple life roles with those of just being a worker, and the developmental processes of one's lifelong sequence of occupationally relevant choices and behaviors (Hershenson & Szymanski, 1992, p. 274)

From these definitions you can see that *occupational choice* assumes that a person will make one choice in early adulthood and remain in that career across his or her lifetime. *Work adjustment* focuses on the work processes and tasks themselves and is slightly broader in its examination of related variables in a particular work setting. *Career development* is the broadest in viewing multiple work and life factors.

These three perspectives have evolved with time. For example, until the last two decades or so, career counselors believed that young adults made one occupational choice prior to entering the workforce, which remained intact and unchanged throughout their lifetime. More recent studies of adult work patterns show that workers make multiple job changes during their work career, and this trend continues to grow. The Bureau of Labor Statistics (1992) reported that an employee typically remains with a particular employer for a median of 4.5 years.

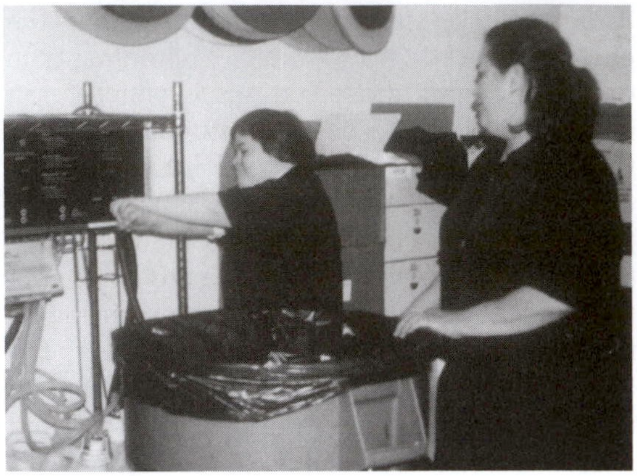

Career development is a lifelong process.

These three perspectives and their related theories have continued to be used and modified to accommodate differences in lifestyles, work, and social conditions. Theories of occupational choice now allow this choice to occur at various times during a person's working life. Work-adjustment theories also may be applied at multiple points in the person's life when a new career decision is imminent. Career development theories have worked to ensure inclusion of diverse populations of workers, including those with disabilities, and have also addressed areas of growth and change that occur throughout adulthood. The team should note how often and when "choice" and change opportunities are allowed.

Critical Point Individuals with disabilities should have the same opportunities to change jobs and careers that individuals without disabilities have.

Another aspect for teams to examine is how each theory defines "success." Some focus only on the individual or one particular aspect of the individual, others focus on the balance between the individual and the environment, and still others focus on multiple interrelationships and factors. Because of the vast array of possible factors, each theory prioritizes and organizes these elements into a particular framework, thereby leading to their differences (Savickas, 1996). New theories also have emerged as our understanding of careers and adulthood has evolved. As the team begins examining the various theories, they also will find that some have been used and tested for several decades and others are much newer with less data on their usage and outcomes. Newer theories also are less likely to have related assessment instruments and curricula and therefore may be of limited usefulness to the team.

The same opportunities for career choice and change have not always been applied to individuals with disabilities, and many career counselors still adhere to the "one choice" set of theories. Pumpian, Fisher, Certo, and Smalley (1997) believe that individuals with disabilities should be allowed the same opportunities for job change and should not be "stuck" in a position that they do not enjoy or do not find challenging and rewarding. This means that the transition team will need to allow for job movement and to view job changes and even negative work experiences (where the student is fired or asked to leave) as important learning opportunities. Ultimately, these experiences will lead to more realistic choices, to jobs that better fit a student's needs and abilities *and* will teach the student how to make these changes more positively.

Critical Point Each career development theory views the individual, the environment, and critical factors differently. "Successful" career development is also defined uniquely.

In describing these theories we will use an organizing system developed by Wolffe (1997), who categorizes theories as being either structural or developmental. In addition to these two major categories, this chapter will describe two work-adjustment theories and one social learning theory—four categories in all. Each of these has important applications for further understanding the multiplicity of influences regarding career development of students with disabilities (Szymanski, Hershenson, et al., 1996). Each theoretical description will include a specific theoretical example, and when available, will list some of the assessment and career instruments that have been developed to implement each theory.

CASE STUDY A

Miguel is a physically active, 18-year-old male who enjoys sports. He has a moderate cognitive delay and his teacher suspects he has some attention deficit/hyperactivity disorder (ADHD) (which has not been diagnosed) because he is highly distractible (noise, bright colors, movement or activity by others) with a short attention span (5–10 minutes is the usual maximum). He communicates best nonverbally with strangers, using appropriate gestures and vocal approximations, although he has approximately 50 spoken words that are understood by family and friends. He has a communication book but frequently forgets to use this when with others. He tends to be easily angered and frustrated when he is not understood. Miguel can be physically aggressive at times, although he is small and thin for his age with a low tolerance for lifting or strength-based activities. He has expressed strong interest in working in an autobody shop and is involved with activities with his family that support this interest (washing cars, observing others doing informal car repair, helping to bring tools).

How would you describe Miguel's career development in terms of Brolin's (1995) four stages described earlier? What are his strengths and needs in terms of these levels according to his age?

CASE STUDY B

Aza is a 15-year-old female who has just entered high school. She has a mild to moderate cognitive delay with moderate vision loss and moderate/severe bilateral hearing loss. She wears glasses but needs nonglare lighting and high-contrast work papers. Her hearing aids frequently bother her (she complains of headaches) but when she takes them out, she hears very few environmental sounds and no speech. She has a spoken functional vocabulary that is adequate for simple tasks and does not use sign language. Aza has not had any work exposure, partly because the prior principal believed she would be a safety hazard. Her parents have not asked her to do many chores up to this point although they recognize that she should start fairly soon. Given her disabilities they are not sure how to teach her to do these things.

How would you describe Aza's career development in terms of the four stages (see previous section, "Stages of Career Development")? What are her strengths and needs in terms of these levels for her age?

Examining for Fit: A Selection of Career Development Theories

What follows is a description of four types of theories: structural, developmental, work adjustment, and learning. Descriptions of each theory will end with a summary of its perspective on the student and work environment and with a list of related instruments. The information in this chapter provides a background in several theoretical models. A team's choice among career theories will influence the types of information the team gathers about a student and the related intervention strategies it uses to promote career development.

Structural Theories

These have been extremely popular at times, with elements still applied to many work and interpersonal situations today. Structural theories categorize characteristics and then emphasize the correspondence or "match" of these characteristics between individuals and work environments. From this correspondence, individuals make an appropriate *occupational choice* that will lead to a satisfactory career. Structural theories date back to the early 1900s, when Parsons introduced the idea of matching client attributes or traits (e.g., aptitudes, abilities, interests, and functional limitations) to workplace demands (Wolffe, 1997). Parson's model became known as the *trait-factor approach* and is still used extensively in modern career counseling and vocational rehabilitation practice (Szymanski, Hershenson, et al., 1996; Wolffe, 1997). His theory examines occupational choice and three variables that are key to this decision:

1. The individual—aptitudes, abilities, interests, ambitions, resources, and limitations
2. The occupation—requirements, conditions of success, advantages and disadvantages, compensations, opportunities, and prospects
3. The relationship between these two groups of factors (Brown & Brooks, 1996; Crites, 1981; Szymanski et al., 1996)

More recent theories have incorporated constructs of midlife career change as well as multiple and lifelong factors impacting individuals and society and have given increasing attention to diverse groups (Brown & Brooks, 1990). These theories view the individual and the environment as a set of variables that should be as similar to each other as possible, in order to ensure job success.

One of the most prominent and popular structural theorists today is John Holland. Holland's (1992) theory of career development categorizes "personality" into six general types, with six corresponding work environments: realistic, investigative, artistic, social, enterprising, and conventional (abbreviated as RIASEC). People are identified as having a dominant personality pattern, with their personalities typically fitting into two or three general types. Holland developed his career assessment instruments to use combinations of each person's three most dominant personality types to identify congruent occupational matches. These instruments include the *Self-Directed Search* (Holland, Fritzsche, & Powell, 1994) and the *Vocational Preference Inventory* (Holland, 1985b).

The team would typically use Holland's proposed three-step process: (1) to identify individual traits according to the six personality types, (2) to classify the work environment by type, and (3) to match the two sets of factors as a basis for establishing congruency and a series of success and satisfaction cycles (Brown, 1990; Spokane, 1996). Personalities and environments also vary along the attributes of consistency, differentiation, identification of strength, congruence, and consistency between the person and the environment. These, in combination with each person's six personality factors (RIASEC), were to match with work environment type in order to establish congruency and satisfaction.

Critical Point Structural theories emphasize matching characteristics of the worker and the work environment.

CASE STUDY

Examine the prior experiential and life opportunity histories of the two students. How would these contribute to, or serve as barriers to, using Parson's or Holland's career theory?

For Miguel: How would his distractibility and verbal skills impact his ability to take or respond to data collection or interviews to determine his personality type? What modifications or adaptations might the team need to make when evaluating results? Would this theory be more of a help or a hindrance in evaluating his strengths as well as his needs?

For Aza: How could her vision needs be accommodated in using instruments related to this theory? What modifications or adaptations might the team need to make when evaluating results? Would this theory be more of a help or a hindrance in evaluating her strengths and needs?

Developmental Theories

Developmental theories tend to divide the lifespan into stages that impact career development. They view occupational choice as *one* aspect of a person's work and adult life, in contrast to the structural theories that focus primarily on this choice. These theories examine career development as the result of lifelong work patterns, change, and the positive interrelationships between the elements of a person's life as leading to a fulfilling career and life. Super (1990) provides one of the more comprehensive and well-known theories. He defines occupational choice as the implementation of self-concepts that unfolds across a lifetime (Brown & Brooks, 1996; Super, Savickas, & Super, 1996). His life-span, life-space approach identifies multiple roles (e.g., child, student, person of leisure, citizen, worker, and homemaker) with five life stages across time (i.e., growth, exploration, establishment, maintenance, and disengagement). The time dimension uses a developmental perspective to address how people change and make transitions as they prepare for, engage in, and reflect upon their life roles, and particularly, their work role (Super et al., 1996; Super, 1984, 1990). Within each stage are recurring roles and transitions as the person changes and develops.

Super (1990) also investigated a number of career patterns in his research to define the concept of "career maturity." This comprises a person's ability to cope with environmental demands, which increases with experience. The complexity of the theory means that specifics regarding personality, life experiences, or the work environment is less specified than some theories, and in particular, structural theories. Since the 1970s, this theory increasingly has addressed changing women's roles, ethnicity, and cultural context (Szymanski, Hershenson et al., 1996). Super also has made a determined effort to make his theory applicable to persons with disabilities (Beveridge, Craddock, Liesener, Stapleton, & Hershenson, 2002; Super, 1957, 1990). Related instruments include the *Career Development Inventory* (Super, Thompson, Lindeman, Jordan, & Myers, 1981) and the *Career Maturity Index* (Super, 1974).

The team's perspective with this theory would view the student as a developing and changing person, who will assume multiple life roles, and move toward increasing career maturity. The description of life stages may be helpful in ensuring that the team considers a range of life roles and career experiences, including the need for coping skills in preparing for lifelong change. This complex and broad theory may help as a checklist to ensure that the variety of life and career experiences are included in planning the strategies and activities that best prepare the student for his or her preferred roles.

Critical Point Developmental theories emphasize multiple and changing roles that shape careers over time.

CASE STUDY

What characteristics of each of the two students might be the most important considerations in planning a career path using this theory? What type of experiences or interventions might be suggested using this approach?

For Miguel: How could this theory be sensitive to his special strengths as well as his needs? How could it help the team look at both his strengths as well as his needs? How might results need to be modified or accommodated?

For Aza: How could this theory be sensitive to her special strengths as well as her needs? What unique insights into her career development might it provide? How might results need to be modified or accommodated?

Work-Adjustment Theories

Minnesota Theory of Work Adjustment

The initial work for this theory was borne out of a focus on persons with disabilities through the Department of Vocational Rehabilitation and the University of Minnesota (Dawis & Lofquist, 1984; Hershenson & Szymanski, 1992). The framework consciously focused on work adjustment and work behavior rather than on occupational choice or career development models because of the authors' concerns with adequately addressing the unique life circumstances that disability status and experience often bring (Hershenson & Szymanski). This and other theories of work adjustment focus on the concept of identifying factors of the worker and the environment that lead to meeting the needs and requirements of each.

The Minnesota Theory of Work Adjustment identifies "work personality" as an important characteristic of each individual that contributes to work satisfaction. Work personality consists of needs that the worker expects to have fulfilled on the job and the specific abilities that he or she possesses to perform required duties. The workplace is analyzed in terms of its ability requirements (knowledge and skills needed by the worker) and its potential to meet a worker's needs. "Work adjustment" is defined as the interaction of two sets of indicators, "satisfaction" and "satisfactoriness." Satisfaction relates to the overall work conditions and to various aspects of the individual's work environment, as well as to the fulfillment of personal aspirations and expectations held by the worker. Satisfactoriness is indicated by the individual's ability to meet the work site's requirements including productivity, efficiency, and his or her evaluation by supervisors, coworkers, and the company (Dawis, 1996; Dawis & Lofquist, 1984; Lofquist & Dawis, 1969; Szymanski, Hershenson, et al., 1996). Job tenure is a product of satisfactoriness and satisfaction.

This theory views the person and the environment as each presenting factors that lead to satisfaction/satisfactoriness when matched. One benefit of using these theories is that several were developed specifically to address the unique needs and coping strategies of individuals with disabilities (Szymanski, Hershenson, Enright, & Ettinger, 1996). This theory may be most useful to a team who has a specific position planned for a student. This would assist the team in examining both the student's and the particular work settings' characteristics, and trying to make an optimal match. If a team had several work options, it could help identify the better match (and the team should also recognize that if none of these positions would fit these categories, then they should continue searching for positions). When minor mismatches occurred (major mismatches would tend to disqualify the position as a "match"), the team could explore ways to accommodate both the student and the environment and achieve better congruence.

CASE STUDY

How would the Minnesota Work Adjustment theory describe the work personality of each of the two students? What type of work-adjustment factors would be important considerations that could lead to satisfaction and satisfactoriness?

How could this theory be applied to Miguel or Aza? Are they ready for such a "match" to be made—why or why not? What unique insights might this theory provide to the team for each of the students?

Hershenson's Theory of Work Adjustment

This theory combines aspects of a career development and work adjustment approach through a focus on two essential elements that evolve over time: the *person* and the person's *environment* (Hershenson & Szymanski, 1992; Szymanski, Hershenson, et al., 1996). It tends to combine the two concepts of lifelong accumulation of roles and interrelated factors, with meeting mutual needs across the worker and the work environment. The personal aspects consist of three domains. *Work personality* is the first domain, consisting of a person's self-concept as a worker and his or her motivation for work. *Work competencies* is the second domain, consisting of work habits, physical and mental skills for work, and work-related interpersonal skills. *Appropriate and clear work goals* is the third domain. The interaction of these three personal domains and the work environment leads to work adjustment. *Work adjustment* also consists of three individual components: *task performance*, *work-role behavior*, and *work satisfaction*.

The three personal domains have certain dominant developmental time periods, although development continues throughout a person's career. Work personality develops primarily during preschool and is influenced by the family. *Work competencies* develop during school years and are modified in response to successes and failures in that environment. *Work goals* are influenced by peer and other reference groups as the individual prepares to leave school and to begin working. Successful work adjustment occurs when the various personal factors and the individual's work components interact successfully with the environment. Hershenson and colleagues have developed several self-rating and observer ratings to assist with evaluating these domains (Hershenson & Szymanski, 1992).

The team may also find this theory helpful in examining the student's "fit" with work and other life environments. More specifically, it can be helpful in developing intervention strategies that focus on specific aspects of the personal domain, and in particular, elements of the work personality, work competencies, or work goals that may need support. Changes in any of these three aspects would then be reexamined in terms of the student's anticipated career outcomes and also in terms of related impacts on his or her environments.

Critical Point Work adjustment theories emphasize the specific skills and attitudes possessed by workers and requirements of specific jobs.

CASE STUDY

Using Hershenson's Work Adjustment theory across the three personal domains, at which stage does each student, Miguel and Aza, appear to be primarily developing? How would you describe the work personality, work competencies, and work goals for each student? For which domain do you need more information? For which domain would you want to develop additional work-life experiences or opportunities?

Learning Theories

The application of Krumboltz's social learning theory to career decision making has its roots in the learning theories work of Bandura. Krumboltz incorporated elements of reinforcement theory, classical behaviorism, and cognitive information processing to Bandura's original theory (Mitchell & Krumboltz, 1996). The origins of a person's career choice are then explained as a result of learning; the career counselor then uses learning theory during counseling and for developing interventions (Mitchell & Krumboltz). Krumboltz's theory is less easily classified by major concept (i.e., occupational choice, career development, or work adjustment), but its lifelong growth and learning focus would make it more characteristic of a developmental category.

This theory proposes two major types of learning experiences that result in individually based behavioral and cognitive skills and preferences. *Instrumental learning experiences* occur when an individual is positively reinforced or punished for behaviors. For example, a student does poorly in assigned household chores and is scolded and reprimanded. *Associative learning experiences* occur when the individual associates some previously affectively neutral event or stimulus with an emotionally laden stimulus. The student is doing the laundry and opens the washer during its cycle and is sprayed with warm water. This recalls an episode when the student spilled boiling water on himself, and thereafter he is very afraid of doing the laundry.

These instrumental and associative learning experiences explain why people enter particular programs or occupations, why they express preferences, and why they may change their preferences at selected points in their lives. In addition, four categories of factors influence career decision-making paths, which include (1) genetic endowment and special abilities, (2) environmental conditions and events, (3) learning experiences, and (4) task approach skills. These four factors interact in infinite ways to form a set of beliefs (Mitchell & Krumboltz, 1996). Individuals develop self-observation generalizations that assess their own performances, and worldview generalizations that predict certain expectations about the future. Faulty self-observations, generalizations, or inaccurate interpretations of environmental conditions can lead to a variety of problems in career decision making.

This theory views the individual as changing through learning. This change is potentially continuous within an appropriate learning environment, with learning strategies used to modify and correct faulty perceptions. The career counselor promotes client learning by assuming roles of educator, coach, or mentor, depending on the situation (Mitchell & Krumboltz, 1996). Interventions may include expanding an individual's capabilities and interests beyond existing characteristics, preparing for changing work tasks, or empowering the individual to take action. This theory may be useful to the team because it emphasizes lifelong learning opportunities; current barriers are addressed through learning and these interventions will then, ultimately build successful career and transition outcomes.

CASE STUDY

How would you describe Miguel's work preference in terms of this learning theory? How would you describe Aza's lack of a preference? Do either one show some potentially faulty beliefs about themselves or the world? What types of interventions and experiences would this theory suggest as the next steps for the students?

To summarize, the theories just described represent a range of those presently used in transition, vocational rehabilitation, or career counseling services. Each theory views students and their interaction with the work and adult world somewhat uniquely. A challenge for the team will be in choosing a theory that best addresses an individual's needs, abilities, and preferences, particularly when the individual is still developing, growing, and changing across these dimensions. As several authors suggested, the team also needs to be careful that the theory adequately accommodates the student's disability.

But what if parts of several theories seem most appropriate, or no one specific theory seems to adequately address a student's unique career profile, even with accommodating unique life and disability experiences? The next section describes two models that attempt to comprehensively organize career theories for a more eclectic use of career theory and, ultimately, for better support of students' career development.

Eclectic Theory Use: Two Models for Applying Multiple Career Development Theories

As we have stated previously, although numerous career development theories have been formulated and tested over the years, many practitioners believe that no single theory, in and of itself, adequately explains the career development of people with (or even without) disabilities (Beveridge et al., 2002; Conte, 1983; Curnow, 1989; Wolffe, 1997). It is also difficult for practitioners to be widely read across multiple theories, and many of us tend to have our "favorites" (Savickas, 1996).

In addition, people with disabilities represent a large and heterogeneous group (Beveridge et al., 2002). The diversity of their abilities and limitations, as well as gender, cultural, and other unique factors, limits the degree to which any single theory is applicable or nonapplicable to their unique situations. As many of us with experience realize, the nature of a person's disability cannot reliably predict how that individual will proceed through the career development process: Two individuals with the same disability may have extremely different life experiences and career concerns.

Suppose that a team can find no one theory that best describes a particular student's career strengths and needs. How should the team proceed? Several individuals have described processes of using multiple models (Beveridge et al., 2002; Savickas, 1996; Szymanski, Fenandez, et al., 1996). We shall describe two of these that take differing approaches to integrate the theories. Both attempt to present a comprehensive theoretical framework whose use leads to specific interventions according to the unique issues of the individual.

Ecological Model of Career Development

Szymanski, Hershenson, et al. (1996) developed an ecological model that examines a vast array of variables across several career development theories. Their model proposes five groups of factors or *constructs*: individual, contextual, mediating, work

TABLE 4–1

Constructs and Processes for an Ecological Model

Five Constructs Used with the Ecological Model of Career Development
Individual factors: The physical and psychological attributes
Contextual factors: All external aspects of the individual's situation
Mediating factors: The individual, societal, and environmental beliefs
Work environment factors: All aspects of the work setting
Outcome factors: The results of the interaction of all the factors
The Six Interrelated Career Development Processes
Impacting the Ecological Model of Career Development
Congruence: The degree of match or mismatch between individuals and their environments.
Decision making: The process of exploring the various work alternatives available in society and then formulating a vocational decision.
Developmental processes: Systematic changes over time that are interwoven with characteristics and perceptions of the individual.
Socialization: The process whereby people learn various life roles (e.g., student, worker, parent, and citizen).
Allocation: The process whereby societal gatekeepers (i.e., parents, teachers, vocational counselors) channel people into or exclude them from specific life directions.
Chance: Unforeseen events that can have a strong impact on career development.

Source: The table is based on the work of Szymanski & Hershenson, 1998. Career development of people with disabilities: An ecological model in Szymanski, E. M. & Parker, R. M. (Eds.), *Work and disability: Issues and strategies in career development and job development* (pp. 79–126). Austin, TX: PRO-ED.

environment, and outcome. These constructs interact to enhance or impede the career development process of people with disabilities (Szymanski & Parker, 1996; Szymanski, Hershensen, et al., 1996). These constructs are described in Table 4–1.

This model is fairly complex: the five groups of constructs attempt to be a comprehensive list for planning across major life issues. Then the framework applies six processes that describe mechanisms by which the constructs can be addressed (see Table 4–1). Table 4–2 uses the constructs and processes to provide a series of related questions and suggested interventions. These include many of the unique characteristics and limitations that students with disabilities may face and interventions for each. Again, the model is complex but so also is planning across the complicated issues of achieving successful adulthood. These tables can serve as a type of checklist to help assure the transition team that major issues are not neglected.

Critical Point Career development is the result of multiple sets of factors (or constructs) and processes.

This ecological framework integrates a number of career theories, including those developed by Hershenson and Szymanski (1992), Holland (1992), Krumboltz (1988), Super (1990), and the Minnesota theory of work adjustment (Szymanski & Parker, 1996). The team may find this most useful in helping to track and account for the myriad of influencing factors and events that have impacted the student to date, and will continue to do so. The annual IEP review that uses the framework can help to identify any new factors that have arisen and how they impact other constructs in the model. This ecological framework has no specific tools of its own but can help the team identify specific need areas, and find a related assessment, then examine the various processes to find or craft some possible career interventions.

TABLE 4–2

Assessment Questions and Interventions for the Ecological Model of Career Development

Questions	Possible Interventions
Individual constructs	
What are current abilities, interests, and limitations?	Active involvement in self-assessment
How are these perceived by the student and family?	Career portfolio
What skills have been learned as a result of education or work experience?	Career portfolio
What values are considered important to career planning by the student and family?	Career portfolio
Has the student had sufficient experiences to foster interest development?	Volunteer and paid work experience
How can individual abilities be enhanced?	Skill training, further education, job supports
How can limitations be lessened?	Assistive technology, job accommodations
Contextual constructs	
How have family background and neighborhood influenced perception of opportunities and responsibilities?	Work role models, mentors, chores, and work experience
How has education facilitated or impeded realization of potential?	Remedial education
What are the financial incentives or disincentives perceived by the individual and family as associated with work?	Inclusion of financial considerations in career planning
Mediating constructs	
How does the student perceive her or his work-related abilities?	Career counseling, successful work experiences
What outcomes does the student expect from employment preparation or rehabilitation?	Appropriate role models, mentors
What are the student's abilities in career planning?	Career classes and workshops, career counseling
What are the student's and family's cultural and religious beliefs that relate to education and work?	Culturally sensitive career planning, culturally sensitive career portfolios
How has the student been impacted by discrimination or stereotypes?	Advocacy
Environmental constructs	
How physically accessible are various target environments?	Consultation on barrier removal, assistive technology, job accommodation, consideration of alternate environments
What is the organizational culture of the target work environment?	Job analysis, social skills training
Does the student understand how to get along in such a culture?	
How has the student gotten along in previous work or school environments?	Social skills training, job coaching
What are the tasks of the environment?	Job analysis
What are the reinforcements?	Job analysis, planning for career advancement

(*continued*)

TABLE 4–2 *(continued)*

Questions	Possible Interventions
Outcome constructs	
How well do the student's skills and behaviors meet the requirements of possible work environments?	Additional training, on-the-job training, social skills training
How well do the reinforcements of the work environment meet the student's needs?	Additional training for career advancement, possible job change
Has the student experienced job-related stress? How well is the student equipped to cope with job-related stress?	Stress reduction techniques, wellness planning, encouragement to use social support, leisure and lifestyle planning
Congruence or correspondence processes	
Is the student aware of potential job accommodations or assistive devices? Have other possibilities been considered?	Discussion and exploration of accommodation possibilities and assistive devices
Have ability scores been lowered by problems of construct validity?	Ecological or qualitative approaches to measurement
Is self-efficacy limiting the types of occupations considered?	Enrichment experiences, role models
Decision-making processes	
What are the cultural practices of the student and her or his family relating to decision making and independence?	Incorporate the student's culture into interventions and goals, involve family members, if appropriate
What are the student's skills and experiences related to making choices or decisions?	Decision-making training, assistance with identifying alternatives and making choices, multiple trial work experiences
Developmental processes	
Has disability limited developmental experiences?	Longitudinal approach to career planning, cautious approach to interpretation of interest measures
Has social skill development been limited?	Social skills training
Has work personality and work competency development been impeded?	Chores, supervised work experiences
Socialization processes	
How have socialization processes affected the student's current role and consideration of future roles?	Role models, psychoeducational interventions
Allocation processes	
Have opportunities been limited by gatekeeping functions in education, rehabilitation, or other service delivery systems?	Remedial education, mentoring, recruitment programs
Do the requirements or processes of current service delivery programs restrict options, create dependency, or otherwise disempower?	Program evaluation, capacity-building interventions

Questions	Possible Interventions
Chance processes	
Is the student prepared to recognize and capitalize on chance opportunities?	Career planning workshops, career portfolios

Source: Based on Career development of people with disabilities by E. M. Szymanski & D. B. Hershenson in Parker, R. M. & Szymanski, E. M. (Eds.), *Rehabilitation counseling: Basics and beyond* (pp. 366–369). Copyright (1998) by Pro-Ed. Reprinted with permission.

CASE STUDY

How would you describe Miguel's and Aza's primary strengths and primary needs in terms of the five constructs: individual, contextual, mediating, work environment, and outcome? In terms of their primary needs, which of the six developmental processes (congruence, decision making, development, socialization, allocation, or chance) would you choose for designing interventions, and why? Which interventions do you suggest as the most important at this point for each student?

Framework for Linking Career Theory and Practice

A second comprehensive career development framework was developed by Savickas (1996). Rather than beginning with a list of possible factors (constructs), he developed his framework based on six key questions. His rationale was to use the primary concerns he had faced as a practitioner and, for each, to provide several useful theories that could best meet the needs of individual clients. Rather than tending to use a few "favorite" theories for all clients, he found this framework helped him to remain focused on the individual's needs.

The framework serves as a problem-solving model to determine which of the theories and interventions best address the individual's issues. For example, a team may try to learn about a particular student's career needs by using several career assessments but may find that the results are not particularly helpful in planning for interventions. This linking framework presents a decision tree across the diverse repertoire of possible intervention techniques and theories. Savickas (1996) poses six types of career questions based on the individual's needs that correspond to specific interventions and career services that best meet these needs. These are shown in Table 4–3.

The first step in using this framework is to assess the student's career issues according to these six questions. This is an important step because the nature of the student's issue should be determined prior to beginning a series of assessments and measurements (Savickas, 1996). These instruments are then more useful for collecting detailed information about the issue, from which the team can design an intervention and transition plan. Savickas begins first with defining the nature of the problem before moving to interventions.

Critical Point Not all career assessments address all issues, so it is important for the team to have a general understanding of the student's career issues first in order to choose the assessments and interventions that are most appropriate.

The team or career counselor would first make a determination about whether or not the student is ready for vocational guidance and has a clear vocational identity. For example, if the

TABLE 4–3
Framework for Linking Career Theory and Practice

Question	Career Intervention Problem	Career Service
Who am I?	Career self	Career counseling
How can work help me to grow as a person?	Drives (fulfilling needs)	Career therapy
How do I shape my career?	Career attitudes, beliefs, and competencies	Career education
What shall I choose?	Vocational self	Vocational guidance
How can I do better?	Occupational stimuli and vocational responses	Position coaching
How do I get a position?	Life roles: work, friends, love	Occupational placement

Source: The table is based on the work of Savickas, 1996. A framework for linking career theory and practice, In W. B. Walsh and M. L. Savickas Ed., *Handbook of career counseling theory and practice*, Palo Alto, CA: Davies-Black Publishing.

student is able to describe or identify his or her interests, abilities, values, and life goals, then he/she is ready to begin identifying and exploring vocational possibilities. If he/she cannot do so, the team can focus on obstacles or issues that are preventing this from occurring. This might include self-concept difficulties, delayed career development, or motivational difficulties. These latter issues are represented in the career self, drives, or career attitudes—the first three rows of Table 4–3.

Students with a clear vocational identity but who have some remaining concerns or confusions about how to achieve this identity suggest issues with achieving a good fit between themselves and their work environment (will they be satisfied and fulfilled, will they succeed and fit in?). These are represented by one of the remaining three rows of Table 4–3 (how to actualize their vocational selves, how to make better decisions and vocational responses, and how to move into a position of choice). The team or career counselor can get additional information by asking the students about their school and work experiences, their perceptions of their successes and frustrations, and their desires to improve or change their current position. These answers can help to identify an area of further focus and intervention.

From identifying which of the six questions best represents the students' issues, the team can select a theory that addresses these concerns, and use the related assessments, interventions and strategies. For example, a student who is unable to describe his or her career beliefs and values may benefit from taking the *Career Maturity Inventory* (Crites, 1978) and examining the results with a career counselor. A student who has a strong vocational identity but is unsure of which career to choose could use the *Self-Directed Search* (Holland, 1985a). A list of theories, related instruments (where available and appropriate), and suggested interventions is described in Table 4–4, based on the six guiding questions (Savickas, 1996).

The list of instruments and assessments are good starting points for data gathering and discussion between the transition team (or career counselor) and the student. These can lead to further experiences and interventions to reaffirm previous responses or to further develop and examine indicated preferences. Those questions with no specified instruments tend to rely upon interaction-based approaches and interventions. For example, questions that reflect concerns about environmental fit and interrelationships between the individual and the environment may be addressed by Super's (1990) life career rainbow

TABLE 4–4
Interventions for the Career Framework

Question	Characteristics of the Individual	Theoretical Models	Career Interventions
Who am I?	Not yet able to articulate self-concepts and wants help in exploring who he or she is and the life goals he or she should pursue	*Focus:* Career patterns and self-exploration *Theories*: Brown and Brooks (1991), Savickas (1989), Super (1954) *Instruments: Career Development Inventory* (Super, Thompson, Lindeman, Joordan, & Myers, 1981), *Career Maturity Inventory* (Crites, 1978), *Career Beliefs Inventory* (Krumboltz, 1988)	*Strategies:* Focus on self-awareness and values with assistance in reflecting upon patterns in his or her life; self-exploration to clarify values and life issues *Interventions:* Self-exploration and values clarification to heighten self-awareness and to increase self-esteem, and elaboration of self-concepts through introspection
How can work help me to grow as a person?	Has significant problems in formulating an integrated and coherent self-concept; he or she wants help in overcoming barriers and conditions that frustrate gratification of his or her needs; tends to feel insecure and often has been discouraged by life experiences	*Focus:* Personal adjustment counseling *Theories:* Blustein (1987), Blustein & Spengler (1995), Meara & Patton (1994), Subich (1993) *Instruments: Vocational Apperception Test* (Ammons, Butler, & Herzog, 1950), card sorts (Slaney & McKinnon-Slaney, 1990)	*Strategies:* Address excessive indecisiveness, anxiety, and conflicts that thwart efforts to form a coherent self-concept and adaptive lifestyle; some benefit from modifying typical reactions to situations *Interventions:* Therapy to work through traumatic experiences, to increase sense of self-worth, and to cope with problematic situations and significant others
How do I shape my career?	Has confusion about careers, he or she wants help in understanding vocational developmental tasks; has issues dealing with career attitudes, beliefs,and competencies	*Focus:* Developmental and educational concepts *Theories:* Blocher (1974), Hoyt (1975), Ivey (1986), Super (1974)	*Strategies:* Educational interventions that emphasize self-control and concentrate on developing adaptive attitudes toward and competencies for designing and managing their own careers; strengthening of self-efficacy and decision-making competencies *Interventions:* Deliberate psychological education and counseling to orient toward developmental tasks and to foster competencies leading to task mastery

(*continued*)

TABLE 4–4 (*continued*)

Question	Characteristics of the Individual	Theoretical Models	Career Interventions
What shall I choose?	Possesses a clear vocational identity but he or she wants help in identifying occupational alternatives	*Focus:* Personality and work setting congruence *Theories:* Holland (1985), Katz (1993), Lofquist & Dawis (1991) *Instruments: Self-Directed Search* (Holland, 1985), *Strong Interest Inventory* (Harmon, Hansen, Borgen, & Hammer, 1994)	*Strategies:* Guidance that translates self-concepts into congruent occupations; exploring matches between self-concept and jobs *Interventions:* Administration and interpretation of interest inventories and ability tests, providing educational and vocational information, prompting exploratory behavior, and identifying career fields for consideration
How can I do better?	Encounters problems in meeting educational or vocational position's demands regarding adaptation to life roles, he or she wants to increase his or her success and satisfaction with work roles	*Focus:* Establishing and adjusting to a career *Theories:* Carden (1990), Dix & Savickas (1995), Hall (1987), Lofquist & Dawis (1969), Savickas (1991)	*Strategies:* Can benefit from strategizing how to get ahead and to get along; emphasize adaptations that improve the fit between the individual and the position through learning about organizational culture, position requirements, and coworkers *Interventions:* Clarify problems, identify relevant attitudes and behaviors, and rehearse and implement new attitudes and behaviors
How do I get a position?	Knows his or her preferred occupation; has made a choice and a commitment; has concerns with the world of work and related behaviors	*Focus:* Successful career placement *Theories:* Herr, Rayman, & Garis (1993), Shingleton & Fitzpatrick (1985), Stevens (1973)	*Strategies:* Reduce job search anxiety, increase assertiveness, encourage exploratory behavior, and increase social skills and self-presentation behavior *Interventions:* Skill training, information gathering, writing résumés, networking, searching for opportunities, and preparing for interviews

Source: The table is based on the work of Savickas, 1996. A framework for linking career theory and practice, M. L. Savickas and W. B. Walsh, in *Handbook of career counseling theory and practice*, Palo Alto, CA: Davies-Black Publishing.

model and concepts of role salience that affect the individual. Mitchell and Krumboltz's (1996) social learning theory may help to examine and address the individual's perceptions and beliefs about his or her relationships with the world. In other cases, educational and vocational experiences and programs are needed to help the person learn necessary work skills and competencies. The linking framework can be a useful tool for the team in identifying a primary issue and in selecting the appropriate vocational instruments and/or interventions that best reflect these issues.

CASE STUDY

Which career question from the linking framework best captures the primary issues of Miguel? Of Aza? Why do you think so?

After the Theories: What Now?

The career theories described earlier offer a variety of perspectives that can be useful to the transition team for supporting educational and career development of students with disabilities. To review: Because individual career theories provide unique perspectives regarding work and the worker, each is not appropriate for every career task or concern, or for every student. Teams may find a particular theory that suits a student very well or may use one of the comprehensive models to examine and organize data across several theories: The ecological model provides a structure for developing a comprehensive profile across multiple factors and allows parents and educators to choose among the processes to develop interventions. The linking framework provides six key questions to guide the assessment and intervention process with specific theories identified for each question.

This chapter's description is a brief look at some of the most popular and comprehensive theories, with a few suggestions regarding their use. Chapter 6 will address curriculum issues across career development; therein providing "part two": implementing career development across career education, life skills, and academic curriculum choices. From the background information in this chapter, the team is better prepared for examining and selecting potential theories across the full range of a student's career development strengths and needs, and also for determining those activities that are most critical in preparing for next steps, or in catching up on missed prerequisite steps. The choice of career theory should coincide with the team's sense of the student's primary issues: A theory's priorities should align with the student's most pressing needs and most explicit interests and preferences.

In general, the better a team's understanding of theoretical career models and their related assessment instruments and intervention strategies, the more likely it will choose a theory that is appropriate to the student's needs. In Chapters 5 and 6 the reader will apply an understanding of different theoretical perspectives to career development and assessment issues, and how these perspectives have been incorporated into an array of curricula, programs, and instruments that now exist. With a more current understanding of these theories, the reader will be better able to choose compatible assessment and intervention programs and to link these to complementary coursework and curriculum options. This will eliminate possible contradictions and conflicts across transition planning activities. Ultimately, this lifelong plan will lead to an individualized career and transition plan that optimizes the development of students with disabilities and leads them to a satisfying and fulfilling adulthood.

Now back to my question from the beginning of the chapter. How does the reader now view the career experiences of successful people who were fired from their first job? Usually, these people ended up learning a lot about how *not* to express their frustrations on the job or to end a working relationship. And they probably got a number of ideas of *better* ways to meet their career and personal needs. So this could represent one aspect of their career exploration/preparation/assimilation along their lifelong path: one experience with a personality or job satisfaction/satisfactoriness mismatch, and an opportunity for significant learning regarding faulty self-observations. So this is not career development gone wrong, but one part of a long process. The same opportunities to experience and to learn (and to occasionally fail as well as succeed) should be afforded to students with disabilities.

Study Questions

1. You are a member of a transition team that is collecting data on the needs, interests, and preferences of a student. How can you use Brolin's four stages of career development to help identify specific aspects for the collection of these data?
2. Choose three of the career development theories from this chapter, one structural, one developmental, and one learning or work-adjustment theory. Identify the perspective that each theory takes in defining key elements of the individual, the workplace, and the interaction between the two. From each of these, determine and compare how you might use important interagency linkages differently to accomplish the primary goal of each theory.
3. Compare these same three theories in terms of planning for a student's movement from school to postschool environments. Based on the theories' perspective of the individual, the workplace, and the individual's interaction, how do the theories differ in prioritizing and organizing potential movement to postschool environments? How would each of these theories fit with your own personal career development up to this point?
4. For each of the three previous theories, determine how they would fit (or not fit) into the ecological model and into the linking framework. Evaluate how useful this incorporation might or might not be to a transition team.
5. Imagine three different students with disabilities who are (a) entering a work exploration experience (observing a series of work sites and spending 2 weeks at each site), (b) beginning a job tryout/job shadowing experience (spending one month working/following a worker in each of several work sites), and (c) beginning a part-time community work experience in an area of his or her preference. Try using first the ecological model and then the linking framework to identify strategies for each that would support a student. For which students does one model seem preferable, and why?

Websites

SCANS: Secretary's Commission on Achieving Necessary Skills:
www.ttrc.doleta.gov/SCANS/

Occupational Information Network—O*NET:
www.doleta.gov/programs/onet/

Occupational Outlook Handbook:
www.bls.gov/oco

North American Industry Classification System—NAICS:
www.census.gov/epcd/www/naics/html

Career Development Competencies at Turner Tech:
http://www.flstw.fsu.edu/online74/instrategies.htm

Career Development Information: North Salem High School Career Services:
http://www.teleport.com./,kcaldwel/index.shtml

High School School-to-Work/Career Development Needs: Sharing Success Programs:
http://www.sharingsuccess.org/code/wsr/stw_hs.html

Vocational Technical Education Consortium of States (V-TECS): *Over 130 published curriculum guides for 250 job titles*

SECTION II

Transition Programs: Creating a Transition Perspective of Education

5

Transition Assessment and Postschool Outcomes

Robert W. Flexer

Pamela Luft

LEARNING OBJECTIVES

The objectives of this chapter are:

1. Explain the major similarities and differences between special education assessment and transition assessment.
2. Describe the types of skills that are tested in each of the three transition domains: current and future work, living, and personal-social areas.
3. Explain the purpose and contributions of formal (standardized) and informal tests (nonstandardized) in transition assessment. Describe the kinds of information each test can provide to support comprehensive data gathering, and describe the advantages and disadvantages with each test.
4. Describe how functional or ecological assessments can be used in each of the three areas of transition assessment and give examples.
5. Describe how academic performance assessment can be assessed for both high- and low-achieving students, and what this

information can contribute to transition planning.

6. Explain your preferred choice in the process of assessment planning and decision making for transition teams.

Introduction

Sitlington, Neubert, Begun, Lombard, and Le Conte (1996) state that transition assessments "should provide the foundation for the transition process" (p. 3) including the information from which the team will identify the student's specific preferences, strengths, and needs. Transition assessments are critical in addressing the IDEA's essential transition element of determining students' needs, interests, and preferences because they can be used to identify career interests, aptitudes, transition goals, curricular needs, or even to assess the environments that students plan to enter. Transition assessments also support implementation of other essential elements of transition in the IDEA. For example, they can provide data on how students will respond to postschool work, education, independent living, and community situtations, thereby supporting an outcome-oriented planning process. In addition, they can help determine whether educational programs and transition activities are actually promoting movement toward students' postschool goals.

Assessment, therefore, provides the informational framework from which all transition planning occurs, and it is critical that the techniques employed are accurate, relevant, and comprehensive in addressing all areas that will be important to the students' adult life. The transition team needs to understand the uses and limits of different types of transition assessments and be able to translate these assessment results into an understandable transition profile. The transition team will have to choose those that best assess students' needs, interests, and preferences and that provide the best information in regard to developing employment and other postschool adult living objectives. Team members need to feel confident that results are valid and reliable and accurately reflect the student's current abilities and future potentials, because the quality of the assessment process will be reflected in the quality of the resulting transition plans and, ultimately, in the student's successful movement into adulthood.

This chapter is organized to provide a foundation in transition assessment practices that are critical for transition planning. The authors will provide definitions and purposes of assessments to make the reader familiar with the variety of assessment approaches that have been developed from several professional disciplines. This breadth of knowledge is needed because the transition to adulthood is a complex process and no one perspective or professional discipline can meet the need of any student in any situation. These transition assessments will then be described in terms of how well they address the essential elements of transition in the IDEA and the three postschool transition domains described by Halpern in 1985 (i.e., employment, residential living, and social/interpersonal adjustment). They will also be classified according to whether they are formal or informal measurement tools, whether they are useful for persons with differing disabilities, and whether they hold predictive validity in regard to how the student will perform in actual situations.

Critical Point The transition profile should synthesize all assessment results in a comprehensive manner to depict accurately the student's abilities, interests, and needs. The transition team must choose assessments that will provide technically sound data to promote the student toward his or her postsecondary goals.

Characteristics of Transition Assessment

Assessment has been defined as the gathering of information for purposes of planning, instruction, or placement to aid in individual decision making (Taylor, 1997). For effective transition planning, assessment strategies must involve the student, the family, and multiple disciplines including educators (i.e., special, general, and vocational), related service providers (e.g., school psychologists, diagnosticians, speech therapists, occupational therapists, and physical therapists), and other individuals involved in the student's transition to adulthood. As the student nears graduation, this list may expand to include personnel from rehabilitation counseling, health or mental health services, colleges or universities, developmental disability services, income maintenance programs, and other assistance or employment services depending on the student's potential future (Halpern, 1994; Sitlington et al., 1996). Transition assessment also needs to also include the evaluations of non-professionals such as paraprofessionals, concerned business leaders, church representatives, or civic group representatives who can be important sources of information about the student and about the community's resources and support (Luft, Rumrill, & Snyder-Marks, in press).

Assessment can serve multiple purposes. However, transition assessment must include some unique approaches and perspectives as well. One of the most important aspects of the assessment process is that it should be ongoing and continuous. Adolescent and young adult students are experiencing tremendous developmental changes. These changes, the impact of their peers, and their learning from transition activities and experiences will clarify and change their values and preferences over time. As the student and the team learn more about these abilities and preferences, they may decide to alter and modify strategies to reach the student's desired adult outcomes. Ongoing evaluation is vital to ensuring that final adult plans represent the accumulation of the student's growth, education, and experiences before leaving high school (Sitlington et al., 1996).

A second important aspect of transition assessment is that it should have a clearly specified purpose. Transition assessment may include some of the same tests as those used by special educators for the development of the Individualized Education Program (IEP) to determine eligibility and to test general areas of achievement, performance, and behavior. However, transition assessment must address abilities and needs related to specific individualized adult outcomes, including the student's success with specific tasks in actual environments. The team therefore needs to assess the student's success in the environments that reflect his or her lifestyle preferences and abilities. This requires clear identification and specification of these environments and of persons who can assess student performance in these settings. Table 5–1 summarizes some major purposes of assessment.

A third important aspect of transition assessment is that it should be individualized. As previously noted, no assessment works well with all students in all situations. The variety of needs and abilities, of career and lifestyle preferences, and the pace of developmental and program-based changes that students experience, require that team members individually select the types of assessments that are most relevant and appropriate. Many assessments were not normed on persons with disabilities resulting in problems of administering or analyzing them. Some newer assessment procedures are less formalized and allow for the

TABLE 5–1
Purposes for Transition Assessment

Category	Description
Determination of development in working, living, and personal/social environments	To find out where the student stands in terms of: awareness, orientation, exploration, preparation, placement, or growth/maintenance. Appropriate for middle school/early junior high and beyond.
Measurement	To identify abilities, interests, capabilities, strengths, needs, potentials, behaviors, and preferences within the areas of personal-social, functional-academic, community-independent living, employment and employability areas. Initial testing appropriate for middle school; more involved analyses appropriate for high school and beyond.
Prediction	To match an individual's preferences and abilities with appropriate program options. Appropriate for high school (Neubert, 1985).
Prescription	To identify strengths and needs and to recommend types of adaptive techniques and/or accommodation strategies that will lead to improved performance. Appropriate for high school and young adults and beyond.
Exploration	To "try out" different tasks or activities and to determine how preferences match abilities for program options and postschool outcomes. Appropriate for high school and young adults (Neubert, 1985).
Skill development	To implement the techniques or strategies that will help a student to explore performance requirements. Appropriate for high school and beyond.
Advocacy	To develop a profile to help students, their families, and others identify concrete ways to assist students in achieving their goals. Appropriate for high school and beyond.

Sources: Adapted from National Information Center for Children and Youths with Disabilities (NICCYD). (1990). *Vocational assessment: A guide for parents and professionals*, Washington, DC: NICCYD.

creation of alternative formats to accommodate students with varying disabilities. Some assessments involve task analyses and situational assessments that contribute more detailed information about the student's success in a specific environment and with a particular set of tasks (Clark, 1996).

A fourth important aspect of transition assessment is the effective summarization and integration of the assessment results into a comprehensive, accurate, and realistic transition profile. Transition assessment involves more than administering, scoring, and reporting tests and results. It involves careful analysis of the assessment results that provide functional, relevant, appropriate recommendations and decisions. The integration of assessments into a understandable profile is a difficult task that generally falls to the coordinator of the IEP team in which transition is discussed. This profile must be free of professional jargon and specifically address student needs, interests, and preferences in a way that emphasizes strengths and that promotes an atmosphere of positive expectations for the student with a disability. Transition planning remains most effective when all members understand these results sufficiently to be able to contribute their own analyses and interpretations. It is particularly important that the student and the family recognize how these assessments can contribute to planning for a positive future.

Critical Point Transition assessments are ongoing, specific, and individualized according to the students' goals and programs. A comprehensive profile can validate needs and preferences and reflect the team's developed "picture" of the students.

Defining Transition Domains

In accordance with the three domains of postschool community adjustment established by Halpern (1985), the CEC Division of Career Development and Transition (DCDT) have defined the important areas of transition assessment as follows:

> Transition assessment is the on-going process of collecting data on the individual's needs, preferences, and interests as they relate to the demands of current and future *working, living, and personal social environments*. Assessment data serve as the common thread in the transition process and form the basis for defining goals and services, to be included in the individualized education program (IEP). (Sitlington, Neubert, & Le Conte, 1997, pp. 70–71)

This definition categorizes transition assessment into three broad areas of current and future environments for the student. The following discussion employs these three transition domains (i.e., current and future working, living, and personal-social environments) to categorize the various types of assessments that can be used in transition planning.

Current and Future Working Environments

Work and career assessments provide information on student needs, interests, and preferences that are designed to lead ultimately to career selection. These assessments may focus on career maturity, development of work behaviors, personality characteristics, cultural factors, or other constructs of career development (see Chapter 4 for a more complete discussion of career models). Some of the most effective assessments for students with disabilities measure career development and maturity, since many of these students lack experiences to help them make career choices. These assessments may focus on general abilities and interests in early stages or may examine specific aptitudes and career attitudes needed for employment success in later stages.

Vocational assessment deals with the role of the worker and demands of the workplace for specific vocations or occupations. When the student's employment goal narrows into a specific job type, the vocational assessment can provide detailed information critical to success in that occupation. The Interdisciplinary Council on Vocational Evaluation and Assessment describes this type of assessment as comprising:

> Services to measure, observe, and document an individual's interests, values, temperaments, work-related behaviors, aptitudes and skills, physical capacities, learning style, and training needs. (Smith, Lombard, Neubert, Le Conte, Rothenbacher & Sitlington, 1996, p. 74)

Vocational assessments focus on work-related characteristics and aptitudes of the student within finite vocational and work-oriented approaches (Le Conte, 1986). Areas that vary with the individual include special aptitudes and special needs, work habits and behaviors, personal and social skills needed for work. Other areas such as values and attitudes toward work, work tolerance and work adjustment, physical abilities, and dexterity are also areas that need to be addressed in vocational assessments.

Critical Point Career assessments look at the life span as a series of stages toward career maturity and measure abilities and interests. Vocational assessments focus on the worker and the demands of various workplace environments and measure work-related aptitudes and characteristics of the student.

Current and Future Living Environments

This second category of transition assessment is extremely broad and variable, depending on the student's lifestyle preferences and potential for independence. The transition team should use assessments in this area to ensure that the student has developed a range of necessary self-care and management skills. When independence is limited, students should have skills that allow a maximum sense of independence and choice within a supported living environment. Some skills that the team may need to assess include basic health and hygiene, medical and dental, home care, safety and community survival skills, and self-advocacy. Some students also may need to learn community travel and transportation skills, shopping, cooking, housecleaning, and money management depending on their current and anticipated levels of independence.

The family, the student's residential staff, or personal care providers can be extremely helpful in providing information about current levels of performance in the area of residential living. Additionally, developmental disability agency staff may provide important information on supported living options as well. All of these individuals can help to define realistic future alternatives and the ongoing monitoring and support that may be needed as the student moves into adulthood. This area of transition is less well defined by testing and assessment instruments; therefore, including the individuals who can assist with gathering relevant data is very important.

Critical Point Assessments for living environments are not well defined; therefore, family and/or support staff involvement is crucial to identify accurately areas of ability, preference, and need.

Current and Future Personal-Social Environments

This third and final category of transition is another area that is highly dependent on the preferences of the student. Most students have desires for friendships, but the number and types of friends they need in order to feel satisfied varies greatly. Consequently, hobbies and community participation, including sports teams or interest groups, should be supported according to the student's preferences. Additionally, some students may plan to marry and have children of their own, so the team may need to address issues relating to dating, sexuality, child care, and possibly, sexual vulnerability in the community. Because friendship, dating, marital, and parenting skills are areas where there are few assessments, teams will need to rely upon gathering information from the student and those individuals who know the student best. Team members who see the student regularly will have valuable perspectives on the student's current abilities in making, maintaining, and, when necessary, ending relationships and friendships with others. The involvement of all important community members on the team can greatly assist in addressing all important transition areas and in better predicting future needs and potential environments.

A unique aspect of the personal/social domain is its influence on success in the two other transition areas, and the team may have to address social skill needs in work and in community living environments as well. A number of assessments address behavioral and interaction aspects of personal-social skills that the team may find helpful. The team may need to develop an integrated assessment approach that identifies related strengths and needs across all three domains with an intervention plan that addresses all simultaneously.

Critical Point Current and future environments, based on student and family preferences, require very specific information that addresses how students function in specific environments.

IDEA Requirements

Well-done and appropriate assessments are the basis for all successful special education and transition programming. In order to ensure appropriate testing practices, IDEA addressed assessment in both 1990 and 1997. The IDEA of 1990 required IEP assessments to be unbiased and given in the native language of the student. In addition, placement in special education was based upon a multifactored evaluation that included multiple assessments across more than one environment (Turnbull, H. R., 1993).

Transition assessments must follow these same guidelines. In addition, the IDEA of 1997 represented a significant shift in assessment processes. It included a greater emphasis on informal assessments that examined the student's performance in specific environments according to each environment's expectations. In contrast, formal assessments tend to be given under strict, neutral conditions; that is, often in a room without distractions, following a standard set of directions, using paper and pencil, or copying or manipulating objects or tools.

Informal assessments allow the team to examine the student's behavior within the variety of environments that are natural to the individual's life, including the anticipated future environments (Clark, 1996; Sitlington, 1996). Formal tests can provide important general information but are usually isolated from critical environmental contexts that frequently either support or create barriers for the student. The greater emphasis on informal assessments also allows greater participation from students and parents in the assessment process because these assessments can be more individualized to better fit their current preferences and visions of possible futures.

IDEA 1997 also specifies that all children who are identified as having special education needs must be considered for assistive technology. Although the law does not clearly specify who obtains technology, it is generally felt that the school team should consider (a) what specific tasks the student is not able to do or participate in because of the disability or suspected disabilities, (b) what has been tried to enable the student to complete the task or to participate, and (c) if a particular strategy or modification enables the student to complete the task or participate within the least restrictive environment.

Critical Point The use of both informal and formal assessments provides the transition team with a holistic view of the student. Informal assessments allow for more variability across environments to create a realistic picture of the student's abilities.

Lastly, an additional aspect of IDEA 1997 that the transition team needs to address is the extent to which the student should be integrated into the general education curriculum and classroom as part of the IEP plan. The 1997 amendments emphasize placement with peers, and if the team does not feel this is appropriate, then it provides a statement as to why this is so. This issue is very important in terms of the preferences of the student and family. Team members may hold contradictory views in terms of what constitutes "peers." Some may believe that integration into a work and community environment with typical adult coworkers represents the ultimate goal of transition and integration and, thus, complies with IDEA. Others may believe that work and community training is "atypical" for most high school students and, thus, represents a "handicapping" placement that contradicts the IDEA. The preferences of the student and family are probably the best gauge of what is most appropriate. Table 5–2 summarizes some specific IDEA requirements pertaining to transition assessment.

Functional Assessments

The assessments that provide information that is directly related to a student's transition outcomes are sometimes called functional assessments. The student's performance or behavior is measured in a specific environment. The standard or criterion of the performance is established to meet that level that is required for success/achievement within that setting. This level is compared to the individual's performance within this setting. Functional assessments were emphasized within the new recommendations by IDEA 1997. Sitlington et al. (1996) suggested their greater use in place of standardized paper-and-pencil assessment.

Gaylord-Ross and Browder (1991) contended that although functional assessment has been defined broadly, it has some of the following characteristics: (a) a focus on practical, independent living/work skills that enable the person to survive and succeed in the real world; (b) an ecological emphasis that looks to the individual functioning in his or her surrounding environment; (c) a process for examining learning and performance; (d) prescriptions for intervention techniques that may be successful; and (e) specification of ongoing monitoring procedures that can evaluate performance progress (p. 45). Table 5–3 provides an example of a functional assessment.

Functional assessments can be either formal or informal assessment tools. Regardless of their respective unique features, they require a relationship between data collection and the transition decision-making process. They must provide information directly related to current or future environments (e.g., regular or special classes, or community, work, or home settings), tasks (e.g., basic work literacy, home care and personal hygiene, soldering integrated circuits onto the mother board), and behaviors (e.g., adhering to medical restrictions, following safety precautions, and taking the correct bus). For transition planning, functional assessments also should relate directly to the student's

TABLE 5–2

New IDEA Requirements for Assessment and Evaluation

Use a variety of assessment tools and strategies to gather relevant functional and developmental information, including information provided by the parent, that may assist in determining whether the child has a disability and the contents of the child's Individualized Educational Program (IEP). Include information related to child's involvement in the general curriculum or, for preschool children, participation in appropriate activities. Other requirements are as follows:

- Increased emphasis on functional and developmental information
- Specific requirement that information from parents is included in the evaluation process
- Results are to be used for determining eligibility for special education services and in developing the child's IEP
- Eligibility determination and IEP development
- Provide information about how the student can best succeed in the general education classroom

Source: Adapted from Taylor, R. L. (2000). *Assessment of exceptional students: Educational and psychological procedures,* Needham Heights, MA: Allyn & Bacon.

TABLE 5–3

Characteristics and Example of a Functional Assessment

Characteristics
- Practical, real-world skills
- Specific individual functioning in specific environment
- Focuses on supporting learning/performance
- Assesses performance progress

Using a laundromat
- Compare students' performance with typical customer
- Identify skills that help performance:
  Watch clock
- Identify distracters that hinder performance:
  Watch others or television
- Identify reminders that work:
  Using picture cue cards
  Going with a supportive neighbor
  Setting a timer
- Identify checkpoints for monitoring:
  Keep checking sorting because colors and whites are still being mixed

transition outcomes. Functional testing typically involves the use of informal procedures, because standardized grade equivalent scores rarely relate directly to functions in the work, living, nor personal-social domains. However, if a student wishes to apply for vocational or postsecondary programs, grade equivalent scores may be a performance requirement and these tests become functional in this context.

Ecological assessments may be "functional" and directly related to transition outcomes. They are used to assess all aspects (e.g., people, places, and things) and interrelationships among these elements within a particular environment that impact a student's performance. Important aspects can include environmental conditions (e.g., heat, light, indoors/outdoors, proximity of others, number of coworkers, size and condition of building, etc.), relationships with others (e.g., impact of the student on coworkers and supervisors, quality of mutual interactions, acceptance and mutual regard, abilities to give and take feedback), and performance accommodations/adaptations. A functional ecological assessment examines the interactive and mutual nature of these relationships to evaluate the student's success in meeting both formal and informal expectations within the setting. Two types of functional assessments are required by IDEA: functional behavioral assessments and functional vocational evaluations.

The purpose of a functional behavioral assessment is to address a problem behavior in a student. A variety of strategies is utilized to identify the purpose of a target behavior and enable the IEP team to identify and individualize an effective intervention. The strategies and techniques most often used to collect data include: questionnaires; interviews with students, teachers, parents; and observations. Quinn, Gable, Rutherford, Nelson, & Howell, (1998) recommend the following steps when conducting a functional behavior analysis: identify and define the problem behavior (start with broad definition and through data collection narrow it down to an operational definition); review data and information from all sources and contexts; examine what has been learned about the behavior (i.e., antecedents, consequences); and develop an individualized intervention. Ideally, the target behavior and intervention will be apparent to the IEP team. In some cases, the IEP team has to work closely in order to find a solution because an appropriate intervention may not be so easily identified.

A team may use a functional vocational evaluation to determine which employment positions are most likely to lead to success within a particular preferred career area for a student. The evaluator may measure functional skills at the work site to determine if the student performs at adequate levels and is able to integrate socially and personally in the work environment. When preparing to seek a specific job, the team may ask for an ecological evaluation at a specific company to ensure that the physical conditions and coworkers/supervisors at that company are compatible with and supportive of the student's needs. Teams will choose to use each assessment to meet their specific needs for information.

Critical Point Functional assessments can be formal or informal. They tend to focus on practical skills, compare student's performance in different environments, examine the process of learning and performance, and specify evaluation procedures to determine progress.

Summary

Transition assessment processes must be broadly inclusive of competencies that are needed for adulthood. These competencies can be categorized into three main areas: current and future work, living, and personal-social domains. The team chooses among a range of formal and informal assessments, including functional and ecological assessments. These provide both general and specific data that are used in planning for desired transition outcomes. The nature of transition means that assessments must be ongoing, have a specific purpose, and should be individualized and effectively summarized.

The assessment process begins with consensus among team members on a student's potential future. They use this to identify the kinds of information that are necessary to assemble a comprehensive transition profile of the student. From this, the team shapes future transition potentials by matching interests and talents with potential job requirements and career profiles, lifestyles and living arrangements, and community participation and socialization opportunities. The next section further describes the types of tests that the team uses in gathering the required information to create the transition profile.

Formal Transition Assessments

Assessments can be classified into two general categories: formal and informal. Standardized or formal assessments are designed for the purpose of determining a person's relative standing within a group for a general trait or characteristic. Typical examples include: intelligence tests (i.e., a number is calculated that compares the student's ability to learn with others of the same age) and achievement tests (i.e., a grade equivalent or stanine score is given that ranks the student's progress compared with others of the same age or grade). Standardized assessments follow formal procedures that were used for developing the test and must be used in giving and interpreting their results. The ability of these tests to compare one individual with another depends on this consistent administration and interpretation. Some tests require prior training with strict rules on who can be assessors.

In addition to intelligence tests and achievement tests, special education and transition programs often use formal adaptive behavior scales, personality tests, and vocational and career aptitudes, interests, worker characteristics, and occupational skills tests for evaluating student ability and progress. Some newer transition tests are being developed that are designed to assess one's knowledge and skills specifically required in community functioning. It has been long recognized that standardized tests give a limited view of the individual (e.g., a focus on deficits) and are not perfectly reliable and valid, particularly for individuals with disabilities. However, there are certain qualities and circumstances that make standardized tests valuable.

Formal, standardized tests go through a development process that strengthens their reliability and validity and allows them to make comparisons between individuals. Reliability refers to stability of scores. For example, a student taking a social skills test should get approximately the same score if he or she takes it again (of course, we hope that training and practice might raise any areas of need). Validity means that a test accurately measures what it is intended to assess. For example, if the results of a vocational abilities test show an aptitude in a particular career area, the student will also demonstrate those aptitudes successfully in a work situation. The difficulty for students with disabilities is that few are included in most test development or in the norming processes that establish the comparison scales. In addition, students who need specific accommodations or who do poorly on certain types of tests (e.g., those that are timed or require transferring answers onto a standardized "bubble" test form) are not likely to perform in ways that represent their true abilities. These comparisons with other students can provide some useful, general information for the team. However, for more specific information about a student's potential in specific environments, the team should combine formal test results with those from informal tests. When both sets of results identify patterns of behavior or gaps and needs for programs, the team can be fairly certain that these are trustworthy and accurate results. Any one test, whether formal or informal, should never be used as the sole indicator of success or difficulty experienced by a student.

Critical Point Formal assessments tend to be standardized and measure a student's skills relative to a norm group of their "peers." These tests have formal procedures for administration and evaluation of the results.

General Skills Tests

A number of instruments provide general assessments of transition skills that can help the team to identify broad strength and need areas. Adaptive behavior scales often are used in multifactored assessments and typically request individuals who know the student well (e.g., teachers, parents, etc.) to rate the individual on the skills required for functioning in the community or school. An example is the *American Association on Mental Retardation* (AAMR) *Adaptive Behavior Scales*. Teachers and parents rate the student's abilities across a number of life-skill areas (e.g., basic academics, self-care, meals, and hygiene). Results provide an age-normed score with 100 as the "average." The *Vineland Adaptive Behavior Scales* is another commonly used instrument with a similar format.

Halpern (1996) developed the *Transition Skills Inventory*, which is completed by the student, parent, and teacher. The skills inventory consists of four broad areas and their respective subdomains, including the following areas:

- Personal life: communication with other people, relating to authorities, relating to peers, responsibility, solving problems, controlling anger, personal safety;
- Jobs: knowing about jobs, finding a job, skills on the job;

- Education and training: reading, writing, math; and
- Living on your own: self-care, nutrition and fitness, money management, home management, community and leisure activities.

Halpern's inventory uses a self-report student form in conjunction with forms for parents and teachers. This helps students to learn about their interests, strengths, and weaknesses and then to use the information obtained to make important decisions that affect their lives. Students can use this to enhance their self-evaluation as a foundation for greater participation with the team in developing their transition plans.

The *Transition Planning Inventory* (Clark & Patton, 1997) is designed to help its user identify and comprehensively plan for the student's transition needs. The instrument assesses employment, education, daily living, leisure, health, self-determination, communication, and interpersonal relationships. There are three forms completed by the school, home, and students. There are over 600 transition goals that are correlated with transition planning statements. Together, these results can assist the team in integrating perspectives from several people regarding the student's needs, preferences, and interests.

Some transition assessments have a more narrow focus. The *Social and Prevocational Information Battery* (SPIB) (Halpern & Irvin, 1986) assesses knowledge of skills and competencies for the vocational and community adjustment of students with mental retardation. The nine subtests examine knowledge of job search skills, job-related behavior, banking, budgeting, purchasing, home management, health care, hygiene and grooming, and functional signs. The battery is intended primarily for junior and senior high school levels and consists mostly of true-false, orally administered items. One important note for team members is that students who have difficulty responding to questions asked in this manner may not give reliable answers.

Daily living skills are an important transition curriculum.

Current and Future Working Environments

The area of work has been fairly well developed for formal assessment through career counseling and vocational rehabilitation programs. Assessment often begins with identification of career interests. The *Becker Reading-Free Interest Survey*, *Career Development Inventory* (CDI), *Career Maturity Inventory* (CMI), *Knowledge of the World of Work Scale*, *Kuder Vocational Preference Record*, *Reading-Free Vocational Interest Inventory*, *Self-Directed Search*, and the *Wide-Range Interest and Opinion Test*

(WRIOT) all provide for some aspects of interest assessment. Additional information about these and other instruments listed in this chapter can help team members to evaluate which, if any, are appropriate for their student (see Clark & Kolstoe, 1995; Gajar, Goodman, & McAfee, 1993; Kokaska & Brolin, 1985; Linn & DeStefano, 1986; Luft, 1999; Sitlington et al., 1996).

Another well-developed area of assessment is work skill and aptitude measurement. Some of these instruments are the *Bennett Hand-Tool Dexterity Test*, *Differential Aptitude Test* (DAT), *Macquarrie Test for Mechanical Ability*, *Minnesota Spatial Relations Test*, and *Purdue Pegboard Test* (Clark & Kolstoe, 1995; Gajar et al., 1993; Kokaska & Brolin, 1985; Linn & DeStefano, 1986; Luft, 1999; Sitlington et al., 1996). The team may want to consult with a vocational evaluator in order to select specific tests that best assess a student's skills in a particular area.

Use of work samples is another popular format that was developed by rehabilitation and vocational education to examine work tasks and performance variables. A work sample is "a well-defined work activity involving tasks, materials and tools that are identical or similar to those in an actual job or cluster of jobs. Work samples are used to assess a persons vocational aptitudes, work characteristics, and vocational interests," (VEWAA, 1988, p. 16). Because a work sample approximates an actual job, the evaluator can observe actual work behavior in a controlled situation (usually a testing room or classroom). Commonly used examples include *Apticom*, *McCarron-Dial Work Evaluation System*, *Singer Vocational Evaluation System*, and *Valpar Work Sample* (Clark & Kolstoe, 1995; Gajar et al., 1993; Kokaska & Brolin, 1985; Linn & DeStefano, 1986; Luft, 1999; Sitlington et al., 1996). These typically involve asking the students to perform certain specific tasks that are evaluated for speed, accuracy, quantity, and quality. A Consumer's Guide discusses and analyzes 30 work sample systems (Brown, McDaniel, Couch, & McClanahan, 1994) and is a good resource for general and specific issues of work sample batteries.

These formal and standardized work samples, like other standardized measures (e.g., intelligence tests, adaptive behavior scales, and the others described earlier), do not predict job success perfectly because they are based on performance of job tasks that only resemble actual jobs and do not occur in a real work environment with typical distractions and conditions. They continue to be used as a means of identifying a student's relative areas of strengths. Although it can change their interpretation and scoring, some experienced evaluators choose to modify these assessments to learn valuable information about a student's rate of learning these tasks, responsiveness to suggestions, and related work behaviors. This can provide helpful information to the team when standardized scores are not necessary.

Current and Future Living Environments

This area has fewer standardized measures although a number of instruments recently have been developed that assess aspects of this broad domain. The ARC's *Self-Determination Scale* (Wehmeyer, 1995; Wehmeyer & Kelchner, 1995) is a formal assessment that is a student self-report instrument designed for use with adolescents with cognitive disabilities, including mild mental retardation and learning disabilities. Through this instrument, students can evaluate their own beliefs about themselves and their self-determination skills or needs, and can assess their progress.

Another important area to assess is whether students have sufficient survival skills to live safely and happily. Several instruments that assess general areas of survival skills include the *Independent Living Behavior Checklist*, the *Street Survival Skills Questionnaire*, and the *Test for Everyday Living*. These typically use an interview or survey format (Clark & Kolstoe, 1995; Gajar et al., 1993; Kokaska & Brolin, 1985; Linn & DeStefano, 1986;

Sitlington et al., 1996). A student's satisfaction is the ultimate measure of transition success. Although there are few such instruments as yet, an additional assessment is the *Lifestyle Satisfaction Scale*, which might provide some useful information for the team.

Survival skill needs may have related effects on personal-social skills and skills needed for work (Menchetti, Rusch, & Owens, 1983; Rusch, 1979). A key feature of survival skill measurement is that the instruments should have social validity and should meet the expectations and beliefs of the community and environments in which the student will live, work, and play. The team may need to interpret some of these standardized tests cautiously; conditions vary considerably between urban, suburban, and rural settings as well as across ethnicity and social class. What meets the expectations of one community may violate those in another community.

Current and Future Personal-Social Environments

Abilities or needs in this domain can greatly impact the other two transition domains. An inability to form satisfactory relationships can lead to unacceptable behaviors in any environment, ranging from social withdrawal to aggression and violence toward others. Not many formal assessments address formation of friendships and dating/marital relationships, but they do address more general social abilities. Some of these assessments include the *Progress Assessment Chart of Social and Personal Development*, *Social and Prevocational Information Battery*, *Waksman Social Skills Rating Form*, and the *Leisure Time Activities Scale* (Clark & Kolstoe, 1995; Gajar et al., 1993; Kokaska & Brolin, 1985; Linn & DeStefano, 1986; Sitlington et al., 1996).

An assessment that combines work with social skills is the *Test of Interpersonal Competency for Employment* (TICE). This is a 61-item survival skill measure that has been validated in terms of important skills that are specific to job tenure (Foss, Cheney, & Bullis, 1986). The student's competence is evaluated in terms of responding to criticisms/corrections, following instructions, and requesting assistance from supervisors; working cooperatively, responding to teasing/provocation, and coping with personal problems as coworker issues. The instrument accompanies a comprehensive training curriculum (Foss & Vilhauer, 1986) so that need areas can be efficiently addressed.

Academic Assessment

Although it is not one of the three transition domains defined by DCDT, transition teams have to do some academic assessment for students with disabilities. However, the extent to which the team addresses academic outcomes will depend on the student's academic potential and career/lifestyle preferences. The *Adult Basic Literacy Assessment*, *Brigance Diagnostic Inventory of Essential Skills*, and *Wide Range Achievement Test* (WRAT) are several general academic tests that can be used to assess basic competencies. The team must also realize that not all students are able to achieve these levels, in which case accommodations and alternative performance options will need to be investigated.

For some students, postschool transition preferences may include 2- or 4-year college or postgraduate and professional training. For other students, postsecondary education will involve further development of transition skills. For many of these individuals with disabilities, there is a need to provide a broader array of experiences and opportunities for attainment of academic skills to allow access to more challenging and advanced jobs. The team members will need to emphasize and build upon these students' academic performance to ensure their success in postsecondary settings.

Although it is normal for all students to be assessed in the realm of academic performance, much of those assessments are more closely allied with classroom curriculum and activities. They may not address the individual student's projected needs in postsecondary environments (Thurlow & Elliott, 1998). Academic assessment for transition purposes must focus specifically on those academic skills that will provide the foundation needed for success in postsecondary education and community and work life. Students who plan to live and work independently in the community also need job-related academic skills as well as functional and survival skills in communication (either written or oral), math, science, social studies, and government/civics. They must be able to budget their income and to balance their checkbook, as well as, for example, to read directions on cleaning products and recipes. Their adult goals will determine the extent and nature of the academic testing that the team needs to pursue.

Many academic tests use formal and standardized procedures although informal procedures also can provide valuable information. Students who wish to enter academically focused postsecondary programs need to develop abilities to take general achievement tests. In addition, they should consider participating in mandatory statewide testing, which is required of regular education students in many states. IDEA requires that students with disabilities should be part of the system of assessment and accountability that is part of school improvement and reform efforts. The type of high school diploma a student receives may depend on his or her ability to take and score well on achievement and state proficiency tests. An academic diploma is increasingly important for assuring entry into postsecondary training facilities. The team may need to be creative devising appropriate accommodations and methods to ensure that this testing reflects the student's actual skills and accomplishments.

Table 5–4 shows the general categories of standardized tests and possible accommodations. Accommodations are necessary in many instances to allow the true abilities of the student to be determined. Because of the technical issues of

TABLE 5–4

Transition-Related Large-Scale Standardized Tests and Accommodations

Types of tests/examinations

Proficiency: Measures on accomplishment of standard curriculum, knowledge, and/or performance in academic subjects at different grade levels

Graduation: Measures on attainment of certain levels of competence to receive a regular diploma

General education development: Tests on meeting high school level requirements in reading, mathematics, writing, social studies, and science in lieu of a diploma

Entrance: Tests on level of preparation for college course work (e.g., ACT, SAT) or graduate/professional school level work (GRE, LSAT, etc.)

Credential: Tests to determine proficiency preparation to enter a line of work/occupation (e.g., BAR, medical boards, teacher license exams, etc.)

Types of accommodations

- Increased time
- Different setting
- Different response types (e.g., oral versus written)
- Revised formats (e.g., enlarged print)

Source: Adapted from Thurlow, M. & Elliott, J. (1998). Student assessment and evaluation. In Rusch, J. R. & Chadsey, J. G. (Eds.), *Beyond high school: Transition from school to work* (pp. 265–296), New York: Wadsworth Publishing Company.

test standardization, the interpretation of the test results is unclear. Tests taken with accommodations are under different conditions so that comparing scores with others (e.g., norm group) is not valid.

Informal Transition Assessments

In the early 1980s, contemporary and functional assessment emerged as an alternative approach to supplement limitations of formal, standardized tests of student characteristics and abilities (Halpern & Fuhrer, 1984). IDEA 1997 emphasizes the use of functional, informal assessment because of these types of weaknesses: "the relevance of traditional intelligence, personality, and neuropsychological instruments and their respective results to the pragmatic educational, work, and community adjustment focus of rehabilitation programs is unclear at best, and may be totally unrelated to the rehabilitation process" (Bullis, Kosko, Waintrup, Kelley, & Issacson, 1994, p. 9).

Informal assessments are used to determine what the students' needs, interests, and preferences are and how well they are progressing in reaching their transition and IEP goals. Informal assessments also can be functional to determine performance on some specific task directly relevant to the educational program of the student. The student's performance or behavior is measured in a specific environment, for example, the classroom or community setting. The standard or criterion of performance is what in fact is required for success/achievement within that setting, in comparison to the individuals' own performance.

One important concern is the potential lack of validity and reliability of informal assessments; in other words, are they really testing what is desired (and not other irrelevant but obscure factors), and are the results reliable (e.g., if different people are observed over several weeks, would the results be the same?). Clark (1996) identified some conditions for determination of valid nonstandardized assessments. He believed that the team's agreement that an assessment is an accurate reflection of a student provides some face validity for an informal assessment. When these results are supported by what is already known (e.g., other informal assessments or formal assessments), then the results may be considered affirmed and useful for program planning.

Informal assessments are a vital complement to standardized test results in transition planning by providing examples of specific successes, strengths, and needs in relation to transition planning and IEP outcomes. Because informal assessments do not meet the technical standards of formal tests, describing how the information was obtained, providing caveats and limitations in their interpretation, and examining the assessments as a whole and among several sources (e.g., different team members in different situations) become very important. Nonetheless, because informal assessments occur in specific environments, their results provide authentic information about how the student performs in these environments and their needs for training, resources, and accommodations in order to be successful. Informal assessments include several types of formats that address all three transition domains depending on the setting in which they are used. Several are described next.

Critical Point Informal assessments are emphasized in IDEA 1997 to supplement the use of standardized tests. Informal assessments provide detailed information on a student's specific successes, strengths, and needs that are directly related to his or her transition and IEP outcomes.

Student School Records

As a preliminary step in developing and updating the students' transition IEP, the cumulative record can be a source of past behavior, attitudes, and performance. School grades, special services, attendance records, performance on group tests, and other information are contained in the student's permanent record. Checklists and anecdotal notes on teacher perceptions of classroom behavior and performance also may be helpful. In particular, patterns of special needs, growth, and development may be detected over time if several teachers noted the same issues from year to year. Since the manner in which information was collected is not known nor are the conditions at the particular time periods, reviewers of records must be careful not to base their current evaluation primarily on past observations.

Curriculum-Based Assessment

One of the most common alternatives to traditional measurement is curriculum-based assessment. These measures assess a student's progress through a particular curriculum, either academic or vocational. Some better curriculum-based assessments also use a criterion-referenced measure that sets a standard reflecting real-world expectations (e.g., the driver's education curriculum expects the same driving and testing performance as found on the state exams).

These assessments are based on the specific activities and objectives within the curriculum, making it a highly accurate test of the student's progress in the program. This type of test was developed because many standardized tests were far removed from the activities of daily instruction and, therefore, were not an accurate measure of "progress" in that program. Curriculum-based assessment also allows for an analysis of content or skills to be completed so that these can be broken down into smaller curriculum objectives or tasks as needed to promote student success.

These assessments require that the student should be taught from an existing curriculum program. Although IDEA 1997 strongly encourages inclusion of all special education students in the regular curriculum, for some students this may not be practical, or may not meet with some of the transition outcomes that are determined to be important by the team. In these cases, curriculum-based assessment may not be practical. However, students enrolled in vocational training programs can be evaluated using curriculum-based vocational assessment, which documents their progress within the training program and ultimately, toward achieving industry-level skills. Case Study A provides an example of a curriculum-based assessment strategy for vocational school settings.

CASE STUDY A

Curriculum-Based Assessment in a Welding Program

A tenth-grade student is enrolled in a welding program. The vocational and special education teacher develop curriculum-based measures in order to determine the student's progress and instructional needs in completing the program. The tasks and activities in performing the welding operations are broken down to assess student learning (e.g., a competency checklist). Additional tests or ratings are developed to measure student interest and motivation, the ability to use equipment and tools in the program, and the ability to communicate with the instructor and other students. In the process of assessing and teaching, the two teachers devise any instructional or equipment accommodations/adaptations that are required for the student to perform welding operations and related or academic tasks. The student and the two teachers are in regular communication while the student progresses through the program.

Source: Adapted from Sitlington, Neubert, Begun, Lombard, and Le Conte, 1996.

The comprehensive *Life-Centered Career Education* (LCCE) curriculum program includes a related assessment program and employs a criterion-referenced measurement (Brolin, 1992a, 1992b;

Brolin, 1995; Bucher & Brolin, 1987). This comprehensive curriculum is designed to prepare students with disabilities with the important skills needed to function successfully as productive workers in the home and community. The three accompanying curriculum-based measures are the LCCE knowledge battery, LCCE performance battery, and competency rating scale. Collectively, these criterion measures make it possible to evaluate the knowledge and skills to determine individually appropriate instructional goals in 22 competency areas and 97 subcompetencies related to the areas of daily living skills, personal-social skills, and occupational and preparation skills.

Criterion-Referenced Assessment

A criterion-referenced standard is used to evaluate mastery with either formal or informal assessments for instruction on objectives and skills. For some work-related and community tasks, there may be specific industry- union- or site-based standards of production quality and quantity that the student must meet. These are examples of socially validated external criteria, which the team will want to follow. Formal assessments including many statewide proficiency tests often use criteria to establish categories of attainment.

School programs typically use criteria in an informal way to measure attainment of IEP and instructional objectives. Some of these standards are arbitrary (e.g., is 70 or 80% an appropriate measure of what is "good" for any particular student?) and others are based on common sense and safety. For example, skills in crossing the street should be mastered at 100%; defining mastery at 80% means that in one out of five times the student will be in danger, an unacceptable level of error in this case. The team should ensure that objectives and programs that use criterion-based assessment reflect upon community and real-world standards as much as possible.

Portfolio Assessment

In some areas of academic performance, a portfolio has been developed to assess student performance. In fact, many institutions of higher education are using portfolios as a means for partial evaluation of a student before receiving a bachelor's degree. The portfolio assessment process is the accumulation of work in the various academic and performance areas to represent the achievement of students. Thurlow and Elliott (1998) have indicated that the purpose of such a process is to document the student's work, to provide knowledge beyond that of standardized assessments and grading processes, and to provide an accountability of educational performance. The portfolio method also has disadvantages in terms of being subjective, difficult for the student who needs a lot of structure, time-consuming, and difficult for establishing reliability and validity. These issues can be addressed particularly if the team knows of specific performance or behavioral standards that are required in a work or community situation. The portfolio can be used as an alternative way of documenting the student's ability to perform at these levels.

Critical Point The portfolio assessment provides an alternative means to evaluate a student's work and improvement over time. The portfolio can include assessment information related to academic performance, job-related skills, independent living, and social skills.

Portfolio assessment with regular and special education students uses student performances (or products) that display accomplishments and improvement over time (Airasian, 1994). Various types of student information or experiences can be included that range from academic to career development to job and community preparation. Through portfolios, a very individual record of the student's growth and development and performance in specific contexts can be recorded, making it somewhat unique (Carey,

1994). Sarkees-Wircenski and Wircenski (1994) recommend portfolio assessment as a good tool for documenting a variety of transition competencies and for directly involving the student in the assessment process. They suggest using videotapes to record students who are successfully performing a variety of tasks. This can be very convincing to a prospective employer or community individual who might not be able to see a student's potential. These types of career or transition portfolios can reflect upon progress over time in critical areas such as:

- Employability skills
- Work-related social skills
- Self-help/independent living skills
- Generalization skills
- Job-specific skills
- Home management
- Independent travel
- Safety and survival skills

Surveys and Interviews

Surveys and interviews are an effective means of gathering information directly from the student and others who are involved with the student in important settings. These individuals include parents, work supervisors and coworkers, group home staff, transportation staff, and a variety of community persons and friends. The team may need to seek out some of these individuals for their help in identifying either factors or conditions that lead to the student's success, or that create barriers.

Interviews are generally conducted face to face or by telephone. Surveys can be either self-administered or completed orally. The value of this method is that the information is obtained directly from the source. Students are the best source for their likes, dislikes, and other transition-related preferences; employers, supervisors, and coworkers are the best sources for what is important in the work environment and how students are performing; parents and families have a unique perspective on the student and their own views on the student's personality and developmental history; and friends and community members have information about interests and participation in other environments.

A number of the instruments listed previously in the formal testing section utilize an interview or survey format. These differ from informal procedures and often include scoring procedures that are based on asking the full set of questions, which are asked in the manner described in a manual.

With informal interviews and surveys, the team members may decide that certain types of information that have not been gathered by other methods are needed and so they design questions to solicit this information. It is important that when creating such an instrument the questions should be relevant, clear, and well designed. Team members may want to have their interview or survey reviewed by several other individuals to ensure its effectiveness. Also, consideration must be given as to how the respondent will answer; that is, yes-no, multiple-choice, or an open-ended format. Students may have difficulty with certain types of questions and answers, requiring that the linguistic structure and conceptual complexity be controlled. In addition, there are dangers with self-report formats because people, for example, may answer in ways that they believe will please the committee or put the student or themselves in the best light. Answers may be well-intentioned but not entirely factual; therefore, it is best to compare interview and survey responses across several individuals to find a consensus. Figure 5–1 provides a sample of a needs and preferences survey.

Situational Assessments

The primary purpose of situational assessment is to observe, record, and interpret a student's

FIGURE 5–1
Transition Needs and Preferences Survey

This survey is designed to help the school determine what type of experiences and education you will need to prepare for life after graduation from high school. It will be used to develop a long-range plan (or transition plan) that will be discussed at the next IEP meeting.

Please answer the following questions based on what you know about yourself (or the student, if filled out by a parent/guardian).

Student name: **Parent/Guardian:**

Student age: **Today's date:**

1. What kind of work or education do you hope to see yourself in after graduation from high school?

Full-Time	Part-time	
❑	❑	University or College—*academically oriented four-year program*
❑	❑	Community/Technical Colleges—*technical/paraprofessional training*
❑	❑	Adult Vocational Education—*advanced job training (e.g., secretary)*
❑	❑	Military Service—*Army, Navy, Air Force, Coast Guard, Marines, etc.*
❑	❑	Competitive Employment—*a job trained by employer (or job coach)*
❑	❑	Supported Employment—*a job with job coach training and then support*
❑	❑	Sheltered Employment—*low pay work activities and training*
❑	❑	Other__________________________________

2. What age do you want to exit school? 18 19 20 21 22

3. Is there a particular kind of work or education that you are currently interested in or other comments? If so, specify:

4. Where do you hope to ultimately live as an adult?

- ❑ Independently in a home or apartment—*generally requires more than minimum wage*
- ❑ Independently in subsidized housing—*usually requires minimum wage or higher income*
- ❑ Wheelchair accessible housing—*ability to live on own or with personal care attendant*
- ❑ Supported living—*staff assist a few hours per day cooking, shopping, budgeting, etc.*
- ❑ Group home/foster care—*staff provide 24 hour care and help in self-care, health, etc.*
- ❑ With parents or relatives—*sometimes with help of support staff or Medicaid services.*
- ❑ Other ______________________________________

5. Is there a neighborhood, city, or locality you hope to live in?

6. What types of community participation do you hope will be available to you as an adult? (check all that apply)

- ❑ Clubs or groups that meet to talk about a common interest (e.g., computers, astronomy)
  Specify, if possible ____

(*continued*)

FIGURE 5–1 (*continued*)

- ❑ Community recreational activities (e.g., YMCA, community centers, out with friends)
  Specify, if possible ______________________________
- ❑ Religious and cultural activities (e.g., church, synagogue, temple, study groups)
  Specify, if possible ______________________________
- ❑ Transportation for work and leisure activities (e.g., car, bus, friends, parents, bicycle)
  Specify type(s) and for what purpose ______________________________
- ❑ Continuing education (e.g., computers, cooking, sewing, home repair)
  Specify, if possible ______________________________
- ❑ Political participation (e.g., voting, involvement in political groups)
  Specify type of participation if possible ______________________________
- ❑ Other/ Comments: ______________________________

7. Check any of the following services that you feel would be helpful to you in achieving your goals.

- ❑ Interest Inventories (e.g., OASYS)
- ❑ In-School Job Placement
- ❑ Work Adjustment Training
- ❑ Community Work Experience
- ❑ Summer Jobs
- ❑ Entrance Exam Training (e.g., SAT)
- ❑ Job Shadowing (i.e., observing a job)
- ❑ Guidance Counseling
- ❑ Vocational Education
- ❑ College Experience
- ❑ Other/Comments: ______________________________

____

- ❑ Transportation and Driver Education
- ❑ Consumer Sciences/Home Economics
- ❑ Money Management Training
- ❑ Sewing and Clothing Care Training
- ❑ Training in Handling Emergencies
- ❑ Training in Cooking and Nutrition
- ❑ Home Repair and Maintenance Training
- ❑ First Aid Training
- ❑ Other/Comments: ______________________________

____

- ❑ Language and Hearing Services
- ❑ Accommodations and Technology
- ❑ Relationships and Marriage
- ❑ Psychology, Social Work, Psychiatry
- ❑ Occupational or Physical Therapy
- ❑ Self-Advocacy Training
- ❑ Vocational Rehabilitation
- ❑ Community Awareness Activities
- ❑ Other/Comments: ______________________________

____

- ❑ *Evaluation(s) (Specify Type Needed):* ______________________________
- ❑ *Referrals (Specify to Whom):* ______________________________

Source: From *Transition planning: A guide for parents and professionals* (p. 9), by R. Baer, R. McMahan, and R. Flexer, 1999, Kent, Ohio: Kent State University. Copyright 1999 by Robert Baer. Reprinted with permission.

general work behavior and adaptation in a specific work or community setting. The assessment provides a measure of the overall behaviors of the student and also provides the opportunity to observe the student's reaction to specific environments. The student and the team member conducting the assessment can learn information on a wide range of behaviors that are important to the student's transition goals.

The open nature of this type of assessment requires that the team provides the assessor with a specific list of behaviors to observe. The team may want information on general interaction or performance in global, descriptive forms. If the team wishes the observer to note specific types of behaviors or responses, it will need to provide specific definitions and examples of what to observe in order that this is clear. Some examples of types of observational goals include:

- Getting along with coworkers
- Accepting criticism
- Following directions
- Punctuality and attendance
- Greeting known neighbors in apartment building and stores
- Crossing streets safely
- Waiting for change when paying for items

Situational assessments can be used across a variety of settings. They also can be used in school to create "simulations" of community environments as a type of training assessment. Their usefulness is in being able to identify variables that may be problematic to the student and those that support their success. When done well (accurate observations of specific behaviors and conditions) by a number of persons who have the same conclusions, these are a useful tool in helping to select potentially successful future environments. See Case Study B for a sample of a situational assessment.

CASE STUDY B

Situational Assessment in a Library Setting

An eighth-grade student is placed in the library for an in-school work situational assessment. The purpose of the assessment is for career exploration and observation of the individual's work and social skills. The librarian and teacher determine that the student will check out books, return books to shelves, and repair torn and damaged books. Over a 3-week period the special education teacher observes the student's social interactions at the checkout desk, ability to catalog books alphabetically and numerically, and ability to work independently repairing books on an intermittent basis. The librarian agrees to supplement these data with information concerning the student's interest level, attention to task, and social interaction. At the end of the situational assessment period, the librarian, teacher, and student discuss the student's interest level, attention to task, and social interaction as well as the student's strengths, needs, and interests noted throughout the assessment. Additional in-school work sites are then discussed and compared in order to further the career exploration process.

Source: Adapted from Sitlington, Neubert, Begun, Lombard, & Le Conte, 1996.

Work Samples

Work samples were described earlier in terms of formalized assessments. When they are developed or modified to accommodate specific work settings, specific student needs and strengths, or to evaluate a specific school or vocational program, they become informal assessments. These measures screen for relevant aptitudes, sample specific components of programs, and identify subsequent assessments that may be more specific. An additional variation to work samples is to build in a teaching component so that rate and style of learning in relationship to specific work tasks are noted. These types of work samples can serve as a basis to match compatibility of student aptitudes and training program requirements or to determine training and accommodation needs within a specific program.

Behavioral Assessment

Behavior assessment is used to assess functional relationships between training and observed behavior. Many of these processes are based on the use of applied behavioral analysis to identify and examine thoroughly factors that are contributing to the existence of certain behaviors. Although this process is quite detailed and deserving of separate study, a brief summary will be included here.

Observation and documentation of behaviors is the basis for much of our work with students with disabilities, with written goals and objectives that are observable and measurable. Many techniques described here can be applied to the range of student behaviors (e.g., improving quantity or quality of work products and improving quality of hygiene practices) and are not limited to undesirable interpersonal behaviors.

Five major recording procedures are employed in behavior assessment. Anecdotal recording is for the purpose of identifying a behavior and its antecedent events, and reinforcing consequences. The behavior must be specifically defined so that all observers know exactly what to measure. For example, a "tantrum" must be defined as the exact series of behaviors that a student demonstrates so that if she just stamps her feet or engages in one aspect but not the full tantrum episode, this can be accurately noted. (When more is known about the behavior, the staff may choose to watch for "early" signs, which have been shown to indicate that a tantrum will soon begin; however, initial observations must first identify all aspects of a sequence.)

Antecedent events are those incidents that happen right before the behavior. They suggest possible causes or triggers and, thus, they are important. The consequences are events that happen immediately after the behavior, such as "time-out," lots of attention from other students and adults, and so on. The following example is based in a case presented by Browning (1997). Through this analysis, an intervention program can be designed around the behavior under consideration: "When Bill has a tantrum at his work site, what occurs immediately prior to that outburst, and what happens immediately following it?" The analysis may show that Bill becomes angered by a certain coworker who won't talk with him (because the coworker is focusing on his work), and the tantrum gives Bill considerable attention from others, which reassures him that he is "likable." Another explanation (depending on which antecedents and consequences are found to be related) is that Bill becomes bored with work (he becomes increasingly agitated, makes increasing attempts to talk with others, or asks to go to the restroom) and the tantrum removes him from the workstation and also reduces the amount of work he has to do.

Observers can use one or more ways to count how often and at what times the target behaviors occur. Event recording assesses the frequency in which the event occurs: "How often does Bill have tantrums on the job-training site?" Time sampling is for the purpose of determining the time period in which the behavior occurs: "Do Bill's outbursts seem to happen in the early mornings/late afternoons, beginning or end of week, when few or many work peers are around?" Interval recording is an observation period that is divided into a number of equal time intervals in which the presence or absence of the behavior (activities) is recorded, especially when the behavior is relatively frequent. Finally, duration recording refers to the length of time that the behavior (activities) occurs. "How long do Bill's tantrums last?" All these types of measurements help to identify specific conditions that lead to the behavior, prolong it, and lead to its happening again. The type of recording depends on whether the behavior occurs frequently or infrequently, or if time-related patterns are suspected. Observing periodic tantrums, how often Bill stopped working to try to talk with a coworker, or how often and long he engaged in "off-task" behaviors would be measured using different techniques.

These observational techniques are used to identify a pattern of behavior and then to document behavioral changes. First, behavioral assessment is used to establish a "baseline" of measurement prior to any training or intervention. This establishes the type, rate, and frequency of the behavior under "typical" conditions. Powell et al. (1991) refer to this baseline assessment as "a process of obtaining information about the worker's current ability to complete an activity before any instruction" (p. 64). From this baseline pattern, the team can gauge if and how much change, if any, has occurred as a result of instruction or intervention.

The area of behavioral change is extremely complex and the team may need to consult a specialist. Improving behavior does not merely consist of reducing or eliminating problematic behaviors but also must teach appropriate replacement behavior. For example, a team may feel successful in reducing Bill's frequency and duration of tantrums. However, this will be short lived if they realize a few weeks later that he has now become increasingly physically violent with training staff and coworkers.

When done consistently and conscientiously, behavioral assessment and management is an important informal assessment tool. It can be used across the range of transition settings to meet the requirements of a variety of work, independent living, and personal-social environments. Powell et al. (1991) provide a practical step-by-step guide for conducting baseline assessments on individuals for supported employment training.

Appropriate Use of Tests

When using any type of assessment instrument, whether a formal device to collect general information or an informal instrument that the team has developed and reviewed to assemble a more complete transition profile of the student, one must follow the intended purposes, technical considerations, and interpretation guidelines. Formal and standardized assessments usually provide this information and expect evaluators to adhere to it. Any change means that the results will not be comparable and the interpretation will need to be modified; the standard interpretation of scores may not be possible.

Informal assessments will not have these guidelines, so the purposes, technical considerations, and interpretation must be carefully determined. Teams who construct their own instruments need to spend time ensuring as much validity and reliability as possible. A more specific set of guidelines for method selection was provided by Sitlington et al. (1997), as shown in Table 5–5. These authors reinforce the need for ongoing evaluation that samples behavior across multiple settings, using several assessors and different methods or instruments. All assessments must be appropriate to the individual and accommodate learning, linguistic, cultural, and technology/assistive device needs. The results must be reported and synthesized into a format that all team members can understand in order to maximize their usefulness in planning.

Critical Point Informal assessments do not have the strict guidelines for administration and evaluation—as do formal assessments. It is very important for transition teams to identify the behavioral goals for assessment as well as the method of data collection to ensure valid results.

In summary, there are a variety of formal and informal assessments that transition teams will use when planning and conducting a series of transition assessments. Tests should be selected

TABLE 5–5

Guidelines for Transition Assessment Processes

- Assessment methods must be tailored to the types of information needed and the decisions to be made regarding transition planning and various postsecondary outcomes.
- Specific methods selected must be appropriate for the learning characteristics of the individual, including cultural and linguistic differences.
- Assessment methods must incorporate assistive technology or accommodations that will allow an individual to demonstrate his or her abilities and potential.
- Assessment methods must occur in environments that resemble actual vocational training, employment, independent living, or community environments.
- Assessment methods must produce outcomes that contribute to ongoing development, planning, and implementation of "next steps" in the individual's transition process.
- Assessment methods must be varied and include a sequence of activities that sample an individual's behavior and skills over time.
- Assessment data must be verified by more than one method and by more than one person.
- Assessment data must be synthesized and interpreted to individuals with disabilities, their families, and transition team members.

Source: From Sitlington, C. L., Neubert, D. A., & LeConte, P. J. (1997). Transition assessment: The position of the division on career development and transition. *CDEI, 19*, 69–79.

based on their ability to provide information that the team needs in relation to potential transition outcomes. Teams may need to ask the advice of diagnosticians in making these choices. Diagnosticians (or school psychologists) may be the only persons who are qualified to give certain types of formal assessments.

When the assessments have been completed, the accumulated results should be synthesized and compiled into a transition profile. This will ensure that team members have a comprehensive understanding of the student's needs, strengths, and preferences and that there are no additional knowledge gaps. This synthesis must be done in a manner that is clear to the student, the parents, and all team members. The assessment results form the basis for all later transition planning and determination of appropriate outcomes and therefore, must be done carefully and used conscientiously.

The assessments that the team chooses to use will have both benefits and drawbacks to consider. Formal assessments provide comparative information but may not measure important specific aspects of performance. Informal assessments may require much more time to develop, use, and interpret but can provide setting-specific information concerning the student's performance. Table 5–6 provides a comparison of types of formal and informal assessments that may be used in secondary special education.

Interdisciplinary Assessment Processes

Collaborative Processes

The process of identifying assessment needs, carrying out the assessments, interpreting the results and compiling them into a succinct profile, and reassessing the information gathered for accuracy, relevancy, and completeness is a very complex task. One important characteristic that makes this process successful is the development of collaborative relationships among team members (Gajar et al., 1993). A trusting and open relationship will allow the many professional

TABLE 5–6

Formal and Informal Transition Assessments

Formal	Informal
• Intelligence, achievement, adaptive behavior • Aptitudes, interests, values, personality • Motivation and affective factors • Work samples • Transition-adaptive behavior assessments • Criterion-referenced • Transition assessments • Norm-referenced transition assessments	• Situational or observational learning styles assessment; • Curriculum-based assessments from courses; • Observational reports from teachers, employers, and parents/guardians; • Situational assessments in home, community, and work settings; • Environmental assessments (specific to student's placement options); • Personal-future planning activities/procedures; • Structured interviews with students; • Structured interviews with parents/guardians/advocates/peers; • Adaptive, behavioral, or functional skill inventories/checklists; • Social histories; • Rating scales of employability, independent living, and personal-social skills; • Applied technology/vocational educational prerequisite skills assessments; and • General physical examinations.

Source: Adapted from Clark, G. M. (1996). Transition planning assessment for secondary-level students with learning disabilities. *Journal of Learning Disabilities, 29*(1), 79–92.

disciplines and community representatives that may be present, including the student, parents, and interested neighbors and friends, to share their perceptions and to participate in providing support and services in planning and achieving transition outcomes.

The amount and variety of information collected across types of instruments and observers/assessors may be difficult to summarize and synthesize. Results may be contradictory or raise additional questions. Team members may be unfamiliar with or doubtful about some types of testing. Establishing and maintaining open communication will allow issues and questions to be addressed early and while there is still time to explore alternatives.

The Assistive Technology Consideration and Assessment Process

As noted earlier, IDEA 1997 specifically indicated that all children receiving special education services must be considered for assistive technology (AT). Each domain area (e.g., physical, communication, cognition) needs to be specifically addressed and considered in terms of potential AT for identified barriers. School personnel then specify what the student is currently using, what the barriers are within each area and what AT might be needed. As with other types of assessment, it is impossible for any single individual to be an expert in all types of AT (Holder-Brown & Parette, 1992). Therefore, the appropriate identification and implementation of AT usually relies upon the knowledge of several disciplines (Holder-Brown & Parette) including occupational therapists, special education, teachers and speech language pathologists. Once there is an agreement that a student should be considered for AT, an AT assessment may occur. There are several models of AT assessment (e.g., Blackhurst, & Cross, 1993; Reed, 1997: Zabala, 1994). Regardless of what AT assessment model one might use, there are three common characteristics that are embedded within all assessment models: (1) the environmental demands placed on that individual; (2) the individual's needs, abilities, and preferences (Chambers, 1997); and (3) the technology characteristics (Thorkildsen, 1994). Additionally, an AT evaluation should be done in a variety of environments to determine the impact on school activities across curriculum areas, in vocational sites, and in community and home settings (Bauder, Lewis, Gobert, & Bearden, 1997).

As an example of AT assessment, Blackhurst (1997) illustrates how assessment can be accomplished through the use of the unifying functional model (see Figure 5–2). The key elements to this model include environment and context, functional demands, exploration of options, personal perceptions, personal resources, external supports, functional response, personal changes, and evaluation and feedback. Using this model as a process for decision making, a school team would be able to make judgments about the use of technology based on a student's functions in response to academic demands as well as in community and vocational environments. Figure 5–3 illustrates use of the model.

Comprehensive Transition Planning

One strategy that may help the team to synthesize assessment data and to prioritize the results into achievable goals is by using a comprehensive planning format. A number of authors have developed holistic procedures to promote comprehensive and cohesive transition planning. Three such programs include the following:

1. Personal Futures Planning (Mount, 1989, 1992; O'Brien, 1987): This program determines activities, supports, and next steps needed.
2. McGill Action Planning System (MAPS) (Forest, Pearpoint, & Snow, 1993; Pearpoint, 1990): Identifies "dreams" and "nightmares," strengths and needs for planning.
3. Circles of Support (Forest & Lusthaus, 1989; Forest, Pearpoint & Snow, 1993; Pearpoint, 1993): Identifies abilities, strategies, and commitments among non-paid supportive peers or colleagues related to an individual's needs.

All these techniques involve collaboration between professional and community individuals who begin with conceptualizing present and/or future life goals for the student. These may best suit transition teams who prefer open-ended and highly individualized approaches. The benefit gained is from the supportive networks that are developed through this process and that can continue well beyond the end of the student's schooling. However, not all agencies and individuals will be equally accepting of a highly student-centered approach (Luft, Rumrill, & Snyder-Marks, in press).

Several curriculum-based transition programs also include frameworks that assist with assembling comprehensive assessment data. The Brolin (1993, 1996) LCCE curriculum described earlier provides detailed and comprehensive curricular planning across 22 domain areas. The Ysseldyke and Thurlow (1994) curriculum and assessment program is similarly detailed and comprehensive. Its goal of ensuring productive and participating students regardless of the presence of a disability may be well-suited for students in inclusive settings.

FIGURE 5–2
Unifying Functional Model

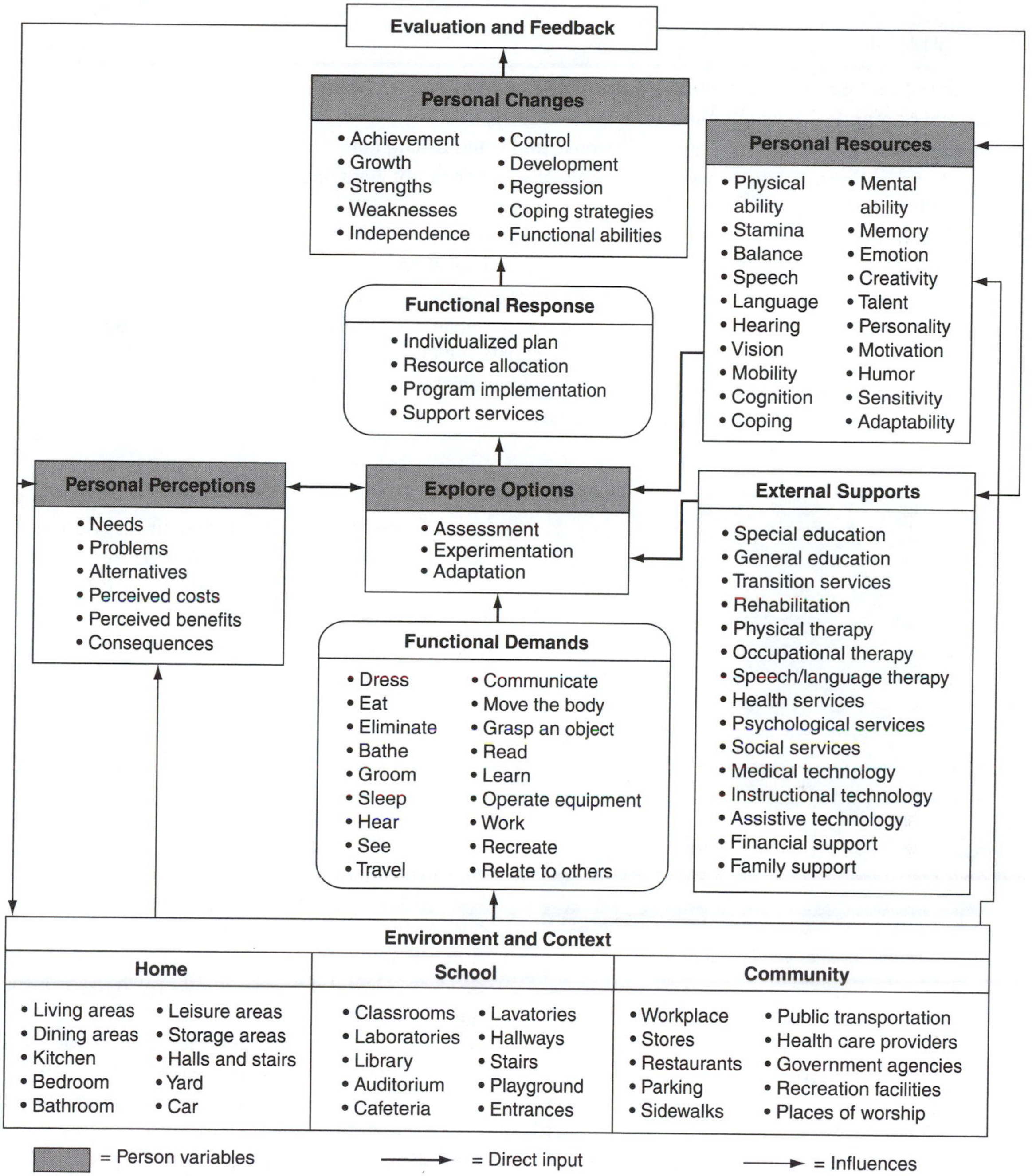

Source: A Framework for Aligning Technology with Transition Competencies by A. E. Blackhurst, E. A. Lahm, E. M. Harrison, N. G. Chandler, *Career Development for Exceptional Individuals*, 22, 1999, p. 159. Copyright 1999 by the Council for Exceptional Children, reprinted with permission.

FIGURE 5–3
Functional Model

Environment and context: Completing written tasks at job site.

Functional demands: Uses left hand, poor fine motor control.

Explore options: Adapted pencil grips, ergonomic pens, and writing cuff.

Personal perceptions: Prefers to work independently and does not want accommodation to "single him out" or to make him look "different."

Personal resources: Willing to try adaptations in order to complete written tasks in a more timely manner.

External supports: Occuptional therapist available for consultation.

Functional response: Weighted ergonomic pen and clipboard.

Personal changes: Accommodation provided support for individual to complete job tasks. Individual satisfied that accommodation did not make him look or act different in order to complete written tasks.

Evaluation and feedback: Follow-up by occupational therapist to review accommodations and to determine the need for other solutions if warranted.

Transition planning includes multiple outcomes.

Teams who use a process approach may prefer this. A curriculum guide by Kohler (1996) provides a comprehensive delineation of elements needed for transition success. Teams who prefer a detailed product focus for planning may wish to use this program.

When teams do not choose to use a comprehensive planning tool, they may wish to make checklists of services, providers, and specific transition goals with more specificity across the three broad transition domains. Wehman, Moon, Everson, Wood, and Barcus (1988) recommend a detailed listing for assessing the student's needs in the following areas: (1) employment, (2) vocational education/training, (3) postsecondary education, (4) financial/income needs, (5) independent living, (6) transportation/mobility, (7) social relationships, (8) recreation/leisure, (9) health/safety, and (10) self-advocacy/future planning.

The task of identifying, carrying out, and synthesizing comprehensive assessment and planning is highly complex. In addition to using one of the comprehensive planning strategies described earlier, the team may need to establish a procedure to ensure that all aspects of the assessment process have been observed. Such a process should include the steps described in Table 5–7.

Use of a comprehensive planning guide or a task-focused process with checklists such as described earlier can assist the team in determining and coordinating the assessment, data synthesis, and needs-prioritizing processes. However, for some students, this is likely to necessitate moving beyond current models and requiring ingenuity and creativity from team members (Luft,

TABLE 5–7

Steps To Ensure Comprehensive Transition Assessment

1. Determine a shared vision of the student's potential future. Use this to identify areas for gathering data.
2. Review past records and existing information for transition-related information. Identify and confirm areas in which additional information is needed.
3. Identify potential formal and informal assessments that can be used for each area above. Use a comprehensive planning or curriculum program, or checklist across the domains of work, living, personal-social current and future environments to ensure coverage of all important areas.
4. Contact diagnosticians and specialized assessors for recommendations on current and additional instruments, if needed. Create additional informal assessments (with assistance/advice from specialists).
5. Schedule formal assessments to be given by qualified evaluators and informal assessments that occur across the student's multiple settings. Present scores and interpretations in written form and discuss with the team. Ensure that all members understand results and their implications regarding potential outcomes and goals.
6. Assemble all assessment information into a comprehensive and clear transition profile.
7. Assess profile for additional information gaps or when information is insufficient, retest and reevaluate contradictory results. Use consensus to reestablish/confirm a shared vision of the student's future.
8. Schedule ongoing assessments, particularly in areas where the student is receiving training or intervention procedures to ensure that the program is successful and that the student is achieving desired short-term goals. Monitor areas that are subject to change as a result of growth and development, maturing interests, and life experiences.
9. Periodically, reevaluate ongoing assessments to ensure their continued usefulness. Examine new procedures and formats if they seem more appropriate.
10. Periodically, reexamine team membership to include additional members who can contribute new information as the student's transition training settings change. Examine the effectiveness of team processes to maintain open, positive communication among members. Make adjustments to assimilate new and changing membership.

1999). Much success of the assessment and transition planning processes depend on the dedication and motivation of the team to meet challenges and to design appropriate solutions.

Conclusion

Transition is a process in special education that combines a common frame of reference with transition-specific requirements for assessment and planning with students and families. Interdisciplinary assessment and planning requirements use student and family-generated transition goals to form a framework for consensus-based planning with professional and community individuals. Assessment processes provide the informational foundations upon which these interdisciplinary processes operate in planning and implementing transition goals.

The multiple-step process that comprises transition assessment processes results in a comprehensive transition profile of needs, strengths, and preferences of the student that is updated and evaluated in an ongoing manner. Transition assessment provides information and data on the important planning, curriculum, and instructional decisions needed by youth with disabilities, their teachers, and other members of their teams. These assessments consist of both standardized (formal) and nonstandardized (informal) assessments that provide the variety of information that the team will need in completing its tasks. Ongoing assessments are needed to modify goals as a result of growth, training, and experience; and to choose programs and guide program and service delivery so that students are supported for success. Interdisciplinary and team process are necessary for effective communication and for ensuring consensus throughout the assessment and planning processes. When effectively and conscientiously carried out, team members will have confidence that their resulting transition plans are based on accurate and reliable data and are likely to lead to the student's successful movement into adulthood.

Study Questions

1. Describe the similarities and differences between special education assessments and transition assessments.
2. What are the three transition domains and the skills tested in each area?
3. Describe the purpose of formal and informal assessments.
4. What kind of information do formal and informal assessments provide?
5. What are the advantages and disadvantages in using formal and informal assessments?
6. What types of information can be gained from the use of functional or ecological assessments?
7. How can academic assessments be used to complement informal assessments?
8. What is the purpose of the comprehensive transition planning approach to informal assessment development?
9. In your opinion, what is the best method of assessment in transition?

Websites

Assessing Students for Workplace Readiness:
http://vocserve.berkeley.edu/centerFocus/cf15.html

Vocational Evaluation and Work Adjustment Association:
http://www.fairaccess.org/vewaa_policy.htm

6

A Curriculum Framework for Transition

Debra Bauder

Thomas Simmons

Robert Baer

LEARNING OBJECTIVES

The objectives of this chapter are:

1. Describe what is meant by the general education curriculum.
2. Identify how the IDEA supports participation of students with disabilities in the general curriculum.
3. Understand how standards-based reforms can benefit students with disabilities.
4. Understand how standards-based reforms can be reconciled with the individualized education programs (IEPs) of students with disabilities.
5. Understand how to develop a high school course of study for a student with a disability.
6. Identify various curriculum access strategies.
7. Describe universal design curriculum approach to education and its importance to student participation in the general curriculum.

Introduction

Curriculum is the foundation of any student's education. Specifically, it has been defined as "a master plan for selecting content and organizing learning experiences for the purpose of changing and developing learners' behaviors and insights" (Armstrong, 1990, p. 4). The curriculum of a school is the centerpiece of the educational programs and opportunities available to the students. It is a statement about the philosophy of the school and about the purpose of education, and it is a reflection of the values of the community. From the student's point of view, the curriculum is all-important because it lays out what the student will be taught and how such subject matter content and educational experiences are organized.

Although this chapter concerns curricular options and programs provided in high school, much of what happens in transition occurs prior to and after secondary education. A career education approach recognizes this long-term view. In the discussion of career theories in Chapter 4, life-span approaches to career development have emphasized the additional importance of the early years as well as adulthood. The general education literature describes these new life-span models, which are more flexible than the traditional high school and based on the developmental needs of youth. These programs can be more than 4 years, can be less than 4 years, and can provide options beyond the required, programmed set of units in core academic subjects.

The authors of this chapter will present curriculum from a life-span career education perspective that focuses on addressing the skills and competencies students need to perform in desired adult roles in the community. The authors will present the general curriculum and standards-based reform in terms that reconcile them with individual student transition needs, interests, preferences, and goals. Program options and the student's course of study will be used as the framework for achieving transition goals and making progress toward adult outcomes (i.e., providing access, participation, and progress in the general curriculum).

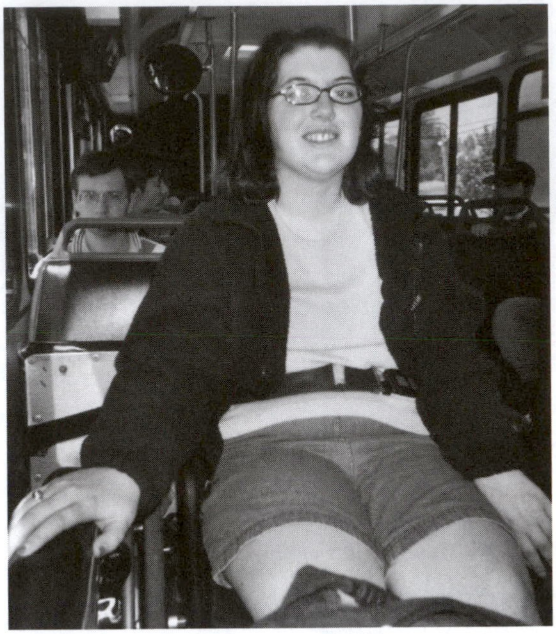

Successful postschool outcomes depend on broad curricular standards.

The General Curriculum and Standards-Based Reform

Given the very subjective character and community-driven nature of schools and curriculum, it is not surprising that there are many opinions and perspectives. A narrow view of curriculum would be a set of books from which teachers teach. Another limited view is that curriculum is the core academic subject content (language arts, math, social studies, and science). The regular education literature on curriculum presents diverse views reflecting a broad range of possible content and organization. In one view, curriculum is viewed as educating students in achieving quality-of-life outcomes (Berman & Roderick, 1977). In another view, curriculum can be simply seen as required courses and subjects. A third view is that curriculum consists of all the experiences a student gets in school including the plans for selecting and organizing those experiences (Armstrong, 1990).

Public secondary school curriculum traditionally has been governed by a "developmental orientation" (Schloss, Smith, & Schloss, 1995) where teaching was organized in a sequential fashion within content domains with each competency built on the mastery of previous content (Schloss et al.,). Typically, planning in this curriculum was based on a set number of units (i.e., Carnegie units) in various content domains such as mathematics, English, social studies, and science, where students were required to successfully complete a set number of academic units in order to graduate (Morse, 2001). Teacher-driven curriculum committees in local school districts controlled how this content was delivered, but had little control over the overall curriculum, which was set by state requirements (Morse).

However, in 1983 A *Nation at Risk* (National Commission on Excellence in Education) had a significant impact on how schools delivered educational services and ushered in 20 years of reform in education. Much of this reform was focused on what was taught and to what standard of performance (Pugach & Warger, 2001). This reform movement led to the development of standards-based curricula that have been adopted by many states and local education agencies. The underlying premise of a standards-based education was to raise the competency or skill level of all children. Since that time, various professional organizations, such as the National Council of Teachers of Mathematics and the National Science Teachers Association have developed and published their content standards.

Standards-based curriculum focused on the outcomes of education in relation to external standards of achievement (Hitchcock, Meyer, Rose & Jackson, 2002; Nolet & McLaughlin, 2000) with the expectation of significantly improved student achievement (Marzano, 2001; Wehmeyer, Argan & Lattin, 2001). However, Thurlow (2002) indicated that there were other reasons for adopting standards-based education. In particular, a predominant viewpoint was that instructional programs would improve (Thurlow, Wehmeyer, Argan, & Lattin) if standards were mandatory. The standards-based curriculum typically included a list of learning expectations that were sometimes referred to as "curricular aims," "common curricular goals," "standards," and "benchmarks" (Ferguson, Droege, Lester, Meyer, Ralph, Sampson, & Williams, 2001).

Under the No Child Left Behind (NCLB) Act of 2001 (P.L. 107–220), all states were required to implement statewide accountability systems that set academic standards in each content area for what students should know and be able to do at various times in their school career. In some cases, standards represented the level of acceptable performance on assessment of a particular skill or in a particular domain (NCLB, 2001). One of the challenges faced by teachers educating students with disabilities was to achieve comparable outcomes, or standards, for all students, (Marzano, 2001). Children with disabilities, however, continued to be excluded from many of these types of educational initiatives (Metheny, 1997; Pugach & Warger, 2001, Thurlow, 2001).

The IDEA of 1997 tried to address this problem by requiring that students with disabilities be involved in the general curriculum (20 U.S.C. § 1414 [d][1][A]). In the appendix to the IDEA regulations (34 C.F.R. Parts 300 and 301) it was noted that:

> In enacting the IDEA Amendments of 1997, Congress found that research, demonstration, and practice over the past 20 years in special education and related disciplines have demonstrated that an

> effective educational system now and in the future must maintain high academic standards and clear performance goals for children with disabilities, consistent with the standards and expectations for all students in the educational system, and provide for appropriate and effective strategies and methods to ensure that students who are children with disabilities have maximum opportunities to achieve those standards and goals. (34.300 58A)

The IDEA of 1997 also supported inclusion in the general curriculum by requiring that all students with disabilities be involved in state and district testing or for a small minority of students, alternative standards-based testing (20 U.S.C. § 1414 [d][1][A]). As suggested by deFur (2002), students with disabilities who were included in the general curriculum would have improved academic performance, and this would be reflected in state and district-wide assessment results. Furthermore, teachers and administrators would use these standard-based assessment results to improve teaching. Figure 6–1 depicts how standards-based reform was designed to improve outcomes.

Full participation in state and district-wide testing became a problem for many students with disabilities when states began using them as a condition for high school graduation and promotion (Curran, 1999; deFur, 2002; Thurlow, 2002). The narrow academic focus of school reform and the NCLB, and the lack of a definition for the "general curriculum" in the IDEA, led many educators to equate the general curriculum with academic approaches (Turnbull, Turnbull, Wehmeyer, & Park, 2003). This narrow focus violated the underlying intent of the IDEA, which stated that all students with disabilities should "be prepared to lead productive, independent, adult lives, to the maximum extent possible" (20 U.S.C. § 1400 [c] [5] [E] [ii]) and that they "participate in extracurricular and other non-academic activities" (20 U.S.C. § 1414 [d][1][A][II][iii]). The appendix to the IDEA of 1997 regulations noted three core concepts in the development of the IEP, including: (a) student involvement and progress in the general curriculum, (b) the involvement of parents and students in decision making, and (c) "the preparation of students with disabilities for employment and other postschool activities" (34.300 57A). Additionally, Part D of the IDEA required that state improvement grants: "clearly define, in measurable terms, the school and post-school results that children with disabilities are expected to achieve" (20 U.S.C. § 1445 [a][6][c]). Turnbull et al. noted that access to the general curriculum was not enough, if it did not address how students with disabilities would achieve quality-of-life outcomes.

Turnbull et al. (2003) have argued for a curricular model that addresses standards-based reforms *and* quality-of-life outcomes. Proponents of standards-based education have argued that this type of education broadens options and post-secondary outcomes for students with disabilities by equipping them with skills that can be used in any setting (deFur, 2002; Greene & Kochhar-Bryant, 2003; Turnbull et al., 2003). Proponents of quality-of-life oriented education point to research indicating that functional curricula, community experiences, and vocational education have been correlated with improved retention rates and employment outcomes for students with disabilities (Blackorby & Wagner, 1996; Greene & Kochhar-Bryant, 2003). The IDEA represented both positions by requiring participation in the general curriculum and the development of an "appropriate education" based on the students unique needs, interests, and preferences.

Critical Point The IDEA described the general curriculum as including a focus on quality-of-life outcomes.

A Model for Transition and Standards-Based Education

The education system of the United States has long recognized the need for a variety of educational approaches. Gray (2002) has described

FIGURE 6–1
Assumptions About Educational Reform

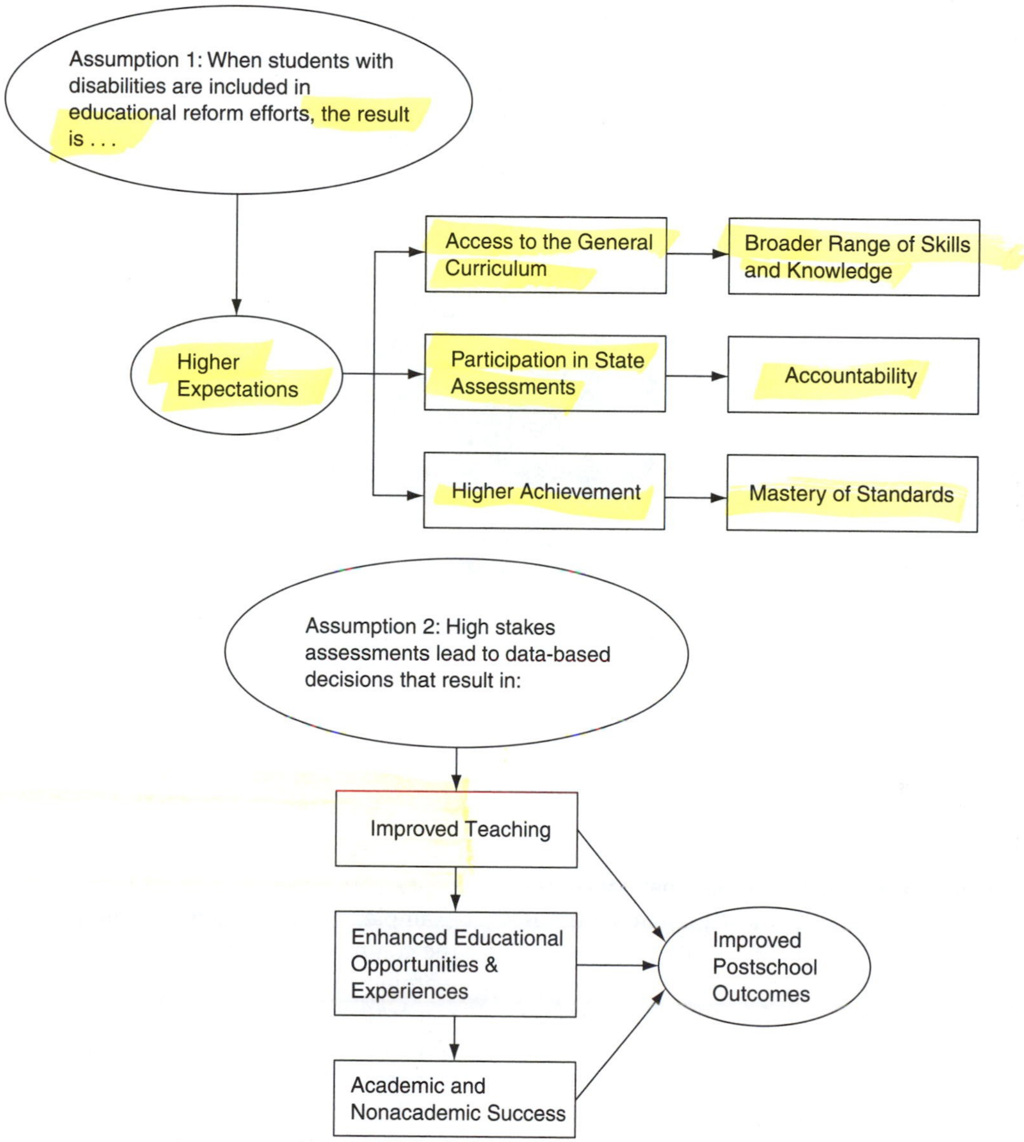

Source: From deFur, S. H. (2002). Education reform, high-stakes assessment, and students with disabilities. *Remedial and Special Education, 23*(4), 205. Copyright 2002 by PRO-ED. Reprinted with permission.

FIGURE 6–2
Standards-Based Curriculum Model

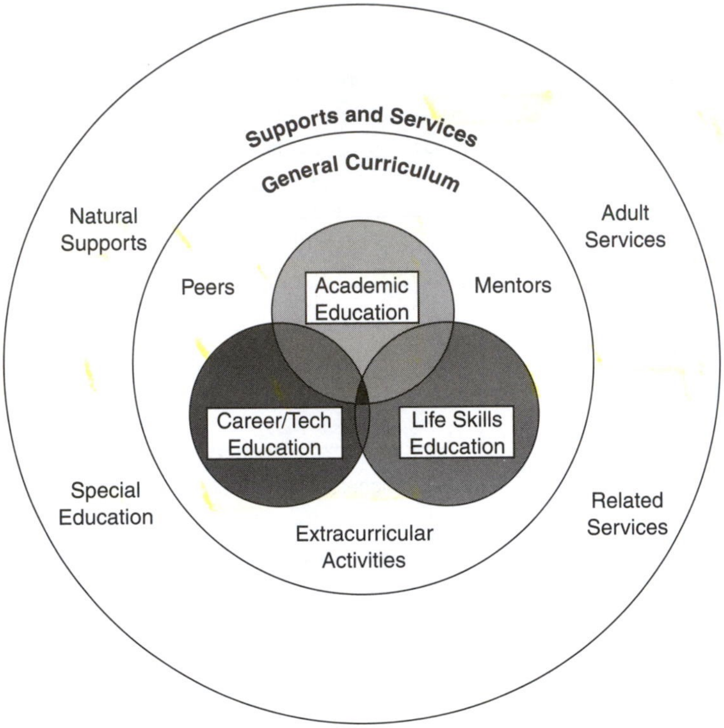

education in American high schools as falling into three typical courses of study: (a) academic, (b) career and technical, and (c) general and life skills. Figure 6–2 depicts a model that conceptualizes these three educational approaches as distinct but overlapping. They are depicted as distinct because they represent career pathways that may be emphasized for students based on their unique needs, interests, and preferences (Greene, 2003). They are depicted as overlapping because under standards-based reforms all students are expected to achieve common core standards in state and district tests (Turnbull et. al., 2003).

It should be emphasized that as a result of the IDEA of 1997 and the No Child Left Behind Act, the three educational approaches depicted in Figure 6–2 no longer represent separate curricula. Now academic, career/technical, and life skills educators must all focus on the same content standards with the only difference being the context in which those skills are taught. For example, in the academic approach, addressing the content standard of addition would entail the learning of rules and abstract processes. A career/technical approach might address this same content standard by having students solve work-related problems using addition. A life skills approach might address the addition content standard by having students balance a checkbook or count out change. Depending on the student, the educator may choose a particular approach based on the student's needs and career interests.

Figure 6–2 also depicts overlap between neighboring educational approaches depicting areas where multiple approaches can be especially beneficial. The overlap between academic and career/technical education suggests the need for combining these educational approaches when academic approaches can be applied to solving career/technical problems and where career/technical approaches can provide experience in applying academic principles. Likewise, academic approaches can be combined with life skills in areas where academic skills can be applied to life problems (such as checkbook balancing) or where life skills approaches can provide practical experiences in applying academic competencies. Life skills and career/technical education may be combined when competencies in these two areas are mutually supportive (e.g., social skill development and workplace behaviors).

The distinct areas of the three circles represent the educational approaches that may be emphasized in a students' particular course of study. These areas could be addressed in a student's IEP. Typically, academic educational approaches might be emphasized for some students seeking a 4-year college degree, while the career/technical educational approaches might be emphasized for students seeking entrance into 2-year colleges, technical schools, or competitive employment after graduation. Life skills educational approaches may be emphasized for students with the most significant disabilities seeking supported employment and/or supported living after graduation (Greene, 2003).

Encircling the general curriculum is the range of support services that help students gain access and that promote movement to postschool settings. These include natural supports, related services, transition services, and adult services. Natural supports include the self-family-friend networks that support both educational and postschool outcomes. Related services include the range of professional services (e.g., special education tutoring, assistive technology, psychology, physical therapy, audiology, mobility training) that help students participate and progress in the general curriculum and function more independently in the community. Transition services include instruction, community experiences, career activities, and other services designed to help students with disabilities achieve their postschool goals. Adult services include vocational rehabilitation, developmental disability services, income support, and other programs designed primarily to support performance in postschool settings.

Critical Point The three typical courses of study in American high schools are: (1) academics, (2) career and technical, and (3) general and life skills.

Academic Education

Academic education represents the most prevalent approach (i.e., academic, career/technical, and life skills) in addressing the general curriculum. Approximately 70% of all students participated primarily in academic education (NCES, 2001), which has typically focused on preparing them to perform in postsecondary academic settings (Greene, 2003). Academic educational approaches have become important for students with disabilities (Baer et al., 2003) because they have been entering 4-year colleges and postsecondary education in dramatically increasing numbers in the past decades (Gajar, 1998). Greene (2003) noted that a typical high school academic education for a student entering postsecondary education included:

- 2 years of history and social science
- 4 years of English
- 3 years of math including algebra and geometry
- 2 years of lab science
- 2 years of foreign language
- 1 year performing arts
- 4 semesters of electives
- Completion of the Scholastic Aptitude Test (SAT)
- The American College Test (ACT)

While academic education approaches have been useful for students entering postsecondary education, they have presented a problem for students with disabilities whose postsecondary goals did not include a 4-year university or college or who learned better through applied educational approaches (Greene, 2003). Many of these students show better retention and postschool outcomes using career/technical and/or life skills educational approaches (Baer et al., 2003; Blackorby & Wagner, 1996).

Critical Point Academic programs represent the largest of the three curricular areas. This is important for students with disabilities interested in postsecondary education because high school requirements have changed to mirror college entrance requirements.

Career/Technical Education

Vocational and career/technical educational approaches were used with about 25% of the secondary school population. Vocational education has been around since the early 1900s (Gray, 2002) and was the precursor to career/technical programs. Generally, vocational educational approaches have been more focused on preparing students for specific occupations than career/technical education, which has adopted more of a career education approach. Cobb and Neubert (1992) developed a broadly defined model for vocational education that is presented in Figure 6–3. In their model, in the middle school years vocational education approaches focus on developing employability skills and awareness of the range of vocational options. Students then enter occupational preparation and learn through work experiences in the secondary school years. These experiences serve as the basis for the student's selection of postsecondary options that then determine the need for ongoing support (Cobb & Neubert, 1992).

Career education began to emerge in the 1970s and provided a broader focus than vocational education (Halpern, 1985). While there were several references to career education prior

FIGURE 6–3
Model for Vocational Education

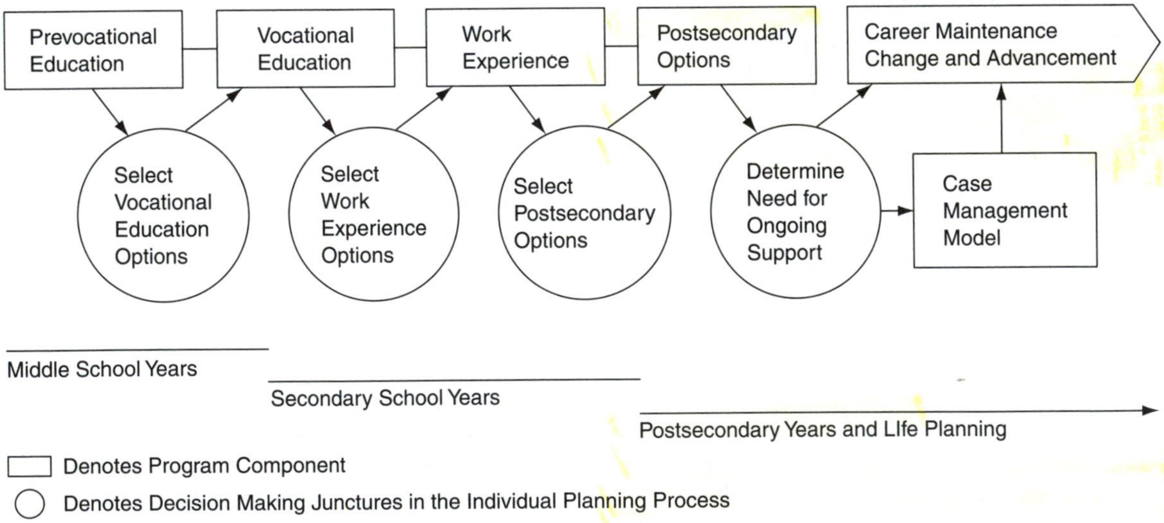

From: Greene, G. (2003). Best Practices in Transition in Greene, G. S., Kochhar-Bryant, C. A. (Eds.), *Pathways to Successful Transition for Youth with Disabilities. (pp. 154-196),* Upper Saddle River, NJ: Pearson Education. Copyright 2003 by Pearson Education. Reprinted with permission.

to this, it was Sidney Marland's work in 1971 when he was the U.S. Commissioner of Education that defined career education as a process of "learning about living" as well as "earning a living" (Brolin, 1997; Clark & Kolstoe, 1995). Kokaska and Brolin (1985) later expanded this definition as follows: "Career education is the process of systematically coordinating all school, family, and community components together to facilitate each individual's potential for economic, social, and personal fulfillment" (p. 43).

In the 1990s, "vocational education" was renamed "career and technical education" (CTE) as these career education approaches were adopted. Career/technical programs were focused on "Tech Prep" programs (Gray, 2002) sometimes called "2 + 2 programs" in the Carl D. Perkins Act of 1990 (P.L. 98–524). In CTE programs, high schools developed specialized training designed to lead into postsecondary job training programs that were, in turn, connected to local labor markets. The CTE model was designed to meet regional employers' labor needs by conducting labor market surveys and by developing specialized workforce training. Table 6–1 illustrates how high school students can move into entry-level jobs, or into postsecondary education and skilled jobs, as a result of high school CTE programs.

Career/technical education was also infused into the general curriculum as a result of reform promoted under the School to Work Opportunities Act of 1994 (P.L. 103–239). This grew out of the work of the Secretary's Commission on Achieving Necessary Skills (SCANS) whose mission was to determine the skills that secondary students needed to succeed in the world of work. The overall goal of the SCANS was to focus on a "high-performance economy characterized by

TABLE 6–1

Examples of Tech Prep Training and Job Outcomes

High School	
Earn a high school diploma and take these high school courses	**Train for these entry-level jobs**
Business Communications, Accounting I and II, Advanced Accounting, Mathematics of Finance, Mathematics, and English	Cashier; Night Auditor/Bookkeeper; Brokerage/Statement Clerk; Billing Clerk; Payroll/Timekeeping Clerk
Receive an *A* or *B* in above course and gain college credit in an articulated program at member colleges and universities	
Community College	
Skill Training	**Skilled Jobs**
Earn an associate degree from a member technical and community college and take required courses in: • Computers and Word Processing • Accounting • International Business • Business Law and Economics • Marketing and Management	Accounting Clerk; Tax Preparer; Internal Auditor; Head Bookkeeper; Assistant Controller; Business Manager; Small Business Owner; Hotel Auditor; Computerized Payroll Accountant

high-skill, high-wage employment" (U.S. Department of Labor, 1991). As a result of their work, the SCANS determined that a high performance workplace required workers to have solid literacy, computational, and thinking skills and positive personal attributes. In their report, *What Work Requires of Schools*: A SCANS *Report for America 2000* (U.S. Department of Labor, 1991), the Commission outlined a three-part foundation of what schools needed to accomplish for individuals to be high performance employees. This foundation is outlined in Table 6–2.

TABLE 6–2
SCANS Foundational Skills

Skill	Description of Skill
Basic Skills:	Reads, writes, performs arithmetic and mathematical operations; listens and speaks
A. Reading	Locates, understands, and interprets written information in prose and in documents such as manuals, graphs, and schedules
B. Writing	Communicates thoughts, ideas, information, and messages in writing; and creates documents such as letters, directions, manuals, reports, graphs, and flowcharts
C. Arithmetic/Mathematics	Performs basic computations and approaches practical problems by choosing appropriately from a variety of mathematical techniques
D. Listening	Receives, attends to, interprets, and responds to verbal messages and other cues
E. Speaking	Organizes ideas and communicates orally
Thinking Skills:	Thinks creatively, makes decisions, solves problems, visualizes, knows how to learn, and reasons
A. Creative Thinking	Generates new ideas
B. Decision Making	Specifies goals and constraints, generates alternatives, considers risks, and evaluates and chooses best alternative
C. Problem Solving	Recognizes problems and devises and implements plan of action
D. Seeing Things in the Mind's Eye	Organizes, and processes symbols, pictures, graphs, objects, and other information
E. Knowing How to Learn	Uses efficient learning techniques to acquire and apply new knowledge and skills
F. Reasoning	Discovers a rule or principle underlying the relationship between two or objects and applies it when solving a problem
Personal Qualities:	Displays responsibility, self-esteem, sociability, self-management, and integrity and honesty
A. Responsibility	Exerts a high level of effort and perseveres towards goal attainment
B. Self-Esteem	Believes in own self-worth and maintains a positive view of self
C. Sociability	Demonstrates understanding, friendliness, adaptability, empathy, and politeness in groups
D. Self-Management	Assesses self accurately, sets personal goals, monitors progress, and exhibits self-control
E. Integrity/Honesty	Chooses ethical courses of action

Source: Adapted from U.S. Department of Labor. (1993) *Learning a living: A blueprint for high performance* (SCANS report). Washington, DC: US Government Printing Office.

In addition to these general competencies, the Commission identified five workplace competency areas: (a) use of resources (e.g., time, money, materials); (b) interpersonal skills (e.g., leadership, team membership); (c) use of information (e.g., acquires and evaluates information and organizes and maintains information; (d) use of systems (e.g., understands social, organizational and technological systems); and (e) use of technology (e.g., selects, applies, and maintains technology).

Critical Point The focus of career and technical programs (renamed in the 1990s from vocational education) is to provide specialized training, based on the local labor market, that will lead to postsecondary training programs and employment.

Life Skills Education

Life skills education approaches provided a direct link between educational standards and the requirements of students' current and future environments, and they were the focus of educational programs for approximately 5% of all students (NCES, 2001). Educational standards were addressed in a life skills approach at the secondary level through functional job-related contexts, daily-living contexts and social contexts. This type of education was typically used for youths who were not going to college; however the use of a life skills approach demonstrated how educational standards can support postschool outcomes for students (i.e., success in their adult lives) (Edgar & Polloway, 1994; Hanley-Maxwell & Collet-Klingenberg, 1994). Life skills education therefore needs to emphasize a comprehensive, life-span approach that is similar to the perspective taken by life-span career development theories. Using a life-span perspective, students would select desired current and future environments based on their current interests and abilities. They would integrate their career choice with other lifestyle choices related to independent living, community participation, leisure activities, continuing education, career advancement, and parenting roles. Although this educational approach was mostly associated with students with disabilities, it did have a small but significant role in the high school curriculum.

Examples of life skills coursework, in the general curriculum, include courses such as home economics, personal finance, or personal

Participants of a college preparation program at Kent State.

consumerism. The focus in all of these courses assumes the need to provide all students with everyday capabilities to function in their own daily life. All individuals need general skills such as writing a check, acquiring a loan, accessing social services, or performing necessary financial accounting. Within this context students gain necessary skills that would support their independence. Linking into this aspect of the life skills would be quite natural because of the general need for all students in preparation for community life.

Critical Point The purpose of life skills programs is to provide a direct and functional link to a student's current and future environments (e.g., independent living, leisure activities, career advancement.)

Universal Design and Access to the General Curriculum

The use of universal design in the development of the general curriculum can have a major impact on its accessibility and whether students with disabilities are able to access it without accommodations. Universal design has its roots in the design of buildings and products to make them accessible to persons with disabilities. Universal design, as it is used in education, implies a design of instructional materials and activities that allows learning goals to be attainable by individuals with diverse abilities (i.e., reading, writing, understanding) (Orkwis, 1999; Orkwis & McLane, 1998).

Extending the concept of universal design to education, Universal Design for Learning (UDL) is based on the premise that "curricular content should be provided in multiple representations or in a transformable format, (i.e., digital/electronic) such that multiple means are built into each learning activity for student expression, control or engagement" (Hitchcock, 2001, p. 8). From their research findings about the brain and learning, the Center for Applied Special Technology (CAST) has found that there are three essential ways that that UDL can be applied to education: (a) recognition networks, which include multiple means of representation to provide alternative formats for presenting information to students tailored to their learning; (b) strategic networks, which include multiple means for student expression and allow students options for demonstrating what they have learned; and (c) affective networks, which include multiple means for student engagement, which provides students curriculum that is interesting and challenging, but with needed supports (Hitchcock, 2001).

Critical Point Universal design, as applied to the general curriculum, creates access to instructional materials and activities and allows learning goals to be attainable by students of varying ability levels.

In order to understand the basic principles of how universal design might help school personnel in developing better access to the curriculum, Wehmeyer (2002) developed a list of principles as illustrated in Table 6–3. It should be noted that these principles align with the CAST UDL principles.

Examples of the equitable use of materials principle include the cognitive rescaling techniques such as autosummarization (see Figure 6–4). The use of e-text, supported text formats, or rebus-supported texts are all examples of the flexible use of materials. It should be noted that there are many e-text sites available for teachers to download materials, such as the *Alex Catalogue of Electronic Texts*, a collection of public domain documents from American and English literature. Examples of the perceptible information principle include the use of captioned videos, alternative text to describe graphics (also known as *alt description* or *alt text*), and scaffold text for comprehension support (Bauder, 2001). Many text-

TABLE 6–3

Principles of Universal Design Applied to Education

Principle	Explanation
Equitable Use	Materials can be used by students who speak various languages, address a variety of levels in cognitive taxonomies, provide alternatives that appear equivalent and, thus, do not stigmatize students.
Flexible Use	Materials provide multiple means of representation, presentation, and student expression.
Simple and Intuitive Use	Materials are easy to use and avoid unnecessary complexity, directions clear and concise, examples provided.
Perceptible Information	Materials communicate needed information to user independent of ambient conditions or users sensory abilities, essential information highlighted and redundancy included.
Tolerance for Error	Students have ample time to respond, are provided feedback, can undo previous responses, can monitor progress, and are provided adequate practice time.
Low Physical and Cognitive Effort	Materials present information in chunks that can be completed in a reasonable time frame.

Source: From Transition principles and access to the general education curriculum, by M. Wehmeyer, In C. A. Kochhar-Bryant & D. Bassett (Eds.) *Aligning transition and standards-based education: Issues and Strategies*. Copyright 2002 by the Council for Exceptional Children. Reprinted with permission.

books combine pictures with print as a way to support comprehension of the topic. However, the picture may not be understandable to a student. Therefore when using a e-text or web site that embeds pictures, the use of alt text that describes what the picture is provides a student with a better understanding. The use of alt text is also especially helpful for individuals who are blind.

There are various curriculum modes that incorporate UDL. Most notable is the Carnine and Kameénui model. Their model is structured around six curriculum design features and was developed primarily to promote learning for students with mild disabilities (see Simmons and Kameénui 1996). These six curriculum design features include:

1. *Big ideas*: targeting concepts, principles, rules, or problem-solving techniques that underlie and/or span critical ideas in the course/curriculum
2. *Conspicuous strategies*: presenting explicit and overt instruction on steps for accomplishing tasks
3. *Mediated scaffolding*: eliciting thoughtful, provocative, and probing questions during instruction that advance students' learning to higher levels of understanding and applications
4. *Strategic integration*: explicitly linking the big ideas across or within curricula
5. *Judicious review*: planning for sufficient review and application of previously taught information
6. *Primed background knowledge*: ascertaining that students have sufficient background knowledge on which to base and build new learning. (King-Sears, p. 70)

FIGURE 6–4
Examples of Universal Design

Autosummarization Example

Text:
A LITTLE more than a hundred years ago, a poor man, by the name of Crockett, embarked on board an emigrantship, in Ireland, for the New World. He was in the humblest station in life. But very little is known respecting his uneventful career excepting its tragical close. His family consisted of a wife and three or four children. Just before he sailed, or on the Atlantic passage, a son was born, to whom he gave the name of John. The family probably landed in Philadelphia, and dwelt somewhere in Pennsylvania, for a year or two, in one of those slab shanties, with which all are familiar as the abodes of the poorest class of Irish emigrants.

After a year or two, Crockett, with his little family, crossed the almost pathless Alleghenies. Father, mother, and children trudged along through the rugged defiles and over the rocky cliffs, on foot. Probably a single pack-horse conveyed their few household goods. The hatchet and the rifle were the only means of obtaining food, shelter, and even clothing. With the hatchet, in an hour or two, a comfortable camp could be constructed, which would protect them from wind and rain. The camp-fire, cheering the darkness of the night, drying their often wet garments, and warming their chilled limbs with its genial glow, enabled them to enjoy that almost greatest of earthly luxuries, peaceful sleep.

Auto Summary of Text:
A LITTLE more than a hundred years ago, a poor man, by the name of Crockett, embarked on board an emigrantship, in Ireland, for the New World. After a year or two, Crockett, with his little family, crossed the almost pathless Alleghenies. Father, mother, and children trudged along through the rugged defiles and over the rocky cliffs, on foot. Probably a single pack-horse conveyed their few household goods. The camp-fire, cheering the darkness of the night, drying their often wet garments, and warming their chilled limbs with its genial glow, enabled them to enjoy that almost greatest of earthly luxuries, peaceful sleep.

Source: Excerpt from *David Crockett: His Life and Adventures,* by John S. C. Abbott.
Available online at the Electronic Text Center, University of Virginia Library at: http://etext.lib.virginia.edu.

Standards Designed to Promote Access to the General Curriculum

The success in developing academic standards for all students, especially at the secondary level, has been a function of the broadness or narrowness of those standards. Kentucky was one state that tried to reconcile academic standards and the individualization of educational outcomes. Due to low and varied academic performance and other inequities, Kentucky passed school reform legislation known as the Kentucky Education Reform Act in 1990 that mandated the development of "benchmarks" (or standards) to improve student performance across the state. In response to this mandate, the Kentucky Department of Education developed a set of standards that were broad and designed to be assessed relative to students' needs in their current and future environments (Kleinert, Kearns, & Kennedy, 1997). These standards were organized into six general categories: (a) basic communication and math skills, (b) core concepts and principles, (c) self-sufficiency, (d) responsible group membership, (e) thinking and problem solving, and (f) integration of knowledge. Within each of these areas, academic standards were broad and related to both general standards and the information needed by students relative to their individual courses of study (Kentucky Council on Postsecondary Education, 1999). Table 6–4 provides an overview of curriculum objectives developed for all students in Kentucky.

In the Kentucky standards, transition goals were embedded into the overall framework of learning objectives. For example, under *Goal 2—Core Concepts and Principles*, the reader can find several transition-related objectives such as employability attributes and postsecondary opportunities. Other transition-related objectives are found under *Goal 3—Self-Sufficiency*, and

TABLE 6–4

Kentucky State Learner Objectives

Goal 1. Basic Math and Communication Skills

1. *Accessing sources of information and ideas:* Students use reference tools such as dictionaries, almanacs, encyclopedias, and computer reference programs and research tools.
2. *Reading:* Students make sense of the variety of materials they read.
3. *Observing:* Students make sense of the various things they observe.
4. *Listening:* Students make sense of the various messages to which they listen.
5. *Computing:* Students use mathematical ideas and procedures to communicate, reason, and solve problems.
6. *Classifying:* Students organize information through development and use of classification rules.
7. *Writing:* Students write using appropriate forms, conventions, and styles to communicate ideas and information to different audiences for different purposes.
8. *Speaking:* Students speak using appropriate forms, conventions, and styles to communicate ideas and information to different audiences for different purposes.
9. *Movement:* Students make sense and communicate ideas with movement.
10. *Using electronic technology:* Students use computers and other kinds of technology to collect, organize, and communicate information and ideas.

Goal 2. Core Concepts and Principles

1. *Nature of scientific activity:* Students understand the scientific way of thinking and working, and use those methods to solve real-life problems.
2. *Number concepts:* Students understand number concepts and use numbers appropriately and accurately.
3. *Mathematical procedures:* Students understand various mathematical procedures and use them appropriately and accurately.
4. *Democratic principles:* Students understand the democratic principles of justice, equality, responsibility, and freedom and apply them to real-life situations.
5. *Structure and function of political systems:* Students can accurately describe various forms of government and analyze issues that relate to the rights and responsibilities of citizens in a democracy.
6. *Structure and function of social systems:* Students observe, analyze, and interpret human behaviors, social groupings, and institutions to better understand people and the relationships among individuals and among groups.
7. *Cultural diversity:* Students interact effectively and work cooperatively with the many ethnic and cultural groups of our nation and world.
8. *Family life and parenting:* Students demonstrate skills that promote individual well-being and healthy family relationships.

(*continued*)

TABLE 6–4 (*continued*)

9. *Consumerism:* Students evaluate consumer products and services and make effective consumer decisions.
10. *Community health systems:* Students demonstrate the skills to evaluate and use services and resources available in their community.
11. *Career path:* Students use strategies for choosing and preparing for a career.
12. *Employability attributes:* Students demonstrate skills and work habits that lead to success in future schooling and work.
13. *Postsecondary opportunities search (jobs, school, military):* Students demonstrate skills such as interviewing, writing résumés, and completing applications that are needed to be accepted into college or other postsecondary training or to get a job.

Goal 3. Self-Sufficiency (This goal is not included in the state's academic assessment program.)

1. *Positive self-concept:* Students demonstrate positive growth in self-concept through appropriate tasks or projects.
2. *Healthy lifestyle:* Students demonstrate the ability to maintain a healthy lifestyle.
3. *Adaptability and flexibility:* Students demonstrate the ability to be adaptable and flexible through appropriate tasks or projects.
4. *Resourcefulness and creativity:* Students demonstrate the ability to be resourceful and creative.
5. *Self-control and self-discipline:* Students demonstrate self-control and self-discipline.
6. *Ethical values:* Students demonstrate the ability to make decisions based on ethical values.
7. *Independent learning:* Students demonstrate the ability to learn on one's own.

Goal 4. Responsible Group Membership (This goal is not included in the state's academic assessment program.)

1. *Interpersonal skills:* Students shall develop their abilities to become responsible members of a family, work group, or community including demonstrating effectiveness in community service.
2. *Productive team membership:* Students use productive team member skills.
3. *Consistent, responsive, and caring behavior:* Students individually demonstrate consistent, responsive, and caring behavior.
4. *Rights and responsibilities for self and others:* Students demonstrate the ability to accept the rights and responsibilities for self and others.
5. *Multicultural and worldview:* Students demonstrate an understanding of, appreciation for, and sensitivity to a multicultural view and worldview.
6. *Open mind to alternative perspectives:* Students demonstrate an open mind to alternative perspectives.

Goal 5. Thinking and Problem Solving

1. *Critical thinking:* Students use critical thinking skills, such as analyzing, prioritizing, categorizing, evaluating, and comparing to solve a variety of problems in real-life situations.
2. *Conceptualizing:* Students organize information to develop or change their understanding of a concept.
3. *Creative thinking:* Students use creative thinking skills to develop or invent novel, constructive ideas or products.
4. *Decision making:* Students use a decision-making process to make informed decisions among options.
5. *Problem solving:* Students use problem-solving processes to develop solutions to relatively complex problems.

Goal 6. Integration of Knowledge

1. *Applying multiple perspectives:* Students connect knowledge and experiences from different subject areas.
2. *Developing new knowledge:* Students use what they already know to acquire new knowledge, develop new skills, or interpret new experiences.
3. *Expanding existing knowledge:* Students expand their understanding of existing knowledge by making connections with new knowledge, skills, and experiences.

Source: From *Futures: Your guide to life after high school*, Kentucky Council on Postsecondary Education.

Goal 4—Responsible Group Membership. Important employment skills are subsumed under *Goal 5—Thinking and Problem Solving* and in *Goal 6—Integration of Knowledge*. Most states have developed academic standards, benchmarks, and assessment tools to indicate the educational expectations and methods of evaluating student performance. When standards are open instead of closed, a variety of means are available for the student to demonstrate proficiency as illustrated in Case Study A.

CASE STUDY A

A special education teacher is team teaching a mathematics class with a general education teacher. One student, with a developmental disability, has an interest in working as a cook after graduation. The goal of the general education mathematics program is for the students to understand and apply mathematical procedures. The student in question has been unsuccessful in comprehending and solving word problems. The special education teacher was able to adapt the lesson to the student's needs by providing a hand calculator and using problems related to measuring and adapting recipes, a skill that this student is capable of accomplishing.

Critical Point Most states have developed academic standards. Kentucky's standards, for all students, were organized into six categories with transition-related goals embedded in the overall framework.

Helping the Student Select a High School Course of Study

Educational approaches for youths with disabilities in the secondary setting must "a) be responsive to the needs of individual students, b) facilitate maximum integration with nondisabled peers, c) facilitate socialization and d) focus on the students' transition to postsecondary settings" (Smith, Polloway, Patton, & Dowdy, 2001, p. 455). As formerly noted, researchers have estimated that 70% of the student population were served primarily with academic approaches, 25% with career/technical approaches, and the remaining 1% to 5% primarily in the life skills education (NCES, 2001). This research also showed that the number of students that went on to 4-year institutions of higher education remained a steady rate of 30 to 40% (NCES, 2001) suggesting that high schools may be oversupplying students prepared in college-preparatory approaches. Of those students that went on to 4-year institutions of higher education, only about half actually acquired their degree within 6 years of entry (NCES, 2001). Other research has suggested that career/technical and academically prepared students equally achieved 4-year degrees (Levesque, Lauen, Teitelbaum, Martha, & Librera, 2000).

Baer et al. (2003) conducted a follow-up study of special education graduates to determine which educational activities were the best predictors of the postschool outcomes of postsecondary education and full-time employment after controlling for other student characteristics. In this study, the educational activities that best predicted full-time employment were vocational education (or career and technical education) and work-study programs in high school. Students with disabilities who participated in vocational education were nearly 2.7 times as likely to report full-time employment within 3 years of graduation. Additionally, students with disabilities who participated in work-study programs reported 2.6 times higher full-time employment rates than students who did not participate in these programs. While the findings were local, they were consistent with the National Longitudinal Transition Study (NLTS) that reported 10% better employment outcomes for students in vocational education and another 5% better outcomes for students who participated in community work experiences.

The course of study that best predicted postsecondary education (i.e., 2- and 4-year colleges and technical schools) was participation in advanced academic classes in the regular education environments (Baer et al., 2003). In this study, students who participated in regular and advanced academics in the high school reported postsecondary education rates of more than 5.1 times the rate of students who did not participate in fully integrated regular education classes. While the findings of the Baer et al. (2003) study were local, they supported the findings of the NLTS that participation in advanced academics was the most important predictor of postschool postsecondary education (Blackorby & Wagner, 1996).

While these statistics may provide some guidance in helping students select their courses of study in high school, it should be emphasized that the local context of the school and the characteristics of the students may play important roles in how the student's course of study impacts his or her postschool outcomes. In the Baer et al. (2003) study, suburban students were much more likely to attend postsecondary education than urban and rural students. Whether this was a result of differing transition goals of students from these school settings, or of the differing career paths offered by these settings, was not determined by this study. Case Study B provides a sequence of planning that identifies a course of study.

CASE STUDY B

Anna's IEP team ensured that she had some career awareness instruction during elementary school. When she entered middle school, the IEP team provided all of her teachers with a list of foundational skills she was working on. Anna received mostly Bs and Cs in her academic classes and the IEP team believed this provided a good program for her. During eighth grade, Anna's IEP team enrolled her in a career exploration course that visited workers in the community and that included activities about work values and habits, and about occupational clusters. In high school, Anna began an animal husbandry program at the local vocational school focusing on her preferred occupational clusters and was taught skills related to animal care and developing dietary plans for animals because her preferred career choice was that of working in the zoo. Anna was also placed in a zoo in her local community where she assisted zoo personnel.

The IDEA of 1997 supported the notion that students' education should be related to their postschool goals and it stated that the IEP must contain:

> "beginning at age 14, and updated annually, a statement of the transition service needs of the child under the applicable components of the child's IEP that focuses on the child's courses of study (such as participation in advanced-placement courses or a vocational education program)." (20 U.S.C. § 1414 [d][1][A][vii][II])

This requirement was in response to the fact that students with disabilities often were not participating in courses that would support their postschool goals (Blackorby & Wagner, 1996). The appendix to the IDEA of 1997 regulations stated that one of the purposes of this clause was to "help reduce the number of students with disabilities that drop out . . . and motivate the student to complete his or her education (34.300–63A). Depending on career choices or the general direction envisioned by the student and the team, a variety of coursework, program, and experiential options may be appropriate for providing a foundation of skills, knowledge, and competencies. Postsecondary education and adult services may also be crucial for students in working toward and achieving their transition goals.

Under the IDEA, the course of study chosen by students by age 14 must be based on their individual needs, strengths, and preferences and should prepare them for current and next environments.

However, the IDEA of 1997 also required that the age-14 statement of transition services needed to specify how the school would support students' courses of study. This meant that the IEP team needed to identify courses of study congruent with students' transition goals and to specify how students were to be provided access to desired courses of study within the general curriculum.

Critical Point Due to the fact that many students with disabilities were not participating in courses that would link them to their postsecondary goals, the IDEA of 1997 stressed the importance of identifying a course of study, and updating it annually, at the age of 14.

Individualized Approaches to Accessing the General Curriculum

Special education students often need individual accommodations in order to access the general curriculum due to physical, sensory, or cognitive disabilities. As noted earlier, access can sometimes be assured by building in open-ended educational standards and by universal designs for learning. At other times, access may require individual accommodations. In considering individual accommodation, it has been necessary to define: (a) the demands of the student's current and future environments, (b) how their disability presents barriers to participation in these environments, and (c) how the environment and the disability barriers can be concurrently addressed.

Educators therefore need to view accessibility issues from an interactive perspective that looks at both individual and environmental factors. For example, people who are hard of hearing cannot access spoken communication under unamplified conditions in a classroom. Someone who uses a wheelchair cannot gain entry into classrooms that are in an inaccessible building. Without enlarged print, people who are visually impaired do not have access to printed material. Without taped texts, the person with a learning disability may not have access to reading material for classes. In all cases, disability and environments interact in a manner that prevents participation, but the specific barriers, even for two people with the same disability, can be quite different. Within each of these disability groups, however, individual experiences can vary, as can needs for accommodations. For example, a person who is hard of hearing needs amplification to gain access to spoken communication, whereas a person who is deaf and uses sign language needs visual communication in order to have access.

The IDEA of 1997, required that the IEP team identify transition service needs related to the student's general course of study by age 14 (20 U.S.C. § 1414 [d][1][A][vii][II]). To identify these transition service needs, Wehmeyer, Lattin, and Agran (2001) depicted a process that looked at student support needs in the following order: (a) assistive technology, (b) curriculum adaptations, (c) curriculum augmentation, and (d) curriculum alteration. This process is illustrated in Figure 6–5. The Wehmeyer et al. approach was designed to be consistent with the "least restrictive environment" requirement of the IDEA by considering less intrusive interventions first. For example, providing a student with an assistive technology (such as a spell-checker) would generally be a less restrictive alternative than adapting the student's entire curriculum.

In using the Wehmeyer et al. (2001) model, it should be emphasized that the accommodation strategies will not always follow the presented sequence. Other factors to consider include the intrusiveness of the interventions at each level and the needs and preferences of the student. In evaluating intrusiveness, "low-tech" solutions should generally be favored over "high-tech" solutions (Blackhurst et al., 1999; Blackhurst & Cross, 1993; Sweeney, 2002), since it may be easier to implement simple adaptations at a later

FIGURE 6–5
Access to the General Curriculum Model

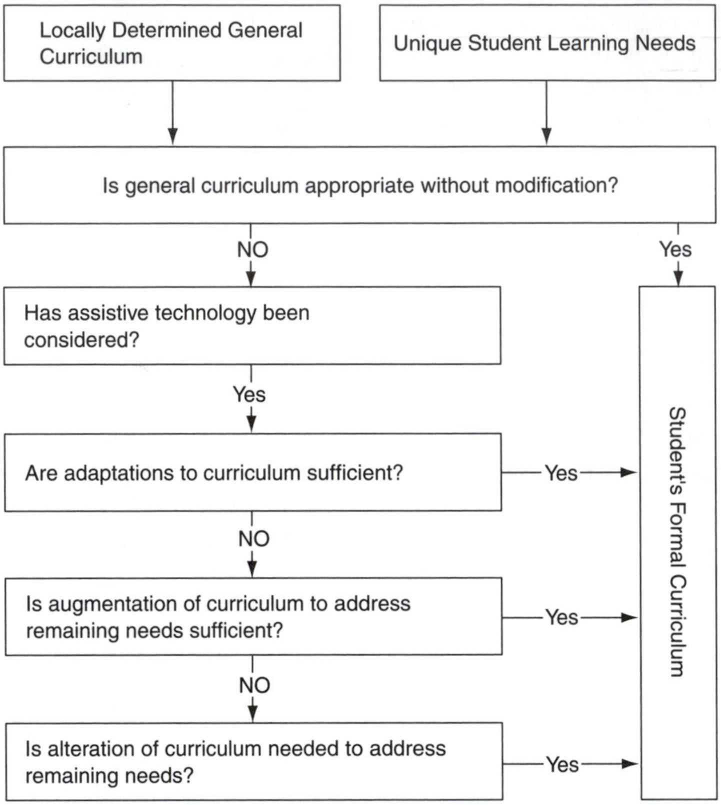

Source: From Wehmeyer, M. L., Agran, M. & Lattin, D. Achieving access to the general curriculum for students with mental retardation: A curriculum decision-making model. *Education and training in mental retardation and developmental disabilities, 36*(4), p. 335. Copyright 2001 by Council for Exceptional Children. Reprinted with permission.

stage of the model than to implement complex ones at an earlier stage. Additionally, student preferences need careful consideration because the effectiveness of accommodation will be highly influenced by the student's acceptance of the approach.

Critical Point The basic question one must ask, of course, is "does the student need any type of modification to the general curriculum?" If the student needs some type of modification then the school personnel need to determine what type of modification must be made that will provide the student with access. There are four general types of access strategies to be considered: assistive technology, adaptation, augmentation, and alteration.

Assistive Technology

It is important to understand that universal design for learning (UDL) and assistive technology (AT)

TABLE 6–5
Examples of Assistive Technology by Functional Categories

Functional Category	Assistive Technology Example
Existence. Technology that provides assistance in basic function areas needed to sustain life	Respirators, feeding devices, and adapted potty chairs
Communication. Primarily consists of augmentative and alternative communication systems, alternative communication (AAC) Augmentative/ alternative communication refers to any technique to enhance or augment communication	Gestures, sign language, nonelectronic augmentative communication systems (e.g., dial scans, communication boards), voice output communication aids, tactile speech aides, visual doorbells, alert and alarm systems
Body support, protection, and positioning. Devices that provide stabilization, body support, or protection to the body	Braces, crutches, standers, walkers, splints
Travel and Mobility. Devices that help a person move about, either horizontally or vertically	Wheelchair, lifts, and electronic travel aids (ETA) with obstacle detection indicators; adapted buses and vans
Environmental interaction. Devices and accessories designed to assist a person perform daily living skills, both indoors and outdoors	Environmental controls that activate appliances such as telephones, lights, TV, and blenders
Education and transition. Devices that support the educational and vocational needs	Computer-assisted instruction software, work-site adaptations, such as electric staplers, switch-activated filing systems, and adjustable desks
Sports, fitness, and recreation. Assistive technology that promotes participation in individual or group sports, play activities, hobbies, and crafts	Bowling ball chutes, audible baseballs, adapted recreational snow equipment (e.g., adapted ski poles and adapted sleds)

are not the same; however, both complement one another. For example, UDL is how curriculum is designed and developed with or without technology. AT is the tools that provide the access to the universally designed curriculum. Assistive technology includes a vast number of devices designed to help individuals with disabilities communicate more effectively, control their environment, and achieve greater mobility (Blackhurst & Shuping, 1990; Raskind, 1997; 1998). To a novice or beginning service provider, the thought of AT can, at best, seem overwhelming. To help individuals better understand AT devices, seven major functional areas have been developed: (a) existence; (b) communication; (c) travel and mobility; (d) body support, protection, and positioning; (e) environmental interaction; (f) education and transition; and (g) sports, fitness, and recreation (Blackhurst et al., 1999). Descriptions of the functional categories and possible AT devices and services are displayed in Table 6–5.

It should be noted that embedded within each of these categories are levels of technology device sophistication, including no technology, low technology, medium technology to high or advanced technology (Blackhurst & Cross, 1993; Blackhurst, 1997). Therefore, AT can be as simple as a pencil grip or as complex as a computer with voice activation capabilities. In addition, it is important to understand the implications of the continuum of AT from low-technology solutions through high-technology solutions. A general principle is that the simplest level of technology that will meet the individual's needs should be considered first. Generally, individuals with disabilities want what will be the most useful for them in providing greater access to their environment (i.e., school, home, and community). The latest, most expensive device is not necessarily the most appropriate or may not meet the needs of an individual. However, the level of sophistication of the device is determined by the needs of the individual.

The process in the selection of AT starts with the assessment process. Several models (e.g., Blackhurst & Cross, 1993; Reed, 1997; Zabala, 1994) have been developed to assist evaluation teams to determine AT devices for individuals. The three important characteristics that are embedded within all assessment models are (1) the environmental demands placed on an individual; (2) the individual's needs, abilities, and preferences (Chambers, 1997); and (3) the technology characteristics (Thorkildsen, 1994). The goal of these models is to address a person's functional responses in light of their environmental demands (Blackhurst, 1997). Using this model as a process for decision making, a school team would be able to make judgments about the use of technology based on a student's functions in response to academic demands as well as to community and vocational demands (Blackhurst, 1997).

A school-based assessment team may be able to assess what is or is not working for a student and determine how AT can be applied to evaluate whether specific AT devices and services are necessary to meet the specific needs of a child (Reed, 1997; Scherer, 1997). However, the IEP team may determine that they do not possess knowledge of resources or do not have knowledge to evaluate AT needs (Chambers, 1997). In these situations, the team would seek additional support from individuals with the level of knowledge or resources necessary to assist the team in evaluating a child's specific educational needs for AT. Additionally, an evaluation to determine appropriate AT should be done in a variety of environments to determine the impact on school activities across curriculum areas, in vocational sites, and in community and home settings (Bauder et al., 1997).

During individual transition planning the team needs to consider all aspects of an individual's life from high school to adulthood, understanding what technology might be required as part of the job and what modifications or adaptations, including determination of the AT, must be part of the planning process (Fisher & Gardner, 1999). One also needs to have a sense of what aspects of postschool environments relate to technology. By looking at each postschool setting in which the person needs to function, and evaluating the nature and needs of the individual for AT that is unique to each of those environments, an interagency team can more clearly sort out what and how each agency should contribute its resources to assure access by the individual to the proper AT for each desired setting.

Critical Point Assistive technology devices are categorized into seven functional areas including: (1) existence; (2) communication; (3) travel and mobility; (4) body support, protection, and positioning; (5) environmental interaction; (6) education and transition; and (7) sports, fitness, and recreation.

Curriculum Adaptations

Curriculum adaptation refers to modifying the representation or presentation of the content in some manner. There are several ways in which the curriculum can be adapted. For example, reading materials can be adapted by modifying the readability level such as highlighting essential information or limiting the amount of information on a page. The vocabulary might also be modified using the "marginal gloss technique". This technique requires the instructor to write terms and their definition in the margins of a textbook page. For some examples of how the presentation of concepts can be modified, Olsen and Platt suggest:

1. Supplement print materials with concept-teaching procedures.
2. Present concepts one at a time.
3. Provide visual supplements, such as transparencies, illustrations, and diagrams.
4. Use modeling and demonstration to clarify concepts.
5. Use games, manipulatives, and hands-on activities to reinforce concepts.
6. Draw upon the different cultural backgrounds and experiences of your students to make concepts meaningful. (p.146)

Additionally, the use of concrete examples, the use of audiovisual aids, and use of supplemental materials are ways in which a teacher can adapt the curriculum. For youths with moderate and severe disabilities, curriculum might be adapted through the use of partial participation. There are four types of partial participation: (a) adapting in sequences through which a students learns, (b) adapting rules, (c) using personal assistance, and (d) using materials and technology.

Outlines and using pictorial representations of the content, such as graphic organizers, were some commonly used accommodations noted by King-Sears (2001). There have been many kinds of graphic organizers such as Venn diagrams, concept maps, and decision-making rubrics. These types of organizers provide a student with a way to manage curricular content. They are not difficult for a teacher to develop or implement.

Cognitive approaches also were used to adapt the curriculum to the needs of students with disabilities. These strategies were defined as a system for learning that actively promotes the comprehension and retention of knowledge) Ellis & Lenz, Deshler, 1996). Some types of cognitive strategies included: (a) activating background knowledge, (b) generating questions, and (c) summarizing, imaging (Deshler, et al.). For example, concept mapping has been considered a cognitive strategy that activates and engages students during all stages of the learning process. To use this strategy, teachers construct a model for organizing and integrating information that they are presenting. By following the outlined procedures (found below), students have been able to organize and integrate information that they are learning through the curriculum.

Concept Mapping Procedure:

1. Choose a key word or topic related to a unit of study.
2. Write the word on an overhead transparency or on a sheet of chart paper.
3. Ask students to think of as many words and ideas as they can that relate to the focal word.
4. Write the words on a map in clusters or categories.
5. Have the students suggest labels for the categories and write them on the map.
6. If there are any key vocabulary words that are important to the comprehension of a reading assignment and students do not mention them, add them to the map with a red marker or pen.
7. Discussion of the concept map is the most important part of the lesson. This helps students become aware of their current thinking and helps them to see relationships between words and ideas.
8. After the reading assignment, or as the unit progresses, new words and categories can be added to the map. Use different colors of ink to show that this information was not known prior to the reading or unit of study.

Concept mapping can be used as a brainstorming activity, during assignments, or as an assessment activity for evaluation purposes. Although considered more of an instructional approach, concept mapping a unit, chapter, or a

Access to the general curriculum can include a personal computer.

course addresses how one can augment the curriculum and provide students with a better understanding of the content.

Content enhancement strategies (Center for Research and Learning, University of Kansas) (an organizational approach) was utilized by the Kent State Transition Center, to develop the Career and Self-Advocacy Program. Briefly defined, content enhancement is an instructional strategy used to enhance the learning of academically diverse students. In addition, it is used to organize a program or class into the various units to be learned. The Career and Self-Advocacy Program is broken down into three primary units, including: (1) postsecondary options, (2) self-awareness and advocacy, and (3) goal setting and IEPs. Each unit is broken down into the specific topics and lessons to be taught to students. The purpose of this program is to get high school students, interested in postsecondary education, to understand the importance of: (a) early planning and research for desired postschool goals (careers and schools); (b) how their disability affects their learning and access to available programs (i.e., knowledge of strengths and areas of needs); (c) the importance of knowing rights and responsibilities (disability and antidiscriminatory legislation); (d) how to effectively advocate for needs; and (e) the importance of understanding, participating in, and writing goals for their IEP. To date, this program has had over 150 participants with varying ability levels. Examples of unit organizers can be seen in Figures 6–6 through 6–8. These figures illustrate how this program has been broken down for student and instructor use.

Critical Point It is important to understand that merely adapting the curriculum does not guarantee improved student outcomes. Teachers need to continually evaluate the changes that they make to determine if adaptations provided students with greater access to the curriculum.

Curriculum Augmentation

Knowlton (1998) refers to curriculum augmentation as an enhancement or expansion of curriculum to teach students strategies that improve their likelihood to succeed. The curriculum may be augmented to include additional content to improve in-school outcomes or additional content to improve postschool outcomes. Examples of the former include the teaching of learning and technology skills to the student. Examples of the latter include career education approaches such as Life-Centered Career Education (LCCE) put forth by Don Brolin and Charles Kokaska (Brolin 1989, 1996, 1997; Kokaska & Brolin 1995); School-Based Career Development and Transition Education Model (Clark & Kolstoe, 1995); and Transition Pathway Model (Greene, & Kochhar 2003).

Learning Strategies

The research conducted on secondary students with learning disabilities indicates that teaching students learning strategies can improve their performance in inclusive settings or on grade-appropriate tasks. Learning strategies have been

FIGURE 6–6
The Unit Organizer I Post secondary Options

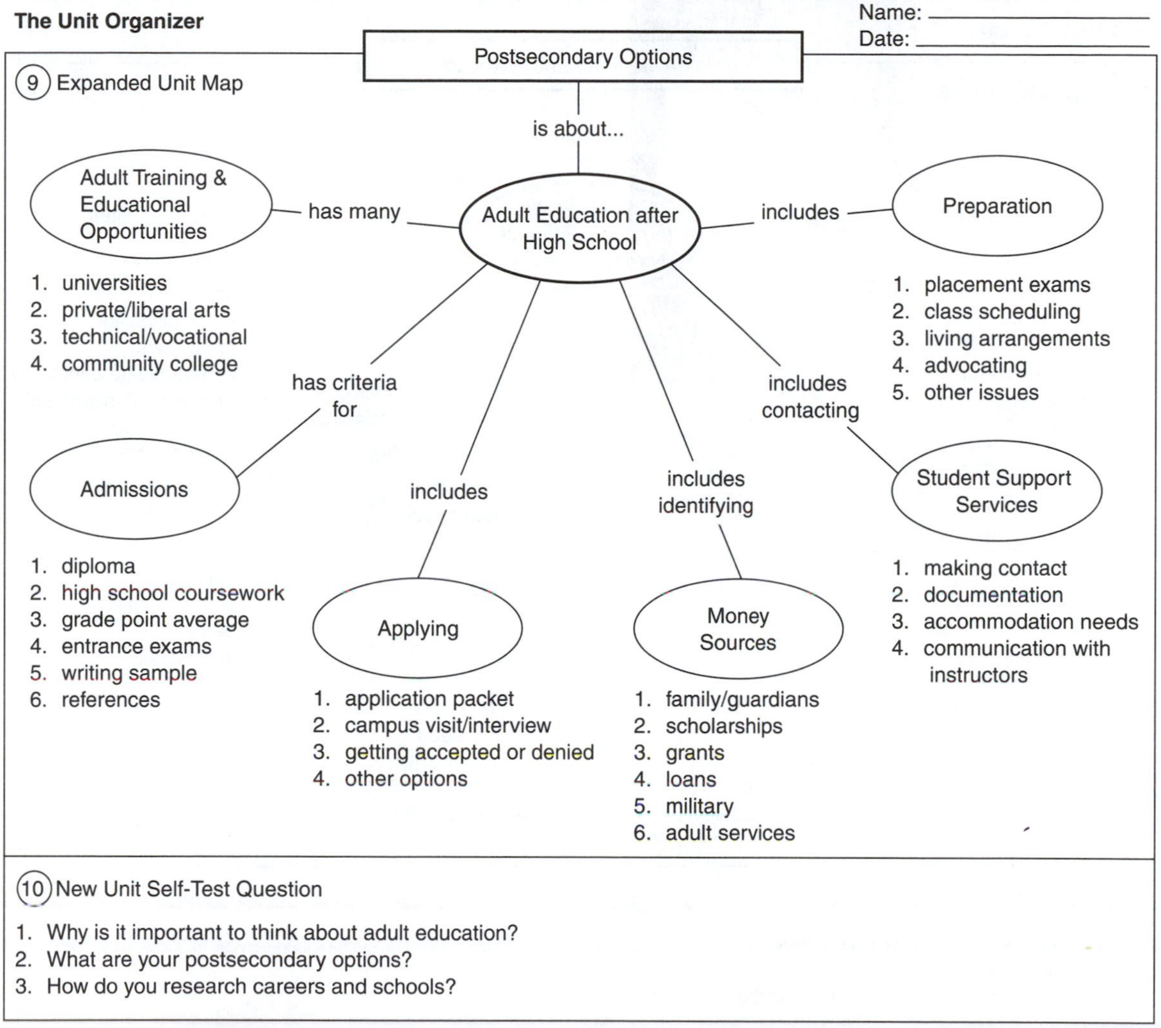

Adapted from *The Unit Organizer Routine*. Copyrights for the template are held by the authors of The Unit Organizer Routine.

Source: From *The Course Organizer* by B. K. Lenz, J. B. Schumaker, D. D. Deshler & J. A. Bulgren, 1998, Laurence, KS.: Edge Enterprises. Reprinted with permission.

generally described as techniques students can use to understand and learn new material or skills, integrate this new information with what we already know in a way that makes sense, and recall the information or skill later, even in a different situation or place (Deshler, Ellis, & Lenz, 1996). According to Deshler, et al., there are five steps to an effective learning strategy: (a) an effective strategy is summarized within a remembering system, (b) the wording of each step in the remembering system is simple and brief, (c) each step of the remembering system begins with an "action

FIGURE 6–7
The Unit Organizer II Self-awareness and Advocacy

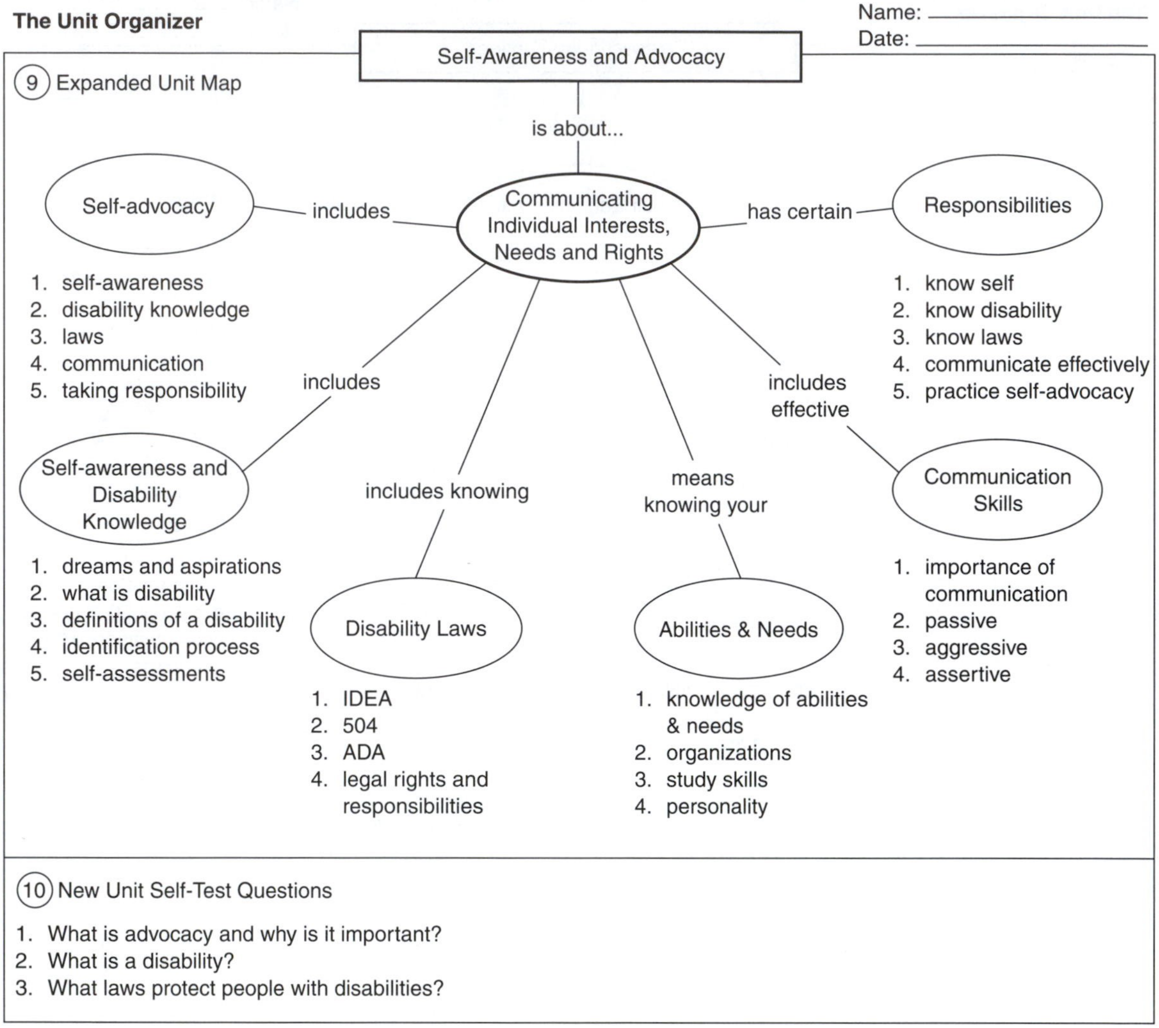

Adapted from *The Unit Organizer Routine*. Copyrights for the template are held by the authors of The Unit Organizer Routine.

Source: From *The Course Organizer* by B. K. Lenz, J. B. Schumaker, D. D. Deshler & J. A. Bulgren, 1998, Laurence, KS.: Edge Enterprises. Reprinted with permission.

word," (d) an effective strategy utilizes seven or fewer steps in the remembering system, and (e) the strategy steps are communicated using words that are uncomplicated and familiar to students. For example, the DISSECT strategy was developed for secondary students to approach multisyllable words within the curriculum content. The steps to DISSECT are:

1. Discover the word's context.
2. Isolate the prefix. Students look at the beginning of the word to see whether the

FIGURE 6–8
The Unit Organizer III Goal Setting and IEPs

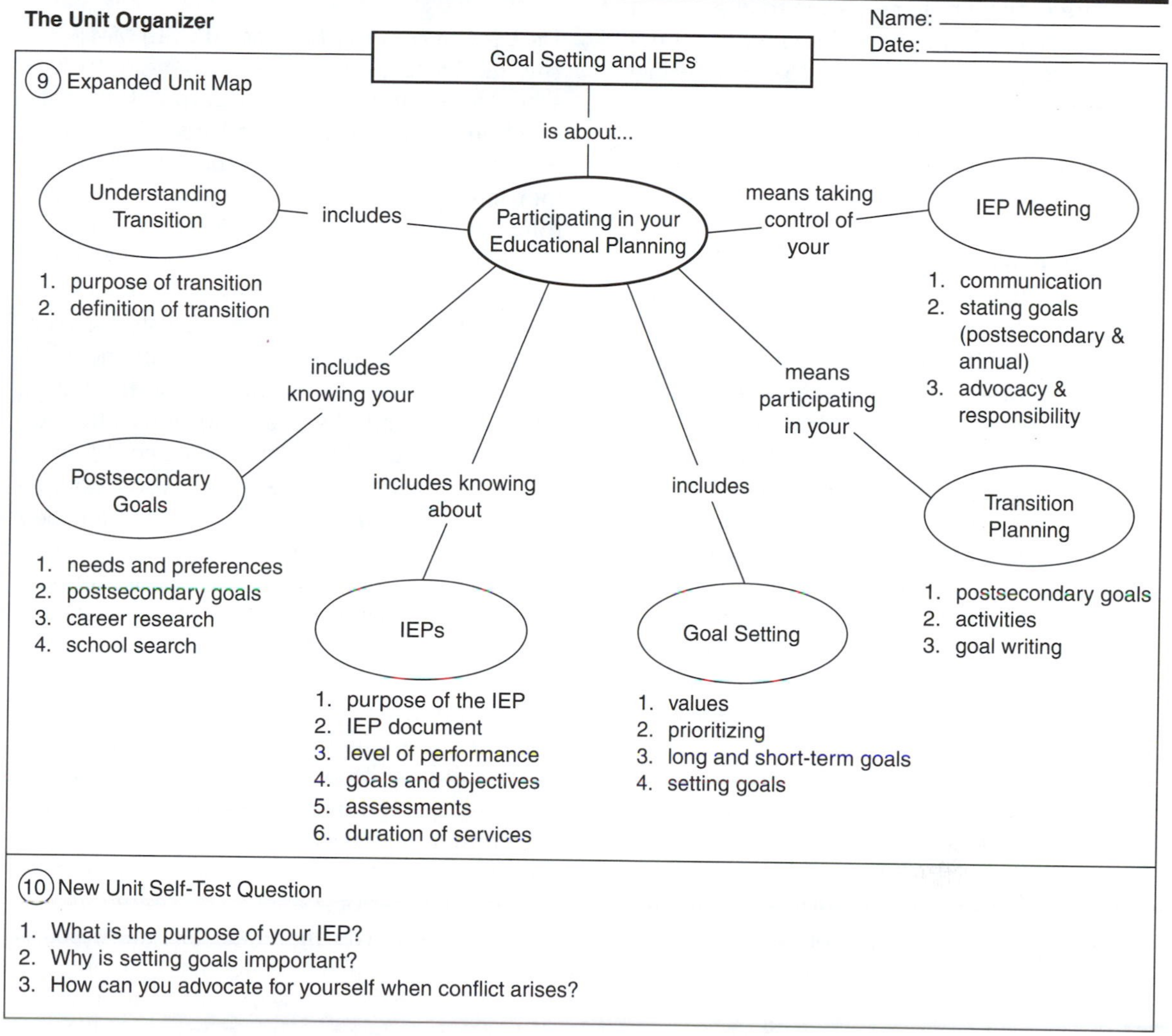

Adapted from *The Unit Organizer Routine.* Copyrights for the template are held by the authors of The Unit Organizer Routine.

Source: From *The Course Organizer* by B. K. Lenz, J. B. Schumaker, D. D. Deshler & J. A. Bulgren, 1998, Laurence, KS.: Edge Enterprises. Reprinted with permission.

initial letter of the word matches a prefix they know. If they do recognize a prefix, they isolate it (e.g., pre/heat). If students do not recognize a prefix, they proceed to step 3.

3. Separate the suffix. Students look at the end of the word to see if the letters match a suffix they know. If they do recognize a suffix, they separate it (e.g., the suffix for the word gladly, students would separate the "ly"); if not, they go on to the next step.
4. Say the stem word.
5. Examine the stem. Students dissect the stem into easy to pronounce parts, two

or three letters at a time. When they can pronounce the whole word, students reread the whole sentence to check their understanding. If students still cannot figure out the word, they go on to the last steps.
6. Check with someone.
7. Try the dictionary. (Vaugh, Bos & Schumm, p. 380–381)

Technology Training

Technology has come to play an increasingly important role in the lives of all individuals. In every aspect of life (e.g., work, recreation, and school), individuals use technology as an effective way to meet the demands of their environment (Behrmann, 1984; Blackhurst & Hofmeister, 1980; Derer, Polsgrove, & Rieth, 1996). For example, every day in some way a person uses technology as a means to perform a function within his or her environment, whether it is to turn on a television using a remote control or to purchase a soft drink from a soda machine. In each instance, technology plays a role for one's convenience, efficiency, or increased effectiveness.

The use of technology is also a tool that educators can use to address the curriculum needs of all students. The use of technology can have an impact for all students in all educational environments. For example, the use of computers is found in the majority of schools today. Computers have word processing programs for students to compose papers. These word processing programs have spell-checkers, thesauruses, and dictionaries that assist students to improve their composition. Some word processing programs also have talking components or voice-out features that allow students with reading difficulties to access the digital text auditorily. Furthermore, voice-input devices allow students with physical difficulties to dictate their composition into the word processing program. Therefore, through just the use of a computer and a word processing program, a full range of needs of both students with and without disabilities can be met to assist them to access the curriculum.

The Life Center Career Education (LCCE) Model

This model focuses on the elementary to high school levels and covers a wide array of skills and experiences. The LCCE is a three-dimensional model that provides competencies across: (a) four interrelated stages of career; (b) key environments of community, family, and school; and (c) three domains with 22 competencies and 97 subcompetencies (Brolin, 1966; Clark & Kolstoe, 1995; Luft et al., 2001). Table 6–6 lists the competencies and curricular areas that are included. The competencies are comprehensive in nature and are designed to prepare individuals for life's future roles. Students are expected to learn about each aspect of the respective 22 competencies and their relationship to daily living, personal social skills, and occupational guidance. The focus of the model is to instate appropriate habits and behaviors, to obtain job skills, and secure employment (Luft et al., 2001).

Instructional objectives, lesson plans, and other supportive materials have been developed both by the original authors and others to provide a full breadth of instructional and learning material. Since this career model does address the life span, the implementation addresses the stages of career awareness, career exploration, career preparation, and career assimilation (Brolin, 1995). The materials include a set of standard assessment materials, implementation and technical assistance information, along with LCCE video training tapes and distance learning programs (Brolin, 1992a, 1992b, 1992c, 1992d, 1993, 1996). Given the broad nature of this model, its inclusion of special education and regular education and the extensive material support, the LCCE appears to be a viable choice for use in transition programs (Luft et al., 2001). Luft et al., although, note that whatever program is used, considerable efforts should be made to match the program to the individual's strengths and needs.

TABLE 6–6
Life-Centered Career Education Competencies

Curriculum Area	Competency
Daily living skills	1. Managing personal finances
	2. Selecting and managing a household
	3. Caring for personal needs
	4. Raising children and meeting marriage responsibilities
	5. Buying, preparing, and consuming food
	6. Buying and caring for clothing
	7. Exhibiting responsible citizenship
	8. Utilizing recreational facilities and engaging in leisure
	9. Getting around the community
Personal-social skills	10. Achieving self-awareness
	11. Acquiring self-confidence
	12. Achieving socially responsible behavior—community
	13. Maintaining good interpersonal skills
	14. Achieving independence
	15. Making adequate decisions
	16. Communicating with others
Occupational guidance and preparation	17. Knowing and exploring occupational possibilities
	18. Selecting and planning occupational choices
	19. Exhibiting appropriate work habits and behaviors
	20. Seeking, securing, and maintaining employment
	21. Exhibiting sufficient physical-manual skills
	22. Obtaining specific occupational skills

Sources: From Brolin, 1989, 1996, 1997; Kokaska & Brolin, 1985.

Career Development and Transition Education Model
Clarke and Kolstoe (1995) proposed a model based upon Marland's original work. Figure 6–9 provides depiction of how their model incorporates age levels and programs to denote services and environments. The model delineates programs and services at the elementary, secondary, and postsecondary levels. It also specifies employment outcomes at the various stages of development (Luft et al., 2001). Clark and Kolstoe (1995) also include programs usually sponsored by vocational rehabilitation programs, community and technical colleges, 4-year university or colleges and graduate or continuing education. This includes postsecondary school options along with cooperative education, work evaluation, and technical education.

At the early years, prekindergarten to grade eight, the model delineates four domain areas: (a) values, attitudes, and habit; (b) relationships; (c) occupational information; and (d) acquisition of job and daily living skills. Each of these levels provides foundational elements that would enable students to gain necessary skills to be able to achieve entry-level employment at the appropriate age (Clark & Kolstoe, 1995). The program further specifies and includes instructional methods, materials, and guidance to assist the implementation of their model. Further, information is included on career guidance and counseling along with a description of needed interagency linkages. Luft et al. (2001) suggest that this model also is potentially relevant for individuals to match themselves for employment outcomes.

FIGURE 6–9
A School-Based Career Development and Transition Education Model for Adolescents with Disabilities

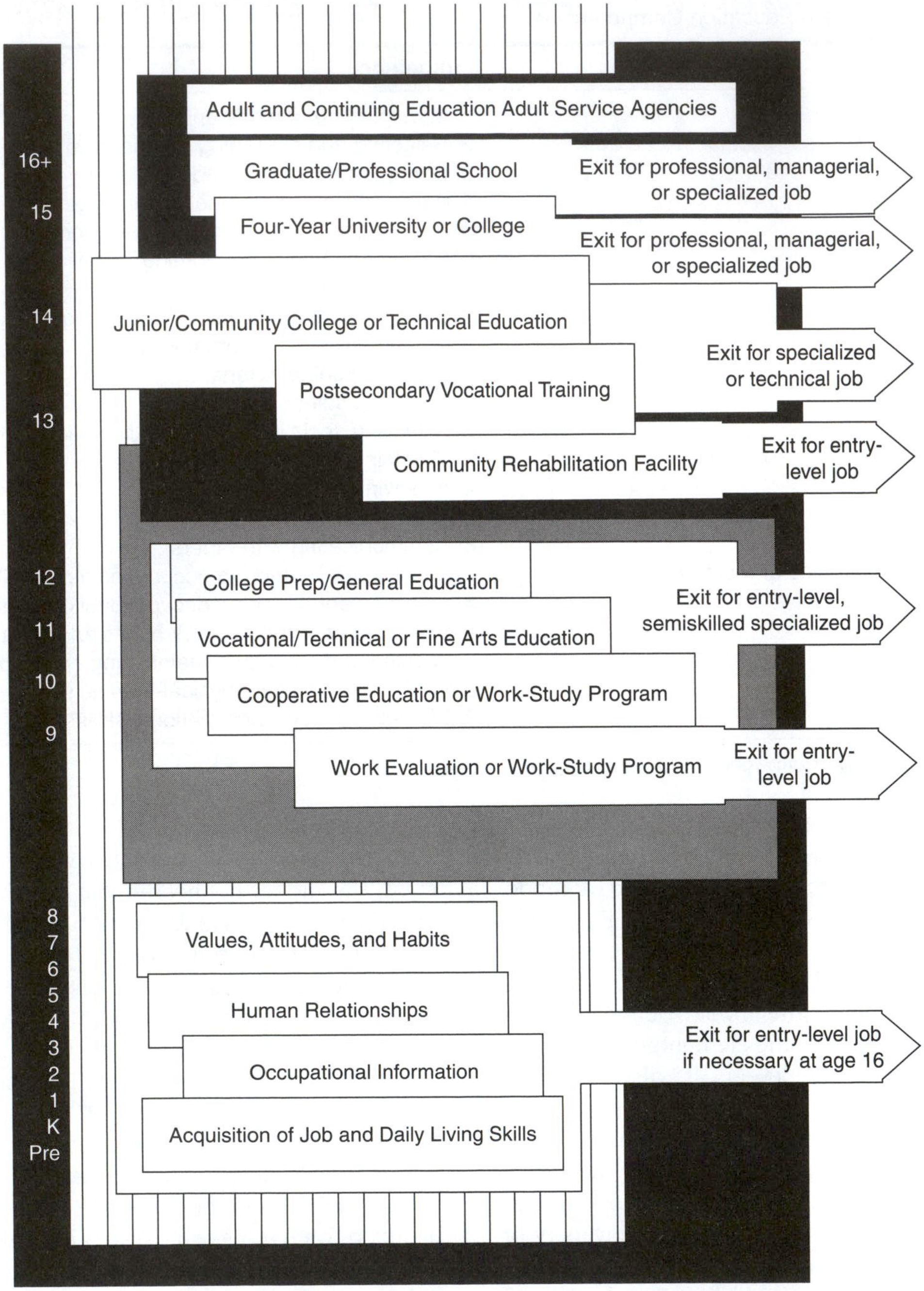

Source: From Clark, G. M., & Kolstoe, O. P. (1995). *Career development and transition education.* Copyright (1995) by Allyn & Bacon, Reprinted with permission.

Transition Pathways

A third career education model is that of Greene & Kochhar-Bryant (2003). The Transition Pathways Model is one that splits the emphasis across differing levels of inclusive settings and projected student outcomes. While Figure 6–10 shows the authors four pathways, Greene and Kochhar-Bryant indicate that the pathways can be modified or expanded based upon varying abilities and academic skills (Greene & Kochhar-Bryant). The model appears to be applicable to the life-span approach; however, the primary target of the model is that of youth at the transition age (age 14 and above). The model was developed around the specific language of the IDEA and consequently allows the school programming to meet the specific guidelines set out by law. It further provides for the course of study specification for youth based upon level of need along with outlining transitional programming components for each pathway. Other unique components of the Transition Pathways Model are its focus on self-determination and access to the general curriculum (Greene & Kochhar-Bryant).

Figure 6–10 also formalizes the transitioning programming components. Greene & Kochhar-Bryant, (2003) split this out in terms of recommended assessment, general education curriculum, instructional setting, related services and supports, transition planning considerations, and transition culmination considerations. The intent of this component is to focus on the practical aspects of getting the needed information and to make transition effective. In a practical way, based upon the individual's needs and the environment the student is in, different services and activities should be implemented in each of the delineated programming components. A case study provided by Greene & Kochhar-Bryant is provided below. It describes an example of Pathway 2, in which a student with a severe learning disability benefits from a Transition Pathway Model.

CASE STUDY C

Alejandro is a 17-year-old student with a severe learning disability. He has been in special education since second grade and is currently functioning at about a fourth-grade level in reading, spelling, and writing skills. His strength is in mathematics, with current functioning around a seventh-grade level. Alejandro was in a resource specialist program through eighth grade, but his academic ability was only moderately progressing. He and his parents decided he would be best served in a high school special day-class program with departmentalized core academic instruction, differential standards for meeting graduation requirements, and emphasis on career and occupational training. Alejandro has received an inclusive education in high school math. He is passing all his courses and is on target to graduate from high school with a diploma next year. Alejandro has a strong interest in automotive repair and wants to work in his father's auto shop business upon graduation from high school and attend community college for advanced training in automotive repair. He is currently enrolled in a high school automotive repair class and works part-time in the parts department his father's shop. His special day-class teachers have taught him about the nature of his learning disability and he has learned to ask for (a) copies of textbooks and automotive repair manuals in advance so he can have them put on tape, (b) peer assistance in note taking, and (c) extended time and a reader for tests. A representative from Student with Disabilities Services from the local community college attended Alejandro's recent IEP meeting and explained how he can enroll in automotive repair courses and receive support from their office. Also in attendance at the meeting was a counselor from the Department of Rehabilitation who explained how Alejandro could obtain support for his education, such as books on tape, and financial assistance with school costs, and purchasing automotive repair tools. Alejandro has a driver's license and will be able to transport himself by car to school and work. He and his parents mutually decided that he would live at home while he attends school. Eventually, he would like to get an apartment and live independently in the community.

FIGURE 6–10
Pathways to Successful Transition Model

IDEA 1997 transition services language requirements	Pathway 1	Pathway 2	Pathway 3	Pathway 4	Transition programming components
Instruction	Fully integrated high school college preparatory curriculum leading to passage of district proficiency exams, graduation requirements, and application requirements for entrance into a four-year university.	Semi-integrated high school curriculum leading to passage, with differential standards applied if necessary, of district proficiency exams, graduation requirements, and all requirements for entrance into a community college or professional vocational school.	Semi-integrated high school curriculum leading to passage, with differential standards applied if necessary, of district proficiency exams and graduation requirements or a certification of attendance.	Semi-integrated high school instructional program that focuses primarily on daily living skills, community-based instruction, and obtainment of a certificate of attendance.	Assessments General education curriculum access and school foundation Instructional setting
Community experiences	Function fully independently in the community.	Function fully independently in the community.	Function semi-independently in the community with necessary supports.	Function semi-independently in the community with necessary supports.	Related services and supports
Employment and other postsecondary adult living objectives	Career exploration and paid work experience in high school; full-time competitive career employment with salary and benefits as an adult.	Career exploration and paid work experience in high school; full-time competitive career employment with salary and benefits as an adult.	Career exploration and paid work experience in high school; integrated paid competitive employment with necessary supports as an adult.	Career exploration and paid work experience in high school; integrated paid competitive employment with necessary supports as an adult.	Transition planning considerations
Functional vocational evaluation and daily living skills	Not needed.	Not needed.	Participate in a functional vocational evaluation that identifies competitive employment skills, obtain daily living skills needed for semi-independent living.	Participate in a functional vocational evaluation that identifies competitive employment skills; obtain daily living skills needed for semi-independent living.	Transition culmination considerations

From: Greene, G. (2003). Transition Pathways. In Greene, G. & Kochhar-Bryant, C. A. *Pathways to successful transition for youth with disabilities* (pp. 198–229), Upper Saddle River, NJ: Pearson Education, Inc. Copyright 2003 by Pearson Education. Reprinted with Permission.

Case study C points out the various components that were relevant to benefit Alejandro. Information had been obtained through a variety of data-gathering assessments to determine his interests and abilities in automotive repair and math skills. Other activities focused on enabling Alejandro to target graduating while the educational setting was addressed through requesting required instruction needs. Related services were determined and the transition planning was accomplished.

Curriculum Alteration

When altering the curriculum, the core content is changed, as distinguished from adaptations and augmentation (Wehmeyer, Agran, & Lattin, 2001). In some cases curriculum may simply be abridged. In other words, for example, the teacher may expect the student with a disability to learn fewer vocabulary terms per week than his or her nondisabled peers and use easy-to-read texts (Mercer & Mercer, 2001). Curriculum alteration can also encompass providing alternative tasks that help the students' comprehend course content, for example, having the student read outlines that highlight the main ideas and pertinent points (Mercer & Mercer, 2001). Curriculum alteration may also include teaching "foundational" content (Turnbull, Turnball, Shank, & Smith (2004). For instance, students with severe disabilities may have a great deal of difficulty reading a general education textbook. However, a textbook that translated into a rebus-enhanced print (i.e., words transformed into meaningful pictures) may provide student with some understanding of the content.

To guide teachers to make these critical decisions, Udvari-Solner (1995) suggested that an alteration is effective if:

- It helps the individual compensate for intellectual, physical, sensory, or behavioral barriers (e.g., student is able to understand major points of lessons).
- It allows the student to use current skills while promoting ways to learn new ones (e.g., student is able to generalize skills in a new setting).
- It prevents a mismatch between the student's skills and the general education lesson content (e.g., student is able to identify key concepts of the lesson).
- It reduces the level of abstract information to make content relevant to the student's current and future life (e.g., content is summarized and student is provided only critical information).
- It creates a match between the student's learning style and the teacher's teaching style.

A functional approach often supports training in life-skills programs because it is designed to "support student learning that leads to success in home, work, and community environments" (McDonnell, Wilcox, & Hardman, 1991, p. 50). However, functional approaches can also be used to support academic and career/technical training as well. Functional training is a backward-planning model because it requires instruction to begin by identifying the terminal behaviors that the student should be able to complete. The choice of instructional settings may be critically important in developing functional programs (especially for individuals who are cognitively disabled) because classroom training often lacks *social validity*, or a close match between training and the requirements of the real-life settings (Kazdin, 1989). Lack of social validity creates problems for students when they try to generalize learned behaviors to the actual environments. Community-based training has many advantages in promoting generalization of learned behaviors because it affords students the opportunity to experience all of the cues, sounds, schedules, and social situations of real settings (Menchetti & Piland, 1998; Patton & Poloway, 1990).

TABLE 6–7

Identifying Activities

1. Select a broad curriculum domain category (i.e., recreation, community, vocational, and domestic) to be analyzed.
2. Identify a list of environments within the home, school, and community settings where students may perform activities related to the identified domain category.
3. Identify additional environments by surveying other professionals, the parents, and the students.
4. Observe these identified environments and list those skills that are essential for competence in each environment.
5. Verify the list of skills with other professionals and with parents.
6. Repeat this process for all domain categories.
7. Review and revise as needed (with minimum of one review annually).

Ryndak and Alper (1996) have noted that some skills cannot be taught in the natural environment. In this case, classroom settings are used to supplement community-based instruction. Krouse and Sabousky (2001) and others (Wehman, 1997; Ryndak & Alper) have suggested that classroom training may need to be considered: (a) when training in the environment does not afford the number of opportunities to gain adequate proficiency and (b) when the required academic content cannot be taught in the community-based setting. Generally, functional programs address five content domains: (a) communication, (b) personal management, (c) social, (d) vocational, and (e) functional academics. Table 6–7 shows how a functional program could be developed for a student with a severe disability across the educational life span.

Wehman et al. (1988) delineated three primary components in the prioritization of functional instruction: (a) identifying functional activities for instruction across life domains, (b) establishing priorities for instruction, and (c) deciding where instruction should take place. Wehman et al. (1988) proposed a seven-step procedure for determining functional goals for students (see Table 6–8). With parent and student input, this process allows the practitioner to select domain categories and environments and ascertain needed skills for students.

With the targeted skills having been selected, it becomes necessary to establish priorities. Using this process it is then possible to identify relevant future environments, compare present and future needed skills, and plan out processes for achieving new skill requirements.

CASE STUDY D

Susan's goal was to live in an apartment with friends after graduation. She currently lives with her parents and knows how to respond in emergency situations. For example, she knows what to do in case of a fire and how to ask her parents for help. She has no budgeting, cooking skills, or ability to use a phone book. She has some vacuuming, cleaning, and dishwashing skills, but requires some prompting. Of these behaviors, it was determined that cooking, phone use, vacuuming, cleaning, and dishwashing were the skills that Susan would perform most frequently in her new environments. Phone use and fire safety skills were considered the most critical for safety, and cooking, cleaning, lunch packing, and dishwashing were considered critical to independence. Home repair and budgeting were lower-frequency behaviors and less critical to independence since they could be provided by the landlord and social service

TABLE 6–8

Prioritizing Activities

1. Identify, with the student and her or his family, the student's performance in each of the transition domain categories. Then, identify desired relevant future environments in which it is projected that the student will be functioning.
2. Identify activities and skills relevant to the student's current environment; identify skills that are necessary to function in projected future environments.
3. Review all relevant current and future activities and indicate those activities that occur in two or more domains and are age-appropriate.
4. List these activities from the most to the least frequent in occurrence.
5. From this list, identify those activities that are crucial for the student's safety. Next, identify those activities that are critical for functioning independently in the identified future environments.
6. Select for immediate instruction:
   a. Those activities that are essential to the student's safety within environments
   b. Those activities that the student must perform frequently in order to function independently within her or his current and identified future environments
7. Select remaining objectives from the list of activities.

agencies. Because phone use was a skill that was critical for Susan's safety in her current environment when her parents were away, this was chosen as the highest priority for instruction. It was determined that Susan did not need to use a phone book since a programmable phone could contain all phone numbers she would routinely need as well as in the case of an emergency. Use of a programmable phone was, therefore, taught first. Because cooking and lunch packing were two behaviors that Susan would need daily to live in an apartment, they were taught next. Because Susan could not read a recipe, the teacher used a microwave oven and illustrated instructions for menu planning. Susan continued to learn the remaining skills based on the prioritized list.

Curriculum adaptation, augmentation, alteration, and the functional approach are typical methods of creating access to the curriculum. They are all used after the curriculum has been developed and implemented in general education. Recently there has been a new trend regarding curriculum access, known as universal design. It should be noted that universal design may also be referred to as universal design for learning, universal design for instruction, and universal design for education.

Conclusion

In this chapter the authors discussed the challenges of aligning transition and standards-based education that stemmed from the IDEA of 1997's requirements that all students with disabilities participate in the general curriculum and in state and district-wide assessments. The authors presented a model that depicted three major educational approaches—academic, career/technical, and life skills as making up the general curriculum. These educational approaches are built around a core set of standards and must share elements of curriculum with each other. The authors noted that accessibility to the general curriculum can be obtained through both systems-level and individual accommodation approaches. At the systems-level, universal design of curriculum and instruction can minimize the need for individual accommodations. When accommodations are needed, the authors recommended the use of least restrictive alternatives and low-tech solutions first, and they presented a model for making these decisions using assistive technology, curriculum adaptations, curriculum augmentation, and curriculum alterations.

Study Questions

1. Discuss standards-based reform and its advantages and disadvantages for students with disabilities.
2. Compare and contrast the various types of curriculum traditionally found in schools.
3. Discuss how universal design and broad standards can make the general curriculum more accessible to students with disabilities.
4. Discuss the IDEA-mandated process to help a student access a high school course of study.
5. Describe the steps described by Wehmeyer et al. in establishing access to the general curriculum.
6. Identify the three important characteristics that should always be considered when determining the need for the use of AT.
7. Compare and contrast curriculum adaptations, curriculum augmentation, and curriculum alterations.
8. Describe the important characteristics of functional alterations to the general curriculum.

Websites

ABLEDATA—
A searchable database of products, devices, and information on assistive technology-related items that puts assistive technology at one's fingertips
www.abledata.com

Alliance for Technology—
The alliance for technology access (ATA) is a network of community-based resource centers dedicated to provide information and to support services to children and adults with disabilities, and to increase their use of standard, assistive, and information technologies
www.ataccess.org/

CAST—
(Center for Applied Special Technology)—Cast provides opportunities for individuals with disabilities through the development and innovative uses of technology
http://www.cast.org/

Closing the Gap—
Closing the Gap is an internationally recognized source for information on innovative applications of computer technology in special education and rehabilitation
www.closingthegap.com

EASI (Equal Access to Software and Information)—
EASI's mission is to serve as a resource to the education community by providing information and guidance in the area of access-to-information technologies by individuals with disabilities
http://www.rit.edu/~easi/

Disability Resources, Inc.—
Information about legal rights, financial resources, assistive technology, employment opportunities, housing modifications, and educational options, transportation, and mobility services
http://www.disabilityresources.org

Project Intersect
http://www.cate.uoregon.edu/ces/intersect/

National Council of Teachers of Mathematics
http://standards.nctm.org

National Science Teachers Association
http://www.nsta.org/index.html

State Online Standards Database
http://www.aligntoachieve.org/AchievePhaseII/basic-search.cfm

Gutenberg Project
http://www.gutenberg.net/

High Tide Project
http://www.ccpo.odu.edu/~arnoldo/hightide/hightide.htm

Window to the Universe
http://www.windows.ucar.edu/tour/link=/windows3.html

Access Standards
http://www.ed.gov/G2K/standard.html

Creating Graphic Organizers
http://www.teach-nology.com/web_tools/graphic_org/

7 Instructional Strategies and Transition Settings

Pamela Luft

LEARNING OBJECTIVES

The objectives of this chapter are:

1. Identify the four organizational categories of instruction and the major characteristics of each in terms of how they can:
   a. facilitate learning, or
   b. creating barriers to learning.
2. Describe the key characteristics of direct instructional methods in terms of:
   a. The role of the teacher.
   b. The role of the learner.
   c. Typical transition learning activities and conditions for which it is most suitable.
3. Describe the key characteristics of non-direct instructional methods in terms of:
   a. The role of the teacher.
   b. The role of the learner.
   c. Typical transition learning activities and conditions for which it is most suitable.
4. Describe how you would vary your use of (a) instructional approaches, (b) instruc-

tional strategies, (c) basic-skill accommodations, (d) independent student practice activities, and (e) evaluation activities to meet the needs of students who have different learning strengths and needs, such as found in students who have:
   a. High incidence disabilities (developmental delays, learning disabilities, and behavior disorders).
   b. Low incidence disabilities (moderate/ severe developmental delays, severe behavior disorders, orthopedic disabilities, health impairments, multiple disabilities).
   c. Sensory disabilities (deaf or hard of hearing, visually impaired, deaf-blind).
5. Describe or develop a transition-focused, interdisciplinary thematic unit that:
   a. Includes at least 2 content areas.
   b. Uses the lesson planning form.

Introduction

Without instruction, what is school? Some people may say it is lunch, recess, assemblies, field trips, fire drills, emergency phone calls, transition meetings, and end of year parties! It is true that frequently school is many things that are *not* instructional. This chapter provides information about instruction to increase the effectiveness of teaching transition skills. Real "hands-on" experience in *doing* transition instruction after reading this chapter will help teachers apply the information presented here. Also, other transition staff will be expected to help IEP and instructional teams develop and evaluate effective teaching, including its application to transition and community settings, so this chapter is also important to them.

Instruction is made up of a very complex set of behaviors. Recent trends seem to define good instruction as higher proficiency test scores. Other people believe it focuses on the "3-Rs." But the purpose of a public education is to prepare children to become working and responsible adults, and participating citizens. The broad goals of education are very similar to transition planning. Yet public and legislative pressures for high test scores raise a conflict: We are mandated to provide transition services by one act, and mandated to link graduation with proficiency scores in other acts.

This chapter is important because, while transition services mandates meet the broad desired outcomes of public education, schools must also regain the public's and politicians' trust that they are instructionally competent. Schools and teachers need to exercise professional judgment in determining and providing the knowledge and skills that students really need in order to be successful adults. Test scores are one potential indicator. The 3-Rs are one set of important content. Educators must implement and demonstrate truly competent instruction, and thereby prove that students can achieve high academic and transition outcomes that go beyond their scores on proficiency tests.

Art and Science of Instruction

Teachers are pressured to accept various notions of what "good instruction" is. Test scores or the 3-Rs are simplistic, one-dimensional definitions. Instruction is complex because it is both an art and a science. It is a science in that good teachers study their students' strengths and needs through records, through conversations with family members and prior teachers and staff, and through observations across different settings. They assess each of their students across the various curriculum options chosen as appropriate by the IEP/transition team. Teachers mentally align each student's learning profile (strengths, needs, interests, age, gender, family and culture, etc.) with these curriculum components and relevant IEP outcomes (annual goals and objectives) to develop an instructional plan for each student. From this plan, and in consideration of the student's learning profile, teachers begin examining the learning environments and the successful instructional strategies they will potentially use. Clearly, this is a complex task for one student; tracking this across multiple students within the same groups, even more so.

Critical Point Teaching is a complex task that consists of integrating science and art aspects.

The "art" of instruction is displayed in teachers' interactions with real students—whose own interactions with best friends, girlfriend/ boyfriends, or parents affect their behaviors on any given day. Each time teachers deliver instruction, and they look those wily, lovable rascals—students—in the eye, the *art* of teaching is performed. Teachers use their personality, appearance, and intellect to effectively motivate and engage the students into trying out, practicing, and mastering a body of knowledge, or a skill. Skillful teachers modify their moods, energy levels, verbal and nonverbal behaviors, and abilities accordingly to stimulate and perpetuate student learning. The interplay of the interpersonal and environmental characteristics that make up this art includes the effective transmission and implementation of our skills in the instructional science aspects. The art skills include being creative and innovative in planning for and implementing these activities.

Within each science and art aspect of teaching, there also are knowledge, skills, and attitudes. Educators need science-based *knowledge*: about curriculum, instructional strategies, student strengths and weaknesses, developing units; *skills*: aligning profiles and curricula, finding and using curriculum and instructional strategies; and *attitudes*: our feelings and beliefs that impact our science-based knowledge and skills, etc. There also is art-based *knowledge*: understanding our own personal strengths and weaknesses as a teacher, using these with those students with whom we seem less effective; *skills*: effective implementation, our abilities to monitor effectiveness, and also modify and adapt while teaching, etc; and *attitudes*: using our own and our students' attitudes to support effective implementation, or modifying accordingly. See Table 7–1 to

TABLE 7–1
Art of Teaching Versus Science of Teaching

	Science of Teaching	Art of Teaching
Knowledge	• Curriculum • Instructional strategies • Student strengths and weaknesses • Developing units	• Understanding own personal strengths and weaknesses as a teacher
Skills	• Aligning profiles and curricula • Finding/using curriculum and instructional strategies	• Effective implementation • Abilities to monitor effectiveness • Ability to adapt while teaching
Attitudes	• Feelings and beliefs	• Ability to use own attitudes • Ability to use student attitudes

examine the comparison between the art and science of teaching.

Good instruction encompasses a broad as well as thorough knowledge and set of skills effectively implemented across the art and science of teaching, with a positive and professional attitude. Because this is very difficult to achieve, good teachers are always learning and striving to improve. Daily practice helps develop multitasking abilities for managing all of these aspects effectively. Good teaching may seem overwhelming at first, but beginners should be encouraged to remember the first day they climbed in the driver's side of the car. As with driving a car, many aspects of teaching will become routine and automatic over time, allowing good teachers to multitask without undue mental stress.

The next section applies transition to instruction, followed by the key components of instruction. Good teaching requires practice, best done under the supervision of a skilled and experienced teacher who provides frequent instructive feedback. Other transition staff can use this information to better understand the complexity and the many aspects and nuances of teaching. Transition team members must be prepared to help generate and monitor the many instructional variations that will ensure optimal learning for each student with unique abilities.

Four Essential Elements of Transition

This section provides a quick review of important transition elements. Psychology classes teach that one way to promote learning is through repetition, which is the strategy used here to help connect transition with instruction. Instruction, like transition planning, should be designed as an *outcome-oriented process* (element one). Good instruction is intimately linked to transition and should lead to positive outcomes for the students.

As with transition activities, good lessons are not carried out in isolation but should also be part of a *set of coordinated activities* (element two). Instruction and transition need to be well organized, sequential, with sufficient repetition and practice for learning to occur—and will likely lead to improved outcomes. Anyone who has sat through disorganized presentations of information knows that they inhibit learning outcomes.

The third element is *promoting movement to postschool activities*. If instruction is developing the knowledge and skills that students need to become responsible and successful adults (also the overall goal of public education), then this element is covered. However, the current focus

TEACHING TIP A

With practice comes automaticity, but herein also lies danger—of becoming a nonthinking, mechanical teacher. Back to the driving analogy: Aren't there a lot of careless drivers on the road who have stopped thinking about driving, or are focused on something else? And maybe there are times when even the best drivers drive on "automatic pilot" and wake up to a near miss. Or they're finding that new CD player, or the cell phone rings; or they're groovin' to a new song and daydreaming about life. We've all had teachers like this too—those on automatic pilot, or daydreaming through each day—or counting down the days until retirement. Teachers have *plenty of challenges* left to keep them energized and enthusiastic, so there's no fear of slipping into a rut!

on testing scores is complicating this process. Despite these pressures it is the responsibility of skilled teachers to develop the knowledge and skills students will need to move successfully beyond school. Instruction is the primary tool for accomplishing this.

None of these three prior transition elements should occur without element four, being *based on student needs, preferences, and interests*. Instruction, transition planning, and most other educational activities are much more likely to be successful when based on the student. Such topics and activities are also called "authentic," and "relevant" (cf. Wiggins and McTighe, 1998). If more instruction had a clear transition focus (i.e., had clear links to successful adult activities) then student motivation (and achievement) would tend to increase.

The process of organizing the myriad science-of-teaching variables upon which teachers overlay the art-of teaching strategies is confusing. Good organization leads to better learning, so this vast array of information about instruction needs a little structuring. This discussion of instruction begins with the classroom environment, using four categories and their elements that are based on Friend and Bursuck (2002) and Wood (1998), with modifications. The four basic categories are: classroom organization, classroom grouping, instructional materials, and instructional methods. These categories are listed and then described in the following sections. A fortunate aspect of these categories is that many can be controlled or modified by the teacher. Therefore, if you realize that one or more of these are interfering with student learning, you and your IEP teammates are probably able to make some changes to improve the situation. The information begins with variables that impact instruction less-to-more directly, beginning with the physical environment. Table 7–2 provides the outline for classroom organization and shows how topics get organized under this category. The outline format used in the table aids the learner to structure new material and promotes better understanding and retention.

Classroom Organization

Physical Structure

The *physical* aspects of the classroom and school environment impact students and teachers. There are pluses and minuses to every environment, whether it is a noisy, inner-city environment or a quiet, rural setting. Some students and teachers do not cope well with specific aspects of each while others cope fine. Physical space and conditions impact people differently, so a teacher needs to be alert to these impacts and work to

TEACHING TIP B

Over the course of 15 years of real-life teaching, I noticed that adolescents' preferences and interests *change*. It happens monthly, weekly, if not daily! And even we, as elementary, middle-school, high-school, and college students changed our friends, our career, and our lifestyle preferences. Student *needs* also vary across environments, by age, across peers/colleagues, and hopefully, as a result of instruction. As team members, we may make transition plans without remembering these changes and then become frustrated. Instead, this is a wonderful opportunity to help students use change as a learning opportunity—how to adapt to and plan for change—a skill they'll need the rest of their adult life.

TABLE 7–2

Outline for Classroom Organization

Classroom Organization
Physical Structure
Space: walls, lighting, floor layout, storage
Classroom appearance and design: decoration, information
Classroom Routines
Academic
Nonacademic
Classroom Climate: Attitudes of individual differences
Classroom Rules and Monitoring
Use of Time
Instructional time
Transition time

optimize them. Watch for nonobvious indicators such as different behaviors across different settings.

Classroom appearance affects each individual differently. Some may thrive in a colorful, lively, and "busy" classroom—others may prefer a minimalist, tidy, Zen-like classroom. Regardless, some students will respond well to the teacher's preferences, and others won't. Lively classrooms may spawn new levels of cognitive achievement or result in frenetic, unfocused behavior. Yet, minimalist classrooms are not necessarily benign either, and may plunge students who are used to high activity levels and noise into lethargy and withdrawal. Keep in mind that, depending upon the impact on the students and the teachers, the classroom environment may need to be altered: space, lighting, appearance, and architecture all make a difference to learning (Friend & Bursuck, 2002; Wood, 2002).

Applying this to transition services, suppose the objective is to teach a student who is highly distractible how to cross an extremely busy four-lane intersection. The instructor will need to begin in less distracting and complex environments and gradually work his or her way to an authentic, real-life outcome. Gradually, the teacher will help the student develop the knowledge and skills, to successfully cross and this may involve teaching compensatory strategies for dealing with the nonessential but highly distracting environmental conditions and intersections that differ (e.g., horns honking in the distance, numerous other pedestrians, nonessental signs, etc).

Classroom Routines

These categories are not mutually exclusive, and have overlapping influences. For example, classroom routines, climate, rules, and use of time all are highly related (including physical structure). Classroom routines should support student learning. All students benefit from some degree of routine, and also from learning to cope with change (nonroutine events). These routines are quite important and include the teachers routine for addressing change. Suggestions include present *change* early in the day or when known; identify how it will impact scheduling; how the class will prepare for and then carry out the change; and how and when class will return to the typical schedule. Advance notice helps even challenging students cope pretty well. Those preparing for work or postsecondary settings need strategies and routines for coping with the unexpected.

Classroom Climate

Classroom routines help to set the classroom climate in terms of how these routines and changes are enforced and implemented, and the interaction patterns (e.g., climate) that result. Certain students will challenge these routines and interaction patterns—and how the challenger is addressed also further reinforces the classroom tone. Climate definitely includes

TEACHING TIP C

Every teacher needs to establish "fair" standards across students of varying abilities, background, and motivation, regardless of class size or alleged homogeneity (no two students are identical!). Students are quite aware of the effort versus achievement conflict, and also accepting of individually defined standards (the teacher must be consistent with this). For nearly identical behavior, a teacher may lavish praise on a highly distractible student crossing a busy intersection, but reprimand a typically calm and attentive student who suddenly engages in distracting, attention-seeking behavior—and the treatment would be "fair" because the calmer student can achieve at a higher standard regarding assertiveness.

how a teacher either supports or discourages acceptance of diversity, an issue that includes ethnicity, gender, and a variety of personal characteristics.

Classroom Rules

A few, positively stated classroom rules that are taught and reinforced consistently through the school year provide the foundation for classroom control (and compliance with instruction). If well conceived, they can be applied equally well to school or community-based settings (e.g., respect other people and their property, try your best, etc., are universally applicable). Clear and effectively implemented rules will also support your classroom routines and climate. The teacher needs to spend extra time and energy establishing these with each new class, but once the rules and routines stabilize, the teacher and students can focus their energies on learning.

Use of Time

All of the above elements influence this one: a well-managed classroom leads to effective use of time during instruction and transition times (between classes or activities). When routines and rules are consistently adhered to and implemented, there is a tremendous reduction in wasted time. It's possible that a teacher could have the previously mentioned aspects designed well but still be unfocused during instruction. The delineation of both instructional and transition times is important (Friend & Bursuck, 2002). Students need to be prompted and trained to end and begin tasks in a timely manner. In addition, they need to leave, change, and return to work areas with increasing amounts of self-monitoring and responsibility in doing so. Teacher will be well-served to remember their own experiences as students, when they manipulated the teacher into wasting class time and when they dawdled and contrived to delay teachers by 5 or 10 minutes between tasks. In remembering, teachers might be better prepared to avoid being manipulated themselves. Once learned, these "time management" skills are easily generalized: to work settings (even coffee and lunch breaks), post-secondary settings (self-scheduling of appropriate homework sessions, time for class preparation and arrival, etc.), and across other adult environments.

A note about behavior systems: It is not within the scope of this chapter to review the many potentially effective systems for encouraging and rewarding positive behaviors. The choice of system depends upon the needs and abilities of the students as well as the

TEACHING TIP D

It is often very difficult to consistently maintain a positive classroom demeanor and to avoid temptations to become punitive. Like television, people often give much more "air time" to problems than to positive events. But we should ask ourselves—when was the last time *we* were nagged, lectured, or berated into cheerful, enthusiastic compliance? It's important to maintain positive routines, climate, and rules, and to be consistent in carrying these out, despite students who challenge you. Positive classroom climates require regular student praise and attention for behaving well, and also a clear sequence of warnings and consequences for defiance. The most effective tool is the teacher's attention and the "air time" given to positive events!

needs and preferences of the teacher—a disregard of either can "break" even the best system. And regardless of what is used—behavior management, token economy, contract, or positive behavioral support systems—all can be quickly made ineffective by inconsistency. Rewards and disincentives work only when they are consistently applied (no matter how tired, or irritated, or inconvenienced the teacher may feel). When designing a behavior system, like other aspects of teaching, one needs to examine the science (analysis) and the art (implementation) components. Begin with a thorough analysis of the behavior (such as a functional assessment; cf., Smith et al., 2001) to determine the exact nature of the behaviors, who and what is contributing to this, and, as much as possible, *why* the behavior is occurring. The student who behaves marvelously on the job but abysmally in the classroom (or vice versa) is telling us something, and it's our job to identify the conditions supporting the *appropriate* behaviors. This analytical and positive framework (looking for when and where the "good" behavior occurs) is part of the strategy of using "positive behavioral supports." Given all of the overlap in the structure category, positive behavioral strategies will reinforce positive rules and a positive, accepting classroom climate. Another point: The ultimate goal of behavior systems is to return to more "normalized" contingencies (i.e., primary reliance on verbal praise, warnings, and reprimands). Once stabilized, the teacher should systematically and gradually decrease the frequency and intrusiveness of the behavior system (much of this depends upon the age, needs, abilities, and prior experiences, in and out of school, of the students). As a student nears the end of his or her schooling, behavior programs need to be adaptable to adult settings. Systems where the student is able to self-monitor and self-check, with periodic oversight (and praise) by a colleague or supervisor, can be a relatively nonintrusive and successfully applied elsewhere.

Critical Point Elements of *classroom organization* can either enhance or impede learning.

Before proceeding to the next section, mentally review how classroom organization—physical structure, routines, climate, rules, and use of time—can be used by the teacher to support instruction in the classroom and in transition environments. Also consider how they should be monitored for possibly obstructing learning (such as impacts of environment and student need mismatches). The next section discusses ways of organizing the *students* for learning.

Classroom Grouping

Whole-Class or Large-Group Instruction

The answer to whether the class should be organized as "one big happy class," groups, or pairs, or individuals, is—it depends. It depends on the students (and their needs), the classroom's physical structure, and so on. Groupings are more variable in general education classes (larger class sizes offer more possible combinations of students), but should be considered in planning *all* lessons. Many students (including those with special needs) require instruction and practice opportunities to learn to work alone, in pairs, in small and in large groups (Friend & Bursuck, 2002; Wood, 2002). In postsecondary and work settings, they will be expected to be able to work alone, in pairs perhaps with a peer or colleague, and in large groups for special projects or at meetings, and they'll probably live with a roommate or two. See Table 7–3 for an outline about classroom grouping.

Students receiving special education who are moving into inclusion settings should not be expected to have the communication and interpersonal skills they may need, despite having appropriate academic skills (or appropriate accommodations). The IEP team should observe grouping configurations in which the student is most and least successful, and design instruction and opportunities to address any needs. Successful skills for each grouping later can be generalized across classrooms, teachers, schools, and potential work and training settings. All students who work with peers will also need some strategies for problem solving and conflict resolution—how to be appropriately tolerant as well as assertive, and when to ask for help (cf. Tileston, 2000).

TABLE 7–3
Classroom Grouping

- Classroom Grouping
  - Whole-Class or Large-Group Instruction
  - Small-Group Instruction
    - Same-skill groupings
    - Mixed-skill groupings
    - Mixed-age groupings
  - Peer-Mediated Instruction
    - Peer tutoring
    - Cooperative learning
  - One-to-One Instruction

Small Group Instruction

When working with large class sizes in general education classrooms, the large group is the most efficient way of providing instruction or information. When some differentiation is required to meet student needs, *same-skill groupings* are fairly efficient. However, students consistently placed in "low" groups are frequently stigmatized—sometimes to the point of impairing motivation and retention for learning. Actually, grouping arrangements are limited only by the teacher's

TEACHING TIP E

Even though putting certain students into groups may present seemingly insurmountable hurdles, this should not be something to avoid. Instead, use *science* to analyze and develop a solution, and use *art* to skillfully implement these groupings. The point is to give students both instruction and practice with different groupings, and in using interaction and learning strategies they will need: for inclusive classrooms, postsecondary settings, and future work and living settings. If students are in a self-contained classroom, they need to collaborate with others to arrange for grouping opportunities.

creativity (and some physical constraints, which also can be creatively minimized).

Teachers also should use *mixed skill, mixed-age groupings* when possible—they provide great opportunities for role change, allowing an older student with special needs to act as a role model to younger students (Friend & Bursuck, 2002; Wood, 2002). This can have enormous side benefits—reinforcing many skills and "maturity" not otherwise seen. Even a notorious class clown is unlikely to be irresponsible with younger students—such students can be highly effective narrators of the real-life *negative consequences* that result from certain patterns of behavior.

A word of caution: Developmentally, adolescents are increasingly peer-focused, and apt to ridicule or ostracize (especially covertly) those who are "different" or don't fit in (cf. Heaven, 2001). Teachers often need to make deliberate grouping choices (particularly at first, to help set the tone and promote positive interactions), and to prepare students with the knowledge, skills, attitudes, and problem-solving strategies to work across these options. Students need appropriate strategies and language for giving corrective and instructive feedback and decision-making tips regarding their use. Students also need practice, strict monitoring by teachers (to detect intolerance), and modeling of acceptance. They need to recognize when their own strategies are failing and when to ask for help. The whole class needs strategies for tolerating distractions and noise (talking from other groups), and to work semi-independently. Self-monitoring checklists (with instructions on how to use them) can help pairs and groups remain focused on essential tasks. By providing task options and choices, groups are able to share resources and still make progress toward their goal.

One-to-One Instruction

This arrangement often is used to remediate or "catch-up" students with knowledge or skill gaps (Friend & Bursuck, 2002). It is best used for students whose skills are quite different from the rest of the group. When combined with self-monitoring, it can help students assume responsibility for their progress. Special education and resource room classes have traditionally used this approach. A final goal should be to return the student to a typical grouping arrangement when the student also can demonstrate strategies for coping with future skill difficulties.

The majority of special education students' access to the regular curriculum will be through inclusive classrooms, and so, students whose classes have been small or individualized, or who are easily distracted, will need preparation for groups. The IEP team may need to arrange for *one-to-one instruction* to build some of these skills. Then the student may need structured practice opportunities with a variety of other students and groupings before inclusion placement occurs.

Peer-Mediated Instruction

All students should have opportunities to give and to receive tutoring, and to perform in a variety of learning roles. Many work settings want students to assist others and to work in groups (e.g., mixed skill and peer tutoring). The SCANS (Secretary's Commission on Achieving Necessary Skills) report (1991) noted that businesses want individuals capable of working and interacting with others—so working positively with peers is an important adult outcome. Peer tutoring (including mixed-skill and mixed-age groupings) and cooperative learning activities offer opportunities for students to develop learning as well as interaction and problem-solving skills (Tileston, 2000).

In summary, teachers should organize their classroom for a variety of grouping options. An added bonus is that due to diverse learning profiles across classrooms (special or general education), varying grouping (and types of instruction) is an effective way to address this. Use of large-group, one-to-one, or small-group instruction exclusively, favors certain students over others. And it doesn't prepare students for work and living settings that require various grouping arrangements.

Critical Point Students should have opportunities to work across all grouping options.

Special educators need to prepare their students for inclusive classroom and adult settings, and general education teachers need to provide a variety of learning/grouping options to meet diverse learning needs. All team members need to collaborate with others in providing these experiences (which give us team members the opportunity to work in pairs or small groups, as well). IEP members should be continually watching for situations and opportunities in which students display strengths and skills, and how these can be used across the many instructional environments within the school or community to vary their standard "role" (e.g., loading/unloading buses, lunch, after-school activities and sports, locker checks, assemblies, homeroom announcements, couriering messages, finding the nearest grocery or bank).

This section is built on classroom organization by adding variations in grouping students—allowing the reader to analyze all of these aspects of instruction sequentially and cumulatively. Before moving to the next section, think of the different groupings and how and when they can be used to support student learning: whole- or large-class, small group (same-skill, mixed-skill, and mixed-age), peer-mediated (peer tutoring and cooperating learning), and one-to-one instruction. Now think of how the physical structure can further support (or hinder) these groupings: the physical structure, classroom routines, climate, rules, and use of time—in school classrooms, assemblies, gyms; in stores, crossing streets, driving, etc. These aspects form the backdrop against which the next section—the primary sources of instructional content—is laid.

Instructional Materials

Textbooks

Table 7–4 lists critical concepts that make up the category of instructional materials. Instructional materials provide the important daily content of instruction. Curriculum provides the long-term organization and goals for instruction. However, curriculum benchmarks and standards are frequently too broad to provide the specifics of daily or weekly planning. Many school districts have identified textbooks or curricula for general education teachers to use. Special education is often much less delineated, particularly for those who cannot be accommodated by the standard curriculum. (Refer to the curriculum concepts of Chapter 6 adaptation, augmentation, and alteration, and first apply these to the curriculum and then look for appropriate textbooks.)

For students in the special education classroom, teachers must be especially concerned that materials are age-appropriate, regardless of the student's current grade-level skills or developmental age. (Be sensitive to the fact that a second grade reading level does not mean that juniors in high school should still be practicing on second grade books. Dating and "Dick and

TABLE 7–4
Instructional Materials

Instructional Materials
Textbooks: basals, content-area textbooks
Manipulatives and models
Technology
Audiovisual aids
Telecommunications
Computers for instruction
Assistive technology

Jane" are not compatible.) All materials should be *authentic* and *relevant* to the achievement of adult living objectives—this may or may not be represented in currently available textbooks. (Special ed teachers generally spend a good part of their at-work and off-work time making appropriate materials. This is part of adapting, augmenting, and altering the curriculum [Wehmeyer et al., 2001]. Vaughn, Bos, and Schumm [2000, p. 474–475] give criteria for reviewing textbooks.

Students in the general classroom need abilities to read, comprehend, and study from the textbooks effectively. These classrooms depend far more on textbook-based instruction; Gunning (2003) estimates that 75% to 90% of learning in content area classes is from textbooks. Therefore, students with special needs require strategies to use texts effectively. Generally, schools do a poor job of preparing students for nonfiction and text reading (Gunning). (The five text structures used in nonfiction writing are: time order, listing, cause-effect, problem-solution, and comparison. Most general education students have to figure out how to read and comprehend these five types on their own). [Cooter & Flynt, 1996; Schirmer, 2000]. Special education teachers (with input from the IEP team) often need to provide skill and practice opportunities (one-to-one tutoring is a good option) to build up student abilities to read, comprehend, and respond to textbooks.

Basal textbooks used to be standard for literacy. Some teachers prefer "authentic" literature and provide reading instruction through use of tradebooks and library books. Basals offer some organizational advantages: they often come with prepackaged workbooks and activities for teachers (Schirmer). Teachers who use same-skill reading groups can assign workbook or activity pages (with a set of answers for easy correction) to one group while providing oversight and intervention to another group. A desire for authentic stories and chapter books, written by highly talented and engaging authors (thereby increasing student motivation to keep reading) has led some teachers to abandon basal texts. It requires organizational skills and energies, but creative teachers use various grouping arrangements (by interest, same- or mixed-skill) with independent journaling and learning center activities to allow rotation among reading groups. Authentic literature also allows teachers to pick topics of interest to students: Urban ghetto settings, runaways, family abuse, and other topics frequently are more motivating and engaging to students. Teachers can easily incorporate transition topics using the same approach (e.g., stories of coping and living independently). A note: Special education students moving from a highly structured, basal-focused reading class into a more holistic and tradebook reading experience will need some preparation.

Content-area textbooks can be a challenge for special education students. As mentioned earlier, schools do a poor job of preparing students to

TEACHING TIP F

When looking for books related to topics of interest, no one can beat a good children's librarian! Within one or two days, they can provide a stack of potential books for the teacher's review. Some librarians are willing to visit classrooms (or arrange regular classroom visits) for read-alouds. Although often ignored by middle- and high-school settings, read-alouds allow students struggling with reading comprehension to equally participate in discussion of sophisticated topics and concepts. Repeated oral exposure to the text structures support all students when they must later read independently—a win-win situation! (cf. Salend, 2001) read across the five nonfiction text strategies. Many special education students struggle in literacy. Students who are still "learning to read" struggle in classes depending upon "reading to learn" and acquire new information. This is where the adaptation, augmentation, and alteration strategies from curriculum design (Chapter 6) should be applied to textbook usage and choice.

Math and science textbooks often are conceptually dense and generally more difficult for students to read (Gunning, 2003). Mastropieri and Scruggs (1994) found that readability of science texts were often higher than the assigned grade level. It can help if students have instruction in unique ways of *applying* various reading strategies to these subjects (Mastropieri & Scruggs, 2000). Unfortunately, we rarely see these teachers instructing students on the appropriate reading strategies. Yet it can't be left *only* to the reading teachers. Strategies in monitoring one's own comprehension and independent strategies to support comprehension (i.e., one's teacher or parent is not always available, sometimes the dictionary is worse than the word itself) are badly needed. Study strategies also can help, and how to choose among them according to conceptual load—or frustration level!

Students moving into work or postsecondary settings need practice reading and responding to commonly used materials and forms. Transition teams should collect a variety of forms and instructions from preferred potential postschool environments and teach the students appropriate strategies. Work settings also may have frequently used customer processing forms that students will need to understand. Computerization means that many of these forms may be on handheld or portable work stations that workers are expected to navigate through (i.e., read and comprehend).

Manipulatives and Models

Manipulatives and models can be helpful for the initial learning of abstract principles and concepts (Friend & Bursuck, 2002) and often help support textbook learning. Teachers must make certain that these materials suit the concept and developmental stage of the student (meaning that someone may need to *make* adapted, augmented, or altered models or manipulatives). To review the meaning of concepts, they are: classification systems that are culturally based, and through exposure and learning, are integrated into each person's unique world schema. Manipulatives and models can be very helpful in bridging understandings. At times and depending upon their unique learning needs, students may also need to be taken to real places and events to build the necessary foundation, or reference to the model. Usage should include teacher demonstration but then move to fluent student use, including abilities to provide a thorough verbal explanation (Friend & Bursuck, 2002).

TEACHING TIP G

When passing out instructional manipulatives or "toys" (from a student perspective) remember that students don't care how much they cost, how long you waited for the order, or any of your other entreaties, pleas, or threats to the contrary. Plan ahead, and make sure to give clear guidelines for their use. Give these guidelines *prior* to passing anything out, *then* distribute them in an orderly fashion (use routines) with your eyes scanning in all directions. Once your prized tools are flinging across the room, boomeranging against the wall, in the latest version of "Class Olympics," it's too late to impose order.

Transition skills are often taught in the community as well as in the classroom.

Sex education offers an engaging example for the use of models. When our teacher shows diagrams of internal body parts, he or she must check that students understand these as *their own* current or future bodies. Even if a teacher is embarrassed about being explicit in demonstrating hygiene or other activities on the models, he or she also needs to be clear! There's the classic story (perhaps an urban legend) of students who misunderstand the teacher's demo and think they are having "safe sex" by putting their condom on a banana, or a broomstick—enough said!

Technology

Developments in technology provide many new ways in which teachers can interact with and instruct students. But technology should be used only to support achievement of an identified outcome, and should never become the goal itself. If the teacher doesn't use purchased technology, essentially the students are being denied access (Gillingham & Topper, 1999).

Audiovisual aids are pretty old but still are useful to enhance learning and retention, and provide images and vicarious experiences that can broaden understandings. Movies and videos (as well as older filmstrips and photos) can vitalize descriptions of countries, peoples, environments, flora, fauna, and so on. Visual (overhead projectors) and auditory media (tape recorders) are powerful additional stimuli to lessons for enhancing retention of new information (kinesthetic and proprioceptive experiences also help). For students who are moving into adult settings, it is critical that they know their own learning strengths, preferences, and weaknesses and can identify these clearly—to future supervisors, or disability office personnel and postsecondary faculty.

Telecommunication capabilities allow teachers, classrooms, and students to establish learning, exploration, and research activities, and to explore issues that are occurring throughout the world—in real-time or asynchronous fashion (at a time convenient to the students). VTEL (video telecommunications) links allow students to enroll in specialized classes (e.g. American Sign Language is taught to several Ohio public school classes from the Ohio School for the Deaf). Many telecommunications capabilities are linked to the Internet, giving students online access to content area experts, to diverse classes around the world, and to overwhelming lists of resources. Transitioning students typically will be expected to have skills in finding and using Internet resources and using email for most jobs and at postsecondary settings. As community and work information is increasingly posted and accessible on the Web, students will need skills in effectively finding and utilizing this information.

Computers also provide new resources for instructional content (Friend & Bursuck, 2002). Drill-and-practice and tutorial software provide endless practice and reinforcement, without human tendencies for frustration and impatience. Simulations are unique ways to present real-life environments to teach knowledge and skills that will be used later. As virtual reality becomes more of a classroom presence, it will be possible for students to have virtual experiences in a variety of careers or job placements, and to "virtually" practice particular work or independent living skills.

These technologies can be highly effective supports of instruction. However, instruction remains the primary path to the goal, and technology is merely a vehicle or tool. A certain path may be quickly and efficiently traversed using a car, but at other times we must walk, or swim, or take a boat. Similarly, computers are not always appropriate for every path. Thoughtful and well-planned technology use is critical to effective teaching outcomes. Spending a lot of money on computers, if they're used only as behavior reinforcements to play games, is a poor investment. Students are happy using earned "free time" in other ways, at much less expense (cf. Gillingham & Topper, 1999).

Assistive technology (AT) has allowed tremendous improvements in access for students with disabilities. Again, if instruction is the path, students who previously couldn't keep up or walk or swim, now have special vehicles to allow them to do so—voice synthesized or manual communication boards, voice-recognition systems, enlarged or specialized keyboards or input devices, more flexible manual or electric wheelchairs, large print, and Braille translations, to name a few. Computer-based AT allows the computer-as-instructional-vehicle to be even further adapted. Digital technology allows a variety of input and output choices by simply changing interfaces (cf. PACER Center, 2002). Voice recognition systems have greatly expanded and improved to allow faster training and a much broader vocabulary. Even use of word-processing and spelling or grammar checkers allows some struggling learners to communicate their thoughts in ways more commensurate with their other abilities. Word-prediction software can greatly help those struggling with English. However the picture is not all rosy: AT adds a level of complexity that is not easily resolved among teams (Todis, 1996) and students with mental retardation underutilize potentially helpful devices (Wehmeyer, 1999).

Making the choices for AT is a complicated process—this field is changing quickly, with far too many options for one section of one chapter (e.g., a wheelchair that can go up stairs). A good decision requires input from specialized software and hardware experts who also are knowledgeable about disabilities. Team education about devices is critical as well because students and teachers can feel stranded when devices break, there are no back-ups available, and repairs can require several days or weeks.

Critical Point Instructional materials and technologies should be carefully selected to support curriculum and learning objectives, and to meet individual student needs and abilities.

The fourth category—instructional methods—builds on the three previously discussed: instructional materials, classroom grouping, and classroom organization. Think again about the benefits as well as concerns in using textbooks (differences in use between special and general education, reading issues, and real-life applications), and the best use of manipulative and models to support conceptual and text learning. Then add technology use to enhance learning and access to materials for students: through audio visual, computer software and hardware, telecommunications, and AT. Sometimes it helps reduce the complexity by thinking of specific students and how they can benefit. Add classroom grouping activities and classroom organization, one element at a time, and then proceed to the core of instruction, instructional methods.

Instructional Methods

Instructional Approaches

We're now at the heart of the teaching process—the choice of instructional methods. Much of the effectiveness of these choices depends upon the teacher's skill in sizing up the students' strengths and needs, and evaluating/analyzing the complexity and organization of the intended content with regard to potentially effective strategies (another *science* aspect). And then teachers have their own personality characteristics that contribute to teaching style and interaction preferences in terms of our implementation (more *art* aspects). This section contains extensive information and detail, because teaching is a complex process. See Table 7–5 for an outline of instructional methods.

Individual

Because of class sizes, individualistic approaches are more often found in resource rooms and in therapy settings (speech, occupational, physical, etc.). It is the one-to-one teaching described earlier under the grouping category. Opportunities for individual instruction are limited by physical conditions (having space to pull a student aside) and numbers of students. Self-contained special education classes can provide individual instruction, depending upon grouping of students, or may use the aide and teacher to switch between individual and group work. In all classrooms, instructional aids often provide individual instruction under the guidance of the teacher. The IEP team can identify specific need areas that are best addressed using this approach.

TABLE 7–5

Instructional Methods

- Instructional Methods
  - Instructional Approaches
    - Individual
    - Competitive
    - Cooperative
  - Instructional Strategies
    - Direct instruction
      - Modeling of processes or skills
      - Skills-based learning
    - Nondirect instruction
      - Conversational approaches
      - Scaffolding
  - Basic Skill-Teaching Accommodations
  - Independent Student Practice
  - Evaluation of Student Performance

Some classroom teachers are able to provide individual learning through centers and self-guided instructional activities. This requires design and set-up time and organizational systems for students (and the teacher) to monitor progress across the centers or stations. Centers can be especially effective with thematic instruction. For example, a theme of "careers" could allow students to individually explore each of the career areas at focused learning stations and provide reinforcement of adult-level vocabulary: education, salary, benefits, schedule, and so on.

Competitive

Competitive and cooperative approaches are more frequently used with special or general education classes of students. In competitive approaches, individuals or teams compete against each other to be the "winner," often by earning the most or least points (tokens, marks, etc.) or by completing a task in the least amount of time. This can be an effective way to reinforce basic skill accuracy. Individually, students chart their own progress to achieve a certain standard. This could include attendance for a frequently absent student, improved hygiene, appropriate social interactions, academic achievement.

Cooperative

These approaches typically assign tasks or projects in which the class or small groups work together to achieve a goal (Friend & Bursuck, 2002; Wood, 2002). Individuals may be assigned specific tasks that are combined into the group's or class's project. Also known as collaborative learning, it can include a community project to clean the neighborhood; to collect research data on the numbers of frogs in a local pond; or to plan, arrange, and carry out on-site interviews with local employers or independent living facilities. You will read later in Chapter 10 on multicultural competence how collaborative learning is preferred by certain cultures. In addition, it has led to more acceptance of students with disabilities than using individualized instruction (Stevens & Slavin, 1995; Reutzel & Cooter, 1999).

Instructional Strategies

There are two major types of strategies: direct and nondirect instruction (Friend & Bursuck, 2002). Direct instruction occurs when the teacher tells or shows how to do something; with nondirect instruction the teacher facilitates and supports students' cognitive manipulation of information that leads to accomplishing a specific goal or achieving a skill. Constructivism is one type of nondirect instruction. The difference between these strategies is succinctly described as: "guide on the side" (nondirect) versus "sage on the stage" (direct). Either approach can be used across the three approaches described earlier; however, direct instruction is more frequently associated with individual/tutoring and competitive approaches, and nondirect associated with cooperative/collaborative approaches. Actually, the association between approach and strategy is dependent upon how the teacher chooses to structure particular activities. Special education classes more often use direct instruction. The recent focus on constructivist learning in general education classes means that students placed in inclusive settings should be prepared for this type of learning.

Direct instruction

Is direct or nondirect instruction better for what, and how do you choose between them? One part of the answer is that *direct instruction* is most effective in promoting mastery of basic skills or fundamental learning processes. For example, when teaching students how to cross the street, or to drive a car, simply arranging an environment in which students "explore and construct" their own knowledge and skill schema is clearly inappropriate. To just "point students toward the nearest crosswalk" or to merely "hand over the car keys" would likely result in a number of fatalities as well as a swift end to our teaching career. First determine if there are procedures or sequences that must be followed without much flexibility (for certifications, licensures, and certain independent living tasks—balancing one's checkbook, doing the laundry, etc.). Then determine the students' current knowledge or skill with these procedures or sequences.

Critical Point Direct instruction is most effective in promoting mastery of basic skills or fundamental learning processes.

Now for the second aspect: How do you implement this approach? The outline in Table 7–6 lists a number of direct instruction components.

TEACHING TIP H

We all have instructional strategies that we do better than others, and some that feel "downright awkward" to us. Once we have experience and have established a style, *any new strategy* feels somewhat awkward—because we haven't practiced it, it's not yet "automatic." We have just answered the question, "Why do some teachers never change, year after year?" The answer is, because (1) it takes work to practice, and (2) it will feel uncomfortable or wrong for a while—and we're not used to that any more! The moral of this tip is: to improve is to change, to grow is to change—and this will always feel awkward at first. The fact that we don't like to change very much, ourselves is something to keep in mind when we tell our students that they need to change.

TABLE 7–6

Element	Explanation	Application
Element 1: Establish the lesson's purpose by explaining its goals and objectives.	Use an Anticipatory Set: introduce content, include a motivation for learning and the lesson's relevance; provide an overview, a schedule, and relevance.	Tell students they will learn how to use the washing machine; ask who washes their clothes, link to when they are on their own. Explain that they will be going to the home-ec room (schedule), then to the laundromat.
Element 2: Review prerequisite skills.	Review previously learned and relevant skills to ensure readiness to proceed.	Ask them to describe parts of a washer, what is needed to wash clothes.
Element 3: Perform a task analysis and introduce content in discrete steps followed by practice.	Present points in small, incremental, sequential steps (base these on students' abilities).	Task analyze: sorting wash, when to wash, steps in loading, turning on, and unloading machine.
Element 4: Give clear directions, explanations, and relevant examples.	Use clear, explicit statements with terminology that the students understand. Rate of presentation will depend on students' skills and content complexity.	Explain each chunked task explicitly and how it fits in the sequence. Have students copy own set of cue cards as needed.
Element 5: Provide time for active and guided practice.	Allow time for practice after covering small amounts of difficult or new material Include a variety of activities that require varying levels of difficulty	Model with self-talk each task chunk; repeat this with students repeating after you; repeat with greater student physical involvement. Put chunks together.
Element 6: Promote active responding and check for comprehension.	Have all students actively respond (active learning), question, and probe.	Each student copies task from instructor, taking turns; other students join in self-talk.
Element 7: Give prompt, specific feedback.	Frequent, prompt, clear, constructive feedback during: lesson, learning checks, and practice; use prompts and praise.	As prompts are withdrawn, give students immediate feedback on performance; praise for success.
Element 8: Offer time for independent activities.	Develop automaticity of skills and knowledge; build on previously learned content; provide examples, divide content into sections, highlight directions and key words.	Assign students to pairs to work independently on washing; have students bring in clothes weekly to wash; demonstrate mistakes. Continue monitoring and feedback.
Element 9: Summarize main points and evaluate mastery.	Summarize main points and follow with 1–5 minute quick probes; maintain skills with weekly, monthly maintenance probes.	Once mastery is attained, add dryer use. When both are mastered, reduce laundry to once each month in a community laundromat.

Based on Mastropieri & Scruggs (2002) and Salend (1998, 2001).

Skill-based learning is a very common application. Driving and crossing streets was mentioned earlier, but many job (establishing and maintaining files, data entry, busing tables at a restaurant) and independent living skills (cooking meals, doing simple household repairs, doing laundry), as well as academic skills (outlining a chapter, performing the four basic math operations, using the scientific method), can be taught very effectively using direct instruction. First, the teacher divides a task into smaller skills and steps, called a task analysis (analyzing the whole into component parts). A complex set of behaviors (such as implementing direct instruction) may require identification of both tasks and subtasks.

One misconception: there is not a "one-size-fits-all" or "best" task analysis. As with any good learning activity, it must fit the learner's characteristics regarding size of the steps and amount of material cued or prompted. For a student who already knows how to vacuum and pick up her bedroom, a task analysis of how to vacuum and clean up a restaurant at closing time would adjust for that. A student who had never used a vacuum would need smaller steps for this same task.

Direct instruction can also be applied to modeling of processes or skills. A teacher may begin with a demonstration accompanied by verbal explanation. Demonstrations can be very effective, followed up with guided attempts then made by the students. After a number of trials by the student (who are demonstrating remarkably increasing mastery), the teacher begins to fade the cues or prompts he or she has been using to guide these trials. One way to help the student monitor him or herself during this fading is to replace the teacher cues and prompts with self-talk—the student learns these to ensure skill or process accuracy. Particularly for complicated processes or skills, or those that involve some judgment in their usage, teachers may use self-talk to narrate their own decision-making processes during the demonstrations. Abbreviated forms of this self-talk can then become the students' own cues. Regardless, the teacher's self-talk can be highly instructive in helping students learn and master these tasks.

To summarize: Task analyses are another of the science aspects of teaching. Teachers examine the students' learning strengths and needs, the size and complexity of the task, develop a system of cues and prompts, and make a decision about whether to use backward or forward chaining—accounting for both the students' characteristics and the nature of the activity to learn.

The third column of Table 7–6 describes a series of steps to be used when implementing direct instruction for using a washing machine, a rather generic task analysis. It is a composite of information from Salend (1998, pp. 244–252; 2000, pp. 322–328) and Mastropieri and Scruggs (2002) to be used as a guide across many potential applications. Within each element, several options or ideas for implementation are described, so be creative!

How can we most effectively incorporate direct instruction into other aspects of instruction? In terms of grouping, direct instruction can be used in combination with individualistic/tutoring, competitive, or cooperative types of instructional approaches, and for large- and small-group instruction. In addition to processes and skills, most instructions for lessons are given through direct instruction—how to complete an activity, how to earn points or rewards for the lesson, or how to work cooperatively in the group and negotiate individual work assignments for the project. Examples of direct instruction are when you are telling, describing, identifying, explaining, listing, and so on. It is highly efficient in transmitting ideas compared to the more exploratory and constructivist (nondirect) approaches. Direct instruction is also appropriate when distributing instructional materials—when it's important to give quick, clear directions (and to avoid students "exploring" their way into yet another version of "Classroom Olympics"). Teachers may give a quick summary (an advanced organizer) to students prior to discussing a new chapter in a textbook. A well-run classroom will use many examples of direct instruction.

Even with driving or crossing the street, there comes a point when the learner needs to experiment with his or her own timing, pacing of procedures, making judgments, and applying the procedures under varying circumstances. A student at this stage may need feedback, but eventually, caring, nurturing and possibly terrified educators will need to allow students independence to make their own mistakes. Even under strict direct instruction, nondirect strategies of coaching and facilitating often are useful in later stages. In fact, many tasks or activities will combine aspects of both direct and nondirect instruction. However, when the instructional goal is to promote learning and development of higher-order thinking and use of problem-solving abilities, teachers need to use primarily nondirect strategies. Remember, this strategy is the "guide on the side."

Nondirect Instruction

Again, how do we choose between using direct or nondirect strategies? The answer: Where direct instruction is efficient and effective, particularly for skill or procedural learning, nondirect instruction is best for higher-order learnings—applying principles and rules, problem solving and conflict resolution, evaluation and synthesis (Friend & Bursuck, 2002; Musston, 1972). These learnings are not just following a set of procedures but also require synthesis of information and evaluation of circumstances that influence use of processes or procedures. Often there is some student exploration of options, and rarely is there just one right answer. Typically, nondirect lessons are done as inquiry or discovery learning, or constructivist activities (Salend, 1998; Mosston, 1972, 1990). The teacher usually assumes a coaching or facilitating role, and challenges the students to consider more complex cognitive relationships or "solutions" to their task.

Critical Point Nondirect instruction is best used to teach higher-order learnings, such as applying principles and rules, problem solving and conflict resolution, synthesis, and evaluation.

Nondirect strategies that the teacher may use include *conversational approaches* such as guided discussion, and role play (including scripting) (Salend 2000; Schirmer, 2000). For example, the teacher may choose to teach students about budgeting for independent living. The teacher facilitates guided discussions regarding how much apartments in their area cost per month, and then guides their awareness of affordable options in contrast to their ideas about preferred lifestyles. Next, the teacher coaches the students' exploration of salary realities of their preferred careers, beginning at entry level (a post-graduation reality). Students collect typical utility and monthly bills, and typical paycheck deductions to help them discover budgeting complexities. The use of role play or drama may help make certain concepts clearer to the students (Schirmer, 2000).

During this exploration, the instructor may use *scaffolding* procedures by giving hints and clues that support key insights. An example of scaffolding their learning of pay concepts would be:

> *gross pay* ≠ *net pay* (your boss is *not* stealing from you), and
>
> *net pay* ≠ *liquid cash* (as in, much of your net pay is encumbered by monthly expenses)

The teacher will first have determined the students' current understanding of these concepts, then develop small teaching steps (a task analysis) that will lead them to these understandings through key questions and discussions. A hierarchical spiral through these two concepts leads to increasingly higher conceptual levels and applications. The example above began with costs of apartments, because many students proclaim a desire to live on their own, in the "lap of luxury." A good way to start this discussion is with a motivating (fits their needs, interests, and preferences) exploration into defining this "luxury." Then, the teacher brings in one level of reality with "typical" entry-level earnings (salary comparison), with a goal of comparing this to typical apartment costs. Students then progress to realize that rent is not the only significant cost. Next, students examine salaries more closely—net versus gross pay—and compare that to apartment plus utility costs. Finally, the teacher helps students fit these figures into an overall budget—and lets them explore if there are ways they can still live the "lifestyles of the rich and famous."

In contrast, direct instruction would *tell* students that their apartment and salary dreams are unrealistic, and then *explain* how and why; or *give* the students a realistic budget to work with, with a brief *explanation* as to why these teacher figures are more realistic. There are definitely times when exploratory, student-focused learning is preferable. Confronting them with unabashed "reality" often results in denial, and prevents important learnings.

Now for the second question: How do you implement nondirect instruction? The example given previously was about budgeting. Here is an application that uses scaffolding to teach *problem-solving skills*. This is not only an important skill for adult living but was identified in the SCANS (1991) report—collaborative problem solving with coworkers. This lesson will also show how instruction may include both direct and nondirect strategies. The first step is to present the new strategy. The most effective and efficient way to do so is through direct instruction; and because problem solving uses a series of steps (procedural learning), it also works well with an introduction using direct instruction. The series of steps include: present the new cognitive strategy, regulate difficulty during guided practice, provide varying contexts for student practice, provide feedback, increase student responsibility, and provide independent practice.

When the instructor *presents the strategy*, students may benefit from a verbal description followed by a demonstration with modeling of all steps. Demonstration with self-talk (to model cognitive processes and decision making) may be highly effective here, again borrowed from direct instruction. Choosing a problem that students find authentic and relevant is also important.

The next step is to *provide guided practice*. The instructor may guide the discussion to choose a relevant problem for the class to solve, or a list of problems for them to try in small groups (guiding is important so that they choose problems appropriate for their current learning—don't have them jump too far in their "zone of proximal development."). Students may need one or two opportunities of full-class guided practice before moving to small group practice. Or the teacher may want students to try a modest problem on their own, then return to guided discussion to attempt a complex problem (expand their application skills). Students need to explore and apply the steps on their own, then return to the group for support. From this point on, the nondirect instructional exploration and inquiry aspects become critical to effective usage. Students need practice in using their judgment and evaluating the process and its outcomes.

The third step expands the situations to which the problem solving is applied, and to *generalize this process* to other issues and settings. The fourth step is to *provide feedback* (always critical—being sure to monitor all groups). The fifth step is to *increase student responsibility*—supporting students (through feedback) and helping them learn to monitor themselves to identify when they are and are not following the procedure correctly. If able to do this in increasingly smaller groups, and with increasing "self-directed" amounts of time, they will be prepared for the sixth step, *independent practice*. During the six steps the class may need periodic refresher "demos" and self-talk. This can further refine their skills if their list of problems becomes increasingly complex.

See Table 7–7 for an illustration of problem solving. The basic set of steps shown in the table can be easily modified to learn conflict resolution (modify step #1 to "identify the problem from all perspectives") or choice making (substitute "choices"—as shown in brackets). Students can learn one basic procedure, from which they can generalize to a number of potentially difficult life circumstances. And their use for transition skills is nearly endless: *problem-solving skills*—waking up on time, finding the best bus route, meeting and making more friends; *choice-making*—deciding if friends are "positive" or "negative", choosing a good career or work place, choosing a hobby; *conflict resolution*—settling an argument with parents, friends, partner, boss, or coworker.

TABLE 7–7
Problem-Solving Model

Problem-Solving Model (also known as conflict resolution/choice making)

1. Identify the problem. [or choice]
2. Consider all possible solutions. [or choices]
3. Identify the pros and cons of each listed solution.
4. Develop a plan of action.
5. Put the plan into effect.
6. Evaluate the success of the plan.
7. Modify the plan as needed and begin again at step #5.

Source: Based on Downing, 1996; Hobbs & Westling, 1998; Jayanthia & Friend, 1992; Nezu & D'Zurilla; Salisbury, Evans, & Palombaro, 1997; Wood, 2002

To summarize, although direct instruction is used to establish certain processes and procedures initially, from then on, the teacher uses nondirect strategies to facilitate student learning through conversations and exploration/inquiry. The teacher leads, guides, and facilitates the development of insights into, and interpretations of, what occurred both during individual or small-group exploration and during larger-group discussions. Examined within terms of other aspects of instruction, for classroom groupings, nondirect instruction is often used with cooperative or collaborative groups, but is not limited to this arrangement. Nondirect instruction often leads to presenting an array of texts or authentic sources, as well as other audio, visual, computer, and Internet resources (again, with guidance) for student use. The Internet allows nearly unlimited resources and opportunities to find experts or educational compatriots.

General education classrooms often do more nondirect instruction than special education classes do—therefore, students moving into inclusion settings need to have some preparation and practice. This can include doing group problem solving in math or using the scientific process (a variation of problem solving). Table 7–8 shows how Mosston (1972, 1990) categorized some types of nondirect and inquiry teaching lessons, and includes some additional classroom and transition examples.

A note about nondirect instruction: Before students can competently engage in inquiry or discovery, they must: (a) have a deep foundation of factual knowledge, (b) understand facts and ideas in the context of a conceptual framework, and (c) organize knowledge in ways that facilitate retrieval and applications (NAP, 2002, p. 4). It makes sense that students must have knowledge and facts before they can use and apply them. Bloom's Taxonomy—knowledge, comprehension, application, analysis, synthesis, and evaluation—is another similar concept. For example, students cannot explore or do inquiry into various career standards or prerequisites without understanding what "work" entails, some critical differentiating aspects among careers (in terms of conditions, educational requirements, and so on), and its importance to adults and families. So before launching into nondirect instruction, it is essential that students have an adequate knowledge and conceptual background—which, in many cases, suggests the need for direct instruction: again these two strategies are intimately linked.

TABLE 7–8

Examples of Nondirect/Inquiry Teaching Lessons

Discovery of facts	About a historical period, about a sport, a career, a lifestyle, etc. . .
Discovery of a relationship among facts	Facts that explain an outcome (cause-effect; relationship between "work" and "pay") Similarities between sets of facts (comparison of civil rights and disability rights movements)
Discovery of concepts	Citizenship rights and responsibilities Ethics Self-determination
Discovery of cognitive behavior skills	Application of problem-solving processes (at work, at home, with friends) Synthesis of information (about careers, utility costs, potential work environments) Drawing conclusions (about budgeting, affordable living) Comparisons and contrasts (among apartment options, career options, friendships) Evaluation using a rubric (fitting lifestyle choices to income realities)

So far, this chapter has discussed: science-based analysis to prepare for teaching—how to use some individualist, competitive, and cooperative learning across different grouping patterns; how to incorporate some of the good materials and resources; how to best use direct and nondirect instruction strategies; how to organize the classroom to support these. Information was also presented to help analyze the instructional materials to optimize the students' learning. But, a worry persists: What if the students don't learn? Or, what if, based on students' learning profiles, the instructor suspects that one or two students are likely to struggle with what is appropriate for the rest of the class?

Evaluation of Student Performance

Despite best efforts, sometimes students fail to learn. The previous sections contained some generic strategies that often help (Friend & Bursuck, 2002), some common-sense ways to adapt the learning activity when the teacher suspects or notices that students aren't learning—and noticing is very important. For fairly comprehensive lists of accommodations by disability, recommendations include: Friend and Bursuck (2002), Mastropierei and Scruggs (2000); Smith, Polloway, Patton, and Dowdy (2001); Vaughn, Box, and Schumm (2000); and Wood (1998). Because all students are unique, the most effective accommodation strategy is individually designed based on observations and analysis of aspects of tasks or procedures, and adaptations, augmentations, and alterations. Observations include the influence of elements of the classroom organization, grouping, materials, and instructional strategies, as well as presentation and response formats (or in digital-processing terms, input and output), and other time, setting, and personnel/people elements impacting the

Transition skills are often taught in the community as well as in the classroom.

students—in effect, all environmental conditions. This is quite comprehensive, which is why it helps to have other IEP team members and parents also observing and providing feedback.

The following examples provide some other generic strategies. For example, if a student is struggling to learn something, check his or her background experiences (also very important when teachers and students do *not* share the same cultural, linguistic, or socioeconomic background). Activate background knowledge to bridge between what students do know and what the lesson requires. In some cases, teachers will need to provide additional background experiences (video and movies help; sometimes field trips are needed). Then build to the needed skill or knowledge mastery—move from the known to the unknown (if students are lost, the instructor has moved too quickly).

If background seems sufficient, check for evidence of the preskills, then teach and review preskills as needed. I identify these preskills as *prerequisites* for my lesson plans. If the cause seems to be weak basic skills, then provide direct instruction, practice, and review for individuals with poorly developed skills. For example, a teacher may be really excited to teach the budgeting unit, but before students can do a budget, they may need to review addition and subtraction—especially regrouping. For some of the more complex learning tasks and processes, the instructor may need to provide some guided nondirect exploratory experiences as well. When selecting these practice examples, the teacher should try to select and sequence instructional examples to fit students' interests and needs—finding personally relevant practice examples can help students stay motivated. This can be hard with rote tasks (basic math facts, spelling lists, housecleaning). This is where competition or self-monitoring for a reward can help. If students have gaps, the instructor will need to modify rates for introducing new skills, going slower at first, and then faster for review. The teacher can mix up the pacing (after mastery) to keep the class lively and interesting.

The strategies above can be used for addressing skill or knowledge gaps—at school, in the workplace, or for independent living. Supervisors in all environments will appreciate information on these basic steps to try—to teach job skills, or living skills. But these are only useful when combined with being an alert, sensitive, and analytical team member or supervisor; a person who observes the conditions that optimize each student's learning, then replicates those across other activities.

A basic fact is that students learn better when given multiple opportunities for practice (Friend & Bursuck, 2002). But often teachers neglect this—effectively or sufficiently. For example, suppose that we had to pass our driver's test based only on the classroom hours, no outside practice allowed. Practice is meaningful and useful (not busywork), even though some days it will be boring and seem senseless. Sometimes practice is

TEACHING TIP I

Some students may do okay in a math text, but can't seem to balance a checkbook no matter how hard they try. It's easy to forget that skills or processes that we teach in isolation are not always generalized to outside or real-life contexts—students need practice with this. That's why incorporating authentic and relevant examples is so important. If students can't use a skill in the real world, then we haven't really *taught* them.

fun, and sometimes it's a grind, but students and instructors alike need to keep their eyes on the goal.

Everyone, at some point, has been given homework that violates many of these recommendations. First of all, homework isn't always just about practice. Sometimes it's simply a means to "finish the rest of this at home" when the teacher ran out of time. This situation often results in the students having no idea what the homework means or how to complete it. What has happened here is that the instructor may have had a great presentation earlier but the students did not master the new information.

Individualizing, being specific and systematic, practicing a few new skills at once (then chunking), and achieving high levels of success—all lead to individual mastery of knowledge or skills. Back to the example of the two students vacuuming and describing task analysis in direct instruction: the girl who frequently vacuumed would be quite annoyed to have to repeatedly practice vacuuming that was needed only by her fellow student who had never vacuumed before. If practice is to be effective, it needs to fit individual needs, be systematic, begin slowly, and work for mastery.

Students should "keep their eye on the prize" regarding their desire to learn what they are practicing, because not every day's practice will be engaging. And feedback should be immediate—teachers should be collecting and analyzing student feedback (groans and grins) on an immediate and ongoing basis, which helps to give relevant and useful, as well as immediate, feedback to students about their work.

Critical Point Independent student practice is critical to knowledge and skill retention; however, material must first have been mastered, and practice should be specific and systematic.

So far, this section has discussed a list of basic accommodations to try if the teachers lessons don't succeed, and some practice strategies to make certain that the lessons presented will be retained and mastered (Friend & Bursuck, 2002). The next step is to ensure that the learning goals were achieved.

Teaching and informal evaluation are interconnected: Good teaching depends on ongoing *observing/monitoring*—while the teacher is teaching, he or she is also observing and monitoring for success (every eye blink, head-nod, foot-shuffle, groan, or shriek tells something about the student's processing of information), which gives more information about how to continue with teaching. Those magic "teachable moments" happen only when the teacher observes, monitors, and notes a unique convergence of student interest and need with a teaching topic or with a link to an experience just described by a student. These are terrific opportunities to illuminate new concepts through other content or events; to demonstrate particular examples, or a new learning or concept; to draw parallels and explore relationships (cause/effect, problem/solution, time sequences, etc.). Through observations a teacher can make and take opportunities for quick practice or review during transitions (between classes) and break times to ask questions, scaffold, practice, and apply some of the cognitive/thinking/problem-solving skills from previous lessons (remember the need for high levels of success).

Many of the other items listed are also covered in Chapter 5. Briefly, about *grading*, it is an institutionalized school-based event intended to measure progress and achievement, and summarize information collected across all of the other formats listed. Some forms include handwritten comments, and some districts use database-driven comments. Teachers and parents may find conferences or narrative grading comments to be better ways of communicating specific information. Some teachers are highly creative and effective in fitting into their district's procedures and responding appropriately to the parents' and students' needs for feedback.

In terms of *testing* procedures, informal testing often gives teachers more classroom and learning-specific information than formal testing, although both types contribute to understanding a student's complete learning profile. Because of the limitations of testing (particularly pencil-and-paper tests), many teachers and schools are using *performance-based assessments* and *portfolios* to evaluate learning processes and outcomes. For many transition outcomes, observing and recording student skills and performance is the only authentic means for truly assessing student learning. To use the street-crossing example, the only verifiable way to confirm that the goal was met is through direct observation; a paper-and-pencil test would not suffice. Videotaping or digital cameras can be excellent ways to document a student's progress and final success. Presentation and multimedia software allow students great ways to build their own portfolios. And these can be very effective tools in convincing potential employers about a student's worthiness. No one said that a "test" had to be a paper-and-pencil event, so teachers should organize evaluation steps and culminating events as best suits their teaching and evaluation needs with regard to their students. Performance-based assessments and portfolios have helped to allow more freedom in how teachers evaluate and "test" students.

The next step is to actually prepare to teach.

Preparing for Instruction

Teacher Preparation

The classroom is arranged; the rules and routines are ready. The teacher has chosen lesson content from the curriculum and identified ways to use various types of students' groupings. He or she has found and made some terrific materials that support active student learning and higher-level learning, and has identified instructional approaches and strategies that have a good chance of being effective as well as some accommodations—with plenty of practice opportunities for all. The teacher plans to be observing and monitoring, and has a rubric for grading and evaluating student work, with specific examples to be added to the students' individual learning portfolios. Laying this groundwork is a tremendous accomplishment.

The challenge to teachers is in keeping of the critical pieces in their head as they stand in front of the class (or move from student to student) every day, all day. There is a tool available—and it is called "lesson planning." A lesson plan summarizes this key information (basically, from across the four earlier categories) so that a plan is in place to achieve intended outcomes. Although all necessary science-based analysis has been conducted and modified as needed across the four categories, the need remains to be very clear and focused for each lesson (and not overwhelmed with considerations). When well done, lesson plans provide a built-in rubric for teachers to evaluate whether or not they have been successful, or if certain portions need to be reviewed and retaught (including helping to evaluate if the strategies used were effective).

Lesson Planning

Essentially, a lesson plan is a tool to assist teachers in making sure that all critical aspects of an instructional lesson will be addressed. With experience, many teachers are able to do much of this mentally, needing only topic listings to remind them of their plans (like a mental macro-command). However, busy teachers will shortcut these processes until teaching becomes a process of "going through" a list of materials or topics, rather than providing experiences that provide for and reinforce *student learning*. "Going through" material is not teaching.

Critical Point A lesson plan is a tool to assist teachers in making sure that all critical aspects of an instructional lesson are addressed, among the myriad of variables that may influence learning.

The lesson plan in Figure 7–1 is very specific and rather lengthy—a format for beginners. With practice (remember that practice should be individualized, specific, and systematic, with high levels of success), much of the lesson planning process will become automatic. Excellent teachers can use their mental "macro-command" topics to call up their objectives, lesson sequence, adaptations, prerequisites, and so on. But when experienced teachers learn new teaching strategies or plan new types of units, then they too must write and plan.

Until teachers have practiced to achieve mastery, they will need to write and review (even several times) the various aspects of this plan. But the plan is to help when things go wrong. For example, misjudging students' preskills and prior learning experience is a chief source of lesson failure in any classroom, and even if the lesson was well planned and well executed some teachers plow ahead until failure. When students look lost, a good teacher reviews the prerequisites in the lesson plan.

Integrated Thematic Units

Even wonderfully planned lessons can be chaotic and fragmented without some link to a larger whole. Of course, lessons should be based on a state or local curriculum that leads to the achievement of standards. But jumping from benchmark-to-benchmark is productive for neither the teacher nor the student. Research shows that organizing knowledge and skills into integrated instructional units is an efficient and effective way to teach (Schirmer, 2000; Siu-Runyan & Faircloth, 1995). Units are organized around central themes, so that repetition of ideas and concepts occurs naturally. Remember the importance of repetition and practice. Teaching based on integrated thematic units helps all students (including culturally diverse; Siu-Runyan & Faircloth) learn concepts, vocabulary, knowledge, and skills at higher levels of mastery (cf., Mastropieri & Scruggs, 2002).

Developing integrated instructional units is not easy—organizing and synthesizing multiple benchmarks and curriculum activities is a very complex set of higher-order thinking tasks. Teaming across content and within grades can greatly help middle and high school teachers who often are assigned subject-specific classes (Siu-Runyan & Faircloth, 1995). Self-contained classes across all subjects may more easily organize such units; however, school support of collaboration, among special educators as well as between special and general educators, is allowing more opportunities for cross-disciplinary or integrated thematic unit planning.

Many transition topics can be easily integrated into thematic teaching units. By including authentic

FIGURE 7–1
Lesson Planning Form

Lesson Planning Form
Name________________ **Grade/Age Level**________________

1. Relationship of lesson to unit or theme: [How does this fit in? Nothing should be isolated from other learnings.]
Students will learn to do their own washing and drying as part of their preparation to live in an apartment.

2. Behavioral objective(s): [1st: Make sure to teach a new concept or skill—you don't need a new plan to review or practice a previously learned skill. 2nd: Write clear, measurable objectives to focus your teaching. If done well, this also is your evaluation step. 3rd : Check this again after you finish the plan—does everything match?]
Each student will sort their clothes, identify proper settings, add soap, load, turn on the washer, and unload the washer with or without using their own written prompts, requiring no teacher prompts on 4 out of 5 trials in the home ec classroom.

3. Materials: [List these to make sure you have them before the lesson.]
Students bring own clothes weekly, classroom purchased detergent, home ec room facilities (already scheduled for Oct – Nov,), note cards of choice (index or smaller), home ec room blackboard to write list of steps.

4. Key teaching strategies and conceptual links: [1st: Think of student needs/abilities and objectives. 2nd: Review procedures under #6 when completed—do they fit student abilities/needs? 3rd: Identify key concepts in this lesson or taught throughout the unit—how will you reinforce them? How will you link them to prior learnings? . . . to the lesson activities?]
Direct Instruction: Explain rationale, steps, outcome, schedule; narrate/use self-talk through demonstration and modeling of decision making—sorting clothes, water temperature and level, amount of soap (small vs. large load); use verbal and physical prompts that are faded—use only as reminders as students demonstrate mastery.
Indirect Instruction: Allow students to work in pairs to sort and wash their clothes—monitor and give feedback. Use guided discussion prior to using laundromat about similarities and differences (what they will expect), then monitor their use in the laundromat facilities.

5. Prerequisite skills, knowledge, and experiences: [What are you assuming the students already know and can remember?]
Have seen their family wash clothes, know some effects of hot versus cold water on clothes (will review), can use measuring cup, read basic detergent and laundry instructions (inside of washer).

6. Procedure: [How are you questioning, facilitating, initiating learning?]
6a. Teaching step(s) to motivate, engage their thinking, review past learnings [present an intriguing idea or authentic/relevant task, link to prior learning and review—to prepare for task]
"Remember our unit on living independently? What was one problem we had with our clothing? Who takes care of your dirty clothing now? How much have you helped? What things were easy . . . were difficult for you when you helped?" (forgot things, got confused, didn't know how to sort or made mistakes with that)
"Tomorrow we're going to the home ec room to do our laundry, but right now we're going to sort—who remembered to bring some dirty clothes from home?"

(*continued*)

FIGURE 7–1 *(continued)*

6b. Instructional strategies/steps to develop target behaviors/skills (how to accomplish the objective): [begin working on the task—1st: Present the problem, identify some solutions (have students participate when possible), 2nd: Model the solution, provide guided/class practice, provide pair or individual guided practice, provide individual independent practice, 3rd: Have students demonstrate the skill according to the objective (if not already accomplished by independent practice).

"Why should we sort clothes . . . what happens if we don't? So how should we sort them?" [Build on past experience]. "Yes, we don't want everything to look pink or gray. That happens because dark colors spread to light colors when they get wet. So we need to divide the clothes into dark and light colors. Everyone show me one light thing . . . one dark thing . . . Now put each in separate piles. Sort the rest of your clothes into these piles. I will check."

Next day: "Who brought their light and dark clothes with them today? Which one is the washer and which is the dryer? What do these buttons/this dial mean?" [Build on past experience.] "Let's read them and see." (Students stand around the washer and read). "The dial (buttons) are for different types of washing. You can see wash, spin, rinse, spin, and off. Look again. What do these words mean for washing clothes?"

"Find some of those words in another place. Yes, if you look below you can see heavy, normal, and spin only. We will use normal. You would use spin only if you needed to rinse something but not wash it with soap—if something gets left out in the rain. You would use heavy for blankets or washable coats or things that were very dirty from being in the mud. Now you need to pick the setting." (Show how to use dial or buttons to select, then continue in this process through steps in getting and adding soap, loading, turning on the washer, and unloading the washer when it's finished.)

---

7. Instructional probe/prompts to summarize, bring closure to the activity, and/or put it in long-term context: [Link to prior and future learning; reestablish relevancy/authenticity—have students demonstrate work, class review their work, have class find additional/authentic examples of this work, present additional or related problems to solve.]

"Who would like to have some help remembering these steps? I have 2 different kinds of cards for you to write down the steps, or you can use another type of paper. Let's first write these on the board to make sure we remember them correctly—who remembers one step?" (Continue to list all steps and ask students to evaluate and correct the full list, have students copy/draw pictures of each step as needed).

"Today we washed one load of clothes and tomorrow we will wash the other. Who can remember one important reason to sort clothes? What is important to remember about the dial/buttons? We will spend this month learning how to wash our clothes each week. Next week we will start washing and drying our clothes. After next month we will go to the laundromat, so we need to practice and remember these things."

---

8. Self-evaluation: [How effective was your (a) planning, (b) implementation? What student, classroom, or setting conditions helped or hindered your success? How could these be better addressed in the future?

(These are instructor's comments about what went well and what was a little rough, which students understood clearly and which need additional practice or prompting, if the steps seem appropriate, or are too big/too small.)

TEACHING TIP J

We start teaching a lesson on grocery shopping but become very frustrated when the students don't remember seeing store "aisles" before. How can this be? What's wrong with them? Maybe they haven't been in stores often. Although last year Mrs. Rodrigues took them on grocery-shopping trips, this class didn't have Mrs. Rodrigues. And several mothers have said they prefer to shop alone (to save time). So maybe they haven't had these background experiences. Lesson learned: We need to be aware of our assumptions. Identifying preskills or prerequisites gives us an immediate checkpoint for floundering lessons. We also need to provide these missing experiences if they are foundational to later learning: a field trip—with cameras and video to help their recall if things begin to flounder again.

and relevant outcomes into all units (cf. Wiggins & McTighe, 1998), units would theoretically *always* support transition outcomes (which are based on students needs, interests and preferences, and therefore authentic and relevant). Figure 7–2 shows two integrated thematic unit examples based on transition needs.

A review: Teachers use lesson plans to help focus their implementation on key strategies and outcomes. Teaching is a complex process so it's all too easy to "overload" on things to consider, manipulate, and address. Lesson planning keeps teachers moving forward to the instructional goal. Thematic unit planning provides a "map" through the current "regions" of the curriculum—a structured path through the content and curriculum standards, to help teachers navigate. The addition of one more instructional step will prevent lesson failure—and that is student preparation.

Student Preparation

The previous section covered how teachers need to be prepared for instruction. To be fair, students also need to be prepared to learn: they must be able to demonstrate the ability to give attention, to comply with directions and commands, and to become motivated (by interests or preferences) and engaged in activities. Often, students will need to be instructed in doing these things, or develop them to a higher level of proficiency; and instructors need to organize the classroom environment in ways that support these behaviors and then try to make grouping decisions that help out. Note how the final categories of good teaching are interdependent with the earlier categories in classroom organization and grouping.

Students with special needs may have difficulties in demonstrating a number of these behaviors. They may not have learned how to give focused attention. (And many teachers, until they observe students work 30 minutes without an eye blink using the latest X-Box or Playstation, don't know that it is possible.) Without first establishing key behaviors, even the best lesson and most prepared teacher is wasting his or her time and energy. Preparing the students to learn makes much better use of everyone's time and skills. And remember the principle of successive approximations—you have a whole year to work on this! Spending 2 weeks to one month on establishing rules and routines, rewards and consequences (e.g., compliance and attention), can yield high save dividends of instructional time throughout the year.

FIGURE 7–2
Thematic Transition Unit

Unit #1: How Can I Live On My Own?

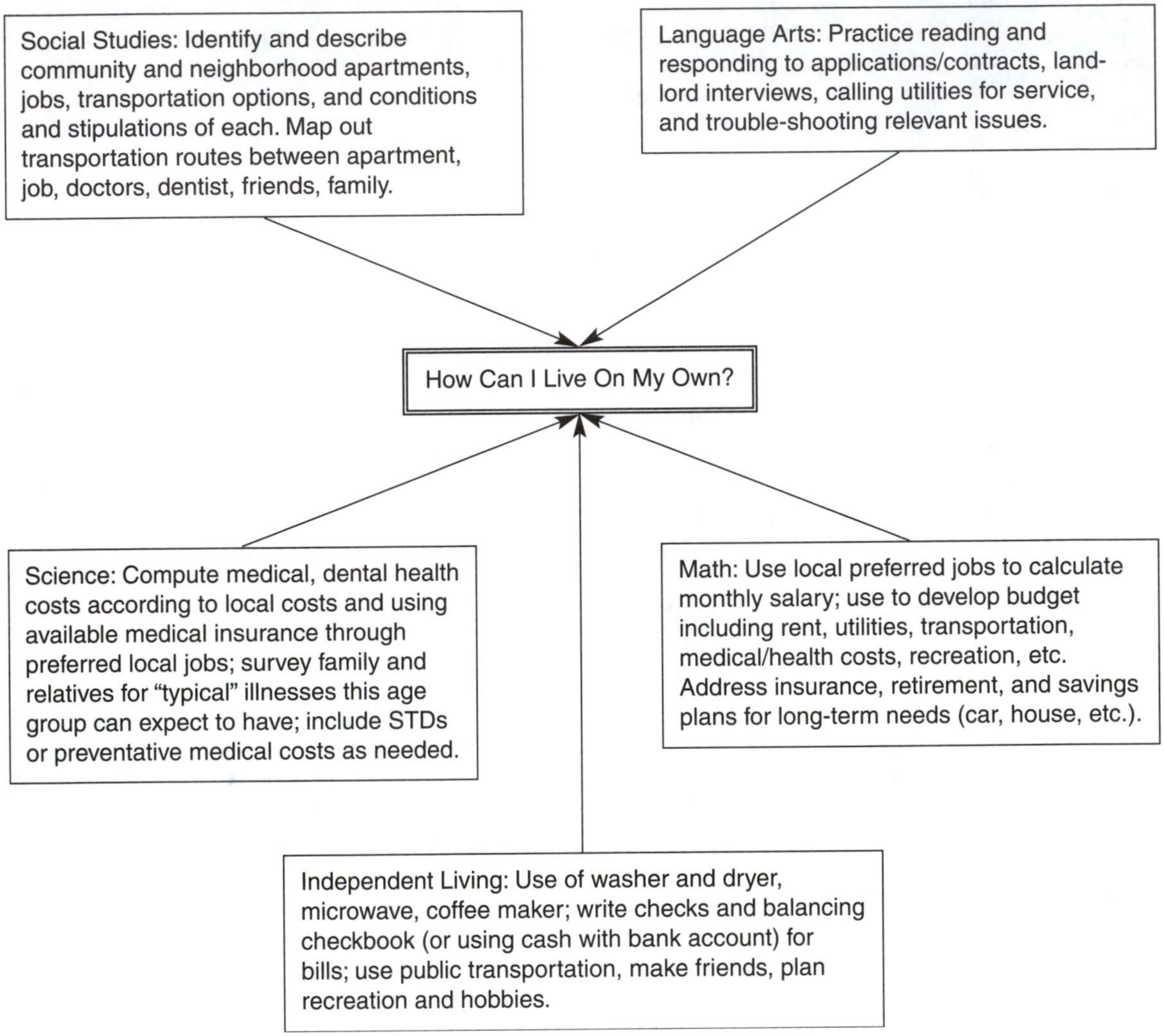

Conclusion

The ultimate outcome of good teaching is student mastery of skills and knowledge. And certainly, the community and politicians are highly aware of this; therefore, teachers are increasingly accountable. Unfortunately, there are mixed messages regarding how students should demonstrate their mastery: from transition legislation that requires

Unit #2: What is Work?

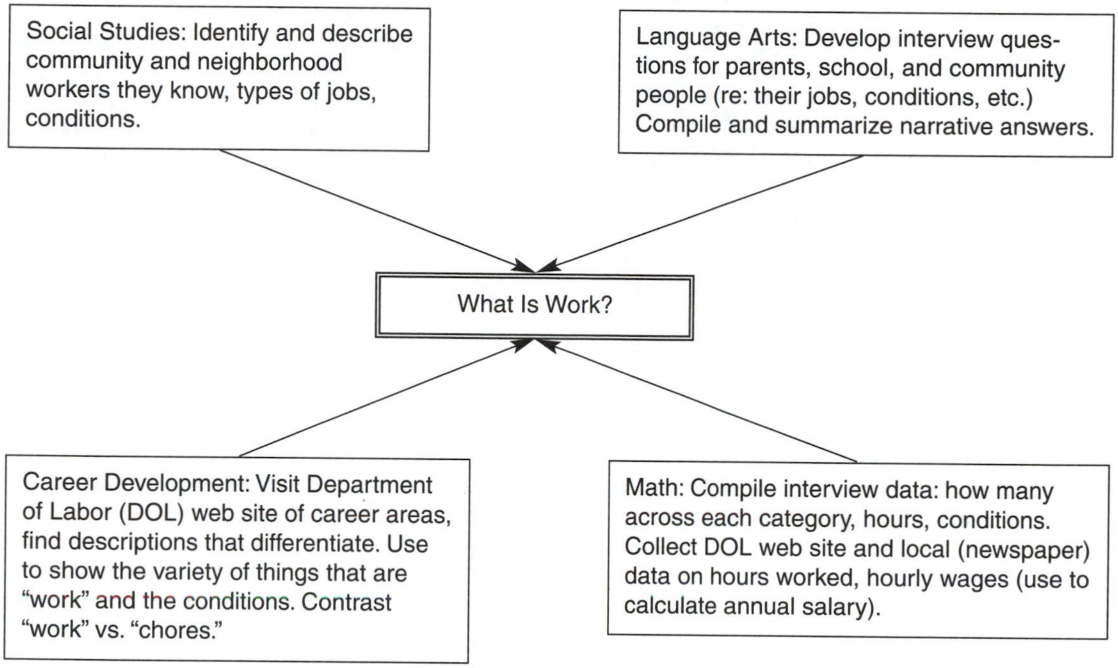

broad and lifelong outcomes, to education legislation that mandates statewide proficiency testing. IEP team members are therefore torn between ensuring that students learn important community-based and transition skills (e.g., using the laundromat or automated teller machines) or demonstrating acceptable levels of progress on annual performance tests.

But what teachers do, and do best, is to provide quality instruction. Although some may accuse teachers of participating in a profession for "lightweights and losers," teaching is too complex a profession to be done well by those who are not committed professionals. Instructors must understand and be able to use a variety of teaching strategies, and evaluate how each can best be used, according to the strengths and needs of students, the settings (including community-based or authentic in-school performance tasks), and types of skills they will be expected to use in each. This chapter's intent has been to present the vast array of variables within what is called "instruction" in a way that readers can better understand their use; and ultimately, to help instructors better implement them in schools.

Special educators are increasingly working in co-teaching or collaborative teaching situations. In these cases, it is essential to not only have the skills to identify appropriate learning strategies for particular students, but to accommodate teaching styles other than their own, and communicate their expertise effectively to partner teachers. Instructors need to articulate and explain what they do, what choices they make, and why they make those choices. They must be sensitive to how best to modify instructional strategies, for themselves, and for other professionals, and how to integrate them within a curriculum that will often need some adaptation or augmentation.

More than ever, teachers must not only be skilled in their own teaching, but must be able to consult and advise others regarding their teaching strategies—with regard to teaching choices and preferences, in their implementation of these strategies, and setting factors (i.e., class and room size, age, noise, resources, etc.). Transition teachers play a critical role on IEP teams in supporting appropriate instructional and curricular decisions and recommendations. They must also be careful listeners: to the students and parents, to general education teachers, and noninstructional team members; and must synthesize their input into identifying specific strategies, or a sequence of strategies, that result in positive instructional outcomes.

Study Questions

1. You are a teacher of a group of students (visualize a diverse group in terms of strengths/needs and ethnicity). What are some of the ways that you will want to modify your (a) classroom organization, (b) classroom grouping, (c) instructional materials, and (d) instructional methods to, first of all, reduce barriers and secondly, to facilitate maximum class learning?
2. You will be utilizing a mix of both direct and nondirect instructional methods in your classroom. What are at least two transition activities you will want to teach your students that are most suitable for direct instruction, and for indirect instruction? For each of these activities, what role will you take as a teacher and prepare your students to take as learners?
3. In your classroom, you realize that your diverse group includes some learners with (a) high incidence disabilities, (b) low incidence disabilities, and (c) sensory disabilities (you get to define these as you like). How will you plan to accommodate these diverse students when teaching your two transition activities, by varying (i) instructional approaches (individual, competitive, and cooperative); (ii) instructional strategies (options within the direct and nondirect choices); (iii) using basic skill accommodations; (iv) independent student practice activities; and (v) evaluation activities? Use the lesson planning form to turn these ideas (from Questions 2 and 3) into a full-planned lesson.
4. Brainstorm your ideas and curriculum links (with others if it helps), then refine and create an interdisciplinary thematic unit using one or both of your transition activities (and lesson) from Questions 2 and 3 above, if possible. Use the lesson planning form to develop another fully-planned lesson.

Websites

Effective Teaching

www.cec.sped.org/conv/zigmund.html

http://curry.edschool.virginia.edu/go/cise/ose/information/interventions.html

Cooperative Learning and Diversity

www.cde.ca.gov/iasa/cooplrng.html

Flaghouse Corporation

www.Glaghouse.com

Global Schoolhouse

www.gsn.org

Problem-Based Learning

The Association for Supervision and Curriculum Development, PBL.NET at

www.ascd.org

Project ASSIST (All Students in Supported Inquiry-Based Science and Technology)

www.edcorg/FSC/ASSIST

Miscellaneous

Center for Teaching and Learning Styles Network

www.learningstyles.net

Online Homework Help

www.hoemworkcentral.com
www.jahl.org
www.searchopolis.com

Virtual Field Trip Sites, ASCD list at

www.ascd.org

8 Transition Services

Thomas Simmons

Robert W. Flexer

Debra Bauder

LEARNING OBJECTIVES

The objectives of this chapter are:

1. Describe categories of transition professional and agency services and practices.
2. Explain how different disciplines and services have an impact on transition outcomes.
3. Explain the transition disciplines and how the interface may affect the delivery of transition services.
4. Describe transition services and the roles and responsibilities of school professionals on the transition team.
5. Describe transition services and the roles of adult services and postschool professionals on the transition team.

Introduction

Chapters 5, 6, and 7 set out the components of assessment, curriculum, and instruction for a secondary transition foundation; described the service delivery system of transition in high schools; and delineated some of the "promising practices." This chapter describes the roles of the principle transition disciplines (special education, vocational education, and rehabilitation) and transition services as provided by a variety of other school and adult service professionals. Each professional service within the individual transition plan needs to provide support to the student and family in clarifying and refining postschool goals. The functioning of the transition team has a great bearing on students making progress each year. The team contributions, both individually and collectively, should promote movement toward the students' postschool goals.

The IDEA of 1997 requires that a variety of transition services be available and that they be provided in a coordinated fashion. The services provided to students would be supportive of student-derived transition goals and promote progress toward those goals. Transition services span a broad spectrum of activities. For example, transition services can be instruction—teaching of content and skills from classes or community activities. These instructional activities should clarify and refine student transition goals and result in concrete learning necessary to achieve the goal. Other transition services that are mandated include: community experiences, development of employment and other postschool living objectives, and related services. Three additional transition services are to be included when needed or appropriate. They include: interagency linkages, daily living skills training, and functional vocational evaluation. Each of these service domains and the respective roles of various professionals are described.

Key Concepts in Transition Collaboration

Because transition services require extensive communication among professionals, collaboration and consultation among school and postschool educators and service providers are required under the IDEA of 1997 (Eber, Nelson, & Miles, 1997). Eber at al. (1997) further described the broad range of skills required of professionals involved in transition and came to the conclusion that individual personnel alone cannot accomplish the requisite desired transition outcomes. As highlighted by deFur and Taymans (1995), the need exists for significant degrees of communication, coordination, and collaboration among vocational rehabilitation, vocational education, and special education programs and staff. As collaborators, team members develop shared values, develop appreciation of unique team member contributions, and derive student- and family-driven transition goals that are consensually developed by the team (Everson & Guillory, 1998). By clarifying who should be involved and their responsibilities, transition teams enable the coordination and utilization of the myriad programs and services available in schools and the community.

The essential element of a *coordinated set of activities* relates directly to the need for interdisciplinary approaches and to the IEP requirement that consensus be obtained from a team. Moreover, transition requirements add services provided by professionals from postschool agencies and environments to the team effort. The uncertainty of the future of the student makes services from these additional team members tenuous and ambiguous at times. For example, although many students may benefit from vocational rehabilitation, few of them will actually receive services, because the need for the service is not the only criterion for eligibility. Similar challenges exist for access to secondary options such as vocational education and school-to-work programs. When transition needs of students are identified, questions of availability and access to an appropriate service usually arise. Often possible options lie in interdisciplinary team functioning. Developing and implementing IEPs based on consensual goal development and interdisciplinary education and services remain both the ideal and the challenge in special education as well as in transition.

The delivery of transition services can be viewed as occurring on three levels. Transition services can be viewed programmatically at a federal, state, and local level. Policies and funds flow from one level to the next within corresponding and mutually supporting structures. Working from the federal structure, statewide and local interagency teams need to be established in order to make transition services accessible and to address barriers. Individual transition teams are another level at which groups of professionals work with students and families in obtaining transition services. Team processes are what the three groups have in common, as well as meeting transition needs through establishing joint values and common goals. An understanding of services as delivered by transition teams is facilitated by a foundation in individual and shared expertise of various professionals involved.

Critical Point Transition services involve the collaboration of many professionals with different philosophies, service delivery approaches, and legal frameworks.

Interface of Transition Collaboration

Integrated services that incorporate the education and expertise of special education, rehabilitation, and vocational education are necessary to meet the comprehensive needs presented by the diverse populations of students with disabilities. All three transition systems are needed, but how they fit together and meet the needs of students in a unified manner requires a working framework among all three systems. An understanding of the relationships among the three systems is necessary to develop such a working framework, which is sometimes referred to as the "interface."

Syzmanski, Hanley-Maxwell, and Asselin (1992) described the interrelationships among special education, vocational rehabilitation, and vocational education as being imperfect and frequently working against one another during these most important stages of the transition process. In general, the history and emphasis of the three delivery systems share similar concerns and emphasis on education and counseling processes. Although complementary, the three systems have distinct features as well. Syzmanski et al. described this interface as follows:

> The three service delivery systems share many common concerns. Specifically, special education and vocational education share concerns for education; special education and vocational rehabilitation specialize in serving people with disabilities; and vocational education and vocational rehabilitation share interests in employment preparation. Nonetheless, these service delivery systems are administered by separate federal agencies, which may or may not facilitate coordinated efforts. (p. 165) (See Table 8–1.)

Syzmanski et al. provided a chronology of the service delivery system interface too. Indicative of the lack of systems interface is the lack of coordination and separate administration. Contradictions grow from these mismatches between systems. One example is the "cessation of matching funds for work study programs on the one hand and the simultaneous promotion of collaboration for transition on the other" (Syzmanski et al., p. 169). Although issues and programs have changed since Syzmanski published her research in 1992, significant differences persist. Examples of these discrepancies

TABLE 8–1
Service Delivery System Differences Among Vocational Rehabilitation, Special Education, and Vocational Education

Category of Difference	Vocational Rehabilitation	Special Education	Vocational Education
Legislation	Rehab Act	IDEA	Perkins Act
Administration	Office of Special Education and Rehabilitative Services, Rehabilitation Services Administration	Office of Special Education and Rehabilitative Services, Office of Special Education Programs	Office of Vocational and Adult Education
Funding	75% federal, 25% state; no local funds	Federal, state, and local; largest share local and state	Federal, state, and local; largest share local and state
Eligibility	Disability, and potential to benefit	Disability, need for special education services	Attendance
Populations served	Adults and adolescents with disabilities	Persons with disabilities from birth through age 21	Adolescents and adults
Scope of services	Range of services for employment and independent living	Range of special education and related services	Vocational assessment, vocational instruction
Service mechanism	District vocational rehabilitation offices/ rehabilitation counselors	Local school districts/ special education teachers and related service personnel	Local school districts, postsecondary programs/teachers, etc.
Evaluation	Numbers rehabilitated; percents with severe disabilities	Compliance with law; service in least restrictive environment	Number of students served
Personnel qualifications	Relevant education in counseling	Usually certified to teach	Usually certified to teach

Source: Adapted from Szymanski, E. M., Hanley-Maxwell, C., Asselin, S. B. Systems interface: Vocational rehabilitation, special education, and vocational education. In *Transition from school to adult life: Models, linkages, and policy* by Rusch, F. R., Destefano, L., Chadsey-Rusch, Phelps, L. A., Szymanski, E. (1992). Sycamore Publishing Company; Sycamore, IL. Reprinted with permission.

include distinctive definitions of severe disabilities for each system; lack of consistency in cooperative efforts between rehabilitation and vocational education; completely different administrative organizations; no more set-aside monies for students with disabilities in vocational education; and, in many cases, lack of emphasis on employment outcomes for special education.

Transition Disciplines

Special education, rehabilitation, and vocational education are the three transition disciplines and comprise one major interdisciplinary framework for understanding transition services. Taken together, they provide the comprehensive support for moving from school to adult environments. The term *interdisciplinary* means that transition services involve a variety of professionals from diverse fields and a number of "service delivery systems." These three concepts of field, professions, and systems are distinctive yet related. For example, concepts of field and professional identity correspond to a service system. A given field and professional identity (e.g., rehabilitation counseling) are tied to a given service system (e.g., a federal-state program of rehabilitation).

The association between the field of study and the profession is also evident in special education and vocational education. Special education and special education teachers are concerned with the delivery of education to students with disabilities within a federal-state-local system of public and private schools. Vocational education and vocational education teachers are concerned with the delivery of specific occupational education to adults and high school students within a federal-state-local system in varied settings. The correspondence of services is the system interface, whereas the interaction of the professionals is an interdisciplinary process (as discussed in Chapter 12). Special education and rehabilitation and vocational education are described as the transition disciplines, with corresponding professional identities and scope of practice and service delivery systems.

Teamwork is critical for coordinated services.

Critical Point Three important transition disciplines are typically involved in transition planning for youth with disabilities: vocational education, special education, and rehabilitation.

Scope of Practice of Rehabilitation Counseling

Rehabilitation counselors' field of study is based in counseling practices and is applied to issues of instilling or restoring function and performance for persons with disabilities in major life activities. The federal-state vocational rehabilitation (VR) system provides services to eligible persons with disabilities to become employed and to live independently. Qualified rehabilitation counselors are the professionals who are at the direct service level in the VR system; however, rehabilitation counselors can apply their practice in any environment or in programs where persons with disabilities are in the process of treatment, recovery, rehabilitation, integration, or reintegration into work and community roles.

Scope of Practice of Vocational Education

Vocational educators' field of study is based on teaching occupational skill development and academics as they apply to particular vocational programs. Vocational educators also can provide a wealth of information, counseling, and assessments pertaining to careers, in addition to apprenticeships or other community-based work training. Vocational educators are concerned with addressing both social and work-related skills and behaviors, as well as the self-determination skills that are vital to the success of all students.

Scope of Practice of Special Education

Secondary special educators' field of study is based on teaching individual students with disabilities specific skills, such as those involved in self-determination, social skills, learning strategies, and, where appropriate, academic content. They also must have an understanding of all the aspects involved in transition planning, including coordinating assessments, setting and evaluating IEP/ITP (individualized transition plan) goals and objectives, collaborating with students, their families and communities, and other appropriate service providers, both within and outside the school, to ensure a smooth transition to adulthood.

Interdisciplinary Identity

Although professional identities for different professionals vary, they also share similarities in their scope of practice. Rehabilitation counselors and special educators both have expertise in disability, but special educators focus on instruction and school settings, whereas rehabilitation counselors focus on counseling and postschool settings. Given the overlap yet distinctive backgrounds and expertise, transition collaboration requires that all team members:

1. Can function in an interdisciplinary context;
2. Are grounded in their own discipline (e.g., special education);
3. Can collaborate with other transition disciplines.

An interdisciplinary transition identity requires that team members understand their own roles and contributions in relation to all other team members, whereas all members understand their own contribution to student transition development.

The characteristics of the three transition systems partly define the professionals' duties. Vocational educators focus on occupational preparation; special educators emphasize transition skill instruction; and rehabilitation counselors use counseling and service coordination as a primary means of delivering transition services. To promote movement toward student goals, the broad background and specialized skills appropriate to transition services must be applied in a team context in which all members speak the same language, share the same assumptions and beliefs, and draw from a common culture (Flexer, Simmons, & Tankersly, 1997).

Effective transition services require that each professional involved make his or her contribution in a way that is supportive of other team members' efforts. For example, consider the roles of the vocational and special education teachers, the guidance counselor (a transition professional from general education), and the rehabilitation counselor. The special education teacher could provide adapted instructional strategies to support performance as required in a vocational program taught by the vocational teacher. The rehabilitation counselor could assess the student in actual or simulated work environments, which could provide information on accommodated performance related to the vocational program. The guidance counselor could provide career assessments to determine if interests and abilities match the jobs and requirements that correspond to careers represented by occupations being prepared for in the vocational program. The level of sharing is such that the implementation of the vocational program is dependent on the expertise of the special education teacher and is necessary for the vocational teacher to instruct the student. The expertise of the guidance counselor and the rehabilitation counselor provides a validity check that shows how to accommodate for the vocational skills learned in the vocational program that will allow performance in the future available work/job environments.

Transition Coordinator

The transition plan process and the coordinated set of activities suggest a role for transition coordination. *Transition coordination* requires that program development and monitoring be provided across all the components of the transition plan. Numerous individual team members and programs may be part of the transition plan. With so many players and programs, oversight and coordination are necessary in order to achieve consistency in program implementation. Kohler (1998) identified the need for a transition coordinator/specialist role. She argued that one person was needed to be responsible for linking the transition services and instruction with broader program issues of schools and community. The transition coordinator role provides a professional that fosters the collaboration, coordination, and communication discussed thus far.

Kohler (1998) further delineated the specific activities subsumed under the role of the transition coordinator/specialist. Under the categories of student-focused planning and student development, she emphasized the need for work experiences and referral to adult service agencies. The transition specialist has key responsibilities for coordinated planning and services, including chairing an interagency coordinating team and ensuring coordinated student assessments. The transition coordinator serves as the resource and training consultant for all team members, including the family. Because transition goes well beyond activities in the classroom, the coordinator is required to keep the diverse activities of the team on a straight course regarding individualized transition plans and schoolwide transition initiatives.

Critical Point The roles of transition coordinators transcend the typical role of the special education teacher and include collaboration and systems change activities.

Asselin, Todd-Allen, and deFur (1998) studied the activities of transition coordinators in Virginia. The outcome of that study corresponded very closely to the outcome of Kohler's study. The various responsibilities that transition staff reported are shown in Table 8–2. A perusal of the roles and responsibilities shows primary responsibilities as including: (1) development of individual student transition plans, (2) development of linkages both within and outside the school, (3) resource development, (4) evaluation, and (5) team education activities.

A transition coordinator role or function shows the major activities involved in developing a coordinated set of activities for students with disabilities. This role draws upon the strengths and contributions of each system and professional expertise for a coordinated effort to effect a meaningful array of transition services. The transition coordinator provides leadership to guide the team and the family/student to accomplish appropriate outcomes. The transition coordinator should be an individual who can organize and facilitate meetings, provide direction for transition programs, and be able to lead and train a variety of professionals in performing the respective aspects of their tasks.

Overview of Transition Services

Instruction, community experiences, development of objectives, and related services are the required transition services that support the various school programs directed toward preparation for life in the community. Interagency linkages, functional vocational evaluation, and daily living skills instruction are provided as appropriate given the student's transition needs and goals. Examples of each transition service requirement include:

1. Instruction: tutoring, employability skills training, vocational education, college entrance exam preparation
2. Community experiences: job shadowing, community work experiences, tours of postsecondary settings
3. Development of employment and postschool adult living objectives: career

TABLE 8–2

Transition Coordinator/Specialist Roles and Responsibilities

I. Intraschool Linkages
  A. Disseminate transition information.
  B. Present in-service training.
  C. Assist families.
  D. Facilitate communication between special education and vocational education teachers.
  E. Facilitate appropriate referrals to school-based programs.
  F. Provide technical assistance to school staff.
  G. Coordinate work/training activities with core content curriculum.

II. Interagency/Business Linkages
  A. Refer students with disabilities to DVR starting at age 16.
  B. Identify, establish, maintain linkages with community agencies (DVR, supported employment agencies), colleges, and businesses.
  C. Educate agencies/schools about programs and procedures.
  D. Facilitate referrals.

III. Assessment and Career Counseling
  A. Identify/refer students for vocational assessment.
  B. Facilitate implementation of recommendations from reports.
  C. Coordinate the development of career awareness and exploration activities as part of the career counseling process.
  D. Collaborate with guidance for student participation in career/job fairs.
  E. Oversee the development of postsecondary employment or training plans.

IV. Transition Planning
  A. Identify transition services provided by community agencies.
  B. Attend/participate in team and IEP/ITP meetings.
  C. Assist in planning/placement decisions.
  D. Help to identify appropriate assistive technology.
  E. Monitor adherence to federal laws.

V. Education and Community Training
  A. Promote self-advocacy.
    1. Develop activities.
    2. Coordinate training for special education teachers.
    3. Train students.
  B. Coordinate school and community work-based learning opportunities.
  C. Examine/identify postsecondary training and education options.
  D. Conduct various tours of employment/training options.

VI. Family Support and Resources
  A. Inform parents/families of community resources/services.
  B. Develop and provide parent training.
  C. Assist families in "navigating the system"/accessing services.
  D. Counsel parents regarding parent/student changing roles.

VII. Public Relations
  A. Disseminate information to employers/parents.
  B. Provide awareness events.
  C. Develop business partnerships (e.g., guest speakers, field trips, and mentorship programs).
  D. Promote work-based learning opportunities.

VIII. Program Evaluation
  A. Carry out needs assessment.
  B. Identify gaps in transition services.
  C. Conduct follow-up study on students who exit the program.
  D. Complete monthly/annual reports.

Source: From Asselin, S. B., Todd-Allen, M., & deFur, S. Transition coordinators: Define yourselves. *Teaching Exceptional Children,* January/February, 1998, 30(3), p. 14. Copyright 1998 by Council for Exceptional Children. Reprinted with permission.

planning, interest inventories, self-determination training
4. Related services: occupational and physical therapy, speech therapy, psychology services
5. Daily living skills training: self-care training, home repair, health training, money management
6. Linkages with adult services: referral to vocational rehabilitation, summer youth employment programs, developmental disability and mental health boards, independent living centers
7. Functional vocational evaluation: situational work assessments, work samples, aptitude tests, job tryouts

A variety of school and postschool collaborators are important for all the services and program options needed to meet diverse student needs and preferences. Involvement ranges from those who directly deliver instruction and services (e.g., teachers, rehabilitation counselors) to those who are responsible for program development regionwide (e.g., administrators). Various staff work together to meet all the transition needs at the high school level.

The many areas of expertise within schools that are relevant to transition are described by duFur and Patton (1999). They indicate that the emphasis on interagency collaboration with adult services may overlook many of the school professionals' transition resources and expertise. High schools deliver many diverse programs and services and have become integral to the successful delivery of transition services to students with disabilities (Wehman, 1992). Today, the school is a place for academics, recreation, athletics, and all sorts of programs that benefit students and society. In order to accomplish the broad goals of schools, school personnel need to demonstrate a diverse array of skills and expertise to enable effective program implementation.

Because transition involves a diverse array of issues and activities requiring skills and knowledge that a single individual cannot accomplish or demonstrate, a significant division of labor is necessary when organizing the efforts to help students with disabilities move from high school to post–high-school independence. For example, a case in point is the classroom teacher. The roles that teachers play can vary widely depending on the school district and staffing issues within that district (deFur & Taymans, 1995). However, Foley and Mundschenck (1997) reported that secondary education professionals expressed that lack of collaboration with other professionals and knowledge about community-based services seems to detract from successful transition. An understanding of various roles and responsibilities of team members provides a foundation for determining school-based personnel's competencies and their type of involvement in the implementation of transition services for students with disabilities.

Critical Point Secondary educators often lack knowledge of community services and collaboration strategies that are critical to transition.

Many of the adult and postschool service providers are counterparts to school-based personnel. They may provide support, services, or instruction in a variety of postschool and community settings and contexts. Often, transition goal attainment occurs after high school graduation. By utilizing counseling, education supports, or community services provided by postschool professionals, students continue along a career development path consistent with their goals.

Instruction

Instruction as a transition service is any instructional activity that promotes access to the general curriculum and movement towards the student's transition goals. General curriculum includes academic subjects, career and technical classes, and life skills, as well as adaptations and accommodations appropriate to unique individual needs. Instructional activities related to transition cover a broad range. They may be tutoring, preparation for college entrance examinations, preparation for proficiency tests, career and technical education, applied academic, employability skills and social skills training, and peer tutoring among others. The transition service concerning the acquisition of daily living skills was not mandated for all students with disabilities but may be incorporated into the instruction of those who need preparation concerning specific life skills (e.g., self-care, money management).

Academic and Career Skill Development

Transition services to support development of both school-based academic and career/vocational competencies are important to students achieving their postschool goals. For example, the acquisition of important work and daily living skills, such as self-monitoring for speed and quality of work, ability to accept feedback and work with peers/coworkers and supervisors/teachers, and ability to follow procedures and rules depend on effective transition instruction. Many of these skills are taught through daily school practices addressing attendance and timeliness, following schedules and routine, working with others, and accepting feedback. However, many students, including students with disabilities, often do not generalize from one situation or setting to another (Westling & Fox, 2000). Transition services provide support for teaching these skills in each of the student's specific work and other transition environments, especially during early career exploration and preparation activities.

Attainment of academic skills may be important to the student's preferred transition outcomes and often need to be given consideration in the planning process. For students continuing on to postsecondary education, particularly in a two- or four-year-college program, high-level academic skills will be a requirement. The students should be placed and supported in inclusive settings and be able to demonstrate success in an academic-based program. Support to meet academic entrance requirements for college and for possible professional licensure or certification may be the transition services that promote movement toward the student's goals. Some vocational-technical programs require specific documented competency levels. Although these may be primarily skill-based, a certain level of academic skills also may be required in the process of becoming qualified. Transition assessments must determine whether the student can realistically meet these expectations, and plan accordingly. At some point, information from representatives from postsecondary institutions and professional licensure or certification groups are required to ensure that the team is addressing all key requirements.

Career and technical programs are a major source of transition instruction. Table 8–3 lists representative career/technical education that may be used to fulfill the student's transition goals. All of these areas listed are broad career clusters that provide vocational education/instruction options for students' goals. Each area can be adapted, altered, or modified to suit the student's needs. While many of the vocational fields may have specified fairly high entrance criteria, students, once accepted, can gain critical skills to help them become more independent and able to find a career.

For effective instructional delivery, special education teachers need to work with content teachers (academic and career/technical) to increase the number of collaborative courses taught within the school. Often the best places for special education students to receive grade-level core-content concepts and socialization skills are in the regular classroom where appropriate accommodations are

TABLE 8–3

Programs That Represent Vocational Career and Technical Education

1. *Agricultural education:* Includes occupations in horticulture, agribusiness, selected food and crop production industries.
2. *Business education:* Focuses on secretarial, administrative, office and business management occupations.
3. *Marketing education:* Includes occupations in retailing, marketing, merchandising, and services, such as real estate, hospitality, and financial.
4. *Family and consumer sciences:* Prepares workers for occupations in the consumer and homemaking occupations, such as day care, lodging, and food service.
5. *Trade and industrial education:* Includes a wide range of occupations in the trades such as graphic arts, metalworking, automotive technology, and manufacturing.
6. *Health occupations:* Focuses on preparation for careers in nursing, medical and dental assisting, nurses aide, radiology, and other medical occupations.
7. *Technology education:* Prepares students to work in a wide assortment of technical occupations related to manufacturing, construction, transportation, and other industries.

Curriculum standards focus on adult outcomes.

provided. Teachers can further foster access to the general curriculum by:

- Scheduling students with disabilities into regular classes where appropriate
- Assisting regular education teachers in understanding and implementing specially designed instruction
- Encouraging participation of students with disabilities in extracurricular and daily social/leisure activities

Content teachers have the responsibility to work with special eduction teachers in order to provide students with disabilities content by using appropriate accommodations, such as the utilization of assistive technology and/or specially designed instruction. This content, as required by the new IDEA rules and guidelines, helps students to develop the skills required for them to live, work, and play as independently as possible in their transition to adult life. Content teachers working with students with disabilities should be active members of the student's transition team. By playing an active part in a student's transition meeting, content teachers will increase their understanding of transition and provide valuable insight into the student's strengths and abilities. They also bring a network of community resources that may provide a linkage necessary for the student's successful transition to adult life.

For students who are following a special education and functionally based academic curriculum, instruction is likely to have a more direct relationship with career and vocational courses. For example, in language arts class, students may be practicing vocabulary from their work sites, refining interaction and communication skills used with coworkers and supervisors, and practicing with forms for self-evaluating their work preferences and performance. In math class, they may sum and average their self-evaluation forms and practice fractions when measuring (1/2, 1/3, 1/4 cup). In science class, they may practice safety rules and procedures for their job, master hygienic procedures used in a restaurant kitchen, or learn how to apply and work with different cleaning chemicals.

For students at these levels, transition services for the acquisition of foundational interpersonal and daily living skills become more important aspects of their personal repertoire of skills. Instruction in functional competencies may include academic skills, such as reading basic directional words, telling time, and following directions, as well as life skills, such as selecting and buying goods, maintaining a healthy body, following directions, and abiding by designated rules and laws. These competencies strengthen many of life's experiences, and failure to acquire them often cannot be isolated from a person's success or failure in the world of work (Clark & Kolstoe, 1995).

Classroom-Based Career Development

Functional academic and regular academic courses can, and should, include many work-related literacy and mathematics skills that students need for successful work. However, not all important information can be covered through academic courses only. All students will need career classes of some type to complete their preparation. These classes should occur at varying levels in a student's career development to reflect the necessary and relevant information at each stage. During *career awareness* and *exploration* phases, classes should focus on the values, attitudes, and habits that comprise a valued employee. They may include investigations into different career domains and encourage students to indicate initial career preferences. These classes should be integrated with career exploration and job shadowing experiences that the students also are having, and focus on related terminology and important job and daily living skills that contribute to successful work evaluations and performance.

During the *career preparation* stage, classes should focus on aptitude and interest descriptions that match with the student's career preferences. Instruction should address specific terminology and concepts that relate to employment, such as payroll deduction, taxes, Social Security, benefits, and the like, according to the student's academic skill levels. The class should include important interpersonal skills, including interviewing, accepting feedback from coworkers and supervisors, maintaining good relationships with coworkers and supervisors, and terminating employment appropriately.

Classes during the *career assimilation* stage may take on a different format. Students may spend much of their day at the work setting and some may be in a postsecondary environment. Course issues would consist of job tenure and maintenance skills, negotiating and resolving interpersonal issues, and the implementation of self-advocacy and self-determination skills for advancement and ultimate career and life satisfaction. Rather than be scheduled as a typical class, these courses may be organized in the form of a job club that meets at the school site, an adult agency, or at a convenient community facility.

Critical Point Individuals with disabilities will frequently need information, strategies, and support to maintain employment, often because they have lacked access to this information and support while growing up.

Community Experiences

Community experiences allow a student to have hands-on experiences in (1) employment, (2) recreation/leisure, (3) postschool adult living, (4) community functioning (e.g., accessing community resources, such as medical, travel, safety, banking). Addressing these domains is important for students who have difficulty generalizing information. Furthermore, special education's responsibility is to develop appropriate community sites in these domains by assessing students' needs.

Community experiences involve a variety of activities and environments. In the employment, career, and job domains, activities range from job shadowing for a few days to exploring occupations or to community job experience or cooperative education, which involves learning knowledge and skills to meet requirements of an occupation. The purpose, intensity, and structure of community experiences for postsecondary education show a similar variety. When students are exploring postsecondary education, tours may be arranged to a number of schools. Some transition programs provide summer activities and programs in colleges or universities to give students a taste of college life and its demands.

Community experiences provide schools with many opportunities to teach students the necessary skills for adulthood as well as to provide exploratory activities. Many skills are taught more effectively in the community, such as: transportation, using community facilities (e.g., stores, laundromats, and public services), learning to care for and maintain personal living space, developing hobbies and recreational and social interaction skills, and using workplace skills related to employment. The community provides an important setting for practicing skills in the environments where students will be when they are living and working in the community.

CASE STUDY A

Durmond is a young man with mild mental retardation just entering high school. He has not had any career awareness or exploration activities to this point in his education. The school teachers and counseling staff decide that Durmond would benefit from some interest inventories; however, those may not be beneficial since Durmond does not really understand potential career/employment possibilities. The school counselor and teacher invite the vocational special needs teacher from the vocational school to attend the IEP meeting. In that meeting a variety of potential jobs are discussed. They also discuss the issues of systematically assessing Durmond's awareness/preferences to deal with his understanding of the work world. The team itemizes a list of potential job skills and places these skills can be attempted. Much effort is placed on a variety of environments and skill performance requirements.

Over the next year or so, Durmond visited local radio stations, metal plating companies, car repair shops, the post office, various clerical and administrative offices, and the local airport. Durmond took notes and was encouraged to ask about the jobs. A plan was also developed and implemented where Durmond would spend longer periods of time at the sites in which he had expressed an interest. In the subsequent year preferred work environments and skills were identified and the team determined to have Durmond job shadow and attempt to perform jobs within the selected work environments. Systematic data was collected on Durmond's performance along with information collected from his supervisors and coworkers. After the initial two years Durmond, with the assistance of the IEP team, decided on a career in metal plating. During his last two years, Durmond was involved in several vocational education classes that dealt with foundational course work that enabled him to understand the issues around chemical acids, etcher solutions, and cleaning materials. Additionally, he began exploring several metal plating companies and eventually was placed in Wayne Metal Works. There Durmond shadowed in greater depth and was assigned to work in the cadmium plating area. After Durmond's third year, a review was conducted to determine whether this job and work environment were appropriate. Durmond seemed to like it and as he progressed in learning skills, management considered him as a candidate for a chrome plating apprentice and potentially working full-time during school breaks and vacations. Upon graduating from high school, Durmond became a full-time employee and was promoted to apprentice a chrome plating position.

Community-based career exploration activities may be the student's first experience away from school. These activities often begin in middle school and become increasingly focused on one preferred career domain as the student matures (Brolin, 1995). Early experiences usually involve visiting a variety of job sites. They may include job-shadowing experiences in which a student observes and follows a worker as he or she goes about his or her job tasks. At the high school level, community experiences often are more focused at providing specific work-adjustment or vocational skill development. These experiences function best when used as an extension of the classroom educational program and can be supplemented by classroom activities. School-based activities can also include business or work simulations in which the students create a business and assume various roles to "run" this company.

As these experiences accumulate, students are able to start developing preferences regarding short- and long-term career objectives. An example of such a program is the Cooperative Transitional Services Program (CTSP) offered at Kent State in Ohio. This program provides career exploration and job skills training to youths with disabilities at various sites on the Kent State campus (Flexer, Simmons, & Tankersley, 1997). Graduate students who are studying to become transition specialists provide the coordination of services and the worksite training. The youths participating in the program "try out" different job categories (e.g., clerical, food service, indoor and outdoor maintenance, library, bus maintenance and mechanics, mail sorting and delivery, and inventory and stock audits) at job sites such as at the bookstore, library, cafeterias, residence halls, groundskeeping department, transportation services, supply center, administrative offices, and the food court. After participating in these various work experience activities, students are better equipped to make realistic decisions and to state preferences regarding long-term job placements.

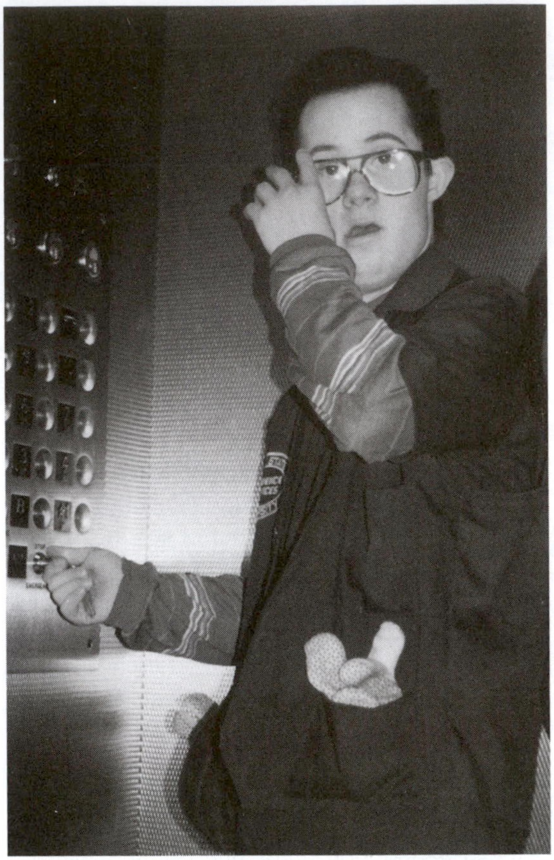

Students learn functional academic skills in the community.

Wehman (1996) suggests a number of principles be followed when planning community-based instruction, as presented in Table 8–4. As with all other educational programs, community-based work experiences should be individualized for the student and should be part of a plan that leads to realistic and preferred outcomes.

An additional caution for professionals developing community work experiences is that they must structure them in line with the U.S. Department of Labor, Fair Labor Standards Act. This Act allows students with disabilities to participate as a "trainee" in unpaid community-based experiences pertaining to school vocational goals. Each of the six criteria presented

TABLE 8–4

Planning Strategies for Community-Based Instruction

1. Individualized and person-centered approach: This tenet requires the development of a specialized set of instructional objectives that are particularly suited to a student's needs and based on the student's desired outcomes.
2. Functional or practical curriculum: The design of subject matter should promote the student's competence at home and in the community.
3. Adaptive curriculum: The course of study should be modified to the specific goals, needs and desires, and capabilities of individual students.
4. Ecologically oriented: A high priority should be placed on skills needed for the activities students want to perform in their major living environments upon leaving high school.

Source: From Wehman, P. (1996). *Life beyond the classroom: Transition strategies for young people with disabilities* (2nd edition). Baltimore: Paul H. Brookes.

TABLE 8–5

Criteria for "Trainee" Status Under the U.S. Department of Labor, Fair Labor Standards Act

1. The training, even though it includes the actual operation of a business facility, is similar to that which would be given in a vocational school.
2. The training is for the benefit of the trainees or students, not the business.
3. The trainees or students do not displace regular employees, but work under close supervision.
4. The business providing the training derives no immediate advantage from the activities of the trainees or students, and on occasion business operations may actually be impeded.
5. The trainees or students are not necessarily entitled to a job at the conclusion of the training period.
6. The business and the trainees or students understand that the trainees or students are not entitled to wages for the period of time spent in community-based vocational instruction.

Source: Fair Labor Standards Act.

in Table 8–5 must be met in order for a student to be considered a "trainee."

Development of Employment and Adult Living Objectives

The transition services that apply to this area deal with transition goals and the processes whereby students develop, test, and finalize their goals. As implied, these transition services are helpful in the process where students gain experience or obtain resources for the purpose of crystallizing their goals—making them more specific and detailed. Again, all transition domains are pertinent—work and school, living, and community participation goals. The activities and resources available in the goal-setting process are numerous and all the transition professionals (special education, vocational education, and rehabilitation) as well as other school and postschool service providers get involved in these transition services. Assessment and planning activities are the major types of activities that assist a student in identifying and clarifying transition goals.

The team needs to ensure that students with disabilities are provided career assessments by the eighth grade and again during sophomore and junior years. Career assessment centers may provide evaluations for regular education students and for students who have a "mild disability." Students with more significant cognitive disabilities require assessment through a functional approach that includes vocational, recreation, and community-related environments.

Various team members have the responsibility to explain the results of these assessments to students and parents. The information gained from these assessments should be embedded into the curriculum, helping students to explore all aspects of specific career interests, as well as to expand possible career choices. This can be done in a variety of ways, including (1) providing speakers from different career clusters, (2) taking students to potential job sites for job exploration, and (3) providing mentoring/shadowing experiences. If vocational or technical education is appropriate, the special education teacher has the responsibility to collaborate with the vocational and technical education teachers to develop accommodations and the specially designed instruction needed to help a particular student succeed.

Critical Point Team members need to work with each other to pull together the expertise to make transition planning successful.

Successful career planning requires both self-awareness and an understanding of the world of work. An important part of this is the transition team's involvement in collecting information that will support the student and team in making appropriate decisions about realistic outcomes. Students also need to be actively involved, according to their abilities, in gathering information about their interests and abilities, in learning about the labor market, in setting short-term and long-term career goals, and in formulating plans for achieving their goals (Szymanski, Hershenson, Enright, & Ettinger, 1996). Teams will need to provide varying levels of support in assisting the students with these tasks.

Monitoring Career Information on Students

Career-related information about the student should be compiled from a variety of sources, including interviews, interest inventories and aptitude tests, work samples, vocational assessment, and portfolio assessment. (Chapter 5 provided detailed information on transition assessment.) Transition services, as defined by the IDEA, include functional vocational evaluations, if appropriate. Like the acquisition of daily living skills and interagency linkages, functional vocational evaluations were not mandated for all students with disabilities—but for those in need of that service. The following discussion presents a brief review of major strategies for supporting the development of transition goals in the planning process.

Interest inventories and *aptitude tests* are important sources of information about student interests, preferences, and skills. Inventories provide a range of career options for students to choose from and define a profile of career characteristics that represent the student's pattern of choices. Work samples provide important information about the student's performance under real-life work circumstances using accurate and reliable observation techniques. Work samples are work situations that are similar to or that reproduce tasks required on a real job. They can provide important information about work behaviors, interpersonal skills, attitudes, and vocational potential (Gajar, Goodman, & McAffee, 1993; Luft, 1999; Sitlington, et al. 1996).

Curriculum-based vocational assessment is an approach that emerged as an effort to improve evaluation relevancy to students and their environments (Gajar et al., 1993; Luft, 1999; Sitlington, et al. 1996). Information is collected directly on the students while they are enrolled in vocational-technical education or other training programs, using identified curriculum goals and standards (Clark & Kolstoe, 1999). Portfolio assessment is a collection of work and can be part of the student's career portfolio. The portfolio documents the student's career interests, academic accomplishments, and vocational skills. As an assessment tool, the portfolio is an extremely valuable tool for assessing the student's progress at developing career-related competencies.

Information about potential work environments should examine the tasks involved in occupations of potential interest, the skills and worker characteristics that are required, and the availability of local job opportunities within occupational categories. State and local job classification resources, job analyses, informational interviews, and job shadowing all can provide information about potential jobs to students and team members aiding in goal development and refinement. The *informational interview*, as seen in Table 8–6, is a strategy that students can use to collect a detailed, up-to-date, and personalized perspective on a specific occupation. In this strategy, the student conducts an interview of a potential job site (which also supports self-determination and empowerment strategies). The list of questions that guide the interview should focus on educational or training requirements, employment outlook, description of a typical day, likes and dislikes about the occupation, appropriate training programs, salary ranges, advice for those interested in pursuing the occupation, and related occupations. Transition team members or teachers can assist the student by providing guidelines for conducting such interviews. *Job shadowing* can be considered an expansion of the informational interview. Used in this way, job shadowing is the process of observing an employee at the work site as he or she performs his or her job. This type of career exploration activity enables students with disabilities to acquire first-hand knowledge about what specific tasks and worker skill requirements are involved in any given job.

TABLE 8–6
Steps the Student Takes to Conduct an Informational Interview

1. Schedule an appointment with someone working in the occupation of interest.
2. Develop a list of questions to guide the interview.
3. Conduct the interview and record interview information.
4. If possible, get a brief tour of the business.
5. Send a thank-you note to the interviewee.

Interventions such as situational assessments and trial work experiences provide opportunities for team members (1) to observe directly how students function in different work situations, (2) to determine the appropriateness of different occupations and living environments, (3) to identify optimal conditions for student success, and (4) to evaluate the effectiveness of different adaptation or accommodation strategies. A *situational assessment* is a means of evaluating student/environment "fit" through direct observation of students in actual or simulated work or living situations. Valuable information about the student's general employability skills and adaptive work behaviors (e.g., task performance, ability to follow directions, grooming, punctuality, openness to constructive criticism, social skills, and reinforcer needs) is gathered by using the situational assessment approach (Chan et al., 1997; Power, 1991). Situational assessments can also be performed in the student's current and future living environments to determine "fit" and readiness for these experiences. Situational assessments examine isolated environments and settings. When collected over the range of potential environments, they are known as *ecological assessments*. They are particularly useful for transition teams in planning across comprehensive lifestyle choices.

CASE STUDY B (PART I)

Katya was diagnosed with cerebral palsy at birth and uses a wheelchair but has good use of her arms. When Katya entered school she was found to have mild mental retardation but has been able to use the regular education curriculum with some modifications. Katya's parents were very concerned that she would have to live at home, but the special education teacher on the IEP team was able to show the parents the impact of ADA on increasing options and accessibility in the environment. Katya's IEP team began integrating basic foundational skills into her classwork and at home. Katya was somewhat shy, so the regular classroom teacher helped to identify two classmates who showed some interest in her. Katya's parents agreed to invite one of these girls to their home once a month. They also began identifying movie theaters and recreation centers that were accessible. Both the teacher and Katya's parents began talking to her about work and work expectations to build her confidence as a future worker. The team developed a list of people who worked in wheelchairs to act as potential role models. Katya's IEP team ensured that she had some career awareness instruction during elementary school. When she entered middle school, the IEP team provided all her teachers with a list of foundational skills on which she was working. Katya was getting mostly Bs and Cs in her academic classes and the IEP team believed this provided a good program for her. During eighth grade, Katya's IEP team enrolled her in a career exploration course that visited workers in the community and included activities about work values and habits, and about occupational clusters. Katya completed her career exploration class with a love of computer work. In high school, her guidance counselor gave her several interest inventories, which confirmed that office work was a preferred option. The IEP/ITP team placed her in a business course and she did well in learning word processing and data entry. Her parents were not sure she could perform for a full day because she complained of fatigue when using the computer at home.

Monitoring Community and Job Placement Information

As transition team members work with the student to explore different employment options, it is especially important to establish community linkages with informal, professional, and employer contacts. Employer linkages are critical to making appropriate job placements that meet the needs of the students. School systems may wish to institute a central clearinghouse for job referrals to support all the transition-age students (Baer, Martonyi, Simmons, Flexer, & Goebel, 1994). Establishing these linkages can occur through job fairs held at high schools and at postsecondary institutions. They also can be developed through community service agencies, including chambers of commerce, and service organizations such as the Kiwanis. Employer advisory boards can be an important means to gain input from local employers about how to better utilize vocational programs for students with disabilities as a labor resource (Baer et al.).

Job development is an important strategy used by transition professionals to identify employment opportunities and secure employment for students with disabilities. The transition professional works to match an employment opportunity with the interests, needs, and abilities of a specific student. Ideally, the student would be able to perform all of the requirements of the potential job but in some cases, due to their disability, they cannot. In this instance, the professional may negotiate with the employer to create or adapt a position that meets the needs of the student and organization. *Job carving* is similar, in that it creates a position that meets the needs of both the student and the organization. The difference is that the transition professional may accumulate parts of several job descriptions to fit the abilities of a student and simultaneously increase organizational efficiency.

Job and career maintance clubs offer support to students and adults with disabilities who are looking for a job or currently working. *Job clubs* utilize a small-group format to provide counselor support, encouragement from other club members, and prospective job leads to people who are actively seeking employment

(Azrin & Philip, 1979). Job seekers meet in groups of 8 to 12 every day for about 2 1/2 hours until employment is secured. The job club method emphasizes group support to club members as they cultivate and follow up on job leads. Lindstrom, Benz, and Johnson (1996) describe a job club model for special education students between the ages of 16 and 21 who are either actively seeking employment or who are already employed. The emphasis of this model is on preparing students for "the transition from the structure of the school environment to the unpredictable and often confusing adult world" (Lindstrom et al., 1996, p. 19).

Whereas job clubs emphasize ongoing support to students participating in a job search, career maintenance clubs emphasize ongoing support to students who have already secured employment but need additional assistance in order to keep their jobs. Group members meet weekly or biweekly to address career maintenance concerns, such as initial adjustment to a new job, employer expectations, appropriate work habits, problem solving, time management, social skills, coworker attitudes, transportation issues, and reasonable accommodations.

CASE STUDY B (PART II)

Katya enrolled in a program for business education taught at the county vocational technical high school. She was very nervous about changing environments and her IEP/ITP team scheduled several preliminary visits to show her where the accessible entrances and facilities were located. The team knew that Katya might not be able to develop competitive level skills, and this was the case. After graduation she met the entrance requirements for the local community college and continued to work on her skills there. The vocational rehabilitation counselor attended the last 2 years of IEP/ITP meetings in the high school and continued to work with Katya while she attended community college. Katya was given the options of possibly job sharing with another worker to split business productivity requirements, or having an employment specialist do job development/ job carving to identify a position that would take advantage of her typing and data entry skills but would not overtire her. Katya completed her community college and moved into an accessible apartment with a cousin. Her vocational counselor found her a part-time job and continued to look for an arrangement that could be full time. Katya found the daily work environment to be challenging despite her preparation in school. When she became overly tired, she was likely to get sick and have to miss one to 2 days of work. Katya decided to join a career maintenance club to help her learn to better gauge her health needs. She also learned some assertiveness and was able to talk to others about barriers she encountered in the environment. After one and a half years, Katya was hired full time at her job. The employment specialist realized there were places in the office that became backed up (e.g., mailroom and filing end-of-month reports). This gave Katya a break from typing and the office made sure that the mail work and filing was accessible to her. A few years later, Katya asked her boss if she could get training to learn the network systems software packages that she saw the office managers using. The boss was reluctant at first and unsure whether she would be successful. She got some books and showed them to her boss to convince him of her sincere interest. Katya knows that she may not become an office manager but this will allow her to increase her skills and work abilities, and probably qualify for a raise.

Students and/or their advocates must possess accurate information about their legal rights under the ADA and be able to communicate their needs assertively to employers. The transition team plays a central role in assisting students to access information about their legal protections, to develop skills at disclosing disability-related information to employers, to identify their accommodation needs, and to request and implement accommodations (Luft & Koch, 1998).

Career classes or job-seeking skills workshops, in which role-playing activities and videotaping are used to facilitate the development of these competencies, provide ideal scenarios for addressing these important topics.

Related Services and Assistive Technology

In Section 1401 (22) of the IDEA Reauthorization in 1997, related services were defined as: transportation, and such developmental, corrective, and *other supportive services* as may be required to assist a child with a disability to benefit from special education, and includes the early identification and assessment of disabling conditions in children with disabilities. Other supportive services encompass speech-language pathology and audiology services, psychological services, physical and occupational therapy, recreation (including therapeutic recreation), social work services, counseling services, including rehabilitation counseling, orientation and mobility services, and medical services, except that such medical services shall be for diagnostic and evaluation purposes only.

When related services were added to the list of required transition services, policy makers wanted transition teams to consider the supports that students may need to benefit from the available transition services. With this requirement, transition teams and related service providers now needed to assess whether this type of support could provide access to more integrated work, education, and living environments, support demonstration of higher level skills, or support objectives for transition goal attainment. This would be consistent with the underlying legislative philosophy of IDEA providing students access to the general curriculum and to integrated settings.

Many related services support the IEP and transition services through either assessment, consultation, or direct services. The National Association of School Psychologists provided an early example for vocational school psychology and transition services, and in fact, incorporated both vocational assessment and intervention practices into its *Standards for the Provision of School Psychological Services* (Thomas & Grimes, 1995). In the case of school psychologists, these support services would involve: psychological and psycho education assessments that focus on career and vocational development, aptitude, and interests (assessment); skill enhancement activities for school personnel, parents, and community members regarding learning, development, and behavior (consultation); and programming designed to enhance cognitive, social, and vocational development (direct service).

The school psychologist, through assessment, consultation, or direct services can provide services supportive of transition instruction, community experiences, and goal development. School psychologists are highly qualified to give and interpret tests and assessments, provide services, and assist others in the use and interpretation of activities directly relevant to vocational and transition goal development and accomplishment. However, Staab (1996) surveyed school psychologists and found that about half felt that their school psychology skills were underutilized in transition activities.

Speech and language therapy (SLP) services also can include assessment, consultation, or direct therapy. To be supportive of transition goals, the related services of SLPs should adhere to the transition services of instruction, community experiences, development of objectives, daily living skills, linkages, and functional vocational evaluation. Table 8–7 provides sample goals and activities conveying how transition services language in curriculum content areas might look in IEPs written by the SLP. From the

TABLE 8–7

IEP Transition Services Language

Transition Service Language (TSL)	Content Area	IEP Goal Example	Sample Activities
Instruction	English/language arts, writing, math	Tommy will identify appropriate vocabulary for completing his resume (education, work experience, interests).	Select vocabulary from sample resume or job application; explore interests.
		Johnny will recognize and identify sequence of events on a daily picture schedule.	Choose and act upon activity from a picture schedule.
Community experiences	English/language arts, writing, social science, health	Tommy will identify and access community and employment resources.	Obtain and complete job application.
		Johnny will walk to an off-campus site and follow safety and traffic guidelines.	Use the vocabulary and concepts for travel and safety issues.
Employment/postschool adult living	English/language arts, social science	Tommy will participate in a prearranged job interview.	Develop language communication scripts appropriate for job interviews; role play mock interview; discussions.
		Johnny will use public transportation with supervision to a work site.	Practice social greeting, vocabulary of transportation.
Daily living skills and functional evaluation	Family life, health, English/language arts	Tommy will appropriately interpret body language/social cues of peers and adults in his community.	Situational role-playing, mock interviews, school office, and so forth.
		Johnny will maintain personal hygiene.	Referral to daily schedule; develop checklist of daily hygiene responsibilities.

Source: From Harrell, P. *Speech & Language Services.* In deFur, S. H., & Patton, J. R. (Eds.). *Transition and school-based services: Interdisciplinary perspectives for enhancing the transition process.* (pp. 77-115). Austin:PROED, Reprinted with permission.

table's sample goals and activities, it is evident that the expertise of language and language development is applied in an instructional context of transition skills (e.g., vocabulary in job resumes).

In addition to speech and language therapy, occupational and physical therapists work with students to ensure access and participation in various environments (e.g., school, home, work, community). Physical therapists evaluate and recommend activities to increase a student's strength, endurance, and ability to maintain postures while participating in his or her chosen environments. Working in conjunction with physical therapists, occupational therapists teach techniques and adaptations to allow student access to daily living activities (e.g., eating, dressing, toileting). Wehman, Wood, Everson, Goodwyn, & Conley (1988) suggested that therapists play a role in the transition process by providing input on student's physical capacities, modifying daily activities, and/or designing, fabricating, or prescribing adaptive equipment to enable performance in community settings. Specifically in work environments, Sowers and Powers (1991) recommended that occupational therapists help conduct job-site and task analyses, develop job-design strategies, and develop supports for job-related activities like eating, drinking, and using the bathroom. Tables 8–8 and 8–9 describe the possible roles in the transition process for occupational and physical therapists.

Assistive technology (AT) services and devices along with occupational or physical therapy are other related services considered. The AT services and devices are usually integrated into the IEP and the student's environment by an Assistive Technology Practitioner (ATP). The ATP would provide necessary AT assessments and appropriate technology if the student required it. Occupational and physical therapists tend to provide the positioning, orthotic or mobility services. Both sets of professionals need to be involved in the placement and services provided in the community. An example of this interaction would be Casey, an individual with a spina bifida. The occupational or physical therapist would attempt to ensure that Casey would have appropriate gait, positioning and ambulation throughout the work environment. The ATP would observe Casey's work environment, determine the most appropriate interface between the student and the job, and integrate the selected technology into the student's job. Related personnel perform their duties on the job integrating their expertise with the job placement or vocational experts. Many ATPs are also trained in positioning and other more-therapy-related issues and might be able to deal with the full range of environmental adaptations.

Fitness, leisure, and recreation are very important for many students served by special education. In not realizing the full benefits of the contributions and interdisciplinary efforts from adapted physical education and therapeutic recreation, students' development as complete human beings and participation in preferred environments are severely compromised. Although instruction in physical education is defined specifically in IDEA as part of special education for students with disabilities, the reality is that appropriate physical education for such students is often missing in public schools nationwide at any level of the curriculum. This is particularly disturbing when noting that a significant number of students with disabilities have marked deficits in physical fitness and motor skills that can adversely affect their life adjustment (Dattilo, 1987; Jansma & French, 1994). Improving physical fitness and motor skills leads to learning lifetime sports skills, with improved health and greater participation in community recreation or sports programs. Professionals trained in adaptive physical education and therapeutic recreation can be major contributors to successful transition through their focus on lifetime fitness, recreation, and leisure skills.

TABLE 8–8

Possible Roles for the Occuaptional Therapist in the Evaluation, Service Planning, or Delivery of Transition Services

1. Teach functional tasks related to temporal aspects (age, maturation, ability/disability, and life stage).
   a. Activities of daily living
      i. Self-care (e.g., dressing, feeding, hygiene, toileting)
      ii. Communication
      iii. Socialization
      iv. Mobility within home, school, community
   b. Home management (e.g., cooking, cleaning, money management)
   c. Work and health habits
   d. Work skills
   e. Leisure
2. Evaluate environmental supports and barriers and recommend adaptations if needed.
   a. Physical characteristics
      i. Accessibility (e.g., terrain, furniture, objects)
      ii. Sensory stimulation (e.g., tactile, visual or auditory cues or distractions)
      iii. Types of objects, tools, equipment
      iv. Temporal cues (e.g., watches with alarms; toothpaste left out on the countertop)
   b. Social characteristics
      i. Activities (e.g., individual or group)
      ii. People
      iii. Role expectations
   c. Cultural characteristics
      i. Customs, expectations
      ii. Values
      iii. Beliefs
3. Adapt tasks.
   a. Change the physical characteristics of the task (e.g., sit instead of stand)
   b. Change the social characteristics of the task (e.g., increase or decrease the number of people involved)
   c. Change the demands (e.g., do part of task; checklists)
   d. Work simplification (e.g., get all items together before shower; reorganize kitchen so able to find objects)
   e. Use instructional techniques (e.g., task analysis, forward and backward chaining, partial participation, positive supports, systematic instruction, natural cues)
   f. Teach compensatory techniques
4. Adapt materials or recommend assistive technology.
   a. Increase or decrease the size, shape, length, or sensory characteristics of materials and objects being used
   b. Adaptive aids (e.g., button hook, reacher, lap board, talking watch, book holder, memory aids, talking calculators)
   c. Switches, computers, appliances, augmentive communication devices, telephones, wheelchairs, environmental control units, positioning devices, alerting systems
5. Develop interpersonal and social skills to support participation in the school, community, home, or work environment.
   a. Awareness of interests
   b. Stress management

(*continued*)

TABLE 8–8 *(continued)*

c. Time management
d. Self-management/coping techniques
e. Leisure activities to promote socialization and develop friendships
f. Assertiveness training
g. Decision-making and problem-solving skills

6. Educate others and learn from others in the home, classroom, community, or workplace.
   a. Student training
   b. Family training
   c. Staff training
   d. Peer training
7. Promote self-advocacy, prevention, and health maintenance.
   a. Legal rights and responsibilities
   b. Disability and health awareness
   c. Talk to others about disability and needs
   d. Promote habits to maintain health (e.g., hygiene, medications, pressure reliefs, birth control, equipment maintenance, etc.)

Source: From Shepherd, J. & Inge, K. J. (1999) *Occupational & Physical Therapy.* In deFur, S. H., & Patton, J. R. (Eds.). Transition and school-based services: Interdisciplinary perspectives for enhancing the transition process. (pp. 117-165) Austin: PROED. Reprinted by permission.

As seen above, these transition services are of critical importance to quality-of-life outcomes for youth with disabilities. Although all possible related services were not discussed, their omission does not mean that they are of less importance. In the past, many of these services have been provided as pull-out programs. As students become actively involved in the transition process, it is essential that the related service personnel work with students within the environments in which they will be living, working, and playing. People involved with a particular student must understand and support this method of instruction. For example, it is obvious that a student receiving speech therapy will benefit from learning how to be understood at his or her job site. A collaborative effort among the speech pathologist, the job trainer or special education teacher, and the employer may make the difference between a successful job placement and a failure.

Critical Point Related service providers must become involved in transition planning and assess and provide interventions in a variety of student environments.

Related service providers form an integral part of the transition team, providing information on the student's strengths, essential instruction in areas of need, and critical resources for overcoming the barriers that students with disabilities often encounter. The aforementioned related service providers are self-explanatory in terms of the types of services provided (e.g., speech therapy: a speech clinician providing interventions that are intended to improve the student's speech production). However, increasingly incorporating interventions within school and community environments requires that activities performed are the basis of the intervention. Services may be integrated into the setting in order to reduce the discrepancy of the student's performance with working peers or to allow learning to occur with little if any disruption to the daily work routine. Consequently, related services must be developed so that the intervention is easily implemented and

TABLE 8–9

Possible Roles for the Physical Therapist in the Evaluation, Service Planning, or Delivery of Transition Services

1. Develop or compensate for skills that support participation in the school, community, or work environment.
   a. Strength
   b. Endurance
   c. Movement patterns
   d. Assume and maintain postures
2. Improve the student's mobility within the home, school, work, and the community setting.
   a. Ambulation
   b. Wheelchair mobility
   c. Climbing stairs
   d. Opening doors
   e. Transfers
   f. Carrying items
   g. Public and private transportation
3. Promote self-advocacy, prevention, and health maintenance.
   a. Exercise
   b. Nutrition
   c. Body mechanics/positioning
   d. Disability knowledge and precautions
   e. Legal rights
4. Adapt tasks and environments so the student can participate.
   a. Accessibility
   b. Position of student and activity
   c. Job-site analysis
5. Recommend or adapt assistive technology.
   a. Mobility aids (e.g., walkers, canes, wheelchairs, standing tables)
   b. Computer access and positioning
   c. Augmentative communication device
   d. Exercise equipment
   e. Accessibility
6. Educate others and consult in the home, classroom, community, or workplace.
   a. Student training
   b. Family training
   c. Staff training
   d. Peer training

Source: From Shepherd, J. & Inge, K. J. (1999) *Occupational & Physical Therapy*. In deFur, S. H., & Patton, J. R. (Eds.). Transition and school-based services: Interdisciplinary perspectives for enhancing the transition process. (pp. 117-165) Austin: PROED, Reprinted with permission.

effectively integrated into the teachers' or coworkers' daily routines.

Much of the input provided by related services personnel provided in the transition meeting will be consultative in nature. However, the related services specialists also may (1) provide services during times of the day that the student is away from the workplace; (2) provide technical assistance to the individual providing the one-on-one training to the student; or, in some circumstances, (3) provide services on the job, demonstrating the necessary training techniques to the direct service provider or coworker. Any of the preceding strategies would have to be implemented based on the needs of the student and the availability or freedom in the workplace.

Interagency Linkages

Transition Services from Adult Service Providers

The public sector (governmental agencies and not-for-profit community organizations) can provide a significant amount of assistance regarding the transition needs of students with disabilities. The primary services that should be considered in the transition process are those provided by:

1. The state departments of vocational rehabilitation
2. State employment services
3. One-stop employment and training (funded under the Workforce Investment Act)
4. The regional adult mental retardation and developmental disabilities provider
5. The regional mental health provider

Transition services are based on the laws of special education, rehabilitation, vocational education, ongoing lifelong supports, higher education, employment and training, and general education. Special education and transition as defined in IDEA is a basic right and as such is described as an entitlement. If a student has a disability, as defined in IDEA, he or she is entitled to an appropriate education and transition services. For services not prescribed by IDEA and those provided in postschool settings, additional criteria may need to be met—making them eligibility-based.

Eligibilty-based transition-related legislation deals with laws that fall into the rehabilitation and the ongoing supports domains, a major service delivery system for postschool services and supports for students who are in transition. A major shift in the status of students in moving to adulthood is that supports and services go from being an entitlement to being based on eligibility criteria. This means that these students may or may not receive services, depending on whether they meet specified criteria. The kind of disability and its severity in some instances constitute the criteria of eligibility.

Rehabilitation services are those that are provided under rehabilitation legislation and deal with supports and services for entry or reentry into the labor market and meet the rehabilitation needs and goals of those found eligible. Generally, a service is viewed as a one-time investment to move an individual into a new or improved role and status (e.g., employment versus unemployment). Thus, rehabilitation services are often referred to as time-limited services.

Other legislation dealing with adults and students who are in transition are adult/postschool services that are assumed to be ongoing. Eligibility in these agencies has specific criteria related to the severity of disability and the need for long-term, ongoing support (in many instances, for the person's lifetime). Still other services and supports are provided primarily only to enable participation and access, not to meet specific disability needs for individuals, such as services that are part of postsecondary education or general community services like employment and training programs.

Regardless, legislation within each legislative area, even those that are not specific to disability, has provisions to protect the rights of persons with disabilities. For example, because employment and training under the Workforce Investment Act (WIA) is a delivery system dealing with preparation for and entry into employment, programs and services are important to some students with disabilities in order to attain or maintain transition outcomes. WIA provides assurances that youth with disabilities will have access to the range and variety of program options where appropriate (i.e., if qualified). Moreover, although transition services for students with disabilities are not referenced in WIA, supplemental aids and services can be provided through IDEA to support participation and program completion. Understanding the unique provisions of legislation and how they are related to transition requirements is part of what transition teams need to know in their role in providing a coordinated set of activities.

Critical Point The essential elements of needs and preferences and postschool goals may require programs outside the purview of special education requiring coordination among special education, regular education, and postschool service providers.

Within various acts and legislation, transition services fall into one of three categories: (1) those provided to students with disabilities in special education who have an entitlement to an education through age 21, (2) those provided to adults who must meet specific criteria and must be found to be eligible in order to receive specialized services, and (3) those provided to any individual with a disability who needs programs and activities that are required to be accessible and not to discriminate against people with disabilities. Transition services in postschool environments are based in the legal and eligibility framework of two or three above.

Federal/State Vocational Rehabilitation Programs

The state agencies of vocational rehabilitation services are available throughout the United States and its territories. The program, originally developed in 1917 (as a result of the Smith-Hughes Act, P.L. 64–347), addressed the employment needs of military personnel who acquired disabilities during World War I (Stodden, 1998). The agency evolved over the years and now provides services to all individuals with disabilities who are impaired enough to restrict their ability to be employed. Vocational rehabilitation (VR) agencies, which have different names in different states, utilize funds via federal and state dollars. At the federal level, the Rehabilitation Services Administration provides oversight and funding for all the state agencies. Furthermore, the federal agency provides these funds to states in a matching process in which the state must match approximately $25 for every $75 the federal VR agency provides to the state. The total amount that a state can receive is dependent on a number of factors, including population size, relative poverty rates, and other characteristics along with the total dollars offered by the state for the match. Some states do not obtain all their potential federal dollars because state VR programs contribute too little.

Acceptance for services from the state VR agency, as it is with almost all adult human service agencies, is not guaranteed. VR agencies follow a process in which all applicants must meet specific criteria to be accepted for receiving services. These are (1) having a physical or mental disability that is expected to last longer than 12 months and (2) this disability results in a substantial impediment to becoming employed. In addition, since the state VR money is not able to serve all people with disabilities, the agency is required to develop a set of criteria that focuses on admitting those individuals whose disabilities are the most severe and who meet certain individualized state needs. This individualized differentiated criterion is called the "order of selection."

Critical Point Vocational rehabilitation providers may have differing definitions of disability and typically are able to serve only a fraction of the students who are eligible for services.

In general, counselors who oversee the provision of services represent the VR agency. The VR counselor conducts interviews, helps to develop an individual plan of employment, provides oversight of financial expenditures for services, and provides counseling. The VR agency provides a variety of services. Although the VR agency and the VR counselor operate differently in each state, the services that are offered and coordinated by the counselor include vocational assessments, career/rehabilitation counseling, job preparation activities, job development, AT and devices, follow-up services, and post-employment services. Other services that a counselor may coordinate include driver's license training, commercial license instruction or heavy equipment operation, college tuition, and treatment for physical or mental health issues. In coordinating these services, the VR counselor must ensure that the services provided be related to an eventual outcome of improving the likelihood of employment.

In accessing VR services, the counselor facilitates the referral process of the individual with a disability. This can take place by either self-referral or referral by another individual. In any case, the individual with the disability (or his or her legal representative) must work with the counselor in completing an application, participating in testing, and transmitting necessary documentation of the disability. The primary method for acquiring the services, once accepted for participation, is through the development of the Individualized Plan for Employment (IPE). This is coauthored by a VR counselor and the individual.

To enable the VR system to work effectively with the public school, school personnel should make initial contacts, indicating the need for the VR agency personnel's participation. Generally, VR has indicated that 2 years prior to graduation is an optimal time for contact and referral. This contact, however, changes based on the severity and the rehabilitation needs of the individual. In some cases, a VR counselor may not be able to participate in every IEP meeting where transition services are discussed. However, the VR counselor should be able to participate via providing written recommendation, verbal communication to the IEP team leader, or in some other manner.

Critical Point Due to large case loads carried by vocational rehabilitation counselors, it is important to use their time wisely and to use flexible means for them to provide input.

The VR agency and counselor should be able to make available a significant amount of help in meeting the employment needs of the individual and in many cases providing primary resources for achieving the eventual job outcome. As was indicated, the VR counselor is able to provide many resources in order to help the individual attain employment. In most cases, the transition services provided to the individual with a disability are purchased by the VR agency. Consequently, there will be a need to involve the professional services purchased by the VR counselor to train or facilitate the career development activities of students with disabilities.

Federal/State Employment Training

Another agency that should be included in the development of transition programs regarding employment is the particular state's employment and training programs (ETP). The federal conduit for this agency is the U.S. Department of Labor (DOL). Again, this agency exists in every state and is titled differently depending on the state. The federal and state agencies generally have oversight of the country's labor laws regarding health and safety, equal employment, labor relations, and employee benefits, along with assisting in the job-seeking process. Each state's employment and training system is designed to assist all people who are unemployed to become employed. As with the VR agency, an individual can access the ETP agency's services through a counselor. Employment service counselors are generally able to provide résumé development assistance and job leads. The counselors also may provide access to testing services and other training programs, depending on how the services have evolved within the state. The counselor generally does not participate in transition meetings. They will, however, work with the VR counselor to coordinate employment-related benefits, and other incentives that might facilitate employers hiring individuals with disabilities.

The former Job Training Partnership Act (JTPA) agencies within each community are another employment service provider. JTPA is now an agency generally subordinate to the Workforce Investment Act agency. The JTPA programs are still being offered; however, in most locations, they are now called workforce services, career one-stop shops, or some other related term. In any event, the services that can be accessed are those that should be taken advantage of when planning for the development of transition services.

Career one-stop-shop programs typically focus on providing services to persons with low socioeconomic status or those who are too disadvantaged to become employed. As with the other agencies, a counselor is the conduit by which services are acquired. The services provided range from skill training to employment readiness training and General Equivalency Diploma (GED) training. In general, the agency functions much like the VR programs in that they fund other agencies or programs that provide those needed services. The general method of distributing funds is through grants to existing agencies or service providers. The potential grantee must submit a proposal that substantiates the need and validates the proposed method. In many cases, the grantee is reimbursed for services rendered or for the accomplishment of their proposed objectives. These same agencies may still operate in communities but under the authority of the Workforce Investment Act. Table 8–10 describes the types of services available to transition-aged youth.

Critical Point Employment training programs typically focus on students and adults from low-income families but may serve students with disabilities under some conditions.

Long-Term Support Agencies

Final groups of agencies that are potential collaborators in the transition process include regional mental health and developmental disability (MH/DD) service providers. These two agencies were covered together because in many locations the agencies are one and the same. Additionally, the two agencies are funded and function, in most cases, in the same manner. The state and regional MH/DD agencies generally receive money from both state and federal funds. In some states, the MH/DD agencies have the authority to collect local taxes. Each agency has a target population for which the agency must provide services and specific guidelines for determining an individual's eligibility. In any case, these agencies are generally not-for-profit. They function by either providing community services or funding other not-for-profit agencies to perform these duties.

In recent years, MH/DD agencies contracted with managed care agencies to provide mental and physical health services to qualifying clients. The types of services that are funded by MH/DD programs include (but are not limited to) employment programs, a range of independent to more closely supervised living programs, case management, counseling and advocacy programs, physical or mental health services, and, potentially, legal assistance. Furthermore, the services that are provided to the eligible participants of the MH/DD agencies can be provided from the moment of eligibility until noneligibility or death. Consequently, a student may have been receiving services since birth.

The MH agency generally deals with people who have significant and persistent mental health problems, such as obsessive-compulsive disorder, schizophrenia, bipolar disorder, and so on. The participants who receive services provided or funded by the MH agency are usually diagnosed

TABLE 8–10

Services Provided by One-Stop Delivery Centers

Services Available to Youth (ages 14–21) and Adults (age 18 and older)

- Local and national job announcements and resource libraries for career research
- Computers, copiers, and fax machines for creating and sending resumes
- Telephone and electronic (computer) linkages to employers and web sites
- Assessment tools to measure skills, interests, and academic levels
- Vocational counseling, job placement assistance, job search, and retention workshops

Services Available to Adults (age 18 and older)

Core Services

- Initial assessment of skill levels, aptitudes, abilities, and supportive service needs
- Financial aid assistance for training and educational programs

Intensive Services

- Comprehensive assessment of skill levels and service needs, group and individual counseling, career planning, and case management
- Short-term prevocational skills, including communication and interviewing skills, punctuality, professional conduct, and other "soft skills"

Training Services

- Job readiness training, on-the-job training, entrepreneurial training, adult education and literacy activities, and cooperative education programs
- Customized training conducted with a commitment by an employer or group of employers to employ an individual upon successful completion of the training

with such disorders by a medical doctor or a psychiatrist and are provided services based on their needs. The range of transition services that would be provided by the MH agency would be case management, housing/independent living, job placement or employment programs, and counseling/drug management services.

The student with mental health issues should have a counselor/case manager assigned to him or her. This individual should participate in the planning of his or her transition services. One could expect that the case manager would participate in most if not the entire IEP/ITP meeting. Additionally, the case manager should provide liaison services with other agencies such as rehabilitation or employment and training. The case manager has broad responsibilities with regard to the student with mental health issues. However, the case manager does not have legal guardianship or any specific ability to cause or force the student to perform certain activities. The services that are provided by the MH agency, and additionally for the DD agency, are generally voluntary. In any case, if the student has potential mental health problems, the local MH agency should be contacted and a request made to include a representative who is involved with the student's mental health services.

Critical Point Mental health agencies typically provide services through the counselor or mental health professional who provides mental health services.

The DD agency operates much like the MH agency. Eligibility is determined through a variety of assessments; however, the primary determination of eligibility is whether the student has significant impairments in three or more of the seven major life activities (i.e., communication, independent living, employment, self-direction, mobility, learning, and self-care). These disabilities should be the result of a physical or mental impairment that occurred before age 22 and are expected to continue indefinitely (Beirne-Smith, Ittenbach, & Patton, 1998). The DD agency is responsible for determining eligibility and should be an active participant in determining goals and services. In many cases, the DD agency will have supported employment programs and/or will provide ongoing support services to enable access to funding from VR for supported employment.

Supported employment is "a job placement and training model designed to prepare people with severe disabilities for competitive employment in regular community settings" (Reed & Rumrill, 1997, p. 238). It evolved in the 1970s as a model that leads to community-based employment after students leave high school. Its key feature is the provision of ongoing support services to assist the individual with job retention. Ongoing support is typically provided by the job coach or employment specialist who is responsible. Job coaches should begin to "fade" (gradually reduce the amount of support they offer) from the work site as natural supports begin to increase in the supervision of the supported employee.

Other services that the DD agency may provide or coordinate are independent living, group homes, and so on. Historically, DD agencies ran or, at the very least, funded sheltered employment programs. Thus, for individuals whose families truly want a sheltered employment setting, the DD agency is usually the agency to contact. Both the MH and DD agencies should be contacted as soon as the school is aware or considers that the student should be eligible for either agency's services. Remember that persons who have a behavior disorder do not necessarily qualify for MH services. Additionally, eligibility for both these programs is limited and the majority of the students served by special education (i.e., students with learning disabilities and many with behavior disorders) qualify, but because of limited funds VR focuses its resources on persons with more severe disabilities. School representatives can improve the chances of a student's acceptance by providing full documentation of the student's disabilities and behavioral tendencies when a release of information is requested by the MH/DD agency. Additionally, any classroom behavioral notes or intervention data also may be useful.

Critical Point Developmental disability (DD) agencies typically serve students with the most severe disabilities although some services (e.g., case management) may be available to students and adults with milder developmental disabilities.

Transition Services of Postschool Education Collaborators

Collaborators from postsecondary programs include people from vocational/technical schools, community colleges, and universities (Gajar, 1998). Training services collaborators could include apprentice programs provided by unions or trade associations and job-readiness training programs. Based on the student's interests and preferences, the placement and IEP teams are the ones to decide which, if any, of these programs will meet the needs of the student. The next step is to allow the student and his or her parents to explore the opportunities and requirements that appropriate programs can provide. This can be done by building the exploration into the student's curriculum, building self-advocacy skills and having the student and parents begin making contacts with postschool collaborators, and/or by inviting these collaborators to the next transition planning meeting.

Critical Point Postsecondary education and training programs should be involved in the development of transition programs at schools and, in some cases, be invited to individual IEP meetings.

All postsecondary institutions receiving federal funds must provide services and accommodations for students with disabilities (Osborne, 1996). Many community colleges and universities have disability centers that provide these services. However, a major difference exists between the services provided at the high school level and those provided in colleges and universities. In most cases, the postsecondary education institution does not provide services unless the service is requested.

Students with disabilities are expected to ask for accommodations and provide proof of their disability. To assure that the student with a disability is capable of maintaining academic performance, the student must demonstrate a significant amount of independence and assertiveness. Thus, after high school the student should be able to (1) contact the postsecondary institution's office of disability services, (2) provide appropriate documentation (usually the latest psychological tests and/or IEP), (3) maintain records that certify the student's disability and his or her needed accommodations, and (4) advocate for oneself. Obviously, in order for students with disabilities to be successful at the college and university level, they must have strong self-advocacy strategies and skills. The special education teacher begins to build these skills as early as elementary school. If students with disabilities leave high school without strong self-advocacy skills, the chances of their success in all aspects of adult life are greatly diminished.

Critical Point Students with disabilities need to learn to advocate for themselves before they leave high school because after graduation, unless the students ask for services, there is no requirement to provide them.

CASE STUDY C

Interagency Agreement

The training of students with disabilities in high school can begin with postsecondary education and training programs while the student is still in high school. Developing such a program takes creativity and planning for the collaborators from each of the institutions involved. An example of such a program is the Steps Towards Educational Progress (STEP) project in Louisville, Kentucky (Simmons, 1996). People with learning disabilities are now working in all kinds of businesses, receiving at least minimum wage and often higher. This change has come from the support of all the transition collaborators, as well as employment agencies. However, planning for these transition supports must start early.

As students, parents, and teachers begin to map out future employment goals, it is essential that collaborators from agencies providing support after high school be active participants in the transition planning process. Together this team delineates the skills needed in the future and begins to build them into the goals and objectives of the student's IEP/ITP. In order to achieve these goals and objectives, additional support may be required. In the state of Kentucky, the collaboration between the Department of Vocational Rehabilitation (DVR) and local school districts has developed a program entitled the community-based work transition program (CBWTP). The program is collaboratively funded by DVR and local school districts. The schools that opt into the program must provide a 25% match to draw down the 75% VR dollars. The CBWTP provides job trainers for students during their last 2 years in school. Job trainers work with local school staff in assessing each student's interests and in placing each student in several different evaluation sites. This gives the student and job trainer the opportunity to see what the requirements of specific jobs actually are, compared with the student's individual interests and abilities. After determining an appropriate job match by the student, parent, special education teacher, job trainer, rehabilitation counselor, and employer, the student is placed in the job and the training component of the CBWTP begins. The goal of this program is for the student to be placed in a permanent job by the time he or she graduates from high school. This level of support is required for many students to be successful after they leave high school.

For other students, additional supports are needed. This is often provided through supported employment agencies. Job coaches or trainers provide ongoing long-term support. These agencies work with employers either to provide additional support required for success in jobs currently available or to help "carve out" a job to meet the specific needs of the client while still filling a need of the business. The goal of supported employment agencies is to find a good match between the client and the job that allows the job coach to pull away slowly while building as much independence as possible for the client. However, some people with the most severe disabilities require even more support. A few school districts around the country have risen to this challenge, developing community-training programs for students. The difficulty with these programs is developing long-term plans that will support the student throughout the student's adult life. Few supported employment agencies have the necessary resources to support people with significant levels of support. At this level, support requires a strong collaborative effort.

Conclusion

A variety of professionals and agencies may be involved in transition planning and services. Each member of the transition team has unique expertise and professional skills that can be applied in the transition process. School-based collaborators need to work together so that education and transition services are effective and relate to the student's goals. General, vocational, career, and transition curricula are delivered in a coordinated manner in high school programs by special, related services, vocational, and regular educators with the support of administrators. Postschool collaborators are involved in the transition process for their contributions regarding future environments. When they contribute to the knowledge of future participation and goal development, they are in a position to provide continuity and to take satisfaction when students achieve the transition to postschool activities. Of utmost importance is that resources of team members should be brought out in support of the student-family determined goals. To accomplish this, the team members must apply their energies in a consistent direction and in a coordinated manner. The team process applied to develop the goal consensus is a prerequisite to transition services that promote movement toward student goals. All members of the team must know the roles and responsibilities of each member in order for the team to achieve the best outcomes for the student. Skills of team membership and, in some cases, team leadership, is requisite for team cohesion: the process underlying goal consensus and productive team interactions.

Study Questions

1. Who should be involved in the transition team? Give at least five examples.
2. What is accomplished through interdisciplinary services?
3. What types of services can a person with a disability receive from a vocational rehabilitation counselor?
4. What are the coordination functions of the transitional coordinator?
5. At what point should a student be referred to adult services?
6. How should related services be included in the transition programming for students with disabilities?
7. Is employment the only goal on which the team should focus regarding postsecondary settings?
8. What are the skills that the transition facilitator should exhibit?

9. How can the school or postschool administrators facilitate or hinder transition practices?

Websites

The Federal Resource Center for Special Education
www.aed.org/special.ed/frc.html

Transition Research Institute
www.ed.vivc.edu/sped/tri/institute.html

School to Work Outreach Project (Exemplary Model/Practice/Strategy)
www.ici.coled.umn.edu/schooltowork/profiles.html

The Office of Vocational and Adult Education
www.ed.gov/about/offices/list/ovae/index.html

National Institute on Disability and Rehabilitation Research
www.ncddr.org

Administration on Developmental Disabilities
www.acf.dhhs.gov/programs/add/

Office of Special Education Programs
www.ed.gov/about/offices/list/OSERS/OSEP/index.html

Office of Special Education and Rehabilitative Services
www.ed.gov/about/

Rehabilitation Services Commission
www.ed.gov/about/offices/list/osers/rsa/index.html

Section III

Transition Planning: Planning for Transition to Adulthood

9

Participatory Decision Making: Innovative Practices That Increase Student Self-Determination

James E. Martin

Laura Huber Marshall

Randall L. De Pry

Your life is the sum result of all the choices you make, both consciously and unconsciously. If you can control the process of choosing, you can take control of all aspects of your life. You can find the freedom that comes from being in charge of yourself.

—***Robert F. Bennett***

LEARNING OBJECTIVES

The objectives of this chapter are:

1. Describe the two major self-determination strands.
2. List the major self-determination components.
3. Describe how federal and state laws and regulations support self-determination-oriented instructional practices.
4. Describe how to infuse self-determination into IEP practices.
5. Show how to establish self-determination as an IEP need area.
6. Explain self-determination assessment.
7. Explain how self-determination fits into a standards-referenced IEP format.
8. Describe the *ChoiceMaker* self-determination curriculum.

Introduction

The previous chapters described the systems and programs designed to help youth in the transition to adulthood and were primarily concerned with developing effective transition programs and services. This chapter addresses the issue of how these systems and programs can be brought under the control of the individuals they are designed to serve. The authors describe self-determination as both a means and an outcome of the transition process. It is described as a means of addressing the essential transition elements of (1) determining the student's needs, interests, and preferences; (2) coordinating activities; and (3) promoting movement from school to postschool environments. Self-determination also is described as both a means of addressing the essential element of developing an outcome-oriented process and a critical outcome of the transition process itself (Field, Martin, Miller, Ward, & Wehmeyer, 1998; Halloran, 1993; Wehmeyer, 1996).

Educators increase students' self-determination by teaching skills and by providing participatory decision-making opportunities where students practice what they have learned. Many typical school functions do not allow student participatory decision making. However, by looking at these typical functions with a self-determination outcome in mind, what are mundane become innovative teaching opportunities: ones that enable students to become participatory decision-makers. As students become participatory decisionmakers, they put into practice their learned self-determination skills.

Critical Point Self-determination must be infused into the teaching process.

Four scenarios shown in Table 9–1 depict how typical school functions convert into innovative opportunities to learn self-determination skills. These examples and nonexamples provide a glimpse into what is possible. Our field is just now beginning to realize the numerous opportunities that exist to teach self-determination every day by converting typical teacher-directed school functions into participatory decision-making opportunities.

Federal Laws, Regulations, and State Practice

Federal special education legislation and regulations include four explicit self-determination statements designed to teach crucial self-determination skills and to provide student participatory decision-making opportunities. First, the Individuals with Disabilities Education Act (IDEA) requires secondary transition-aged students to be invited to attend their IEP meeting. Second, IEP transition goals and activities must be based on *student* needs, interests, and preferences. The spirit of IDEA implies that students of transition age, with support from the IEP team, should determine and implement their own goals, objectives, and activities based on *self-perceived* needs, preferences, and interests—not simply those expressed by parents and educators. Third, the U.S. Congress declared with the Rehabilitation Act amendments of 1992 (P.L. 102-569) that the presence of a disability does not diminish the rights of individuals to enjoy self-determination. Fourth, the Rehabilitation Act mandates that all programs and activities funded by the federal and state offices of vocational rehabilitation must promote the principles of self-determination.

Critical Point The IDEA and the Rehabilitation Act amendments specifically address self-determination.

In addition to federal regulations, each state must minimally implement its special education practices to match the expectations established in the federal laws and regulations. States, however, may exceed the federal minimum requirements.

TABLE 9–1
Case Scenarios

Scenario	Typical Functions	Innovative Opportunities
Scenario 1: The IEP Meeting	The special education teacher invites a student to his IEP meeting, but he is not provided with any instruction about the IEP or what to do at the meeting. The student does not want to attend and does not come to school the day of his meeting. Teachers, support staff, and parents talk about the student's interests, skills, needs, and last year's IEP goal performance. They make plans for this year without any direct student input.	Prior to the IEP meeting, Sean learns about the IEP, the meeting, and prepares a script of what to do and say. During the meeting, Sean actively participates and even directs part of *his* IEP meeting. He begins by stating the purpose, introduces everyone, talks about his interests, skills, and how he did on accomplishing last year's IEP goals. He asks for teacher and parent support to accomplish his goals.
Scenario 2: IEP Goal Attainment	The special education teacher assumes responsibility for attaining the IEP goals. The teacher builds supports, implements strategies, and collects data. The student does not know her IEP goals or how she is progressing toward accomplishing them.	Bekah shares the responsibility for attaining her IEP goals. The teacher educates Bekah on how to accomplish her goals. Each week Bekah completes a plan to accomplish a portion of her goals and then evaluates the success of her plan at the end of the week.
Scenario 3: Course Scheduling	The special education team determines what classes students take for the next semester. The team considers their perception of student skills, limits, and interests in building the student schedule.	Students build their own schedule in consultation with their teachers. Students learn what classroom characteristics they like and learn their school skills and limits. The students next consider their needs and goals, then match their interests, skills, and limits to required and optional courses.
Scenario 4: Functional Assessment	The special education team conducts a functional assessment in reaction to a persistent behavior problem, then develops a behavior support plan.	Sean actively participates in the functional assessment process, helps to analyze and interpret data, and develops a support plan in collaboration with the team. Sean shares responsibility in accomplishing the goals of his behavior support plan.

The transition vision of the Ohio Department of Education, Office of Exceptional Children, for example, implements the spirit of the law. Special education practice in Ohio could satisfy the minimum requirements by only *inviting* students to their IEP meetings, but instead, students are *expected* to be present at their IEP meeting and to participate actively in the planning and implementation of their transition to adult life educational program (Ohio Department of Education, Division of Special Education, 1999). To this end, special education transition practice in Ohio:

- Expects students to lead their own IEP meetings
- Expects students to describe and discuss their postsecondary transition goals
- Teaches students about their transition process
- Expects students to develop postsecondary goals based on their interests and preferences

To document this transition vision, Ohio school districts must report the number of student-led IEP meetings, documentation of efforts to develop postsecondary goals based on student interest and preferences, the number of students who discuss their postsecondary goals, and a listing of the programs or strategies used to educate students about transition.

Self-Determination

Since the late 1960s, special educators have discussed self-determination. One way to understand self-determination is to view it as two strands that have evolved over time: (1) the choice strand and (2) the goal-setting and attainment strand. The self-determined learning model of instruction (Wehmeyer, Palmer, Agran, Mithaug, & Martin, 2000), and the self-determined learning theory (Mithaug, Mithaug, Agran, Martin, & Wehmeyer, 2003) exemplify how our field's understanding of the concept has matured and merged from two strands into one.

The Choice Strand

The earliest, and a few modern self-determination definitions, cluster into the choice definitional strand. Within these conceptualizations, choice becomes a right that people with disabilities exercise (Ippoliti, Peppey, & Depoy, 1994). Self-determination begins with choice and motivates action. A few of these definitions include:

- Nirje (1972): Self-determination is a critical component of the normalization principle. Choices, wishes, and aspirations of people with disabilities must be considered when actions affect them.
- Deci and Ryan (1985): Self-determination is the capacity of individuals to choose and then have these choices be the driving force behind their action.
- Deci and Ryan (1994): Individuals are self-determined to the extent that they freely choose their behaviors.
- Wehmeyer (1992, 1994): Self-determination refers to the attitudes and abilities required to act as the primary causal agent in one's own life and to make choices regarding one's actions free from undue external influence.

The trend in special education is toward greater involvement of students in their own education by providing them opportunities to make their own choices (Smith, 1994). Opportunities to engage first in simple, then increasingly complex choice making must be infused throughout students' education (Winup, 1994). When educators provide individuals choice-making opportunities, students express their individuality, and teachers show that they value and respect their students (Coupe-O'Kane, Porter, & Taylor, 1994). Belief in choice making impacts practice, as the following three examples demonstrate. First, when teachers provide students task choice opportunities, disruptive behavior significantly decreases and learning increases (Munk & Repp, 1994). Second, when students are given a choice of vocational tasks, their productivity increases (Mithaug & Mar, 1980). Third, when students read text materials that interest them, the students comprehend and enjoy the task better than with material they do not enjoy (Ryan, Connell, & Plant, 1990).

Critical Point Self-determination practices improve learning and productivity because students are engaged in tasks they have chosen and that are meaningful to them.

Special educators said in a statewide survey that they consider choice as the primary self-determination strategy. When asked what strategies constitute self-determination, 91% of the special education teachers identified choice making (Agran, Snow, & Swaner, 1999). They identified goal setting as the second ranked strategy.

The Goal-Setting and Attainment Strand

This second self-determination strand includes choice but emphasizes goal setting and the goal attainment process. Ward (1994), who champions this view, wrote that the optimal outcome of the self-determination process is setting a goal and achieving it. A few of the goal attainment definitions include:

- Ward (1988): Self-determined individuals define goals for themselves and take the initiative in achieving those goals.
- Martin, Marshall, and Maxson (1993): Self-determined individuals know what they want and how to get it. From an awareness of personal needs, self-determined individuals set goals, then they doggedly pursue their goals. This involves asserting their presence, making their needs known, evaluating progress toward meeting their goals, adjusting their performance as needed, and creating unique approaches to solve problems.
- Wolman, Campeau, DuBois, Mithaug, and Stolarski (1994): Self-determined individuals know and can express their own needs, interests, and abilities. They set appropriate goals, make choices and plans in pursuit of their goals, and make adjustments as needed to achieve their goals.
- Field and Hoffman (1994, 1995): A self-determined person defines and achieves their goals from a base of knowing and valuing themselves.

Critical Point Goal attainment strategies are critical in ensuring that students with disabilities are truly self-determined.

When goal attainment defines self-determination, certain practices result. Martin and Marshall (1995) suggest that students should identify their needs and interests across different transition domains; establish goals that match their interests, skills, and limits; develop a plan to accomplish their goals; evaluate their progress toward meeting their goals, and make adjustments in their support, strategies, or goals. An opportunity for this to occur, for example, exists within the IEP process: getting ready for the meeting, the meeting itself, and the subsequent goal attainment process. When typical school functions change to become participatory decision-making opportunities, students actively participate as an equal team member to help establish goals.

The Strands Merge

Just having the opportunity to make choices and decisions does not ensure that a person will be self-determined (Wehmeyer, 1997, p. 36). Self-determined individuals *choose* goals that match their interests, skills, and limits (Martin & Marshall, 1995). The goal attainment strand includes choice but goes much further. Goal attainment strategies empower individuals to achieve their choices (Wehmeyer, Agran, & Hughes, 1998).

The self-determined learning model of instruction (Wehmeyer et al., 2000) brings the two strands together with the premise that once a goal is chosen, learning to adjust to attain the desired goals is necessary for a successful transition. The self-determined learning theory (Mithaug et al., 2003) extends the model and postulates that learning is adjustment and that people learn when their attempts to attain goals are blocked. To attain goals, choices, actions, and beliefs may need to be adjusted. Students learn by adjusting and adjust to learn. When students learn to align their choices, actions, evaluations, and adjustments with their self-identified needs and interests, the likelihood of attaining desired goals increases (Martin, Mithaug, Cox, Peterson, Van Dycke, & Cash, 2003).

Self-Determination Components

Martin and Marshall (1996a) interviewed adults with disabilities, parents of children with disabilities, conducted a multidiscipline literature review, and undertook a national survey to determine a set of self-determination skills. This resulted in seven self-determination constructs (see Table 9–2). These include (1) self-awareness, (2) self-advocacy, (3) self-efficacy, (4) decision making, (5) independent performance, (6) self-evaluation, and (7) adjustment. These seven constructs break down into 37 additional components.

TABLE 9–2
ChoiceMaker Self-Determination Constructs

1. *Self-awareness:*	Identify needs; identify interests; identify and understand strengths
	Identify and understand limitations; identify own values
2. *Self-advocacy:*	Assertively state wants and needs; assertively state rights; determine needed supports
	Pursue needed support; obtain and evaluate needed support; conduct own affairs
3. *Self-efficacy:*	Expects to obtain goals
4. *Decision making:*	Assess situation demands; set goals; set standards
	Identify information to make decisions; consider past solutions for new situation; generate new creative solutions
	Consider options; choose best option; develop plan
5. *Independent performance:*	Initiate tasks on time; complete tasks on time; use self-management strategies
	Perform tasks to standards; follow through on own plan
6. *Self-evaluation:*	Monitor task performance; compare performance to standards; evaluate effectiveness of self-management strategies
	Determine if plan completed and goal met
7. *Adjustment:*	Change goals; change standards; change plan
	Change strategies; change support; persistently adjust
	Use environmental feedback to aid adjustment

Source: Adapted from a table originally published in: Martin, J. E., & Marshall, L. H.(1996a). ChoiceMaker: Infusing self-determination instruction into the IEP and transition process. In Sands, D. J. & Wehmeyer, M. L. (Eds.), *Self-determination across the life span* (pp. 215–236). Baltimore: Paul H. Brookes. Used with permission from University Technology Corp.

Other goal attainment definitions of self-determination include similar conceptualizations. These definitions consider goal setting, planning, evaluation, and adjustment as central components. Field and Hoffman (1994) developed a self-determination model consisting of five areas: (1) know yourself, (2) value yourself, (3) plan, (4) act, and (5) experience outcomes and learn. Mithaug, Wehmeyer, Agran, Martin, and Palmer's (1998) self-determination learning model poses questions that students ask, then answer across three phases: (1) setting learning goals, (2) constructing a learning plan, and (3) adjusting behaviors. The Mithaug et al. (1998) model also provides teacher objectives to facilitate answering the questions. We present these questions and selected teacher objectives in Table 9–3.

The Importance of Self-Determination

A growing number of studies indicate the positive impact of self-determination skills upon postschool outcomes. Wehmeyer and Schwartz (1997) collected self-determination measures on students with learning disabilities and mental retardation prior to their exiting from high school. After leaving high school, the former students who had higher levels of self-determination while in high school had higher employment rates than those who had lower self-determination scores. Wehmeyer and Palmer (2003) replicated their 1997 study and found that once again students with learning disabilities and mental retardation who had higher levels of self-determination in high school had more positive postschool outcomes than students with lower self-determination scores. Their data also showed that from the first to third year following graduation, students with higher levels of self-determination experienced additional positive outcomes than those who had lower self-determination scores.

Critical Point Self-determination has been linked to better postschool outcomes for persons with disabilities.

Martin, Mithaug, Oliphint, Husch, and Frazier (2002) determined that job choice options and adjustments support increased vocational success. These researchers compared the employment outcomes of almost 600 individuals with disabilities who completed a systematic "choose and adjust" process to 200 workers who did not. Those who completed the self-directed employment choice process retained their jobs significantly longer than those who did not.

Gerber, Ginsberg, and Reiff (1992) interviewed a group of adults who were identified as learning disabled during their school years, to determine why some were successful and others were not. They found that successful individuals with learning disabilities had:

- Control of their lives and surroundings
- A desire to succeed
- Well-thought-out goals
- Persistence
- Adapted to their environment
- Built a social support network that facilitated their success

After conducting the interviews, Gerber et al. (1992) realized that successful individuals decided, long before they became successful, that they would be successful. The authors concluded that successful adults with severe learning disabilities wanted to succeed, set achievable goals, and confronted their learning disability so that appropriate measures could be taken to increase the likelihood of success. One highly successful young man explained it like this: "Successful people have a plan. You have to have a plan, goals, strategy, otherwise you are flying through the clouds and then you hit the mountain" (Gerber et al., 1992, p. 480). These findings, when combined with what we know from other disciplines, strongly suggest

TABLE 9–3

Self-Determination Learning Model

Phase 1: Setting a Learning Goal

Student Questions

- What do I want to learn?
- What do I know about it now?
- What must change to learn what I do not know?
- What can I do to produce that change?

Selected Teacher Objectives

- Enable student to identify specific strengths and instructional needs in a specific area.
- Enable student to evaluate and communicate preferences, interests, beliefs, and values that relate to this area.
- Assist student to gather information about opportunities and barriers in physical and social environment.
- Teach student to prioritize need.
- Teach student to state a goal and identify criteria for achieving that goal.

Phase 2: Constructing a Learning Plan

Student Questions

- What can I do now to change what I do not know?
- What will prevent me from taking action now to produce that change?
- What can I do to remove these obstacles?
- When will I take action and remove these obstacles?

Selected Teacher Objectives

- Enable student to self-evaluate progress toward goal achievement.
- Enable student to determine plan of action to bridge gap between self-evaluated current status and self-identified goal status.
- Enable student to identify most appropriate instructional strategies.
- Enable student to identify and implement strategies to overcome barriers and obstacles.
- Support student to implement student-directed learning strategies.
- Enable student to determine schedule for action plan.
- Enable student to self-monitor progress on implementing action plan.

Phase 3: Adjusting Behaviors

Student Questions

- What actions have I taken?
- What obstacles have been removed?
- What has changed about what I do not know?
- Do I know what I want to know?

Selected Teacher Objectives

- Enable student to self-evaluate progress toward goal.
- Collaborate with student to identify if action plan is adequate or inadequate given revised goal.
- Assist student in deciding if goal remains the same or changes.
- Assist student to change action plan if necessary.

Source: Excerpts taken from Mithaug, D. E., Wehmeyer, M. L., Agran, M., Martin, J. E., & Palmer, S. (1998). The self-determined learning model of instruction. In Wehmeyer, M. L. & Sands, D. J. (Eds.), *Making it happen: Student involvement in education planning, decision making, and instruction* (pp. 299–328). Baltimore: Paul H. Brookes.

the beneficial outcome of increased self-determination skills.

Infusion of Self-Determination into the IEP

Self-determination skills make a difference in the postschool outcomes of people with disabilities. Unfortunately, students with disabilities possess far fewer self-determination skills than do secondary students who do not have an IEP (Wolman et al., 1994). Only a few IEPs include self-determination goals, even though teachers value self-determination skills. For students to learn and use self-determination behaviors in their everyday life, self-determination skills must be taught and opportunities provided for students to practice self-determined behaviors.

Critical Point States and local education agencies need to go beyond the minimum requirements for self-determination established by federal legislation.

Educational practice appears to reflect this view. Agran et al.'s (1999) survey of special education teachers found that 77% considered self-determination as an important curricular area, with only 3% of the teachers rating self-determination as a low priority. However, a discrepancy exists between the teachers' expressed importance and their inclusion of self-determination into most of the IEPs they write. The Utah teachers said that:

- 14% include self-determination skills on most IEPs
- 61% include self-determination skills on some IEPs
- 25% include self-determination on few or no IEPs

What can be done to create more of a match between the perceived importance and the inclusion of self-determination goals into students' IEPs? One answer to this question begins with considering self-determination as a need to be discussed at the IEP meeting.

Establishing Self-Determination as an IEP Need Area

Educators and parents must consider self-determination as an educational necessity, one to be pursued as seriously and systematically as any other skill area we value (Agran et al., 1999, p. 301). The route to making self-determination an educational necessity begins with establishing its need in the IEP's present level of performance section (Sale & Martin, in press). Assessments, either formal or informal, typically document the present level of performance and establish the need. Self-determination assessment tools may assist with this process.

Three published self-determination assessments may help to determine students' self-determination strengths and needs. These include The ARC's *Self-Determination Scale* (Wehmeyer & Kelchner, 1995) the *Self-Determination Knowledge Scale* (Hoffman, Field, & Sawilowsky, 1996); and the *ChoiceMaker Self-Determination Assessment* (Martin & Marshall, 1996b). Each tool provides a unique perspective and reports the results in different ways (see Field, Martin, Miller, Ward, & Wehmeyer, 1998; Sale & Martin, in press, for detailed descriptions of the three assessments). The *ChoiceMaker Self-Determination Assessment* singularly produces suggested IEP goals and objectives.

The *ChoiceMaker Assessment*, as a curriculum-referenced assessment, matches the *ChoiceMaker* curriculum (see Table 9–4). It consists of 54 items that evaluate student self-determination skills and the opportunities at school to exercise these skills. The *ChoiceMaker Assessment* contains three sections: choosing goals, expressing goals, and taking action. The "choosing goals" section assesses goal setting based on students'

TABLE 9–4

Sample ChoiceMaker Assessment's Expressing Goals Questions

	Student Skills	Opportunity at School
Section 2: Expressing Goals	(Does the student do this?)	(Does school provide structured time?)
E. *Student Leading Meeting—Does the student:*	(not at all) (100%)	(not at all) (100%)
E1. Begin meeting and introduce participants?	0 1 2 3 4	0 1 2 3 4
E2. Review past goals and performance?	0 1 2 3 4	0 1 2 3 4
E3. Ask questions if student does not understand something?	0 1 2 3 4	0 1 2 3 4
E4. Ask for feedback from group members?	0 1 2 3 4	0 1 2 3 4
E5. Deal with differences in opinion?	0 1 2 3 4	0 1 2 3 4
E6. Close meeting by summarizing decisions?	0 1 2 3 4	0 1 2 3 4
	Subtotal _____	Subtotal _____
F. *Student Reporting—Does the student:*		
F1. Express interests.	0 1 2 3 4	0 1 2 3 4
F2. Express skills and limits.	0 1 2 3 4	0 1 2 3 4
F3. Express options and goals.	0 1 2 3 4	0 1 2 3 4
	Subtotal _____	Subtotal _____
	TOTAL (E + F) _____	TOTAL (E + F) _____

Source: Excerpt taken from: Martin, J. E. & Marshall, L. H. (1996b). *ChoiceMaker self-determination assessment.* Longmont, CO: Sopris West. © 1997 University of Colorado. Used with permission from University Technology Corp.

knowledge of their interests, skills, and limits across school, employment, and post-high-school education domains. The "expressing goals" section assesses students' participation and leadership in IEP meetings. The "take action" section measures students' goal attainment skills (see Table 9–4 for sample questions).

Teachers evaluate each of the 54 items using a five-point scale across both the Student Skills and Opportunity at School columns. The raw scores for each of the three sections are summed, graphed, and compared to the total points available to find the percent of available self-determination skills and opportunities. Items assessed as zero, one, or two become possible IEP goals and objectives.

CASE STUDY

Zeke, a 14-year-old high school student, receives special education services due to the impact his learning disability and emotional problems have upon his educational performance. The special education team at Zeke's high school believes in teaching self-determination skills and in providing many opportunities to practice learned self-determination skills. In preparation for Zeke's first high school IEP meeting, Mrs. Gomez and Zeke jointly complete the *ChoiceMaker Assessment* to document his present level of educational performance.

Zeke's *ChoiceMaker Assessment* profile (see Figure 9–1) shows that Zeke's high school provides 33% of the choosing goal opportunities, 100% of the expressing goals opportunities, and 99% of the taking action opportunities. Zeke's skill profile depicts low and variable self-determination levels: a 30% choosing goals skills level, a 10% expressing goals skill level, and a 38% taking action skills level. The skill levels differ significantly from the opportunities provided by his high school program.

Critical Point Self-determination should be measured in terms of choosing goals, expressing goals, and taking action.

In preparing for Zeke's annual IEP review meeting, Mrs. Gomez writes the results of her assessment into the IEP form's transition present level of educational performance and needs section (see Table 9–5). She then sends a copy of her self-determination assessment and a draft present level of performance section home for Zeke and his parents to review and discuss prior to the IEP meeting.

At the IEP meeting, Zeke (with coaching by Mrs. Gomez) showed the team his self-determination assessment profile, then described his strengths and a few of the self-determination skills he has not yet mastered. Mrs. Gomez then reviewed the school's self-determination expectations. The team realized a large discrepancy existed between Zeke's current performance and the expectations to engage in self-determination activities. Zeke and the team decided he needs to:

- Choose education, employment, and personal goals based on an understanding of his skills and limits
- Learn to lead his educational meetings
- Learn the goal attainment skills needed to take action on his IEP goals

Mrs. Gomez wrote these into Zeke's "transition need" section of his IEP, and then wrote a self-determination IEP goal and related objectives:

Goal

Within the next 20 weeks, Zeke will increase self-determination skills to an average of 83%.

Objectives

1. Within the next 10 weeks, Zeke will increase taking action skills to 90% as measured by the *ChoiceMaker* self-determination assessment.
2. In the next 15 weeks, Zeke will increase choosing goals to 70% as measured by the *ChoiceMaker* self-determination assessment.
3. Within the next 20 weeks, Zeke will increase expressing goals skills to 90% as measured by the *ChoiceMaker* self-determination assessment.

FIGURE 9–1
ChoiceMaker Assessment Profile

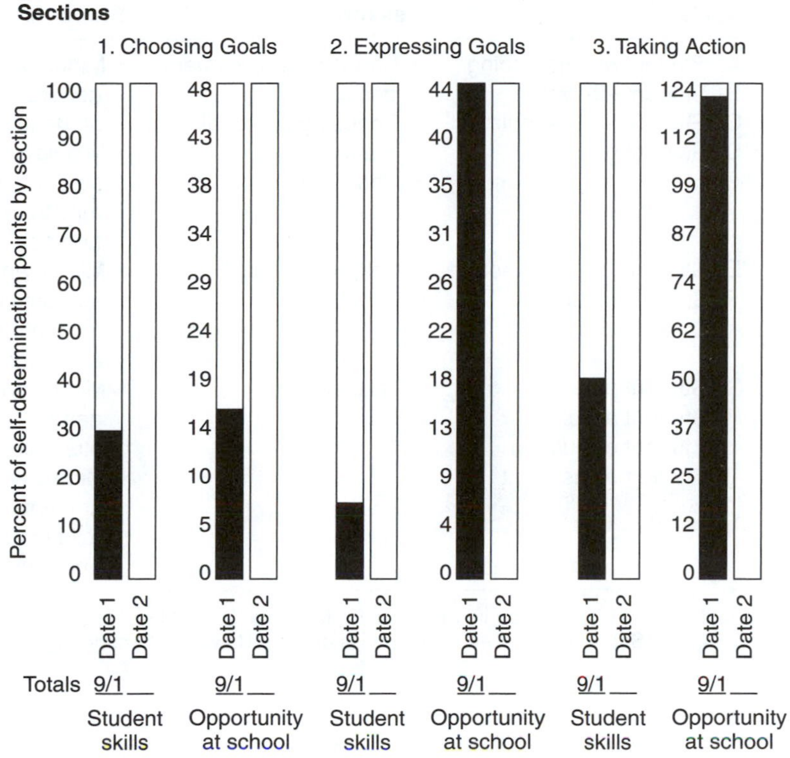

Teaching Self-Determination and Creating Participatory Decision-Making Opportunities

Once self-determination goals are written into the IEP, special education teachers need to make teaching self-determination skills a priority. Teachers may develop their own lessons, or choose to use or modify already-developed lesson packages in order to teach self-determination skills to their students. (See Field et al., 1998 for a review of numerous self-determination lesson packages or go to *http://www.uncc.edu/sdsp/sd_curricula.as*). Teachers across the country use the *ChoiceMaker* self-determination instructional packages to teach basic self-determination skills and to practice learned self-determination behaviors.

The *ChoiceMaker* series consists of the *ChoiceMaker Self-Determination Assessment* and six instructional packages. The instructional packages include:

- *Choosing employment goals* (Huber Marshall, Martin, Maxson, & Jerman, 1997)
- *Choose and take action: Finding the right job for you* (Martin, et al., 2004)
- *Choosing education goals* (Martin, Hughes, Huber Marshall, Jerman, & Maxson, 1999)
- *Choosing personal goals* (Marshall, Martin, Hughes, Jerman, & Maxson, 1999)

TABLE 9–5
ChoiceMaker Lesson Matrix

Section	Goals	Lessons	Students
Choosing Goals	A. Student understanding B. Student interests C. Student skills and limits D. Student goals	• Choosing employment goals • Choosing personal matters goals • Choosing education goals	• Middle and high school general education students • Middle and high school students with an IEP and mild to moderate learning and behavior problems
Expressing Goals	E. Student leading meeting F. Student reporting	• Self-directed IEP	• Middle and high school students with an IEP and mild to moderate learning and behavior problems
Taking Action	G. Student plan H. Student action I. Student evaluation J. Student adjustment	• Take action	• Middle and high school general education students • Middle and high school students with an IEP and mild to moderate learning and behavior problems

Source: Adapted from a table originally published in: Martin, J. E., Marshall, L. H., Maxson, L. & Jerman, P. (1996c). *Self-directed IEP.* Longmont, CO: Sopris West. Used with permission from University Technology Corp.

- *Self-directed* IEP (Martin, Huber Marshall, Maxson, & Jerman, 1996).
- *Take action: Making goals happen* (Huber Marshall, Martin, Maxson, Hughes, Miller, McGill, & Jerman, 1999).

Each instructional package teaches specific goals and objectives of the *ChoiceMaker* curriculum (see Table 9–5). The *ChoiceMaker* curriculum, which operationalizes the self-determination constructs identified in Table 9–2, contains three strands, nine broad teaching goals, and 54 objectives.

Development of the ChoiceMaker *Lesson Packages*

The development of each lesson package followed the same process (see Table 9–6). A team comprised of university faculty, public school special educators and administrators, parents, students with an IEP, and adults with disabilities jointly worked on conceptualizing, writing, and field-testing the materials. The development teams wrote the lessons to attain specific *ChoiceMaker* goals and objectives. The teams repeatedly took the draft lessons into middle and high school programs to field-test. Feedback from the teachers and students resulted in numerous revisions. Researchers then conducted rigorous studies to demonstrate the programs' effectiveness. We will describe the results of these studies when we explain each lesson package.

Critical Point *ChoiceMaker* was developed and field-tested in collaboration with educators, students, adults with disabilities, and parents.

TABLE 9–6

ChoiceMaker Self-Determination Curriculum Matrix

Sections	Teaching Goals	Teaching Objectives							
1: *Choosing Goals* (through school and community experience)	*A. Student interests*	A1. Express ***education*** interests	A2. Express ***employment*** interests	A3. Express ***personal*** interests	A4. Express ***daily living, housing, and community*** interests				
	B. Student skills and limits	B1. Express ***education*** skills and limits	B2. Express ***employment*** skills and limits	B3. Express ***personal*** skills and limits	B4. Express ***daily living, housing and community*** skills and limits				
	C. Student goals	C1. Indicate options and choose ***education*** goals	C2. Indicate options and choose ***employment*** goals	C3. Indicate options and choose ***personal*** goals	C4. Indicate options and choose ***daily living, housing, and community goals***				
2: *Express-ing Goals*	*D. Student leading meeting*	D1. Begin meeting by stating purpose	D2. Introduce participants	D3. Review past goals and performance	D4. Ask for feedback	D5. Ask questions if don't understand	D6. Deal with differences in opinion	D7. State needed support	D8. Close meeting by summarizing decision
	E. Student reporting	E1. Express interests (from A1–A4)	E2. Express skills and limits (from B1–B4)	E3. Express options and goals (from C1–C4)					
3: *Taking Action*	*F. Student plan*	F1. Break general goals into specific goals that can be completed now	F2. Establish ***standard*** for specific goals	F3. Determine how to get ***feedback*** from environment	F4. Determine ***motivation*** to complete specific goals	F5. Determine ***strategies*** for completing specific goals	F6. Determine ***support*** needed to complete specific goals	F7. Prioritize and ***schedule*** to complete specific goals	F8. Express ***belief*** that goals can be obtained
	G. Student action	G1. Record or report performance	G2. Perform specific goals to ***standard***	G3. Obtain ***feedback*** on performance	G4. ***Motivate*** self to complete specific goals	G5. Use ***strategies*** to perform specific goals	G6. Obtain ***support*** needed	G7. Follow ***schedule***	
	H. Student evaluation	H1. Determine if goals are achieved	H2. Compare performance to ***standards***	H3. Evaluate ***feedback***	H4: Evaluate ***motivation***	H5. Evaluate effectiveness of ***strategies***	H6. Evaluate ***support*** used	H7. Evaluate ***schedule***	H8. Evaluate ***belief***
	I. Student adjustment	I1. Adjust goals if necessary	I2. Adjust or repeat goal ***standards***	I3. Adjust or repeat method for ***feedback***	I4. Adjust or repeat ***motivation***	I5. Adjust or repeat ***strategies***	I6. Adjust or repeat	I7. Adjust or repeat ***schedule***	I8. Adjust or repeat ***belief*** that goals can be obtained

Source: Adapted from a table originally published in: Martin, J. E., Marshall, L. H., Maxson, L., & Jerman, P. (1996c). *Self-directed IEP*. Longmont, CO: Sopris West. © 1996 University of Colorado. Used with permission from University Technology Corp.

Self-determined choices enhance postschool outcomes.

Use of the ChoiceMaker *Lesson Packages*

Each *ChoiceMaker* lesson package may be infused into existing educational programs. Because the *choosing goals* and *taking action* materials are compatible with middle and high school content area courses, they may be used for general education students *and* with students who have an IEP. The *self-directed* IEP materials, which teach the *expressing goal* section of the curriculum, are designed for students with an IEP. The *Choose and Take Action* multimedia software package uses a repeated measures design within a situational assessment to teach and assess entry level vocational choices of students and adults who cannot read, have more moderate to severe cognitive disabilities, and have limited to no previous work experience. All other *ChoiceMaker* lesson packages teach students who have at least minimal reading and writing skills.

Teaching and Creating Opportunities for Choosing Goals

The choosing goals section of the *ChoiceMaker* curriculum provides students the skills and knowledge needed to express their interests, skills, limits, and goals across different transition areas. The choosing goals lesson packages include *choosing employment goals*, *choosing education goals*, and *choosing personal goals*. As exemplars of the choosing goals lesson packages, in this section, we review the general choosing goals process and samples from the *choosing employment goals* lesson package. We then briefly describe the *choosing education goals* and *choosing personal goals* instructional packages.

Choosing Goals Process

Each of the choosing goals lesson packages includes methodology for students to determine quickly their goals across transition areas. A student video included in each of the three lesson packages, entitled *Choosing Goals to Plan Your Life*, introduces the choosing goals process by showing actual high school students learning and using the choosing goals process.

After watching the video and completing the choosing goals lessons, students complete a choosing general goals worksheet. Figure 9–2 presents a sample section of a choosing general goals worksheet from the *choosing employment goals* lesson package for a high school student who wants to work as an autobody repairman. After the student knows how to complete the form, he simply reads each question and writes in his answer. If he does not know the answer, then that becomes his goal. In this example, Cal does not know the requirements to become an autobody repairman. So, learning the requirements to be an autobody repairman becomes his goal. Once completed, students may use the form for discussions in their transition class, with their parents, or in their IEP meeting. If students do not know their goals, the lesson packages teach students to identify their goals based on an understanding of their interests, skills, and limits. Cross, Cooke, Wood, and Test (1999) found that the choosing goals process enabled

FIGURE 9–2
Choosing General Goals

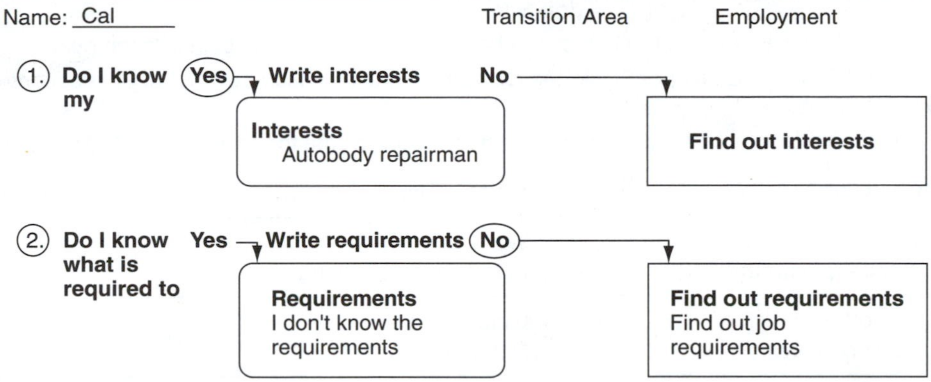

Source: Excerpt taken from: Marshall, L.,H. Martin, J., Maxson, L., & Jerman, P. (1997). *Choosing employment goals.* Longmont, CO: Sopris West. © 1997 University of Colorado. Used with permission from University Technology Corp.

students to provide information on vocational and other transition domains so that they could actively participate in their IEP meeting. When compared to the *McGill Action Planning System*, the results favored the use of the *ChoiceMaker* choosing goals process.

Choosing Employment Goals

The *ChoiceMaker* curriculum objectives (see Table 9–6) addressed by *choosing employment goals* are:

Objective A2: Express employment interests.
Objective B2: Express employment skills and limits.
Objective C2: Indicate options and choose employment goals.

The *choosing employment goals* lesson sequence is flexible and designed to be mixed and matched with the content and opportunities of existing school curriculum, classes, and schedules.

The lesson activities, which take place at community job sites and in the classroom, teach students to reflect upon their experiences, draw conclusions about themselves, and learn about community opportunities. Students collect and assimilate this information over time so that they can make informed career decisions. The *choosing employment goals* lesson package consists of three parts: (1) choosing general goals lessons (discussed earlier), (2) experience-based lessons, and (3) dream job lessons.

Experience-Based Lessons

Teachers use these lessons and materials with students who are involved in on-the-job activities through work study, on-the-job training, volunteering, or in an after-school job. These lessons teach students to draw meaningful conclusions about their interests, skills, and limits based on their own work experience.

Students learn the job characteristics and job duties they like by completing the *Job Characteristics I Like Worksheet* (see Figure 9–3) and *Job Duties I Like Student Worksheet* process. To examine their on-the-job skills and limits they complete a *Work, Social, and Personal Skills* (see Figure 9–4), and a *Job Duties—How I Did* process. When done repeatedly across time, the results yield a self-directed

FIGURE 9–3
Job Characteristics I Like Worksheet

Name: ______________ ***Job Site*** ______________ ***Date:*** __________

Directions: WHAT I LIKE column: Circle the job characteristic that you like best in each box.
WHAT IS HERE column: Circle the job characteristic in each box that best describes what is at this job.
MATCHES column: Circle YES if the first two columns are the same. Circle NO if they are not.

	What I Like	**What is Here**	**Matches**	
1.	Work alone Lots of people around	Work alone Lots of people around	Yes	No
2.	Quiet workplace Noisy workplace	Quiet workplace Noisy workplace	Yes	No
3.	Work close to home Distance to job doesn't matter	Work close to home Distance to job doesn't matter	Yes	No
4.	Weekdays only Weekends too	Weekdays only Weekends too	Yes	No
5.	Easy job Challenging job	Easy job Challenging job	Yes	No

Source: Excerpt taken from: Marshall, L. H., Martin, J. E., Maxson, L., & Jerman, P. (1997). *Choosing employment goals.* Longmont, CO: Sopris West Publishers. © 1997 University of Colorado. Used with permission from University Technology Corp.

vocational profile that may be shared with others (see Figure 9–5). Students save their results to develop a self-directed vocational portfolio, which they can show at their IEP meeting to add data to the IEP's present level of performance section.

Dream Job Lessons

With the dream job lessons, students in a general education academic or a transition class gather information about a variety of jobs, then research those they think they would like. Students determine how their interests, skills, and limits match those jobs. The lessons may be used sequentially or separately. There are four lessons in the dream job section: (1) job clusters, (2) dream job research, (3) dream job interviews, and (4) dream job shadowing.

Choosing Education Goals

The *choosing education goals* lesson package teaches students to choose high school and postsecondary education goals that match their interests, skills, limits, and available opportunities. The *ChoiceMaker* self-determination transition curriculum objectives addressed by the *choosing education goals* lessons include:

Objective A1. Express education interests.

Objective B1. Express education skills and limits.

Objective C1. Indicate options and choose education goals.

The *choosing education goals* lesson activities all take place in the classroom. The lessons teach students to reflect upon their experiences,

FIGURE 9–4
Work, Social, and Personal Skills Student's Worksheet

How I Did column: Circle 3, 2, or 1 whichever best describes your performance.

Supervisor Thinks column: From the *Work, Social, and Personal Skills Supervisor Worksheet*, copy the numbers that your supervisor chose to describe your performance.

Matches column: Circle Yes if yours and your supervisor's evaluations are the same. If they are not the same, circle No.

Skills	How I Did	Supervisor Thinks	Comments	Matches
1. Follows company rules	Very good **3** OK **2** Needs improvement **1**	Very good **3** OK **2** Needs improvement **1**		Yes No
2. Comes to work on time or calls if late or absent	Very good **3** OK **2** Needs improvement **1**	Very good **3** OK **2** Needs improvement **1**		Yes No
Social				
8. Talks the right amount	Very good **3** OK **2** Needs improvement **1**	Very good **3** OK **2** Needs improvement **1**		Yes No
9. Behaves appropriately	Very good **3** OK **2** Needs improvement **1**	Very good **3** OK **2** Needs improvement **1**		Yes No
Personal				
12. Works independently	Very good **3** OK **2** Needs improvement **1**	Very good **3** OK **2** Needs improvement **1**		Yes No
13. Good grooming	Very good **3** OK **2** Needs improvement **1**	Very good **3** OK **2** Needs improvement **1**		Yes No

Source: Excerpt taken from: Marshall, L. H., Martin, J. E., Maxson, L., & Jerman, P. (1997). *Choosing employment goals*. Longmont, CO: Sopris West Publishers. © 1997 University of Colorado. Used with permission from University Technology Corp.

FIGURE 9–5
Job Characteristics I Like Graph

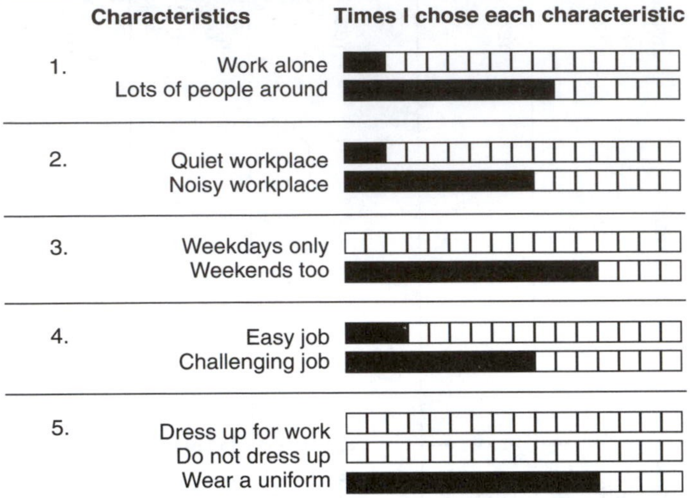

Source: Excerpt taken from: Marshall, L. H., Martin, J. E., Maxson, L., & Jerman, P. (1997). *Choosing employment goals.* Longmont, CO: Sopris West Publishers. © 1997 University of Colorado. Used with permission from University Technology Corp.

draw conclusions about themselves, and learn about education opportunities. Students will collect and assimilate this information over time to make informed decisions about their secondary and postsecondary education plans. Peterson, Van Dycke, Borland, and Crowover (2003) found that students who participate in *choosing education goals* lessons can create their own plan of study and can provide most if not all of the plan of study components needed for their IEP.

While using the *Choosing Education Goals* lessons, students complete a variety of activities that are designed to help:

- Determine what students hope to do at different stages of their lives.
- Identify the school subjects that students like.
- Complete a personalized graduation checklist.
- Develop an individualized education performance summary.
- Learn postsecondary education terminology.
- Complete study habits, work habits, and academic skills self-assessment.
- Maintain a study habits log.
- Develop an individualized postsecondary education options information table.
- Choose secondary and postsecondary education goals.

Choosing Personal Goals

The *choosing personal goals* lesson package teaches students how to develop satisfying personal lives and how to spend their free time in safe, legal, and healthy ways. The *ChoiceMaker* self-determination transition curriculum objectives (see Table 9–6) addressed in the lessons include:

Objective A3: Express personal interests.

Objective B4: Express personal skills and limits.

Objective C5: Express options and choose personal goals.

While using the choosing personal goals lessons, students complete a variety of activities designed to help them:

- Consider how they interact with other people.
- Evaluate the interactions of the groups in which they are involved.
- Identify the activities they do in their free time to further their relationships, hobbies, talents, recreation; or health and wellness.
- Decide if they would like to make changes in the way they interact with people or in the activities they do and identify ways to make those changes.
- Investigate activities, events, and services that are available in the community or school that can help them to make those changes (e.g., classes, clubs, teams, art groups or activities, sports, counseling, and community events).
- Consider their interests, skills, and limits in relation to the opportunities and choose personal goals of activities they want to try.
- Try their chosen activity and evaluate the results.

Summary

Once students identify their goals based on an understanding of their interests, skills, and limits, they then need the skills to express their goals at their IEP meeting.

Teaching and Creating Opportunities for Students to Lead Their IEP Meeting

More than two decades after the passage of the first federal special education laws, students, parents, and general education teachers finally must meet to develop the students' IEPs. IDEA mandates that students 14 years old and older must be invited to attend their IEP meetings, and that the IEP discussions and decisions must reflect student interests and preferences (Storms, O'Leary, & Williams, 2000). Implementation of these reforms has been slow, with most states failing to achieve even minimal levels of compliance (Grigal, Test, Beattie, Wood, 1997; Hasazi, Furney, & DeStefano, 1999). The National Council on Disability (2000) reported that "88% or 44 states failed to ensure compliance with transition requirements" (p. 89). Williams and O'Leary (2001) found that many schools do not invite students to their own IEP meetings. Johnson et al. (2001) indicated that secondary education must improve student attendance at IEP meetings, and prepare students to actively participate in their meetings so they can lead discussions about their plans and goals. The U.S. Dept. of Education's Office of Special Education Program Expert Strategy Panel Report indicated that today's secondary schools provide too few opportunities for students to learn and practice IEP leadership skills prior to their IEP meeting (U.S. Department of Education, 2001). Even so, a growing number of students do attend their IEP meetings. Many of the statewide transition system change grants sponsored by the U.S. Department of Education encouraged student involvement in their IEP meetings (Williams & O'Leary, 2001).

Research suggests that when students attend their IEP meetings without specific IEP meeting instruction, they do not know what to do, lack understanding of the meeting's purpose or language, feel like no one listens to them when they do talk, do not know their goals or other outcomes of the meeting, and think that attending the IEP meeting would be a meaningless activity (Lehmann, Bassett, & Sands, 1999; Lovitt, Cushing, Stump, 1994; Morningstar, Turnbull, & Turnbull, 1995). Powers (1997) discovered that if students attended their IEP meetings with no prior instruction in what to do, they did not enjoy their IEP meetings and they did not understand the language or the meeting's purpose. She also found that students (and parents) believed that IEP team members did not talk to the student or ask for student input. Martin, Huber Marshall, and Sale (in press) conducted a survey of almost 1,770 IEP team members who attended middle and high school meetings over a 3-year period. They found that when students attend their meetings, the students talked less and understood less about the reason for the meeting than did all other participants.

Critical Point Students' presence at the IEP meeting is not enough. They must learn their role and how to participate meaningfully.

Presence at the IEP meeting without knowledge of the process and skills in what to do achieves very little. Clearly, to make student-directed IEPs a meaningful educational experience, students should learn their role in the IEP process and what they can do to become a meaningful part of that process.

The expressing goals section of the *ChoiceMaker* curriculum provides students the skills and knowledge needed to become actively involved in and to direct their own IEP meeting. While at the meeting, the students learn how to discuss their interests, skills, limits, and goals across different transition areas.

Five available lesson packages help educators to teach students the skills required to participate in and direct their own IEP meetings. These include the *Self-Advocacy Strategy for Education and Transition Planning* (Van Reusen, Bos, Schumaker, & Deshler, 1994); *Whose Future Is It Anyway?* (Wehmeyer & Kelchner, 1995b); *A Student's Guide to the* IEP (McGahee-Kovac, 1995); *Next Steps* (Halpern, Herr, Wolf, Lawson, Doren, & Johnson, 1997); and the *Self-Directed* IEP (Martin, Huber Marshall, Maxson, & Jerman, 1996c). The *Self-Directed* IEP specifically teaches students to attain the expressing goals section of the *ChoiceMaker* curriculum.

The Self-Directed IEP

The *Self-Directed* IEP teaches students to become active participants in their IEP meetings and to chair the meetings to the best extent of their ability. It teaches students the two goals and 11 objectives that are crucial for student involvement in their own education planning process (see Table 9–6). Through the use of the self-directed IEP materials, role-play practice prior to the meeting, and participatation in their actual meeting, students learn the leadership skills that they need to manage their IEP meeting. The *Self-Directed* IEP contains several different instructional materials. These include:

- *Self-Directed* IEP *in Action Video* (7 minutes). This video shows students with different disabilities using the self-directed IEP lessons in their classes and talking about their experiences. This video is used to introduce the self-directed IEP to students, parents, teachers, and administrators.
- *Self-Directed* IEP *Video* (17 minutes). This video shows a student named Zeke, using each of the 11 steps to lead his IEP meeting while describing the process to a younger, reluctant friend. Zeke's meeting provides a model for each of the 11 steps needed to lead an IEP meeting (see Table 9–7). The meeting depicted in the video shows an ideal meeting, in which the student viewers focus upon the steps that are necessary to lead an IEP meeting.
- *Teacher's Manual*. This book provides background information, detailed lesson plans, and a teacher answer key to the quizzes and activities. Lessons include a variety of activities to teach each step, including a mnemonic learning strategy, vocabulary-building exercises, role-

TABLE 9–7

Eleven Steps to the *Self-Directed* IEP

1. Begin the meeting by stating the purpose.
2. Introduce everyone.
3. Review past goals and performance.
4. Ask for others' feedback.
5. State your school and transition goals.
6. Ask questions if you do not understand.
7. Deal with differences in opinion.
8. State what support you will need.
9. Summarize your goals.
10. Close the meeting by thanking everyone.
11. Work on IEP goals all year.

Source: Excerpt taken from: Martin, J. E., Marshall, L. H., Maxson, L., & Jerman, P. (1996c). *Self-directed IEP*. Longmont, CO: Sopris West Publishers. © 1997 University of Colorado. Used with permission from University Technology Corp.

playing, discussion, and brief reading and writing activities. The lessons are all presented in a model, lead, test approach.

- *Student Workbook*. This consumable workbook provides students an opportunity to apply each step to their own IEP. A script, summarizing all the steps, is completed at the end of the lessons for students to use at their IEP meeting.

Instructional Considerations

The IEP is the one unique aspect that defines special education. If educators and families are serious about involving students in their IEP process, then students must be taught their role. This means that even in fully included schools, students who have an IEP must receive instruction about the IEP process and their role in it.

The Self-Directed IEP contains 11 sequential lessons that can be taught in six to ten 45-minute sessions. The lessons may be taught in a resource room, study skills class, or other settings. To teach students who are fully included in general education classes may involve meeting with individuals or with a group during study hall or other convenient times. The lessons also may be taught in an elective class.

Impact of the Self-Directed IEP

Sweeney (1996) undertook a pre-post-controlled group study to measure the impact of the *Self-Directed* IEP upon Florida high school students with learning disabilities and mental retardation. In comparison to the students in the control group who did not receive instruction, Sweeney (1996) found that the students who completed the *Self-Directed* IEP lessons:

- Attended more of the IEP staffings
- Had more parents attend IEP staffings
- Talked more about their interests
- Shared more of their dreams for the future
- Talked more about the job they wanted
- Felt like they were the boss of their IEP meeting
- Felt more confident in reaching their IEP goals

Snyder and Shapiro (1997) and Snyder (2002) found that the *Self-Directed* IEP taught adolescent students with emotional and behavior problems the skills needed to direct their own IEP meeting. Allen, Smith, Test, Flowers, and Wood (2001) and Arnold and Martin (2003) showed the functional relationship between the *Self-Directed* IEP and increases in participation by students with mental retardation and learning disabilities in their IEP meetings.

Summary

The goals and objectives are the most important instructional outcome of the IEP meeting. In a *Self-Directed* IEP meeting students play a major role in determining the goals. But after the meeting, how are the goals attained? Typically, goal attainment becomes an educator's duty. However, do educators need to be the only people responsible for goal attainment? What about the student?

Teaching and Creating Opportunities for Attaining Goals

Currently, special education teachers feel it is their responsibility to attain students' IEP goals. However, is this really the best education practice? To us, something is wrong with a practice in which the student is absolved of any goal attainment responsibility. After all, whose education is it, and whose goals are on the IEP? If goal attainment is the most important part of being self-determined, then why are students not more responsible for their own goals? Are educators really acting in the student's best interest if teachers carry the entire burden of responsibility for goal attainment?

We do not think so. We believe that students should have at least equal, if not greater, responsibility for achieving their own IEP goals. Our dream is that once the IEP meeting is concluded, the goal attainment process begins. Our dream is for students to meet weekly with their teachers in order to develop plans to achieve their own IEP goals, after evaluating the progress they made the previous week in achieving the past week's plans. We cannot think of a better way to make the IEP process a student-centered, living document. *Take Action: Making Goals Happen* is the *ChoiceMaker* instructional program that teaches goal attainment.

Critical Point It is believed that students should take as much responsibility as possible for their own IEP goals.

Take Action Overview

The *Take Action* lesson package teaches students a simple, yet effective goal attainment process. As with the other *ChoiceMaker* lesson packages, this lesson package is introduced with a student-oriented video demonstrating the take action concepts. *Take Action* lessons teach students to plan how they will attain their goal by deciding (1) a standard for goal performance, (2) a means to get performance feedback, (3) what motivates them to do it, (4) the strategies they will use, (5) needed supports, and (6) schedules. This leads to student action, evaluation, and adjustment. These lessons can be applied to any goal or project and, thus, are excellent for use in content classes.

Take Action Lessons

By using a model-lead-test approach, the *Take Action* lessons systematically teach students an easy and effective goal attainment process. Here we discuss four lessons:

- *Lesson* 1. Introduces the *Take Action* process for accomplishing goals. Students watch the 10-minute *Take Action* video, which shows students developing plans and working on attaining their own goals. The students in the video assisted in writing and creating the video. The goals you see them working on in the video use goals from their own lives. Introduced in this lesson are the four major parts of the take action process: plan, act, evaluate, and adjust.
- *Lesson* 2. This lesson begins the process of teaching students how to break long-term goals into short-term objectives. To do this, students participate in an example process showing what a student must do to get her driver's license.
- *Lesson* 3. Students are introduced to plan making. Here they learn the parts of a plan that is needed to attain their goal. Hands-on activities are used to demonstrate each plan part. One of the concluding activities is for students to match the question being asked to the correct part of the plan (see Figure 9–6).
- *Lesson* 6. Students learn the importance of evaluation and adjustment to goal attainment.

FIGURE 9–6
Take Action Review

Name ______________________ **Date** ______________________

Find the question that explains each part of a plan. Write it under the correct part of the plan.

Questions

How will I get information on my performance?	What help do I need?	When will I do it?	What will I be satisfied with?	What methods should I use?	Why do I want to do this?

Parts of a Plan

Standard	Motivation	Strategy	Schedule	Support	Feedback

Source: Excerpt from: Marshall, L. H., Martin, J. E., Maxson, L. M., Miller, T. L., McGill, T., Hughes, W. M., & Jerman, P. A. (1997). *Taking action.* Longmont, CO: Sopris West, Inc. © 1997 University of Colorado. Used with permission from University Technology Corp.

They examine the evaluation and adjustments of earlier plans.

- *Remaining lessons.* The remaining lessons teach students how to develop their own plans for sample goals, then for their own goals. The last lesson teaches students how to use the take action goal attainment process in other settings, and with a wide range of goals.

Impact of *Take Action* Lessons

German, Martin, Huber Marshall, and Sale (2000) undertook a study to determine the effectiveness of *Take Action* in teaching goal attainment to six students with mild to moderate mental retardation. After completing the *Take Action* lessons, all the students had significant increases in the attainment of specific daily goals. The students went from achieving 0 to 25% of their daily goals during baseline to 80 to 100% after instruction in the *Take Action* lessons. Walden (2002) demonstrated that university students with learning disabilities could learn the *Take Action* goal attainment process and that the strategy generalized.

Teaching and Creating Opportunities for Students with Severe Cognitive Needs

Most available lesson packages teach self-determination skills to students with mild learning and emotional challenges. Only a few materials exist to help educators teach self-determination skills to students with more severe cognitive needs (Field et al. 1998). Martin, Mithaug, Oliphint, Husch, & Frazier (2002) use illustrations to develop a self-directed vocational assessment and to establish self-directed goal attainment (see Figure 9–7). In their *Self-Directed Employment Program* students complete a repeated-measures situational assessment process to determine preferred job characteristics, tasks, and locations. Second, students learn an on-the-job problem-solving system that utilizes written or illustrated contracts to improve social, personal, and work performance. Third, students engage in job adjustment and career advancement decisions. The procedures capitalize upon discrepancy problems that workers must solve. During assessment the students need to resolve the discrepancy between what they like and what may or may not exist at a job site. In placement, this discrepancy exists when the workers self-evaluations do not match their supervisors' evaluation. The *Self-Directed Employment Program* provides opportunities for students to resolve these discrepancies.

The *Choose and Take Action* program combines interactive software, classroom lessons, and community experiences to enable individuals with developmental disabilities to make practical career choices. Students watch video segments, select a job that matches their interests, try the selected job at a community site, evaluate the experience, and then make new choices based on what they learned. The *Choose and Take Action* instructional activities are designed to teach students numerous self-determination skills, including:

- Choosing from a variety of work options
- Planning whether they want to watch or do the activity
- Completing the plan in the community setting
- Evaluating what they liked and did not like about the setting, activity, and work-site characteristics, and how the students did while they were at the setting
- Using the information gained in the experience to make the next choice

The *Choose and Take Action* software also introduces students to a variety of job and career possibilities and teaches them to identify what is most important to them about a job: the setting, the activity, or the characteristics.

Target Population

Choose and Take Action is designed for students and adults with developmental disabilities, brain injury, and autism who are unable to read and write. The characteristics of students for whom this program will work the best include:

- Students with moderate to significant cognitive needs
- Students who have difficulty getting information from print
- Students who can attend to a computer screen
- Students who can follow simple verbal instructions
- Students in middle and high school
- Students with limited work experience

How *Choose and Take Action* Was Developed

The development of the *Choose and Take Action* software program involved numerous steps. First, a group of teachers, adult-service-supported employment personnel, former students with a disability, parents, advocates for students with disabilities, and university faculty met to brainstorm. The group identified critical self-determination skills. Next, a project advisory panel (made up of transition specialists, teachers, former students, parents, agency and university personnel, and school administrators) voted on the relative importance of each skill area. Third, the development team along with representatives from three states spent several days creating a rough draft of the software specifications and functions. Fourth, the advisory panel reviewed and finalized the software plan. Fifth, the software plan underwent

FIGURE 9–7
Characteristics I Like Versus What Is Here Form B

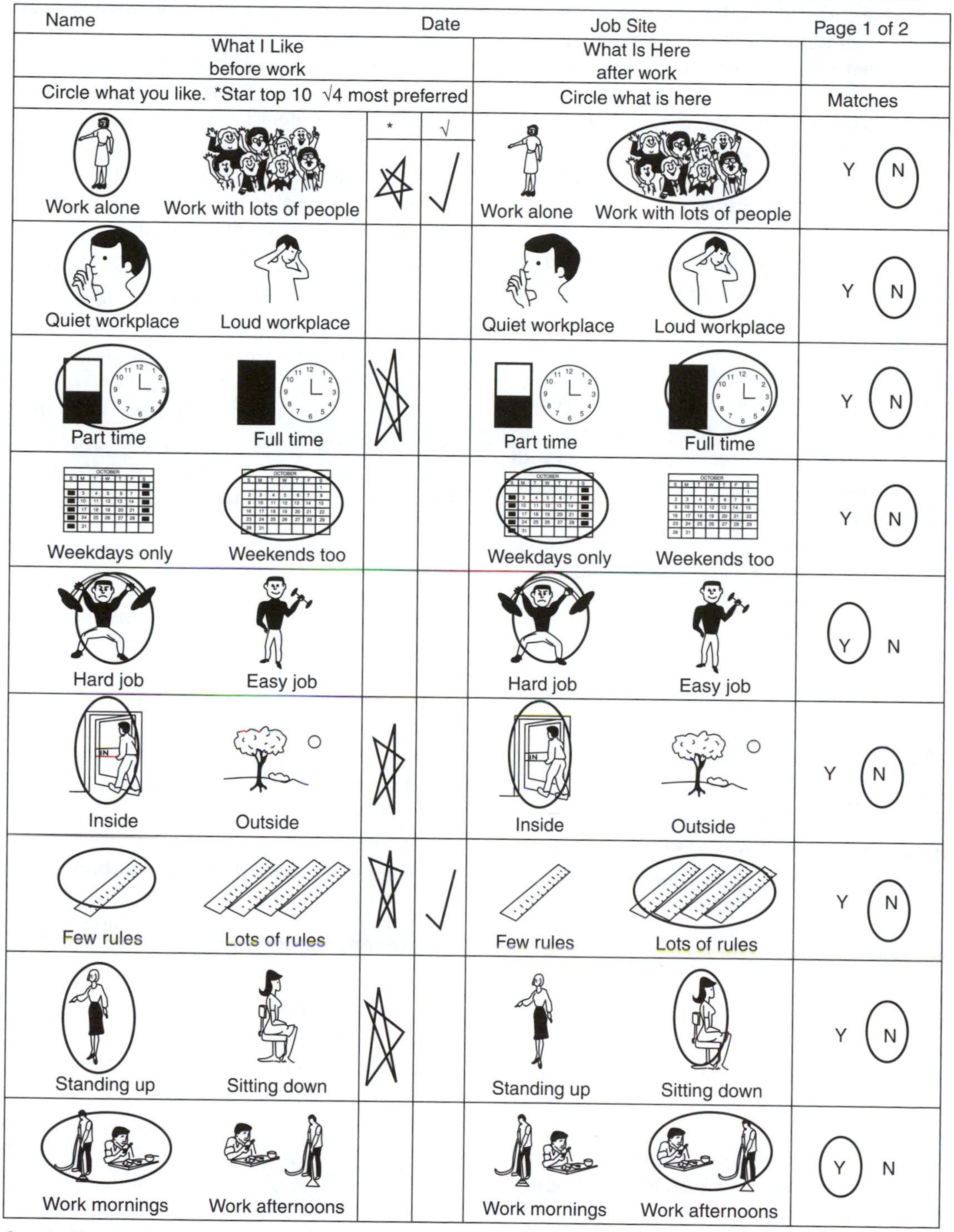

___ EXPLORING CHOICES
✓ TESTING CHOICES

Name	Date	Job Site	Page 1 of 2

What I Like before work		*	√	What Is Here after work		Matches
Circle what you like. *Star top 10 √4 most preferred				Circle what is here		
Work alone	Work with lots of people			Work alone	Work with lots of people	Y N
Quiet workplace	Loud workplace			Quiet workplace	Loud workplace	Y N
Part time	Full time			Part time	Full time	Y N
Weekdays only	Weekends too			Weekdays only	Weekends too	Y N
Hard job	Easy job			Hard job	Easy job	Y N
Inside	Outside			Inside	Outside	Y N
Few rules	Lots of rules			Few rules	Lots of rules	Y N
Standing up	Sitting down			Standing up	Sitting down	Y N
Work mornings	Work afternoons			Work mornings	Work afternoons	Y N

Source: Excerpt from: Martin, J. E., Mithaug, D. E., Oliphint, J. V., & Husch, J. (2002). *ChoiceMaker employment: A self-determination transition and supported employment handbook.* Baltimore: Paul H. Brookes.

a nationwide social validation process. Experts in transition, self-determination, employment for individuals with disabilities, individuals with disabilities, and parents reviewed the plan. Then, the comments and suggestions were incorporated into the software and lessons. Sixth, the software and lessons underwent extensive field-testing in four states, with their findings incorporated into the final product.

Daviso, Ackerman & Flexer (2003) found that the choices students make using the *Choose and Take Action* program correlates highly with the results of the *Becker Reading Free Interest Inventory*. Students chose the same types of jobs from both picture assessments. Student with severe disabilities demonstrated stable choices supporting the value of preference assessments with these students. Sylvester, Martin, Woods, and Christianson (2003) discovered that student-chosen job characteristics, tasks, and setting preferences do not match their caretakers' choices.

The *Choose and Take Action* Cycle

The *Choose and Take Action* cycle includes four steps. Students complete the first two cycle steps, choice making and plan development, in one session.

> **Step 1: Choice Making.** During choice making, students view pairs of randomly presented videos showing different employment settings, activities, and job characteristics. From each pair, students select the one they like the best. After they have viewed all the videos once, the ones they chose the first time are paired and the students choose again. This continues until students choose one final video option to try. Then, students develop a plan.
>
> **Step 2: Plan.** During the plan part of the program, students determine if they want to *watch* someone do the activity at their selected setting or if they want actually *to do* the activity. Printed plans are produced and shown with pictures that students chose: the setting, activity, two characteristics, and whether they want to watch or do the activities. The evaluation questions regarding these choices are also printed on the plan.
>
> **Step 3: Try It.** Based on the plan, the student goes into the community to "try it" at the chosen setting. Students will interact with the workers at the site as much as possible as they watch or do the activity.
>
> **Step 4: Evaluate.** Students, with the instructor's guidance, evaluate the experience, then they enter that information into the computer.

With each step, the teacher provides only instruction that the students require to complete the step independently. Of course, an educator will need to arrange the detail involved in visiting a "try-it" site. The *Choose and Take Action* software is designed for students with limited work experience; therefore, it is critical for students to complete the process a number of times in order to try many different things.

Video Clips

The software contains 31, 20-second video clips, across 14 employment settings and 15 activities. Twelve characteristics, each shown at least four times, are also included in the 31 video clips. Each video clip shows an employment setting, an entry-level activity, and two characteristics of the job. For each setting, there are two or three video clips showing a different activity, and each activity is shown in at least two settings.

The teacher may limit the number of video clips that a student will see in one session. The settings and activities shown in the video clips represent entry-level jobs and cover most job categories in the Department of Labor's *Occupational Outlook Handbook*. The jobs represent opportunities that are available in most communities. See Table 9–8 for a listing of video settings, activities, and characteristics.

Importance of Try-It

Students in the target population may have difficulty generalizing from what is depicted in the

TABLE 9–8
List of Setting, Activities, and Characteristics Included in the Video Clips

Settings	Activities	Characteristics
Auto dealer/mechanic	Assemble and disassemble	Spacious
Construction site	Bag items and bring in carts	Cozy space
Factory	Bus tables	Noisy
Florist/Green house/Nursery	Care for animals	Quiet
Grocery store	Care for people	Inside
Hospital/Nursing home	Care for plants	Outside
Hotel	Heavy cleaning	Wear own clothes
Janitorial service	Laundry	Wear a uniform
Landscape/Outdoor maintenance	Light cleaning	Many people
Office	Move materials	Few people
Restaurant	Filing	Messy
Retail	Paperwork	Clean
School/child care	Stock shelves	
Vet office/Kennel/Grooming	Wash dishes	
	Yard work	

video to a real setting. The videos give more information than a text or pictured version of an employment interest inventory, but they still do not exactly replicate the community settings students will visit. Students must go to the settings and try it to make their choices meaningful.

Reports

The software records students' choices throughout the program and creates reports indicating the students' choices in the choose, plan, and evaluate sections. There is also a place for instructors to record their observations and notes about the students' experiences and their discussions. Students will be able to graph their results on simple bar graphs. The reports and graphs will help students and the IEP teams to see the students' emerging interests and skill trends. These reports, including the instructor's evaluations and observations, may be included in a student portfolio. This provides information about students' preferences for IEP meetings and vocational assessments. This will give students a starting place for employment decision making.

Summary

The *Choose and Take Action* lesson package infuses the best of what is known about teaching self-determination with available technology. The use of interactive video software provides an additional means for students with severe needs to show teachers what they want.

Creating Opportunities to Practice Self-Determination Skills

Students with emotional and behavioral disorders (EBD) present a unique challenge to the transition process. Students with EBD have the lowest graduation rate of all students with disabilities, the highest dropout rate, and a high rate of contact with the criminal justice system (Blackorby & Wagner, 1996). Innovative practice for students with behavioral challenges provides the opportunity to combine self-determination instruction *and* effective behavioral support planning. The following examples show what we mean.

Traditional Approach

William, a 12th-grade student at a local high school, acts out chronically at his community-based vocational placement. The teaching team decides that a functional assessment is needed, and they spend several hours collecting data and observing William across settings, using both indirect and direct functional assessment methodologies. Upon completion of the functional assessment, the team convenes and develops a behavior support plan outlining a replacement response and teaching strategies to establish new and more appropriate behavior. After 3 weeks of implementing the support plan, the team becomes frustrated—William's acting-out has actually increased.

Student-Directed Functional Assessment and Behavior Support Planning

William's teaching team is more concerned than ever about William's increased chronic acting-out at his community-based vocational placement. This time, rather than using a traditional teacher-directed functional assessment, they involve William. The team meets with William over a morning snack to determine his beliefs regarding the problem behavior. William talks about his behavior at the vocational setting. With this new information, the team—with William as an equal member—conducts indirect and direct functional assessments. The collected data identify the perceived function or purpose of William's problem behavior. Following the functional assessment, William leads his behavior support planning meeting and shares with the teaching team what he learned. During the meeting, he identifies his interests, skills, and goals. The teaching team (with William as an equal member) writes a behavior support plan with instructional and support strategies, and environmental modifications to help William learn a new replacement response to his acting-out behavior. The behavior support plan is also incorporated into William's IEP.

Data are collected for several weeks by the teaching team *and* William. After 3 weeks the data clearly shows that the problem behavior has decreased and William's replacement behavior is being demonstrated consistently at his vocational placement and across other environments.

Opportunity for Participatory Decision Making

O'Neill et al. (1997) writes that a functional behavioral assessment is the result of an information gathering process that includes an analysis of the person's schedule, activity patterns, curricula, staff support, and physical environment, as well as the observation of the person's behavior in targeted settings where the problem behavior occurs and does not occur. When collected, this data is used to develop alternatives to the problem behavior that are functionally equivalent to the behavior of concern, while at the same time being more appropriate in targeted settings. O'Neil argues that functional behavioral assessments create a context for understanding problem behavior and are best used as a method to "maximize the effectiveness and efficiency of behavioral support" (p. 3).

Critical Point Students can participate in functionally assessing their own behaviors and in developing intervention strategies.

In most cases, educators and support staff complete the functional assessment and implement the behavior support plan without direct student input. But, there is an alternative that includes the student as a key person in this process. Students with emotional or behavioral disabilities who have learned to choose and attain goals have the skills that are necessary to set goals about their behavior, make plans to adjust their behavior, take action on their plan, self-monitor and self-record targeted behavior, and adjust goals and plans as the situation dictates. As students learn these important self-determination skills, they can become an increasingly effective member of their behavior support team.

Students with emotional or behavioral disabilities, or other students who exhibit chronic or persistent problem behavior that prevents them or their peers from receiving a reasonable educational benefit from the general curriculum, can and should participate in their own behavior support planning process. Important outcomes result when students participate in their behavior support planning, implementation, and evaluation processes. For example, students will: (a) *choose goals*—identify needs and interest based on the functional assessment data; (b) *express goals*—lead the behavior support planning meeting, which results in the development of a behavior support plan; and (c) *take action*—implement their behavior support plan, evaluate progress toward goal attainment, and make adjustments to their plan as needed.

Conclusion

Self-determination skills contribute to a successful transition. Since most students with an IEP lack well-developed self-determination skills, teaching these skills must become a priority in the transition process. For this to occur, self-determination must be considered as a transition need. Once the need becomes established, self-determination teaching goals detail what must be taught. Educators, then, must teach students self-determination skills and provide opportunities for students to practice and generalize their learned skills.

Study Questions

1. You are a member of a high school IEP team and believe that self-determination skills need to be taught to your students. How will you include self-determination in the IEP process?
2. From your knowledge of what takes place in secondary programs, identify at least three different ways that each self-determination concept depicted in Table 9–2 can be taught and practiced by students with high incidence disabilities.
3. Write a letter to your Congressional representative detailing how IDEA needs to be modified when the act is again authorized to make its self-determination emphasis even stronger than it is today.
4. Your team has a budget of $1,800 to purchase new materials. Go to the web sites of different educational publishing houses and build a purchase request document to submit to your principal. Include a description of the material, its use, how it will help to meet your students' IEP goals, and purchasing information. (See the list of web sites at the end of the chapter.)
5. Using your state's academic standards, write a standards-referenced IEP goal and objectives to teach a self-determination construct from Table 9–2.

Websites

Selected list of publishers that distribute self-determination materials:

Sopris West for *ChoiceMaker* materials
www.sopriswest.com

Brookes Publishing Company
www.pbrookes.com.

Pro-Ed
www.proedinc.com

Council for Exceptional Children
www.cec.sped.org/

Self-Determination Synthesis Project Homepage
www.uncc.edu/sdsp

10

Multicultural Competence for Working with Families

Pamela Luft

LEARNING OBJECTIVES

The objectives of this chapter are:

1. Describe at least two major reasons that transition team members can expect to work with culturally different families and students.
2. Compare some of the major differences between identified U.S./American beliefs and values and minority group beliefs and values in the areas of worldview, personal identity, disability, and relationships.
3. Explain cultural differences that may impact team processes for identifying and addressing the student's needs, interests, and preferences in the transition process.
4. Explain cultural differences that impact goal-setting and outcome-oriented processes of transition planning, including movement from school to postschool activities.
5. Describe potential conflicts in developing participatory decision making with families who are not acculturated into the American interaction style (e.g., represent culturally different groups) and culturally competent

and appropriate approaches to support such decision making.

6. Describe strategies for preparing staff and families in culturally competent interaction processes.

Introduction

It is increasingly likely that residents in the United States will work with and live near those who are culturally different from themselves. Minority populations in the United States are increasing in size (Bose, 1996; Garcia & Yates, 1986; Knopp & Otuya, 1995; Wald, 1996). This is confirmed by U.S. census data showing that between 1980 and 2000 average, minority populations grew 11 times as rapidly as the majority Caucasian population (U.S. Census Bureau, 2002, November). And within the past 10 years (1990 to 2000), although there was a 13.2% increase in overall population, minority populations grew more quickly: 15.6% increase in African American, 26.4% increase in American Indian/Alaska Native, 48.3% increase in Asian, and a 57.9% increase in Hispanic or Latino population. Of the total population, those of Hispanic or Latino descent now represent 12.5%, those who are African American are 12.3%, those who are Asian are 3.6%, and those who are American Indian and Alaska Native 0.9% (U.S. Census Bureau, 2001, March). Regardless of ethnicity, everyone is increasingly likely to have "close encounters" with those who are different from themselves.

This impacts work on IEP and transition teams in that team members are increasingly likely to work with minority students and families, as well as other team members. In addition, many of the legal mandates and transition components described in Chapters 1 and 2 are based on American cultural beliefs about disability, optimal outcomes for all people, and how best to achieve these outcomes. These are not shared by all cultural traditions so that in some ways, by complying with these mandates, people are being set up for cultural conflicts. A pervasive problem is that most individuals are most effective in working with those who are culturally similar to themselves (Lareau, 1989). Yet, professional team members are responsible for providing quality services to *all* students, families, and clients. How, then, can a team learn to move beyond its own cultural habits, as well as some of the legally proscribed education practices, to provide effective services to culturally different families (this means anyone who is culturally different from *themselves*)? This is not easily answered; it can be helpful to look at what culture means to people's daily lives.

Culture and Country Issues

People who live in the United States often think of themselves as supporting and accepting cultural diversity—the country, after all, is populated primarily by generations of immigrants. The Statue of Liberty publicly displays a welcome to the world, and the United States is viewed as the "melting pot" of cultures and ethnicities from around the globe (Bull, Fruehling, & Chattergy, 1992; Cordeiro, Reagan, & Martinez, 1994; DeVillar, 1994; Hanson, 1998a). In truth, harmony is not always achieved—ethnic violence and intolerance erupts periodically and is not easily resolved. As Bull et al., state, "contact between cultures—whether in inner-city New York, between ethnic groups in eastern Europe, among the tribes of Nigeria, or between religious factions in India—has long been the source of profound human suffering as well as mutual enrichment (p. 131)."

It is obvious that, in fact, tolerance for diversity is difficult—and it is because of human nature. People have an instinctive preference for cultural homogeneity in their daily lives (Brislin, 1993; Green, 1999). They wish to be with, and interact with, others who are like them. People who are alike tend to feel comfortable together, understand each other, and associate easily because they share general lifestyle and beliefs. Often it is a struggle to understand and interact with people who may have significantly different practices and beliefs from their own. Rather than a "melting pot," a better analogy of the United States is that of a "salad bowl" consisting of complementary but different elements, because diverse cultural groups don't often completely "meld" together (Cordeiro et al., 1994; DeVillar, 1994). By reading and examining culture and its omnipresence within our thoughts, feelings, behaviors, and interactions, the reader will better understand how and why conflicts occur and then acquire some strategies for positively negotiating potential differences. This chapter's overall goal is to help the reader begin the journey toward becoming culturally competent: to begin understanding cultural differences, to become more sensitive to their occurrence, and to better mediate between one's own beliefs and those that are highly dissimilar.

One fascinating aspect of culture is how its beliefs are translated into practices. The following section examines the four essential elements of transition in terms of cultural practices. The reader saw these in Chapters 1 and 2 and now will reexamine them through a different cultural lens. This will provide a sense of some of the conflictual situations into which teams and families are placed when making transition plans.

Cultural Perspectives and Transition Mandates

Legislation and policy are ways in which societal and cultural ideals and values are formalized (Cordeiro et al., 1994; Nieto, S., 2000), and the IDEA's four *essential elements* of transition represent a number of these values. The first essential element—*consideration of the student's needs, interests, and preferences*—mandates that the transition team individually assess the students' preferences for their future career and lifestyle. In the United States, an important cultural value is that of being independent and self-reliant as a means of achieving personal and social success (Althen, 1988; Dunn & Griggs, 1995; Green, 1999; Hammond & Morrison, 1996; Hanson, 1998a; Harry, 1992a; Hobbs, 1975; McPhatter, 1997; Pinderhughes, 1995). However, a number of other cultures place greater value on belonging to a group and do not prefer to be highly independent or self-reliant (Chan, 1998a; Hanson, 1998a; Harry, 1992a; Joe & Malach, 1998; Lynch, 1998b; Pinderhughes, 1995; Zuniga, 1998). These cultures believe that the needs, interests, and preferences of the group (e.g., the extended family, the neighborhood, the community, or the tribe) are more important than those of the individual. Some may not accept the notion of "student choice" but, rather, that the group's needs should be addressed before those of an individual (i.e., if the group is functioning effectively, then the individual's needs will be met). We need to be cautious in how we implement this "individualized" planning process and do so in a way that includes the parents and other family (or group) members, and values their input.

The second essential element of transition planning is to use an *outcome-oriented process*. Outcomes that are considered "positive" or "successful" are highly culturally defined (Nieto, 2000). For example, many people who are acculturated into the American value system (are accepting of these values) are likely to have personal goals for earning more money (Americans value financial success), buying a nicer car or home (accumulate material possessions), and having important or successful friends (social status) as ways to improve their quality of life. Achieving these things leaves Americans feeling successful and content. They may very much want transitioning students to have a well-paying job, to have a nice car and apartment or home, and to make friends with key coworkers and supervisors—these are often valued as "high expectations." In contrast, the student's family members may prefer that she or he live and work within the family or community (value on being with the group) and remain loyal to people in the community (personal worth gained through being honorable, respectful, and loyal) who were helpful in the past. These latter outcomes are valued much more highly by the family than are high salaries, social status, and so on (Harry, 1992a, 1992b; Turnbull, 1993; Turnbull, Barber, Kerns, & Behr, 1995). Therefore, the family's preferred outcome may be for their child to live at home because of her or his disability and to take a job with a long-time family friend. Team members must be careful that they do not impose *their* preferred outcomes or culturally defined "high expectations" on the student or family.

The third essential element of transition planning is *coordinated interagency responsibilities or linkages*. School personnel are mandated to invite individuals from adult service agencies and other community service organizations who are or will be assisting the student and family after the student leaves school. However, families may prefer to work within their extended family and community group. Some cultures have great difficulty in seeking help or in disclosing a need for help, and may not feel comfortable with a large group of individuals ("outsiders") discussing their or their child's "needs." Interagency personnel who attend one meeting annually with the parents may be viewed with some suspicion, and families may resist accepting advice or programming support from these individuals who "don't know the family." Teams need to be sensitive to the family's feelings regarding numbers of professionals at these meetings and the sometimes frequent "turnover" of positions.

The fourth essential element of transition is *movement from school to postschool activities*. As team members, one may not have thought of successful transition outcomes as cultural values—to live independently (or with a roommate), to have a job, to have friends outside of the family, and so forth. These expectations may create conflicts with families who view having single, unmarried children living outside the home as indicative of parental dysfunction and failure (Turnbull et al., 1995). Other families may expect all income earned by unmarried children to be given to the parents, without question, out of loyalty. The transition team needs to first ask the students and their families about postschool preferences and make no assumptions otherwise.

Because parent involvement remains a critical element in transition success (Salembier & Furney, 1997), teams who create conflictual situations may be puzzled later to find that transition plans are not succeeding. It is always important to engage the family in identifying mutually agreeable goals *before* moving into the planning phase. Team members need to watch for assumptions they may have about achieving a "high-quality" life, or "high expectations" and what "success" means, or whether self-determination or self-advocacy interventions correspond with the family's vision. For example, cultures that value group harmony and identity (through family, community, tribe, etc.) may not subscribe to American values of independent decision-making or advocacy skills. Such cultures have great faith in the group's ability to respond to the needs of the individual, in contrast with many middle-class Americans who have much more faith in the individual's ability to take care of himself or herself. The family may even view the team's advocacy suggestions as undermining their family and community harmony. Therefore, the transition team members should never presume that specific transition values are necessarily shared by the family (in fact, it's a good idea to ask *all* families first).

Critical Point Legislated and mandated transition practices often represent beliefs and values of mainstream society more than they represent those of diverse cultures. Professionals need cultural competence in successfully negotiating between these mandates and ethnically diverse families.

Now the reader has seen how cultural differences can lead to tremendous barriers in effective transition planning, and some of the cultural "traps" have been identified: in the legislation, the essential elements of transition, and in assuming that these values are shared by the family. The next sections will address why analyzing culture can be both difficult and frustrating, and its pervasiveness within societies and organizations.

The Problem of Cultural Awareness

One significant problem with studying and analyzing culture is that it remains largely invisible. Culture consists of the "ideals, values, and assumptions about life that are widely shared among people and that guide specific behaviors" (Brislin, 1993, p. 4). It is also "the complex, changing nexus of values, attitudes, beliefs, practices, traditions, and social institutions . . . of a community" that includes religion, language, foods, history, and dress (Cordiero et al., 1994, p. 20). These fluctuating attitudes, ideals, and assumptions remain largely internalized until a person calls upon them to guide his or her behavior. When values are not challenged, there are no visible behaviors that lead anyone to think about or remember a particular value. For example, cleanliness and personal hygiene habits generally are not an issue in a person's daily life until challenged by someone who, through physical appearance or smell, does not meet expected cultural standards (Brislin, 1993). When confronted by this difference, one's typical response is to "protect" the cultural value and to reaffirm how important it is. In this example, a person might reaffirm his or her belief in this value by describing how much "better" people are when they practice regular and thorough hygiene (e.g., they will experience negative consequences at work, socially, to their health, etc.).

Critical Point Our own cultural beliefs and values are generally invisible to people until those beliefs and values are challenged.

Cultural values often remain covert because people are socialized into their culture as children and guided into a particular set of behaviors and beliefs without considering them (Brislin, 1993; Lewis, 1997). These early, formative experiences make it difficult to distance oneself enough to analyze them. In addition, people who share the same culture rarely discuss their values and assumptions, reinforcing their hidden nature. For example, only when religious or democratic values are challenged (e.g., through the United States' engagement in the Middle East) do Americans discuss values and assumptions (such as, what it means to be a Christian, an American Muslim, or a Jew).

With much of culture nicely hidden away, when faced with a conflict, people often respond by reaffirming their own beliefs and behaviors as being "better," rather than "unearthing" the underlying core values and analyzing them and the contrasting value accordingly. Without training, these cultural conflicts may become intensified with each future encounter. In fact, people often find violations of their culture to be emotionally upsetting and vivid (Brislin, 1993). Such feelings are not likely to be aired or recognized at a team meeting, and therefore, may never be resolved.

The good news is that learning about cultural differences has been found to decrease negative emotional responses and discomfort when faced with a culturally conflicting situation (Brislin, 1993). Cross-cultural knowledge and skills allow people to feel more relaxed in these situations. Transition team members may not know much about a particular family's culture but by using more open and communication-fostering strategies, families will sense that the team is working to create a comfortable and positive interaction climate. This is an important first step for establishing open and trusting relationships with culturally different families, and ultimately, to more collaborative and effective interactions among all team members.

Control Issues and American Cultural Forces

By their very nature, societies use cultural values to proscribe and structure their interactions (male to female or female to female, adult to child, and so on) and how certain processes or tasks are organized (e.g., making decisions and solving problems) (Brislin, 1993; Lewis, 1997). In these ways, culture acts as a mechanism for social control (Gray, 1997). Societies also organize themselves by assigning power—through status and leadership roles. This same process occurs when two people of differing cultures meet: One culture will dominate, creating a high-status versus lower-status interaction (Althen, 1988; Green, 1999; Hanson; 1998a). It is the dominant culture that receives the higher status: Maintaining equality between diverse cultures is not typical. So another important factor in becoming culturally competent is recognizing the status and leadership role one often will be accorded when meeting a student or family member. One's status may be allocated based upon how strongly he or she represents the dominant culture, or in response to the family's own cultural beliefs about schools, school professionals, and what they believe a school professional's role should be in terms of their child's education. A family will accord a school professional a certain status and expect him or her to take on certain leadership roles. "Pretending" to be equals will not lead to honest and open communication; instead, one's role can help to ensure that the family feels listened to and respected with regard to their own experiences and beliefs, including cultural values.

Cultural Diversity and Conflicts

As stated previously, transition team members are likely to work with families and other team members who are culturally different from themselves. Because of increasing globalization and fluctuating immigration patterns, it is also likely that team members will meet certain families about whose cultural background they are moderately uninformed (regardless of how much of an expert they become). *Multiculturalism* is a concept used in this chapter that recognizes the diversity of cultures and ethnicities within the people of schools and community services, and the competencies across these diverse cultures that are important for professionals in these services. Professionals who learn the understandings, concepts, and strategies that support "cultural pluralism" will be better able to develop harmonious coexistence among the different cultures with whom they work (Green, 1999). *Cultural pluralism* is a belief that indicates an acceptance of cultural diversity as a valuable and worthwhile facet of a society. However, it is *cultural relativism* that holds that it is neither possible nor desirable to evaluate or judge cultural patterns, practices, or beliefs of a community by using the standards of another community (Cordiero et al., 1994, p. 20). Developing a resistance to "evaluating" other cultures is one of the first precepts of cultural competence.

Cultural competence, then, begins with an understanding of, and respect for, cultures and ethnic backgrounds and their impact on ourselves and others (Green, 1999; Lynch, 1998b). It does not consist of a single set of skills or knowledge for working across all cultures, because "culture" and "competence" vary with the situation and those people involved (Green, 1999; Lynch, 1998b). Like culture itself, competence evolves and is flexible, to support "the ability of service providers to respond optimally to all children, understanding both the richness and the limitations of the sociocultural contexts in which children and families as well as the service providers themselves, may be operating" (Barrera & Kramer, 1997, p. 217). Just as there is no "one" right answer, there also is no "one" correct culture, or set of beliefs or behaviors (that is *cultural relativism* in practice). The next section discusses some of the special challenges of trying to maintain a multicultural, and cultural relativistic perspective in our schools.

Critical Point Cultural competence is built upon an understanding of, and respect for, the many different cultures of the world. It leads to the ability to respond in optimal ways with all children and their families, within both the richness and limitations of our current sociocultural environments.

Cultural Diversity in Special Education

The context of schools and special education offers strong beliefs in supporting children and their families but also offers some contradictions. These can greatly complicate people's efforts to become culturally competent and support all families, especially if they are unaware. For example, many individuals have entered special education and disability services because they enjoy helping others who have special challenges. However, the history of the special education profession has not been altogether altruistic.

One ongoing problem for special education programs has been their tendency to have minorities overrepresented in comparison to their proportions within the larger society (Donovan & Cross, 2002; Sarason & Doris, 1979). The first compulsory education laws passed during the 1880s, were attempts to socialize immigrant Catholic children in what was a traditionally Protestant country (Hobbs, 1975). Special education programs at this time were used to classify and segregate immigrant Irish, Italians, Hungarians, Germans, Russians, and other groups and to isolate them from the more established American children (Sarason & Doris, 1979). Intelligence tests were used to show that these children were inferior and needed special classroom placement; professional educators realize now that these tests and their procedures were highly biased.

Students are identified for special education through referral and assessment processes; however, several lawsuits have documented that these processes can become biased and unfair (Turnbull, 1993). Therefore, Public Law (P.L. 94-142) and IDEA require that these decisions be based on multiple measures (not just on one test) and that all assessments be done in the child's primary language or mode of communication, administered by trained personnel, with each instrument testing specific areas of educational need (Turnbull, 1993; van Keulen, Weddington, & DeBose, 1998). At least one person on the multidisciplinary team must have knowledge in the area of the suspected disability. Essentially, schools refer students who aren't progressing and succeeding as expected, for a number of reasons. But because definitions of "success" and "typical expectations" are highly culturally-bound, children from culturally different families are at high risk for referral. In fact, this has been the pattern found.

The U.S. Department of Education Office for Civil Rights (OCR) has monitored ethnic proportions in special education classes since P.L. 94-142 was passed, and results consistently show an overrepresentation of minorities in special education programs. Until 1985, twice as many African-American students were placed in classes for mild mental retardation, and 1.5 times as many were placed in classes for severe behavior disorders (U.S. Department of Education, 1987). Latino students in Texas were categorized with learning disabilities at a rate of 315% relative to their population (Holtzman, 1986). More recent data (U.S. Dept. of Education, 1994, 1997) still showed high placement rates for Native American and Latino students in classes for students with mental retardation. The Committee on Minority Representation in Special Education recently evaluated OCR and Office of Special Education Program (OSEP) datasets (1997 and

1999) and still found patterns of racial overrepresentation in many disability categories: African American and American Indian/Alaskan Native children remain at an increased risk of identification for mental retardation and emotional disturbance, and males were more likely to be in all high-incidence disability categories. There also was significant placement rate variation among states (Donovan & Cross, 2002), again suggesting that certain mandated processes are not applied equitably. In general, despite mandates for fair assessment and placement processes, minority students continue to be placed into special education programs at a higher than expected rate (Burnette, 1998; Greenberg, 1986; Harry, 1992a; Markowitz, 1996; Reschly, 1997; Russo & Talbert-Johnson, 1997; Sarason & Doris, 1979; U.S. Dept. of Education, Office of Civil Rights, 1987, 1994, 1997).

This, then, creates a compounded problem: Special education shows a pattern of overrepresentation of minority children *in addition* to the increasing size of previously identified "minority groups." Van Keulen et al. (1998) predicted that by the year 2000, minority children would constitute one-third of all children, and that by 2030, this figure would be 41% of the child population. In fact, in the year 2000, 62.5% of the school-age population (or five-eighths, and less than two-thirds) was white alone (non-Hispanic) with 14.9% African American, 14.9% Hispanic or Latino, 4.3% Asian, and 1.1% American Indian/Alaskan (U.S. Census Bureau, 2003, August). This suggests that increasingly large numbers of students are at risk of being placed in special education (Greenberg, 1986).

What are some of the cultural differences that lead to placement? Differences in behavioral and personal interaction styles and in learning styles (global and holistic versus linear and analytic), and, as a result of bilingual communication, may be misinterpreted as evidence of a disability (Burnette, 1998; Turnbull, 1993). Few school professionals are trained to provide multicultural special education assessments or classroom interventions (Burnette, 1998; Obiakor & Utley, 1996; Talbert-Johnson, 1998). Consequently, referral teams rarely examine classrooms or schools for cultural factors that may contribute to a child's difficulties, nor do they consider culturally specific attributes and skills that the child *is* able to perform successfully (Burnette, 1998; Cummins, 1986; Obiakor & Utley, 1996; Simich-Dudgeon, 1986; Willig, 1986). These same behavioral, interpersonal, learning, and communication concerns apply to transition teams. Therefore, when plans and interventions are not progressing as expected, we should examine if prerequisite behaviors or beliefs are present, or even valued, in a culturally different child.

Critical Point Lack of cultural competence in identifying and assessing ethnically diverse children who demonstrate authentic disabilities continues to lead to high rates of referral and placement in special education programs.

For many reasons, public schools and agencies often are organized along the lines of mainstream American beliefs and values. Therefore, it also is likely that culturally different families and students may already have experienced cultural barriers and conflicts during referral and assessment processes; during classroom interactions and activities; and in their previous communications with teaching, administrative, and agency personnel. By middle and high school, families have had years of working with schools and services. The general lack of cultural training for many public service professionals means that transition team members will not be equipped with awareness, information, and strategies for building trust and negotiating these types of difficulties.

Critical Point Ethnically diverse families and children may have had poor prior experiences with professionals who did not recognize or value their cultural differences. They may have difficulties trusting and communicating with the team until members demonstrate their cultural competence and sensitivity.

Setting the Stage for Cultural Conflicts

The high rate of minority group presence in special education classes means that transition teams are likely to work with families who are culturally different (Wald, 1996). A further complication is that the demographics of personnel in education and other public services (e.g., counselors, social workers, etc.) show that teachers and professionals are primarily white, middle class, and female (Burnette, 1998; Eubanks, 1996; Moores, 1996). Proportionally fewer members of minority groups become special educators and the number of African-American personnel is expected to continue to decline (Sexton, Lobman, Constans, Snyder, & Ernest, 1997). The result is that few students of color, or who are male, can expect to have teachers of similar backgrounds (Knopp & Otuya, 1995; Simpson, 1997).

Individuals who are socially or culturally different usually have much greater difficulty in achieving equal levels of societal access to its rewards. This gets back to the issue of comfort and ease of communication. For example, parents who are middle or upper-middle class have been found to be more successful in creating genuinely individualized IEPs for their child that represent a broader range of options than typically made available to minority and lower- or working-class parents (Lareau, 1989; Lynch & Stein 1987; Mehan, Hertweck, & Meihls, 1983). One of the reasons this occurs is that middle- and upper-middle-class parents interact more easily with school and agency staff; and when individuals feel more comfortable with each other and share the same basic values, their interactions tend to be much more successful. So minority parents and their children are unlikely to work with personnel who are ethnically like them, and are also less likely to be successful in their IEP and planning meetings.

Add to this the fact that minority groups are overrepresented in the lower-income and among the country's poorest groups (Dennis & Giangreco, 1996; Fujiura & Yamaki, 1997; Harry, 1992a; Janesick, 1995; Miller & Roby, 1970; Rose, 1972). For example, 31% of African Americans, 26% of Hispanics, and 10% of white Americans lived below the poverty level in 1989. In 1999 these figures were 24.9%, 22.6%, and 8.1%, respectively with an overall rate of 12.4%—not a big improvement (U.S. Census Bureau, 2003, May). Immigrants who do not move into an existing and well-established support system can experience lower social status as a result of being a minority, which can result in poorer income potential. Families who struggle with both language and cultural barriers also are likely to have poor wages and limited employment opportunities. In summary, minority families are statistically more likely to be poor. In addition, they are more likely to have their children placed in special education and to work with professionals who are culturally different than themselves, and also less likely to have a successful IEP plan.

Critical Point Those who represent a national or ethnic "ideal" tend to have the most prestige and power; those who are further from this ideal are frequently marginalized, with decreased power over their own lives.

Because the majority of professionals are white, middle-class females, they may not be able to evaluate accurately the quality of services when working with culturally different families. This is because perceptions of services and family satisfaction often are gauged through culturally-based behaviors. For example, family members may smile, greet, and interact with team members pleasantly and appear to have few questions or concerns. Yet, this may not reflect their satisfaction with services. A comparison of African-American and Caucasian early intervention specialists found that the

Caucasian personnel rated their services to African-American parents higher than did their African-American peers (Sexton et al., 1997), including:

1. Openness to input from parents.
2. Establishing positive relationships with parents.
3. Actively encouraging parents to be involved in their children's program.
4. Services were a positive experience for children and their families.

The families did not concur with these evaluations. This is compounded by frequent lack of training in this area (Markowitz, 1996). Professionals need to be cautious and ascertain satisfaction in other, less culturally bound ways. Minority parents clearly have some issues to contend with when working with our schools.

Examining American Cultural Values

American Values and Beliefs

Despite the (continuing) history of diverse immigration waves in the United States, there is a set of identified American values and norms. These are the typical standards for behavior within American culture and are primarily reflected in the lifestyle of the white, middle, and upper-middle class (Althen, 1988; Dunn & Griggs, 1995; Green, 1999; Hanson, 1998a; Harry, 1992a; McPhatter, 1997; Pinderhughes, 1995). This group holds a majority of powerful societal positions and uses its class-based power to influence government, legal, and social processes: Its tax base supports the country; it lobbies for changes in laws; it serves on public school boards that decide curriculum and teaching practices; and it provides the majority of civil servants, such as police, teachers, and government workers.

Many American cultural values were brought with the pilgrims and reinforced by pioneer movements into the unknown West. Values include industry, success and achievement, civic-mindedness, usefulness, individualism and personal choice, self-reliance and independence from others, privacy, equality, informality, future orientation and progress, and a focus on efficient management (Brookhiser, 1991; Hammond & Morrison, 1996; Hobbs, 1975; Stewart, Danielian, & Festes, 1969). These translate into behaviors such as keeping busy, setting personal goals, reading self-help books (i.e., independent self-improvement), rating importance of an activity and giving time according to immediate "relevance," expecting meetings to follow an agenda and a time schedule, successfully competing against others (for individual honors, grades, salaries, etc.), addressing problems succinctly and rationally, and using day planners to maintain organization and efficiency (scheduling leisure and family activities as well as professional meetings and appointments; leisure should be goal oriented to achieve fitness or health).

Assimilation and Acculturation of Values

Professionals who work with and study immigrant people often view them in terms of steps they have made toward "assimilation" or "acculturation" (Green, 1999; Lynch, 1998a; Joe & Malach, 1998). These steps categorize individuals in terms of their acceptance of the dominant cultural characteristics of a particular society, in contrast with those who retain their native language and habits (considered to be "traditional"). These same concepts can be applied to educator professionals. As "successful" individuals, educators have acquired certain of the standard American cultural values, or live within these expectations. They may display more or less of the typical values depending upon the situation and its context.

Green (1999) proposes an alternative view that defines the entire concept of ethnicity and acculturation as "situational" rather than absolute, and is modified to suit the needs of various types of cross-cultural encounters. For example, a family may adhere to ethnic patterns while in their community by celebrating festivals, eating traditional foods, and socializing with others; however, they may accept the dominant culture's standards about work, housing, and traumatic health care (Green, 1999; Hanson, 1998a). In addition, degree of acculturation depends on many factors, including Socio-economic Status (SES), generational status, religion, age at immigration, language ability, education level, gender, cultural attitudes, length of residence in majority language country, and personality factors (Lynch & Hanson, 1992).

This perspective allows family members to become increasingly bicultural, according to situational demands. They may retain traditional values that they believe are important, but they also can learn to use IEP/ITP meetings in a more "Americanized" way to support their child's development. This view also allows professionals to support families who may wish to learn specific skills that will increase their sense of success at these meetings, without feeling that they have to address the full range of culturally different behaviors and values.

A family's affiliation with their cultural group may change with their acculturation into American lifestyles. This will depend on a number of factors described earlier, including if they live within a strong minority community, if they have American relatives nearby, if they had previous exposure to American cultural values, if they are recent immigrants, and if they desire to accept American values. A family's level of acculturation also may change over time and between generations. The child may have different perspectives on the American lifestyle in comparison to his or her parents or extended family members. These perspectives may change as the child develops and has either positive or negative interactions with American cultural values. The transition team will need to know how the family interprets and reinterprets adulthood for their child in terms of these ongoing bicultural issues (Harry, 1992a).

One further note: Our profession requires us to obtain advanced levels of education in order to deliver services. For successful professionals, this also attests to a certain level of "acculturation" achieved, perhaps unconsciously and regardless of ethnicity. This educational and professional status often is perceived by others as power, which becomes important in interaction with families. Those who are recent immigrants are likely to have less education and lower income-earning power, while professionals are likely to have a higher social status than the families they work with (Green, 1999). These differences need to be considered carefully when interacting and negotiating plans with these families.

Contrasting Transition Values

Table 10–1 lists some of the differences between American and other cultures regarding several transition practices. For example, interaction differences impact how team members establish open, trusting, and collaborative relationships with families. The other ideals, values, and beliefs that are mandated and expected in the transition planning process can lead to cultural conflicts. The following sections describe some of the key contrasting values to alert the reader to potential difficulties.

Contrasting Values of Identity

Several cultures emphasize group identity rather than individualism, and the child's future roles may be defined as his or her place within the family or group structure. The family also may disagree with, or see as destructive and undermining, transition team goals to develop their child's independence, self-reliance, and abilities

TABLE 10–1
Key Cultural Differences Between U.S./ American and Other Cultural Groups

Cultural Characteristic	U.S/American Cultural Value	Culturally Contrasting Value
Cooperation versus competition	Society (and public schools) encourage doing better than others as proof of mastery; games are based on having a winner and loser; winners in a variety of activities are regularly rewarded.	Cooperative societies work together to achieve a mutual goal; children may be taught to wait until everyone has finished so that no one is embarrassed; individual achievement is likely to be less motivating in comparison to roles as family member and group or community pride.
Individual versus family or group orientation	Standard value on small, nuclear family units with little reliance on the extended family. Use of professional assistance and services when issues cannot be resolved within the nuclear family unit.	Importance of extended family or group and blood kinship lineage, with respect for elders and ancestors. Child's achievement (or disability) may reflect upon the entire family. Family and group identity may be of primary importance and contribute to the family's reputation, status, cohesiveness, and sense of collective (group) responsibility.
Time orientation	Time is measured and used efficiently; punctuality is expected and rewarded. People wear watches and professionals use appointment calendars; wasting time or lateness is viewed negatively. Monochronic orientation for doing one thing at a time—for example, "business before pleasure," and students work without talking or distractions.	Time is "given" in many other parts of the world and is generously shared; quality of interpersonal relationships takes priority. Polychronic time orientation handling several interactions and activities simultaneously, encouraging business and pleasurable activities together; appear to have several individuals talking at the same time with intermittent listening, laughing, and commenting.
Gender roles and responsibilities	Traditional nuclear family remains the ideal with a working father and stay-at-home mother who cares for the family's emotional and physical needs; this is responding to increased single-parent homes and working mothers with greater role and gender flexibility.	Some cultures have strict gender-based roles with pampering of young males and girls caring for younger siblings with home responsibilities and limited independence. Some discourage conversations between children/adults, or males/females until appropriate times. Some groups have highly adaptable family roles among parents, extended family, and older children.
Interaction style	Tendency to be direct with a topic, factual and impersonal. There is an expectation to identify and address difficulties and conflicts	May use indirect means to address a topic with requirements to begin serious discussions with initial, interpersonal, and social interactions. May use a more

(continued)

TABLE 10–1 *(continued)*

Cultural Characteristic	U.S/American Cultural Value	Culturally Contrasting Value
	directly, including expression of related concerns and use of a highly verbal style. Laughing and giggling are expressions of enjoyment. Typically, focus on one topic or activity at a time. Americans tend to prefer more interaction space than many Latinos, southern Europeans, and Middle Easterners; less than African Americans and Asians.	emotive style or an unobtrusive, nonemotive interaction style depending on group. Status, authority, and roles of interaction partners may be very important and dictate specific styles. Southeast Asians may see laughing and giggling as a sign of extreme embarrassment or discomfort. Loud talking or personal contact may be rude or offensive; others see it as natural expression and friendliness. May be comfortable with multiple conversations simultaneously. Interpersonal space preferences vary widely with culture.
Fate versus individual	There is very little that cannot be controlled—cars, services, utilities, or medical interventions. Emphasis is on individual rights and responsibilities, self-determination and autonomy. Is rewarded for taking care of one's own needs independently.	May believe that control lies outside the individual, with external forces largely responsible for what happens to people. Value on harmonious existence with surroundings and circumstances. May feel responsibility toward oneself as is reflected in terms of family and group roles, not through own achievements.

Source: This table is based on Chan (1998a, 1998b), Green (1999), Hanson (1998b), Harry (1992a, 1992b, 1992c), Joe and Malach (1998), Lynch (1998a, 1998b), Sharifzadeh (1998), van Keulen et al. (1998), and Willis (1998).

to make his or her own decisions and choices. Several cultures have very different values about young adult independence from parents with age expectations that are both younger and older than typical American youths.

Contrasting Views of Disability

In the United States, we tend to believe in a "medical model" for diagnosing and curing disabilities. The result is an ever-growing list of identified disabilities (Ysseldyke, Algozzine, & Thurlow, 1992). Not all cultures recognize this variety and number of disabilities. For example, some cultures focus only on obvious physical or mental disabilities (Harry, 1992a; Zuniga, 1998). Many mild disability categories are what other cultures perceive as part of a normal range of behaviors. Families may have great difficulty in understanding why their child is being identified as "problematic" and placed in specialized programming. Their religious or cultural beliefs may result in much less of an urgency for intervention planning and remediation because it is their "fate" or a result of "God's plan".

In terms of transition planning outcomes, the family may be completely committed to allowing their child with a significant disability to remain at home under their protection and love.

For a child with a mild disability, the family may believe that the school's elaborate transition plans are unnecessary and that their child will be a successful adult within the community and its support system. Families may not view transition planning as important because they do not foresee a future that is problematic. They believe that the family or community structures will provide the necessary supports. Other families may believe that the disability reflects poorly upon the family, and they are very uncomfortable discussing these issues in the detail that Americans prefer.

Contrasting Values for Family Relationships

American families remain focused on the nuclear family as the center of all primary relationships. Other cultures that utilize wide kinship or community webs may not view parents as the primary decision makers or caretakers. Such parents may even view their signatures on IEP/ITP documents as meaningless because they lack the formal approval of their extended family or community group. Another difference is that child-rearing practices are culturally based; some do not focus on independence and self-reliance, or reflect development milestones that include the age at walking, talking, and toilet training (i.e., these are often viewed as a *critical* event by both American professionals and parents). In many Asian cultures, young children are not diapered but are expected to relieve themselves freely and are washed as needed. Older children and adults may feed young children for an extended period because caring for a younger child, or also a child with a disability, is not viewed as a burden (Lynch, 1998a). These are viewed as part of the normal interdependence (versus American independence) of family members on each other.

Table 10–2 summarizes key aspects of transition planning and their impact on families. The table also suggests potential negative impacts when professionals are unaware of the impact of their own values and behaviors and ways to resolve some of these differences. For example, schools and agencies often schedule IEP/ITP meetings in one-hour blocks to promote efficiency and rational decision making, with little time spent in building a relationship with family members. Schools may not invite key family or community decision makers, which can confuse and insult them.

When cross-cultural conflicts are not resolved, families and professionals may become increasingly confused and distrustful of each other. Initial barriers are likely to become more solidified as each responds in culturally appropriate, but cross-culturally offensive, ways. Culturally diverse families may withdraw out of respect or to allow the school to save face, or they take steps within their own family or community that address their child's issues that are very different from school expectations. Families may be puzzled and hurt that school personnel spend so little time establishing relationships with the extended family and their community as well, which would demonstrate their commitment to a genuine understanding of their child. They may interpret meetings based on rapid decision making and problem resolution as rude, overbearing, and controlling (Harry, 1992a).

Schools, however, are expecting families to comply with the signed documents (Harry, 1992a). Personnel may conclude that the family is either unable or unwilling to follow the plans. They may be evaluating them to be "bad parents," who lack both caring and commitment to their child (Harry, 1992a, 1992b, 1992c). In these cases, personnel often limit the information and choices presented to parents (Lynch & Stein, 1987; Mehan et al., 1986). Across 12 studies, Harry (1992a) found that minority parents were less involved and less informed, and parents felt that the professionals implicitly or explicitly discouraged their participation.

TABLE 10–2
Potential Impacts and Resolution of Cultural Differences

	ITP Legislative Mandates and Practices	Contrasting Cultural Values	Results of Unresolved Conflicts	Culturally Competent Responses
Goals of the IEP/ITP planning processes	Identify student's skills, needs, preferences, achievement levels. Identify goals and plan steps to achieve desired outcomes.	Contribute to group and family needs, and listen to others. Build relationships that value communication, harmony, and personal/family honor.	Schools limit the information or choices given to families. Families are offended that key members are excluded from meetings Families may not voice concerns out of respect or due to status differences.	Be alert to goal and outcome differences; begin with personal interactions (visiting). Establish a trusting relationship with family (regarding cultural preferences for formal/informal, gender, and role-consciousness).
Transition outcomes for students	To develop independence, self-reliance, assertiveness, and economic success for work, ability to live alone (with minimal support), and satisfying leisure activities.	To develop group interdependence, social harmony, and extended support networks that contribute to the family and community. To develop non-competitive attributes and skills with a focus on relationships and respect for others.	Schools judge families as unable or unwilling to work toward critical goals. Families withdraw or "ignore" advice from school; may not attend future meetings.	Gradually begin to solicit from family members their description of preferred adult outcomes (in a culturally appropriate manner). Negotiate differences by suggesting a variety of alternatives and explain rationale for professional suggestions in a culturally appropriate way.

Examining Cultural Beliefs of Other Groups

Thus far we have examined some typical American values and how they impact transition services planning, at times developing into conflicts and uncomfortable encounters. Without training and intervention, it is likely that neither the professional personnel on the team nor the families will have the skills to resolve this situation. The next section moves toward providing information on some of these skills by describing key information about, and values of, a number of cultural groups within the United States. This will help in realizing that any resolutions must be done in appropriate interaction styles, and that account for key areas of difference in worldview, family structure, child rearing, and beliefs about disability.

These descriptions should be read within a paradigm of diversity: Each family and individual chooses to ascribe to, and to express, each value or belief in potentially unique ways; acculturation is situational and families and individuals may or may not choose to adhere to more Americanized beliefs or values at any point in time; and culture is continually evolving (Cordiero et al., 1994; Green, 1999; Hanson, 1998a; Lynch & Hanson, 1992). So these descriptions are only starting points, to help expand cultural referencing during the ongoing process of monitoring for cultural conflicts.

Native American Values and Beliefs

These groups in the United States include 517 separate tribes or nations with over 150 languages. There is tremendous diversity and cultural differences that exist particularly among the Navajo, Eskimo, and Cherokee peoples (Dunn & Griggs, 1995). General tribal interests and life pathways often are similar although tribal customs and languages, and life practices frequently are unique (Hanson, 1998b). Their existence has been significantly influenced by life on the reservation, although more than one-half do *not* live there. Native Americans live in most major U.S. cities and although many are part of mainstream society, many also retain their traditional beliefs and values to some degree.

Levels of affiliation with tribal members and traditions may vary greatly; however, tribes often continue to provide a strong level of personal and cultural identification. Much of the Native American culture of today has been influenced by adaptive and acculturation strategies from three centuries of contact with a highly dissimilar and somewhat hostile U.S. government, lifestyle philosophy, and social organization. The Bureau of Indian Affairs continues to exert a strong influence and exists as a separate governmental body in the United States (Hanson, 1998b; Joe & Malach, 1998).

Wide cultural belief and value differences exist between Native American people and U.S./American perspectives on relationships with and dominance over nature, paths to harmonious lifestyles, family structure, child rearing, interaction and communication, and causation of disabilities. This can lead to profound differences in goals for transition planning and definitions of an optimal adult lifestyle. Communication styles are much less direct with times for silence: American values of communication directness and efficiency with meetings, according to a time line and agenda, can very negatively affect trust, communication, and participatory decision making.

African-American Values and Beliefs

This group includes people from West Africa, the Caribbean, and those who have lived in the United States for many generations, resulting in many different cultural patterns, lifestyles, and beliefs. As a whole, these people have distinct patterns of thinking, feeling, and acting, some of which have developed as an adaptation to discrimination and their history of slavery. The family, marriage, and kinship bonds are extremely important and the impacts of slavery on relationships can still be seen. African American family members may or may not live together (often misinterpreted by American culture as family instability). Great value is placed on the extended family, blood relatives, and strong kinship networks with multigenerational social networks for relatives, friends, and neighbors.

Family remains the source of their culture, providing socialization and guidance with a great value on communication. The family provides members with a sense of who they are, including their relationship with the dominant white culture. Family structure is significantly impacted by socioeconomic class (lower versus middle or upper class) and rural versus urban location. There is comparatively higher unemployment, which impacts families in terms of health and poverty despite a higher rate of working mothers, than found among many white Americans. Family structure is more flexible with collective responsibility and sharing of child care across family and community relationships. The American meeting and communication styles that focus on direct, assertive, and nonemotive recitation of "facts," with expectations of timely decision making can all negatively impact effective collaborative planning with the family. If the team is primarily white, the family may be suspicious and challenge opinions and educational options recommended by the team.

Latino People's Values and Beliefs

Latinos include people from Mexico, Puerto Rico, Cuba, and Central and South America, with specific cultural characteristics that are unique to each geographic area. Puerto Ricans are the second largest Latino group in the United States (Mexicans are the largest), with Central and South Americans the fastest growing group. Cubans tend to have more economic success; Central Americans immigrate for job opportunities but often experience greater levels of poverty. Family commitment is of paramount importance to all, including loyalty to family, a strong family support system, and a view that the child reflects upon the honor of the family. There may be a strongly hierarchical order among siblings with a duty to care for members who have a disability, are ill, or are elderly.

Ethnic networks and supports are very important for teaching families about resources, procedures, and mechanisms of organizations in the United States. This is especially important for Latina women when they no longer have family or community networks from home; the barrio church often provides important sources of help. Many communities offer support groups for parents with some of the more common disabilities (e.g., cerebral palsy or Down syndrome).

Strong cultural differences with American values may occur in the strong focus on the family and community for a sense of identity and appropriate life roles (gender and age-specific). Planning processes and outcomes may be influenced by interaction styles that expect greater attention to group issues and familial well-being than to individuals within the group. Relationships are very important and support personal values of trustworthiness, loyalty, and respect.

Asian-American Values and Beliefs

An older term, "Asian-Pacific Americans," has been separated to differentiate between the many widely varying beliefs and values (Pacific Island Americans are described separately). Asian Americans include ethnic groups that originate from: east Asia—China, Japan, and Korea; Southeast Asia—Burma, Cambodia, Indonesia, Laos, Malaysia, the Philippines, Singapore, Thailand, and Vietnam; and south Asia—India, Pakistan, Sri Lanka, Bangladesh, Bhutan, and Nepal (Chan, 1998a; Dunn & Griggs, 1995). Although several Asian-American groups are known for their industriousness and economic success, other refugees (e.g., from Cambodia, Laos, and Vietnam) tend to have high rates of unemployment and low wages.

These diverse groups represent a variety of religions, beliefs, and lifestyles. Hindus believe in reincarnation, a respect for all living things, and the worship of many gods. Muslims believe in one God and strive to live in accord with the five pillars of their religion, including daily confessions of faith, praying five times daily, charity to those less fortunate, fasting during the ninth month, and a pilgrimage to Mecca at least once during their lifetime. The majority from Southeast Asia practice Buddhism, which believes in peace, harmony, strong family commitment, nonmaterialism, and avoidance of extremes. Those from east Asia practice either Confucianism, Taoism, or Shintoism, which follow a set of ethical standards, including obedience to authority, honesty, kindness, and respect for elders. Refugee groups may retain tribal beliefs such as spiritualist and animist practices.

All these religions share deference to authority, emotional restraint, specified roles defined in paternalism (i.e., men and elders enjoy greater status than women and children); a hierarchical, extended family orientation; interdependence; harmony with nature; and commitment to learning and academic achievement. Although these groups are primarily and strongly patriarchal in their families, there are several strong matriarchal groups.

Wide differences with American culture occur in these religious practices and worldviews, including peace and harmony (nondominance over nature and others), strong family commitments that extend to previous generations, and strong social roles and proscribed relationships. These impact transition outcome goals and self-determination and also often conflict with American preferences for communication that is flexible in role, informal, assertive, and direct.

Pacific Island-American Values and Beliefs

This group includes the Pacific Rim islands (people from the Philippines, Indonesia, and Polynesian islands of Hawaii, Samoa, and native New Zealanders) as a separate cultural group. Indonesia is strongly influenced by Muslim and Asian religions; however, there also is a strong Christian presence. For example, Filipinos are primarily Catholic, and Hawaiians are strongly Christian (Chan, 1998b; Mokuau & Tauili'ili, 1998). The Christian religions emphasize brotherly love, justice, and charity as strong values. The influence of Asian religious beliefs encourages obedience to authority, honesty, kindness, and respect for elders with strong links to ancestors. There is a tendency toward paternalism in certain cultures, although Polynesian cultures have strong matriarchal structures. The influence of native folk beliefs and Asian religions are the most contrasting cultural differences and include social structure and child-rearing practices.

Filipinos tend to be highly educated with professional backgrounds but experience underemployment when their professional training is not recognized in the United States. Native Hawaiian and Samoan families value education, but economic and social factors have led to a lower success rate.

Becoming Culturally Competent

Developing Cultural Skills

To put this new cultural learning in some cultural context: U.S. culture likes the "facts" about things, and so these "facts" about the cultures have been duly provided. It is important that educators use these "facts" carefully and thoughtfully with children and families; otherwise they may contribute to more historical prejudice and superficial overgeneralizations (Bull, Fruehling, & Chattergy, 1992). Any summary description, of course, neglects the diversity within these groups. And any immigrating group to a particular area of a country will emerge as somewhat different from those who immigrate elsewhere, despite their common origins. For example, the culture of descendants of Japanese immigrants to Hawaii will be different from those who settled in California as a result of their different experiences (Bull, et al., 1992). So we must use these as a starting point, a way of enhancing our cultural perspective toward cultural pluralism (with no judgments or evaluations).

When reading these descriptions the reader may have had moments of feeling highly similar and compatible, as well as feeling highly dissimilar. The process of becoming culturally competent starts with a clear understanding of one's own beliefs and values and an acknowledgment that they will differ from those of others (Dennis & Giangreco, 1996; Fradd & Weismantel, 1989; Hanson & Carta, 1996; Harry, 1992a; Lynch, 1998a). Next should come an examination and awareness of one's own personal levels of acculturation, and the impact of cultural learning on one's personal and professional behaviors and expectations. Some of the most worthwhile personal introspection and learning can occur through honest and open communication with families; however, they should not be placed in a role of becoming the primary source of cross-cultural teaching. It is very important to continue interacting with culturally different individuals and reflect on the results. Green (1999) recommends a three-step plan that includes background readings and research, which also depends on personal cross-cultural interactions through the use of a chosen cultural guide. This guide is to explain and interpret what should be frequent visits to ethnic communities. Pinderhughes (1995) also suggests a model for cultural competence and adds important qualifying characteristics of being (a) comfortable with difference, (b) willing to change previously held ideas, and (c) flexible with one's own thinking and behavior (see Table 10–3).

Wolfe, Boone, and Barrera (1997) recommend a six-step strategy to guide reflection

TABLE 10–3

Becoming a Culturally Competent Professional

Steps to develop cultural competence

1. Background preparation: Read descriptions in journals, make a series of visits to the community to learn about the social interactions and characteristics and the resources that are available.
2. Use of cultural guides: These are ordinary people who may or may not be community leaders but who can articulate what is going on around them.
3. Participant observation: This is a long-term commitment to learning in detail about the life of a community with minimal intrusion into the day-to-day activities of the residents by participating in community activities with simultaneous observation of all interactions and details about community life.

Questions to ask in evaluating your cultural competence

1. How much personal and social time do I spend with people who are culturally similar to or different from me?
2. When I am with culturally different people, do I reflect upon my own cultural preferences or do I spend time openly learning about the unique aspects of another person's culture?
3. How comfortable am I in immersion experiences, especially where I am in a numerical minority?
4. How much time do I spend engaged in cross-cultural professional exchanges?
5. How much work have I actually done to increase my knowledge and understanding of culturally and ethnically district groups?
6. What is my commitment to becoming culturally competent? What personal and professional sacrifices am I willing to make?
7. To what extent have I nondefensively extended myself in approaching professional colleagues with the goal of bridging cultural differences?

Source: Adapted from Green, J. N. (1999). *Cultural awareness in human services: A multi-ethnic approach.* Boston: Allyn & Bacon, p. 76.

and inquiry to ensure culturally relevant transition planning:

1. Awareness of culture-related issues that influence collaborative transition planning—knowing one's own attitudes, beliefs, values, and cultural preconceptions;
2. Identification of personal values regarding adult life—including autonomy, independence, interdependence;
3. Perception of family values related to cultural diversity and adulthood—finding out what the family values;
4. Congruence and incongruence among educator and family values—assessing congruence among all team members;
5. Communication with the family to verify perceptions and obtain additional information—also regarding role family prefers that they and the team take during the transition process; and
6. Reflection on family meeting and future plans—identifying sources to help resolve disagreements and to promote mutually satisfying outcomes.

The first three steps focus on identifying and understanding values. The last three steps support communication and using mutual problem solving to resolve important differences: it begins with problem identification (assessment of congruence), then opens up communication between team and family members for problem solving. The last step evaluates the team's success; but culturally different personnel often misinterpret family perceptions regarding satisfaction.

Taking courses in cultural differences also can help. Bellini (2002) found that enrolling in multicultural graduate courses or participating in workshops had a positive impact on rehabilitation counselors' multicultural counseling competencies. Although data were self-reported, workshops and courses benefited all persons—from those without a great deal of multicultural experiences or formal training to those with a great deal.

Among the most difficult aspects of cross-cultural learning is that of personal discomfort, which can arise when confronting oneself with differences or when realizing that one needs to change. And the conflictual situation itself often causes strong emotional pain (Brislin, 1993). Therefore, it can be helpful to have a cultural guide to help mediate and debrief (particularly from painful experiences). This person should be competent, both as a member of a minority group and one who is articulate and knowledgeable about his or her own culture. Involving the whole team, or at least a few other colleagues, can be very helpful in providing support and encouragement through frustrating or troubling situations . . . which leads to the next section, about school-based cultural activities.

Schoolwide Professional and In-Service Training

The more people on the transition teams and throughout the district and school who have received training and experience in cross-cultural skills, then the less likely it is that culturally different children and families will be misdiagnosed and poorly treated by the schools or the special education and IEP/transition processes. It can be very reassuring to do some of the activities with others who are known and trustworthy. The best solution would be for schools and districts to implement effective training, ensuring that all professionals share the same perspectives on cultural pluralism and working with culturally different families. School and agency personnel certainly have needs for information about, and access to, culturally competent practices (Burnette, 1998; Markowitz, 1996; Obiakor & Utley, 1996).

Bellini's (2002) research suggests that courses and workshops are helpful. This would suggest that all team members could similarly benefit from courses and workshops. All individuals would need to express their commitment and begin with becoming aware of their own values and cultural beliefs. Other key professional competencies include (1) involvement with parents and (2) an understanding of the cultural and linguistic background of the family (Rodriquez, 1994). It is important to note that *personal involvement* is the first listed competency. Although relationships with families are not typical of American values (the medical model believes that noninvolvement maintains objectivity and, therefore, greater accuracy in diagnosis and treatment), several cultures consider this essential to receiving satisfactory services from professionals.

The school needs to be prepared to address members who are not equally supportive of multicultural competence. Sue (1996) described four types of resistant beliefs: (1) there is no need to change because current practices are equally appropriate for all populations, regardless of race, culture, ethnicity, gender or otherwise; (2) multicultural competencies are unrealistic for any one individual given the multitude of knowledge and skills that are necessary; (3) we must wait until appropriate standards and guidelines are developed for *all* underrepresented groups including gays and lesbians, and women; and (4) cultural diversity represents reverse racism and quotas, is biased and unbalanced (Middleton et al., 2000, p. 220). This is where school- or district-wide policies can be helpful: They establish a standard that all are expected to achieve.

School- and agency-based in-services and workshops are an excellent starting place; however, they will never be sufficient unless they are continuous and ongoing, with mechanisms that allow for feedback and evaluation (Green, 1999; Hanson, 1998a). Typically, in-services and workshops are designed to address one or a series of narrow topics through informal or formal training programs. Often they have little or no sufficient follow-through and reinforcement of learnings in order to achieve significant change. Those who are resistant often take advantage of the short-term nature of such programs.

A more complete planning process would include schoolwide and agencywide planning that involves potential restructuring or revising of building mission statements and policies (Fradd & Weismantel, 1989). In order to be truly effective, this type of change should address multicultural issues and needs for *all* staff, and not just "key" personnel or faculty. Such a comprehensive approach is the best way to address institutionalized processes and procedures that may create cultural barriers. An organizationwide program is the best means for providing cultural competence across the range of personnel that can interact with culturally different families and clients (e.g., bus drivers and office staff also should have "a cultural clue" when families arrive). The IEP and transition teams also need information about culturally fair assessment and referral/eligibility processes, identifying and building upon cultural strengths and resources in carrying out IEP/ITP plans, and developing appropriate expectations regarding students and families (cf. Markowitz, 1996; Obiakor & Utley, 1996). Everyone needs information about cross-cultural interaction styles when making contacts, setting up appointments and meetings, or soliciting information to be used in files. And each school or agency consists of unique cultural strengths, needs, and challenges that are best utilized and addressed through a school- or agency-focused program. Ongoing feedback allows the training to be modified to address unrealized challenges, and to set new goals with new activities across subsequent years. Again, a one-shot, one-year, hurry-get-it-over-with approach will not have many long-lasting results (even though it fits so well with U.S. cultural values of efficiency and time management).

Schools and agencies should recognize parents as a potential source of cultural expertise (Brame, 1995; Harry, 1992a), for example, as members of advisory groups and in assisting with cross-cultural training. Of course, this is best done outside of the IEP/ITP meeting and when the parents don't have something personal at stake. Schools and agencies may have minority staff and faculty who are also valuable resources, and who may have excellent strategies for successfully balancing two or more cultures (Harry, 1992a; Obiakor & Utley, 1996). However, they cannot be expected to know about the range of *all* cultures within an area (Luft, 1995). Each locale may have highly specific immigrant populations with distinct cultural values that are unknown to nonmembers. Parents and community leaders are the best resources in these instances (Harry, 1992a).

An important consideration in planning multicultural training programs is that program administrators themselves may not have an extensive background. A survey of 30 special education administrators in Ohio showed that although most believed that teachers should participate in multicultural education training, only 4 of the 30 had received any such formal training (Ford, 1992). It can, in fact, be left to individual members of schools and agencies to raise issues about the need for cultural competence and to assist in assuring comprehensive and appropriate planning and training procedures. Using an organization-wide training program can also help to ensure that administrators as well as all other levels of faculty and staff receive this important training.

Parent and Family Training

Families also need basic information and assistance in becoming culturally competent (Brame, 1995; Burnette, 1998). For parents, this includes information about the special education system and transition planning processes, as well as how to find support from peers. Peer parent groups are a very important and "user-friendly" resource for providing training, advocacy assistance, and increased participation in educational planning. These have been a highly effective tool because families often feel more comfortable in learning from each other and through the social ties they form (Dybwad, 1989; Harry, 1992a; Gliedman & Roth, 1980). This is especially true if the peer parent groups are of the same cultural group and social/educational status. Transition team members also may be included in family groups to provide important assistance and liaison support. Parent-focused transition workshops or in-service programs also have been used successfully. Turner (1996) studied 30 parents and found that an inservice program increased parents' understanding of transition, of their role and its importance, their confidence in participating, and helped them to communicate and advocate during meetings.

Minority families may want to use school resources and support in learning to better understand American culture and services. In this case, combination of professional and family training could also develop and support cultural competence learning for all team members, and including parents (Correa, 1989). Family members could be included with the organization's training plans to serve as individual cultural guides, to serve on professional development planning groups in order to provide comprehensive training to both staff and families, and to help ensure ongoing feedback between parents and professionals to assure mutual trust and communication. This type of inclusive and comprehensive training would thus include all key stakeholder individuals who are involved in educational and transition service planning to develop the cross-cultural skills needed to work effectively with each other. Each member would be valued for the skills and experiences they share with others, providing everyone with opportunities to develop new cultural insights.

Working with Culturally Different Families

In the best situation, the school/agency is working to identify potential cultural barriers and eliminate or minimize them. This means it is not just us individuals, or the team, who is solely responsible for giving families information and support in negotiating institutionalized and interpersonal cultural conflicts. The first challenge is ensuring that educators interact and communicate appropriately with culturally different students. This is an appropriate starting place because, although it may not be culturally correct for a particular instructor, he or she is obligated to provide services to the student, based upon the student's individual needs, preferences, and interests. The "i" in "individual" takes on new meaning.

Supporting Student Participation

As discussed earlier, mandates to address the student individually can be seen as undermining and insensitive to some cultures' social and family order. So when working with families that value the group (rather than the individual), the team must use considerable delicacy in balancing these mandates with the family's desires. The team should also ascertain information about the acculturation levels of the family members and the student, to help determine the strength of potentially conflicting transition outcomes and processes. In many cases, indirect probing and comparing answers to family/group-centered versus student-centered questions can help. It is helpful to remember that acculturation can vary across work, living, socialization, and recreational areas so that there can be strong family-team consensus on some, if not all, aspects.

Students may feel highly supported by, and comfortable with, their culture and community with interests and preferences that align closely with what their family prefers. The difficulty can be if team members strongly disagree with these perceptions; however it is important to remember that parents are often critical to successful transition outcomes and, essentially, the family's involvement is lifelong. Most young adults require some, if not extensive, cooperation from their family and community to complete the process of becoming successful adults, long after the transition team has relinquished responsibility.

Teams may also have difficulty when a student expresses certain preferences that do not align so closely with that of the family. Sometimes these differences can be negotiated on a step-by-step approximation process that allows all team and family members (including the student) to feel comfortable with the new preference. For example, if a student wishes to work outside the community in a position different from that envisioned by his or her family, the team may be able to negotiate for trial work in a similar position inside the community, and then move to a position outside, but near the community. Both the family and student can use this to learn about how comfortable they are, or are not, with this situation. It also is typical of adolescents to require a number of trial learning experiences before being able to make realistic decisions about their future; therefore, everyone benefits (and the student gains experience and time regarding the decision).

Another potentially conflictual aspect of transition planning is the need for individually based interest assessments, to ensure better student decision making. It is important to explain these instruments and their rationale to the family. The team may wish to assign activities and exercises to be carried out jointly with the family and community so that the child is not placed in a position of engaging in activities that could create difficulties or conflicts.

At no point does the team wish to set up the student for increased family conflict, or to support the student's acculturation in a way that leads to conflicts. Again, the team may need to identify a series of steps that the family, student, and team can agree upon, and that can be used to evaluate everyone's comfort level with specific paths toward adulthood. And the team certainly wants to avoid being in a position of mediating an escalating conflict between a highly "Americanized" student and culturally traditional family members. Although U.S. culture views some teenager/parent conflict as typical, the team would be wise to use its cultural skills to avoid additional pitfalls resulting from bicultural and acculturation issues.

Just a note here about assessments: Transition team members rely upon a variety of assessment processes (described in Chapter 5) to identify transition strengths, needs, interests, and preferences. Design of tests that are culturally neutral has been extremely challenging and difficult, with accurate and culturally fair testing difficulties still unresolved (cf. Markowitz, 1996; Reschly, 1997; Russo & Talbert-Johnson, 1997; U.S. Dept. of Education, 1987, 1994, 1997). Transition team members must be very cautious about the accuracy and interpretation of these tests when making decisions about appropriate futures for culturally and linguistically different students. Assessment items may need to be modified both when presenting the item (the stimulus) and with the required responses from the student. Culturally appropriate interaction styles can greatly impact on how well children understand directions for each task and their ability to respond to specified testing protocol. Table 10–4 provides suggestions that may be helpful to the transition team in addressing these issues (Keitel, Kopala, & Adamson, 1996; van Keulen et al., 1998).

Supporting Family Participation

It is appropriate to follow information about avoiding and/or addressing student-family issues with a discussion of family issues with parental rights. Many states have developed brochures and packets to ensure that families receive standardized and thorough information. Yet clearly, if parents are not fluent in English and there are no translated versions available, written materials are of no help. In addition, embedded cultural values and processes (including due process, equal opportunity, etc.) may not be recognized for what they are by culturally different families. Sharing information may require personal contact, and a period of time that begins with culturally appropriate "visiting" and getting to know each other. Of greatest importance is that team members learn to be sensitive to cultural dissonances and when communication appears to break down or expectations are widely discrepant, they stop the meeting process to begin probing "gently" in order to ascertain potential cultural conflicts. This type of process is the best way to ensure that families understand their rights, but also the referral-diagnosis-placement process, and program and placement options. The team needs to begin with what the family currently understands about these issues, relative to their values and beliefs (even though it often doesn't fit with our U.S. efficiency and time-management values).

Participatory Transition Planning

One of the most important aspects of collaborative planning is to begin with shared goals and values (Friend & Cook, 1990). This fits well with any transition team, whether or not there are culturally different members. A good place to start is with how the family defines their child's ultimate adult outcomes. This may lead to a discussion of related beliefs and values regarding the student. Again, soliciting family input should be done in a culturally supportive manner rather than the typically "direct" and efficient American style. Just a note: when one initially uses culturally different interaction styles they may seem quite awkward and uncomfortable, and the family's response may be difficult to gauge as well. As trust and comfort develops between all members, the communication and negotiation processes will become increasingly easier.

Once the team has obtained a fairly comprehensive description of the family's vision, it can begin to suggest and then establish some mutually agreeable goals. This vision should include, as

TABLE 10–4

Suggestions for Modifying Assessments with Culturally Different Students

Modification of the item stimulus

1. Repeat the instructions using different words, repeat them more often than recommended, or use sign language.
2. Change the pronunciation of words to reflect the child's culture.
3. Use different pictures when getting unexpected responses; use more culturally appropriate pictures as needed.
4. Modify item wording, probe for related responses, and include additional items to give the student every opportunity to respond.
5. Allow the parents or a trusted adult to administer test items.
6. Administer only a portion of the test; complete the testing in several sessions.

Modification of the item response requirements

1. Allow more time than recommended by the test.
2. Accept responses that are different from allowable responses but that are appropriate for the child's language or culture.
3. Allow the student to change responses.
4. Allow the student to clarify responses and ask questions.
5. Allow the student to respond using sign language, a foreign language, or a gesture.

Scoring

1. When altering a standardized test in any way, this must be described in the report and with the results of the testing; be certain to include this.
2. Do not use the modified results to present normed scores, percentiles, or grade equivalents; changes in assessment procedures always impact normed scoring procedures.
3. Use the modified results to explain your findings and results in terms of the student's abilities; this may have helped you to learn that the student possesses certain skills or knowledge that were masked by cultural differences, and explain how these modifications helped you to learn these things.

Source: Adapted from Keitel M. A., Kopala M., & Adamson W. S. (1996). Ethical issues in multicultural assessment. In Suzuki, L. A., Miller, P. J., & Ponterotto, J. G. (Eds.). *Handbook of multicultural assessment* (pp. 29–48) San Francisco: Jossey-Bass; and van Keulen, J. E., Weddington, G. T., & Du Bose, C. E. (1998). *Speech, language, learning and the African–American child.* Boston: Allyn & Bacon, pp. 123–125.

much as possible, if and where their child will work, live, and participate in leisure and recreational activities, and with whom. Some of these may be very different from the team's vision because of views of disability, gender, or family honor. A good point to begin negotiations may be to present a potential alternative, but with a similar outcome. The team may need to present a rationale for the outcome in terms of its benefit to the child and family/community (i.e., from their cultural perspectives) and why this is a good alternative (i.e., when the student goes to their job, the boss will typically expect . . .). An alternative is to agree on some initial steps rather than ask the family to support an entire program. Over time the family may see the benefits to themselves, their community, and their child that they at first had difficulty envisioning. Developing consensus on aspects of this vision can lead to further consensus later. In terms of equality, the same can be said about the team: They may need to try part of the family's vision, and, over time, come to understand how it best fits with the child's anticipated future.

When describing a vision of adulthood, one must guard against a temptation to present only one, optimal "American" set of outcomes as the transition program, or to limit options one presents to families, especially if the family seems to be struggling. This can be particularly challenging with cultures that have difficulty expressing their goals (long-term planning is not an activity valued by all cultures [Lewis, 1997]) or are reticent in discussing these topics. Families may not be able to express this directly to team members, but also may be comfortable with this ambiguity (not typical of American values). They may see our attempts at decisiveness as being pushy and overbearing, which then further reduces their willingness to participate in decision making.

Another potential conflict: Some cultural and family groups need more time to make decisions than is typical for American IEP/ITP meetings. They may need to share meeting suggestions with their larger community group or particular leaders who are not present and so, the meeting may have to be continued later. This can present a problem, particularly with some school administrators who prefer not to end a meeting without a parental signature. This type of "American" pressure must be negotiated carefully—just one more reason why involving the entire school or agency can be very helpful.

Working with All Families

This chapter has focused on issues related to culturally different students and families. However, the sensitivity and willingness to suspend cultural expectations will help one be more effective with *all* families, regardless of ethnicity. In fact, many parents of children in special education have experienced difficulties in IEP and transition processes.

Kohler (1993) examined research on outcomes from parent involvement to determine how much parents and families contributed to transition outcomes. She found that although multiple studies implied that parent involvement was important, many fewer identified specific positive transition outcomes. Schalock, Wolzen, Ross, Elliott, Werbel, and Peterson (1986) did an analysis that showed when families were moderately to highly involved with their children's programs, the children were more successful on employment-related outcome variables. Hudson, Schwartz, Sealander, Campbell, and Hensel (1988) found that of 40 successfully employed young adults aged 19 to 25, 94% of the subjects felt that family support (with friends, school program and staff support) was important in completing their education, and 90% felt family support was an important personal resource for successful transition. Heal, Gonzalez, Rusch, Copher, and Destefano (1990) studied factors discriminating between successful and unsuccessful employment with home support being one of several significant factors. Halpern, Doren, and Benz (1993) reported on a 3-year follow-along study that indicates that most students found jobs either on their own or with the help of family or friends. Thus, informal supports were more important than the program supports for this key employment outcome. Morningstar, Turnbull, and Turnbull (1995) studied transition outcomes and found that the students' families highly influenced and shaped their career goals.

So there is research that indicates that families contribute to positive transition outcomes. Yet another line of research indicates that parents are *not* very involved in IEP or transition planning meetings, or in making decisions, despite legislative mandates to the contrary. Turnbull and Morningstar (1993) found that parents were likely to participate only passively in IEP and other educational decision-making meetings. Gilmore (1974) supported this by finding that parental involvement in decision making received a low priority rating by educators, and parent involvement itself was considered to be desirable but not very important. Although there has been some improvement in the past two decades since P.L. 94-142 was enacted, professionals still generally do not use suggested parent involvement practices to ensure active participation (Hilton & Henderson, 1993), nor do they consider parents as having equal weight in decision-making processes (Dinnebeil & Rule, 1994; Lynch & Stein, 1982; McNair & Rusch, 1987; Pruitt & Wandry, 1998; Repetto, White, & Snauwaert, 1990; Tilson & Neubert, 1988).

Further research examined the types of roles that parents were able to take during IEP and education decision-making conferences. Gartner and Lipsky (1987) reviewed studies on student participation in the IEP process and noted that many parents are minimally involved in providing information, making decision, and advocating for their child's needs (Vaughn, Bos, Harrell, & Lasky, 1988). Vaughn et al. studied interactions within meetings, characterizing such conferences as one of decision *telling* rather than decision *making*.

So it appears that there is room for improvement in significantly involving families of students with disabilities, regardless of their ethnicity. Are there other concerns that make this involvement difficult for families? An important issue is family resources and meeting time. For example, not all families have cars for transportation, or have work schedules that can accommodate meeting times during typical school hours and schedules (Brame, 1995). This is true for many families, regardless of ethnicity. Lynch and Stein (1987) also found that 54% of minority families were unable to attend their last school meeting because of work, time, transportation, or child-care conflicts. Therefore, teams may want to consider holding meetings in the family's home and in the evenings or weekends to show their commitment to the family and supporting their involvement (Brame, 1995; Lynch & Stein, 1987). Such an arrangement would not be appropriate for all cultural groups, and team members must meet with the comfort level of the family. However, involving community resources and leaders as well as being flexible regarding times and days will greatly help the team and families learn to trust and respect each other.

Conclusion

The cultural understandings described in this chapter impact cross-cultural relationships that go far beyond transition and IEP planning meetings. In fact, the need for cultural competence impacts all aspects of family and student interactions. Every conversation with the student or his or her parents, every note, telephone call, written report, and meeting convey beliefs and opinions, many of which unintentionally convey culturally based expectations. The team should be aware of potential differences in learning styles that can impact the effectiveness of instructional training programs that have been selected to implement transition plans. Many classroom instructional tasks expect analytical and cause-effect thinking that differ from cultures that support global and holistic perspectives (for information about culturally different learning styles, see Dunn & Griggs, 1995).

The steps toward becoming culturally competent are gradual and require time and perseverance. Each person must learn to recognize the power of our own cultural beliefs and values and to understand the ways in which these differ from the families with whom we work. These differences frequently include race, educational level, economic level, and social status. The process of learning about culture requires being flexible, having a willingness to abandon previous ways of thinking, and becoming culturally challenged through interacting with those who are different from one by visiting their communities and reading and studying about these differences. Although one is likely to feel awkward at first, positive intentions may allow one to become increasingly comfortable and effective.

Skills in cross-cultural interaction will become increasingly important with the continuing immigration and changing demographics of the United States. Many families with whom transition teams will work have neither the English skills nor the cultural competence to interact effectively with American institutions. The unique adult-focused and outcome-oriented nature of transition planning and its requirements for participatory decision making create a situation that can lead to substantial cultural barriers and conflicts between families and transition team members. The current lack of cross-cultural expertise in many schools and agencies makes the skills acquired by educators even more valuable.

This chapter has provided a starting point with information and insights for improving cross-cultural transition planning and team interactions. This is a time of opportunity and change, with U.S. public services becoming more willing to recognize cultural difference as an area of need. Readers of this book may become the few members of their workplace with a background in cultural competence. Schools also need organizational leaders who can live in, between, and beyond cultures (Gray, 1997). Those who continue to develop their competence can play an important role in seeing that all members of the transition planning team, and the workplace, have the necessary knowledge and skills to provide high-quality and effective services.

Case Study Introduction

Asian-Pacific Americans represent one of the largest groups of immigrant peoples in the United States (Chan, 1998a, 1998b). Examine your cultural competence by planning how you would work with these two students and their families. Use Table 10–3 as a start.

CASE STUDY A

Tru Lang is a 15-year-old Vietnamese student who has a visual impairment and mild/moderate developmental delays. He once showed you a scar on his chest that he said was from a camp. You know that as a child he spent some time in a war orphans camp separated from his parents and had moved to the United States to stay with an uncle. He was reunited with his parents and siblings when they were able to leave Vietnam a few years later. He is very outgoing and animated, with strong vocational interests in working outdoors. He seems very interested in being like other American teenagers. You know little about his family at this point but believe that his uncle and aunt lived here for several years and may be important acculturating factors and bicultural interpreters for the family.

CASE STUDY B

Crystal is a 17-year-old Cambodian girl who lives with her family, which includes an older sister. She has developmental disabilities and had little or no language until she entered school here at age 11. You know little about the family and they have not shared much in past interactions or in school records. You have been told that her "parents" are really her aunt and uncle although it is her real sister. She and her sister were able to escape but you believe that her real parents were killed. You do not know whether or not she and her sister witnessed this. Crystal, like her family, expresses little about herself or her activities. Although her name is Americanized, she does not seem to have strong desires to act like other American teenagers. She does not have strong friendships with the other students (girls or boys) and does not talk much about the TV shows she watches. Only occasionally have you seen her express strong anger, which surprised you, perhaps as the result of someone doing something culturally offensive to her. Crystal has done job shadowing and trial work experiences across the major occupational categories, but it has been difficult for you and the other team members to get a strong sense of any of her preferences. She is a very compliant and pleasant student to work with in other ways; however, it is becoming important for her to make a vocational choice soon.

Study Questions

1. What are the reasons and processes that lead to overrepresentation of minority students in special education programs? From your experience in schools and agencies, what could you do as an individual that would help to correct these patterns?
2. What are the major differences among white, middle-, and upper-middle-class values and minority group beliefs and values in the areas of identity, disability, and relationships? What are your beliefs and values, and how closely do they align with some of these cultural values?
3. How can team processes accommodate culturally different families in terms of (a) determining student needs and preferences, (b) setting goals, (c) determining appropriate outcome-oriented processes, and (d) in moving from school to postschool activities? Where would you start and then how would you proceed if you began to sense a difference in values on these areas?
4. A family does not speak during the annual IEP/ITP meeting and even does not respond to direct questions from team members. What are (a) some of the culturally appropriate reasons that this family might not do so and (b) how would you approach the family to support their greater participation in a future meeting?
5. One of the interagency members of your transition team has a very directive approach that you believe is causing the family to withdraw emotionally from the team. This agency member has informed you that the family is poor, a minority, and, from what they can see, uncaring and uninterested. You disagree with this conclusion. How would you try to keep the communication open with this person and then further engage him or her in considering some less judgmental conclusions?
6. Your principal/supervisor has asked you to help plan a program to increase cultural sensitivity and appropriateness in your school/agency. How would you begin such a program, whom would you include in the planning process, and what would be your specific outcomes of this training?

Websites

Council for Exceptional Children
http://www.cec.sped.org

Division for Culturally and Linguistic Diverse Exceptional Learners
http://www.cec.sped.org

Standing Committee on Ethnic and Multicultural Concerns
http://www.cec.sped.org

Ethnic Studies at USC
http://www.usc.edu/isd/archives/ethnicstudies/

Council of the Great City Schools
www.cgcs.org

The Center for Research on Education, Diversity, and Excellence (CREDE)
www.cal.org/crede

Intercultural Email Classroom Connections (IECC)
www.stolaf.edu/network/iecc

11

Transition Planning

Robert Baer

LEARNING OBJECTIVES

The objectives of this chapter are:

1. Develop a general concept of transition planning as it relates to youth with disabilities and the Individuals with Disabilities Education Act (IDEA) of 1990 and 1997.
2. Identify some common myths about transition planning that have emerged since it has become IDEA policy.
3. Understand the process of preparing for the IEP/transition meeting and the many models, assessments, and considerations that must be addressed before the actual meeting occurs.
4. Understand the process of implementing the transition plan from the development of the IEP/transition plan to the assessment of progress.
5. Develop a general understanding of common questions that may be asked by families in the development and implementation of the transition plan.

Introduction

This chapter examines transition planning from the perspective of the educator who is responsible for creating a choice-rich and supportive environment for individual students in transition. It will provide a blueprint for combining the previously discussed transition policy, the best practice, and self-determination strategies into a comprehensive process known as "transition planning." Specifically, this chapter describes a step-by-step method for developing an individualized transition planning process that involves students and their families in: (a) the determination of their needs, interests, and preferences, (b) the creation of an outcome-oriented transition process, (c) the development of a coordinated set of transition activities, and (d) the promotion of student movement to desired postsecondary settings.

Transition Planning and the IDEA of 1990 and 1997

The Individuals with Disabilities Education Act of 1990 (IDEA; P. L. No. 101-476) mandated transition planning in response to studies that showed poor postsecondary outcomes for students graduating with individual education programs (IEPs) (Hasazi, Gordon, & Roe, 1985; SRI International, 1990). The "statement of needed transition services" in the IEP (also known as the individual transition plan or ITP) was designed to improve postsecondary outcomes by assuring that students' IEPs supported their postsecondary goals." The IDEA of 1990 was the first piece of legislation to mandate transition planning by requiring a statement of needed transition services in the IEP for students no later than age 16, which was to be reviewed at least annually.

The IDEA of 1997 (P.L. 105-17) extended the notion of transition services to include the transition into a high school course of study related to students' individual career interests. It mandated that by no later than age 14, student IEPs must specify transition services that are necessary for them to participate in their desired course of study (e.g., career and technical [or vocational] education or college preparation). This provision was added in order to deal with the concern that students with disabilities often were unable to access educational and vocational programs related to their transition goals. In promulgating regulations for the IDEA of 1997, the committee noted, "the IEP provisions added by P.L. 105-17 are intended to provide greater access by children with disabilities to the general curriculum and to educational reforms [such as school-to-work programs] . . . " (p. 55091).

Critical Point The IDEA of 1990 and 1997 mandated transition planning for all students with IEPs, at first aged 16 or younger, and now aged 14 years or younger.

The IDEA of 1990 and 1997 promoted four major criteria for designing transition services. First, they must be based on students' needs, taking into account their preferences and interests. Second, they must be developed through an outcome-oriented process and identify a series of steps toward reaching students' desired employment and adult living goals. Third, transition services must be a coordinated set of activities encompassing a broad range of services and supports, including those provided by the school, the family, the community, the adult service system, and the postsecondary environments. Finally, they must be designed to promote student movement from school to postschool activities by developing bridges of generic, time-limited, and ongoing supports that extend into early adulthood (Will, 1983).

Determining Student Needs, Interests, and Preferences

The IDEA of 1990 resulted in a number of federal regulations relative to assuring the consideration of student needs, interests, and preferences in transition planning. Section 300.344 required that, "if the purpose of the meeting is the consideration of transition services for a student, the public agency (school) shall invite the student." If the student does not attend the IEP meeting in which transition is discussed (or the IEP/transition meeting), the IDEA required that the school "ensure that the student's preferences and interests are considered." Section 300.345 specified that the notice of the IEP/transition meeting must inform parents that the student will be invited to the meeting. The IDEA of 1997 strengthened the focus upon student self-determination by adding the requirement that the IEP include a statement that students and their parents have been notified in writing of the transfer of IDEA rights to students upon reaching the age of majority (section 615 [m]).

Outcome-Oriented Transition Planning

The IDEA of 1990 and 1997 regulations addressed outcome-oriented planning by strongly recommending provision of transition services in the area of "development of employment and other post-school adult living objectives." The IDEA described employment and postschool adult living objectives as including "postsecondary education, vocational training, integrated employment (including supported employment), continuing and adult education, adult services, independent living, or community participation" (section 602). By requiring transition services in the area of development of employment and other postschool adult living objectives, the IDEA promoted both the identification of postsecondary goals through career exploration and the development of postsecondary goals through career development activities. Additionally, the IDEA's inclusion of independent living and community participation as possible postschool objectives suggested that transition services needed to focus upon more than just school-to-work activities.

Coordinated Set of Activities

The IDEA mandated that each student's IEP/transition plan include, "if appropriate, a statement of each public agency's and each participating agency's responsibilities or linkages, or both, before the student leaves the school setting." It required that each meeting include "the child's teacher, a regular education teacher (if the student is or might be in regular education) and . . . a representative of the public agency other than the child's teacher who is qualified to provide, or supervise the provision of, special education. . . ". The IDEA also specified that "the public agency shall invite . . . a representative of any other agency that is likely to be responsible for providing or paying for transition services" and went on to stipulate that "if an agency invited to send a representative to a meeting does not do so, the public agency must take other steps to obtain the participation of the other agency in the planning of any transition services." The IDEA placed the responsibility for coordination of transition plans with schools and required that:

> If a participating agency failed to provide agreed upon transition services contained in the IEP of a student with a disability, the public agency responsible for the student's education should, as soon as possible, initiate a meeting for the purpose of identifying alternative strategies to meet the transition objectives and, if necessary, revise the student's IEP. (Section 300.348)

Promoting Student Movement to Postschool Activities

The IDEA required that transition services be designed to move students toward their desired postschool activities and suggested that they should be initiated early enough to achieve those outcomes. The IDEA of 1997 required that, "beginning at age 14, and updated annually, a statement of the transition service needs of the child . . . that focuses on the child's courses of study (such as participation in advanced-placement courses or a vocational education program)" be included in the IEP (Section 300.347). The IDEA mandated by no later than age 16 a statement of needed transition services in the IEP that addresses the need for transition services specified in the definition, including "instruction, related services, community experiences, the development of employment and other postschool objectives, and, when appropriate, acquisition of daily living skills and functional vocational evaluation" (Section 300.29).

Common Myths in Regard to Transition Policy Implementation

Stowitschek and Kelso (1989) warned that making transition plans part of the IEP would cause them to take on many negative characteristics of the IEP, including lack of year-to-year continuity and low-quality objectives. Research indicates transition plans often lack vision, linkages, and methods for coordinating services (Gallivan-Fenlon, 1994; Grigal, Test, Beattie, & Wood, 1997; Krom & Prater, 1993; Lombard, Hazelkorn, & Neubert, 1992). Four common myths have become prevalent in schools where educators have focused upon transition "paper compliance" (Baer, Simmons, & Flexer, 1996).

Myth One: There Is One Transition Planning Process for All Students

Transition planning as a career planning process must be individualized and suited to the cognitive and career needs of individual students with disabilities. Some students may choose to participate in regular education career planning processes as part of transition planning (Clark & Kolstoe, 1995; Menchetti & Piland, 1998), whereas others may prefer person-centered planning approaches such as Personal Futures Planning (Mount, 1994; O'Brien, 1987). The principles of self-determination and appropriateness must be concurrently applied in the selection of transition planning approaches.

Students with disabilities should be able to take an active role in transition planning, but they also must be provided with planning that is sophisticated enough to address the complexity of school and adult service systems. Consequently, no one transition planning process fits all students. In fact, some students may need multiple planning approaches (e.g., person-centered planning and career planning).

Myth Two: Planning Occurs Only in the IEP/Transition Meeting

Transition planning involves much more than a short meeting at the beginning or end of an IEP meeting. In a comfortable environment, students and families should be given time to discuss their needs and desired postsecondary outcomes, and to plan activities for several years at a time. This generally requires a discussion of these issues prior to the IEP/transition meeting because students with disabilities and their families have been shown to participate much less in larger meetings with many professionals in attendance (Pumpian, Campbell, & Hesche, 1992; Whitney-Thomas, Shaw, Honey, & Butterworth, 1998). The planning process, Choosing Options and

Accommodations for Children (COACH), has suggested that the initial interview limit participation to the teacher/facilitator, family members, and the student to assure meaningful student and family input (Giangreco, Cloninger, & Iverson, 1993).

Myth Three: Transition Plans Cover One Year

Transition plans are by definition long-term plans since they are focused upon postschool outcomes. The IDEA requires that these plans be reviewed annually, but that they should not be discarded each year and started anew. Unfortunately, this presents a logistical problem when the transition plan is part of the IEP. As part of the IEP, transition services are subject to the same requirement as other IEP services, and it has been argued that multiyear transition plans obligate the school to provide services too far in the future to assure that they will be available when the time comes. Yet, without multiyear planning, the transition statement in the IEP becomes nothing more than a list of short-term functional activities. Many schools have addressed this dilemma by developing a long-term transition plan that is passed along from year to year and is used to provide continuity in IEP planning.

Myth Four: Transition Teams Meet Only Annually

The IDEA requires that the transition team be reconvened as soon as possible if transition services cannot be provided as planned. General principles of good planning require monitoring, evaluation, and revision of plans whenever major changes occur, including: (a) change in student goals, (b) problems in student performance, (c) failure to obtain services as planned, or (d) new opportunities or programs that may benefit the student. Yet, research indicates that less than 25% of secondary schools have a mechanism

Computer-assisted assessments support the determination of career interests.

for reconvening the IEP/transition team if services cannot be provided as planned (Baer et al., 1996; McMahan & Baer, 2001). Some schools have addressed this problem by developing computer-linked planning, interagency teams, or conference calls to assure regular communication (McMahan & Baer, 2001).

Critical Point Implementation of IDEA's transition mandates should go beyond minimum or "paper compliance" requirements.

Preparing for the Transition Meeting

Choosing Transition Planning Processes

Transition planning must address the unique planning capabilities and needs of students with disabilities and their families. To some degree, all transition planning approaches should be: (a) person-centered, (b) self-determined, and (c) career-oriented. Planning approaches emphasizing person-centered planning have been used primarily for individuals who have difficulty developing career goals due to both the extent of their disability or a difficulty in expressing preferences (Menchetti & Piland, 1998). Although typically used with students with severe disabilities, these planning approaches may also benefit students with milder disabilities who have no postsecondary goals or direction to their IEPs (Rojewski, 1993). Person-centered planning approaches usually involve a facilitator, a recorder, the student, and various family, friends, classmates, and coworkers who work together to answer questions regarding the student's (a) history, (b) dreams, (c) nightmares, (d) relationships, (e) abilities, and (f) plan of action (Holburn & Vietze, 2002). Person-centered planning approaches include:

1. *Personal Profiling* (O'Brien, 1987). A planning approach that uses graphics to determine in relation to the individual: (a) important people, (b) important places, (c) critical events, (d) health issues, (e) daily life choices, (f) ways to gain or lose respect, (g) support strategies, (h) hopes and fears, and (i) barriers and opportunities.
2. *Personal Futures Planning* (Mount & Zwernick, 1988). A type of person-centered planning that addresses issues in the areas of: (a) home, (b) work or school, (c) community, (d) choices and preferences, and (e) relationships.
3. *Essential Lifestyle Planning* (Smull & Burke-Harrison, 1992). A person-centered planning approach that focuses upon seven areas: (a) non-negotiables, (b) strong preferences, (c) highly desirables, (d) personal characteristics, (e) personal concerns, (f) needed supports, and (g) action steps.
4. COACH (Giangreco et al., 1993). A form of person-centered planning that stands for choosing options and accommodations for children. This approach includes the family's values and dreams in IEP planning.
5. *Making Action Plans* (formerly McGill Action Planning System (MAPs) (Vandercook, York, & Forest, 1989). A form of person-centered planning that develops "road maps" by defining personal history, identity, dreams, nightmares, strengths, and gifts.

Self-determination is an important focus of transition planning. Good person-centered and career-oriented planning processes address the need for students to make their own decisions, but self-determination models may enhance student participation by developing self-awareness and leadership skills. Self-determination approaches typically focus upon improving the student's ability (a) to self-advocate, (b) to make decisions, (c) to develop goals, (d) to demonstrate leadership, and (e) to take an active role in IEP/transition meetings. Self-determination approaches include:

1. *ChoiceMaker* (Martin, Huber Marshall, Maxson, & Jerman, 1996). A self-determination approach that focuses upon (a) choosing goals, (b) expressing goals, and (c) taking action.
2. *Group Action Planning* (Turnbull & Turnbull, 1993). A self-determination approach that helps students to take charge of personal futures planning.
3. *Whose Future Is It Anyway?* (Wehmeyer & Kelchner, 1995). A self-determination curriculum that is designed for persons with cognitive disabilities consisting of 36 lessons that address (a) having self-awareness, (b) making decisions, (c) obtaining supports and transition services, (d) writing and evaluating transition objectives, and (e) learning leadership skills.
4. *Next* S.T.E.P. (Halpern et al., 1997). A student-directed transition approach consisting of 16 lessons that address: (a) getting started, (b) self-exploring and evaluating, (c) developing goals and activities, and (d) putting a plan into place.

5. IPLAN (Van Reusen & Bos, 1990). A form of person-centered planning focused on students with learning disabilities that stands for Inventory, Plan, Listen, Ask, and Name your goals.
6. TAKE CHARGE (Powers et al., 1996). A student-directed collaborative approach focused on students with physical disabilities that pairs youth with adults of the same gender with similar challenges, and uses four primary strategies: (a) skill facilitation, (b) mentoring, (c) peer support, and (d) parent support to develop student skills in achievement, partnership, and coping.

Career planning approaches can be effective for many students, especially students who plan to enter postsecondary education and technical careers. Career development approaches tend to be: (a) systematic, (b) developmental, (c) focused on self-awareness, and (d) oriented to a wide range of occupations. Career planning approaches include:

1. *What Color Is My Parachute* (Bolles, 1995). This publication provides an overview of career development and some useful exercises and examples related to identifying interests, researching jobs, developing résumés, and conducting interviews.
2. *Life-Centered Career Education* (LCCE) (Brolin & Schatzman, 1989). This career development approach delineates 22 major competencies that can be infused into primary, middle, and secondary curricula to address the major life domains of work, home, and academics.
3. The *Career Maturity Inventory* (Crites, 1978). This assessment, along with the Career Development Inventory (1990), can direct counseling (or the use of a computerized DISCOVER program) to address competencies in related to the roles of student, leisurite, citizen, worker, and homemaker.
4. The *Myers/Briggs* (Myers & McCauley, 1985). This assessment identifies four personality temperaments that can be used to develop self- and career-awareness (e.g., extroverted, intuitive, feeling, perceptive, or EIFP).
5. *Employability Life Skills Assessment* (Weaver & DeLuca, 1987). This criterion-referenced checklist may be used yearly to assess a student's level of performance in 24 critical employability skills areas in the domains of personal, social, and daily living habits.
6. The *Self-Directed Search* (Holland, 1985b). This instrument identifies six personality types and matches them with six matching categories of jobs to help students make a career choice related to their needs and preferences.

The *Self-Directed Search* is particularly effective for transition planning since it provides information on student personality types and matches it with occupations that have a high probability of being a good career choice (Simmons & Baer, 1996). However, this structural approach may not work as well with students with low career maturity. It is recommended that this and other instruments be used under the supervision of a person who is qualified to administer them.

Critical Point Transition planning approaches should be selected with the student and the family and should emphasize self-determination, person-centeredness, and career orientation.

Time Lines for Transition Planning

Like all people, persons with disabilities go through many transitions in their life (Brolin & Schatzman, 1989; Repetto & Correa, 1996). In proceedings related to the current reauthorization of the IDEA, it is likely that educators will be expected to address a number of *transition points* in the educational life-span, including the transition to school (currently addressed in Part C of the IDEA), transition to middle school, transition to high school (currently addressed in the IDEA's requirement to address the student's course of study by age 14), and the transition to postsecondary environments (addressed in the IDEA of 1990 and 1997). In the context of this book, transition planning is focused upon the transition from school to postsecondary environments. However, it is important to view transition in the context of the student's total learning experience since transition planning at the secondary level must build upon the student's developmental experiences up to that time. Table 11–1 shows how transition choices should be developed and formed from primary school on.

Forming the Transition Planning Team

The composition of the transition planning team is a primary consideration in the development of a transition plan. Selection of team members should be a collaborative effort with the student and the family integrally involved (O'Brien, 1987). This is important because research indicates that self-friend-family networks account for more than 80% of the jobs obtained by students after graduation (Hasazi, Gordon, & Roe, 1985; SRI International, 1992). The selection of the transition team also should include representatives from high school and postsecondary environments desired by students so that they can establish contacts and become familiar with the requirements of the programs they want to enter.

Critical Point The transition team should be developed with the student and the family and should include core members, natural supporters, adult service providers, and representatives of postsecondary environments.

Core transition team members are persons who should always be involved in the development of the IEP/transition plan. According to the IDEA, core members include:

1. The student with a disability
2. Parents and guardians
3. The special education teacher
4. A representative of the local education agency who is knowledgeable about the general education curriculum
5. An individual who can interpret evaluation
6. A regular education teacher (if the student is or might be in regular or vocational education classes).

In addition to these core members, individual students may have specific needs or preferences that require the involvement of other transition stakeholders. These include but are not limited to: (a) work-study coordinators and transition specialists, (b) related service providers, (c) vocational rehabilitation counselors, (d) adult service providers, (e) employers, (f) representatives of postsecondary education programs, and (g) community supporters and advocates. These and other team members should be identified in the process of assessing the student's desired environments related to work, education, community participation, and residential living. The respective roles of transition team members are outlined in Table 11–2.

Transition Assessments

The IEP/transition coordinator should assure that students and their families have all the information they need to make informed choices regarding student postsecondary goals, course of study, and necessary transition services. Prior to the meeting, the educator should collect and obtain the assessments needed for the IEP/transition meeting. These may include a range of vocational and life skills assessments that can help students to identify their strengths, needs, interests, and preferences. It also can include student and family surveys that assess the student's career maturity and family-student agreement on postsecondary goals. The following list includes some types of assessments that may be useful for specific students (Clark & Patton, 1997):

- Interest inventories (computer and written)
- Transition surveys

TABLE 11–1

Timelines for Transition Planning

Primary Level: Grades 1–4

Goals: Employability and independent living skills and attitudes

Objectives:

1. To develop positive work habits
2. To appreciate all types of work
3. To develop an understanding of how to cope with disability

Possible Activity Areas:

- Inclusion activities
- Responsibility activities
- Work sample activities
- Career field trips
- Discussions about work
- Discussions of interests and aptitudes
- Exploration of technology
- Decision-making and problem-solving activities

Middle School: Grades 5–8

Goals: Career exploration and transition planning relative to course of study

Objectives:

1. To understand the relationship of school to work
2. To understand interest, aptitudes, and preferences
3. To understand work, education, independent living, and community options
4. To determine a general secondary course of study
5. To identify needed accommodations and supports for secondary education
6. To specify transition services needed to participate in a desired course of study by no later than age 14

Possible Activity Areas:

- Visits to vocational and technical schools
- Visits to high school
- Complete interest inventories
- Functional vocational assessment
- Career fairs
- Survey transition needs and preferences
- Employability assessment
- Daily living skills classes
- Money and budgeting classes
- Community awareness classes
- Political awareness classes
- Job shadowing
- Career guidance
- Self-determination and advocacy training
- Training in use of disability technology and related services
- Computer training
- Mobility training
- Counseling
- Employability skills training
- Decision-making and problem-solving activities

(continued)

TABLE 11–1 *(continued)*

High School: Grades 9–10

Goals: Career exploration and transition planning
Objectives

1. To develop meaningful and realistic postsecondary goals
2. To develop work, education, residential, and community participation skills and supports relevant to goals
3. To learn to manage disability technology and request accommodations

Possible Activity Areas:

- Technology assessment
- Make agency referrals
- Update transition goals
- Self-determination training
- Develop IEP/transition plan
- Vocational education
- Placement in advanced classes
- Work experiences
- Job shadowing
- Job placement
- Job clubs
- Linkages with adult services

High School: Grades 11 and up

Goals: Transition and overlap into postsecondary environments desired by the student
Objectives:

1. To test goals through experiences and activities
2. To secure options for postsecondary education and/or employment
3. To develop residential and community participation supports and contacts
4. To develop linkages with adult services
5. To empower students and families to function in adult environments

Possible Activity Areas:

- Review and revise IEP/transition plans
- Involve adult services
- Self-determination training
- Apply for adult services
- Apply for postsecondary education
- Financial planning
- Visit relevant postsecondary environments
- Develop job seeking skills
- Job placements
- Community memberships
- Transfer transition coordination
- Develop follow up supports
- Transfer transition plan to family or adult services

Source: From R. Baer, R. McMahan, & R. Flexer, 1999. *Transition planning: A guide for parents and professionals* (p. 9), Kent, OH: Kent State University. Copyright 1999 by Robert Baer. Reprinted with permission.

TABLE 11–2
Responsibilities of Transition Team Members

Team Members	Responsibilities
Student*	Identifies needs, strengths, preferences, and interests
	Takes a leadership role in planning with supports
	Participates in all planning activities
	Identifies friends, family, and community members who can be part of the transition team
	Assumes IDEA rights at the age of majority
Parent/Guardian*	Provides information regarding student needs, strengths, preferences, and interests
Also:	Participates in referrals to transition programs and adult services
Siblings	Assists in procuring social security numbers, identification cards, and transportation passes
Friends	Plans for long-term financial support, social security, trust funds, or other supports
Advocates	Asks for assistance in obtaining community and residential services as needed
	Provides opportunities for the student to try out adult roles and responsibilities
	Identifies the person who will coordinate the transition plan
	Identifies friends, family, and community members who can be part of the transition team
Special education teacher*	Helps students to identify postsecondary goals and to obtain needed transition services
Collaborating with:	Identifies school or community agency personnel to be included in transition planning
Vocational education	Prepares the student and the family for participation in the IEP/transition team
Work study	Writes the statement of needed transition services in the IEP transition plan
Related services	Coordinates transition services and activities in the IEP/transition plan (may delegate)
Guidance counselor	Provides information and assists families in developing referrals for adult services
	Links the IEP to the student's course of study and required testing
	Collects and monitors information about student progress
	Provides or obtains accommodations and supports for all education services
Regular education teacher*	Connects the IEP to the general education curriculum
	Helps students to identify postsecondary goals and needed transition services
	Provides classroom instruction to support the student transition to adult environments
	Collects and monitors information about student progress
	Adapts curriculum and provides or obtains accommodation for regular education

(continued)

TABLE 11–2 *(continued)*

Team Members	Responsibilities
	Obtains or provides accommodations for state and regional proficiency tests
An individual who can interpret evaluations*	Provides assessment information regarding student needs, interests, and preferences Provides assessment information regarding student strengths and aptitudes Interprets assessments and evaluations for the student and the family Identifies limitations of assessments and additional assessment needs Works with the student and family to identify assessment options
Representative of the local education agency familiar with the curriculum*	Provides information about programs offered throughout the school Identifies how the student with a disability can be included in general education programs Assists in obtaining technology, accommodations, and supports for inclusion and transition Helps to identify how to address general education curriculum and competencies Assists the transition team in obtaining accommodations and supports for student graduation, and for participation in state and regional proficiency tests
Adult service providers, Including:	May provide job training and placement before and after graduation May provide case management and service coordination services
VR services	Determine eligibility for Supplemental Security Income and Medicaid (generally VR and Social Security)
MR/DD services	May provide independent living services
Mental health	May provide functional vocational assessments and job counseling
Bureau of employment	May provide health services and supports
Social security	May provide technology and accommodations
Independent living center	May help to fund postsecondary education or vocational training
Employers	May provide recreational and leisure opportunities
Postsecondary educators	May provide counseling and behavioral supports
Human services	May assist in developing peer and coworker supports
	May provide opportunities to try out postsecondary environments
	May provide child support

*Core member
Source: From R. Baer, R. McMahan, and R. Flexer, 1999. *Transition planning: A guide for parents and professionals* (p. 11), Kent, OH: Kent State University. Copyright 1999 by Robert Baer. Reprinted with permission.

- Employability skills inventories
- Personal futures planning
- Structured situational (i.e., home, community, and work) assessments
- Assessments of postschool environments desired by the student
- Curriculum-based assessment
- Structured interviews
- Social histories
- Adaptive behavior inventories
- Life skills inventories
- Assessment of prerequisite skills for vocational education
- Aptitude tests

- Personality scales
- Social skills inventories
- Vocational skills assessments
- Professional assessments (e.g., psychology, medical, vision, speech, and mobility)
- College entrance examinations
- Assessment of technology needs
- Career portfolios

Care must be used in selection of standardized assessment instruments and in presentation of their findings. Assessment information should be: (a) valid for the type of student being tested, (b) related to actual and desired student environments, (c) understood by all members of the transition team, and (d) focused upon student strengths. Research indicates that standardized assessment procedures often lack validity for students with disabilities because they do not consider the effects of supports, technology, and training on student performance (Menchetti & Piland, 1998). Hagner and Dileo (1993) point out that standardized assessment procedures may have little use for students with severe disabilities since they lack the pressures, cues, sights, and sounds of the environments in which students will have to perform. These researchers advocate strongly for the use of situational assessments, or assessments that are conducted in the actual environments in which the student is expected to perform.

Critical Point Transition assessments should be valid for the type of student tested, individualized, strength-focused, functional, and socially referenced.

Backward Planning

The transition coordinator should employ a technique known as "backward planning" in developing transition services and the IEP (Steere, Wood, Panscofar, & Butterworth, 1990). Figure 11–1 shows how backward planning would work for a student desiring supported employment in a clerical situation after graduation. Starting with the final year prior to graduation, the student is established in the environment of choice—in this case, supported employment—to assure that the necessary services and supports are in place prior to graduation so that he or she could be simply transferred to the adult service system. Two years before graduation, the student is moved toward transition into supported employment through job placement, job club, and follow-along services. Three years prior to graduation, transition services are focused upon community experiences and vocational education that lead to supported employment. Four years prior to graduation, the focus of activities is career exploration with a focus upon job shadowing, guidance counseling, and employability skills training. This backward planning approach should be used for each student's

Varied transition services are required to meet mandates.

FIGURE 11–1
Backward Planning Worksheet

Postsecondary Goal: Supported Employment in a Clerical Setting
Current Age: 18
Age to Graduate: 22

Needed transition service	Age 19	Age 20	Age 21	Age 22
1. Supported employment in a clerical setting			X	X
2. Follow-along support			X	X
3. Job placement services and job club		X	X	
4. Transportation training	X	X		
5. Develop social security work incentive plan		X		
6. Vocational education in clerical skills	X	X		
7. Community work experiences during the school year		X		
8. Summer jobs	X	X		
9. Job shadowing	X	X		
10. Guidance counseling	X			
11. Employability skills training	X	X		
12. Apply for social security benefits—done at age 18				
13. Referral to vocational rehabilitation—done at age 16				
14. Referral for MR/DD services—done at age 16				

Source: From R. Baer, R. McMahan, and R. Flexer, 1999. *Transition planning: A guide for parents and professionals* (p. 17), Kent, OH: Kent State University. Copyright 1999 by Robert Baer. Reprinted with permission.

postsecondary goals, including postsecondary education, independent living, and community participation. A general rule of thumb for backward planning is, the more severe the disability, the more overlap that will be needed between school and postschool environments. Figure 11–1 shows a sample backward planning worksheet for a transition employment goal.

Critical Point The development and implementation of postsecondary goals should drive the student's educational experience each year until graduation.

Preparing for Student and Family Led IEP/Transition Meetings

Prior to the IEP/transition meeting, the transition coordinator should go over the summary of assessment-identified transition service needs with the student and the family in order to develop consensus on: (a) general postsecondary goals, (b) the student's course of study, (c) the types of transition services needed, and (d) the student's self-determination needs. Backward planning can be done with the student and the family to test the feasibility of postsecondary goals and to help them understand the amount of effort that will be necessary to achieve those goals. The results of this discussion should be summarized so that they can be used by the student and the family to drive the IEP/transition meeting. The student and the family also should be acquainted with the terms that may be used in the IEP meeting, and the use of ChoiceMaker or other student-led IEP curricula may aid in this process. A sample glossary is included in Appendix B.

An IEP/transition meeting agenda should be developed with time allotted for the student and the family to lead the discussion. The meeting agenda should specify meeting activities, the time allotted for each activity, and the desired outcomes. At the start of the IEP/transition meeting, there should be time for all transition team members to introduce themselves, to identify their role, and to state how they know the student. The following is a sample 2-hour IEP/transition team meeting agenda. Times and agenda items may vary depending on the number of meeting participants, the student transition service needs, and the level of consensus among team members prior to the meeting. The team may want to appoint a timekeeper at the start of the meeting to notify members when the discussion is exceeding the allotted time. Figure 11–2 shows a sample agenda for an IEP/transition meeting.

Critical Point Educators must plan ahead to ensure student and family participation in the IEP meeting in which transition is discussed.

Implementing the Transition Plan

Writing the IEP with a Transition Plan

The way the statement of needed transition services is written into the IEP may vary according to both the organization of the IEP and the needs of individual students. Typically, a transition IEP should include: (a) a vision statement, (b) the student's current level of functioning, (c) the student's course of study and related transition needs, (d) the student's postsecondary goals in regard to work, postsecondary education, residential living, and community participation, and (e) needed transition services and the persons who are responsible for each.

1. *The Vision Statement*

The vision statement is the opportunity for the student and the family to put their goals and aspirations in their own words. In thinking of a vision, it may be helpful to ask the student and the family to think of a typical day, week, month, and year that would describe the desired goals. For example, a typical day might include work activities, time for rest and leisure, transportation concerns, and communication with friends and family. A typical week might include weekend outings, church, shopping, housework, and visits with friends and family. A typical month might include shopping for clothes, personal items, recreational items and such. Finally, a typical year may include holidays, vacations, time with family, and educational pursuits. The following is an example of a vision statement:

> *John would like to work as an auto mechanic after graduation. He would like to live in an apartment and spend his days working and his evenings with friends or a spouse. During the week, John would like to go to movies, shop for groceries, take walks, exercise at the YMCA, and attend church. Periodically, he would like to shop at the local mall and travel to his aunt's house about 30 miles away. During the year, John would like to take driving vacations, attend holidays with family, and spend two weeks camping in the summer.*

2. *Present Levels of Performance*

According to the IDEA, present levels of performance should be based on a range of formal and informal assessments. This part of the IEP should

FIGURE 11–2
Sample IEP/Transition Meeting Agenda

Cindy—Age 16		
Agenda Item	**Time—Presenter**	**Outcome**
I. Introductions	5 minutes—Teacher	Team sharing of names, relationship to student
II. Overview of agenda and meeting rules	5 minutes—Teacher	Team understanding of meeting purpose and process
III. Presentation of student/family postsecondary goals and course of study	10 minutes—Student and Family	Team understanding of student postsecondary goals and preferred course of study
IV. Presentation of student transition service and activity preferences	10 minutes—Student and Family	Understanding of student transition service and activity preferences
V. Discussion of transition service needs/preferences	15 minutes—Team	Consensus on needed transition services
VI. Assignment of responsibilities and timelines	20 minutes—Team	Completed IEP/transition plan
VII. IEP development	60 minutes—Team	Completed IEP

Source: Adapted from R. Baer, R. McMahan, and R. Flexer, 1999. *Transition planning: A guide for parents and professionals* (p. 19), Kent, OH: Kent State University. Copyright 1999 by Robert Baer. Reprinted with permission.

be written in a functional manner that describes strengths and refers to needs in terms of what the student must do to succeed in a given area. For example, an IQ test is nonfunctional because it gives no direction to the team regarding planning of the student's course of study. Additionally, the current level of performance needs to specify what the student needs in order to progress in the general curriculum. The following is a sample level of performance statement:

> *According to a 9/2002 reevaluation, teacher reports, work samples, and parent input, John has strengths in the areas of mathematics skills of addition, subtraction, multiplying, and dividing using a calculator. He still needs help in converting metrics. John needs to learn to work more quickly and efficiently related to his goal of being an auto mechanic. John also needs to learn to ask for help when frustrated. Grade level expectations of John's peers consist of basic math calculations as well as the application of math calculations in word problems. In order to participate in the general curriculum John will need the help of a tutor, use of a calculator and spell-checker, and curriculum modifications to focus math and English on applied mathematics and reading of technical manuals.*

3. *Statement of Transition Service Needs (or Course of Study Statement)*

After completing the vision statement and identifying the student's current level of functioning it should be possible to determine what course of study would best move a student from his or her current level of function to the desired postsecondary goals. The course of study statement needs to have two components: (a) the desired course of study and (b) the transition services needed to support the student in that course of study. In determining the course of study some general guidelines are that:

1. Four-year college = advanced college-level classes
2. Two-year college = regular and advanced classes, college courses, and vocational training
3. Technical school = advanced vocational training and related academics
4. Employment = applied academics, vocational training, and school-supervised work experiences
5. Supported employment = functional academics, vocational training, and school supervised supported employment

As noted in Chapter 6, students may need assistance in accessing these classes including: (a) assistive technology, (b) curriculum adaptations, (c) curriculum augmentation, or (d) curriculum alteration. These accommodations or "transition service needs" should be included in the statement of transition service needs (or course of study statement). An example of the course of study statement would be as follows:

> *John will need tutoring, curriculum adaptations, a calculator, and a spell-checker to participate in vocational education leading to employment after graduation.*

4. *Statement of Needed Transition Services (or Individual Transition Plan)*

The statement of needed transition services was first required in the IDEA of 1990. This statement has also been known as the Individual Transition Plan (ITP). The transition plan should include: (a) general postsecondary goals and (b) a list of transition services to reach those goals. Postsecondary goals could include goals in the areas of work, education, residential living, and community participation. When the student is younger, these goals may be broad (e.g., competitive employment, postsecondary education, etc). As the student nears graduation these goals may become more specific (e.g., working with autos, 4-year college, etc.). If the student has not formed postsecondary goals, the transition goal may be the identification of these goals.

The second part of the statement of needed transition services (or transition plan) are the activities that will promote movement to the student's desired postsecondary goals. According to the IDEA of 1997, transition services include: (a) instruction, (b) community experiences, (c) development of employment and other postschool adult living objectives, and (d) related services. If appropriate, the IEP/transition plan also should include transition services in the areas of: (a) daily living skills, (b) functional vocational evaluation, and (c) interagency linkages. The seven major categories of transition services outlined in the IDEA of 1997 can be described as follows:

1. *Instruction*. Includes tutoring, employability skills training, vocational education, social skills training, college entrance exam preparation, preparation for taking state and regional proficiency tests, and placement in advanced classes.
2. *Community experiences*. Includes job shadowing, community work experiences, tours of postsecondary education settings, and residential and community tours.
3. *Development of employment and other postschool adult living objectives*. Includes career planning, guidance counseling, interest inventories, person-centered planning, futures planning, self-determination training, job placement, and job tryouts.
4. *Related services*. Includes occupational and physical therapy, speech therapy, social services, psychology services, medical services, rehabilitation technology, and other professional supports to move the

student toward postschool outcomes. Related services also include special education services to help the student participate in the general curriculum.

5. *Daily living skills training*. Includes self-care training, home repair, health training, home economics, independent living training, and money management.
6. *Linkages with adult services*. Includes referrals or assignment of responsibility for services to vocational rehabilitation (VR), summer youth employment programs, mental retardation and developmental disability (MR/DD) services, mental health services, social security, independent living centers, and agency fairs involving a range of adult services.
7. *Functional vocational evaluation*. Includes situational work assessments, work samples, aptitude tests, and job tryouts.

Many IEP formats include a transition page where postsecondary goals can be identified and then related activities listed below them. For example a transition plan for the goal of working with automobiles might appear as follows in the IEP:

Postsecondary Goal: Working with Automobiles

Transition Activities	***Person Responsible***	***Due Dates***	***IEP Goal***
• Auto mechanics classes	VOED teacher	9/1/03 – 5/1/04	1.1
• Automotive work experience	Work study	1/1/04– 5/1/04	2.2
• Referral to VR for job coach	Work study	9/1/03	n/a

5. *Annual Goals*

Now that the course of study statement and the transition plan has been completed, it is important to tie transition activities into the goals, objectives, and activities in the IEP. The first step in this process is the development of measurable annual goals. For example, the automotive activity from the above transition plan refers to IEP goal #2.2. This annual goal could be written as follows:

- 2.2. *Work experience—John will successfully complete a work experience in auto mechanics.*

6. *Objectives*

The IEP objectives should be specific components of the IEP annual goal that can be measured. For the above annual goal, the following objectives would help the team determine whether the IEP goal #2.2 has been reached:

1. *John will independently complete the 10 duties of his job.*
2. *John will have no behavior outbursts on his job.*
3. *John's work will be of a quality acceptable to the employer.*
4. *John will convert fractions to decimals while using socket wrenches.*

7. *Assessment of Student Progress*

The assessment of student progress should be specified in regard to the procedures being used, who will do it, the target levels, and the schedule of assessments. Assessments must occur at least as frequently as assessments for students without disabilities. For the four objectives stated above the assessment of student progress may be written as follows:

- *Procedure—task analysis* (#1), *behavior reports* (#2), *employer interviews* (#3), *and class work* (#4)
- *Who—work study coordinator* (#1–3) *and classroom teacher* (#4)
- *Criteria*
  1. *John successfully completes 10 steps in task analysis for five consecutive days.*
  2. *John requires no behavioral intervention from employer for two consecutive weeks.*
  3. *Employer rates work quality as acceptable for a regular employee for four consecutive weeks.*

4. *John successfully converts decimals to fractions and vice-versa at 95% accuracy.*

- *Schedule*
  1. *John will be assessed on completion of his task analysis weekly.*
  2. *John's behavior will be discussed weekly with his employer.*
  3. *John's work quality will be discussed weekly with his employer.*
  4. *John's math teacher will assess decimal/ fractions skills weekly.*

8. *Needed Services*

Once the objectives and assessment procedures have been identified, the IEP team should identify services that will be needed to achieve each of the objectives under the annual goal. For the previously listed objectives needed services may be delineated as follows:

1. *Employer/employee training* 12/1–12/30/03 *by work study*
2. *Job coaching* 1/1–1/30/04 *by vocational rehabilitation*
3. *Evaluation and follow-along by work study* 2/1–5/1/04
4. *Training and assessment by math teacher* 9/1/03–12/1/04

9. *Least-Restrictive Environment(s)*

Discussion of the least restrictive environment to provide the proposed education and services should commence only after the student's education and support needs have been identified. The least-restrictive environment should never be discussed at the beginning of the IEP meeting, because this may result in the student being slotted into a program before consideration of the student's educational needs. An example of the least-restrictive environment statement for the above student would be:

- *The least-restrictive setting for John's automotive work experience is an integrated school supervised community work experience site. The least-restrictive setting for John's classroom training in applied mathematics is a regular education class.*

This completes the process of writing John's work experiences into his IEP. This process should be repeated for major transition activities (e.g., auto mechanics class) but may not be necessary for one-time transition services (e.g., referral to VR).

Assessing Transition Progress Using a Career Portfolio

The career portfolio is an important tool for assessing competencies, especially during the transition years. The career portfolio may serve several functions: It can provide a standardized form of assessment that can be used for all students, including those with the most severe disabilities. It also may help students to job match and to go on job interviews by providing documentation of skills desired by employers (Sarkees-Wircenski & Wircenski, 1994).

The basis of a career portfolio is a set of competencies that can be applied to student high school experiences and activities. The student demonstrates these competencies in a number of environments, including the home, school, work, and community. Documentation of competencies may include examples of the student's work, photographs, supervisor's comments and evaluations, and even videotapes. The assessment of the career portfolio may be done by the teacher in collaboration with family members, other educators, related service providers, adult service providers, or employers.

The competency areas addressed by the career portfolio may be drawn from a number of sources. A widely recognized source of career competencies is the Secretary of Labor's Commission on Achieving Necessary Skills (commonly referred to as SCANS). An example of a SCANS career portfolio assessment appears in Figure 11–3.

FIGURE 11–3
Sample Career Portfolio Assessment Using SCANS Competencies

Student Name:	*Code amount of support needed*			
Date: Evaluator(s):	**(C) Continuous, (H) Hourly, (D) Daily, (W) Weekly, (M) Monthly, (I) Independent (NO) No Opportunity. Append photos, samples of work, videos, or comments**			
SCANS Competencies	**Home**	**Work**	**Class**	**Leisure**
1. Organizing, Planning, and Resource Allocation				
1.1. Selects relevant activities				
1.2. Prioritizes activities				
1.3. Allocates time				
1.4. Follows schedule				
1.5. Handles money effectively				
1.6. Budgets money				
1.7. Uses materials effectively				
2. Working with Others				
2.1. Contributes to group effort				
2.2. Communicates with friends and coworkers				
2.3. Is courteous toward others				
2.4. Initiates activities and provides leadership				
2.5. Resolves conflicts				
2.6. Works with persons from diverse backgrounds				
3. Acquires and Uses Information				
3.1. Acquires new skills by reading or seeking help				
3.2. Organizes and maintains information				
3.3. Interprets directions or requests clarification				
3.4. Uses computers to process information				
4. Understanding Complex Interrelationships				
4.1. Understands tradition and culture of environment				
4.2. Understands role of self in environment				
4.3. Suggests ways to improve environment				

A Case Study on Transition Planning

Cindy was a student who had autism with pervasive support needs relative to self-care, learning, self-direction, communication, and independent living. Her autism was often exhibited in the form of irrational fears, aggression, stereotypical behavior, and rituals. In middle and early high school, it was determined that Cindy was not responding to traditional educational approaches as evidenced by her distractiveness and aggression toward teachers and peers in this environment. At age 14, her parents determined that Cindy should pursue a course of study leading to employment after graduation with transition services in the areas of behavioral supports, direct instruction, and psychiatric consultation. This was written into Cindy's IEP at age 14.

Jill, Cindy's special education teacher, was charged with developing a new IEP/transition plan for her since she was turning 16 this year of school. After consultation with Cindy's parents and observation of Cindy's interests and preferences, it was determined that Cindy would benefit from personal futures planning, a psychology assessment, and a variety of situational assessments to determine her needs, interests, and preferences. These assessments were arranged with the help of the guidance counselor, the work-study coordinator, and a futures planning consultant from a local university.

Critical Point Assessment approaches are to be developed in conjunction with the student and his or her family.

As a result of Personal Futures Planning (Mount & Zwernick, 1988), it was determined that Cindy and her parents wanted her to work in competitive employment and to live in a supported living situation after graduation. Jill had some concerns that these postsecondary goals may be rather ambitious because Cindy had such extensive behavioral concerns. However, Cindy's parents pointed out that most of these behaviors were exhibited in the classroom and, therefore, could be controlled by the selection of a calm and nondistracting environment for employment after graduation. After some discussion, Jill agreed to support Cindy and her mother in presenting these postsecondary goals to the IEP/transition team.

Psychology assessments showed Cindy having considerable difficulty with changes in routine and a history of developing rituals that interfered with daily routines. A variety of situational assessments showed that Cindy preferred quiet and nondistracting environments and was quite interested in matching and organizing things. She did very well in the hospital records room filing records, although she had one outburst when maintenance workers had to work on the lights. She also did very well in delivering magazines and mail to patients. Transitional service needs were identified as follows:

1. *Instruction.* Cindy needed social skills training, behavioral supports, job skills training, and direct instruction approaches.
2. *Community experiences.* Cindy needed community work experiences related to working in nondistracting clerical settings, experiences in getting to and from the bus, and experiences in living away from her parents.
3. *Development of employment and other postschool adult living objectives.* Cindy needed extensive job placement services and a plan for ongoing behavioral supports in both supported employment and supported living.
4. *Related services.* Assessment showed that Cindy needed related services in the areas of psychology services and augmented communication technology.
5. *Daily living skills training.* As reported by her parents, Cindy needed help to use public transportation.

Student Name:	*Code amount of support needed*			
Date: Evaluator(s):	**(C) Continuous, (H) Hourly, (D) Daily, (W) Weekly, (M) Monthly, (I) Independent (NO) No Opportunity.** **Append photos, samples of work, videos, or comments**			
SCANS Competencies	**Home**	**Work**	**Class**	**Leisure**
5. Working with a Variety of Technologies				
5.1. Chooses proper tools or procedures				
5.2. Understands proper setup and operation of equipment				
5.3. Prevents, identifies, or solves problems with equipment				
6. Basic Skills				
6.1. Uses written information critical to environment				
6.2. Communicates ideas in writing				
6.3. Uses mathematics critical to environment				
6.4. Effectively listens and responds to verbal directions				
6.5. Effectively communicates verbally				
7. Thinking Skills				
7.1. Generates new ideas				
7.2. Uses good judgment				
7.3. Recognizes and solves problems				
7.4. Uses blueprints or drawings				
7.5. Knows how to find information				
7.6. Uses concepts and values in problem solving				
8. Personal Qualities				
8.1. Works hard and perseveres				
8.2. Maintains a positive view of self				
8.3. Is friendly, adaptable, and polite				
8.4. Exhibits self-control				
8.5. Is ethical and honest				

Source: From R. Baer, R. McMahan, and R. Flexer, 1999. *Transition planning: A guide for parents and professionals* (pp. 24–25), Kent, OH: Kent State University. Copyright 1999 by Robert Baer. Reprinted with permission.

6. *Linkages with adult services*. Assessment showed that Cindy would benefit from supported employment through VR and DD services, and a Social Security PASS (plans for achieving self-support).
7. *Functional vocational evaluation*. Evaluations emphasized the need to do situational assessments in a variety of environments.

Critical Point Assessments must be summarized in a manner that is understandable and focused upon student support needs and strengths rather than upon student deficits.

Jill worked with Cindy and her parents to develop a list of who should be invited to the IEP/transition team meeting. Cindy had shown preferences for Jeff Plant, an older friend who had taken her to many community activities and who was the facilitator of Cindy's futures planning meeting. Jill reported that Jeff Ringles, the work-study coordinator, had suggested involving VR services, Social Security, and MR/DD since these agencies would be needed to provide support for community work experiences and supported employment. Cindy's mother recommended Jackie Speaker, an occupational therapist who evaluated Cindy for augmented communication technology, and Leonard James, a behavioral specialist who had worked with Cindy. As required by IDEA, Jill also invited a district representative who was knowledgeable about the general education curriculum, Cindy's regular education teacher, and a vocational-education teacher who was able to interpret evaluations.

It was determined that, because Cindy was nonverbal, Cindy's mother would start the meeting with a review of Cindy's preferences in regard to employment, residential living, and community environments. She would also discuss transition services that would address Cindy's needs and environmental preferences, including community work experiences, supported employment (before graduation), and vocational education. A meeting agenda was developed and a meeting was set for a time that was convenient for Cindy, her mother, and Jeff Plant, Cindy's friend.

Critical Point Prepare the student and the family to participate in the IEP meeting and to lead parts of the discussion.

At the meeting, Jill asked team members to address themselves to Cindy and her mother and to identify themselves, their role, and how they knew Cindy. Jill emphasized that the purpose of the first part of this IEP meeting was to generate a plan that would lead to the types of postsecondary outcomes desired by Cindy. The rules for discussion were that the team must start with Cindy's environmental preferences and then brainstorm needed transition services to establish her in those postsecondary environments. These transition services, then, would be allocated the year prior to graduation.

Jill appointed a recorder and led the IEP/transition team in brainstorming the types of transition services that Cindy would need to move into her preferred environments of a quiet nondistractive work setting, a small family-type residence, and leisure activities with her friends and family. To develop supported employment and independent living options, the adult service representatives suggested (1) the development of a PASS plan with Social Security, (2) job placement and training through VR, and (3) ongoing employment and residential supports from MR/DD. Fred Fryman, the MR/DD representative, suggested that their case managers could help to coordinate these services and to obtain residential services for Cindy.

The school representatives identified the need to involve Cindy in applied mathematics, English, and vocational education since Cindy showed interests and aptitudes in these areas. The regular education teacher agreed to give

Cindy assignments that would help her to identify words and numbers that were critical to working in the clerical and library settings she seemed to prefer when she job shadowed at a number of locations. The vocational educator agreed to see about getting Cindy into the school's secretarial training program with supports and accommodations provided by her behavioral support specialist and occupational therapist. The work-study coordinator agreed to develop community work experiences and supported employment prior to graduation. The district representative agreed to obtain a waiver on some entry requirements for vocational education so that Cindy could attend.

The team suggested, and Cindy's mother concurred, that Cindy should stay in school as long as possible to assure that she had the needed training, technology, and supports to achieve her postsecondary goals. It was determined that she would remain in school until age 22. Using backward planning, transition services were planned as follows:

1. Last year in school (age 21). It was determined that Cindy would need to be established in supported employment with supports from both the school and adult service providers. Due to Cindy's concerns about changes in routine, it was decided that this placement should carry on into adulthood.
2. Two years from graduation (age 20). It was planned that this year should focus upon the development of the postschool objectives with needed transition services provided in the areas of job placement, development of ongoing supports including a PASS plan, and continued community and career exploration.
3. Three years from graduation (age 19). It was determined that this year should focus upon the development of community work experiences, situational assessments, and the use of technology and accommodations related to Cindy's desired postsecondary settings.
4. Four years from graduation (age 18). This year was focused upon completion of vocational education and academics with continued assessment of Cindy's performance and preferences in regard to work and residential and community settings. Intake for all critical adult service program services also should have been completed.
5. Five years from graduation (age 17). It was decided that Cindy's transition service needs for the coming year would be mainly in the areas of academics, vocational education, development of employability skills, social skills training, daily living skills training, and mobility training. It also was determined that Cindy must be trained as soon as possible in order to identify technologies and accommodations that she would need for work.

As a result of this discussion, the following transition plan was developed. Each member was given a list of names, phone numbers, and addresses (including e-mail) to facilitate networking. Jill, then, took the time to address Cindy and her mother in order to explain the plan and to ask if they had any questions. The following IEP/transition plan (Table 11–3) was developed as a result of this planning.

Upon completion of the meeting, Cindy and her parents were given a copy of the IEP/transition plan and the major points were explained to them. They were informed that the IEP/transition team would be reconvened if any problems emerged, and they were encouraged to communicate any questions or concerns to Jill as their transition coordinator.

In the following year, Jill monitored provision of transition services and reconvened the team as needed. She also called each transition

TABLE 11–3

Sample IEP/Transition Plan

Statement of Needed Transition Services

Name: Cindy Doe — Date: 5/1/00

Age: 16 — Age to Graduate: 22

Person Responsible for Coordinating Transition: Jill Smith, Teacher

Postsecondary goals: Supported employment in clerical setting; supported living in hometown; Involvement in integrated clubs and religious organizations; more friends

Course of study and needed transition services: Vocational education (clerical) with direct instruction and behavioral supports. Also classes in consumer sciences, applied academics

Transition Area and Related Activities	Responsible Person	IEP Goal	Start: End:
1. Instruction:			
1. Applied math and English	Pat Claire-math teacher	1.1, 1.2	9/00–6/01
2. Clerical vocational education	Joe Gonzalez-VOED teacher	3.3	9/00–6/01
3. Employability skills	Jill Smith-SPED teacher	3.2	9/00–6/01
4. Social skills training	Joe Lyon-teacher	4.1	9/00–6/01
2. Community Experiences:			
1. Job shadowing in clerical settings	Jeff Ringles-work study	3.4	9/00–6/01
2. Visits to clubs and church groups	Julie Doe-parent		9/00–6/01
3. Community work experiences	Jeff Ringles-work study	3.5	9/01–6/03
4. Supported employment	Jack Point-VR counselor		9/03–6/04
5. Summer camp	Julie Doe-parent		8/00–9/00
3. Development of Employment and Adult Living Objectives:			
1. Job placement and training	Jack Point-VR counselor		5/03–9/03
2. Development of a PASS plan	Sally Fort-social security		5/03–9/03
3. Development of residential plan	Fred Fryman-MR/DD		9/02–5/03
4. Development of ongoing supports	Fred Fryman-MR/DD		5/03–9/03
4. Related Services:			
1. Behavioral plan	Leonard James-Beh Spec.	4.2	By 9/00
2. Augmentative communication training	Jackie Speaker -O.T.		9/00–5/01
5. Daily Living Skills:			
1. Provide mobility training	Jeff Plant-Friend		4/01–5/01
2. Provide training in home safety	Jill Smith-SPED teacher	4.4	1/01–5/01
6. Linkages with Adult Services:			
1. Vocational rehabilitation services	Jack Point-VR counselor		Age 16
2. Developmental disability services	Fred Fryman-MR/DD		Age 16
3. Social Security	Sally Fort-Social Security		Age 16
4. Residential services	Fred Fryman-MR/DD		Age 18
5. Case management services	Fred Fryman-MR/DD		Age 16

(continued)

TABLE 11–3 *(continued)*

Transition Area and Related Activities	Responsible Person	IEP Goal	Start: End:
7. Functional Vocational Evaluation:			
1. Situational assessments in a variety of class, home, work, and leisure environments	Jeff Ringles-work study coordinator		9/00–5/01
2. Career portfolio	Sam Smith-guidance counselor		

Comments: Cindy will need a calm and nondistracting environment and ongoing supports.

Source: From R. Baer, R. McMahan, and R. Flexer, 1999. *Transition planning: A guide for parents and professionals* (p. 30), Kent, OH: Kent State University. Copyright 1999 by Robert Baer. Reprinted with permission.

service provider and Cindy's parents every three months to determine how Cindy was progressing. At the end of the year, Jill forwarded the IEP/transition plan to Joe Lyon, who was to take over as Cindy's special education teacher the following year.

As Cindy moved through high school, there were a number of changes in the transition plan. Cindy was in a variety of work experiences in a library setting, delivering mail, and photocopying for a bank. Despite her success in a couple of her work experiences, she continued to need a great deal of supervision. Collectively, the transition team had to advocate for provision of supported employment because Cindy's MR/DD caseworker felt that she would be safer in a sheltered workshop. After considerable work and support from her family, Cindy was able to obtain a supported employment placement at a government agency delivering mail in-house with ongoing supervision. Her ongoing need for a job coach was partially funded and deducted from her earnings as an impairment-related work expense (IRWE), thereby maintaining her eligibility for Social Security and Medicaid. Cindy's parents set up a PASS plan to help her purchase a car so she could be driven to work by her job coach. Cindy also was able to obtain a supported living situation and to participate in community activities with the help of Medicaid funding.

Questions Families Frequently Ask

The educator who is responsible for coordinating the IEP/transition team meeting should be prepared to answer frequently asked questions of parents and students. Although it is impossible to know about all the agencies and services, the coordinator should have a basic working knowledge to assist the student and the family in determining who should be invited and involved in transition planning. The following are questions that are frequently asked by parents in regard to IEP/transition meetings.

1. ***What employment services are available in the community?***

   There are agencies in each community that provide youth and adults assistance in finding and maintaining employment. These include:

- Vocational rehabilitation (VR) services: Provide or pay for vocational assessment, job placement, job training, postsecondary education, technology, and other time-limited services.
- Mental retardation and developmental disabilities (MR/DD) programs: Provide ongoing supports for students with the most severe disabilities in the areas of sheltered employment, supported employment, residential services, and case management.

- Workforce Investment Act (WIA) programs: Provide time-limited youth employment programs and a variety of job programs, generally for economically disadvantaged students.
- Mental health programs: Provide case management and occasionally supported employment for students with psychiatric disabilities.
- Nonprofit agencies such as United Cerebral Palsy, the ARC, and Goodwill Industries: Provide sheltered employment, supported employment, and other services for youth and adults with disabilities, often through contract with VR.
- Youth services programs: Generally provided to youth who have been in trouble with the law, often through contract with VR.
- Employment agencies: Provide job placement, generally on a fee-for-service basis. Sometimes this service can be paid for by VR.
- Postsecondary education programs: Often provide job placement and career services for their students. Vocational rehabilitation may pay part or all of the cost of these programs for eligible students.

2. ***What employment services do school districts provide students with disabilities?***

School districts may provide a number of services that are available to students with disabilities. These are provided through general, special, and vocational education. Some examples of programs designed to provide work experience or vocational training are (a) work-study or transition coordinators, (b) occupational work-adjustment staff, (c) vocational educators, (d) school-to-work program staff, and (e) guidance counselors.

3. ***What should my child do to get into postsecondary education after high school?***

There are four major types of postsecondary education: (a) vocational/technical schools, (b) community colleges (2-year), (c) liberal arts colleges, and (d) state universities. Every postsecondary program has academic requirements that must be met. However, community colleges often have remedial programs for students who have had difficulty in general areas of course work such as mathematics and English. Postsecondary options should be explored early in high school to select the proper course work and to choose a postsecondary program that provides the services and supports that will be needed by the student after graduation. The student also should receive training in asking for needed accommodations and supports and visits and/or audit classes from desired schools (Turner, 1996). College and other entrance exams should be taken early and applications sent out in the final year of high school.

4. ***What can I do to help my son or daughter get a job?***

Parents have a very important role to play in their child's getting and keeping a job. The expectation that their son or daughter will work is important to convey to their children as they grow. Supporting the school district's efforts to provide job preparation also is essential. Parents can assure that meaningful vocational goals are written into their child's IEP and transition plans and provide opportunities for their child to develop important work skills, habits, and attitudes by giving them chores and responsibilities. Parents also can assist job placement professionals by providing them with leads and introducing them to employers they may know.

5. ***How do I apply for adult services?***

Generally, a student with an IEP will be eligible for vocational rehabilitation (VR) services, and the school can initiate a referral at the parent's or student's request, but typically only students with the more severe disabilities obtain VR services. MR/DD programs often serve only students with the most severe developmental disabilities and the family generally initiates referral. Summer youth employment programs often serve students with milder disabilities who are economically disadvantaged, with referrals typically coming from the school. Mental health job programs are commonly accessed through the mental health counselor and generally reserved for students with the most severe psychiatric disabilities.

6. ***Is there an alternative to sheltered employment for students with severe disabilities?***

Supported employment is designed to serve students who have traditionally gone into sheltered workshops and day activity centers. This is competitive paid work that is performed in an actual job site by individuals who, because of their disability, need ongoing support services to perform that work. Supported employment has four characteristics: (a) paid employment, (b) integration with nondisabled coworkers, (c) ongoing support after job training, and (d) driven by student career goals. Supported employment models include:

- *Individual placement approaches* that include structured assistance in job placement and job training. A job developer develops a job of interest to the student and a job coach trains job skills and provides other training to maintain employment (e.g., social and travel skills). Once the job coach phases out, a professional, coworker, or family member provides follow-along services at the job site.
- *Mobile work crews* of three to eight persons are transported to perform contracted work such as janitorial and landscaping services at area businesses. These crews operate under the supervision of one or more employment specialists.
- *Cluster placements* or enclaves of three to eight persons are supervised by employment specialists and work in a business or industry doing the same job as other nondisabled workers.

7. ***Can a student have a job coach while still in high school?***

VR or the school can provide job coaches for students with intense support needs while they are still in high school. School districts may choose to hire their own job coaches or to use VR services for eligible students. It is important to establish eligibility and to involve adult service providers in transition planning, if they are providing or paying for job coaches.

8. ***What are ongoing support services and follow-along services?***

Ongoing support services or follow-along services are provided throughout the term of employment after the job coach is phased out. The purpose of these services is to enable the individual to continue to perform the work required by the employer. They may include services that occur at or away from the work site, such as transportation, personal care services, counseling, and behavioral supports. Typically, ongoing support services are provided through MR/DD programs or long-term mental health programs, but employers, family members, or other agencies also may provide them.

9. ***What is Supplemental Security Income (SSI)?***

Supplemental Security Income (SSI) is an income support program run by the Social Security Administration. Monthly benefits can be paid to youth or adults with disabilities if their individual or family income falls below a certain level, and if their disability is severe and expected to last at least 12 months. SSI can be helpful in supplementing student income while in postsecondary education or entry-level work. Generally, SSI is applied for at age 18 when family income is no longer considered.

10. ***What is the difference between SSI and Social Security benefits?***

Social Security Disability Insurance (SSDI) is a government insurance fund that is typically paid to a young person with a disability who has a retired, deceased, or disabled parent who paid into Social Security. Social Security benefits are applied for in the same way as SSI; they may amount to more than SSI, or they may be supplemented by SSI if they are less than the SSI amount.

11. *What information is needed to apply for SSI and SSDI?*

Application should be made in person at the local Social Security office. The Social Security representative will need to see the following items:

- Social Security number
- Birth certificate
- Information on income and resources: payroll slips, bank books, insurance policies, car registration, burial fund records, and other information about assets
- Mortgage papers and lease arrangements
- Impairment-related information: name, address, and phone numbers of all doctors, hospital or medical facilities where the student has been treated or tested, and any medical reports in your possession
- Work history (SSDI only)

12. *When can SSI benefits be applied for?*

SSI benefits may be applied for at any age if the child has a significant disability and if the income of the child and that of the family are very low. After age 18, students may be considered a family of one and receive SSI benefits if their income falls below SSI guidelines and if the total resources of the student amount to less than $2,000.

13. *How can my son or daughter get Medicaid benefits?*

People who meet the eligibility requirements for SSI benefits are usually eligible for Medicaid benefits as well. Medicaid benefits are applied for at the local office of the U.S. Department of Health and Human Services. An individual may be eligible for Medicaid and not receiving SSI if he or she is working and needs Medicaid to maintain health benefits.

14. *If students work, does this cause them to lose SSI?*

SSI programs encourage recipients to work through a number of allowances and work incentives. For students, several thousand dollars of earnings can be allowed without affecting benefits by using the Student Earned Income Exclusion. Students may also set up a Plan to Achieve Self-Sufficiency (PASS) where (through an agreement with Social Security) earnings may be placed in a bank account to save up for an item that makes the individual more independent (e.g., college, car down payment, etc.). These savings and this income are not counted against benefits.

Generally, SSI recipients lose only $1 for every $2 they earn and are allowed to exclude $85 of earned and unearned income and any impairment-related work expenses (IRWEs) before these SSI deductions are figured. For example, a person who earns $385 dollars a month will lose only $150 of SSI benefits ([385−85]/2). SSI has other work incentives, including deductions for (a) impairment-related work expenses (IRWEs), (b) student earned income exclusion, (c) blind work expenses, (d) plans for achieving self-support (PASS), (e) property essential to self-support, and (f) continued payment under a VR program. These should be discussed with a Social Security representative.

15. *What about Medicaid and work?*

Unless recipients earn more than double their SSI check plus $85, Medicaid benefits will be continued automatically. Even if a recipient is no longer receiving an SSI payment, he or she can continue to receive Medicaid if:

- The disabling condition continues.
- There is a need for Medicaid to work.
- A person cannot afford medical coverage.

16. *Why do I need to plan for residential living options?*

Whether the student plans to remain at home or to move out, parents should assure that necessary residential supports are provided to ensure that the individual with a disability is cared for after the parents retire or become ill. Depending on eligibility, the student can maintain independence through family supports, Medicaid waivers, low-income housing, personal care attendants, supported living services, or other residential programs. It should be emphasized that residential services often involve long waiting periods and, therefore, should be applied for many years before they are needed.

17. *Why do I need to plan for community participation?*

Research indicates that students with disabilities can become more isolated as they grow older. Due to lack of mobility, income, and social networks, they may have difficulty making the right friends and meeting the right people to assure a good adult quality of life. Membership in religious/cultural affiliations (e.g., church or synagogue), clubs, and recreational programs provide natural and ongoing support networks that can assist persons with disabilities to maintain friendships throughout their life.

18. *Can I have a transition plan without an* IEP?

If a student has a substantial mental or physical impairment but does not qualify for special education, a transition plan can be developed under Section 504 of the Rehabilitation Act, which requires access to appropriate education for all students with handicaps. Section 504 does not require an IEP, but it does require a plan for any area needed by the student to gain an appropriate education. This can include a transition plan.

Common myths about transition plans have emerged as they have become part of the IEP, including the need to standardize the process for all students, to limit planning to a small part of the IEP meeting, to plan year to year, and to meet annually as part of the IEP meeting. At most schools, much of the transition planning process must occur outside the IEP meeting in order for the transition coordinator to individualize planning approaches, to conduct planning in a relaxed and creative atmosphere, to conduct multiyear planning, and to meet regularly.

The process of transition planning, therefore, extends far beyond the process of developing a transition statement as part of the IEP transition meeting. Preparation involves consideration of the method of planning and assessment, forming the transition planning team, exploring service options, and planning for student and family involvement. The implementation of the transition service plan starts with the IEP/transition meeting and continues through implementation of the IEP, assessment of progress, and coordination of transition services. There are many questions and problems that will arise as part of this process that will require the transition coordinator to continuously update knowledge about adult service options, supported employment, financial support, and postsecondary education.

Conclusion

Transition planning was developed in response to studies that showed poor postsecondary outcomes for graduates of special education programs. The IDEA of 1990 and 1997 developed a legal definition of transition planning that included four major criteria: (a) based on student needs, taking into account interests and preferences; (b) developed as part of an outcome-oriented process; (c) a coordinated set of activities; and (d) designed to promote movement into employment and other postschool environments.

Study Questions

1. There are four major criteria for transition planning. Discuss one in detail, outlining IDEA's legal requirements and how schools should address this area.
2. Compare and contrast the transition requirements of the IDEA of 1997 and 1990.
3. Discuss how the transition plan has become part of the IEP, and how this has had unintended consequences for transition planning.
4. Discuss how a school can help students and families to become involved in the IEP transition planning process.

5. Discuss what a teacher should do to prepare for the IEP/transition meeting, and how this process might differ for students with mild and severe cognitive disabilities.
6. Describe a transition goal and write it into the IEP.
7. Discuss how transition progress can be assessed using standardized approaches.

Websites

National Center on Secondary Education and Transition:
http://www.ncset.org/

Transition Planning—NICHCY:
http://www.ldonline.org/ld_indepth/transition/nichcy_TS10.html

What Is Person-Centered Planning?:
http://www.reachoflouisville.com/person-centered/whatisperson.htm

In-Depth Discussion of Person-Centered Planning:
http://soeweb.syr.edu/thechp/everyday.pdf

ERIC: Self-Determination and the Education of Students with Disabilities:
http://ericec.org/digests/e632.html

National Coalition on Self-Determination:
http://www.oaksgroup.org/nconsd/

Self-Determination: Position Statement of CEC:
http://www.dcdt.org/pdf/self_deter.pdf

Self-Determination: Selected Bibliography:
http://www.isdd.indiana.edu/cedir/selfadvobib.html

ChoiceMaker:
http://www.coe.unco.edu/TRAC/choicemaker.pdf

Self-Directed Search: Web-based:
http://www.self-directed-search.com/browser.html

Self-Directed Search: Overview:
http://www.learning4liferesources.com/special_orders.html

Meyers-Briggs: Overview:
http://www.discoveryourpersonality.com/MBTI.html?source=looksmart

ERIC Digest: SCANS Competencies:
http://www.ericfacility.net/ericdigests/ed339749.html

12

Coordinating Transition Services

Robert Baer

LEARNING OBJECTIVES

The objectives for this chapter are:

1. Identify four major approaches to service coordination and their underlying philosophies.
2. Understand how student and family expectations define service coordination.
3. Define the five major responsibilities of the transition services coordinator.
4. Identify the 11 major job duties of the transition services coordinator.
5. Identify competencies needed by the transition services coordinator.

Introduction

Special education's involvement in providing transition services under the requirements of the IDEA has required educators to work with a staggeringly complex adult service system (Baer, 1996; Paulson, 1993), with differing legislative foundations, eligibility requirements, intake procedures, service definitions, and philosophies (DeStefano & Snauwaert, 1989; Szymanski, Hanley-Maxwell, & Asselin, 1992). Ward and Halloran (1989) suggested that this system represented a serious disconnect between the entitlement philosophy of school programs and the availability driven philosophy of adult services. Szymanski et al. noted that these differences were rooted in history, definitions of disability, funding differences, and differences in evaluation standards. Kochhar and Deschamps (1992) maintained that adult service and special education policies were often at odds in assuring services for learners with special needs, and Kortering and Edgar (1988) emphasized the need for more cooperation between special education and vocational rehabilitation.

The complex array of school and adult services has pointed to the need for transition services coordinators who can address both the individual and the systems level transition needs of students with disabilities (Kohler, 1998). At the individual level, transition coordinators need to assure the development of a coordinated set of activities designed to promote student movement to postschool environments. At the systems level, they need to address barriers related to intake and referral, information gathering, planning, service delivery, and evaluation (Baer, 1996). This chapter has been designed to discuss these issues by starting with a review of a range of service coordination strategies. It then applies these strategies to the categories of transition activities developed by Kohler (1998), and the job duties of transition coordinators as defined by job audits (Asselin, Todd-Allen, & deFur, 1998; Baer, 1998). The chapter closes with an extended case study to show how these transition activities and job duties were applied in a single case.

The Range of Service Coordination Strategies

Much of what has been published about service coordination (or case management) has emanated from the fields of rehabilitation and mental health, which have had a long history of dealing with fragmented service delivery systems. Service coordination models have ranged from *broker* models on one end of the continuum to *full support* models on the other (Hagen, 1994; Hodge & Draine, 1993). Broker models of service coordination have often been used by service coordinators (or case managers) with large caseloads (Hodge & Draine). Typically these models consisted of an expert case manager who linked the individual to needed services and then intervened only as new services were needed or when a crisis situation arose (Hodge & Draine). Because of the broker model's focus on stabilization in the community and on appropriate use of services (Hodge & Draine), transition coordinators using this model tended to focus their services on assertive individuals and on individuals in crisis (Intaglia & Baker, 1983).

At the other end of the continuum, full support models used ecological approaches to service coordination. These models required much lower caseloads because the service coordinator functioned as part of the interdisciplinary team and provided proactive services that included assertive outreach, development of environmental supports, and promotion of self-determination (Hodge & Draine, 1993). Services and supports were assessed in these models through what Brown, Nietupski, & Hamre-Nietupski (1976) called the *criterion of ultimate function* and Vincent et al. (1980) described as the *criteria of the next environment*. Full support approaches to service coordination have been identified as best practice in both education and rehabilitation programs (Asselin, Todd-Allen, & deFur, 1998; Baer, 1996) but have remained difficult to implement due to their labor intensiveness.

In between these two extremes, two other service coordination models have been identified in the literature: (a) rehabilitation models and (b) personal strengths models (Hodge & Draine, 1993). A unique feature of the rehabilitation model was the use of functional assessments to determine strengths, deficits, skills, and abilities and then the application of this information to help individuals succeed in specific environments (Robinson, 1991). Typically, this included strengthening individual skills and making adjustments in the living and working environments to facilitate independence. The service coordinator in this model served as a buffer between the individual and the service system and success was measured based on individual satisfaction in the environment of choice (Robinson). This model was less time-intensive than full support models because it targeted specific environments (usually work or education) and focused interventions more on the individual than the environment.

Under the personal strengths models, the service coordinator served as a mentor who assisted individuals in identifying personal strengths that could be used to achieve desired goals. This model has been typically used with individuals with greater career maturity and the ability to identify and develop their personal potential. The advantage of this model was that the focus on strengths and individual resources provided new perspectives about the person with a disability. Evaluation of success under the personal strengths model was based on the individual's ability to identify and obtain personal goals (Hodge & Draine, 1993). It had the advantage of being most closely aligned with the philosophies of the independent living and student self-determination movements.

Family expectations also played a role in the choice of service coordination strategies. Research has found that family expectations of professionals typically fall into one of four general categories: (a) expectations for support and emotional guidance, (b) expectations for cognitive guidance and evaluation, (c) expectations for assuming personal initiative with professional feedback, and (d) expectations for collaboration (Koch & Rumrill, 1998b). It is important that transition coordinators negotiate rather than impose coordination strategies, since congruence among youth, family, and professional expectations has been shown to be positively related to ratings of the working alliance (Al-Darmaki & Kivlighan, 1993). Additionally, families may have many other concerns and stressors that limit their ability to assume service coordination responsibilities (Hayden & Goldman, 1996).

A number of factors influence the expectations that students with disabilities and their families have regarding the transition process, including the individual's career maturity, availability of resources and natural supports, and the preferences of the individual. The "helping" and formalized culture of the disability service system may not fit well with individuals or families who view disability from the perspective of the emerging consumer culture of the independent living movement, which has defined lack of civil rights, societal responses to disability, and dependence on professionals as the primary concerns in disability service provision (Shapiro, 1993; Tower, 1994). The independent living movement has stressed self-management of services by persons with disabilities through collective advocacy, self-help groups, generic support services, and access to the community (DeJong, 1984; Tower).

In some cases students with disabilities and their families may expect greater involvement of professionals in service provision. Hayden and Goldman (1996) suggest that the caregiver's marital status, the youth's level of cognitive disability, frequency of maladaptive behaviors, and the health status of the adult family members are important considerations in determining support strategies. Care should be taken in using service-oriented models such as the broker model because an over-reliance on services may create problems for students with disabilities who move from a service-rich environment in high school to little or no services after graduation (DeStefano & Snauwaert, 1989; Ward & Halloran, 1989).

The Responsibilities of Transition Coordinators

Kohler (1998) conceptualized transition activities as falling into five categories: (a) student-focused planning, (b) student development, (c) family involvement, (d) collaboration, and (e) development of program structures and attributes. This transition model went beyond the four essential elements of transition in IDEA, and provided a means for organizing the activities of the transition coordinator. Kohler's categories of student-focused planning and family involvement primarily addressed the IDEA's essential element of determining student needs, interests, and preferences, but they extended this notion to include the family. The categories of collaboration and of development of program structures and attributes addressed the IDEA element of developing a coordinated set of activities, but they extended this notion to include interagency collaboration. Finally, the category of student development was highly related to promoting movement to postschool activities, but it included a range of activities to promote in-school results as well as postschool outcomes. From Kohler's research, the Council of Exceptional Children's (CEC) Subcommittee on Knowledge and Skills and the CEC Division on Career Development and Transition (DCDT) identified "transition coordinators" as:

> . . . an individual who plans, coordinates, delivers, and evaluates transition education and services at the school or system level, in conjunction with other educators, families, students, and representatives of community organizations. (Division of Career Development and Transition, 2000, p. 1)

Within Kohler's overall framework, transition coordinators performed a number of specific duties. Asselin, Todd-Allen, and deFur (1998) and Baer (1996) used a job audit process known as Developing a Curriculum (DACUM) to identify the major job duties of a transition coordinator. These were identified by practicing coordinators as:

1. Linking services and instruction
2. Identifying postsecondary opportunities and competency requirements
3. Developing community worksites and work experience programs
4. Coordinating referrals
5. Scheduling and facilitating transition meetings
6. Promoting student self-determination
7. Monitoring fulfillment of transition team member responsibilities
8. Chairing the interagency coordinating body
9. Developing communication strategies, methods to release and share information
10. Developing methods to identify future service needs of families and students
11. Coordinating student follow-up studies

The following discussion will examine each of these duties within the general categories of transition services developed by Kohler (1998).

Student-Focused Planning

Each member of any working alliance enters the process with unique expectations (Koch &

Rumrill, 1998b). These expectations need to be identified at the outset so that any discrepancies among the expectations of the transition coordination, the individual, and the family can be resolved and a mutually acceptable set of expectations can be established (Koch & Rumrill). These expectations may evolve over the working alliance and include expectations about outcomes and expectations about roles. Koch & Rumrill described a five-step process in developing a working alliance:

1. Address individual expectations routinely as part of the intake process.
2. Clarify expectations about professional roles, goals, and services of the rehabilitation process.
3. Identify discrepancies between what individuals hope will occur and what they expect to occur.
4. Determine if there are differential expectations among members of the working alliance.
5. Reassess expectations at various stages of the process.

Before the IEP/transition meeting, the transition coordinator should develop consensus among key transition stakeholders, including the youth, family, school, service providers, and natural supporters regarding what is to happen at the meeting. Typically, IEP/transition meetings do not allow time for extensive debate or disagreement and should not be held if a deadlock issue is imminent. If the transition coordinator disagrees with the goals and services selected by the youth and their families, the issue should be resolved prior to the meeting. At the IEP/transition meeting, the transition coordinator should almost always support the choices of youth with disabilities and their families.

In some cases, students may disagree with their families or guardians regarding career choices, services, or supports. In this situation, the transition coordinator should mediate by providing students and their families with additional information or career exploration experiences. This could include involving the student and family in informational meetings with guidance counselors, employers, postsecondary educators, community members, or service providers. In the few instances where students and their families cannot reach consensus, the transition coordinator generally should follow the wishes of the family while supporting the student before the age of majority, and vice versa, after the age of majority.

Prior to the IEP/transition meeting, the transition coordinator should define the role of students and their families in the meeting itself. For students and families with a high degree of career maturity, the transition coordinator may want to encourage them to assume the role of directing the IEP/transition meeting. This active student/family role can be supported developing an agenda, script, or PowerPoint presentation prior to the meeting. The student and/or the family can use these aids to present their transition goals and service preferences at the start of the IEP meeting in which transition is discussed. The transition coordinator can assist them in this role by serving as the timekeeper, notetaker, and prompter. In some cases, the transition coordinator may need to act as an advocate for the student and the families by reading their transition goals and service preferences and by helping the student and family defend these choices.

Scheduling and Facilitating Transition Meetings

The transition coordinator should work with special and general educators to schedule meetings in a way that maximizes student and family participation. Approaches include the use of personal invitations to students and family members, offering alternative times for meetings, holding meetings in alternative locations, and helping to arrange transportation for families. The transition coordinator should also develop strategies for maximizing participation of adult service providers using strategies that include grouping IEP meetings to be attended by an adult service provider and by arranging alternative ways for adult service providers to provide input.

The transition coordinator also needs to accommodate the schedules of families, while at the same time assuring maximum participation of key educators and adult service providers. This may be difficult because adult service providers and educators may be reluctant to meet outside their regular work schedules, while families may find day meetings difficult to attend. This issue can be partially addressed by identifying those times that families are free during the day or times that educators and adult service providers are available on the weekends and in the evenings. These key times can be reserved for families that have difficulty meeting during regularly scheduled hours.

The invitation to the IEP/transition meeting should consist of a written invitation with an enclosed meeting agenda and a simple way to RSVP (e.g., phone call or self-addressed stamped envelope). The transition coordinator may need to make follow-up phone contacts to encourage students, key adult service providers, community members, and families to attend. Families, and even adult service providers, may avoid participation in IEP/transition planning as a result of previous experience where their input was not valued, or where the IEPs were essentially developed prior to the meeting. The transition coordinator needs to assure families and adult service providers that their role in the meeting will be critical. One method of doing this is to develop a meeting agenda that includes time allotted for the student, family, and adult service providers to present issues of concern to them.

The IEP/transition meeting should be conducted in a way that presents the youth with disabilities and their families in the best light. Starting with seating and introductions, students and their families should be given priority in their IEP meetings. The meeting should not start with a discussion of students' weaknesses or disabilities because this will limit the possibilities envisioned for the student by the team. If any student background is provided at the start of the meeting, it should focus upon positive experiences and strengths. Otherwise, the meeting should start with a discussion of the postsecondary goals that have been developed with the students and their families, preferably with each student or the family presenting these themselves.

The second item on the agenda should be a discussion of what services and supports students will need to achieve their goals. This is another critical phase of the planning process because team members may challenge the feasibility of the student's goals at this stage. Unless students and families request input in this regard, discussion and reappraisal of goals should not be allowed to drag on. The coordinator may need to redirect the team from reappraisal of goals to noncritical brainstorming and generation of solutions at this stage (Koch & Rumrill, 1998b). This process may be aided by providing a list of commonly used services and supports and then allocating these services and supports year by year using the backward planning process discussed in Chapter 11. At this stage, it also is useful to develop contingency plans for services and activities (such as summer programs) that may or may not be available due to eligibility, waiting lists, or lack of funding.

The transition coordinator should anticipate positive outcomes by asking questions such as, "When will this service be provided?" and "Who will provide this service or activity?" (Koch & Rumrill, 1998a). In addition, the transition coordinator should ask the question of how the transition plan will be connected to inclusive classroom activities and the student's particular course of study by asking questions such as, "How will transition services and activities be supported by class work?" or "How will the student learn the math or spelling needed to participate in this program or activity?" The outcome of this stage of the meeting should be a list (or statement) of needed transition services and activities with time lines for their completion, contact persons, and reference to supportive classroom activities. The student, family, or transition coordinator may thank the team for their efforts at this stage and hand the meeting over to the student, family member, or teacher who is responsible for developing the remainder of the IEP.

Coordinating Referrals

Student-focused planning may also require the development of linkages to planning conducted by adult service agencies. The transition coordinator needs to develop linkages with adult service and the range of educational programs. The Social Security Administration and the Rehabilitation Services Administration are the two most common referrals for funding and services for youth with disabilities. Transition coordinators need to become familiar with Social Security and its work incentives programs, such as plans to achieve self-sufficiency (PASS), impairment-related work expenses (IRWEs), and student income exclusions. They must become familiar with the programs of the vocational rehabilitation (VR) services and with the services it funds, including postsecondary education, vocational school, assistive technology, computers, and job placement and training. Coordinators also should be aware of when students may apply for and begin receiving services since many adult service programs also serve youth and even children. The coordinator should know that adult services vary widely for different disability groups, from location to location, and from year to year.

The transition coordinator may want to sponsor an agency fair where students, teachers, and families can sign up for adult services at the school. As part of an agency fair, each agency representative and representatives of postsecondary environments can fill out a questionnaire. Figure 12–1 presents an example of such a questionnaire. These can be typed, alphabetized, and put together to make a directory that the school can give to students, community members, and families for easy reference. Additionally, the adult service providers can be invited to present to parents, students, and teachers as part of a panel presentation, which is followed by the opportunity for participants to meet with agency representatives and fill out referrals.

The transition coordinator should be aware that student and family preferences need to be respected in making referrals for adult services and that some referrals may need to be initiated by the student or the family. Referrals for mental health and developmental disability (or mental retardation) services may be resisted by some students for fear of being stigmatized as "retarded" or "crazy." Additionally, families may have misinformation about adult service programs that need to be addressed. For example, many students and families believe that developmental disability programs provide only sheltered workshop services, when these programs can actually provide supported employment and supported living services in the community.

Student Development

Siegel (1998) suggested that because there was no single transition program that served all students with disabilities, all programs should maximize accessibility. According to Siegel (1998), youth with profound disabilities and extremely challenging behaviors should have access to supported employment services, day treatment, residential, and immersion programs and should have follow-along services that extend for up to five years. Youth with mild learn-

FIGURE 12–1
Outline for Panel Presentation

1. **Your name:** ______________________________ **Title:** ______________________________
2. **Your agency:** ______________________________ **Phone:** ______________________________
3. Please provide a brief overview of the purpose of your agency:

____
____
____
____
____

4. Briefly, what transition services are available to students with disabilities before age 18?

____
____
____
____
____

5. Briefly, what transition services are available to students with disabilities after age 18?

____
____
____
____
____
____

6. Generally, what types of students are eligible for your services and how should they be referred?

____
____
____
____
____

ing or emotional disabilities should be involved in job shadowing and have access to work experiences during the last two years of school. They also may need to have access to team teaching, vocational special education, community work experiences, participation in career/technical and vocational clubs and organizations, linkages with adult services, and support in accessing a community college program.

Critical Point Students with disabilities should have access to all educational and career/technical and vocational programs with supports.

Linking Services and Instruction

Transition coordinators can link services and instruction by assuring that students' courses of study relate to their postschool goals. As noted earlier, the IDEA mandates that by age

14, student IEPs should include a "statement of transition services needs" related to students' desired courses of study. There are two important components of this IDEA requirement: (a) identifying a course of study and (b) identifying transition services needs related to that course of study. Courses of study could include specific classes or training related to student postschool goals, but the author recommends identifying general courses of study such as vocational education and advanced academics, because these programs have been shown to promote positive postschool outcomes for students (Blackorby & Wagner, 1996). Transition service needs would generally include the provision of assistive technology, curriculum adaptations, curriculum augmentation, or curriculum alterations that would allow the student to progress in this course of study (see Chapter 6).

Access to the general curriculum may be resisted by general education teachers who feel unprepared to teach students with disabilities, so the coordinator may need to advocate for inclusive practices such as team teaching. Additionally, students with disabilities may experience difficulties in accessing career/ technical and vocational education programs that require them to complete all regular education programs before entering. Transition coordinators must therefore become familiar with academic standards and develop strategies for the student to address these standards while still working toward desired postschool outcomes (Greene, 2001; Wehmeyer, 2002). This would include planning for student participation in high-stakes tests required for graduation and promotion. Additionally, transition coordinators should assure that students with postsecondary education goals complete the courses required for entry into the postsecondary education programs of their choice and take college entrance examinations.

Identifying Postsecondary Opportunities and Competency Requirements

A primary role of the transition coordinator is providing linkages to services and supports needed for the development of employment and other adult living objectives for youth with disabilities and their families. Prior to the IEP/transition meeting, the coordinator needs to develop linkages with postsecondary educators and adult service providers who can aid in the development of the transition plan; and with natural supporters, employers, secondary educators, and service providers who can assist in its implementation. The transition coordinator should assist youths and their families in identifying and inviting potential postsecondary meeting participants. This requires out-of-school activities such as touring area businesses and educational programs, meeting with employer groups, having students conduct informational interviews with employers and schools, and meeting with vocational educators. The coordinator can also invite employers to consult as part of individual IEP teams or as part of a school-wide interagency transition team.

It is important to establish the right contact person for each program. It may be much more effective to use a representative of student disability services or learning centers from a 2- or 4-year college than an admissions officer who is unfamiliar with disability issues. For employers, it may be more effective to establish contact with employee assistance personnel than with personnel managers who are more inclined to screen than to welcome applicants with disabilities. The general rule for selecting contacts is that they should: (a) be able to represent the postsecondary program, (b) be as knowledgeable of disability issues as possible, and (c) be supportive of persons with disabilities.

It is critical that the transition coordinator establish linkages with 2- and 4-year colleges, vocational and technical schools, employers, continuing education programs, residential programs, transportations, parks and recreation, YMCAs, independent living centers, neighborhood organizations, cultural centers, and a myriad of other community programs. Key contacts from each of these programs should be on file and easily accessible, and the coordinator should establish new contacts as needed by individual students. Each contact should be cultivated and rewarded for participating in meetings or providing consults. Rewards can include thank you letters, invitations to school events, recognition dinners, or providing useful information of interest to the contact. It is important to understand that many of these contacts provide consultation on their own time, so their input should be used efficiently and effectively. The coordinator can use career fairs, group together IEP/transition meetings that postschool providers are to attend, and use conference calls to maximize participation of postsecondary contacts while minimizing time demands.

Developing Community Work Sites and Work Experience Programs

Wehman (1990) stated that an employer advisory board was a critical element of a successful transition program. Halloran (1992) asserted that education-industry collaboration was an important strategy for ensuring that students with disabilities had access to employment training opportunities. Rhodes, Sandow, Monk, Buckley & Albin. (1991) noted that involving employers would be the major source of training in a future in which special education and adult service budgets were expected to show little or no growth, and they noted that employer resources already dwarfed those available through special education and rehabilitation. Phelps and Maddy-Bernstein (1992) found that the benefits of business-education partnerships included additional resources, employment opportunities, increased personal attention, improved facilities, and better teacher morale. Other researchers pointed to the importance of employer support for students with mild disabilities who were not eligible for adult services (Scuccimarra & Speece, 1990).

In addition to advisory boards, several researchers have developed mechanisms for forging individual partnerships with employers. Rhodes et al. (1991) noted that employee assistance programs were a potential support mechanism for the worker with a disability, and suggested that new legislation such as the Americans with Disabilities Act would enhance transition as employers expanded existing employee support programs to meet the needs of persons with disabilities. Hagner, Rogan, and Murphy (1992) identified strategies for facilitating natural supports in the workplace by using a consultant approach with employers. They found that it was important to get employers to take ownership of services for employees with disabilities, rather than having service providers offer to do it all.

The development of community work sites and work experience programs for youth with disabilities requires the ability to use both the individual's and the school's network of contacts. Some common practices might include hosting an agency or business advisory committee, becoming a member of a business-oriented community group, maintaining a "job bank" with other agencies, or hosting a career fair (Baer, Martonyi, Simmons, Flexer, & Goebel, 1994). It is also important to survey staff, board members, former and current employers, and consumer supporters to develop job leads. The most efficient way to develop job leads is through personal referrals from a person known to the prospective employer.

In developing community work experiences, the transition coordinator needs to be aware of child labor laws and of the Fair Labor Standards Act. Work experiences need to be addressed in students' IEPs to protect schools and employers from liability. Work experiences must be voluntary with no expectation of remuneration and

Support needs may vary over time.

they must not result in immediate advantage to businesses or to displace workers. Students should spend no more than 5 hours at a work site for career exploration, no more than 90 hours for assessment, and no more than 120 hours for unpaid training. Students should receive training by staff while in work experiences and should not work with power equipment before age 18 (Petric, 2002).

Promoting Student Self-Determination

Transition coordinators need to encourage and provide opportunities for self-determination and decision making in the transition process. Many students with disabilities and their families will have had previous experiences with IEP planning that lead them to define their role as passive, uninvolved, or dependent. To promote self-determination, the transition coordinator should assess factors affecting the student's ability to make informed choices. Informed choice assumes that the youth with a disability is: (a) free from coercion, (b) has the necessary information and experience, and (c) is able to make choices that have a reasonable expectation of positive outcome (Dinerstein, Herr, & O'Sullivan, 1999).

Assuring that students are free from coercion in setting goals and choosing services is an important role of the transition coordinator. Coercion, unlike persuasion, is based on force rather than information and may be both covert and overt. Overt coercion may come from professionals or family members (Dinerstein, Herr, & O'Sullivan, 1999). It may come from professionals in the form of threats to discontinue support services if youth with disabilities choose to participate in settings that make provision of these services inconvenient to providers. Overt coercion may also come from family members who pressure the student into accepting services that are more convenient for the family (e.g., the convenience of regular day activity programs versus supported employment).

A more difficult concern for the transition coordinator is covert coercion. Covert coercion may include questions such as, "You want to work in a restaurant, yes?" Apart from leading questions such as this, research indicates that even yes and no questions can be coercive since many individuals with disabilities have learned to answer yes to questions posed by persons in authority (Wehmeyer & Kelchner, 1995b). Transition coordinators need to avoid yes and no questions in interviews, whenever possible. Open-ended questions are preferable, with comprehensive lists of well-defined choices provided as support. Covert coercion can also be avoided by developing a script or PowerPoint presentation with the student prior to the meeting. This assures that the student's goals and service preferences are clearly stated and less subject to distortion.

A second consideration in assuring informed consent is that students need the necessary information and experience to make informed choices about their education program and the IEP planning process. Martin, Huber-Marshall, Maxson, & Jerman (1996); Wehmeyer & Kelchner (1995), Van Reusen & Bos (1990); Powers et al. (1996); and Halpern et al. (1997) and others have developed self-determination curricula that may be useful in this regard (see Chapter 11). Transition coordinators should be aware of these self-determination curricula and encourage their use with students. Additionally, students should be aware of service, curriculum, and support options available in their school system.

Determining the reasonableness of the outcome of student decisions regarding the education program is perhaps the most difficult aspect of assuring informed consent. A student who makes choices that do not have a reasonable chance of outcome may be considered unable to provide informed consent (Dinerstein, et al. 1999). However, a student who is not allowed to make some "unreasonable" decisions may never develop the maturity to give informed consent. The transition coordinator, therefore, must support the right of students and families to make low feasibility choices early in transition planning, while at the same time assuring that these choices do not result in substantial harm. For example, a failing student who chooses a college preparatory career path could meet with teachers of college preparatory high school courses, college admissions officers, and college disability services to discuss the reasonableness of his or her choice. If the student chooses to proceed with a well-informed but possibly unwise decision, the transition coordinator should support this decision while minimizing the harm of failure. For, example the transition coordinator could enroll the student in advanced academics but provide frequent follow-up to assure that progress is being made. If the student succeeds, expectations should be reshaped accordingly, but if the student fails after all supports have been tried, the IEP team should be reconvened promptly to discuss alternative strategies. In some cases, students may succeed against all odds. In other cases, students or families may need to revise transition goals.

Critical Point The transition coordinator needs to assess student decisions relative to voluntariness, knowledge, and reasonableness of outcome and to provide self-determination training and opportunities to make choices.

Promoting student self-determination becomes a critical issue as the student approaches the age of majority under state law. The IDEA of 1997 requires transfer of IDEA rights and control of the IEP team at that age unless the student has been determined incompetent or unable to give informed consent about the education program (IEP). If the student has become increasingly self-determined and has had opportunities to demonstrate informed consent in the early years of transition planning, she or he is much more likely to be ready to be given IDEA rights at the age of majority. On the other hand, if this issue is not addressed, it is likely that the student will never have the opportunity to assume this role.

In keeping with the concept of self-determination, the transition coordinator should provide opportunities for students to practice advocacy skills in supported situations. Students should know about their disability, the accommodations they need, and how to communicate these needs with educators, employers, and community members. They should request accommodations and services on their own with the support of the transition coordinator. Self-advocacy is a critical skill that may make the difference between a student succeeding or failing in postsecondary education, employment, or social interactions. These self-advocacy skills can be developed through a number of approaches including self-determination training, mentoring from successful individuals with disabilities, or development of advocacy groups.

The advocacy role of the transition coordinator should not be confused with the advocacy role of the student and the family. Webster's dictionary defines advocacy as "speaking for or on behalf of a person." Advocacy in this sense can be empowering and disempowering. If the coordinator speaks on behalf of youth with disabilities and families who can speak for themselves, it is disempowering. On the other hand, the transition coordinator may be able to assist individuals and families in communicating with service providers whose culture and technical jargon may be foreign to the layperson. In this sense, advocacy by the transition coordinator may be seen as empowering.

Family Involvement

Families can provide critical insight into student interests, abilities, history, and preferences and may act as surrogate decision makers for students who are unable to give informed consent (Dinerstein, et.al, 1999). They also play a critical role in improving student performance and attendance in school and in supporting the individual's transition after leaving school. Family involvement in transition planning and programs also can help the parents form realistic expectations for the students as they observe them performing competently in classroom and community environments with supports.

Carney and Orelove (1988) noted that parental influence toward community integration depended on parent beliefs about their children's needs and capabilities, and their beliefs about the availability and appropriateness of community services. They developed a grid that showed how parental perceptions were formed. This grid appeared as follows:

	Know Available Services	Don't Know Available Services
Believe in child's capability	1. Parents know community options and believe they are appropriate.	2. Parents don't know community options but believe they are appropriate.
Don't believe in child's capability	3. Parents know community options but do not believe they are appropriate.	4. Parents don't know community options and don't believe they're appropriate.

Carney and Orelove (1988) suggested that parent involvement promoted student independence only when their beliefs and knowledge fell in Cell 1. They found that parental ability to make informed decisions related to six factors: (a) knowledge of the range of options, (b) ability to evaluate options, (c) knowledge of child's skill, (d) knowledge of child's preferences, (e) knowledge of how to get services, and (f) knowledge of how to advocate for services not available (Carney & Orelove, 1988).

The transition coordinator should therefore be aware of the difficulties that families have in participating in the transition process. They may find transition planning ambiguous and confusing; be reluctant to discuss their child's disabilities in front of a group; and may lack clear, relevant, and timely information about transition services. The transition coordinator needs to address these issues by making families more knowledgeable, connected, and supported. The coordinator can support them in this regard through development of joint family-professional transition training, resource fairs, a single point of contact for all services, support groups, information materials, and networking activities (Kohler, 1998).

Cultural issues can result in discord and conflict when the culture of a service delivery system differs greatly from the culture of the individual and the family (Hanley-Maxwell, Pogoloff, & Whitney-Thomas, 1998). Some cultures depend more heavily on support from extended families, neighborhoods, and churches, while other cultures may reject the idea of social services, altogether. For example, a transition services coordinator in rural Ohio or Pennsylvania should know that many Amish communities will not accept social services, but may use them if they are termed educational services. Service coordinators in urban settings must be sensitive to extreme dissonance between social service agencies and minority cultures, while recognizing the great potential of neighborhood and religious affiliations (Hornstein, 1997). Service coordinators need to understand the youth's culture, explore alternative service and support approaches, discuss individual needs and preferences, and provide choices regarding service providers and supporters.

Critical Point The transition coordinator should develop a variety of options for families to participate in transition planning and the development of transition programs.

Collaboration

The transition coordinator should promote collaboration in a way that minimizes the barriers among the student, family, and professionals; and that also improves collaboration among the professionals themselves (Baer, Goebel, & Flexer, 1993). In this regard, the transition coordinator must foster transition team processes that move team members from a multidisciplinary approach (where professional roles are rigid and specialized) to an interdisciplinary or transdisciplinary approach where professional, student, and family roles are less circumscribed. Multidisciplinary models of service delivery are more prevalent in medical programs where professionals typically work in a professional/patient relationship with only limited consultation with other disciplines. Interdisciplinary approaches are more prevalent in nonmedical disability programs where professionals typically work in a professional/consumer relationship as part of a team. Table 12–1 compares and contrasts these models and their implications for assessment, planning and service delivery.

More than any other approach, personal strengths models of service coordination imply the need for a transdisciplinary approach to service provision. In this approach, professionals work as consultants to individuals with disabilities and to other professionals on the team. Both services and planning are provided collaboratively. *Role release* is an important characteristic of the transdisciplinary model where team members work as part of an integrated program providing services and supports that are organized around individual needs rather than professional services (Baer, Goebel, & Flexer, 1993). In this approach, students, family members, and other professionals may participate in implementing physical therapy, behavior programming, and training as part of an integrated community program focused upon individual goals.

Critical Point The transition coordinator should develop a team process that equalizes relationships between families and professionals and that minimizes barriers between the disciplines.

In directing collaboration, the transition coordinator should be familiar with laws pertaining to youth with disabilities. These include the IDEA, Section 504 of the Rehabilitation Act, the Americans with Disabilities Act (ADA), and other civil rights legislation. Transition legislation and regulations can be difficult to read and interpret, so the coordinator should attend in-service programs and obtain publications by the National Association of Special Education Directors (NASDE) and other publications of professional and parent organizations.

TABLE 12–1
Comparison of Service Models

Multidisciplinary	Interdisciplinary	Transdisciplinary
Participation of the student is limited to a professional-student relationship.	*Participation* of the student is as a member of a team.	*Participation* of the student is as a member of a team.
Assessment is done or interpreted by the professional seeing the individual student	*Assessment* is based on needs and preferences as seen by the student and each team member, including nonprofessionals.	*Assessment* is based on needs and preferences, as seen by the student and each team member, including nonprofessionals.
Planning is confined to organization of individual treatments provided by the professionals.	*Planning* is based on functional needs within professions, coordinated to obtain outcomes desired by the student and the family.	*Planning* is based on functional needs and preferences, across disciplines, in which activities are shared to obtain outcomes.
Implementation consists of a series of individual treatments.	*Implementation* consists of services and activities coordinated by the transition coordinator.	*Implementation* consists of services and activities collaboratively provided by professionals and team members.
Evaluation is based on progress in regard to year-to-year goals.	*Evaluation* is based on progress toward individual postsecondary goals set by the team and the student.	*Evaluation* is based on progress in achieving the student's total quality of life before and after graduation.

Source: Adapted from R. P. Baer, G. Goebel, & R. W. Flexer (1993). An interdisciplinary approach to rehabilitation. In R. W. Flexer & P. L. Solomon, *Psychiatric rehabilitation in practice.* Boston: Andover Publishers.

The transition coordinator is likely to encounter conflict in efforts to promote collaboration. A common myth about any collaborative process is that collaborators will agree, have shared values, and develop consensus without conflict (Koch & Rumrill, 1998b). Strong working relationships with transition team members should assure that conflict and disagreement can occur without destroying the relationship. Koch and Rumrill (1998b) define a four-step process for resolving conflicts: (a) accurately defining the conflict, (b) clarifying misconceptions, (c) generating options, and (d) implementing and evaluating resolutions. It is important to identify conflicts and resolve them as they arise to avoid breakdown in relationships and disruption of decision making and team process.

Transition coordinators should deal with conflicts discretely, preferably outside student or agency meetings. If a conflict threatens to disrupt an IEP/transition team meeting, the coordinator should recess or adjourn the meeting until the conflict is resolved. The coordinator should set up a meeting between the conflicting members, preferably in a relaxed neutral setting, and follow the four-step process for conflict resolution. In conflict resolution, the coordinator should assume the role of mediator and periodically reassure participants that conflict is normal in a good working alliance (Koch & Rumrill, 1998b). If the coordinator is directly involved in the conflict, he or she may bring in an outside person as an arbitrator.

Developing Communication Strategies and Methods to Release and Share Information

In the 1980s the Office of Special Education and Rehabilitation Services (OSERS) began to focus on interagency agreements as a way of bringing the transition disciplines together. Heal, Copher, and Rusch (1990) studied the characteristics and perceived value of these agreements in 29 demonstration projects. They found that while several agencies were involved (average 3.93 per agreement) less than half (11) involved vocational education. Heal et al. (1990) also found that interagency agreements did little to address the problem of fragmented transition services. Generally, the respective agencies invested minimal time and resources in interagency collaboration and collaborative efforts tended to focus on information and referral, rather than developing a truly coordinated set of activities (Heal, et al., 1990).

To address this need, authors of best practice have recommended the development of school-interagency transition teams to develop channels of communication and to iron out policy differences (Everson, 1990; Halloran, 1992; Halpern, 1992b; Heal, Copher, et al., 1990; Phelps & Maddy-Bernstein, 1992; Wehman, 1990; Wehman, Moon, Everson, Wood, & Barcus, 1988). These teams may focus on a number of issues. Heal, et al. (1990) suggested that transition teams focus on service overlaps and gaps, while Wehman et al. (1988) recommended that they be formed to address the need to: (a) share referrals, (b) do local needs assessment, and (c) share funding. Everson (1990) suggested that transition teams address local obstacles (such as funding and lack of parent participation) through collaborative efforts designed to empower parents and students.

Communication among the many programs serving youth with disabilities can be challenging for transition coordinators who spend much of the time out of the office. Ohio's systems change project for transition explored this issue by funding a number of pilot sites to address shared intake, referral, and transition planning. Approaches varied among the sites and included:

- Sharing the IEP/transition plan with all agencies serving a given youth, with the agencies then using it as the base of all plans concerning the youth
- The development of a password protected computer site where general information on students could be stored and released to agencies
- The development of common intake and referral sheet used for all agency services. (Baer, 1996)

Release of information restrictions can be a major impediment to communication. The transition coordinator may need to look into how information can be shared among transition providers without violating the privacy of youth with disabilities and their families. Collaborating agencies may fall under the jurisdiction of privacy laws pertaining to medical information (HIPPA) or educational information (FERPA). A blanket release of information that allows the sharing of information among all transition agencies for a limited time can facilitate information sharing. This can help students and families who often have to answer the same questions repeatedly to different transition services providers. Some considerations in the development of a blanket release of information form include the option for students and families to control:

1. What information is to be released: identifying information, case information, financial information, sensitive medical information (e.g., HIV and AIDS)
2. How long the release of information is in effect (e.g., 180 days, 360 days, etc.)

3. What agencies can receive student information (all agencies, specific agencies)
4. How information is protected by all agencies covered by the blanket release
5. How the student or family can revoke the release of information at any time
6. Assurances that refusal to sign the blanket release will not affect services (Baer, 1996)

In addition to the blanket release of information form, each participating agency will need to sign a member agreement for information sharing. This member agreement needs to specify: (a) how information will be used, (b) information will not be used in criminal manners, except as required by judicial order, and (c) members will maintain information in a secure manner. Both the blanket release of information and the member agreement should be shared with legal experts at each of the agencies to assure that they comply with the law and agency regulations. (See Appendix C for a sample blanket release of information and member agreement.)

Monitoring Fulfillment of Transition Team Member Responsibilities

The transition coordinator needs to develop mechanisms for monitoring services in IEP/transition plans. This is an area of particular concern since research indicates that less than 25% of IEP/transition teams were reconvened when adult services could not be provided as planned (Baer et al., 1996). This lack of concern for maintaining planned transition services indicated to transition team participants that transition planning had little importance or relevance to what the student was actually doing in school.

The transition coordinator monitors service provisions by establishing benchmarks and contacting service and support providers periodically to assure that they are on schedule. It is important that the transition coordinator make contacts with key service providers well in advance of transition services deadlines to allow time to correct problems or to revise time lines before deadlines are missed. Additionally, periodic contact with members of a student's IEP/transition team allows the coordinator to gather information and to cement relationships. This investment in relationships with team members is a valuable resource when things go wrong or mistakes are made. If services cannot be provided as planned, the coordinator should reconvene the student's transition team. Reconvening the team offers the student and the family the opportunity to discuss alternative ways of addressing transition objectives.

Critical Point The transition coordinator needs to assure that transition planning drives provision of student services and to reconvene the student's transition team if services cannot be provided as planned.

Development of Program Attributes and Structures

Often the transition system at a given school lacks the program structures to promote student-focused planning, student development, family involvement, or interagency collaboration (Kohler, 1998). Relative to the transition planning, this may be manifested in limited time for youth and family input in the development of the IEP/transition plan, use of technical language, inviting only preferred service providers to transition meetings, inconvenient meeting times and places, and excessive bureaucracy. There also may be lack of critical transition programs, such as life skills instruction, career and career/technical and vocational education support services, and structured work experiences (Kohler, 1998).

To deal with these program issues, the transition coordinator must be able to mobilize transition stakeholders in adopting exemplary transition practices (Everson & Guillory, 1998). The transition coordinator may address these issues by forming a schoolwide interagency transition team. The membership of the school-level interagency transition team should include all transition stakeholders, including families, adult service providers, administrators, educators, employers, and transition specialists. The makeup of the team may vary from meeting to meeting, depending on the students or issues to be discussed, but it should generally address issues such as:

- Community supports
- Better access to vocational services
- Curriculum enhancement and life skills instruction
- Cross-training for students, parents, and professionals
- Development of work experiences
- Strategies to empower youth with disabilities and their families
- Strategies to empower minority youth with disabilities and their families

A number of surveys have been developed to self-assess transition policy compliance and the best practice (Baer, McMahan, & Flexer, 1999; Johnson, Sharpe, & Sinclair, 1997; McMahan & Baer, 2001; Morgan, Moore, McSweyn, & Salzberg, 1992). Appendix D contains a survey that school-based interagency transition teams have used in Ohio to assess policy compliance and the best practice. This survey examines both current and the team members' perception of the most promising practice in relation to 36 criteria.

The school-level interagency transition team also can be an effective mechanism for maintaining current information on transition services by bringing school and adult service providers together to discuss the ever-changing system of services available to transition-age youth. Key representatives from major programs such as rehabilitation services, developmental disabilities programs, WIA (Work Incentive Act), Social Security, mental health, and the Department of Job and Family Services (formerly the Department of Human Services) may be able to provide information pertaining to many other programs in the community.

Critical Point The transition coordinator should support or develop a schoolwide interagency transition team to address systems issues, planning, and program development.

Generally, the transition coordinator needs to be familiar with group process skills to manage effectively the school-level transition team. Tuckman and Jensen (1977) suggest that groups go through five rather predictable stages of development: forming, storming, norming, performing, and adjourning. In the forming phase, the coordinator needs to recruit representatives of critical transition stakeholder groups and to convince them of the importance of addressing transition issues for youth with disabilities. In the storming phase, the coordinator needs to lead the group in a noncritical generation of ideas about desired transition outcomes and the best practices to achieve those outcomes. In the norming phase, the transition coordinator needs to develop an action plan that outlines who is to do what by when. In the performing stage, the transition coordinator as the leader needs to monitor performance, reward success, and problem solve failures. At the adjourning phase, the team members are given an option of leaving the team or renewing commitment. Often this is determined by the terms of membership.

Developing Methods to Identify Future Service Needs of Families and Students

The transition coordinator needs to develop a method of determining how many students and families need specific types of transition services prior to and after leaving high school. This information can be shared with programs and agencies that provide these services so that they can plan accordingly. The coordinator can use a number of approaches to identify these needs. These approaches include (a) a review of IEP/transition plans; (b) a survey of students, families, and professionals; or (c) focus groups.

Once the coordinator has obtained the information, it should be shared with all concerned providers and agencies. The school-based interagency transition team can assist the coordinator in this regard by providing a forum where the information can be discussed. The interagency transition team should address questions, including: (a) Are services being utilized effectively?; (b) Does the current service capacity meet the future needs of students?; and (c) How can service capacity and service needs be addressed?

Coordinating Student Follow-Up and Follow-Along Studies

Follow-up and longitudinal (or follow-along) studies of students who have exited school provide information on the problems that students encounter after graduation and on the effectiveness of the transition services they received before graduation (Baer et al., 2003). Follow-along studies follow a cohort of students over time, whole follow-up studies collect information on outcomes at a single point in time (Halpern, 1990). These studies may be conducted for all students or for a random sample of students. Typically, follow-up and follow-along studies look at student outcomes 1, 3, and 5 years after leaving school. Questions commonly addressed by these studies include:

1. The person's age and date of leaving school (typically from school records)
2. The type of disability (typically from school records)
3. Ethnicity (typically from school records)
4. Employment information (e.g., duration, type, wages, benefits, hours, etc.)
5. Support information (e.g., adult services, financial supports, natural supports, etc.)
6. Community activities (e.g., civic, volunteer, recreation, etc.)
7. Transportation (e.g., car, bus, walking, family, etc.)
8. Living arrangements (e.g., family, independent, supported living, etc.)
9. Postsecondary education enrolled 2-year, 4-year, other) postsecondary education completed
10. Transition and school programs that were especially helpful
11. Transition and school programs that were unavailable or unhelpful

A Case Study in Transition Services Coordination

As a transition specialist at an urban school, Ellen and her mother came to me this June to discuss her educational program as she entered high school. Ellen's eighth grade teacher, Ms. Middleton, had informed them that, since Ellen was 14 years old, her IEP meeting would include a discussion of what she would be doing after graduation and how she would get there. The teacher also told them that we would be talking about other agencies and programs that might help Ellen to reach her goals. Ms. Middleton noted that they were very confused about what "transition" was and what this had to do with Ellen.

Ms. Middleton and I met Ellen and her mother outside the school and had coffee, soft drinks, and donuts while we discussed Ellen's transition to high school and what she would like to do after graduation. Ellen responded "yes" when her mother said "You want to go to school to be a nurse's aide, don't you?" but it was clear that Ellen had no concept of what a nurse's aide did. Ellen clearly was looking for emotional support and guidance, so I surveyed both Ellen and her mother regarding what they saw Ellen doing both before and after graduation. Through this survey, it was clear that Ellen would need a lot more information and that her mother would need to give her more freedom in regard to her choices. We discussed the importance of self-determination and how it could be developed through functional and vocational evaluations, community experiences, informational interviews, and job shadowing. Ellen seemed to be interested, but her mother was concerned that she would miss out on class work. After some discussion, we suggested that Ellen and her mother meet with the guidance counselor and the work-study coordinator to explore this issue further.

Critical Point Keep student-focused planning by scheduling meetings at alternative sites and by assuring the student is giving informed consent.

After meeting with the guidance counselor and the work-study coordinator, Ellen and her mother agreed to do the functional-vocational assessment, which identified an interest in library work and a number of areas in which Ellen would need services and supports to pursue this course of study. Ellen had poor spelling skills and no typing skills. It also was clear that while Ellen expressed an interest in library work, she based this decision on the fact that she had no other work experiences. However, it was clear that Ellen liked that type of work environment and enjoyed books. The guidance counselor provided Ellen with a tentative list of classes and the work-study coordinator discussed some areas that might be explored through community work experiences and job shadowing.

Ellen and her mother preferred that I act on their behalf in the first IEP/transition meeting. In the meeting, we focused upon career exploration and the transition services and supports that Ellen would need to participate in her course of study. The guidance counselor, the vocational evaluator, and the work-study coordinator were invited to the meeting. The guidance counselor agreed to enroll Ellen in business-related English, typing, and math classes. The vocational evaluator suggested a hand speller to help Ellen with her spelling problems. The work-study coordinator agreed to arrange some job-shadowing experiences around office work and related occupations. We discussed time lines and responsibilities for each service and I said that I would be calling monthly to check on Ellen's progress.

Critical Point Promote student development by integrating academics and transition activities.

During the ensuing year, assessment information needed by other agencies was collected. Everyone involved with Ellen was encouraged to help her identify interests and needs, not only in regard to employment, but also in her home and the community. After a series of job-shadowing experiences and a very positive experience with her typing teacher, Ellen decided that she really wanted to do office work. However, Ellen was having extreme difficulty in English and math courses and it was feared that she would not be able to do the academic work to get into a 2-year business school. Ellen and her mother were becoming excited about her new goals, however, and agreed to present their vision at the second IEP/transition meeting. We went over postsecondary goals and needed transition services point by point and rehearsed how their plan would be presented at the meeting. After the discussion, it was decided that Ellen and her mother would like to see her get a chance to try out a community work experience when she turned 16.

It now became clear that Ellen would need an IEP/transition plan that addressed instruction, community experiences, and development of her employment objectives in the following year. She also would need linkages with adult service providers to provide the supports she needed to pursue a 2-year college degree. Also, the issue of Ellen's low English and math scores would need to be addressed in light of her postsecondary goals. Therefore, I contacted and discussed Ellen's upcoming IEP/transition meeting with the rehabilitation services, the work-study coordinator, local business schools, and Ellen's math and English teachers. Some difficulties were encountered with the math and English teachers who used a curriculum that focused upon preparation for a 4-year college. We finally generated the option that Ellen's grade could be partially based on math and English competencies demonstrated on the job and that her class work would focus upon applied math and English.

Critical Point Promote collaboration and resolve conflict outside the IEP/transition meeting whenever possible.

All involved transition stakeholders were invited to Ellen's IEP/transition meeting. Due to a conflict, the counselor from the rehabilitation services could not make the meeting, but she provided written input and committed the agency to developing an individual plan for employment (IPE) so that Ellen could receive accommodations and job coaching in her community work experience. Other members attending the meeting included the special education supervisor, the typing teacher, the work-study coordinator, the guidance counselor, Ellen, her mother, a reading resource teacher from a local business college, and the English teacher. At the start of the meeting, an agenda was distributed, as well as a copy of the survey that Ellen and her mother were going to present to the team. I explained to the team that each member should work toward Ellen's goals and share information and outcomes.

In her IEP/transition meeting, Ellen and her mother enthusiastically presented a vision of Ellen working in an office setting and living in an apartment after attending a 2-year school. It was noted that Ellen had done very well in typing classes with the help of her speller and enjoyed her job-shadowing experiences in office settings. The English teacher was skeptical of this goal and suggested that a vocational program may be more appropriate. After a brief goal reappraisal, the team was brought back to a discussion of how to support Ellen's goal. The reading resource teacher from the business school suggested that they would consider Ellen's work experience in her admission and that they could provide notetakers and tutors to assist her in doing the academic work. The work-study coordinator volunteered to provide work experience. The English teacher brought up our previously discussed idea of allowing Ellen to receive credit for English and math skills that she demonstrated on the job and to incorporate these into instruction.

The family agreed to develop an IPE with the vocational rehabilitation counselor and list business college and community work experience as vocational goals. The special education supervisor agreed to work with the principal on allowing the English and math teachers to alter their curricula. The IEP/transition plan reiterated the need for Ellen to have classroom accommodations in regard to spelling and note-taking. Needed transition services were also identified in regard to instruction (applied math and English), community experiences (work-study), development of postschool objectives (meeting with the business college), and linkages to adult services (referral to VR). One concern was raised that it was school policy that Ellen would have to pass the state and regional proficiency tests without accommodations in order to graduate. This issue could not be addressed by Ellen's transition team and was referred to the school-level interagency transition team.

The school-level interagency transition team consisted of parents, students, professionals, administrators, and adult service providers. When Ellen's issue regarding proficiency testing was brought to the team, several other parents agreed that this was a major concern of students with disabilities. It was noted that many students were dropping out of school due to frustration with proficiency tests. One administrator stated that it was a state policy that could not be changed. Using conflict management approaches, it became clear that school policy was based on a misperception of state policy on proficiency testing and that the school was not complying with the accommodation requirements outlined in the IDEA of 1997 and section 504 of the Rehabilitation Act. The administrators and parents worked together to generate options regarding accommodations for testing that would match accommodations being provided to Ellen in classes. The team also recommended the development of a career portfolio assessment as an alternative way of having Ellen demonstrate skills required by the school. (This eventually helped Ellen get into business school despite poor grades.)

Critical Point Promote development of transition programs and structures through linkages with administration and other transition stakeholders.

The following year, Ellen was assigned a new transition coordinator. Ellen, her mother, the new coordinator, and I met over coffee, soft drinks, and donuts to discuss where to go from here. Ellen expressed interest in getting into a vocational program focused upon business, but she was experiencing difficulties in getting the required credits. Her expectations for her new transition coordinator would be that he would collaborate with her to address her educational needs. I bid farewell to Ellen and her mother and offered to keep in touch. I gave Ellen a self-addressed envelope and my phone number for her to contact me and let me know how she was doing. I was confident that Ellen was on the road to a meaningful future, regardless of the barriers that she would encounter along the way.

Critical Point Develop ways of following up with students after graduation.

Conclusion

In this chapter, we have discussed four models of service coordination—brokerage, personal strengths, rehabilitation, and full support models. The full support model of service coordination was defined as an ecological model of planning that involves an array of professional and natural supports from the student's current and future environments. The personal strengths service coordination model aligns well with independent living models of service delivery by minimizing dependence on professionals and to limit intrusion into the lives of persons with disabilities. This chapter also emphasized how the transition coordinator needs to consider individual and family preferences, cultural concerns, and support options in determining which of the service coordination models to emphasize. The objectives of service coordination were identified as (a) student-focused planning, (b) student development, (c) family involvement, (d) collaboration, and (e) the development of transition programs and structures.

Study Questions

1. Discuss four models of service provision that are considered state of the art for individuals with disabilities.
2. Discuss how student needs, preferences, and cultural background impact upon how services should be provided.

3. List and define the five major goals for transition programs and transition services coordination.
4. Describe why student self-determination is an important objective of transition services coordination.
5. Describe two strategies for developing ongoing linkages and sharing information with adult service providers.
6. Describe how to prepare a student and the family for the IEP/transition meeting.
7. Describe how you would set up a schoolwide interagency transition team. Whom would you invite? What would you discuss? How would you involve families and students?

Websites

Transition Research Institute
http://www.ed.uiuc.edu/sped/tri/institute.html

Center for Innovation in Transition and Employment
http://cite.educ.kent.edu/archives.html

National Center for Learning Disabilities Inc.
http://www.ncld.org/

National Center for Research in Vocational Education
http://www.ncld.org/

Independent Living Movement
http://www.acils.com/acil/ilhistory.html

Ecological Curriculum
http://www.ttac.odu.edu/articles/ecolog.html

The Office of Vocational and Adult Education
http://www.ed.gov/about/offices/list/ovae/index.html?src=mr

The National Center for Children and Youth with Disabilities (NICHCY)
http://www.nichcy.org/

The National Longitudinal Transition Study
http://www.sri.com/policy/cehs/nlts/nltssum.html

National Institute on Disability and Rehabilitation Research (NIDRR)
http://www.ncddr.org/

Administration on Developmental Disabilities
http://www.acf.dhhs.gov/programs/add/

IDEA Practices
http://www.ideapractices.org/

Office of Special Education Programs (OSEP)
http://www.ed.gov/about/offices/list/osers/osep/index.html?src=mr

Model Transition Projects—The Transition Institute
http://www.ed.uiuc.edu/sped/tri/projwebsites.html

Federal Resource Center for Special Education
http://dssc.org/frc/

DCDT Transition Specialist Competencies
http://www.dcdt.org/pdf/trans_educators.pdf

SECTION IV

Transition Outcomes: Achieving Quality Outcomes

13

Transition to Employment

Darlene Unger

Thomas J. Simmons

LEARNING OBJECTIVES

The objectives of this chapter are:

1. Identify and indicate the services that are offered by state and local agencies that can provide employment-related services to persons with disabilities.
2. Describe how the persons with disabilities can gain access to services that those state and local agencies provide.
3. Understand the unique features of community-based vocational services for students with disabilities.
4. Understand the importance of developing valued cultural roles for people with disabilities.
5. Compare and contrast the effectiveness of supported employment and congregate/segregated programming, including the elements of generic supports versus traditional placements.
6. Describe the elements of person-centered job selection, the formation of personal

network in finding work, and the concept of target job development.

7. Identify job carving and job sharing as a concept in enabling people with disabilities to go to work.
8. Describe the importance of a career path for people with disabilities.
9. Describe the differences between social welfare and social entitlement programs along with two key social security incentive programs.

Introduction

During some point in their lives, the vast majority of our nation's youth will enter the working world and seek to develop careers with opportunities for advancement. However, the paths that youth with disabilities take to the workforce vary depending on one's career goals, support needs, and the extent to which individuals participated in work-based learning and employment experiences while in school. Some students exit public school programs competitively employed, while others pursue postsecondary education and training prior to beginning their careers. Regardless of the path to the labor force, competitive employment, defined as compensation at or above minimum wage for work performed on a full- or part-time basis, should be a transition-related employment goal for the vast majority of students with disabilities. It is a well-documented finding that students with disabilities are more likely to be employed after exiting school if they have participated in community-based work experiences or were employed competitively while in school (Blackorby & Wagner, 1996; Morningstar, 1997; Wagner, Blackorby, Cameto, & Newman, 1993; Wagner, D'Amico, Marder, Newman, & Blackorby, 1992; Wehman, 2001). Opportunities for work-based learning and the transition of youth with disabilities to employment is a critical component of any effective transition program.

How have youth with disabilities fared in the competitive labor market? Findings from follow-up studies of youth with disabilities who exited secondary special education programs provides evidence of the importance of transition planning and programming related to employment. Findings from an extensive national longitudinal study of school exiters with disabilities, revealed that employment rates for youth with disabilities lagged significantly behind their peers without disabilities (Wagner, D'Amico, Marder, Newman, & Blackorby, 1992). Similar findings were reported by Fabian, Lent, and Willis (1998) in that 3 to 5 years after high school slightly more than half of young people with disabilities were employed, compared with 69% of their peers. The severity of one's disability has also been linked to higher rates of unemployment. For instance, a survey of 398 high school graduates with severe disabilities showed that 48% were not employed or pursuing postsecondary education. Of those employed, slightly more than one-third (34%) held competitive jobs (Johnson, McGrew, Bloomberg, Bruininks, & Lin, 1997). In fact, relatively few individuals with severe disabilities work competitively in the community. The community-based employment rates reported in several studies varied from 0% to 20% across studies (Edgar & Levine, 1986; Edgar, Levin, Levine, & Dubey, 1988; Haring, Lovett, & Smith, 1990; Hasazi, Gordon, & Row, 1985; Wehman, Kregel, & Seyfarth, 1985).

Underemployment, or chronic unemployment, remains a serious problem for many Americans with disabilities. The most recent National Organization on Disability (NOD)/Lois Harris and Associates survey of Americans with Disabilities (2000) indicated that two out of three persons with disabilities are not working. Despite the implementation of school-to-work transition programs, progressive laws designed to remove barriers to employment, and advancement in rehabilitation technology, employment rates for people with disabilities have changed very little since the 1980s. Increasingly, educators, rehabilitation professionals, students with disabilities, and their families are collaborating to promote awareness of, and access to, comprehensive employment supports in order to facilitate community employment.

The purpose of this chapter is to describe employment options for individuals with disabilities and the array of services and supports available to assist with the transition from school to employment. Though employment options for people with disabilities have evolved since the early 1960s, many of the vocational programs and services that were prevalent during that time still exist today. The current focus of employment programs for people with disabilities emphasizes providing customized employment services, which involves individualizing the employment relationship between employees and employers in ways that meet the needs of both. The information that follows analyzes employment options for people with disabilities both before and after the passage of the Americans with Disabilities Act of 1990. Lastly, in order to facilitate competitive employment for young adults with disabilities, a description of comprehensive employment supports for people with disabilities, including agency-mediated, business-mediated, government-mediated, and student and family-mediated supports is presented. The reader will gain knowledge of the various services and supports available to facilitate employment and retention for individuals with disabilities.

Employment Options for Individuals with Disabilities Prior to Americans with Disabilities Act

Historically, the continuum of employment options for people with disabilities has ranged from segregated vocational settings (e.g., adult activity centers and sheltered workshops) to competitive employment in community-based businesses. The problems inherent in the continuum model of service delivery for people with disabilities were well documented (Will, 1984). The employment continuum was based on the "readiness" mentality meaning that students with disabilities must earn their right to less segregated employment options by demonstrating the skills and abilities needed to compete in the work force. Many individuals with disabilities are kept in segregated day services because they are viewed as "not ready to leave" and the belief that people need to be taught work or social skills in artificial, stimulated environments in order to prepare for the real world of work. Thus, few people actually move, or progress from the most restrictive, most costly end of the employment continuum to the least restrictive, least costly level—competitive employment. Segregated facilities have proliferated as the primary day services option for adults with disabilities since the 1960s.

During the early 1980s, a great deal was learned about the abilities of people with severe disabilities to work in competitive employment, with job coaches in supported employment, or with adaptive aids, compensatory strategies (e.g., Kreutzer, Wehman, Morton, & Stonnington, 1988), and rehabilitation engineering at job sites. Since the 1990s, inclusive work opportunities in competitive employment arrangements have gained increasing popularity as the vocational option of choice (Wehman, 2001) in addition to competitive employment for people with disabilities being declared a national priority. Due to a variety of factors, including structural changes in the economy, recent legislation, diversion of funds allocated for segregated settings to community-based alternatives, and an increased emphasis on consumer choice in the design and delivery of services, there is a movement towards providing customized employment services for individuals with disabilities.

The following section describes the evolution of employment options for people with disabilities.

Adult Day Programs and Sheltered Workshops

In the 1960s and 1970s vocational options for individuals with disabilities included an assortment of adult day-program activities and sheltered workshops. Adult day programs offered activities of daily living, training, prevocational training, "make-work" vocational activities, field trips, recreational activities and other types of special education-related curricula (Wehman, 2001). The programs were typically operated through the local mental retardation and development disabilities agency. The philosophy of these programs is that adults with disabilities should learn skills in center-based programs and, ultimately, generalize those skills into competitive employment and independent residential life. Yet, findings demonstrate that people who are placed into these centers do not leave them and never "graduate" to workshops or into competitive employment (Buckley & Bellamy, 1985).

Another option that attempted to meet the needs of individuals with disabilities included specialized work training in what has been termed "sheltered employment" (Whitehead, 1977). The general underpinnings of the sheltered work process was to provide individualized environments to "habilitate" (habilitate, meaning to train versus the term "rehabilitate", meaning retrain) individuals with disabilities, offering the individual a long-term protective environment for learning work skills. The specialized sheltered employment genre, which included a three-step process to attain competitive employment, provided little in the way of relief for persons with disabilities (Bellamy, Rhodes, Bourbeau, & Mank, 1986). Although at the time, sheltered workshops represented a substantial leap forward in the design of early vocational programming for people with disabilities, these programs ultimately failed (Bellamy et al., 1986).

Generally, characteristics of sheltered employment included pay that is less than minimum wage, limited opportunities for daily interaction with nondisabled people except for paid staff who work at the facility, and limited instruction or training on work skills that transfer to real jobs in community-based businesses. Individuals with disabilities were not hired to work in sheltered employment settings. Instead, they were placed in these sheltered employment settings to receive training, yet very little training on work skills occurred. In the vast majority of sheltered workshops, individuals earn less than minimum wage and are paid on a piece-rate basis for contractual work secured from local businesses. However, the work performed in these environments has little relevancy to preparing people for work in today's labor force.

The greatest failing of adult day programs and sheltered employment was that very few people move from segregated programs to real employment opportunities. Research findings that compare employment outcomes of people with disabilities across employment programs (i.e., sheltered workshops, competitive employment) demonstrated that individuals with disabilities earn more money, experience greater opportunities for interaction with nondisabled coworkers or customers while employed in community-based businesses (Gilmore & Butterworth, 1996; McCaughrin, Ellis, Rusch, & Heal, 1993; Rogan, Grossi, Mank, Haynes, Thomas, & Majad, 2002; Wehman, Revell, & Kregel, 1998). Yet, it is estimated that 70% of individuals served in rehabilitation programs are either in sheltered workshops or segregated nonwork day programs (McGaughey, Kiernan, McNally, Gilmore, & Keith, 1994). Public policy makers, disability advocates, and individuals with disabilities continue to demand the phasing out of segregated employment options in favor of competitive employment.

Through the delivery of employment-related transition services and the development of comprehensive employment supports all youth with disabilities, including those with intensive support needs, should transition directly into integrated jobs or postsecondary education, thus bypassing the readiness mentality of segregated facilities. There is no justifiable reason for the continued transition of students with disabilities, who have participated in community-based work experiences during their secondary school years, into segregated employment settings, such as sheltered workshops. Those who might argue that segregated vocational options should continue to remain as part of the continuum of employment choices for students with disabilities need only review the findings from the plethora of research (e.g., Gilmore & Butterworth, 1996; McCaughrin, Ellis, Rusch, & Heal, 1993; Rogan, et. al., 2002; Wehman, Revell, & Kregel, 1998), which demonstrates that quality of life outcomes are better for those in competitive employment compared to their counterparts in segregated settings for individuals with disabilities. Furthermore, segregated employment settings do little to foster the implementation of student choice and self-determination in the transition process. Rarely are individuals with disabilities given choices about the types of work they engage in, the hours they work, the time they have breaks, or the type of supports they need in segregated settings. This is in direct opposition to the principles of student or consumer choice inherent in the reauthorization of the IDEA in 1992 and 1997 as well as the Rehabilitation Act Amendments of 1992.

Transitional Employment

Transitional employment has been defined within the supported employment regulations in the reauthorization of the Rehabilitation Act Amendments in 1992 and 1998, as a "series of temporary job placements in competitive work in integrated settings with ongoing support services for individuals with the most significant disabilities due to mental illness" (706[18][A & B]). Historically, transitional employment has been used as an effective vocational placement option for individuals with mental illness (Ford, 2001; Gervey & Shafer, 1995; McCarthy, Thompson, & Olson, 1998). The program has expanded as an option of choice for individuals with physical disabilities and sensory impairments.

In transitional employment, an employment support provider or rehabilitation counselor provides specialized help on job sites with the understanding that there will be limited follow-up activity and that the employer will be able to maintain supervision (Wehman, 2001). The amount of assistance that the worker with a disability receives from the employment support provider will last 2 weeks to no longer than 3 months. In many instances, the employment support provider works with the employer and worker with a disability to identify potential support needs and secure accommodations that will help the worker perform his or her job. Oftentimes, the goal of transitional employment is to analyze the experience and use the information to make subsequent decisions about career choices and support needs (Ford, 2001).

Supported Employment

Supported employment (SE) is an employment service option that originated in the early 1980s because of the dissatisfaction with segregated vocational options available, such as day activity centers and sheltered workshops. Since its inception as a federal program through the 1986 Rehabilitation Act Amendments, the number of people participating in supported employment in the United States has increased from 9,800 to over 140,000 (Wehman, Revell, & Kregel, 1998b). Supported employment has proven to be an effective vocational service delivery option for many individuals with severe disabilities including individuals with mental retardation (Rusch, 1986; Wehman & Hill, 1985; Wehman, Hill, Brooke, Pendleton, & Britt, 1985), traumatic brain injury (Wehman et al., 1993), physical disabilities (Baer, Simmons, Flexer, & Smith, 1994), and psychiatric disabilities (Bond, Dietzen, McGrew, & Miller, 1995; Collignon, Noble, & Toms-Barker, 1987; MacDonald-Wilson, Revell, Nguyen, & Peterson, 1991).

The 1992 and 1998 Rehabilitation Act Amendments (P.L. 102-569) defines supported employment as:

> (i) competitive work in an integrated work setting, or employment in integrated work settings in which individuals are working toward competitive employment, consistent with the strengths, resources, priorities, concerns, abilities, capabilities, interests, and informed choice of the individuals with ongoing support services for individuals with the most significant disabilities.
>
> (A) for whom competitive employment has not traditionally occurred; or for whom competitive employment has been interrupted or intermittent as a result of a significant disability; and
>
> (B) who, because of the nature and severity of their disability, need intensive supported employment services . . . and extended services . . . to perform such work. (706[18][A & B])

In its formative years supported employment was characterized by the use of a job coach or employment specialist who worked with a person with a disability to secure employment, provide on-the-job training to the individual, and provide long-term follow-along or ongoing support to the worker for the duration of his or her employment. This did not mean that the employment specialist provided training and assistance on a daily basis for the duration of the worker's employment. Instead, the job coach trained the employee to perform the job and then gradually and systematically faded from the work site. The provision of long-term support is one of the distinguishing features of supported employment over other vocational rehabilitation service options. The most widely implemented SE model involved an employment specialist working one-on-one with an individual with a disability. Although, supported employment service delivery also incorporated group placement (e.g., enclaves, mobile work crews, and cluster placements) of individuals with disabilities who received fairly constant support and monitoring. Today, supported employment is much more broadly defined to include not only the intervention of a rehabilitation professional, but also the involvement of (1) family and friends; (2) community organizations and service groups; (3) coworkers and supervisors who serve as mentors, trainers, and providers of ongoing support; (4) existing human resources and employee assistance programs within the hiring company; and (5) training and support through internal, corporate-driven models of supported employment.

Components of supported employment service delivery are included in Table 13–1. The employment specialist and the individual with a disability and his or her support people work collaboratively during all aspects of SE service delivery (Parent, Unger, Gibson, & Clements, 1994). For instance, the job coach may have the individual with a disability identify job leads in the local newspaper or network with family and friends to identify potential employment opportunities. Long-term or ongoing support may be provided by coworkers or other employment supports instituted at the work place.

In addition to increased opportunities for integration, wages, and choice, other important differences between supported employment and segregated vocational options revolve around the ideas of "work readiness" and long-term or ongoing support. Supported employment service delivery is based on a "place and train"

TABLE 13–1
Components of Supported Employment Service Delivery

Component	Description
Developing a Customer Profile	A planning tool that provides a "snapshot" of the individual that includes his or her strengths, interests, needs, and expected outcomes. Information is gathered from a variety of sources and across multiple environments including: home, school, and recreational settings, and formal assessment records.
Job Development	Involves working collaboratively with the individual with a disability and key people in his or her life, such as family members, teachers, and friends to network and identify employment opportunities based on student's likes, preferences, and abilities.
Job Placement	Identifies supports to address preemployment questions and concerns such as securing uniforms, employer tax credits, addressing SSI/SSDI concerns, and facilitating the completion of preemployment paperwork (e.g., I-9 form, job application, etc.).
Job Site Training and Support Development	Employment specialist works collaboratively with the employer in developing and implementing employee training. Oftentimes, the employment specialist will have to provide systematic instructional procedures to train the employee with a disability. Assists in determining employee support needs and arranging accommodations. Facilitates the social integration of the employee with a disability.
Ongoing Support	Identify and facilitate the use of long-term supports for the worker with a disability. Assist in the development of a long-term support plan. Assess employer satisfaction.

approach in which employment is secured for an individual with disability based on an individual's unique abilities, needs, and preferences and then the individual is trained to do that job in the business where the actual job is located. The employee begins receiving compensation for his or her work from day one of his employment, the same time that he is being trained to perform the job. As was discussed previously, the segregated vocational options operate on a "train and place" approach and individuals are required to demonstrate certain skill competencies before they are referred for community employment placements.

The advantages of supported employment are that individuals with disabilities benefit from training in the environment where they are actually working. Supported employment participants perform real, meaningful work in integrated settings with ongoing supports. The positive employment outcomes of supported employment participants have been well documented in a number of important areas including: employee satisfaction (Test, Hinson, Solow, & Keul, 1993), job placements (Mank et al., 1997), wages and benefits (Kregel, Wehman, & Banks, 1989), favorable employer perceptions (Kregel &

Unger, 1993), and effective support strategies (Parent, Unger, Gibson, & Clements, 1994).

The unfortunate reality in many communities is that employment service delivery for individuals with disabilities still is based in an employment continuum and the readiness model despite the inherent flaws with the continuum. Though public policy initiatives are moving the field toward customized employment for individuals with disabilities, competitive employment for many Americans with disabilities remains an elusive dream. Increasingly, local education agencies are providing a variety of work-based learning experiences, including paid internships and competitive employment (e.g., Luecking & Fabian, 2000). When students with disabilities experience success in working at community-based business, then why is it necessary for students to transition into segregated employment options? If students are competitively employed while still in school, then we must critically examine our employment-related transition programs to identify the factors that contribute to the transition of students into segregated employment settings. Furthermore, with the emergence of comprehensive employment supports for people with disabilities we must ask ourselves if the continued transition into these segregated settings is warranted for the vast majority of youth with disabilities. Special educators and transition specialists must continue to increase their knowledge of, and experiences with, the variety of employment supports for individuals with disabilities in order to develop and implement transition programming that promotes student choice and ensures access to community employment. For some students further education or career training may precede competitive employment, for other students transition into competitive employment may occur during their secondary school experiences or immediately following.

Emerging Employment Options for Individuals with Disabilities

Customized Employment

One avenue for circumventing the "readiness" mentality of the employment continuum involves delivering "customized employment services." Customized employment means:

> ... individualizing the employment relationship between employees and employers in ways that meet the needs of both. It is based on an individualized determination of the strengths, needs, and interests of the person with a disability, designed to meet the specific needs of the employer. It may include employment developed through job carving, self-employment, or entrepreneurial initiatives, or restructuring strategies that result in job responsibilities being customized and individually negotiated to fit the needs of individuals with a disability. Customized employment assumes the provision of reasonable accommodations and support necessary for the individual to perform the function of a job that is individually negotiated and developed. (Federal Register, June 26, 2002, Vol. 67, No. 123, pp. 43154–43190)

Certainly, supported employment has emerged as a proven approach to delivering customized employment services. Many special educators and transition specialists are familiar with supported employment and are quite comfortable in communicating information regarding SE services to students and their families. Furthermore, through their experiences in developing community-based work experiences, many special educators have modified existing jobs or taken tasks from several jobs within one business to create a position that meets the unique knowledge, skills, and abilities of an individual with a disability while simultaneously addressing a business need. However, they are less familiar with other forms of vocational options that emerged from the customized employment approach that can assist students with disabilities in pursuing careers of their choice, such as self-employment and entrepreneurial initiatives. A brief description follows.

Supported Self-Employment for Individuals with Disabilities

Though people with disabilities have not traditionally been viewed as candidates for self-employment or small business ownership, *supported self-employment* for individuals with disabilities is gaining increasing popularity across the country as a vocational option for individuals with disabilities (Doyel, 2000; Griffin & Hammis, 2001). An outgrowth of supported employment, supported self-employment has adopted many of the same tools used in supported employment while enlisting the assistance of new community partners such as state Developmental Disability Planning Councils, the Small Business Administration, and financial institutions.

The three core disability employment programs, the federal/state vocational rehabilitation system, the Social Security Administration, and the Workforce Investment Act agencies represent avenues for financial resources for financing a small business start-up or entrepreneurial initiatives. They have the capacity to fund a small business start-up for someone with a disability with free, individual grant-type funds and services as well as pay a small amount to a business consultant to assist in developing a business plan for a prospective business owner with a disability (Griffin & Hammis, 2001). It is important to note that these funds are grants and not loans that the person has to repay. Examples of self-employment and entrepreneurial initiatives that people with disabilities have pursued include the operation of: a cleaning business; vending machines, in which the individuals purchase and then place vending machines in businesses, schools, organizations, which they are responsible for restocking and keeping operational; a kettle korn franchise; and window washing service. It is important that individuals involved in transition planning and programming recognize that supported self-employment may be a viable employment option for students with disabilities.

Competitive Employment with Supports

Significant numbers of students are exiting special education and secondary education classrooms unable to fully participate in our society. People with disabilities represent an overlooked and untapped employment resource. Many students lack basic skills necessary to find a job, or know what resources and incentives are available to assist in the job search. The students who do find work and are employed in the competitive market are underemployed.

Competitive employment with supports, while not being a truly recognized category or designation, fits within the new efforts distinguished as *customized employment*. In many cases students with disabilities who are more capable of independent work still don't have the skills to find work. Lack of these critical transition skills often limits their career development. In most cases, unless otherwise trained or assisted, students don't have the job-seeking skills, interview skills, or the ability to represent their skills in a way that fosters truly competitive employment. This additionally results in limited career advancement and perpetual low-paying positions. The venues that have historically been developed for individuals with career goals requiring more advanced training have been traditional employment structures such as Office of Employment Services and One-Stop-Shops (Simmons & Whaley, 2001). It is also important to note that, if students are provided with appropriate career guidance and planning along with a future plan for postsecondary training, students are better prepared to move on to more challenging careers. In addition to traditional structures for securing employment, students who may need time-limited support to obtain and retain employment could benefit from other categories of individualized or group support mechanisms.

Business Advisory Councils

Business advisory councils (BACs) have been in use for over 20 years (Rusch, 1990). In fact, BACs have been mandated by programs funded through the Projects with Industry (PWI) program of the Rehabilitation Services Administration since the early 1980s (P.L. 93-112). BACs are placement and employment programs that intricately involve employers in their development and oversight. Business advisory councils afford a close relationship with employers by engaging them in the actual implementation aspects of programs and services. While BACs have been required within the PWI programs for numerous years, the degree of involvement of the BACs has varied quite significantly (Hagner & Vander-Sande, 1998).

Critical Point Business advisory councils (BACs) may be utilized to increase employment of persons with disabilities.

Baer, Martonyi, Simmons, Flexer, & Goebel (1994), for example, implemented a BAC that was focused on a specific program but utilized the employer participants to market and provide services to individuals with disabilities. Baer, Martonyi, et al. (1994) focused on a systemic approach by enabling the employers to choose the amount of involvement in addressing the community's needs regarding employment of persons with disabilities and utilized a traditional team process approach that focused on stages of team development. The stages included forming, storming, norming, performing, and adjourning phases. These stages were used to both understand the processes and facilitate ongoing development. Baer, Martonyi, et al. (1994) found that their BAC was able to develop marketing and business connections that had a significant impact on the employment of persons with disabilities. Further, they found that the marketing activities cost the disability related employment agencies far less to develop. In addition, the BAC became so involved that employers developed services that were not in existence before the BACs inception.

Critical Point BACs, as with all committees or groups, follow certain developmental stages. The phases are forming, storming, norming, performing, and adjourning.

Job Clubs

A job club is a program that uses group dynamics and mutual support to enhance employment prospects (Malone, 1996). Azrin and Besalel (1979) developed a job club approach that focused on training in job skills seeking with the expectation that participants in the club would also be strongly involved in seeking and soliciting job leads (Azrin and Besalel, 1979). In fact the job club approach requires the participant to utilize these job-seeking efforts on a daily basis. Primary to this focus is the intensive nature of the job club approach (Azrin & Philip, 1980). Baer, Martonyi, et al. (1994) developed two job club programs meeting the needs of persons with both mental illness and physical disabilities. These respective programs fostered job-seeking skills, making contacts with friends, family members, and potential employers on a daily basis. Further, the job clubs were continued beyond the point of individual placement to facilitate ongoing supports. Baer et al. (1996) found that a higher percentage of placements and maintenance of employment was attained as compared to other local community employment programs.

Employer input is key to socially valid curriculum.

Critical Point Job club programs have been found useful in developing and maintaining employment. The primary reason seems to be the training of employability skills and ongoing group supports.

Mentoring

Mentoring has become a significant programmatic effort in recent years (Siegel, 1998). Mentoring is a process that involves matching the person with a disability with an individual knowledgeable and skilled in work and job-getting strategies (Hagner & Vander Sande, 1998). In fact, one can implement the mentoring role through several methods. One can be a mentor that discusses and counsels the individual, much like the Big Brother and Big Sister programs. Further, one can be a mentor in the workplace (Hagner & Dileo, 1993; Smith & Rojewski, 1993). The coworker-mentoring role has been most extensively utilized with persons with disabilities (Mank, Oorthuys, Rhodes, Sandow, & Weyer, 1992). Hagner & Dileo, (1993) suggest that selection of the mentor be someone who has worked at the place of employment for at least several months, is well liked by his coworkers, is scheduled to work at the same time as the individual with a disability, and is a willing mentor.

Critical Point Utilizing a mentor allows for a more typical approach to job training and ongoing support for people with disabilities (Mank, Cioffi, & Yovanoff, 1997).

Summary

There are several reasons why it is necessary for special educators and transition specialists to be able to communicate to transition-age youth and parents the differences between vocational options for people with disabilities. These include: limited awareness of and experiences with adult service agencies by students and parents; the difference between the entitlement-based special education service delivery system and the eligibility-based adult service programs; and the high unemployment rate of individuals with disabilities. Though many students with disabilities may further their education before beginning their careers, it is also important for them to realize the supports and employment services available to them, not only in completing their postsecondary education, but also in beginning their careers upon successful completion of their college degree program, or changing their educational and career goals after leaving high school.

Resources for Customizing Employment

In providing school-to-work transition services for youth with disabilities, special educators and transition providers have a tendency to rely almost exclusively on their own school or program resources to develop community-based training and employment sites and provide support to young adults who may require assistance in securing or maintaining employment. Similarly, human service agencies have relied on a paid job coach or perhaps natural supports to provide assistance or support to individuals seeking competitive employment. Unfortunately, educators and human service professionals have not utilized the variety of vocational options and work supports that exist to facilitate community employment for young adults with disabilities. In some instances, special educators and human service professionals may be unaware or unable to access these supports and in other instances programmatic or administrative barriers (e.g., lack of interagency collaboration) may prohibit effective implementation of workplace supports. Comprehensive employment supports for individuals with disabilities are typically classified into four categories: agency mediated, business mediated, government mediated, and consumer and family mediated supports (see Table 13–2) (Wehman & Bricout, 2001).

It is beyond the scope of this chapter to include a detailed description of the variety of employment supports in each of these categories. For a more detailed analysis of comprehensive employment supports the reader is referred to the work of Wehman & Bricout (2001). It is important for special educators and transition specialists to be aware of the variety of employment supports available to assist in facilitating competitive employment. The following section will identify the most commonly utilized and accessed employment supports, agency mediated for youth transitioning from school to employment.

Agency-Mediated Supports

Agency-mediated supports are typically originated through a human service agency such as the Federal/State Vocational Rehabilitation Program. As you can see from the examples presented in Table 13–2, agency-mediated supports can be in the form of direct assistance from a paid professional such as a job coach or may be in the form of a service authorized or implemented by a human service agency, such as securing assistive technology or developing compensatory strategies that are implemented at the job site. Since agency-mediated supports are widely utilized a brief discussion of the most frequently utilized adult service agencies that

TABLE 13–2

Comprehensive Employment Supports for People with Disabilities

Employment Supports	Description and Examples
Agency-Mediated Supports	Job coach assistance, specialized assistance, compensatory strategies, assistive technology, counseling, substance abuse services, VR counselor
Business-Mediated Supports	Job restructuring, workplace accommodations (including environmental modifications, assistive technology, task modification, schedule modification), coworker mentoring, job creation, employee assistance programs
Government-Mediated Supports	Social security work incentives, employer tax credits, Medicaid waiver, Ticket to Work, and Work Incentive Improvement Act
Consumer/Family/Community Mediated Supports	Personal care attendant, peer mentors, family members as job developers, friends and neighbors used for transportation

are involved in facilitating employment for individuals with disabilities is warranted.

To facilitate the development of postsecondary employment outcomes, the school personnel should be aware of the general structure and function of adult service agencies involved in facilitating employment outcomes. The agencies that are there to help in the process generally consist of approximately seven different but, in some cases, related agencies. Examples of the adult service agencies are vocational rehabilitation (VR) programs, developmental disabilities (DD) agencies, mental health (MH) programs, employment and training programs, and community and human service programs.

In general, no state offers or requires a postschool employment agency to provide services to all people who apply for services. In general, the agencies that help persons with disabilities to gain employment provide services through a selection or priority basis. One must either meet the agencies' criteria for providing services or the individual receives services once others who are higher on the agencies' priority list are served. In contrast to special education services, adult service programs are eligibility-based.

It is important to note that no individual is guaranteed access to adult services. Programs such as the VR, DD, and MH are primary programs in that they fund or provide the basic resources to accomplish employment. Secondary programs, such as employment and training programs and community and human service programs, usually receive funding from the primary programs, so that the secondary programs can provide their services. In any case, all of these agencies or programs should be involved in the development of employment services for the student who meets the respective agencies' criteria for providing services. Referral to these agencies should be discussed in the initial ITP team meeting as early as possible in the student's educational programming, and a team representative should be given the responsibility to make the initial contact and referral.

Vocational Rehabilitation Agency

Each state and the U.S. territories have a vocational rehabilitation (VR) agency. Both state and federal money jointly fund the states' VR programs. The VR programs are operated by the state with rules that must meet federal guidelines regarding expenditure of money and resources. As described in Chapters 2 and 3 of this book, VR is a federally designed program. Vocational rehabilitation programs are authorized through the federal legislative process, specifically the Rehabilitation Act amendments of 1998 (now embodied within Title IV of the Workforce Investment Act). This act authorizes federal funding of VR services throughout the states, with each state providing 25% of the operating costs and the federal government providing the remaining 75% of the match. The primary emphasis of VR programs is employment. Consequently, any individuals who are accepted for service must have a disability related to performing work.

To apply for services, one must either be referred or self-referred. Once referred, a potential client (a person with a disability) meets with the VR counselor and an application is taken and processed. The counselor must determine the potential client's needs and probable acceptance for receiving services. In order to qualify for services, the client must be of legal employable age and have the following characteristics: a physical or mental impairment which results in a substantial impediment to employment. If an individual meets this criteria, he or she will be determined eligible unless there is clear and convincing evidence that the individual cannot benefit from or does not require vocational rehabilitation services (Wehman, 1997a). Additionally, most VR programs suggest that the potential client should be referred to them only 2 years before the student is projected to leave public schools. This, however, could change based on the individual needs of the student and the severity of the disability to employment (Wehman, 1997). There have been increasing concerns voiced by parents and transition and rehabilitation professionals regarding the need to have rehabilitation counselors more actively involved with transition age youth prior to the student exiting school.

To determine eligibility and to fulfill his or her part of the cooperative relationship, the client must provide evidence of disability, agree to be tested to ascertain employment support needs, participate in a rehabilitation planning process, and be actively involved in training/job seeking. Generally, the initial component of assessment and determination of acceptance should take no longer than 30 days. Once accepted, the client and the VR counselor jointly author and agree to an individual plan of employment (IPE). This plan should spell out exactly what the client's targeted employment goal is and what the counselor and client will do to help the client attain that goal.

The types of services that a VR agency offers are vocational and career counseling, employment training, job skill training, job coaching, money for employment-related expenses, and other employment-related services. All services are provided or purchased by the counselor based on the agreement formulated in the individual plan. Whereas services are provided based on the individual plan, the cumulative success and rehabilitation of the client is based on the client's movement through the VR system and gaining employment. Counselors are evaluated based on the number of their clients that move through the system.

To achieve these outcomes, the counselor usually has a single pool of money to be spent for the caseload of their clients. The determination of the dollar amount that each counselor has is based on the number and severity of the clients in the caseload and the basic amount of dollars coming into the state. The counselor must use his or her best clinical judgment to determine what services will be procured and at what cost for each client. Thus, it is important for special educators and rehabilitation providers to convey the idea that services offered through the VR program are based on program eligibility requirements and just because a student is determined eligible for services it does not guarantee that the student will receive those services at no cost to the individual.

Visual Impairment Rehabilitation Program

Another agency that may or may not be part of the state VR system is a program that serves persons with *visual impairment* (VI). In some states, the VI agency is separate from the primary VR agency, and the agency uses a differentiated term such as the Department for the Blind or Rehabilitation Services for Visual Impairments. These VI agencies or services are authorized under the same VR Rehabilitation Act amendments, but the services are exclusively offered to persons with visual impairments. These services may begin as early as elementary or middle school. In addition to having an employment focus, the VI agency also focuses upon providing services related to independent living and mobility. Otherwise, the services that are provided by the VI agency are essentially the same as those provided by the VR agency.

Developmental Disabilities Agencies

Developmental disabilities (DD) agencies are also found in all the United States and its territories. These agencies are supported by state and federal dollars, most of which come from federal sources. Some states also add a significant amount of funding to the federal funding. In states such as Ohio and Texas, additional funds are added at the local level through levies and other taxing methods. This increases the pool of money available for services.

The legislation on developmental disabilities and other legislation (e.g., Medicaid, Social Security, etc.) have provided the impetus for developing programs and services across the country for persons with more significant or developmental disabilities (Scheerenberger, 1983). The various laws generally provide proportional funding to each state based on the population size and the number of individuals with developmental disabilities. Each state develops differing methods for delivering these resources. In some states, there are separate entities that are sometimes called Mental Retardation and Developmental Disabilities (MR/DD) programs. Other states combine the DD agency with their mental health services. However, each state and territory has some mechanism for delivering services and providing supports to individuals with DD.

In general, each state has both state and local offices that are contact points for acquiring services. The state-level agency generally provides administrative and programmatic support. The DD legislation also provides for the operation of an advisory council (typically named a Developmental Disabilities Planning Council) and an advocacy agency (typically named protection and advocacy) to help in assuring appropriate service development throughout the state (Braddock, 1987). At the local level, there are agencies that either fund or provide funds for services to be developed. The local-level agencies distribute state flow-through dollars that meet the individual's needs. These local agencies generally have case managers, direct service staff, and/or counselors, who provide for assuring appropriate services to persons with DD (Braddock, 1987). The staff within these local agencies is required to develop *individual habilitation plans* (IHP) that meet the individual needs of the person with DD. Each IHP is developed in a similar manner as an IEP (individualized education program) or an ITP (individual transition plan). There is a requirement to involve the individual with DD with a team of needed professionals, and to focus upon improving outcomes for the individual with DD in work and in other areas, such as living, recreation, relationships, communication, and personal skills. The programs that are provided to the individual vary depending on the plan.

To qualify for services under the DD act, the individual must have a disability that occurred before age 22 and significantly impairs three of seven major life activities. These life activities are language, capacity for independent living, economic self-sufficiency, self-direction, self-care, learning, and mobility (Wehman, 1997a). Regarding the diagnosis, it is important to note that the DD agency serves individuals based on their capability as opposed to diagnostic labels.

Services that are provided by DD agencies vary according to the local and regional governing board that oversees the individual agencies. Each agency is either a not-for-profit self-administered program (with oversight provided by the state) or a state office directly representing the state. Services that can be provided include independent living programs, highly structured residences (institutions), supported living, various types of employment programs, a range of recreation and community experiences, counseling, and other community and institutional services. These services are again either offered or funded through the DD agency's resources. However, in either circumstance, the local and ultimately the state DD agencies are required to provide oversight and assurances that the delivery of services is appropriate.

Mental Health Agency

The mental health agency functions much like the DD agency/services that was explained earlier. There are state and local agencies: The local agencies can either be a private not-for-profit entity with an oversight board or the state may represent itself through offices and staff employed by the state. Mental health agencies are funded through a combination of funding options. Medicaid, Social Security, health insurance, and a variety of state and federal mental health funding mechanisms are used to support state MH services (Baer, Goebel, & Flexer, 1993; Cook & Hoffschmidt, 1993; Stroul, 1989).

Qualifying for MH services requires that an individual be diagnosed with a *severe and persistent mental illness* by a qualified clinician. Generally, the phrase "*serious and persistent mental illness*" is the term that is used to describe (SPMI) the disability. A diagnosis of SPMI is defined as:

> Certain mental or emotional disorders (organic brain syndrome, schizophrenia, recurrent depressive and manic depressive disorders, and paranoid and psychoses, plus other disorders that may become chronic) that erode or prevent the development of their functional capacities in relation to three of their primary aspects of daily life "personal hygiene and self-care, self-direction, interpersonal relationships, social transactions, learning and recreation". (Goldman & Manderscheid, 1987, p. 13)

Other more specific criteria can be found in the American Psychiatric Association's DSM-IV codes for psychiatric diagnosis. However, key to diagnosis and differentiation from developmental disability is the fact that the delay in three major life activities should be due to a psychiatric cause (Lawn & Meyerson, 1993).

The services that one can receive also are similar to those one receives in the DD system. The key mechanism that guides the delivery of services is what Stroul (1995) calls a *community support system* (CSS). The CSS is designed to help maintain the individual with SPMI in the community. Consequently, services are determined based on the need of the individual to live successfully and independently in the community. The individual is able to receive the following services: mental health treatment, client identification and outreach, protection and advocacy, rehabilitation services, family and community supports, peer support, income support and entitlements, housing, health and dental care, and crisis response services (Stroul, 1995, p. 49).

In general, services from an MH program is offered at any time that a diagnosis is made. However, most mental health diagnoses are not made until later in the student's life, so it is uncertain when would be the most appropriate time to make a referral. However, if the individual is exhibiting significant problems and has an initial diagnosis, the student should be referred.

Contract Agencies

The availability of training and employment programs and services can vary in different localities. As described earlier, the training and employment programs might be part of one of the primary service or program providers (VR, DD, or MH). Or independent programs may receive funding from those agencies to provide the placement and employment service. Employment and training programs are generally private not-for-profit agencies that have an executive director and an advisory board for administrative oversight. The programs are funded in part or on the whole with fee-for-service contracts with the primary providers. The employment and training programs are generally small organizations with small specialized staffs. The staff usually has special training in either community placement and employment or an expertise in a specific skill area. The employment service providers will perform the tasks of assisting the person with a disability in either gaining the skills to find a job or training the individual with a disability in a particular job. The employment and training staff also may perform a combination of the two components.

Another hybrid of the traditional employment and training agency is that of a business, such as a coffee shop or some other service or manufacturing business, that operates primarily to benefit the individual with a disability. Bond and Boyer (1988) have termed these employment agencies *client-employing programs*. These operate as a service or manufacturing business and employ only persons with disabilities. Other similar organizations also may operate a business that employs a mixture of persons with and without disabilities. Additionally, still other employment and training programs will use the client-employing business as a training site for initial skill training. The site is used to facilitate future permanent placements in other similar settings. Although the client-employing business does perform a service and benefits to persons with disabilities, Bond (1991) and others (Simmons, Selleck, Steele, & Sepetauc, 1993) have criticized the model due to business and inclusionary factors.

Other community programs and human service agencies provide employment services that help persons with disabilities to gain access to employment; however, these programs are not targeted only to meet their unique needs. These programs include the state's agencies of employment services and job training partnership programs. Each of these programs offers employment and skill-related training to address the needs of individuals who are either not employed or in need of being reemployed.

State Bureau of Employment Services

The state's bureau or office of employment service is a workforce development program that has been in existence since the early 1900s (Droege, 1987). This program is funded through federal and state tax money. The primary focus of this agency is to meet the needs of each state's economic development and to match employers that are looking for employees with individuals looking for work. As with the VR, DD, and MH agencies, there are state and local offices. Local offices of employment services can be found in nearly every state and municipality. The services provided by the state employment agencies include computerized tracking of available jobs, centralized advertising, and referral of those jobs. Additionally, large special training programs are provided that meet individual employer needs, authorizing tax incentives to motivate employers to hire special classes of people and training programs that enable individuals to gain their high school equivalency diploma (GED, a general education diploma) and job-seeking skills classes. Although they are not the primary targets of the state offices of employment, persons with disabilities are one of the targeted populations that the agencies have a priority to serve. Consequently, state employment services will provide resources for special programs to meet the needs of the individual with disabilities. These special programs, however, differ in various localities.

Accessing services also is similar to the other primary service providers. In each locality, there are counselors, program specialists, employer liaisons, and training specialists. To gain access to the services, one must apply for services and go through some testing to determine the best job skill match. A referral will be provided if there is a match between the individual's skills and available jobs in the community. The tests that are provided have been developed by the U.S. employment services (USES) and are quite beneficial for individuals who assimilate well into the mainstream of individuals without disabilities. Some problems have been noted about the USES tests for persons with disabilities (Droege, 1987).

One-Stop Career Centers

One of the primary elements of the Workforce Investment Act of 1998 (see Chapter 2) was the expansion of *One-Stop Centers* (OSC). The centers are intended to unify education, vocational training, and employment programs into a single system in each community. There are several principles that guide the development and implementation of OSC, including: univeral access, consumer empowerment, streamlining services, increased accountability, business involvement, state and local flexibility, and improved youth programs. One-stop centers are based on the idea that there should be a single point of entry to various employment services and training programs for all job seekers. Thus, an individual could go to one location and have access to various employment and training programs or services that had traditionally been offered at different locations (e.g., Vocational Rehabilitation Services, State Bureau of Employment Services, etc.). Three levels of services are available through the OSC:

- *Core services*—job search skills training, interviewing techniques workshops, résumé development preparation, work exploration and referral to employers with job openings
- *Intensive services*—may target specific groups, such as youth, people with disabilities and those with limited income, and include the development of an individual career plan, career counseling, and case management
- *Training services*—targeted for indivduals who are not able to become employed through the use of core and intensive services; training may include occupational skills training, adult education, on-the-job training, and customized training for the employer

Social Welfare, Social Entitlements, and Work Incentives

Most people with significant disabilities rely on programs administered by the Social Security Administration to provide supplemental income and entitlement income. Most importantly, these programs include Medicaid and Medicare benefits. Most people who attain employment through supported employment work part time. Parent (1996) found that 67% of supported employees received no employer sponsored health benefit. Johnson, et al. (1997) reported that nearly 75% of students exiting public school special education programs received Supplemental Security income (SSI) and consequently, Medicaid. Sixteen percent received Social Security Disability Income (SSDI) and Medicare coverage.

Social Security/Disability Insurance

The SSDI program strictly limits income for disabled participants to $700.00 per month (effective July 1, 1999). Wages over this amount are considered trial work months. Social Security allows for a 9-month trial work limit and an extended period of eligibility. At the end of this time the Social Security Administration makes a determination of Substantial Gainful Work Activity. This implies that the person with a disability is earning a wage for providing something of economic benefit to an employer. If it is determined that the individual can work in spite of their disability then SSDI benefits are terminated.

Supplemental Security Insurance

The SSI program is a federal welfare subsidy and provides for work incentives to allow people to work. Under Public Law 99-643, SSI cash benefits to recipients are determined on a flexible scale based on countable income. As wages increase, cash benefits decrease. Under Section 1619b, when the cash benefit reaches zero, recipients continue on the Social Security rolls, allowing them to continue working. Medicaid benefits also continue under Section 1619b (extended Medicaid coverage). Medicaid benefits continue so long as wages fall below the federal threshold amounts for earnings. These incentives have allowed thousands of people to go to work. Unfortunately, there is a great deal of confusion as to how to use these benefits. Many people who can go to work do not, due to ignorance of these work incentives or misinformation provided by service providers.

Additional Work incentives

Two additional work incentives are emerging as effective work incentives: *Plans for Achieving Self Support* (PASS) and *Impairment Related Work Incentives* (IRWE). These programs are designed to set aside earned income in order to reduce "countable income" and maintain social security eligibility. These programs enable people to purchase equipment or services necessary for individuals to work. West, Wehman, and Revell (1996) determined that 57% of supported employment programs use PASS or IRWE to assist participants. The most frequently purchased services include transportation to work, job coach services, and work site modifications.

Model Employment Practices

While supported employment has been a primary focus in the employment field for persons with moderate to severe disabilities for many years, the authors feel that the four features of supported employment are a pragmatic means for envisioning all employment practices for young adults with disabilities. Consequently, the four features are described in terms of method and involvement practices that relate to all people, including persons with disabilities.

The four features of supported employment services include: individualized assessment, job development, on-the-job training, and on-going support. Individualized assessment is a process by which the supported employment provider learns about the unique skills and abilities of the person for whom a job search is being done. There is a similarity between this process and the process described by Richard Nelson Bolles' *What Color is Your Parachute* (1999). Bolles discussed five effective job-hunting methods. Among these was the "creative job hunting approach." This method urged the job seeker to figure out what his/her best skills and favorite "knowledges" are. This notion of learning what the job seeker has to offer is parallel to the idea of developing an individualized assessment or a person-centered approach to job selection. A person-centered approach begins with the premise that we all have unique skills and interests that define what a good job would be for us. For people with disabilities, the disability can prevent us from getting to know who someone is and what their interests are. Knowing what someone is good at is the first step in creating a job match rather than placing someone at a job site that is available.

Person-Centered Job Selection

Person-centered job selection relies on the use of nontraditional assessment exercises for determining an appropriate job match. As opposed to standardized, norm-referenced testing that is designed to assign a diagnostic category, employment based on needs, interests,

The environment is a powerful teacher.

and preferences takes a personalized approach to learning about the individual. Where standardized tests can describe what someone cannot do, person-centered activities allow the employment professional to learn the work preferences of the individual. By investing time in getting to know the individual's dreams, interests, and unique skills, the evaluator or team can look beyond the person's disability and develop the "right job" for the individual. By investing the time to get to know a person's dreams, interests, and skills, the evaluator can perform an assessment in a balanced, trusting, and reciprocal way. By spending time in getting to know the person in typical environments, the evaluator can make an assessment of what considerations need to be made in order for the person to be successful at his or her job. This type of assessment is different than finding a job and hoping the person will be successful. Too often jobs for people with disabilities have centered on food service and cleaning jobs with little regard for matching skills and preferences with the requirements of a given job. In fact, the emerging criticism of employment programs is the overreliance on entry-level food service and janitorial jobs. These types of work are characterized by high turnover and low wages. Jobs of this type are an easy job placement for staff trainers who have not taken the time to assess what a "good job" would look like for the participant (Mank, Cioffi, & Yovanoff, 1997). When a person-centered approach is utilized, the job match is individualized and the job more fulfilling for the participant.

Critical Point Person-centered assessment and placement can be defined as the opposite of norm-reference assessment and placement.

The most important consideration in a person-centered approach to job selection is to ensure that the activities used for evaluation are meaningful and occur in everyday life. If the evaluation relies on artificial tasks or environments then the individual will quickly realize the message that the task is not real or relevant. If there is no sense of purpose to the task then what a sad message this must send to someone who, for their entire life, has always faced a life of lowered expectations. What message does this send to family members, employers, and the general public? Tasks used in evaluation should have a suitable level of challenge, should offer the appropriate amount of decision-making, and should be appropriate for the age of the individual.

A person-centered approach to job selection leads to a job development approach that places faith in the power of friends and family of the job seeker. A group of friends and family have a personal stake and want to see good things happen for the person seeking work. As opposed to a formal group of therapists and paid professionals, the individuals who participate in a person-centered group are there voluntarily. Paid professionals will be involved in the planning but a balance of nonpaid people can be beneficial. This type of planning group places emphasis on the knowledge and resources of a job-seeker's personal network. This is similar to Bolles (1999), who lists friends and family as the third and fourth most effective job-hunting method. Our friends and family form a personal network. Very few jobs in our culture are found by looking in the want ads or making phone calls to employers. Bolles (1999) lists classified ads as a least effective method of job seeking. According to Bolles, answering blind ads in newspapers leads to employment for only 5% to 24% of job seekers. Utilizing our network of friends, family, and acquaintances fills most jobs. In many circumstances the axiom is true that "it's whom you know, not what you know." For too long human service professionals have discounted the power and efficacy of the job seekers personal network in their job development efforts. See Case Study A for an example of social network job finding.

Critical Point The most important consideration in a person-centered approach to job selection is to ensure that the activities used for evaluation are meaningful and occur in everyday life.

CASE STUDY A

Within the most recent year, a man with a disability was looking for work at a plastic factory. The staff of a local community employment agency made several contacts but after 2 months the man had no firm job offer. One Sunday night at a church service the congregation was encouraged to stand up and say whatever was on their minds. As Mark, the man with the disability, looked around the church he noticed the owner of the plastics molding company. Mark took this opportunity to stand up and tell the congregation that he had been unemployed for some time and needed a job. He stated "he always thought he'd like to work at a plastic formulating plant." Mark went to work the next week.

Once a job outcome has been targeted for the individual, the work of job development begins. As with any job seeker, an organized plan will be established for getting a job. As a means of preparation, a decision needs to be made early regarding how much the job seeker will do and how much representation will be required by the service provider. The key is to develop a job-seeking strategy where the individual is empowered in the process and is taking an active role consistent with his or her ability. If too much assistance is provided, the job seeker may be stigmatized by the presence of the service provider. If too little support is provided, then the job search may not be successful. For instance:

- How much assistance will the job seeker need in contacting employers?
- Does the person represent him- or herself well enough that the service provider should not sit in on the interview?
- Should the job seeker, due to the complexity of his/her disability, not attend the initial employer contacts?
- Can the job seeker develop or participate in developing a résumé as part of the job search?
- Has the job seeker been adequately prepared for what to do and say in a job interview? Does the job seeker need more skill training?
- Do the jobs that have been selected allow for career growth?

For some job searches, the paid professional will take the lead in making job contacts and meeting with potential employers. For people who are more capable, the role of the staff person may be to organize the search and provide advice and counseling to the job seeker. For others all that might be needed are supports such as a job club or informal mentor. Regardless of the amount of representation needed to get someone employed, it is essential that the staff person and the job seeker be aware of the accepted protocol for contacting an employer. The first question to consider is "how would anyone contact this employer?" Is it best to send a letter with a résumé before a contact is made? Is it customary to walk in on an employer and make an unannounced "cold call?" Should a formal appointment be made; with whom? Generally, the more typical the contact is to that of any job seeker, the greater likelihood of success.

Job Design

Creativity is essential in job design. One size does not fit all. Targeted job development requires a great deal more flexibility and creativity than typical job acquisition activities. *Targeted job development* means that marketing activities are designed to benefit one person and not designed to sell the services offered by an agency. When an individual interviews for a job the individual's skills and abilities are being sold. The same should be true for people who require a little extra attention in order to go to work. Service professionals should be acutely aware of this fact when they are representing someone at risk of being seen in a devalued role by an employer or the community. The ultimate goal is, of course, to match the skills, preferences, and conditions for work with the setting, task, and decision-making complexity of a particular job. We all have individual requirements in regard to where we work, how we work, and when we work. Creativity in job design cannot be undersold when someone goes to work. Flexibility may include job carving or job sharing.

Job carving involves negotiating with an employer to construct a new job description from two or more standardized job descriptions at the business. An example of this process is provided in Case Study B. Within the job carving process Dan's skills and interests were reviewed. Once the analysis was completed, employment was sought that allowed for Dan to perform either a majority or separate components of presently available jobs. Employers are generally heavily involved in the development of job carving practices. It is the employer that knows his or her jobs and with the assistance of a community employment specialist, a variety of jobs could be developed.

Critical Point Creativity is essential in job design.

CASE STUDY B

Dan works at a laboratory run by the U.S. Geological Survey (USGS). His job is to sanitize sample bottles used by field workers taking water samples from Maine to the Mississippi River. The bottle sanitizing job is a time-consuming, complex operation and involves dangerous chemicals. Prior to Dan's employment, this job was part of the chemist's job description. With Dan fulfilling these functions, the chemists have more time to devote to testing samples, preventing the typical spring and summer backlog of work. Dan is employed in a challenging job where he can demonstrate his competency. Additionally, Dan has taken on more complex tasks since he went to work at the lab. The staff of the community employment agency went to USGS with the purpose of designing a job that is specific to Dan's skills rather than trying to have Dan "fit" an existing job description. In developing a carved job, the community employment staff had to spend time in getting to know Dan and what his unique skills were. The community employment staff also had to get to know the employer and the business to learn what tasks would fit Dan's abilities. Close attention was paid to the environment, coworkers, tasks, and culture of the business.

Job sharing arrangements are effective when individuals with disabilities are primarily interested in working part time (Granger, 1996). Job sharing arrangements, as the name implies, allow for two people to share a single part-time job. Two people with disabilities or a person with a disability and a nondisabled person may share a job. This arrangement is most effective when the amount of earning is restricted or when personal issues or responsibilities prevent someone from working full time.

Shared jobs or carved jobs can be effective for any job seeker. Job flexibility has found its place in our business culture. People work for a variety of reasons and have different requirements for what defines a good job for them. Salary alone is not the only factor people consider in accepting a job. Issues like child care, proximity to home, flexibility in scheduling, geographic area, and job satisfaction all are issues job seekers consider. This same flexibility is key to a quality job match and positively correlates with job satisfaction and job longevity (Dentzer, 1992).

In some instances, job seekers do fill an existing job description. Many people with disabilities, at an early age, have indicated that their expectations were high for having a career path. The role of the service provider in these situations is to work with the individual to develop a "road map" on what vocational steps should be taken to get the person to their ultimate job target. A career path involves competency building by working at a series of jobs that lead to the ultimate job target. See Case Studies C and D for two examples of how this can be accomplished.

CASE STUDY C

Jean is a good example of someone who has succeeded at her career path. Jean graduated from high school in 1969. For the next 11 years, she found herself working at a segregated sheltered workshop. In all those years, she never gave up her dream of working in an office setting. Jean began her career track volunteering at a local university library. At this job , she learned how to organize tasks, how to file, and how to conform to the culture of a business. After a short time, she went to work part time at a steel factory as a file clerk for the sales staff. Jean learned to organize and manage a complex filing system. She also was responsible for taking phone orders and making appointments for the sales staff. After several years, she left the factory to work for the local county clerk's office. This was a full-time position with comparable benefits and wages to her nondisabled coworkers. Jean is responsible for a variety of duties, including processing vehicle registrations, license plate renewals, and vehicle liens. Her present job is challenging and fits the requirements of her dream job of 15 years ago. She works in an office setting performing complex tasks. She works in a downtown office setting where she has contact with professional people. She has the opportunity to develop friendships with her coworkers and to attain respect for her job competency. After going to work at the clerk's office, Jean was able to move from the family home into her own apartment. She has an active social life and is making plans for her retirement.

CASE STUDY D

Another example of a career track has been the experiences of Trevor. Trevor experienced a brain injury while in college. After several years of rehabilitation services, Trevor was eager to enter the workforce. He worked for an industrial lighting company as a data entry operator. He later worked as an inventory control specialist for a major retail distribution warehouse. These clerical skills allowed Trevor to develop competencies that led to his ideal job, working as a runner for a large downtown law firm. Trevor has returned to school, pursuing an associates degree as a paralegal.

Natural Supports

The most significant development in the field of employment services is the way people are trained and supported to perform their job. In the early years of employment programs, the accepted method of job training was to develop a job that required no extra planning to teach the new hire to do his or her job. The job developer would analyze requirements at the job site several days before the new employee would begin. This would allow the job developer to develop a training strategy in preparation for the employee to go to work. As employment programs evolved, we have learned that there are distinct liabilities in viewing job sites in a narrow fashion.

With supported employment, a job coach is employed by a supported employment program, but this is ultimately artificial to the job environment. The presence of a job coach on site too often draws attention to the worker with a disability and can stigmatize the individual. Other employees notice the presence of the job coach and look upon the supported employee differently than if the person was trained in a more typical fashion. The presence of a job coach sends a faulty message to other employees at the business that special skills and knowledge are required to work with and relate to the employee with a disability.

The focus of job training has shifted from external job training to the reliance of generic supports that naturally occur at the workplace (*natural supports* in the workplace). Many businesses have training programs in place for their employees (Nisbet & Hagner, 1988). All businesses have a unique culture that enables a new employee to learn their job and to become assimilated into the workplace. The strength of generic supports is to work within the accepted framework of the business to allow the person with a disability to be accepted into the workplace culture, as any other employee would be. The role of the employment staff, in these instances, is to act as a consultant or advisor to the business during the training period. Employment staff will act as advisors to the training staff providing information on teaching strategies, task organization and other issues that may arise during job training. This role can be more difficult than the traditional job-training role because the job trainer is not always present at the business. The results of this type of training are of tremendous benefit to the individual with a disability at work.

Critical Point The most significant development in the field of supported employment services is the way people are trained to perform their job.

In a landmark study of supported employment, Mank, Cioffi, & Yovanoff (1997) investigated the relationship of employment features and outcomes for supported participants and the use of natural supports in the workplace. The analysis applied to the data in this research studied the relationship between the level of job site integration and seven variables: type of work, level of disability, monthly wages, hourly wages and the "typicalness" of the employee's circumstances in relation to that of nondisabled coworkers. Mank et al., (1997) found that work site interaction with nondisabled coworkers was positively correlated with higher wages and longer job retention. Most strikingly, it was found that the correlation holds regardless of the severity of disability of the employee. Conversely, the study concluded that the more atypical someone's conditions are at the start of employment, the more atypical conditions continue regardless of time on the job or complexity of the task (Mank et al., 1997).

An example can be found in a central Kentucky employment agency through which a man named Terry gained a job. Terry has significant disabilities that prevented him from entering the work force. His disabilities included total blindness, midrange deafness, and selective mutism and presumed mental retardation. The central Kentucky agency's staff found that Terry had a tremendous interest in radio and music. His hobby was a music collection composed of thousands of recordings. When initially encountered, Terry worked four days per week at a day activity center putting toys in gumball machine eggs. Terry's ambition was to work in radio. It would have been impossible for the agency staff to learn to operate a radio station and provide the training Terry needed. A radio station was located that employed a disc jockey, Edmund, who was also blind. He agreed to work with Terry in the role of a mentor. By utilizing Edmund's expertise, Terry went to work in an occupation that would have been impossible if traditional job training techniques were utilized.

Employment with supports makes a commitment to each person served that they will receive a level of support that is consistent with their needs. Supports are personally designed in order to enable the person to work with maximum independence. Too much support may further stigmatize the individual with a disability. Too little support may jeopardize the person's job. This balance is not stagnant but fluid, allowing for support to change based on circumstances. The provision of support on the job site is essential for both the employer and employee, and includes the following:

1. Addressing management and coworker changes at the business
2. Retraining, consultation and new task introduction

3. Advocating for raises, benefits, and job advancement
4. Facilitating job changes as the result of termination, advancement, lay-off, or business closure
5. Modeling appropriate work behavior
6. Developing appropriate social interaction skills

Without this valuable service it would be unlikely that many people served in community-based vocational services would be successful. This is especially true for people with long-term mental illness, brain injury, mental retardation, and autism.

Services and Agency Delivery Matrix

Table 13–3 provides an overview of services that generally are needed to support employment outcomes for students with disabilities. The row across the top of the table indicates agencies, with the initial side column showing the potential services that could be provided. A legend is provided to describe the generic or usual categories of disabilities that one would refer to in delivering services. Although these categories do not match the categories delineated by IDEA, the terms generally are used across the country when referring to diagnostic categories.

The purpose of Table 13–3 is to provide the reader with a quick reference to where an individual with a particular disability could acquire certain services. As was described in prior sections of this chapter and book, all the services are available but all potential participants may not be able to qualify for access to the service. For instance, in row two, "Career Planning," one can look across and see that all the agencies would provide career services. However, each agency may have differing restrictions as to whom may receive the service. Further, case management, employer benefits (e.g., targeted job tax credits and reduced wage options) are limited to very few agencies. Other access issues include the particular agencies' conditions on providing services. To make the point, the VR agency may be required to offer various training and employment programs and the individual may qualify for receiving these services; however, the individual may not fit within the VR agencies' priority service categories. Consequently, the individual would not be able to access the service. One can use Table 13–3 as a guide for asking for services, but differences do exist in the practical application of those who might be able to receive the employment-related service.

Conclusion

In order to facilitate competitive employment for the millions of Americans with disabilities who desire it, we must be more effective in disseminating information and linking students and parents and other participants in the transition process to these workplace supports. By familiarizing oneself with the numerous employment supports, we can more effectively identify and implement resources or accommodations that will assist more students with disabilities in participating in community-based work experiences and ultimately competitive employment, via further postsecondary education and training or immediate entry into the labor force. Our description presented only a small component of comprehensive employment supports for people with disabilities, agency-mediated supports. However, there are many supports that students transitioning from secondary education or college and universities can access and utilize to help them achieve their career goals. By identifying the appropriate mix of supports for a student with a disability, we are better able to inform students, parents, and potential employers of the appropriate resources available. It is important that special educators know the resources that are available in one's local community so that

TABLE 13–3

Transition to Employment Service Providers

PROVIDERS → SERVICE V	**Community Employ-ment Agency**	**Public School**	**Voca-tional Educa-tion**	**Work-Study Voc. Sped Coord**	**Job/WIA/ State Employment Agency**	**Voc. Rehab./ VI Agency**	**Mental Health Agency**	**MR/DD Agency**	**Post-secondary Education Agency**	**Adult Vo-Tech Agency**
Functional vocational evaluation		All	All	All		All	PD	MD, OH		
Career planning	All	All	All	All	All	All	PD	MD, OH	All	All
Job shadowing	All	All	All	All		All	PD	MD, OH		All
Job search training	All	All	All	All	All	All	PD	MD, OH		All
Job placement	All	All	All	All	All	All	PD	MD, OH		All
Technology/AT		All		All		All	PD	MD, OH		
Transportation		All	All	All		All	PD	MD, OH		
Job training	All	All	All	All	All	All	PD	MD, OH		
Follow-along							PD	MD, OH		
Employer benefits					All	All	PD	MD, OH		
Case management						All	PD	MD, OH		
Independent living skills		All					PD	MD, OH		
Residential-home services							PD	MD, OH		
Financial supports							PD	MD, OH	All	All
Recreational services		All					PD	MD, OH	All	All

Legend: LD = learning disability, BD = behavior disorder, OH = orthopedic impairment, MD = multiple disability, PD = psychiatric disability, SI = sensory impairment.

Source: Adapted by permission: Baer, Simmons, & Flexer, 1996.

they can more effectively tap into the array of employment supports. By discussing and distributing information during IEP meetings, students working with their parents or advocates can make informed choices about the type and degree of supports they wish to access.

Furthermore, students and their parents may be more inclined to access services and supports if they are provided with specific contact information, including agency name, contact person, phone number, and eligibility requirements for specific vocational-related postsecondary programs. We know from our discussion on interagency collaboration that representatives from many of these programs should be present at the IEP transition planning meetings. However, the sad reality is that in many localities the seemless transition from school programs to adult service programs or postsecondary education does not occur.

Workforce Recruitment Program

The Workforce Recruitment Program for College Students with Disabilities (WRP) is a resource for businesses nationwide to identify qualified temporary and permanent employees from a variety of fields. Applicants are highly motivated postsecondary students and recent graduates eager to prove their abilities in the workforce. To get names, background, and contact information on candidates whose skills match your needs, call Job Accommodation Network (JAN) at 1-800-526-7234.

Project EMPLOY

The President's Committee on Employment of People with Disabilities is seeking to expand employment opportunities for persons with mental retardation through Project EMPLOY. Project EMPLOY was initiated as a result of research on best practices. The findings indicated that employment barriers inherent in negative stereotyping can be eliminated through a program of demonstration, outreach, and education when coupled with technical assistance.

Study Questions

1. Make a list of the various service providers that could assist an individual with a disability in getting a job. Then list the services that the individual might need. How might you as a school transition related teacher or specialist work with those respective agencies and services?
2. Describe the history of employment for persons with disabilities. What kinds of things were right or wrong with respect to the various aspects of employment services?
3. What is a career path and how can students with disabilities successfully navigate through such a process?
4. What social service programs exist and to what degree can people with disabilities make use of such programs?
5. How can one use the relative plethora of employment supports to facilitate competitive employment for persons with disabilities?
6. What is community-based vocational training and how does it differ from traditional vocational training?
7. Describe supported employment and how it differs from the more traditional methods? Are there advantages to either? Which model appears to be better for students that you have encountered? Why?

Websites

Job Accommodations Network:
http://www.jan.wvu.edu/

West Virginia Research and Training Center:
http://www.icdi.wvu.edu/homepage.htm

Office of Special Education and Rehabilitation Services:
http://www.ed.gov/about/offices/list/osers/rsa/index.html?src=mr

The Association for Persons in Supported Employment (APSE)
http://www.apse.org/index.html

The US Department of Labor, Office of Disability Employment Policy
http://www.dol.gov/odep/welcome.html

Career One-Stop
http://www.careeronestop.org/

U.S. Department of Labor
http://www.dol.gov/index.htm

Rehabilitation Research & Training Center on Workplace Supports
http://www.vcu.edu/rrtcweb/

Worksupports.com
http://www.worksupport.com/

Rehabilitation Research and Training Center (RRTC) on Workforce Investment and Employment Policy for Persons with Disabilities
http://www.comop.org/rrtc.htm

Training Resource Network, Inc.
http://www.trninc.com/

The Center on Education and Work
http://www.cew.wisc.edu/

Heath Resource Center—The National Clearinghouse on Postsecondary Education for Individuals with Disabilities
http://www.heath.gwu.edu/

Employment Support for People with Disabilities
http://www.ssa.gov/work/

Ticket to Work
http://www.socialsecurity.gov/work/Ticket/ticket_info.html

Mainstream Inc.
http://www.mainstreaminc.org/

National Federation of the Blind
http://www.nfb.org/

Closing the Gap
http://www.closingthegap.com/

America's Job Bank
http://www.ajb.dni.us/

Job Openings EdHIRES
http://www.ed.gov/about/jobs/open/edjobs.html?src=gu

Office of Special Education and Rehabilitative Services (OSERS)
http://www.ed.gov/about/offices/list/osers/index.html

Job Web
http://www.jobweb.com/

The ARC
http://www.thearc.org/

YAI/National Institute for People with Disabilities Network
http://www.yai.org/

14

Postsecondary Education and Career Paths

Deborah Durham Webster

Greg Clary

Penny L. Griffith

LEARNING OBJECTIVES

The objectives of this chapter are:

1. Describe the function of preparation and planning in meeting postsecondary transition goals.
2. Recognize the importance of academic requirements, social and independent living goals, and planning in achieving postsecondary education goals.
3. Be aware of the various postsecondary education options and their differences in demands and charactertisics (i.e., size of school, admission requirements, racial/gender makeup, cost, support services available, etc.).
4. Be aware of various ways to explore career interests and to understand the role career exploration activities play in matching potential postsecondary schools to the individual student's interests, needs, and preferences.
5. Know and understand legislation that applies to the postsecondary sector (i.e.,

section 504 of the 1973 Vocational Rehabilitation Act and the Americans with Disabilities Act), how it differs from IDEA, and the importance of transmitting that knowledge to their students.

6. Develop skills to empower students by increasing the understanding of their disability and the ability to self-advocate, and by increasing their knowledge of their rights and responsibilities in postsecondary settings.
7. Be sensitive to the impact that cultural values, attitudes, and beliefs may have on the students and their families when promoting postsecondary educational goals, as well as issues that may arise for first-generation college students or those who come from a rural background.
8. Know and understand how postsecondary education and training goals relates to IDEA's four principles inherent in transition planning and services.

Introduction

The last chapter addressed issues related to the transitioning process to employment settings. For many students, postsecondary education and training is an important step in reaching employment and career goals. Therefore, this chapter provides an overview of the information needed to guide students and their transition team members in preparing for and succeeding in postsecondary educational environments. The transition from high school to adulthood tends to be a difficult time for all adolescents, but especially for many students with disabilities (Halpern, 1992; Rusch, DeStefano, Chadsey-Rusch, Phelps, & Szymanski, 1992). This process may require greater planning for students with disabilities because they may not have had the supports and experiences necessary to develop confidence, self-determination, social judgment, or self-management skills (Loewen & Iaquinto, 1990), all of which are needed to succeed in postsecondary learning environments (Webster, 2001). Actually, succeeding in postsecondary education can be hard work for anyone. For a student with a disability, it means that many things have had to fall into place. Most sources of information say that planning must begin "early," defined as late middle school or ninth grade, when high school course selection occurs (Cowen, 1993; Turner & Simmons, 1996).

Continuing education after high school is only one option that a student might choose in the developmental process toward adulthood. However, this further step along the road to lifelong learning is a positive choice for obvious academic reasons and because completion of postsecondary education and training enhances job prospects. In addition, continuing education can provide social opportunities that expand upon a student's interests and knowledge of various recreational activities. It also provides students with a potential postponement of adult obligations, such as complete financial independence, marriage and family, and job performance. Obtaining postsecondary education is correlated with higher income, lower rates of unemployment, and better overall quality of life (Dohm & Wyatt, 2002; Francese, 2002). Education and a satisfying career are key means to quality of life and desired lifestyle.

Various postsecondary options are described with a focus on matching these settings to *student needs*, *interests*, and *preferences*, in addition to specific methods used to assess and explore career options based on cultural values and beliefs. For example, a 4-year college or university is just one alternative among many types of further education and training available after high school. Vocational and career technical institutions, in addition to community and junior colleges, can all lead to enhanced quality of life and a variety of rewarding employment opportunities.

The importance of identifying goals and preparing students for postsecondary outcomes through *backward* transition planning is also examined along with coordination and bringing necessary stakeholders to the team process. Academic as well as nonacademic preparation, including community-based experiences, are viewed as vital for students' success in postsecondary education and promoting movement toward goals. The chapter concludes with an overview of issues that will enhance the participation of students with disabilities from a wide variety of environments in continuing education/lifelong learning.

In summary, this chapter provides an overview of the current literature regarding access to postsecondary environments for students with disabilities, postsecondary options and supports available to students with disabilities, and curricular planning and processes at the secondary level and beyond, which adhere to the IDEA principles regarding transition services.

Postsecondary Programs and Students with Disabilities

Participation and Outcomes in Postsecondary Programs

Employment demands of the future will require further training beyond secondary school (deFur, Getzel, & Trossi, 1996). The high skill, high wage jobs of the future will demand a workforce with good critical thinking and academic skills, who also have good problem-solving and interpersonal skills and the ability to learn constantly on the job (Getzel, Stodden, & Briel, 2000; Hoye, 1998). Many jobs that once required completion of high school vocational and technical programs, now call for some type of postsecondary credentials (Gray, 2002). Studies have shown that high school career and technical education programs not only result in preventing students from dropping out, and thus graduating from high school (Plank, 2001; Gray), but that students from those programs that were integrated with an academic component have a 60% probability of going on to college (versus 72% for those students who followed an academic only or "college prep" curriculum) (Gray). Clearly job opportunities exist for students with vocational and technical training. For instance, Department of Labor projections state that by the year 2010 there will be a demand for 380,000 computer software engineers, a position that requires a bachelor's degree, while nearly half a million computer support specialists, a job which requires an associate's degree, will be needed (Gray). In addition, there is a critical shortage of technicians, while a global surplus of engineers currently exists (Gray).

Critical Point The students who began to approach the employment rates of their nondisabled counterparts were more likely to have taken a concentration of vocational education in high school. (Wagner & Blackorby, 1996)

Though many vocational/technical programs can meet a student's transition goals and lead to gainful employment, a study conducted by the National Center for Educational Statistics (1993) found that while 95% of high school students planned to continue their education, 85% of those surveyed planned to obtain a 4-year degree.

Ernest Boyer (1987), who conducted a nationwide interview of college students, found that the vast majority thought that going to college was necessary if an individual wished to earn good money in a satisfying career and to obtain the "good life." Even though there is evidence to suggest that many college graduates are underemployed (Gray, 2002; National Center for Educational Statistics, 1993), according to the U.S. Census Bureau's 2001 population survey, the average household headed by a person with a bachelor's degree earned a median annual income that was nearly twice that of one headed by a high school graduate (Francese, 2002). Individuals with graduate degrees have even more earning power. The median household income headed by someone with a professional degree is nearly three times that of a high school graduate. A contributing reason for this income differential is that college graduates and those with professional degrees tend to intermarry and to maintain their careers (Francese). As well as higher earnings, college graduates also had more career options, better promotion opportunities, and lower rates of unemployment (Dohm & Wyatt, 2002).

College graduates with disabilities also appear to have higher employment rates than persons with disabilities who do not have a postsecondary degree (DeLoach, 1992; Harris & Associates, 2001). However, when compared to students without disabilities who have obtained a college degree, students with disabilities are still at a disadvantage in terms of securing employment (Rumrill, 1994).

Critical Point When compared to high school graduates, graduates from higher education institutions enjoyed better health; had higher self-esteem, greater career mobility, and better interpersonal and problem-solving skills; were more tolerant in their views of others and more open to new ideas, more politically active, and more likely to participate in community affairs and to become leaders at work and in their communities (Knox, Lindsay, & Kolb, 1993; Pascarella & Terenzini, 1991).

The National Longitudinal Transition Study (NLTS) found that postschool outcomes were better for students with disabilities who had a transition plan that included a specified postschool outcome, such as postsecondary education (Wagner, D'Amico, Marder, Newman, & Blackorby, 1992). However, a gap still exists between the postsecondary experiences of students with disabilities and their peers in the general population. To begin with, one out of every four students will drop out of high school between the 8th and 12th grade (for Latino students the ratio increases to one out of every two) (Gray, 2002). Youth with disabilities drop out of high school at twice the rate of their peers without disabilities (American Youth Policy Forum/Center on Education Policy, 2002). For those who attain a high school diploma, approximately 63% attended some type of postsecondary institution, compared to 72% of the general population (American Youth Policy Forum/Center on Education Policy, 2002). The majority of high school seniors expect to attend some college, and almost half expect to complete at least a bachelor's degree (Gardner, 1987; Gray, 2002). However, data shows that retention and completion rates in postsecondary programs are significantly lower for students with disabilities compared to their peers in the general population (American Youth Policy Forum/Center on Education Policy, 2002; Wagner et al., 1992). These gaps in postsecondary education participation between persons with disabilities and their nondisabled peers not only lead to significant gaps in lifelong income earnings but also with such related issues as diminished independent living opportunities and more reliance on public assistance benefits (NIDRR/SSA, 1999). Clearly, successful postsecondary education transition planning for students with disabilities is a critically important area to be considered and planned.

Student Voices

"It is amazing to me how much a society can contribute to the perception of the masses. People with disabilities are viewed as childlike and dependent, so therefore we are—self-fulfilling prophecy becomes true when hopelessness sets in. Yet when someone comes along and challenges these societal views they may be glorified for fighting to overcome their limitations yet shunned by the disability community because they set up high expectations for others in similar circumstances. What we all want is just to be accepted for who we are, but society sets up these expectations (or most generally a lack of expectations) to keep us in a different place. We are not generally held to the same standards as others. This really bothers me. I have always liked to prove I could do something when others said I could not. However, everyone with a disability should not have to prove anything; we should be accepted on the basis of our humanness."

Critical Point Postsecondary students with disabilities are more likely than the general population of college students to have family and financial obligations (such as dependents, other than a spouse) that may interfere with their schooling. (National Center for Education Statistics, 1999a)

TABLE 14–1

Percentage of Postsecondary Enrollment by Disability Type, 1988 to 1994

Disability Type	1988	1991	1994
Health impairment	15.7	14.6	16.4
Hearing impairment	11.6	10.5	9.7
Learning disability	15.3	24.9	32.2
Orthopedic impairment	13.8	13.5	10.2
Other impairment	18.5	18.3	18.8
Speech impairment	3.8	5.4	3.5
Visual impairment	31.7	25.2	21.9

Source: Henderson, C. (1995). *College freshmen with disabilities: A statistical profile.* HEATH Resource Center, American Council on Education, U.S. Department of Education.

Postsecondary Participation of Students with Disabilities

In spite of the obstacles numerous students with disabilities face in postsecondary programs, many of these students have demonstrated a resiliency that enabled them to succeed on their own (Webster, 2001). The number of students with disabilities enrolling in postsecondary institutions has continued to increase over the past few decades (American Youth Policy Forum/Center on Education Policy, 2002; Blackorby & Wagner, 1996; Henderson, 1992, 2001; U.S. Department of Education, 1996). For example, the number of full-time college freshmen reporting disabilities has more than tripled, from 2.6% in 1978 to 8.8% in 1991 (Henderson, 1992), increasing slightly to over 9% in 1998 (American Youth Policy Forum/ Center on Education Policy, 2002). As shown in Table 14–1, the kinds of disabilities reported by freshmen also has changed over the years, with learning disabilities now accounting for approximately 40% of all college students with disabilities in 2- and 4-year institutions, as opposed to 15% in 1985 (HEATH Resource Center, 1995; Henderson, 2001; National Center for Education Statistics, 1999a). There has also been a substantial increase in the numbers of students reporting psychiatric disabilities (Eudaly, 2002).

Critical Point Compared with their nondisabled peers, college students with disabilities were more likely to be men, to be older, and to be white, non-Hispanic. (National Center for Education Statistics, 1999a)

The increase of students with disabilities in postseconedary education has been attributed to the following four factors: (1) compensatory services received in high school by students who are now enrolled in postsecondary education; (2) disability advocacy groups lobbying postsecondary institutions for increased services; (3) the impact of federal legislation, such as section 504 of the Rehabilitation Act (P.L 93-112) of 1973 and the Americans with Disabilities Act (ADA) (P.L. 101-336) of 1990 (which requires postsecondary institutions to make reasonable accommodations and to provide access for persons with disabilities); and (4) as enrollment of "traditional" students decline, postsecondary institutions are recruiting "nontraditional" students to keep their enrollment numbers up (Gajar, 1998).

Although colleges and universities have made significant progress over the last 20 years to promote educational access and opportunities for students with disabilities (Rumrill, 1994), availability does not guarantee access to or success in a chosen program of study (Getzel & Kregel, 1996). The increase in the number of students with disabilities who actually graduate from college with a bachelor's degree or higher has been less dramatic than the increase in enrollment, rising from 14% in 1986 to 19% in 1998 (American Youth Policy Forum/Center on Education Policy, 2002; Harris & Associates, 1994). However, since 1998 there has been a disturbing decline from 19% to 12% among persons with disabilities who have graduated from college (American Youth Policy Forum/Center on Education Policy, 2002). Far too many students with disabilities enter postsecondary programs with little or no preparation and a significant number of qualified students do not attend at all (American Council on Education, 1996; Blackorby & Wagner, 1996; Marder, 1992; National Center for Education Statistics, 1999a; Newman & Cameto, 1993). For example, students and their families, teachers, and agency personnel may assume that because a high school student is academically prepared for a postsecondary education, little else is needed in terms of preparation for success in a postsecondary institution (deFur et al., 1996). However, the higher standards imposed by colleges with less administrative and social supports, in addition to a greater emphasis on independent functioning (Siperstein, 1988), means that effective transition planning for many students must involve more than just focusing on academics.

Critical Point Findings reveal that among 8th graders in 1988 who finished high school by 1994, the majority of students with disabilities (56%) were less likely to be even minimally qualified for admission to a 4-year college, compared with their peers in the general population, of whom 37% did not meet minimum admission requirements (National Center for Education Statistics, 1999a).

Students and their transition teams need to become aware of factors that will hinder or enhance a student's postsecondary choices so that they can prepare accordingly. The topics presented in the following sections of this chapter provide the reader with information and skills that have been found to assist students in being successful. Transition teams need to access curriculum resources and to develop individualized intervention plans to focus preparations upon:

1. Dealing with a different legal status as a student with a disability
2. Spending time in activities that will be required later in college
3. Choosing from the many postsecondary alternatives that are available

Options and Supports

Types of Postsecondary Programs

Students with disabilities and their transition teams should be aware of the differences among the types of colleges, universities, and vocational, technical, and proprietary schools. For example, 4-year colleges and universities offer programs of study that lead to a bachelor's, master's or doctoral degree, whereas junior and community colleges offer courses that can lead to a certificate, license, or associate's degree, often taking at least 2 years to complete the prescribed program of study. Community colleges, which are publicly funded, offer a variety of classes, including vocational and occupational courses and have either no or low-cost tuition; whereas junior colleges are usually privately supported, more expensive, and offer a liberal arts program of study. Technical or proprietary schools can also offer certificates, licenses, and associate's degrees and focus on a particular trade or technical career.

Community and technical/ proprietary schools exist in or near most communities and generally require only a high school diploma or equivalent as an entrance requirement. Local colleges, both community and colleges of continuing education within universities and 4-year colleges, have an additional advantage of offering opportunities for lifelong learners to explore all kinds of subject matter, thus enriching the learner's quality of life. Further information on differences among traditional postsecondary programs is shown in Table 14–2.

The purposes, programs of study, entrance criteria, requirements for licenses or certifications, and associate's or baccalaureate degrees will all vary (HEATH Resource Center, 1995) between and among the different types of institutions. In addition, the individual strengths, needs, and interests of the student also will vary and educational goals may change over time. Therefore, an important step toward a successful outcome is matching the individual's overall needs and goals to the appropriate learning institution.

TABLE 14–2

Postsecondary Educational Options

Four-Year Colleges and Universities

Colleges provide general academic programs leading to a bachelor's degree in the arts (BA) and sciences (BS). Universities offer the bachelor's degree in addition to professional and graduate programs leading to advanced degrees such as a master's degree or a doctorate. Tuition, room and board, and books are generally more expensive per year than at other types of postsecondary programs (HEATH Resource Center, 1995). Some have open admissions (i.e., anyone over the age of 18 and/or with a high school diploma or GED), but most have selective admissions based on high school GPA, class rank, SAT/ACT scores, letters of recommendation, personal interviews, and other evidence of achievement (HEATH Resource Center, 1995). Ninety-five percent of public and private colleges and universities offer "remedial" courses, taken by 40 to 70% of entering freshmen (Gray, 1996), which assist students in developing compensatory skills and strategies for learning, help them to identify necessary accommodations, and to gain confidence.

Community, Junior, Vocational, and Technical Colleges

Community colleges are nonresidential institutions which offer programs less than 4 years in length, generally 2 years or less. Programs can lead to a license, a certificate, an Associate of Arts (AA), Associate of Science (AS), or an Associate of Applied Science (AAS). The cost is generally thousands of dollars less than a 4-year college and allow students to take a few selected courses in an area of interest. Most of them are open admission, but they may require students to take a placement exam (i.e., ASSET). Students who are not academically prepared may be required to take some "developmental" course work. Usually this course work prepares students for the fastest growing jobs identified by the U.S. Bureau of Labor Statistics, such as computer engineers and technicians, dental hygienists, medical technicians, and paralegals (Kent, 1997).

Technical colleges have a special emphasis on training for specific careers in technical fields such as data processing or mechanical trades. Some offer programs leading to an AA or AS degree. They often operate in conjunction with local industry, business, and public and other service organizations (Mitchell, 1997). Some programs are formally linked to programs that students begin during their last 2 years of high school. Such partnerships are frequently referred to as tech-prep, school-to-career, or two plus two programs.

Proprietary schools are run-for-profit institutions that offer courses in such areas as secretarial, bookkeeping, or culinary training. Credits from these programs may or may not transfer to 2- or 4-year institutions.

Critical Point Self-determination skills are vital in order for students to clarify their preferred postschool transition outcomes. (Steere & Cavaiuolo, 2002)

Consider the following. Although more students continue to enroll in our nation's 4-year colleges and universities, roughly half will fail to graduate and 43% of those who do leave with a bachelor's degree report being underemployed 2 years after graduation; the rate of underemployment is 67% for arts and science majors (Gray, 1996, 2002). In a survey reported in the *Chronicle of Higher Education* (International Survey of Faculty Attitudes, 1994), 80% of the faculty thought that incoming freshmen were not academically prepared in written and oral communication, and 85% thought students were not adequately prepared in mathematics. This is not surprising given that it has been estimated that 50% of high school students who enrolled in college did not complete an academic, nor a vocational curriculum integrated with academics (Plank, 2001). Therefore, unless a student is academically and socially prepared, as well as highly motivated to succeed, a 4-year college or university may not be the appropriate choice after high school.

Critical Point Only 12% of students with disabilities had taken any advanced math courses before graduating, which are often required for college entrance. (Wagner & Blackorby, 1996)

There is some research to suggest that earnings are not affected by whether a student attended a 2- or 4-year college (Pascarella & Terenzini, 1991). In fact, one of the fastest growing bodies of students in higher education are "reverse transfers" (i.e., students with a bachelor and/or graduate degree who enroll in 1- and 2-year certificate or associate degree programs) (Gray, 1996). Jobs in technical and occupational fields can lead to high-paying careers that equal or are greater than those earned by graduates from 4-year colleges and universities (Gray, 1996, 2002). "Nontraditional" students now account for over 60% of overall higher education enrollments (Aslanian, 1996).

Critical Point Nearly 60% of all students with disabilities going on to a postsecondary education enrolled in 2-year (or less) institutions compared to one-third of students without disabilities. Students without disabilities were more likely to enroll in 4-year institutions (62%) compared to students with disabilities (42%). (American Youth Policy Forum/Center on Education Policy, 2002)

The Carl D. Perkins Vocational and Applied Technology Education Act of 1990 (P.L. 101-392) mandates that students with disabilities have access to the full range of vocational and technical programs, such as tech-prep, which links vocational courses of study in the last years of high school with a program of study in local community or technical colleges (Lombard, Hazelkorn, & Miller, 1995). However, in their national study on state policies and practices in tech-prep Lombard et al. (1995) found that few states had implemented the equal access provisions, even though 4 years had elapsed since the Perkins Act had become law and funding was available. In addition, most students with disabilities who are enrolled in vocational courses in high school take the traditional vocational/career and technical programs of study, which lack an academic component and therefore decrease the likelihood of going on to postsecondary education and training (Gray, 2002).

Requirements of Postsecondary Education

Understanding Legal Rights and Responsibilities

Legally, postsecondary institutions must not discriminate in the recruitment, admissions, or treatment of students with disabilities. However, students with (and without) disabilities often lack knowledge regarding the civil rights of students with disabilities (Pitman & Slate, 1994;

Stageberg, Fischer, & Barbut, 1996). In order for students with disabilities to navigate and advocate successfully in postsecondary settings, they must be aware of their legal rights and responsibilities (Frank & Wade, 1993; HEATH Resource Center, 1995). Under the Individuals with Disabilities Education Act (IDEA), the school is responsible for identifying and assessing the student with a disability and for providing appropriate education instruction and related services. However, IDEA does not apply to students in postsecondary education, as the students themselves become responsible for many services that were once provided for them. The three pieces of legislation that impact postsecondary education are the Rehabilitation Act of 1973 (especially section 504), the Americans with Disabilities Act (ADA) of 1990, and the Family and Educational Rights and Privacy Act (FERPA) of 1974 (see Table 14–3).

Student Voices

"Advocacy to me means speaking up for oneself, knowing the rights granted to you, and making sure you get those rights. To be a good advocator for oneself you need to know about your disability and know your needs. One can't be afraid to speak for oneself if a problem comes about. If one feels they are not getting the rights they deserve they need to speak up. Knowing one's rights is important as well. If you don't know your rights how can you stand up for yourself? A self-advocator must be knowledgeable about their rights as a person with a disability."

The Rehabilitation Act of 1973 was the first piece of civil rights legislation for persons with disabilities (Jarrow, 1992). Section 504 states that no *otherwise qualified* individual with disabilities be excluded from participation in, or denied the benefits of, or subjected to discrimination under any program receiving federally funded assistance. Although colleges and universities do not have to offer special education courses, subpart E, which focuses specifically upon higher education, further requires that both public and private institutions make appropriate academic adjustments and reasonable modifications to the colleges' procedures and policies. This is to ensure that students with disabilities can fully participate in the same programs and activities that are available to students without disabilities (Flexer, 1996).

Critical Point While disclosing a disability is a personal choice, students who choose not to disclose to their college office of disability services may not receive the accommodation and modification to which they are entitled.

Adjustments, Modifications, and Accommodations

The term *otherwise qualified* means that the person meets the requisite academic and/or technical standards required for admission to the postsecondary institution's programs and activities (Heyward, 1996). Section 504 also led to the promotion of disability resource programs in postsecondary institutions in order to provide appropriate academic adjustments such as the extension of time permitted to complete a degree (Flexer, 1996). Reasonable modifications ensure that students with disabilities are not excluded or segregated from the general student population and apply to areas such as housing, financial and employment assistance, physical education and athletics, counseling, placement services, and social organizations (Flexer). ADA upholds and extends the Rehabilitation Act's civil rights protection to all public and private colleges and universities, regardless of whether they receive federal funds (Flexer; Frank & Wade, 1993).

FERPA protects the confidentiality of student records at the postsecondary institution. Only persons with a legitimate reason can view the student's records or those given express permission by the student to do so. FERPA also gives the students the right to access their records and

TABLE 14–3

Comparison of Federal Legislation Guiding Services for Persons with Disabilities

	The IDEA	Section 504	The ADA
Purpose of law	To provide a free, appropriate, public education (FAPE) in the least restrictive environment through federal funding to states, with substantive requirements attached to funding	A civil rights law which protects persons with disabilities from discrimination and requires reasonable accommodations to ensure nondiscrimination with no authorization for funding	A civil rights law which provides all persons with disabilities broader coverage than section 504 in all aspects of discrimination, with no authorization for funding
Scope and coverage	Applies to public schools and covers students ages 3 to 21 who have a disability that impacts their education	Applies to any program or activity that is receiving federal financial assistance and covers all qualified persons with disabilities regardless of whether special education services are required in elementary, secondary, or postsecondary settings	Applies to public or private employment, transportation, accommodations, and telecommunications regardless of whether federal funding is received and covers all qualified persons with disabilities, and qualified nondisabled persons related to or associated with a person with a disability
Disability defined	A listing of 13 disability categories is provided in the act, and all must adversely affect education performance	No listing of disabilities, but inclusionary criteria of any physical or mental impairment that substantially limits one or more major life activities, having a record of such an impairment, or being regarded as having an impairment	No listing of disabilities provided. Same criteria as found in section 504. HIV status and contagious and noncontagious diseases recently included

(continued)

TABLE 14–3 *(continued)*

	The IDEA	Section 504	The ADA
Identification process	Responsibility of school district to identify through "child find" and evaluate at no expense to parent of individual	Responsibility of individual with disability to self-identify and provide documentation. Cost of evaluation must be assumed by the individual, not the institution	Same as section 504
Service delivery	Special education services and auxiliary aids mandated by child study team and stipulated in the IEP	Services, auxiliary aids, and academic adjustments may be provided in the regular education setting, arranged for by special education coordinator or student disability services	Services, auxiliary aids, and accommodations arranged for by the designated ADA coordinator. Requires that accommodations do not pose an "undue hardship" to employers
Enforcement agency	Office of Special Education and Rehabilitative Services in U.S. Department of Education	The Office for Civil Rights (OCR) in the U.S. Department of Education	Primarily the U.S. Department of Justice, in conjunction with the Equal Employment Opportunity Commission and Federal Communications Commission. May overlap with OCR
Remedies	Reimbursement by district of school-related expenses is available to parents of children with disabilities to ensure FAPE	A private individual may sue a recipient of federal financial assistance to ensure compliance with section 504	Same as section 504 with monetary damages up to $50,000 for the first violation; attorney fees and litigation expenses are also recoverable

Source: Adapted from: *Handicapped requirements handbook* (January) 1993. Washington, DC: Thompson Publishing Group.

to challenge information contained in the record (HEATH Resource Center, 1995). Although section 504 and the ADA require postsecondary institutions to provide equal access to their regular programs and prohibits the institution from making preadmission inquiry regarding a student's disability, once the student has been admitted, the student *alone* is responsible for self-identifying and providing the required documentation. Postsecondary institutions are not under any obligation to provide accommodations *until the student* contacts the college Office of Disability Services (ODS) (or the person on campus who is responsible for providing services) *and* provides the required documentation. Typically, this procedure must be followed at the start of each term/quarter/ semester. Decisions concerning the exact accommodations to be provided are determined on an individual basis. Accommodations are then negotiated between the postsecondary service provider and the student. The law states that the institution should provide effective accommodations based on the identified needs of the student, which means that the student's individual preference for a particular accommodation does not define the nature and level of services that should be provided (Heyward, 1996). However, students who are aware of the accommodations they need and who have the ability to self-advocate are in a better position to have their individual needs met.

Student Voices

"It is my responsibility, being the person with particular needs, to make my needs known to others. It is not their responsibility to assume what I may or may not need, this can lead to problems. I prefer to do as much as I possibly can for myself even if it would be easier for me to let someone else do it. I have found that the more I do for myself the better I feel about myself, and the more difficult the task, the greater the sense of accomplishment I feel. I thrive off of my challenges and my struggles and when a person attempts to help me when I haven't asked for their help I take offense to it. I know they're only trying to be helpful but in my opinion they are actually hindering me in many ways."

Demands and Supports in Postsecondary Environments

Understanding legal foundations, rights and responsibilities, and the postsecondary options that are available to students provide the transition team with a basis for developing some transition goals leading to the outcome selected by the student (Webster, 1999). As the team studies the various options, they should help the student also become aware of the ways in which the various postsecondary environments differ from one another and from the high school environment. An example of differences between high school and college demands is shown in Table 14–4.

In addition to assisting the student in understanding her or his own disability and knowing that she or he will have to self-identify and seek out support services in postsecondary settings, the team's understanding of the performance expectations of the individual in postsecondary environments forms the basis for additional transition goals. As the information provided under the legal rights and responsibilities section, as well as in this section suggest, students seeking postsecondary degrees will have to be much more independent, responsible, and self-motivated in college than they were in high school. Institutional support services are available, in accord with the federal requirements discussed, but students will have to know what each school offers and how to access the various resources. The students need to understand that they will no longer have a team guiding them; will probably not have an IEP (individualized education plan, although some colleges do provide these); may have to pay for extra help, such as tutoring services; and will need to understand all the other differences between their current

TABLE 14–4
Differences Between High School and College

	High School	College
Responsibility	Teachers, counselors, and principals are responsible for providing students with support services.	The student is responsible for requesting assistance and advice when needed.
Class time	Students sit in class for 6 hours per day for 180 days, which totals 1,080 hours per year.	Students sit in class 12 to 15 hours per week, 15 weeks per semester. This totals about 450 hours per school year.
Tests	Tests are given weekly or at the end of a chapter, and quizzes are given frequently.	There will be fewer tests, 2 to 3 each semester per class and they will cover more material, perhaps 4 to 6 chapters.
Study time	Homework ranges between 1 to 3 hours per day.	A general rule of thumb is at least 2 hours of homework for every hour spent in class; 3 to 5 hours of homework daily.
Knowledge acquisition	Information is provided mostly through in-class resources, assigned reading, and classroom discussion. Out-of-class research is minimal.	Course work requires more library work and writing; longer papers are required as well as research.
Assignments	Assignments are broken down into step-by-step tasks.	Instructions may be less specific and some may only be given on the syllabus at the beginning of the semester. Students decide how they will complete the task.
Grades	Classroom attendance and participation contributes to grades with numerous quizzes, tests, and homework assignments. Class may be changed for some students with IEPs.	Grades are based on fewer tests and assignments. Attendance is not always a requirement. Students may need a certain GPA to move ahead. All students meet same class standards.
Teachers	Teachers often take attendance, check notebooks, put information on the chalkboard. They monitor progress and will offer assistance when needed. They directly impart knowledge and facts.	Instructors often lecture nonstop and do not always teach from the text. Students are expected to learn from outside readings and research. Students monitor their own progress and need for help.
Parent role	Parents are often advocates and work with teachers and counselors to assure the student is being supported academically.	Parent is a mentor and works with the student to offer support and guidance.
Freedom	Much of the student's time is structured by parents, teachers, and other adults.	Students structure their own time among academics, work, and extracurricular activities. They make their own decisions about schedules, class attendance, and studying.

Source: Adapted from: MacKillop, J. (1996). *Ladders to success: A student's guide to school after high school.* Puget Sound, WA: Puget Sound Educational Service District.

environment and the various postsecondary settings available.

Critical Point Many school systems destroy records of special testing once a student graduates from high school. Therefore students need to request those records not only in order to provide documentation of their disability to colleges and adult service providers, but also to make sure they complete an assessment battery shortly before leaving high school. If the testing is relevant and current, colleges may accept the documentation, hence saving the cost of a private evaluation. However, it is best to check with the postsecondary institution(s) the student plans to attend to see what types of documentation they require.

CASE STUDY

Succeeding in College Requires More Than Mere Academics—Michelle's Story

Due to my situation, which is a so-called disability known as cerebral palsy, my schedule and life have always been very structured. Therefore, I have been forced to develop time management skills. I need assistance with daily personal hygiene and eating. I am not able to take early classes or late night classes, unless I am enrolled in the same class as my attendant. To make it easier on both of us, the attendant either works the shift before or after that class.

I have 11 personal attendants who assist me in my everyday life. It is very difficult to find people to work the early and late hour shifts, due to the fact that everyone needs sleep. We all have our own lives and I don't want to impede on other people's lives because the people who work for me most of the time are also my friends. I care about their lives as a friend and not only as an employer. Those special bonds that I form with assistants (because I need so much help with personal things) don't grow unless you are forced to work with them a lot or to take the time to spend quality time with one another. If that kind of friendship does not exist, I feel that it takes a toll on the working relationship, which leads me to my next point. I had to terminate someone's position today.

Lucky for me, I did not really consider her a close friend as of yet. It is very hard to reprimand my friends or to terminate their employment. I terminated her employment because this is the first semester she had worked for me, and she had already asked for approximately 6 days off, only giving me 4 days' notice. They were all out-of-town trips, so she knew about them ahead of time. Normally, what we do when a person wants to take off is post a note in my room and then whoever chooses can sign up to take the shift. But for some reason, this person did not understand this concept. At the beginning of every semester, I give each attendant a phone list of all the other attendants' numbers. When they want to take off, they either post a sign or call each other.

The situation today affected my time management plan for the day. That is, because I had to take time out of my schedule to e-mail several attendants to explain the situation and to find someone to fill the shifts. The person whose employment was terminated works both Saturday and Sunday mornings. That shift is really important because I need to get out of bed. For the time being, I am going on a week-to-week basis with that shift. It may get a little harder to manage my time as I get further into my college career, due to class times. However, I made it this far, so I feel that with the help of all my friends and family, I can do pretty much anything.

I do most of my homework on my computers. I am able to type myself, but only six words per minute. In order to utilize my time in a better fashion, I normally dictate to my personal attendants, while they type for me. I also have all my textbooks on audiotapes through the Library for the Blind and Dyslexic. I have a visual perception problem, which means I cannot follow one line of text. It is caused by the cerebral palsy. The muscles in my eyes are weak, so they tend to stray off the line. Sometimes bigger print helps, but not always. It depends how close the lines are to each other.

As for my books on tape, my nightly attendant shift is from 7 to 11 P.M. During that shift I have to eat dinner, dictate any typing, and take a shower. So, usually, when I have a chapter to listen to, I listen to it after my attendant leaves. I leave a little light on and over the 3 years I have been at Kent, I have programmed myself to stay awake. That is just another challenge that comes with cerebral palsy and having to manage my time. During the day, I'm able to spend up to 4 hours alone in my room, although there are always people in the hall. Those times when I'm alone in my room is another chance I get to listen to my books on tape.

During the day, I either take the vans from class to class or have my attendants walk with me. I don't like to walk by myself because of my visual perception problems. I also have trouble seeing curb cutouts and different elevations of land. Also, because I have been in an electric wheelchair since I was 7 years old and drive it so much, I have developed tendonitis. Therefore, when I have an attendant with me, I normally train her to drive for me. My tendonitis has gotten worse this semester, so having someone drive for me now is basically a requirement. We all have those instructions from my physical therapist at the health center. That is another thing that I am required to fit into my schedule. I go to therapy twice a week, for an hour each session. It helps me to assist my attendants when they are doing a transfer or helping to move me from one place to another. It also helps me with my stress level. A big part of cerebral palsy is something called "spasticity." It is the contraction and loosening of muscles. How tight my muscles are depends greatly on my mood or how much stress I'm under. My muscles also contract when I get excited or scared. They even contract when I just talk in general because my stomach diaphragm muscles don't work. So, it takes lots of effort to get air out. To get words out, I have to put every muscle into the effort of talking. Cerebral palsy is caused by a lack of oxygen to the brain, which occurred sometime during the birthing process. There are several different variations of it, but in my case, of course, I am not affected cognitively.

There are a lot of people on campus affected with cerebral palsy and I just happen to be one of those who are the most affected physically. To go out with friends also is hard, if I don't go out with someone who works for me, during the normal time that person is scheduled to work, or with someone who's just a friend and doesn't work for me. I have to schedule people around times when I want to have fun. This is very maddening sometimes, but it's an everyday part of life! It's also part of life that some of my friends and I can't drive. All of these things I feel and know because I live my life, and it greatly affects the way I manage my time!

Another part of managing my time in my social life is something I do with a group of friends who are known as the GPC. It stands for Gimp Power Coalition. A "gimp" is slang for someone with a physical challenge, to put it simply. I rely on this coalition throughout my everyday life at Kent to support me in any good times and bad that come along with the challenges that we have. Once a month, our GPC has a movie night; sometimes we end up watching the movies we rent and sometimes we don't because that is the one time in the month when we all get together and just talk or vent if we need to. I feel that I'm a very lucky person because I'm one of the few people whom I know is a part of two coalitions. I have a very strong GPC at home for all through school I was integrated with other people with physical challenges. Some of my friends who are part of the Kent GPC come from different backgrounds and don't have a very strong GPC at home. That is why I feel very fortunate; otherwise, I would not be able to go through my everyday life anywhere at this time in my life without being a part of either one of my GPCs. As a result, being a part of these groups is so important in my life, which is just one more thing that affects my time management in everyday life.

(*Michelle Marcellus, Senior, Consumer Studies Major, Kent State University*)

Support and Services in Postsecondary Settings

Although legally all colleges and universities must provide access and reasonable accommodations, the ways in which the services are provided vary greatly among institutions (HEATH, 1997; Scott, 1996). These services range along a continuum from those where services are practically nonexistent to campuses that offer extensive, comprehensive services (Brinckerhoff, McGuire, & Shaw, 2002; Scott, 1996). Some colleges offer "college experience" summer programs for high school students with disabilities (HEATH Resource Center, 2003; Serebreni, Rumrill, Mullins, & Gordon, 1993) in addition to summer orientations for incoming freshmen (Scott, 1996). As postsecondary institutions and programs can differ in a variety of ways, as can the individual student's strengths, interests, and needs, the key lies in finding a good match between the two.

Critical Point Research has shown that services and accommodations provided vary by type and size of the postsecondary setting. Public 2- and 4-year colleges were more likely to provide a service or accommodation for students with disabilities than their counterparts in the private sector, as were medium and larger sized institutions compared to smaller ones. (National Center for Education Statistics, 1999b)

Students who are knowledgeable about their legal rights and aware of the mandated services available for them will have a more realistic expectation about what kinds of help they may expect in college. For transition planning purposes, it is important for prospective students to contact the Office for Students with Disabilities (OSD) at each school that they may be considering in order to determine the best fit. The Council for the Advancement of Standards in Higher Education (Miller, 1997) described the mission of disability support service programs as being twofold:

1. Assurance that qualified students with disabilities have equal access to all institutional programs and services.
2. Advocate responsibly the needs of students with disabilities to the campus community.

Types of Services Offered

The array of services to students, staffing patterns, and the degree of administrative support varies widely among institutions of higher education. One issue common to all colleges is that their requirement to provide disability-related services begins when students request services. Types of services and accommodations specifically for students with disabilities cited in the literature include: (a) summer or presemester specialized orientation programs; (b) individualized counseling and advising; (c) priority registration and/or reduced courseloads; (d) course substitutions, course waivers, and modified materials, program, or degree requirements; (e) taped textbooks, lectures, and the allowance of tape recorders in the classroom; (f) services of adjunct personnel such as notetakers, proofreaders, typists, readers, interpreters, mobility guides; (g) alternative testing accommodations such as untimed, individualized, or oral examinations; (h) assistance with study skills, self- and time management; (i) adaptive and regular technological assistance (e.g., calculators, Braille devices, reading machines, computer keyboard modifications, augmentative communication devices, modified word processors, modified telephones); and (j) accessibility adjustments, such as the removal of architectural barriers, designed parking areas, transportation assistance, and barrier guide sheets (Gajar, 1998, p. 391).

Institutional resources that are available to all students also may provide benefits to students with disabilities. For example, Offices of Career Services can assist students in defining and accomplishing personal and academic goals through career counseling, occupational information, including internships and part-time jobs, job placement and referral, assistance with résumés and on-campus interviews, information on graduate schools and programs, and services specifically designed for students with disabilities. In addition, many other resouces are available on most campuses that can provide valuable resources such as academic advising, counseling services, learning assistance centers, office of student activities, office of financial aid, and student orientation programs.

While proprietary and private technical institutions typically do not have offices of disability services, they too are subject to the Americans with Disabilities Act (1990) and so cannot discriminate against students due to their disability.

Critical Point While roughly all postsecondary programs enrolling students with disabilities provide supports to help them succeed (American Youth Policy Forum/Center on Education Policy, 2002), the range of services differs among various postsecondary settings on a continuum from minimal to extensive.

Student Voices

"I am puzzled as to why information related to disabilities is not included in the freshman orientation class. This would be a great way to integrate both those with and without disabilities and increase awareness of the barriers that both groups face, as nondisabled people are crippled by their ignorance as well as their prejudice. Those of us with disabilities struggle with self-esteem and self-confidence issues that can easily be made worse by the negative attitudes of others."

College Climate

Colleges vary widely in terms of their missions, admission requirements, costs, accessibility, faculty and staff, student body, courses and programs offered, community and financial resources (including opportunities for financial aid), size, location, athletics, and social activities (HEATH Resource Center, 1995; Kezar, 1997a; Scott, 1996). For example, research has suggested that a student's cognitive and academic gains are enhanced in an institution where there is greater interaction between faculty and peers and where teaching, as opposed to research, is a priority (Astin, 1993). Traditionally, faculty with a research orientation tend to be in larger public universities, which often place less emphasis on student development and undergraduate education in general (Kezar, 1997b). However, according to Kezar (1997b), many of these institutions have recently begun to focus more upon undergraduate education and student development. More important than the actual size of the university or college is the degree to which a student participates in clubs, organizations, and activities and the ties they develop with a specific department (Pascarella & Terenzini, 1991). Research has also shown that one of the strongest predictors of a student's satisfaction with his or her postsecondary experience is leaving home to attend college (Astin), as students living away from home tend to be more involved in their campus activities. This correlation, however, does not apply to many students from ethnic minorities (Astin). The racial and gender makeup of an institution also may impact upon the college experience. There is evidence to suggest, for example, that women's colleges enhance students' career attainment and socioecomic aspirations (Pascarella & Terenzini, 1991). Also, although historically black colleges and universities enroll only 16% of all African-American students, each year roughly one-third of all African Americans who earn a college degree graduate from these colleges (Gray, 1996). In addition, the 31 tribal colleges in the United States and Canada provide academic, vocational, and technical programs (similar to those at mainstream institutions) to over 25,000 Americans from 250 federally recognized tribes (Monette, 1997). Attending these types of schools also may offer more mentors and role models and a greater likelihood of completing degrees (Kezar, 1997a). However, perseverance and social support can facilitate the success of minority students in institutions where the majority of students are from a different culture.

Many lifelong skills are developed at college.

Critical Point Students need to match their personal preferences and needs to the characteristics of the institution. For example, students with physical challenges may benefit from a campus that does not have environmental barriers and has a climate that is welcoming to students with disabilities (Wilson & Getzel, 2001).

Finding the Right Fit

Research has shown that a student's motivation, interactions with faculty and other students, and involvement in campus activities have a greater impact upon educational outcomes than the type of institution one chooses (Kezar, 1997a; Tinto, 1993). Although selecting an institution depends on the student's interests, strengths, and needs, some institutions may better provide the types of environments in which an individual will thrive and succeed. Many high schools have college counselors who may assist the student and his or her team in choosing a postsecondary school. The key is finding a good match between the setting and the individual.

Awareness of the types of postsecondary options available, the student's rights and responsibilities, and the demands of college life is a first step toward providing an outcome-based transition program for students with disabilities. With this background knowledge in place, the transition team, including the student, can begin the process of devising a secondary curriculum that fits the chosen goal. Initially, selected goals may change or be modified along the way, but team members continue to have in mind what choices are available. The process of helping a student to reach her or his goal is grounded in the four principles of IDEA: *Transition services must* (1) *be based on students' needs, taking into account their preferences and interests*; (2) *be designed within an outcome-oriented process*; (3) *be a coordinated set of activities*; and (4) *promote movement from school to postschool activities*. These principles form the bases of assessment, curriculum, instructional methodology, experiential activities, and formative/summative evaluation of the transition student's secondary education.

Critical Point Many postsecondary professors and instructors are unfamiliar with various types of accommodations. Therefore, students who have the knowledge and ability to self-advocate will be more likely to get their needs met.

Student Voices

"Any student with a disability (or disabilities) should meet up with a student with similar disabilities at that college. I feel it is important to talk to a mentor as much as possible so that the high school student would get the understanding and impression of what it is like to go to college there. In order to make a successful transition, he/she might want to stay at the college for a weekend and 'shadow' the individual around for like maybe one or two days' worth of classes and see what it's like. Then, the student would be able to have a better understanding of what the college will provide in terms of their disability. The student should also meet with the director of SDS and talk about what kind of accommodations would be provided. Be sure to have on hand documentation or any medical records and notes from the doctors."

Preparing for Postsecondary Education

The transition planning process should be guided by the interests, needs, and preferences of students and their families. Family participation in this process is crucial as families not only influence career aspirations (Super, 1990; Symanski, 1994), but they also play a powerful role in developing future visions, which are related to career and lifestyle options (Morningstar, Turnbull, & Turnbull, 1996). Educators also must be aware of attitudes, values, and beliefs from the students' and families' cultural perspective in order to develop strategies to promote success in postsecondary educational settings (Association of Higher Education and Disability [AHEAD], 1998). For example, some cultures may value collectivism or the group more strongly than individualism (Greenfield, 1994; Kim & Choi, 1994). Therefore, focusing upon how a postsecondary education could increase the status and standard of living for the extended family or group may increase the students' and families' motivation more than emphasizing the benefits to the individuals.

Student Voices

"When I went to camp for a week in my younger years, I got a feel of being independent without the safety net of my mother. When I was nine I took a shower only once that week because I didn't ask for one. The next year I had one every day that I was there, because even with the constant push from the greatest mother in the world, I realize that nobody is going to take care of me but me. . . . If I had been pampered and nurtured all the time while at home I wouldn't have lasted the first semester in college."

Determining Student Need and Interest

Interest Surveys and Needs Assessments

Determining the student's needs, interests, and preferences should begin early and continue throughout the student's school career. Teachers who effectively identify students' expectations, choices, and preferences through observations, conducting interviews and assessments with the students and significant others, are more successful in facilitating a positive transition to adulthood (Wehmeyer, Agran, & Hughes, 1998). Formal assessments can provide an introduction to the idea of matching information about careers to an individual. These include, but are not limited to instruments like *The Self-Directed Search* (Holland, Fritzsche, & Powell, 1994) (a self-rating instrument that aids the individual in determining career options that best match his or her personality, interests, values, skills, and abilities); and *Discover* (ACT Test Administration) (a computer program that assesses where the student is in personal career planning and includes Career Journey Inventory, Abilities Inventory, Uniact Interest Inventory, and Experience Inventory). The assessment process begins in the ninth grade, or earlier if appropriate, and is completed by the twelfth grade.

Critical Point Career choices are influenced in part by exposure to a range of oppportunites in school and in the workplace. Therefore students from at-risk groups, such as lower SES family status, ethnic minorities, and women may well have a narrow range of interests merely due to lack of opportunities. (Lindstrom & Benz, 2002)

Assessment of student needs and interests also can be incorporated into a student's academic performance by (1) using checklists based on subject areas and the strengths, needs, experiences, and skills needed to be successful in both high school and postsecondary education settings; (2) obtaining and recording information through observation of the student by teachers, family members, and others who are well acquainted with the student; and (3) recording information through interviews concerning academic, functional academics, and vocational and community experiences (Duffey et al., 1996); and (4) having student-teacher conferences regarding ongoing classroom work as it applies to team-selected goals that will facilitate the transition to postsecondary education.

Student-Directed IEP/ITPs

As stated throughout the text, students' active participation in the team process is central to transition planning and decision making, especially if students' needs and interests are to be taken into account. By providing opportunities for students to make meaningful choices and to demonstrate preferences in what, how, and why they learn, students can acquire the skills of self-determination (Aune, 1991, Halpern, 1994; Sitlington & Frank, 1990) that are crucial for success in postsecondary education. For example, research has suggested that when learners are provided a rationale for why they are learning, student motivation and participation in activities increases (Deci & Chandler, 1986). Participation in meaningful transition planning and student satisfaction with school instruction is a strong predictor of participation in postsecondary education (Halpern, Yovanoff, Doren, & Benz, 1995). Although the mere physical presence of students at their IEP/ITP meetings may meet the statutory requirements of IDEA on its own, it fails to meet either the spirit or the intent of IDEA (Wehmeyer & Ward, 1995), which calls for student participation to the greatest extent possible. Actively participating and having responsibility for developing transition goals will increase the opportunity for students (1) to become knowledgeable about the functional limitations of their disability; (2) to develop a sense of independence and perseverance; (3) to engage in problem solving and conflict resolution; (4) to develop self-advocacy and self-determination skills (deFur et al., 1996); and (5) to develop greater self-discipline and self-management skills (Shaw, Brinkerhoff, Kistler, & McGuire, 1991). Several examples of student-directed IEP programs are available and could be adapted as needed or used as guides in helping teams to learn how to empower students.

Student Voices

"Self-advocacy is something that needs to be taught to us long before we reach college. It should begin at around 14 years of age when we are *supposed* to become an active participant in our IEP meetings. Unfortunately, most school administrations and other involved professionals . . . and parents . . . pay mostly lip service to this 'ideal' situation. Most people with disabilities sit in those meetings while everyone else decides our fate. This encourages and perpetuates 'learned helplessness.' Then, we reach college . . . or the workforce . . . and have no idea what to do, let alone how to do it!"

Critical Point Persistence is an essential component of self-determination. Within 5 years of beginning a postsecondary education, 41% of students with disabilities had earned a degree or credential, and another 12% were still enrolled. (American Youth Policy Forum/Center on Education Policy, 2002)

Far too often students become the passive recipient of instructions and services and have no role in determining their learning needs and goals, or in evaluating their progress (Van Reusen & Bos, 1994). The disservice this does to students who will soon find themselves in a postsecondary program cannot be overstated. At the postsecondary level, the students themselves bear a significant responsibility for the impact of their own college experience (Pascarella & Terenzini, 1991) and, therefore, students who have taken a more active role in their high school education will be in a better position to succeed in a postsecondary program. The different social, academic, and independent living expectations demanded in most postsecondary settings (Shaw et al., 1991) means that students who are college-bound, for example, will require more than just academic preparation to meet the challenges that lie ahead. Becoming actively involved in the transition process provides an ideal venue for students to become knowledgeable about the functional limitations of their disability; to develop a sense of independence and perseverance; and to engage in problem solving, which is essential in developing the crucial skills of self-determination and self-advocacy (deFur et al., 1996); as well as greater self-discipline and self-management (Shaw et al., 1991). If students are to succeed in postsecondary programs, they must be provided with the appropriate training that will enhance their skills in self-determination, identifying postschool goals, and choosing appropriate educational experiences (Aune, 1991; Halpern, 1994; Sitlington & Frank, 1990). Participation in meaningful transition planning and student satisfaction with school instruction is a strong predictor of participation in postsecondary education (Halpern et al., 1995).

Critical Point Research has shown that students who are more self-determined in high school are more likely to be employed (and at at higher rate of pay) after high school than students who were less self-determined (Wehmeyer & Schwartz, 1997).

Career Exploration and Planning

The School-to-Work Opportunities Act (STWOA) of 1994 calls upon schools to provide instructional programs and career guidance and planning that will result in assisting students in determining a career major that integrates academic and occupational content, with a view to enhancing the students' chances of succeeding in postsecondary programs and future employment (Benz & Kochhar, 1996). In his analysis of high school career and technical education, Gray (2002) found that although students who chose an academic concentration were initially better prepared when they entered high school than those who chose a vocational concentration that integrated academics into the program of study, the achievement gap was insignificant by the time they graduated. Whereas students who went the traditional vocational route that excluded an academic component, were the least prepared when they entered high school and had the lowest achievement upon graduation. Students need to have the opportunity to combine academics with career exploration activites such as:

- Service learning programs that provide community service in nonpaid voluntary positions.
- Job shadowing where the student can get a more realistic view of the essential functions of occupational areas of interest.
- Work experience opportunities where the student works at a particular job for a set period of time, generally two to six weeks.
- A part-time or summer job, which also can teach the student responsibility, reliability, and interpersonal skills, as well as provide a way to save and learn how to manage money for college.
- Informational interviews where the student meets with people working in careers in which the student has expressed an interest.
- Establishing mentors and networks in the local business community as well as encouraging the student to discuss career options with family and friends.
- Working with school guidance or career counselors who should have access to a variety of career interest inventories and vocational assessments; using the Internet and school

and public libraries as a resource that can provide information on a variety of careers (e.g., *Dictionary of Occupational Titles*, or *Occupational Outlook Handbook*) and the latest trends in the labor market, as well as describe different types of college programs.
- Develop a career portfolio.
- Link student's hobbies or leisure activities to potential careers.
- Explore postsecondary programs that offer internships that provide limited intensive learning experience outside the traditional classroom and/or cooperative education programs that work with students, faculty, and employers to help students clarify career and academic goals and expand classroom studies by participating in paid, practical work experiences.

In addition to the various career interest inventories and strategies for career exploration discussed earlier, a vocational assessment also can aid students in deciding upon an appropriate postsecondary program to facilitate their future employment goals.

Student Voices

"My advice to perspective students is to examine and really think about what their ten-year plan is going to be for themselves, because the less time figuring out their career path the more likely they will get funding, especially if they want the government to help. So they [really need] to do research on what they want for themselves by themselves. If people tell the student what they should do, the less likely their heart will be in it to follow through. Therefore, this is a totally independent decision for the student, and once decided they should be ready to give up their whole life for their plan, which may or may not include college. Being happy in life should be the goal no matter how they get to that point."

Critical Point In their study on the career development of young women with learning disabilities, Lindstrom & Benz (2002) concluded that opportunites and counseling are meaningless unless they lead to a self-directed decision-making process.

Although career development should begin as early as elementary school (Benz & Kochhar, 1996; Clark, Carlson, Fisher, Cook, & D'Alonzo, 1991), students should begin formally exploring the world of work no later than middle school, as they begin to discover their own talents and abilities, as well as career areas of interests or career majors. By exploring career options, reflecting upon career interests, and engaging in a gradual process of eliminating choices that are not a good fit (Lindstrom & Benz, 2002), students will be in a better position to understand what kinds of postsecondary programs can best meet their individual needs. In addition, students and their transition teams need to be aware of trends in the labor market and future employment opportunities in their areas of interest and strengths. In order for career planning to be effective, the transition team must develop partnerships among the student, educators (including career guidance services/school counselors), and community-based service providers, such as vocational rehabilitation personnel (deFur et al., 1996).

Identifying Goals and Preparing Students for Postsecondary Outcomes

Since Will (1983) first defined transition as a bridge to adulthood, the main goal of the transition process has been achieving positive postschool outcomes (DeStefano & Wermuth, 1992; Halpern, 1992). In order to accomplish this successfully, goals must first be identified, along with the necessary instructional activities, supports, and services that will facilitate making those goals a reality. Once a student and family have identified a potential postsecondary

TABLE 14–5

Roles and Responsibilities for Students Involved in Planning Postsecondary Outcomes

Student Roles and Responsibilities
Understand the nature of their disability, including its effect on learning and work.
Establish realistic goals after identifying strengths, needs, preferences, and interests.
Present a positive self-image by stressing strengths while understanding functional limitations due to the disability.
Know how, when, and where to discuss and request appropriate accommodations.
Develop personal qualities, such as self-assessment, risk-taking, and perseverance.
Develop and work on the use of appropriate social skills.
Develop and use effective studying, test preparation, test-taking, time management, and note-taking strategies.
Explore a range of postsecondary options and entrance requirements and deadlines for admission.
Select courses that will meet the necessary requirements.
Actively participate in and prepare for the postsecondary application process.
Maintain an ongoing personal file or portfolio that includes school and medical records, IEPs, résumés, and samples of academic work. Consider people to ask for recommendations, such as teachers, counselors, employers, and so on.
Identify and access resources that will provide needed support such as getting to know your career or guidance counselor and other college resources available at your school that can provide assistance.
Investigate different ways to save money for a postsecondary education.
Investigate the availability of financial aid from federal, state, local, and private sources, as well as scholarships.
Talk to adults in a variety of professions to see what they like and dislike about their jobs and what kind of education is needed for different kinds of jobs.
Get involved in school and/or community-based extracurricular activities that you find interesting or that enable you to explore career interests.
Practice self-advocacy in your classrooms and at your IEP meeting.

Source: Adapted from *Latest Developments.* (1994). AHEAD.

program as a primary transition goal, and understand what demands and supports are available, the student and the transition team can begin to identify further the activities needed in order to reach that goal. The roles and responsibilities of students, teachers, and parents shown in Tables 14–5, 14–6, and 14–7 suggest a coordinated curriculum that goes beyond course work and ensures that the student acquires skills in other developmental areas. Such a curriculum requires careful planning and ongoing communication among team members, and means that student learning and practicing skills must take place outside the school, as well as in the classroom. In addition, some role-release by teachers and parents must occur so that the student takes on more responsibility.

Critical Point Self-determination skills are lifelong skills, as evidenced by the legal requirement that individuals with disabilities be included as participants

TABLE 14–6

Roles and Responsibilities for Families Involved in Planning Postsecondary Outcomes

Parent/Guardian Roles and Responsibilities
Encourage their child to develop independent decision making and self-advocacy skills.
Become involved in transition planning and ensure that their child is also involved and actively participating in the process.
Help their child to identify their strengths, needs, preferences, and interests and to develop realistic goals.
Encourage their child to develop future education plans and to explore realistic postsecondary options.
Help their child to select high school courses that meet postsecondary requirements.
Collaborate with secondary and postsecondary staff in making decisions concerning programs, services, and resources.
Help their child to collect and maintain their ongoing personal file or portfolio that includes school and medical records, IEPs, résumés, and samples of academic work.
Encourage their child to read independently, as well as to explore career interests through work or community service experiences.
Help their child to investigate the availability of financial aid from federal, state, local, and private sources, as well as scholarships.
Communicate confidence in their child's ability to be successful in a postsecondary environment.

Source: Adapted from *Latest Developments.* (1994). AHEAD.

in developing their Individual Plan for Employment (IPE).

Backward Planning Based on Identified Postschool Goals

Once postschool goals have been identified, the student and his or her transition team must begin to ask questions, such as (1) What knowledge and skills are needed to make a successful transition to a postsecondary academic or technical/vocational program? (2) What knowledge and skills does the student have at present? (and how will they be assessed?) and (3) What knowledge and skills does the student need to acquire? (NICHCY, 1993). As postsecondary programs build upon the skills and knowledge acquired in earlier years, planning the necessary strategies to achieve the student's ultimate goal must start early. For example, a student who does not plan ahead for a college education may have difficulty in completing all the required or recommended courses that are necessary to qualify for a 4-year college or university. In addition, students may need to work on acquiring more effective independent study skills or arranging accommodations that are needed for college board or SAT testing. The key lies in the student and transition team first determining the kind of postsecondary program that best fits the student's needs and then planning backward to incorporate activities that will facilitate the achievement of that goal.

Critical Point As of October 2003, the College Board, source of the SAT test, can no longer flag the test scores of students with disabilities who take the standardized aptitude exams with accommodations. This follows a similar decision by the Educational Testing Service to stop flagging the scores of several other standardized exams for which accommodations were administered. Information regarding accommodations on the SAT can be found

TABLE 14–7

Roles and Responsibilities for Educators Involved in Planning Postsecondary Outcomes

Secondary School Personnel Responsibilities
Encourage students to look beyond high school toward postsecondary education by initiating, designing, and evaluating effective transition plans and coordinating services that are consistent with federal and state laws, rules, and regulations.
Form a transition team consisting of a coordinator, the student, the parent(s) and/or other family members, administrators, teachers, counselors, and related service providers.
Develop an appropriate packet of materials to document the student's secondary school program and to facilitate service delivery in a postsecondary program.
Provide administrative support, information/resources, and time to foster collaboration among team members.
Inform the student about laws, rules, and regulations that ensure her or his rights.
Provide the appropriate course selection, counseling, and academic support services to meet the individual student's needs.
Ensure the student's competency in literacy and mathematics.
Ensure that the student learns effective studying, time management, test preparation, and test-taking strategies.
Ensure that the student has the skills to self-advocate effectively and to provide opportunities for practicing these skills.

Source: Adapted from *Latest Developments.* (1994). AHEAD.

at: *http://www.collegeboard.com/disable/student/html.accom.html* and for the ACT at: *http://www. act.org.aap/disab/policy.html*

Interagency Responsibility and Linkages

Many services and experiences that students with disabilities will need in order to make a successful transition to postsecondary education will require the input of persons beyond the immediate personnel in schools. Establishing interagency linkages may be one of the most integral components in developing successful transition services (Halpern, Benz, & Lindstrom, 1992). Therefore, it is imperative that the transition team draw upon the expertise of all relevant school, family, and community agencies (DeStefano & Wermuth, 1992) to ensure a seamless and successful transition to postsecondary programs. Depending on the individual student's interests, preferences, and needs, this could include vocational rehabilitation personnel, transportation agencies, disability-specific agencies, personal care attendants; Job Training Partnership Act (JTPA) personnel and vocational and/or regular education teachers; career guidance counselors, recreational therapists, employers, social workers, health (including mental health) care professionals; and representatives from the relevant postsecondary program. As a student's entitlement to education and related services end once the student has left the public school system, establishing needed linkages not only benefits the student during transition planning, but makes a smooth transition to adult life (NICHCY, 1993).

Critical Point Almost three-quarters of postsecondary institutions that enrolled students with disabilities, worked either formally or informally with their state VR agencies (National Center for Educational Statistics, 1999b).

It is especially important that transition teams network with relevant postsecondary personnel who may be able to provide a wealth of information on the kinds of preparations and requirements needed to make the transition to their particular programs. This could include persons such as admission counselors, financial aid officers, and student disability service providers. Table 14–8 provides a list of resources and activities that postsecondary personnel may be able to provide.

Student Voices

"My advice is to start with Vocational Rehabilitation (VR) services as early as possible. Meet with your counselor and see if you feel comfortable with him/her and also you should know what you plan on doing during college. I was never told about VR when I graduated from high school . . . I found out about it much later after I had already started college and I would hate for another person to go through that too!"

Promoting Positive Postsecondary Outcomes

Appropriate instructional and other transition-related services always should be designed bearing in mind promoting movement from school to postsecondary activities (NICHCY, 1993). In order to achieve the desired postschool outcomes, the transition team must remember the nature and demands of the selected postsecondary program and setting and design appropriate experiences that may go beyond the mere academic (DeStefano & Wermuth, 1992).

Selecting Courses that Meet Postsecondary Requirements
Although effective transition planning for a postsecondary program involves a wide range of activities, such as facilitating the student's development in self-advocacy and socialization skills (Gartin, Rumrill, & Serebreni, 1996), the student also must be academically prepared for higher education programs. Individual programs and institutions vary in their specific entry requirements, which is why it is important to establish links early with the perspective institution's postsecondary personnel (see Table 14–8). Additionally, it is important to start planning for high school classes toward the end of middle school or junior high so that the student will have a greater opportunity to complete all the necessary courses needed to qualify for the postsecondary program of his or her choice. Therefore, the transition team should work with the school guidance counselor to ensure that the student takes the appropriate required and elective courses that are needed to meet the student's postschool goals. A typical college preparatory curriculum required for admission to most 4-year institutions follows (AHEAD, 1987; HEATH Resource Center, 1997; Turner & Simmons, 1996):

- Four years of English (e.g., English, American literature, English literature, English composition, world literature)
- Three years of mathematics (e.g., algebra I and II, geometry, precalculus, trigonometry, calculus, analytic geometry, probability)
- Three years of science (e.g., earth science, biology, chemistry, physics)
- Three years of social sciences (e.g., American history, world history, American government, state history, principles of democracy)
- Two years of a foreign language (e.g., Spanish, French, German, Latin, Russian, Japanese)
- One to two years of the arts (e.g., art/studio art, visual arts, photography, music, dance, drama, speech)
- One to three years of appropriate electives (e.g., economics, psychology, statistics, computer science, communications)

For students who are interested in pursuing careers in vocational and/or technical fields,

TABLE 14–8
Roles and Responsibilities of Postsecondary Personnel

- Provide linkages to high schools through outreach efforts.
- Inform secondary school personnel of the prerequisites necessary for the successful transition to postsecondary options.
- Disseminate information about college preparation and the expectations associated with various postsecondary environments.
- Provide opportunities for prospective students and their families to visit the campus and to provide information about the unique features of the specific postsecondary program.
- Help students to effectively negotiate postsecondary environments.
- Offer summer orientation programs on the admissions application process, admissions requirements, and general college survival skills.
- Clarify roles of the student and the service provider in a postsecondary setting.
- Offer comprehensive orientation programs to students who have chosen to attend a particular institution.
- Help the student to use a range of academic accommodations and technical aids, such as electronic advanced organizers, texts on tape, grammar and spell checkers, and other word processing programs.
- Assist the student in evaluating her or his dependence on external supports and adjust the level of assistance when appropriate.
- Work with the student to develop appropriate social and interpersonal communication skills.
- Facilitate the development of the student's self-advocacy skills, including a realistic understanding of the functional limitation due to the disability, and how to use this information for self-understanding and advocating in a postsecondary setting.
- Foster independence through increased responsibility and opportunity for self-management.
- Encourage the student to participate in the campus social life and extracurricular community and campus activities.
- Promote the student's self-esteem and self-confidence.
- Inform the student and their families about services that postsecondary institutions provide, such as student disability services, academic, and other specialized services.
- Ensure the timely development of documentation materials in keeping with application deadlines.
- Advocate, when appropriate, on behalf of students to ensure their rights under section 504 and ADA are safeguarded.
- Negotiate "reasonable academic adjustments" with faculty and administration that will maintain the integrity of the curriculum.
- Establish written policies and procedures concerning admissions, diagnoses, accommodations, curriculum requirements, and service delivery to students with disabilities.
- Work closely with admissions officers to ensure that students with disabilities are fairly considered.
- Act as a liaison to the greater college community and inform them about serving students with disabilities.
- Provide faculty and staff development on students with disabilities.

Source: Adapted from *Latest Developments.* (1994). AHEAD.

some of the preceding courses should be integrated with vocational or technical courses in the student's area of interest. Since almost all two-year programs require basic skill knowledge in science, mathematics, English, and computer awareness, it is wise to integrate vocational/technical programs of study with academics (Gray, 2002). Again, it is best to work with the school guidance counselor and personnel at the institution that the student wishes to attend.

Student Voices

"It always has amazed me that society recognizes how hard women and blacks have fought for equal rights but barely recognizes how hard people with disabilities fought. It also amazes me that in school you are taught about African Americans and slavery and Martin Luther King, etc., but there is not one class that teaches you about disabilities, ADA, Section 504 or IDEA, etc., or about the leaders involved in fighting for equal rights for people with disabilities. I think that school systems need to include these issues in their curriculums."

Critical Point The transition team is responsible for developing a coordinated set of school to postschool activities, focusing upon curricula as well as community-based learning.

Most college instructors will not accept handwritten papers so that students who possess keyboard and word processing skills will be at an advantage when starting a postsecondary program. In addition, classes in study skills, time management, and assertiveness training may prove helpful because how a student's time is spent when in a postsecondary setting is the sole responsibility of the student, not of the institution.

Community-Based Experiences

For many students with disabilities, awareness of postsecondary options and the demands to succeed in those environments may not automatically enable the student to make valid judgments of preference (DeStefano & Wermuth, 1992). However, when linked to direct community-based activities, the students, their families, teachers, and other service providers will be in a better position to determine the needs, preferences, and interests. For example, in a postsecondary institution, the students will be faced not only with academic demands, but also with different social and independent living demands, such as managing finances, buying clothing, food, and other personal needs (deFur et al., 1996). Therefore, community-based activities might involve developing interests outside school, such as engaging in work or volunteer experiences, which can teach students responsibility, reliability, interpersonal skills, and teamwork. Connecting school-to-work activities (a cornerstone of the School-to-Work Opportunities Act [STWOA] of 1994) contributes to a more meaningful education experience for all students (Benz & Kochhar, 1996), as well as facilitates the development of career interests and goals. Working part time, which also is a good way to earn money for a postsecondary education, and extracurricular activities in and outside school, can help students to explore and develop their talents and interests (in addition to being an asset to a college application). Although too many students often are forced to choose between a traditional academic college-prep track or more functional community-based learning experiences, the restructuring of schools, implicit in STWOA's "concepts and principles, offers hope that this artificial dichotomy can be reduced, if not eliminated altogether" (Benz & Kochhar, 1996, p. 43).

Inclusive School Environments

Postsecondary environments, although varying in the number of supports offered to students with disabilities, basically are inclusive environments. If students are to make a successful transition, it is important that they have experiences interacting with their peers in the general population. The NLTS found that 70% of students who participated in postsecondary academic programs spent 75% of their time in regular education high school classes (U.S. Department of Education, 1995). However, research, using the same database, found that more time spent in regular education also was associated with an increased likelihood of course failure (Hebbeler, 1993). Because course failure is one of the strongest predictors of dropping out of school, the relationship between inclusive school environments and positive postschool outcomes is complex. Therefore, students with disabilities in regular education settings must be given opportunities to succeed and the necessary supports if the results are to be positive. If instruction is based on student-determined interests, preferences, and needs, then the likelihood of success in inclusive settings is greatly enhanced (Halpern, 1994; Wehmeyer et al., 1998).

Although determining social integration outcomes for postsecondary environments is value-driven (Haring & Breen, 1989), many students who experience problems in the social/interpersonal domain in high school will continue to face similar types of problems in postsecondary settings (Chadsey & Sheldon, 1998). In a study of college students who were deaf, Brown and Foster (1991) concluded that natural existing opportunities were the most ideal settings in which social integration was more likely to occur. In other words, there is a greater probability of integration occurring if the social interactions are secondary to the task rather than artificially imposed. Students with disabilities who identify a need in this domain, therefore, may have to be encouraged to take advantage of these naturally occurring activities.

Student Voices

". . . understanding by the teacher not only helps the student academically by having the extra time and use of special services, but it also helps the student integrate socially within the class time. An example of this is my 10th grade English class when I first receive my Liberator, and the beginning of my continuing 'motor mouth' habit. So I was typing out every answer in the discussion of the classic epic *Beowulf*, and the first few classes it was hard to get time to fully answer the questions partly because of me getting use to presetting my answers before raising my hand. Also, in part, for everyone, including myself, getting use to me having a voice. Because, before that I had a bliss board which is just a monopoly board covered with 500 words where I had to point and have the person follow building the sentences as they went along. Using the bliss board was very frustrating during class discussions because someone had to come over to see what I was saying, and if [they] got it the first time and kept up with my hand speed it was a miracle. So after 2 weeks of having the Liberator in school, I learned how to type my answers in before raising my hand and all my [teachers] adapted to calling on me to give answers. My teacher Ms. Barr especially integrated me and my new found voice into the flow of the discussions by lingering on the subjects a little longer when she sees me frantically typing. She asked me questions more than two times unlike most of my other teachers did or still do. When I [was] going to say her name I always used one 'r' to pronounce it right, but one day of class I wasn't thinking and I put the extra 'r' in the name, and when I spoke I said 'Hey, Ms. Bear,' and the whole class burst out laughing at how I said her name using my Liberator. Everybody started calling her 'Ms. Bear,' and it made me feel so good to hear the whole class, including the teacher, incorporate me into the personality of the class."

Critical Point Students with disabilities may need access to instruction in social/interpersonal relationships in an inclusive environment.

Self-Advocacy

Self-determination also includes characteristics such as self-advocacy, creativity, and independence (Durlak, Rose, & Bursuck 1994). Although well meaning in intent, persons with disabilities often are encouraged to hide their disability (Field & Hoffman, 1994) by professionals and parents alike. In addition, a desire to conform and fit in with one's peers is natural for most adolescents and young adults, and the movement to a new postschool setting provides an opportunity to escape previous labels and the stigma associated with special education and being different (deFur et al., 1996). According to Ball-Brown and Frank (1993), the latter is a major reason that many students with disabilities of color do not access support services at postsecondary institutions. However, as the students alone are responsible for disclosing their disability at postsecondary institutions, they must learn to self-advocate effectively (Brinckeroff, Shaw, & McGuire, 1992; deFur et al., 1996; Lynch & Gussel, 1996; Scott, 1996) and to realize that it is to their advantage to "own" the diagnosis of their disability, especially "hidden disabilities," such as a learning disability (Brinckeroff et al., 1992).

Critical Point Self-determination in adult life is based on skills related to self-knowledge, self-acceptance, and self-advocacy.

Research has shown that when the skills involved in self-advocacy are systematically taught and the students are given immediate and specific feedback, along with the opportunity to practice these skills in both training and natural environments, students with disabilities can acquire, maintain, and generalize these skills (Aune, 1991; Durlak et al., 1994). Again, active participation in transition planning is one of the best ways that students can develop their self-advocacy skills (deFur et al., 1996; Webster, 2001). For example, if the student and his or her transition team decides that the student needs extended time to complete tests, then he or she should request the required accommodation with the appropriate mainstream teacher.

Self-determination involves assuming responsibility for one's goals and accomplishments (Ward, 1988). Providing students with disabilities the opportunity to self-advocate and make choices is an empowering experience and enhances the student's perseverance (deFur et al., 1996). However, self-determination also involves assuming responsibility for one's setbacks (Ward, 1988). In their study of successful adults with learning disabilities, Gerber, Ginsberg, and Reiff (1992) found that the participants gained a sense of control over their professional lives by engaging in a process of "reframing" situations in which they recognized, accepted, and understood the impact of their learning disability and how to use their unique abilities to overcome potential obstacles. The participants in the study also had developed a strong desire to succeed, along with the ability to set realistic goals and to persevere in achieving them (Gerber et al., 1992).

Student Voices

"Self advocacy is something that comes with knowing yourself and taking risk to stand up for yourself. It is a process and takes time. I think self-advocacy is something that someone grows and gets better in over time. Sometimes it is helpful to have others as role models in self-advocating. Sometimes one is just getting taken advantage of so much and it is the last straw that there is no choice than to advocate for oneself. Besides, who knows me better than I do? Self-advocacy is sort of a neat thing, you can feel the empowerment."

Enhancing Participation in Postsecondary Education

Social Aspects of a Postsecondary Education

Although the institution may provide many supports for students with disabilities, students are more likely to persevere in working toward their degree when socially integrated into the community life of the college or university as well as when they are engaged in academics (Astin, 1993; Tinto, 1993). Even though any programs or activities supported by the college, such as sporting events or artistic performances, must be accessible to students with disabilities, as must campus transportation systems (Scott, 1996), the onus is on the student to get involved. Involvement fosters integration (Astin, 1993), so it is important that students take advantage of the variety of activities that are available on campus and in the surrounding community. Research suggests that adult students with disabilities may have poor self-esteem and interpersonal and socialization skills (Brinckeroff et al., 2002; Vogel & Forness, 1992) that may result in social isolation. Studies of interactions between college students with various disabilities and their peers without disabilities (Fichten & Ansel, 1988; Fichten, Robillard, Tagalakis, & Ansel, 1991) found that whereas students with disabilities felt comfortable around their peers without disabilities, both students with and without disabilities had more negative thoughts about *interacting* with students with disabilities. Although there is a lack of research regarding effective interventions for the social integration of college students with disabilities, students who are persistent, yet adaptable (Gerber et al., 1992), and who are aware of their strengths and needs in social as well as academic areas (deFur et al., 1996), may find it easier to integrate socially in campus life. Personal and group counseling (Getzel & Kregel, 1996; Vogel & Forness, 1992) also may be effective social interventions as are involvement in student support groups (Getzel & Kregel).

Critical Point College students with disabilities were equally likely to participate in cultural and recreational activities as their nondisabled college peers (13%) (National Center for Education Statistics, 1999a).

When students start college, their new independence, new environment, and new intellectual changes often will impact the student's sense of self (Fox, Zakely, Morris, & Jundt, 1993). The opportunity arises to question some values and norms that were accepted in their family and previous environments (Fox et al.). For example, experimenting with drugs and alcohol is a reality at many colleges. Although risk-taking is an essential component of self-determination (Wehmeyer et al., 1998), research has shown that persons with mild disabilities are at greater risk for substance abuse than persons without disabilities (Gajar, Goodman, & McAffee, 1993). In addition, many students with disabilities do not receive awareness education in this area (Wehmeyer et al.). Therefore, it is important that students with disabilities receive information on the potential problem of substance abuse so that they will be in a position when in college to make informed decisions.

Critical Point Students with disabilities may need specific information regarding high-risk behaviors and choices.

First-Generation College Students

First-generation college students (i.e., the first person in the family to attend college) are growing in number (Mitchell, 1997) as the need for an education beyond high school is reflected in the current labor market. Many of these students come from ethnic minority and working-class families (Fox et al., 1993). For all students, making it through the first year is critical to college success and eventual graduation. Seventy-three percent of freshmen who entered a college or university in the fall of 1995 did not return to the same institution a year later (Geraghty, 1996). For students with disabilities who are the first-generation college students, the challenges are greater, as many are less academically and psychologically prepared for college than their peers from college-educated families (Mitchell, 1997). According to Mitchell, some challenges facing the first-generation college students include effectively balancing their time between school and work (as many come from low-income families and must work out of necessity); lack of skills in time management, budgeting, and dealing with education bureaucracies; and the tension created between the student and his or her family and friends who may have difficulty in understanding the demands and rewards of college. In order to aid the transition of these students, parents need to become familiar with the academic, financial, and social demands of higher education. In addition, the transition team should investigate bridge programs (which involve partnerships among high schools, community colleges, and universities) and other services such as special tutoring, counseling, mentoring, and peer support programs that are designed to facilitate the success of first-generation college students. School guidance counselors, as well as colleges, will have information on programs offered to this population of students.

Critical Point Two thirds of American school districts and 33% of the nation's children are located in rural areas of the country (U.S. Department of Education, 1995).

Student Voices

"A mentoring program would help a number of incoming students with disabilities. I keep looking back and telling myself that if I had a mentor of any kind when I first came to college I would not have had such a dramatic first year. I could have used a mentor to help me to better understand college life. I am the first one in my family to come to college and I had no idea what to expect. To make a long story short I had a long and terrifying year at college. But I survived and I am still here. If I can help in any way to prevent this kind of experience for another student I will help in any way possible."

Rural Students

While students from rural communities also may face similar types of challenges, researchers have primarily focused on employment and service provision issues rather than transition into postsecondary education (Clary, 2001). Fitcher (1991) proposed several reasons for this limited attention given to rural issues, including (a) urban problems seem so much bigger, with greater support to a much larger segment of the population; (b) the problems of rural America as portrayed by the media seem vague and of little relevance to most Americans, who themselves have only a rudimentary knowledge of rural America; (c) rural problems often are characterized by the unique factors of a particular locale, thus the similarities and interconnectedness of rural problems often go unnoticed.

While definitions of rural vary somewhat, all are characterized by fewer people living in a particular geographic area. It is important to realize that there is a wide array of rural subcultures and rural geographic traits that, in turn, impacts the educational systems of their respective communities (Helge, 1984a; Khattri, Riley, & Kane, 1997). Helge (1984b) noted that such factors as geographic barriers (e.g., mountains, roads), climatic barriers (e.g., seasonal flooding, extreme heat/cold); language spoken in the community, population scarcity, cultural diversity, economic lifestyles of the community; and relationship of school district governance systems to external sources of funding all need to be considered when designing educational services in general, and services to students with disabilities, in particular.

The majority of jobs in rural areas are changing; as in most other jobs, they now require skills beyond those acquired by high school graduates (HEATH Resource Center, 1996). Too often rural high school students face limited access to information on postsecondary options. In addition, research has shown that students with disabilities in rural areas frequently must deal with fear, low aspirations, attitudinal barriers such as low expectations from parents, teachers, and the community;

lack of counseling and information; lack of family support (and at times family opposition); rural ecology issues such as geographic location, transportation needs, proximity to postsecondary institutions; and need for financial assistance (Clary, 2001; HEATH Resource Center, 1996). To overcome these barriers, the transition team should address the same principles of good transition planning previously discussed in this chapter, in addition to educating students and families about and encouraging them to pursue postsecondary options. Additional recommendations include: developing a parent network; holding parent/student transition planning events with appropriate guest speakers; providing opportunities for students to acquire experience with adaptive/assistive technology; sponsoring field trips to postsecondary institutions for students with disabilities; and creating mentor programs that pair rural students with college students or college graduates (either in person, as pen pals, or through e-mail connections) (Clary, 2001; HEATH Resource Center, 1996).

Critical Point Section 508 of the Rehabilitation Act of 1973, as amended 29 U.S.C. § 794 (d), requires federal agencies to ensure that technology is accessible to employees and members of the public with disabilities to the extent it does not pose an "undue burden." Section 508 speaks to various means for disseminating information, including computers, software, and electronic office equipment using the principles of universal design. Although Section 508 directly applies to federal agencies, questions have been raised regarding its applicability to postsecondary institutions. However many colleges are working towards applying this universal technology design to their campuses. At any rate, the accessibility standards developed by the federal government should serve as a model for all educational institutions. For further information on Section 508 go to: *http://www.access-board.gov/* 508.*htm* and for assistive technology in your particular state go to: *http:// www.resna.org/taproject/ at/statecontacts.html*

Specialized Programs

Postsecondary opportunities also exist outside the traditional academic college path. Many community colleges have a mission to promote opportunities for a diverse body of students. However, the NLTS found that of the 14% of all students with disabilities who went on to a postsecondary education two years after leaving high school, only 5.8% were students classified as having mental retardation and 3.8% as having multiple disabilities (Wagner, 1989). In a study of students with mental retardation who attended a community college, Page and Chadsey-Rusch (1995) found that although the students had not made significant academic gains, they had achieved interpersonal and social benefits, such as enhanced self-esteem.

Some community, vocational, technical, and 4-year colleges offer specialized programs for students with disabilities. For example, Taft College and Monterey Peninsula College, both part of the California Community College system, offer a range of courses for students with developmental disabilities (Mertz, 1997). Taft's "Transition to Independent Living Program" offers a residential 22-month independent living skills curriculum (i.e., managing money, self-advocacy, and building and maintaining relationships) in conjunction with working on campus and participating in campus activities. Landmark College, a private coeducational institution in Putney, Vermont, specializes in serving students with dyslexia, attention deficit hyperactivity disorder (ADHD), or specific learning disabilities (SLD). It offers noncredit foundational courses along with an Associate of Arts (AA) degree in General Studies and has articulation agreements with a variety of four-year colleges (Mertz, 1997).

Some four-year colleges also offer specialized programs for students with disabilities, such as Lesley College's Threshold Program (a residential program in Cambridge, Massachusett's, for students with severe learning and cognitive disabilities). The nondegree program aims to develop the skills that are necessary for independent living through practical courses and field placements in the areas of early childhood and human and business services (Mertz, 1997). Others, such as Beacon College in Leesburg, Florida, offer students with learning disabilities the opportunity to earn AA and BA (bachelor of arts) degrees in Human Services and Liberal Studies (Mertz, 1998). Although not commonplace, many colleges and universities have comprehensive programs designed for students with disabilities, such as Ohio State University; Southern Illinois University at Carbondale; Wright State University, Ohio; the University of Minnesota; and Ball State University, Indiana (HEATH Resource Center, 1995; Scott, 1996); and include services, such as independent tutoring in content areas or study and organizational and time management skills, which are beyond those the institution is required to provide under section 504 or ADA. In addition, there are a growing number of nondegree college-based transition programs for students with cognitive disabilities such the College Campus Based Transition Program at Buffalo State College. This program is a collaborative effort between Buffalo Public School, the college, and parent groups, and serves students who have completed their high school education but are still eligible for public school services until the age of 21. Students receive their education in inclusive college settings with their nondisabled peers. Similar programs can be found at many community colleges throughout the country as well.

Critical Point Specialized programs in community, vocational and technical schools, and colleges are also available as postsecondary options for students with disabilities. College guidebooks such as *Peterson's Colleges and Programs for Students with Learning Disabilities* (Mangrum & Strichart, 1997) and the *K & W Guide to Colleges for the Learning Disabled* (Kravets & Wax, 1995) can assist the transition team in finding specialized postsecondary programs. Understanding what each institution requires and has to offer, the student with his or her team can select among those environments that best fit the student's needs and goals from a variety of backgrounds.

Conclusion

Transition planning for college is really a subset of planning for adult life because postsecondary education is not an end in itself; it is one choice that a student might make in preparing her- or himself for adulthood. If students and their families are to make informed choices, they must be aware of the options and the pros and cons of the various options, and be given opportunities for making meaningful choices based on a self-knowledge of their strengths, interests, and needs. With appropriate preparation and continuing supports, postsecondary education provides an extended educational opportunity for developing social, interpersonal, and cognitive problem-solving skills, as well as academic and career skills that are becoming increasingly necessary in today's society for *all* our citizens.

Student Voices

"We should learn to examine our disability and accept its limitations within our particular culture and society . . . learning to celebrate what we do have . . . our differences . . . without humiliation . . . without trying to fit into the mainstream . . . to celebrate our piece of the mosaic is what empowerment is all about. I would never accept an operation to be 'normal' . . . to have a slight chance of thinking and processing information like the nondisabled . . . I like the kaleidoscope in my head. . . . differences are essential to beauty."

Study Questions

1. Explain the reasons why it is important to incorporate postsecondary goals and objectives into the transition plans of students with disabilities.
2. Why should effective planning for a postsecondary education include more than just academic goals?
3. Discuss why each of the following is crucial to the student succeeding in a postsecondary environment:
   a. Self-awareness of one's interests, needs, and preferences, including understanding the functional limitations of one's disability
   b. Knowledge of the rights and responsibilities of students in a postsecondary environment and how they differ from IDEA
   c. The ability to self-advocate
4. How can teachers assist students and their families in finding the right fit between the student's interests, preferences, and needs and potential postsecondary institutions?
5. Discuss why it is important for students to have meaningful opportunities to take an active role in their transition planning, including leading IEP/ITP meetings.
6. Discuss how issues, such as cultural values of the students and their families, first-generation college students, and students from rural backgrounds can impact the transition planning process.
7. Why are community-based experiences and appropriate linkages to other service providers (including adult services) necessary for a smooth transition to postsecondary education settings?
8. What should teachers be doing to ensure that the postsecondary education and training goals of their students meet the criteria of best transition planning and services, as defined by the four principles in IDEA?
9. Make a list of the things that need to be in place before a student can successfully transition to college.

Websites

College Is Possible:
http://www.CollegeIsPossible.org/index.html

Getting Ready for College Early: A Handbook for Parents of Students in the Middle and Junior High School Years:
http://www.ed.gov/pubs/GettingReadyCollegeEarly/#step1

Preparing Your Child for College:
http://www.ed.gov/pubs/Prepare/index.html

The Student Guide: Financial Aid from the U.S. Department of Education:
http://www.ed.gov/prog_info/SFA/StudentGuide/1998–9/index.html

College Board Online:
http://www.collegeboard.org/

The Education Testing Service Network:
http://www.ets.org/

African American Global Network: Historically Black Colleges & Universities:
http://edonline.com/cq/hbcu/

NICHCY (National Information Center for Children with Disabilities):
http://www.nichcy.org/

The National Center for Learning Disabilities (NCLD):
http://www.ncld.org/

Gallaudet University:
http://www.gallaudet.edu/

AHEAD (Association on Higher Education and Disability):
http://ahead.org/

National Clearinghouse on Postsecondary Education for Individuals with Disabilities [HEATH Resource Center]:
http://www.heath.gwu.edu/

Education Resources Information Center Clearinghouse on Disability and Gifted Education
http://ericec.org/ (then click on links to other information sources; also link to laws)

Disability Access Information and Support (DAIS)
http://www.janejarrow.com

The Council for Opportunity in Education
http://www.trioprograms.org/

PEPNet (Postsecondary Education Programs Network for Individuals who are Deaf/Hard of Hearing
http://www.pepnet.org/

Closing the Gap: Computer Technology in Special Education and Rehabilitation
http://www.closingthegap.com/

DO-IT (Disabilities, Opportunities, Internetworking and Technology
http://www.washington.edu/doit/

Alliance for Technology/Assistive Technology Advocates
http://www.ataccess.org

Information on Assistive Technology
http://abledata.com

Division on Career Development and Transition (DCDT)
http://www.dcdt.org

Job Accommodation Network (JAN)
http://www.dol.gov/odep/programs/job.htm

National Center for the Dissemination of Disability Research
http://www.ncddr.org

Independent Living, USA
http://www.ilusa.com/

15

My Home and Community: Developing Supports for Adult Living

James A. Knoll

Carolyn Bardwell Wheeler

No American should have to live in a nursing home or state institution if that individual can live in a community with the right mix of affordable supports.

—Donna Shalala, Secretary of Health and Human Services July 28, 1999, National Conference of State Legislatures

LEARNING OBJECTIVES

The objectives of this chapter are:

1. Explain the factors that have contributed to the emergence of supported living and personal assistance services as the preferred organizing frameworks for residential services.
2. Explain the limitations inherent in the traditional services continuum as the organizing framework for residential services for people with mental retardation and developmental disabilities.
3. Define supported living and contrast it with group homes and other "facility-based" approaches.
4. Describe the emergence of the independent living movement.
5. Define personal assistance services and link increased demand for universal access to these services to the disabilities rights movement.
6. Describe legislative and legal developments that are contributing to increased

access to supported living and personal assistance services.

7. Describe the use of vision, skills, resources, and supports as a framework for planning for successful transition to independent adult living.

Introduction

Much of the literature on transition has preparation for employment as its primary focus. For the vast majority of people with disabilities, this is as it should be; just as for many other Americans, the principal determinant of the good life is a secure job that pays a decent salary. Historically, the education system and the adult services system have failed to emphasize paid employment as an expected outcome for people with disabilities. This was one of the factors that led to the mandates for transition planning being written into IDEA. However, it is a major mistake to limit discussions of transition to employment. For many people with disabilities, particularly individuals with severe disabilities, issues of employment must be linked with other aspects of adult life. The place of residence, access to transportation, a range of recreation opportunities, a network of relationships, and needed specialized supports and services are all connected to the opportunity to work, enjoy an acceptable quality of life, and contribute to the life of the community.

This chapter examines some issues that are critical if students are preparing to live as independently as possible *in their own home* as adults. At the outset, it is important to emphasize that a focus on independent adult life is critical in the education of all students with disabilities. It is a serious error to assume that just because someone has a so-called mild disability, educators should not be concerned with assisting him or her to develop independent living skills. The question of independent community living becomes much more complex when the focus shifts to students with moderate to severe disabilities, who need some form of assistance with activities of daily life. This chapter attempts to provide a reasonably balanced presentation of the multiple issues that must be addressed in this area of transition. We begin by examining the challenges that students with disabilities and their parents face as they focus upon independent adult life. We then explore the evolution in supports for home living for adults with severe disabilities that has occurred in the last several decades. This discussion presents the reader with some planning and service delivery issues that continue to confront people with disabilities in many areas today. This discussion is followed by an examination of the current best practice in community living for people with severe disabilities. The concluding section of the chapter presents catalogs of the range of concerns that should be addressed in planning for the transition to adult home life for all students with disabilities.

Certainly, most authors and teachers will contend that preparation for "independent living" is at the heart of the transition process. Unfortunately, the experience of parents and people with disabilities has been otherwise. This area is frequently one where there is a high degree of disconnect between what the schools do and the challenges people confront once they are no longer eligible for a free appropriate public education (FAPE).

The Parental Perspective: Life Is More Than a Job

Most parents of young adults with a disability see employment as an important consideration as they look to the future. However, for many parents, particularly those of students with moderate to severe disabilities, a job is a secondary consideration. Knowing their son or daughter as they do, parents are confronted with the question, "Who will look out for them when I am gone?" (Knoll, 1992). In this lies the critical question that all parents at some level ask the education system. "Are you preparing my child to make a smooth movement into adult life?" "Are you building a foundation for future security?" To the extent that the school system fails to have this real-world focus upon transition, it fails to address this truly valued outcome; to that extent, the system is deficient. This is where the central meaning of transition becomes apparent. For some parents, a narrow emphasis on employment can be at odds with their basic fears about lifelong security for their child. The promise of employment is a chimera—a wisp of smoke—that can vanish with the next economic downturn, corporate acquisition, or change of supervisors. Why should the relative security of Social Security disability be abandoned for the mere promise of a possibility?

Critical Point Parents often define their hopes for their children with disabilities in terms of assurances of long-term safety and security.

This sense of social insecurity is further intensified by the day-to-day battle that most families experience to obtain the most rudimentary services. Families are not looking for absolute certainty, but they are searching for a sense of stability and commitment to the long-term support of their son or daughter (McNair & Rusch, 1991). Traditionally, this type of security often was tied to the bricks, mortar, and real estate of the old institutions and group homes. As we move into the 21st century, the fundamental challenge of transition for students with a disability is the need to develop the necessary skills and to mobilize the resources for the future so that the family can envision stability and security ahead for their child. Lack of knowledge about available resources, referrals to a waiting list, endless application forms to complete, complex interagency agreements, conflicts over responsibilities, and mere paperwork plans create anxieties, not assurance.

So, for many families, the centerpiece of the transition process and the foundation for all other outcomes, even the possibility of employment, is the development of a vision of a person's home as an adult. Home, "a place of safety and security, my place, the base of operations, where I'm in charge" is not usually on the top of the agenda for the typical young adult. This is something that takes on meaning and reality as the person becomes emancipated from his or her parents' home and forms an independent identity. In some ways, the establishment of our own household is the line of demarcation for true adulthood (Ferguson & Ferguson, 2000). We set up housekeeping; we define our place in the world. The absence of this vision for the future of their children with severe disabilities leads many parents not to see transition as a time to broaden horizons. Rather, they experience new limitations, as the entitlement of free appropriate public education seems to be replaced by the uncertainty of adult life.

Thus, parents who often have struggled long and hard with the reality of a child's disability may view transition to adult life in a different light from that of the professional who is involved with the family. Not surprisingly, the young adult with a disability may have an experience and a perception of this whole process that differs from the perspective of both parents and professionals.

Transition to a New Vision

The "story" in this chapter is not really about the students with disabilities but is about us—teachers, administrators, and adult service workers—and how we have learned to listen to all the students with disabilities we encounter.

We have to create the concept of transition to help us support people with disabilities as they face the challenge of growth and change that comes with movement toward becoming an adult in our society. The challenges were always present, but, for a long time, our preconception about what was possible for people with disabilities has limited our ability to act. So, this chapter is about "transition," not so much as mandated by IDEA, but as a fundamental reorientation in the thinking. The real story here is about how *we* learned to listen and see.

The evolution of a positive vision of the future does not emerge overnight. A vision of possibilities after high school for students with disabilities comes from their life experience, just as it does for all young adults. The presence or absence of a vision of possibilities ultimately revolves around a series of questions that go to the heart of education quality:

- Are teachers and the school systems clear from the time a student enters school that the ultimate measure of education quality and success is how the individual does after graduation?
- Has the total education program been guided by a long-term vision of possibilities?
- Has transition toward a meaningful adult life been a facet of education from day one?
- Have teachers and administrators promoted values of independence, contribution, and community participation for all students?
- Or, has the focus of education for students with disabilities been one of low expectations and restricted opportunity that leads to a vision of life on public assistance, dependency, or providing employment for human service workers?

As every chapter in this text makes clear, a long-term systemic approach to transition is critical to shaping positive outcomes for all students with disabilities. The reality is that a vision of possibilities is only partially dependent on opportunities provided by the school and the advocacy of parents and others. Unfortunately, the legitimate hopes and ambitions of people with disabilities in this country and throughout the world are, in fact, subject to societal and community forces that have little to do with personal motivation or vision. Generations of people with disabilities have seen their hopes and the hopes of their families shattered against the hard realities of service agencies and a public that has no vision of possibilities. Indeed, even today students who have received a free, appropriate public education in the least restrictive environment with an appropriate focus on transition toward meaningful adult outcomes can be frustrated. It is still true that even with a successful education experience, some students and their family members will experience the blank stare of an absent vision as they look to adult agencies to support them in their home, job, and community.

A History of Residential Approaches for People with Disabilities

To understand what is possible for young adults with disabilities today, we must review the evolution of residential services during this century. As ADAPT (Americans Disabled for Attendant Programs Today) points out:

> The 20th century began with eugenics taking a primary place in US and world history (it could be called the "Century of Eugenics"). But, it will end with a "qualified" victory for the integration of people with disabilities in all communities . . . [in] the 1920's and 30's when states not only sterilized and legally terminated the lives of people with disabilities, but their creation of institutions for people with disabilities became widespread; and as the century grew so did these

> institutions from nursing homes, to institutions for people with psychiatric or developmental disabilities. . . . Yesterday the question was should people with disabilities live in the community? Today it is how are we to provide services for people with disabilities in the community? (ADAPT, 1999b, p. 1)

The critical lessons that emerged from this movement from "special places for special people" to "an individualized system of support for home living" have relevance for all people with disabilities.

From State Institutions to Group Homes

By the late 1960s the rationale for segregation of people with disabilities based on the ideology of the eugenics movement was long dead. However, the professional practices and the facilities developed in the first half of the century loomed over people with disabilities and their families. Basically, the only publicly funded resources available for people with extensive disabilities existed in institutions, nursing homes, rehabilitation centers, and other long-term care facilities. A fundamental reorientation of services occurred in the United States during the late 1960s and 1970s. The most visible sign of this transformation has been the downsizing of publicly financed residential institutions for people with mental retardation and psychiatric illness into the 1970s. The exposé of life in these facilities and the associated lawsuits required states to begin the development of the so-called "community-based services." Although this relocation of services has had a far-reaching impact, it merely set the stage for what some have regarded as a true revolution. This revolution has changed both the modes of service delivery and the underlying philosophy that guides the thinking of providers. This essential reexamination of basic principles is at the heart of a new way of thinking about disability and the roles of the organization and the individuals who work with people with disabilities.

The profound nature of this change notwithstanding, in the public eye, the issue is simply "relocation." It continues to be controversial as the state department announces plans to close a large congregate care facility and to move the residents to smaller community homes. Indeed, this process of relocation provides a foundation for asking the basic questions that led to the transformation.

The controversies surrounding institutional closure and relocation have made the fundamental transformation largely invisible to the general public. For example, even today large segments of the general public continue to see people with developmental disabilities in terms of the prejudices and beliefs of the past. Indeed, the very idea that, in 1999, eight states (New Hampshire, Vermont, Rhode Island, Maine, New Mexico, West Virginia, Alaska, and Hawaii) and the District of Columbia no longer had a state institution for people who were labeled as mentally retarded and that several other states had reduced their institutional population to the point that the one remaining facility has a total population equivalent to a large group home has come as an absolute revelation. Many in the general public still accept it as axiomatic that special people need special places. Yet, this relocation of services that has gradually captured the public unaware is not the core of this chapter. What we want to explore is the next wave of this change that is even today challenging the "new" structure put in place by the previous generation's efforts at deinstitutionalization.

The public outcry at the abysmal conditions in the old institutions led to an effort to rectify the problem by developing smaller "homelike" settings in "typical neighborhoods." The group homes, board and care homes, adult foster care homes, and "independent living apartment programs" of the 1960s and the 1970s laid the foundation for the new community system of services. These networks of residential services were and often are still called "community alternatives," as an alternative to institutions. For the general public, the entire effort has, perhaps, been best captured under the rubric of "group homes." This is not surprising since group homes were and still are central to this effort. The last two decades have seen the emergence of a massive national system of small facilities housing three to 16 individuals. National chains of for-profit provider organizations that contract with states or local community mental health organization manage many of them.

Because a good part of this reform of services was paid for by federal money, under the Medicaid program, much of the guidance was provided by federal regulations. It is important to realize that these regulations were initially designed to address the myriad of problems in the old large congregate care institutions. So-called "small ICF/MR" (intermediate care facility for the mentally retarded) regulations often were adopted by states to govern group homes that were not Medicaid funded. This footnote on federal congregate care policy is an instructive artifact that helps to guide any student who wishes to understand the underlying tensions in the field of adult services today.

Essentially, the federal regulations took the guidance provided for the management of a facility that is designed for hundreds, if not thousands, of inmates and "simplified" them for facilities serving 16 or less and located in community settings. The underlying model that shaped these regulations was medical in focus and sought to provide quality care and treatment for "patients" who were defined by regulation as being dependent and "incompetent" to care for themselves. This gross simplification of a complex series of historical events serves to capture an important fact that goes to the heart of our central discussion in this chapter. *The "traditional" approach to community residential and vocational services for people with developmental disabilities is based on the largely uncritical translation of the institutional model into a community environment*. This reality notwithstanding, thousands of people in these community programs have a life experience significantly better than that of people who continue to reside in institutions. A generation of people had been the beneficiary of the "community-based model" of service. Perhaps, more importantly, the next phase in the conceptual revolution would have been impossible if the process of relocation had not occurred.

Critical Point Initial efforts to reform residential services for people with developmental disabilities focused on regulations for "cleaning up" institutions and using these new rules to guide the establishment of smaller facilities located in residential neighborhoods.

Through the 1970s and into the 1980s, two currents intertwined to provide a critique of the rapidly developing system of community services for people with disabilities. As group homes, adult care facilities, and nursing homes proliferated, the principle of normalization and the independent living movement emphasized that simply being smaller was not sufficient to be better. Together these two related philosophies of service pushed for a fundamental reexamination of practice in all organizations and agencies serving people with disabilities.

Normalization

Integral to the ongoing process of change was the vision of possibilities nurtured by the principle of *normalization*. First articulated in the late 1960s and early 1970s, normalization attempted to provide a coherent framework for planning services (Wolfensberger, 1972). It offered a positive response to the demeaning and dehumanizing conditions found in most institutions. At its core, normalization was premised on respect for the basic humanity of individuals with disabilities. It was based on the assumption that, like all human beings, people with cognitive disabilities would mature, develop, learn, and change based on their life experience. Further, it adopted an ecological perspective on human development by holding that the interaction between the person and the environment must be consciously examined in the design and management of human service organizations. In essence, "normalization" means making available patterns and activities of everyday life for people with disabilities that are as close as possible to those experienced by their same age peers. If you wanted people to grow, you could not provide them with narrowly constricted opportunities; you needed to provide them with the same range of possibilities as anyone else. The apparent simplicity of normalization led many critics to contend mistakenly that it denied the reality of disability. This did not mean, "making people normal." It acknowledged that a special set of guiding principles was required because people with disabilities often need extraordinary resources in order to achieve the most typical goals. Normalization provided a way for professionals to consider how they provided these extraordinary resources.

Thankfully, from a current vantage point in the 21st century some of these ideas seem self-evident. Yet, in the 1970s and 1980s, normalization had a revolutionary effect on services for people with developmental disabilities. It provided the generation of people coming into the field of human services in the decades with a critical framework from which to examine themselves and the agencies for which they worked. It was no longer acceptable to attribute less than optimal programming to the limitation of the "clients." Increasingly, there was a call for organizations to be accountable for assisting people to achieve meaningful quality-of-life outcomes.

Critical Point Normalization provided a context for critical thinking about services for people with disabilities.

Only after relocation had occurred were advocates, parents, and progressive service providers able to confront the contradictions inherent in the "community-based services system." Eventually, the principle of normalization led many individuals who had built group homes to confront the structural problems inherent in these minifacilities. Increasingly, it became apparent that regulations and structures which were premised on the smooth running of large-scale congregate care facilities had little to do with assisting people to achieve their legitimate aspirations as a citizen. On a daily basis, service providers, advocates, and family members found themselves struggling to balance the tension inherent in the interplay of the individuals' hopes and fears, human relationships, and the bizarre requirements of state and federal regulations. All of this just so that people with disabilities could live a "normal life." It seemed so simple, yet the implementation was quite complex.

Independent Living

As it evolved, the principle of normalization moved from being seen exclusively as a framework for services for people with mental retardation and developmental disabilities. Professionals in many other areas of disability service saw its value as a critical framework. Additionally, an emerging group of people with disabilities viewed it as a valuable tool to use in their challenge to the status quo. In the late 1960s and early 1970s, groups of people, primarily with physical disabilities, around the country (most notably in Berkley, California, and in Denver, Colorado) began to organize to challenge the barriers they encountered in daily life (Shapiro, 1993). This beginning of the disability rights movement saw normalization as one tool that could assist people with disabilities in their struggle to gain control of their own lives.

This effort, which became known as the *independent living movement*, grew out of the social change of the 1960s. As racial and ethnic minorities and women came together in mutual support to challenge institutionalized discrimination, so did these pioneers with disabilities. They looked at the struggles of these other groups and saw that they too were the "victim" not of physical conditions, but of societal prejudice. Historians of this movement (McDonald & Oxford, n.d.) point to its linkage to five social movements: (1) deinstitutionalization, (2) the African-American civil rights movement, (3) the "self-help" movement as seen in organizations such as Alcoholics Anonymous, (4) the demedicalization movement toward more holistic approaches to health care, and (5) the consumerism movement toward greater responsiveness on the part of providers and manufacturers. Central to this movement was the idea of control by consumers of goods and services over the choices and options that were available to them. People with disabilities were not to be seen as passive recipients of "care" or patients, but, rather, as self-directed individuals making the decisions that were needed to manage their own lives. This way of thinking quickly evolved beyond the management of one's own life to direct control and management of the services.

The development of independent living was synthesized in the late 1970s by Gerben DeJong (1979) when he presented independent living as a fully developed alternative to the medical model. Disability was neither abnormal nor a tragedy that transformed the person, but it was a natural part of the human experience. As DeJong articulated on independent living, the problems or deficits were found in the society, not the individual. Within this framework, people with disabilities were not sick or broken; they did not need to be "fixed." The real problems were the social and attitudinal barriers that they faced. What was in need of repair was society, not the people with disabilities. Finally, and most importantly, in the independent living model, control must be exercised by the individual and not by the medical or rehabilitation professional. From an independent living perspective, people with disabilities are self-determining individuals who are not passive victims, objects of charity, cripples, or incomplete people.

Critical Point Consumer control is the centerpiece of the independent living movement.

The independent living movement found a focus for its philosophy in the programs of Centers for Independent Living (CILs), which was established and funded by the Rehabilitation Act of 1973 (see Table 15–1). This legislation provided for a high degree of direct consumer control in these new centers. As might be anticipated, many of these new programs initially were found to be closely linked to traditional rehabilitation centers. As the network expanded and the mandate for true control by people with disabilities was underscored by subsequent reauthorization of the Rehabilitation Act, this ideal became a reality. Simultaneously, the political wing of the movement joined with other disability organizations to mobilize for federal passage of a civil rights act that recognized the reality of discrimination in the lives of Americans with disabilities. With the passage of the Americans with Disabilities Act in 1990, the movement was able to turn its attention to the reality of segregation of people with disabilities, specifically, the thousands of people with a wide variety of disabilities who were confined against their choice in nursing homes and other long-term care facilities. It became clear that the next target was the bias in favor of congregate care facilities that existed in professional practice and the federally funded program for people with significant disabilities (Medicaid).

The Supported Living Movement

Initially, the independent living movement focused primarily upon its traditional core constituency of people with physical disabilities.

TABLE 15–1

Guiding Principle for Centers for Independent Living

As outlined in the Rehabilitation Act of 1973, as amended, Title VII, Chapter 1, Part C, Section 721, there are seven (7) standards for the center for independent living.

1. *Philosophy.* The center shall promote and practice the independent living philosophy of
   a. Consumer control of the center regarding decision making, service delivery, management, and establishment of the policy and direction of the center;
   b. Self-help and self-advocacy;
   c. Development of peer relationships and peer role models; and
   d. Equal access of individuals with severe disabilities to society and to all services, programs, activities, resources, and facilities, whether public or private and regardless of the funding source.
2. *Provision of services.* The center shall provide services to individuals with a range of severe disabilities. The center shall provide services on a cross-disability basis (for individuals with all different types of severe disabilities, including individuals with disabilities who are members of populations that are unserved or underserved by programs under this act). Eligibility for services at any center for independent living shall not be based on the presence of any one or more specific severe disabilities.
3. *Independent living goals.* The center shall facilitate development and achievement of independent living goals selected by individuals with severe disabilities who seek such assistance by the center.
4. *Community options.* The center shall work to increase the availability and to improve the quality of community options for independent living in order to facilitate the development and achievement of independent living goals by individuals with severe disabilities.
5. *Independent living core services.* The center shall provide independent living core services and, as appropriate, a combination of any other independent living services specified in section 7(30) (B).
6. *Activities to increase community capacity.* The center shall conduct activities to increase the capacity of communities within the service area of the center to meet the needs of individuals with severe disabilities.
7. *Resource development activities.* The center shall conduct resource development activities to obtain funding from sources other than this chapter.

Source: From the Rehabilitation Act of 1973 as amended, Title VII, Chap. 1, Pt. C, Section 721, Rehabilitation Services Administration, Office of Special Education and Rehabilitation Services, U.S. Department of Education.

With the growth of the movement, it became more inclusive involving people with conditions such as traumatic brain injury and psychiatric conditions. However, many individuals in the movement continued to see the issues of services for people with mental retardation and developmental disabilities as different. After all, these latter groups had a cognitive disability. Could they really manage their own lives? During the early 1990s, this changed as the self-advocacy movement and the emergence of "supported living" demonstrated that fundamentally all people with disabilities confronted the same barriers.

For people with developmental disabilities, the traditional approach to services was fairly successful at achieving deinstitutionalization. True community membership occurred less easily. By 1986, the majority of individuals who were receiving residential services were living in community facilities and residences (Lakin, Hill, White, & Write, 1988). However, it is important to note that although most individuals with developmental disabilities were living in communities, this did not mean that they actively participated in community life (Kregel, Wehman, Seyfarth, & Marshall, 1986). Programs and residences can easily be physically located in the community without being socially integrated (Biklen & Knoll, 1987a). The aforementioned Medicaid regulations told providers to focus upon preparing staff to manage the facilities and failed to make community membership a clear priority (Knoll & Ford, 1987). These regulations led many traditional group homes to institute practices that actually erected barriers between the residents and the neighbors (Biklen & Knoll, 1987b).

These community-based group facilities were better than the old institutions. However, they continued to be *facilities* and *not homes*. The distinction between a home and a facility was an important one. Few people would choose to live in a facility. With few exceptions, persons living in housing provided by social service agencies did not choose where they lived or with whom they lived. Within this system, the type of facility determined the services. A change in service needs necessitated a move by the individual, and individuals were denied the opportunity to establish permanency or roots in their communities. Furthermore, with housing owned and controlled by service providers, residents developed neither a sense of ownership nor a feeling of "home" about where they lived.

Critical Point Supported living reflects a new way of thinking, which abandons the preconceptions of traditional facility-based approach, about how to meet the needs of people with severe disabilities.

In the mid-1980s, the supported living movement began to emerge in the field of developmental disabilities. This did not occur in a university think tank, a state administrator's office, or a federal agency, but rather in small organizations that decided to work around the rules (Taylor, Racino, Knoll, & Lutifyya, 1987). Initially called the "nonfacility-based" approach to services, these local efforts challenged the typical way of doing business. They quickly helped to define a new state of the art in "community support" or just "support" rather than "community-based services."

The supported living movement language reflected a new way of thinking in the field of developmental disabilities (Minnesota Governor's Planning Council on Developmental Disabilities, 1987). Support was a new organizing framework in the mental retardation and developmental disabilities field and was the engine of change in the late 1980s and early 1990s (Bradley, Ashbaugh, & Blaney, 1994). The inclusion of the support of disability concept in the 1992 revision of the definition of mental retardation published by the American Association on Mental Retardation (AAMR) reflected a new paradigm for thinking about mental retardation (Luckasson & Spitalnik, 1994; Schalock et al., 1994).

Community "services," as developed during the era of deinstitutionalization, were based on the "continuum" model. This continuum of residential services stretched from the traditional institution on one end to "independent living" at the other end. Along the way, the system offered various types of group living arrangements. These small facilities often were described as offering residents a range of "residential settings" that were "homelike" and "normalized," primarily because they were smaller and geographically less isolated than the large institutions of the past. The emphasis was on the development of programs, a predefined package of services, into which people could fit based on an assessment of their functioning level. The concept of supported living offered an alternative to the continuum of services' emphasis on program slots. Rather than focusing upon putting people into community programs, the attention was on building the individual network of formal and informal supports that a person needed in order to meet the day-to-day demands of his or her home and community (Ferguson & Olson, 1989; Taylor, 1988; Taylor, Racino, Knoll, & Lutifyya, 1987).

In effect, this supported living approach emphasized the separation of housing from support services. Because initial efforts at the development of community programs for people with developmental disabilities usually were deinstitutionalization efforts, it was assumed that the two needs, housing and services, were linked. Experience showed that this was not so and was contrary to the experiences of in-home health programs serving populations such as the aged. In these programs, people received needed services by using community providers and/or specialized assistance on an as-needed basis in their own homes. Changing needs did not necessitate a change of residence.

Closely connected to this conceptual breakthrough was another, still controversial, insight: the rejection of the continuum of services as a viable vehicle for organizing services for people with disabilities (Taylor, 1988). The concepts of the least restrictive environment and the continuum of services were not useful for the transition of adults with disabilities into the community. As a result of focusing upon programs and a limited number of options rather than upon the individual, the services based on these concepts unduly limited the opportunities for people to achieve true membership. Membership was best served when supports were brought into a person's home or other regular community setting, instead of configuring a "setting" around a predefined array of services.

In the area of policy and practices, supported living has moved from small local efforts to being touted as the "New Jerusalem." Many policy analyses see it as the cost-effective salvation for federal agencies, state departments, and local providers who are overwhelmed by demand for services (NAPRR, 1991, 1992; Smith, 1990). Additionally, the federal government explored supported living in eight Medicaid community-supported living arrangement (CSLA) demonstration projects (Lakin & Burwell, 1995).

Critical Point A supported living program delivers the individually needed services and supports to people in their home rather than requiring them to move into a facility that provides a preestablished menu of services.

Living in My Own Home

The current generation of students with moderate to severe cognitive disabilities, multiple disabilities, and physical disabilities is the first that does not have to accept arbitrary limitation on the desire to live in their own home as adults. In the 21st century, it should no longer be necessary to use euphemisms such as "homelike setting" or "least restrictive residential alternative" to justify less than optimal living situations. People with significant needs for supports in daily living have the right to expect the same adult outcome as any other member of our society: life in a home of their own. This is really a new phenomenon. Achieving this outcome still requires substantial knowledge and action on the part of educators, parents, and advocates. The following is a discussion of the two related efforts that are increasingly making "a home of my own" a reality for people with varied types of disabilities. Supported living has emerged to provide the service framework for people with developmental disabilities. *Personal assistance services* (PAS) is emerging as the "umbrella" term that may eventually encompass supported living; but historically, it has been seen as a service for individuals with physical disabilities.

CASE STUDY A

Supported Living in Our Own Words: Julie Allen

"Supported living is one of the three greatest things that have happened in the lives of persons with disabilities! The other two are *personal futures planning* and *supported employment.* All three are person-centered supports, not services as defined by the social service system. They all set a person with disabilities free to make a life of his or her own, which is exactly what is happening to Julie and to us, her parents.

However, our life has not always been filled with such opportunity. When Julie graduated from public school at the age of 21, there were no adult services in our community that addressed Julie's needs and preferences. She sat home with Mom and Dad for a year, and the future looked bleak.

But now, with the help of supported living resources and a planning process called personal futures planning, we are well on our way for Julie to have an independent life of her own (with support). Our initial intent has been for Julie to have opportunities to be integrated into the community where she lives and to learn new living skills. To accomplish this, our family has utilized supported living resources to employ an "attendant tutor." With the help of her attendant tutor, Julie does volunteer work at the local spouse abuse center and at her church. She is also learning basic housekeeping skills, such as dusting, sweeping, preparing meals, and more.

We are planning for Julie to live in an apartment of her own with a housemate in the near future. The funds to pay for a housemate have been approved. We have found an apartment, and we are in the process of interviewing potential housemates. Boy, are we excited (and a little anxious)! We also are looking for Julie to have a paid job in the community in the near future. We have learned that it is very important to find a good job match for Julie. Supported employment is helping in this area.

In our experience, the most challenging thing about supported living is putting your vision into practice. It is like recruiting the people who help to make the plan work and deal with the personnel problems that all small businesses have. That is really what a supported living plan is, the business of giving a person the support he or she needs to live in the community. You also have to define the dream in specific terms in order to put it in practice. Over time the dream becomes a reality through trial and error. If you make mistakes, or something doesn't work as you anticipated, you have the opportunity to keep adapting supports. There is no agency that decides whether you can have this service but not that one or that you are no longer eligible (or appropriate) for the program."

Person-Centered Planning and Services

A review of the literature on person-centered planning and services presents a perspective on some basic challenges in human services (see, e.g., Hall & Walker, 1998; Hulgin, Shoultz, Walker, & Drake, 1996; Klein, 1992; O'Brien & O'Brien, 1992; Racino, Walker, O'Connor, & Taylor, 1992; Taylor, Biklen, & Knoll, 1987; Taylor, Bogdan, & Racino, 1991). In particular, focus on people who are usually identified as the "most difficult to serve" or the "residual institutional population" requires an unambiguous examination of what it means to provide help. The common characteristic of person-centered programs is an absolute commitment to the individual and the belief in a common group of principles. Central to these principles is an uncompromising commitment to the community as the place where all people should live (Taylor, Racino, Knoll, & Lutifyya, 1987). The central message of person-centered planning literature is that the keys to developing an agency that supports community membership are conceptually very simple: It takes commitment, individualization, flexibility, and concern for human relationships. This vision is conceptually very simple but amazingly complex when it comes to instituting these values as the enduring basis of a publicly supported system of supports. Some of the key components of person-centered planning are:

1. *Real Life, Not "Programming"*. Support personnel need to see the mutual interdependence of housemates and the demands of each individual's daily routine determining the needs for skill development or supports (Klein, 1992; Knoll & Ford, 1987). Development and learning should occur in the course of the normal daily routine, not in contrived and artificial programs.
2. *Commitment*. People with the greatest degree of disability and their families need reassurance that there are individuals who have made a long-term commitment to support them. The individuals and organizations that work with them must be willing to stick with them in good and bad times, and during periods of erratic behavior (O'Brien & O'Brien, 1992b).
3. *Personal Advocacy*. People with the most complex needs also are likely to be the ones with the greatest number of agencies involved in their lives. Everyone may have shuffled them around in the service system because no one was willing to make a commitment to provide them with what they need. This means that an agency that decides to accept a long-term responsibility to a person has to work both formally and informally to bring about change in other agencies. This also means advocating for new and innovative services that meet the specific need of the individual and for collaboration that crosses over agency lines of responsibility (Johnson, 1985; Lippert, 1987; O'Brien & O'Brien, 1991).
4. *Choice*. People with disabilities often have had few opportunities to experience making decisions, even small ones, throughout their lives. This indicates that support personnel must know how to assist people in making real choices in areas of daily life and to be comfortable with balancing the risks involved (Johnson, 1985; Klein, 1992; Knoll & Ford, 1987; O'Brien & O'Brien, 1991).
5. *Flexibility*. Supports must be developed to match the strengths and needs of the person, to build on natural community resources, and to attune to the realization that life can be chaotic at times. People change over time and the supports they need must adapt to match their changing life situation (Johnson, 1985: Klein, 1992; Minnesota Governor's Planning Council on Developmental Disabilities, 1987; O'Brien & O'Brien, 1991, 1992b).
6. *Relationships*. Being part of a community means that people have enduring relationships with people other than those paid to be with them. With real friendships come natural systems of support that often are able to forestall or prevent relatively minor problems from becoming insurmountable difficulties that escalate into a crisis. Most people have these systems, but people whose lives have been constrained within the human service system frequently have few natural networks. Often the most that the "formal" service system can do is to provide opportunities for people to develop relationships. For good or ill, friendships cannot be planned or controlled (Bartholmew, 1985; McKnight, 1987; O'Connell, 1988). (See Table 15–2.)

The focus on "support" has led many organizations and individuals to change their vocabulary; yet, the actual operation of agencies and the style of individual professionals remain substantially the same. Much of this can be attributed to the well-established nature of the system of group homes and the strength of the existing provider network. As the failure of vocational services to convert to supported

TABLE 15–2

Key Concepts in Supported Living

- The majority of people with developmental disabilities have always lived at home with their families or on their own.
- People with disabilities need to be able to move out of the family home and to establish their own identity as adults.
- Control over your own life—particularly where and how you choose to live—is essential to the definition of adulthood in modern America.
- Despite great progress, reform efforts of the last 30 years continue to place control in the hands of human service organizations.
- Support of families and for adults requires a new role for human services built on a problem-solving partnership and recognition of the primacy of consumer control.
- The array of supports that an individual is provided for his and her needs in daily life is far different from a continuum of residential options or developing individualized service plans.
- "Supported living" has provided a useful framework for exploring how housing can be separated from supports.
- Individuals with the most severe disabilities can be supported in their own homes.
- Housing must be separated from supports.

employment has demonstrated, it is very hard for a facility-based agency to give up its real estate and to redefine its mission. This confusion has been furthered by the seeming ease with which the term "support" can be appropriated to a wide range of activities that have little relationship to the conceptual underpinnings of supported living and person-centered planning. This phenomenon, similar to the many ways that normalization was distorted, has led some authors to develop lists of nonexamples (e.g. see Table 15–3).

The belief in personal choice and control and full community participation for people with developmental disabilities requires the transformation of professional practice. The promise of these approaches will be lost if the field does not systematically reeducate itself. Professionals entering the field must be both imbued with this new way of thinking and have the skills needed to undertake the far-reaching changes that lie ahead. More than a decade ago Smull and Bellamy (1990) concluded that the supported services paradigm has primarily occurred as a result of the "creativity and effort of local service providers . . . the challenge for government is to sustain these gains, encourage further development, and make the benefits of the support paradigm more widely available. . . . Specific solutions to the policy challenges must be developed in the political context of existing state and federal programs" (p. 11).

Access to Supported Living

As might be anticipated from the history of supported living, it takes many forms in states and communities around the country. What is consistent and unique about supported living is adherence to the key principles outlined earlier. Within the formal system of service, it is critical to appreciate the importance of these guiding principles as the vocabulary of support proliferates, sometimes in the absence of practices that fit the language. Nonetheless, a growing number of organizations are really implementing an individualized person-centered approach to supported living.

TABLE 15–3
Supported Living is NOT . . .

- A "program" to fix or change people
- People forced to live the way we think is good for them
- A test to see if you can live with no problems, and if not, you get sent back to group living
- An incentive or reward for good behavior
- Being assigned roommate(s)
- Compatible with services that congregate and control people
- A way to avoid responsibility for careful decisions about threats to people's vulnerabilities
- Another stop on the service continuum
- A funding stream used to do more of the same kinds of services
- Having permission to live in an agency-controlled apartment
- Another name for "downsizing" existing facilities into smaller units; otherwise, renaming existing services
- Isolation and loneliness

Source: From O'Brien, J. (1993). Supported living: What's the difference? Responsive Systems Associates, Inc.

Critical Point Recently some organizations and regional agencies have begun using the term "supported living" as the generic term for all residential services for people with disabilities. It is important to examine what an agency is doing to determine if it fits the definition of supported living.

Throughout the country, there are small local providers that exemplify the roots of supported living and use a variety of traditional funding mechanisms to assist people in their own homes. Although the supported living organization typically has been small, size no longer is an essential characteristic. A growing number of fairly large organizations have begun to struggle with how to convert a well-established system of group homes into supported living.

Most states have a regionalized approach to adult services for people with developmental disabilities and this can contribute to significant within-state variation in the experience of people with disabilities and their families. Although they receive significant guidance from the state department, regional and county authorities enjoy considerable autonomy. This means that in one state neighboring communities may have very different access to supported living. Some regional entities have converted completely to supported living as a guiding philosophy. So, it is possible that a person in the next county may have no access to in-home supports. There, the experience of planning for transition may entail putting an individual's name on an endless waiting list for one of the rare slots in the region's six-person group homes.

As noted, early on federal Medicaid had a significant impact upon the development of community services. This continues to be true in the area of supported living. As yet, the successful federal experiment with the community supported living arrangements (CSLA) has not led to a total revamping of the federal Medicaid long-term care program. At present, a number of serious proposals for a fundamental reworking of "long-term care policy" have been presented and are being debated (see the subsequent discussion of MiCASSA). Currently, individual states are given a great deal of flexibility under the home and community-based waiver (HCBW) options to use Medicaid in a variety of flexible and individualized ways. This also has contributed to wide variation in what is available in a particular state. Some states have opted to use supported living as the guiding framework for all Medicaid long-term care funds for people with developmental disabilities. In these states, the total system is moving toward supports for individuals. On the other hand, some states have made limited use of waiver programs or have developed plans that reflect a very traditional approach to service. In these states, individuals who are dependent on Medicaid to purchase their services will likely find the opportunities for supported living severely restricted. Additionally, the federal government has limited states in the use of Medicaid waiver slots by requiring a cap on these slots in their applications for federal matching funds.

Finally, it is important to remember that significant portions of services for people with developmental disabilities were funded exclusively by state funds. This meant that some of the earliest innovations in supported living were financed with moneys that were not trapped in the complexities of the federal system. A variety of innovative efforts were designed and continue to be implemented using state funds, but many states have converted their state-funded programs to Medicaid. As with much information discussed in this chapter, it is important to keep in mind that, unlike access to public education, there is no entitlement to supported living or most other adult services. It is true that if a person with a disability meets the criteria, he or she is entitled to Medicaid; but, as previously explained, that is not a guarantee of access to supported living. In the typical state program, a procedure exists to restrict access to limited state dollars. Once the money is gone, the next person who comes "through the door" requesting supported living will be told to come back during the next budget period.

The point of this discussion was to underscore that although supported living provides a framework for a basic reworking of the system of long-term care for people with developmental disabilities, we are a long way from seeing the promise of this change fully realized. Whereas the concept and descriptions of effective programs have been widely disseminated for over a decade, there are regions where supported living is still a totally novel concept. One can still hear the objection: "What are you talking about? He (or she) is too severely disabled to live outside a facility." It matters little that we can point to numerous examples that provide ample evidence of the efficiency, effectiveness, and quality that mark supported living.

In the case of supported living, like supported employment, long-term planning for transition is critical. The teacher must start early to build expectations for students with disabilities to have meaningful adult life. By shaping attitudes and expectations, educators also contribute to moving service systems toward becoming more responsive. Raising expectations early in life so that parents and family members of people with disabilities see what is possible and desirable is a critical tool in changing the look of adult services. On a certain level, transition planning that reaches back into the early grades is a form of marketing. It is about creating consumer demand for the best quality products. It is about helping parents to have the highest expectation for the person with a disability as an adult: "Yes, we expect he or she will work and live in his or her own home. The person will choose how to define home for him or herself."

CASE STUDY B

Supported Living in Our Own Words—Tim Scott

"It was September 20, 1995, I was working in my office when the phone rang. I figured it to be another applicant or possibly an employer calling to make a job-related inquiry. But, instead, to my surprise, it was the Governor's Office asking if this was the Tim Scott who is doing such a fine job working with people with disabilities and advocating for supported living and supported employment in Kentucky.

After a few comments regarding the upcoming general assembly and briefly discussing my letters and my efforts to influence the members of Kentucky's Health and Welfare Committee to expand supported living, we hung up. I really didn't think about what had actually happened at the time of the call, but at the end of the day while driving home, it occurred to me that all the letters I had recently sent off may actually make a difference in some way, particularly the one to Governor Jones to thank him for supporting and setting up the regional councils for supported living.

I had been involved in an intense letter-writing campaign after graduating from UK (University of Kentucky). My purpose then was in regards to getting attendant care, or the means thereof, into western Kentucky due to my declining sense of self-worth and the overall well-being and mental health of myself and my mother who was providing the majority of my attendant care. I was a 29-year-old quadriplegic; how was I to get up daily and retain a job and attendants on $432 a month SSI? My family was my primary caregivers and main source of support for the last 12 years. To make things worse, my mother's arthritis was getting worse, which only added to the constant growing feelings of dependence. The aggravation and worry turned into depression and anger, and I started wondering about my self-esteem and my future due to the dissonance I was creating within my family.

With a strong religious conviction and a lot of patience, grace, and forgiveness, I fought on looking for answers. Vocational Rehabilitation (VR) and our local MH/MR (mental health/mental retardation) respite program had done all they could do pertaining to attendant care, and my situation was looking pretty bleak. In 1992, I had acquired a job but was still desperately exploring all avenues for attendants so that I could use my earnings to get out of my parents' home. Eventually, I was put with a gentleman who works for Kentucky MH/MR out of Western State Hospital, which is where I might end up if I didn't find help soon! But, anyway, this wonderful individual had some new and exciting news about a program called "supported living." He explained to me that if I would jump on board by making phone calls and writing letters to our state representatives, there was a good chance that help was on the way.

I didn't realize it at the time, but this man and his understanding and intentions would change my life forever. I was introduced to the "supported living" concept. Kentucky's MH/MR's intentions were to form a pilot program across Kentucky in its efforts to pass a bill in the general assembly to implement supported living. I didn't have anything to lose. I immediately thought it a wonderful idea and one that I wanted to be a part of. Supported living became a reality in early 1993. Since then, supported living has grown to become one of the best things this great state has done with its tax dollars. Supported living is a dream come true for those who might otherwise not have a chance to prove themselves.

I was one of the first to be awarded a small amount of supported living money due to my needs and my efforts on its part. Without it, I would not be able to retain my position as a Regional Placement Manager doing vocational counseling for Heartland Projects with Industry in Western Kentucky, which I have worked successfully for the last 4 years now. Supported living has allowed me to hire adequate attendant care and even provides work-related assistance to help me perform my job duties, and it has helped with some assistive devices that are needed for both my job and daily living.

Although I work in a professional position, my income is not high enough to surpass the Social Security criteria for substantial and gainful activity due to impairment-related work expenses (IRWE); that is, vehicle loan, medicine, and medical supplies and equipment that my insurance won't pay. Keeping your supported living plan and IWRE or PASS (plans for achieving self-support) expenses separate and distinguishable is important. Supported living funds are not considered as income and can be utilized with family members, a big plus over other programs, but participants must pay all applicable taxes.

Thanks to supported living, all my income isn't being taken for my primary care. In 1994, I was able to buy a computer, which I needed for my work. Also, I just built a nice ramp to access my residence and am now able to get in my bathtub due to a used overhead lift I was able to purchase. In addition, I have been blessed to have been married recently and have purchased a house, which three years ago was only a dream. Although supported living moneys can't be used to purchase homes and automobiles directly, it has allowed me to save some of my income for the down payment toward the purchase of my house. Supported living is proof to me that God truly helps those who strive to help others and themselves. . . . Amen.

I witness firsthand every day how supported living helps others because of my job responsibilities. I have seen it change family despair into delight. It has helped people to start and hold onto small businesses by building ramps and allowing tools to be purchased. It provides attendant care and security for countless individuals. And, most importantly, it allows individuals to get out of their houses and to become a part of a community.

Supported living is broad based in its ability to provide services and it works on a personal futures planning motto, which allows for personal choice. In my 16 years of dealing with disability issues, I personally believe that supported living is a true blessing and the wave of the future."

Personal Assistance Services

As the movement toward supported living was developing in the field of developmental disabilities, a consensus was developing around access to high-quality personal assistance as being critical to independent living for most other people with disabilities (Racino & Litvak, 1999). When these two movements are carefully reviewed, it becomes apparent that they are both sides of the same coin; that is, they are both built on the same foundations of self-determination, choice, and community participation. The two movements are offered as positive alternatives to congregate care placements. The primary difference lies in the fact that people with developmental disabilities often require a greater degree of support in problem solving and making choices. Once the advocates in the independent living centers saw this difference as a legitimate support need and not as characteristics that made people with developmental disabilities qualitatively different from other people with disabilities, the linkage of these two efforts was achieved (Racino & Litvak).

Critical Point Access to personal assistance services (PAS) is seen by many people with disabilities as a civil rights issue. The ability to obtain personal assistance can be the factor that enables many people to live and work in the community rather than face nursing home placement or isolation within the home.

According to a blue-ribbon panel assembled by independent living research utilization (ILRU) and the Robert Wood Johnson Foundation (Dautel & Frieden, 1999), personal assistance services (PAS) are the key to quality of life for the people with a wide range of disabilities. Racino (1999) outlines how PAS has moved from an almost exclusive focus on physical disability to provide an essential service to people with a very wide range of disabilities, including psychiatric conditions, brain injury, and mental retardation, in essence merging with supported living. Reviewing the research on PAS, the blue-ribbon panel (Dautel & Frieden, 1999) found that access to these services is associated with maintenance of good health and functional capacity; productivity (Richmond, Beatty, Tepper, & DeJong, 1997); employment (Nosek, 1990); independence in living arrangement (Human Services Research Institute, 1991); and community integration (HSRI, 1991). The panel notes that the ability to manage one's own life has a profound impact on anyone's mental health status. It affects the ability to work, engage in family and social activities, and otherwise be actively involved in life. Although personal assistance is defined as a health care issue, ultimately access to this service can shape self-image.

According to Litvak, Zukas, and Heumann (1987):

> Personal assistance services (PAS) are tasks performed for a person who has a disability by another person that aim at maintaining well-being, personal appearance, comfort, safety, and interactions within community and society as a whole. In other words, personal assistance tasks are those tasks which the individual who has a disability would normally do for himself or herself if the person had no disability (p. 1).

The type of tasks that they are referring to include: (a) assistance with personal care activities, such as dressing, grooming, feeding, toilet, and so forth; (b) assistance in moving around the home and the community; (c) assistance with home maintenance, including cleaning, shopping, cooking, laundry, and repairs; (d) help in caring for infants and children; (e) aid in cognitive life management, such as finances and decision making; (f) assurance of personal and home security; and (g) assistance in communication services, such as interpreting or reading. In 1991, the Consortium of Citizens with Disabilities, a Washington-based coalition of the major disability organizations, developed a cross-disability statement of policy guidelines for PAS. This list of principles presents a picture of PAS as critical for people with disabilities to attain "life, liberty, and the pursuit of happiness." The guidelines said that PAS should be designed:

- To be guided and directed by the choices, preferences, and expressed interests and desires of the individual.
- To increase the individual's control over life based on the choice of acceptable options that minimize reliance on others in making decisions and in performing everyday activities.
- To enable PAS users to select, direct, and employ their own paid personal assistants, if desired.
- To enable PAS users to contract with an agency for these services, if desired.
- To foster the increased independence, productivity, and integration of these individuals into the community; to be easily accessible and readily available to all eligible persons where and when desired and needed.
- To meet individual needs irrespective of labels.
- To allow payment to family members for the extraordinary personal assistance they provide.
- To be provided in any setting, including in or out of the person's home.
- To be based on an individual service plan.
- To offer PAS users of all ages the opportunity and support needed to assume greater freedom, responsibility, and choice throughout life (Consortium of Citizens with Disabilities, 1991, p. 3).

Based on an extensive review of the PAS literature and interviews with PAS users, Connie Lyle O'Brien and John O'Brien (1992a) have developed a checklist for evaluating personal assistance policies and programs. This checklist is structured around what they see as three essential qualities of effective personal assistance services: availability, comprehensiveness, and controllability. Table 15–4 provides a summary overview of the information provided in this instrument.

The National Blue-Ribbon Panel on Personal Assistance Services (Dautel & Frieden, 1999) notes that, at present, access to PAS is just about as erratic as access to supported living. Litvak (1995) reports on the unduly complex and uncoordinated nature of the service system. With no coherent national policy, there continues to be a nationwide predisposition toward

TABLE 15–4

Checklist for Evaluating Personal Assistance Services (PAS) Policies and Programs

Available

PAS are available to people:
"of all ages, based on functional need . . . regardless of incomes."

PAS do not create disincentives:
"to employment, to eligibility for other benefits and services, to marriage and child rearing."

PAS encourage and supplement natural supports.

PAS funding comes through a long-term, stable source.

PAS funding provides fair pay and benefits for assistants.

Comprehensive

PAS are negotiated based on individual needs, preferences, and circumstances.

The program does not arbitrarily limit what the assistants can agree to do.

Participants can get the assistance needed with:
"personal routines, household routines, travel, communication, cognitive assistance, raising children, assuring security."

The program provides emergency backup.

Participants can get assistance with no limits:
"Assistance is available . . . in the home . . . outside the home, at work, at school, to participate in community life, to travel."

The program offers as much assistance as needed when it is needed:
"up to 24 hours a day, 7 days a week, . . . The amount of assistance can change as the participant's needs change."

Controllable

Participants can decide how much control they want to exercise by choosing:
"to get cash or voucher to hire and supervise assistants."
"to hire a business agent or agency to manage personal assistance system for them."
"to use assistants employed, trained, and supervised by an agency."

The medical supervision is not required.

Assistants can perform any and all health care routines that the participant would perform if able.

Participants can provide all training if they desire.

Participants can be family members if they desire.

The program provides participants with access to information on how both to manage assistants and to perform daily routines and their personal assistance system.

The program provides mechanisms to mediate conflicts and disputes.

The program provides vehicles for participants to share information.

Source: Derived from O'Brien & O'Brien, 1992a.

facility-based care and a catch-as-catch-can approach to delivering home and community services. In most locales, it is still easier for a person with a disability to obtain a bed in a nursing home than to obtain demonstrably more cost-effective PAS. According to ADAPT (1999a), the average annual Medicaid expenditure for a person using community-based services is

$7,276, whereas expenditure for nursing home residents averages $23,225. At the present time, over 80% of our Medicaid dollars ($40 billion) spent on long-term care are used for institutional services, leaving only 20% ($10 billion) for all community services (ADAPT, 1999a). In 1995, 22 states reported that they did not make use of the Medicaid personal care optional services (Winterbottom, Liska, & Obermaier, 1995).

A year after the passage of the Americans with Disabilities Act, a group of leaders from the disabilities rights movement came together in Oakland, CA, under the sponsorship of the World Institute on Disability to begin the next phase in their campaign for full access. Out of this meeting came a resolution on personal assistance services, which said in part:

> People with disabilities are entitled to be enabled to achieve the highest possible level of personal functioning and independence through appropriate education, health care, social services and assistive technology, including, as necessary, the assistance of other people. . . . We consider independent living and the availability of services to be critical to the exercise of our full human and civil rights, responsibilities and privileges.
>
> To this end, we condemn forced segregation and institutionalization as direct violations of our human rights. Government policies and funding should not perpetuate the forced segregation, isolation, or institutionalization of people with disabilities of any age. The Americans with Disabilities Act was passed into law to promote the equalization of opportunity. The passage of comprehensive federal personal assistance legislation is essential to realizing the historic promise of the Act (World Institute on Disability, 1991).

Critical Point Legislation and litigation remain necessary to challenge the institutional bias that exists in federal and state long-term care policy for people with disabilities.

This effort culminated in the introduction of the Medicaid Community Attendant Services and Supports Act (MiCASSA, S1935) by Senators Harkin and Specter on November 16, 1999. This legislation was designed to provide a real basis for addressing the nationwide lack of access to personal assistance services and supported living. It reflected a consensus across the disability community of an effective vehicle for finally reversing the institutional bias that has dominated disability policy in this country for the last century. Table 15–5 provides an excerpt from the introduction to MiCASSA.

Additional impetus was given to MiCASSA and other efforts to improve access to individualized community supports for people with disabilities by an event that occurred a few months earlier. On June 22, 1999, the U.S. Supreme Court delivered an opinion in the case of *Olmstead v.* L. C. *and* E. W., 119 S.Ct. 2176 (1999). Two women with mental illness and mental retardation brought this lawsuit in a Georgia state psychiatric hospital. They requested services in the community so that they could live outside the state hospital. The professionals on their treatment team agreed with them. However, the state was very slow in developing community living arrangements and, as a result, the state had essentially an endless waiting list. Hence, the plaintiffs found themselves on the waiting list for years, so they sued Tommy Olmstead, the Commissioner of Georgia's Department of Human Resources. In their lawsuit, they charged that the state of Georgia violated the Americans with Disabilities Act (ADA) integration mandate by failing to provide services in the most integrated setting appropriate to meet their needs, which in their case was the community, not an institution.

The Supreme Court agreed with the plaintiffs. It stated clearly that denial of community placements to individuals with disabilities was precisely the kind of segregation that Congress sought to eliminate in passing the ADA. The

TABLE 15–5

MiCASSA, the Medicaid Community Attendant Services and Supports Act

Purposes

The purposes of this Act are as follows:

(1) To provide that States shall offer community attendant services and supports for eligible individuals with disabilities, and

(2) To provide financial assistance to the States to support systems change initiatives designed to assist each State to develop and enhance a comprehensive consumer-responsive statewide system of long-term services and supports that provides real consumer choice and direction consistent with the principle that services and supports are provided in the most integrated setting appropriate to meeting the unique needs of the individual.

Policy

It is the policy of the United States that all programs, projects, and activities receiving assistance under this Act shall be carried out in a manner consistent with the following principles:

(1) Individuals with disabilities, or, as appropriate, their representatives, must be empowered to exercise real choice in selecting long-term services and supports that are of high quality, are cost-effective, and meet the unique needs of the individual in the most integrated setting appropriate;

(2) No person should be forced into an institution to receive services that can be effectively and efficiently delivered in the home or community;

(3) Federal and State policies, practices, and procedures should facilitate and be responsive to, not impede, an individual's choice; and

(4) Individuals and their families receiving long-term services and supports must be involved in decision making about their own care and be provided with sufficient information to make informed choices.

Source: S1935, 106th Congress, MiCASSA: The Medicaid Community Attendant Services and Supports Act, p. 2. (Introduced November 16, 1999.)

Court noted that segregation and institutionalization, unless required because of a person's condition, constituted discrimination and violated the ADA's "integration mandate." There was much more to the decision as it outlined other considerations for the state. Nonetheless, it presented an important new lever to be used in expanding community supports for people with disabilities.

Within the context of this text, it is important to note that *Olmstead* had implications for students currently in school who will potentially be on a waiting list for community support services. The National Association of Protection and Advocacy Systems (NAPAS) (October 1999) feels that the *Olmstead* decision extends to people who are or will be on a waiting list. In the decision, the Court stated that one defense a state can offer against lawsuits such as *Olmstead* is that it has a comprehensive effective working plan for placing qualified persons in less restrictive settings. In other words, the state can defend itself by showing that it is thinking and planning ahead to meet the needs of those at risk of institutionalization. The implication currently for people who are not in facilities is that, "If an individual is on a waiting list to receive community supports, the state can presume that person is not currently receiving adequate community supports. If a person is not receiving appropriate community services, then they are at risk of institutionalization" (NAPAS, 1999).

Transition to Interdependent Life as an Adult

Increasing access to supported living and PAS is breaking down barriers that historically have kept people with severe physical disabilities, cognitive disabilities, and multiple disabilities from living in their own homes. This transformation of adult services underscores the role of education in preparing *all students* for "assuming emergent adult roles in the community" (Halpern, 1994, p. 116). So, although the individual considerations may vary from person to person, public education has a responsibility to all children that begins when they walk through the door of a preschool program. It means all of education is about transition, that is, a lifelong process of growth as we learn to cope with an ever-changing world. The outcome of education is the development of lifelong learners who are prepared to live together and to contribute to the life of the community. This vision of *interdependent* living is the goal for all students.

The experience of the students with disabilities who are receiving special education strongly suggests that this goal requires increased attention from the education system. Four items must be on the planning agenda as students, parents, educators, and service providers look to an adult life with maximal personal independence and community contribution for all students with disabilities. These items are not checkoffs on a form to be completed as the student has his or her 14th birthday. The preparation of lifelong learners starts the minute that the education system first meets the child and parents by addressing vision, skills, resources, and supports.

Vision

As we discussed at the beginning of this chapter, people with disabilities have long found their lives defined in terms of limitation. This makes it very difficult for the person and members of his or her family to think about meaningful adult outcomes when they reach transition age. Often they have been taught to avoid thinking about the future. Is it any wonder that discussion of employment or of home living are rejected as not making any sense? It is critical that from the beginning of a student's education career a long-term focus on adult outcomes should be nurtured. Families and people with disabilities must be encouraged to explore possibilities, just like every other student and family. This process begins, as it does with all students, with the earliest discussions of, "what do you want to be when you grow up?" This requires that professionals adopt a positive tone and demeanor in the interaction with even the youngest children. As the principal professionals, the disability experts, in the family's life for perhaps as long as 18 years, have a major responsibility to contribute to forming a positive vision.

Critical Point Educators must start early to assist families to develop a positive long-term vision of adult life for children with disabilities. This should include informing them, even at the elementary level, about the "best practices" in adult services and the strengths and limitation of what is currently available in their locale.

Develop Supports and Skills

Perhaps the principal lesson of the movement toward supported living has been a rejection of the "readiness model." This traditional approach to planning was based on a developmental approach and embedded in the traditional education, vocational, and residential services continuum. Under this model, there were certain specific skills that were a necessary prerequisite before a person could move on to the next less restrictive step in the continuum. Organizations that have used "support" as an organizing framework have demonstrated the fallacy in this logic. They have consistently demonstrated that an appropriate support can be mobilized to bridge the gap between a person's ability and the demands of a setting. Does this mean that educators and adult providers should not worry about developing skills? The response to this question is a resounding no! Educators and others must continue to put as much (or more) energy into assisting people to develop the skills that are necessary to maximize their independence. Teaching, although not specifically highlighted in the taxonomy of supports outlined in the 1992 AAMR definition manual (Luckasson et al., 1992), continues to be a crucial support. Independent or at least partial mastery of a skill is a valuable asset to any person. Skill development is not an excuse for failing to support the development of relationships, but if appropriately focused, it can actually contribute to the nurturing connections.

Critical Point Educators must have a longitudinal perspective on skill development, so that valuable instructional time is not wasted teaching and learning skills that have little or no long-term value or use to the student.

Develop Usable Skills

The last 25 years of progress in the education of students with severe disabilities has taught all educators an important lesson about skill development. The skills we choose for targeting during our valuable and limited instruction time must have ecological validity. They must be responsive to the needs of the students' present and future environments. They must be useful. They must contribute to achieving prioritized education outcomes. This lesson applies to all education, but it is particularly relevant to the education of student with disabilities.

This point needs to be emphasized: *As we think about the challenges confronting all students with disabilities, we need to examine what we teach to assure ecological validity.* This is as much a consideration for students with so-called mild disabilities and emotional and behavior disorders as it is for students with severe and multiple disabilities. Although this point refers to all areas of the curriculum, its greatest area of relevance is the preparation for independent living as an adult. Students with mild disabilities will not be eligible for support services such as their peers with more obvious disabilities. Therefore, it is critical that their teachers examine the curriculum and their IEPs in order to assure mastery of the skills that the students need to make it as an adult.

Teach Skills in Inclusive Settings

Some educators feel that there is an inherent tension between the need for students with disabilities to develop independent living skills and inclusive education (Fuchs & Fuchs, 1995). One of the rationales traditionally given for resource room and special class placement has been that these placements provide the opportunity to

Families play important transition education roles.

teach skills that are not part of the regular curriculum. Increasingly, this logic is being challenged on several fronts. First, the opportunity for positive social interaction and connections that have the potential to develop into sustained relationships outweighs the value of the separate placement (Strully & Strully, 1985). Second, the mainstream setting proves the opportunity to learn and master skills in an authentic setting, thereby providing ecological validity and increased likelihood of generalization (Brown et al., 1989). Third, efforts at reform in general education are providing increased opportunity for authentic instruction for all students (Baker, Wang, & Walberg, 1995). Fourth, differentiated instruction within the general education classroom can be effectively designed to assure that basic skills are addressed for students with disabilities (Kearns & Dryer, 1997). Finally, some systems are demonstrating how students with disabilities experience a high degree of inclusion in the early grades and then move into a program with a heavy emphasis on life skills when they are in the latter years of high school. At that point, the varied schedules of all students mean that the special education pullout will be less obvious as many students engage in co-op and other out-of-school activities. Using this approach, some systems provide full-time community-based skills training for students with moderate to severe disabilities in the post-18-year age group, after their peers of the same age have graduated from the public school system. In this approach, the students with disabilities also graduate from the high school building and their program is based at a college campus or other community setting (Hall, Kleinert, & Kearns, 2000; Jorgensen, 1998).

Teach Priority Skills

The hallmark of special education is the design of an instruction program that addresses the unique needs of each student. However, the multiple competing priorities within the school and the numerous skills for independent living found in resource manuals and curriculum guides mean educators must thoughtfully decide how to use limited instruction time (see, e.g., Cronin & Patton, 1993; Dever, 1988; Falvey, 1989; Ford, Schnorr, Meyer, Davern, Black, & Dempsey, 1989). Educators need to establish clear priorities for each student. This process requires careful assessment, effective communication with the student and family, and a clear picture of how the student's disability impacts upon participation and independence in the present and future environments. A major contribution to this decision-making process is the long-term vision of the future which each student and family have developed. Rather than attempting to provide a comprehensive community living curriculum guide, in Table 15–6 we have used the nine adaptive skills areas (other than "work") found in the 1992 AAMR definition manual (Luckasson et al., 1992) in order to generate a series of suggestive questions to assist in planning for student skill development.

Resources for Independent Living

Within the framework presented here, resources are potential sources of funding, services, informal supports, or equipment that will enable a person to maximize his or her independence. The organizations and agencies outlined subsequently should all be explored in the planning for transition to independent living. In many cases, these potential sources of support can provide the lever needed to make things happen. These supports are discussed in the following sections.

Income Maintenance

Unfortunately, it remains true that many people with disabilities are poor and thus are dependent on some form of public assistance. These programs are currently in a state of

TABLE 15–6
Assessing Skills and Supports for Community Living

1. *Communication.* Does the student:
   - Initiate the interaction with someone else?
   - Use an alternative or augmentative communication system that is easily understood by a stranger?
   - Engage in a reciprocal conversation?
   - Communicate choices?
   - Make requests?
   - Ask for assistance?
   - Make others aware of special communication needs?
   - Effectively respond to complex directions?
2. *Self-care.* Does the student:
   - Follow acceptable personal hygiene?
   - Maintain personal appearance throughout the day?
   - Carry and care for personal hygiene items?
   - Care for hair?
   - Wear clean clothing?
   - Demonstrate acceptable dental hygiene?
   - Dress appropriately for situation and weather?
3. *Home living.* Does the student:
   - Take care of belongings?
   - Pay bills?
   - Use appliances and utensils safely?
   - Keep household material organized?
   - Perform simple repairs?
   - Make shopping lists?
   - Plan a nutritious diet?
   - Prepare meals?
   - Recognize household safety concerns?
   - Demonstrate appropriate manners?
   - Store perishables, appropriately?
   - Clean up after meals?
   - Perform household cleaning?
4. *Social skills.* Does the student:
   - Share tasks with others?
   - Take turns?
   - Initiate interactions appropriately?
   - Cope with negative feedback?
   - Recognize social boundaries?
   - Recognize and apologize for mistakes?
   - Participate as a group member?
   - Recognize varied social roles?
   - Recognize site-specific rules or expectations?
   - Follow rules?
   - Help others?
5. *Community use.* Does the student:
   - Drive an automobile?
   - Have access to public transportation?
   - Use public transportation?
   - Understand a bus schedule?
   - Call taxicabs or paratransit provider to arrange travel?
   - Walk safely around the community?
   - Find locations in the community?
   - Give others directions?
   - Cautiously interact with strangers?
   - Ask for help if lost?
   - Solve problems if lost?
   - Use restaurants?
   - Use stores?
   - Use various community services?
   - Use churches?
   - Use health care facilities?
   - Ask for help in a community setting?
   - Locate desired items in stores and other settings?
6. *Self-direction.* Does the student:
   - Manage a personal schedule for:
     - a day?
     - a week?
     - a month?
   - Consider alternatives in making personal decisions?
   - Organize activities with others?
   - Plan ahead?
   - Regulate his or her behavior?
   - Actively direct personal assistants?
   - Understand his or her support needs?

(continued)

TABLE 15–6 *(continued)*

7. *Health and safety.* Does the student:
   - Follow safety rules?
   - Exit a building when hearing an alarm?
   - Inform others when ill or injured?
   - Take medicine as directed?
   - Use the telephone to obtain help?
   - Avoid alcohol, drugs, and tobacco?
   - Know simple first aid?
   - Avoid sexual abuse?
   - Report abusive or threatened situations?
   - Manage birth control?
   - Inform others of plans?
8. *Functional academics.* Does the student:
   - Maintain a checkbook?
   - Manage a bank account?
   - Maintain a monthly budget?
   - Budget money for planned purchases?
   - Effectively manage money when making a purchase?
   - Use reading:
     - to plan purchases?
     - to shop?
     - to obtain information?
     - to communicate with others?
     - to understand printed notices received in the mail?
     - for recreation?
   - Seek assistance when unable to understand written information?
   - Use writing to:
     - manage household?
     - communicate with others?
     - keep records?
     - fill out forms?
   - Seek assistance when a written document is required?
   - Use computer technology to help with:
     - financial management?
     - written communication?
     - accessing information?
   - Telling time?
9. *Leisure.* Does the student engage in:
   - A variety of recreational activities?
   - Activities that enhance physical fitness and health?
   - Provide an opportunity for developing relationships with other members of the community?
   - Active recreation activities?
   - Passive recreation activities?
   - Recreation activities:
     - alone?
     - with a group?
     - at home?
     - in the community?

Source: Derived in part from Ford, A., Schnorr, R., Meyer, L., Davern, L., Block, J., & Dempsey, P. (1989). *The Syracuse community-referenced curriculum guide for students with moderate and severe disabilities.* Baltimore: Paul Brookes.

evolution with an increasing emphasis placed on providing incentives for recipients to go to work. For people with disabilities this has meant the gradual removal of actual disincentives to employment. Many people with disabilities will make some use of Social Security Income (SSI) and Social Security Disability Insurance (SSDI) to contribute to their support as they establish themselves in their own home. Additionally, various traditional group living situations use Social Security funds to cover some of their residential cost. It is very important to make contact with the Social Security office to explore how these programs can most effectively support the students desired future. It is important to obtain the most current information about opportunities like PASS (plans for achieving self-support), which allows for a certain degree of flexibility in these massive programs. The same office is also the source for information and applications for the food stamp program.

Critical Point People with disabilities have an increasing array of options related to where and how they live as adults. Unfortunately, for them moving out of Mom and Dad's house still requires more than finding an affordable apartment. Transition planning must focus on identifying and accessing the resources and supports needed for students with disabilities and their families to have a life experience that parallels that of their nondisabled siblings and friends.

Resources for Home Ownership

Even with the reality of poverty, there are a number of ways for individuals with disabilities to achieve the dream of home ownership. The range of programs and strategy that make this possible have expanded substantially in the last few years as supported living and PAS have gained increasing notice in the area of public policy. Several national projects have compiled resource guides for home ownership (Home of Your Own Project, 1995; Hulgin, Walker, Fisher, Handley, & Shoultz, 1995). Some of these strategies are summarized in Table 15–7. An important source of information and resources is the local or state office of the U.S. Department of Housing and Urban Development (HUD).

Community Mental Health and Developmental Disability Programs

In many states, the entry to supported living and PAS is found in the county or regional community mental health (CMH) center or regional developmental disabilities center. In some

TABLE 15–7

Housing Strategies

It is unfortunately true that many people with disabilities have very limited financial resources. So, as we increasingly delink the provision of services and supports from the provision of housing, we need to identify sources of funding to pay for housing. A report to the President's Committee on Mental Retardation identified the following strategies.

Federal programs:

- Section 8 housing certificate from HUD
- Public housing programs funded by HUD
- HUD's section 811 and PHA section 515 program provides capital housing grants to nonprofit organizations
- McKinney Act permanent housing funds develop housing for people at risk of becoming homeless
- HUD's community development block grants help local communities to develop urban areas including housing
- Low-income tax credits provide benefits for owners/investors in low-income housing

State/local efforts:

- Bridge subsidies for people on waiting lists
- Grants for closing costs, down payments, and setup costs
- Nonprofit housing corporations supported by state bond issues
- Programs of technical assistance and financial consultation
- Bank community reinvestment obligations
- Cooperative housing arrangements

Source: From Research and Training Center on Residential Services and Community Living. (1994). *Housing policy and persons with mental retardation.* Minneapolis, MN: Institute on Community Integration.

cases, these entities are a branch of state government. In other cases, they are semiautonomous organizations that contract with the appropriate state agencies. In approaching these organizations, you must know what to look for since these organizations often are large and offer a variety of very different services. They may provide developmental disabilities and mental retardation services, child and adult mental health services, substance abuse services, and/or early intervention services. Depending on where you live, the CMH center may be the principal or only provider of services for a particular population or provide no direct service other than service coordination (case management). Most CMHs centers are principal gatekeepers for adult services, and, thus, also are the place where you will encounter a large waiting list for services. All these factors mean that they are an early contact, and the development of good working relationships with representatives of these organizations will be able to help you and your students better prepare for moving into adult life.

Public/Home Health Services

Access to affordable health care is one of the major challenges confronting people with disabilities in the United States. This problem of access and the medical management of many residential programs have been, perhaps, the greatest barriers to independent community life for many people. As noted earlier, there are currently several initiatives that will reform the federal health care program for people with disabilities (Medicaid). Many students with severe disabilities will already be eligible for and receiving Medicaid. As other students become adults, they may become eligible for Medicaid. This reality and the range of services provided under this program mean that the local office of this agency should be on the planning agenda for most students. It should be noted that in some states people with developmental disabilities would access Medicaid through the developmental disabilities program of the CMH program. As indicated in our discussion of MiCASSA, Medicaid is an important potential source of PAS. In this same area of planning, the local public health office, the Program for Children with Specialized Health Care Needs, the Visiting Nurse Association, home health agencies, and durable medical equipment providers may all have a role to play in assisting students with physical disabilities to obtain assistants and services for their homes.

Centers for Independent Living

Traditionally, schools have not had many interactions with Centers for Independent Living (CILs). This is unfortunate since these organizations, as shown in Table 15–8, have a wide array of services for individuals with all types of disabilities. This lack of connection has begun to change as CILs increasingly are dealing with people who have graduated from special education programs. Recently, the beginning of a discussion about the relationship of CILs to parent resource centers has started. This groundbreaking initiative follows on the CILs' increased opening to people with developmental disabilities. As educators increasingly deal with preparing their graduates with disabilities for independent and supported living and the use of PAS, the CILs should grow into an invaluable link for the students to maintain as they move out of the school system.

Community Living Organizations

Most communities have independent private for-profit and not-for-profit organizations that provide services for people with either developmental disabilities and/or mental health diagnoses. Most

TABLE 15–8

Centers for Independent Living

As described by the Rehabilitation Services Administration (RSA) (1999) centers for independent living (CILs) are consumer-controlled, community-based, cross-disability, nonresidential private nonprofit organizations. They provide services for individuals or groups of individuals with significant disabilities that promote independence, productivity, and quality of life.

Currently, there are approximately 250 centers for independent living across the country, with at least one CIL in every state, the District of Columbia, U.S. Virgin Islands, Puerto Rico, and American Samoa. Annually, over 100,000 individuals with significant physical and mental disabilities receive direct services. Many additional individuals benefit from the centers' systems advocacy to increase the services of the communities to meet the needs of individuals with significant disabilities.

CILs provide a varied combination of services, including the core services of information and referral services; independent living skills training; peer counseling (including cross-disability peer counseling); and individual and systems advocacy. As appropriate, additional services also can include the following:

- Counseling
- Services related to securing housing or shelter
- Rehabilitation technology
- Mobility training
- Life skills training and interpreter and reader services for individuals with significant cognitive disabilities
- Personal assistance services
- Consumer information programs
- Education and training necessary for living in the community and participating in community activities
- Supported living
- Transportation
- Physical rehabilitation
- Therapeutic treatment; prostheses
- Individual and group recreation services
- Training to develop youth with disabilities to promote self-awareness and esteem
- Develop advocacy and self-empowerment skills, and develop career options
- Services to children
- Services to benefit individuals with significant disabilities in enhancing their independence, productivity, and quality of life
- Preventive services
- Community awareness programs to enhance the understanding and integration into the society of individuals with disabilities
- Other services that may be necessary and consistent with the provisions of the Rehabilitation Act of 1973, as amended

Source: From Rehabilitation Services Administration (RSA) Programs: Centers for Independent Living. Office of Special Education and Rehabilitation Services, U.S. Department of Education, 1999.

of these organizations trace their roots back to efforts at deinstitutionalization. Therefore, many of them are firmly "wedded" to the traditional continuum of service. However, it is important to note that the first examples of supported living were developed by small private organizations. Most of the "best" examples of supported living continue to be found in this sector. Recently, though, an increasing number of larger private and public sector organizations have begun to implement a supported living approach. Many of these organizations also will provide other services and supports, such as supported employment and other day programming. Depending on the nature of the organization and the structure of your state service system, you may be able to involve these types of organizations directly in planning for an individual student. In other states, the community mental health agency or the state mental retardation/developmental disabilities services office is the only authorized entrée into these organizations.

Regional Transportation Authorities and Paratransit

In a world dominated by the automobile, people who do not drive are at a distinct disadvantage. The Americans with Disabilities Act has improved access by people with disabilities to public transportation, but transportation must remain a priority when planning for independent home living. For many students with a disability, access to public transportation will be the factor that ultimately determines where they can live. Regardless of the fact that regional transportation authorities are not on a state's interagency group on transition, the local school system should open a clear channel of communication with the transportation agency in its region.

Self-Advocacy

Throughout this book and especially in this chapter, the emphasis is on full membership and participation in the life of the community for all students with disabilities. The self-help movement and particularly the independent living movement have demonstrated that sometimes the best support for integration is taking time with people who share your experience of being treated "differently." The critical fact is that people choose to come together in mutual support. They are not placed into a self-advocacy group as part of their treatment plan. The opportunity to come together as a peer to learn from others, to assist others in problem solving, and to participate in group mobilization, for change truly can assist a person to achieve that most elusive goal: empowerment. The role of the school is to support self-advocacy and to offer the students the opportunity to participate.

Other Supports

In essence, supports are a unique array of resources that are mobilized to bridge the gaps that exist between the skills and the abilities of the person and the demands of everyday life. Supports can include specialized services from agencies; assistive technology; personal assistants; service facilitation; adapted environments; and help from family, friends, roommates, and neighbors. As outlined previously, a philosophy of support is distinguished from a service mentality by the rejection of assuming that there is a prepackaged solution to addressing a person's needs. In fact, each network of supports will be uniquely tailored to each individual situation. The other distinguishing characteristic of this approach is the assumption that supports built on personal relationships are more reliable than those contracted from an anonymous public agency.

The simplest way to develop a support plan is to use a planning matrix similar to the one illustrated in Table 15–9. Here the adaptive skill areas outlined earlier form one axis with the possible sources of support along the other axis. Using this tool, the circle of support and the transition planning team can identify priority needs under each skill area. These priorities are critical skills that the student has not mastered or cannot perform because of the disability. The bulleted topics in Table 15–9 are

TABLE 15–9

A Simplified Supports Planning Matrix

	Sources of Support				
Adaptive Skill Areas	**People (family, friend, neighbors, housemate)**	**Technology**	**Environmental Modification**	**New Skill to Be Learned**	**Formal Service Agency**
Communication					
Self-care					
Home living					
Social skills					
Community use: • Travel					
Self-direction • Managing supports					
Health and safety					
Functional academics: • Managing finances					
Leisure					

specific skills that are problematic for many young adults with disabilities and are highlighted. After the critical skills, the ones that in another time would have been seen as requisite for independent living are identified and the appropriate source of support can be explored. The person and his or her supporters must ask a series of questions: Does a new skill need to be learned? Who in the network can offer assistance? Can the environment be modified or a more accessible setting found? Is there technology available that will make independent performance possible? Does a formal support need to be mobilized to meet this need? At this time, it can be determined which of the resources outlined earlier must be mobilized to provide additional assets to aid in achieving the student's independent living goals.

Conclusion

Transition is an interesting concept with multiple layers of meaning. Fundamentally, transition is about the ongoing process of change. It captures a sense of movement from one reality to another. This chapter has cataloged a transition in American society, not of people with disabilities into adult life. Today we are experiencing a fundamental transformation in which the assumptions and beliefs of just a few years ago are being left in the "dust of time." A new reality for Americans with disabilities, particularly those with the most severe disabilities, is on the horizon. Public policy and public opinion are both slowly but profoundly being transfigured by the tenacious advocacy of people with disabilities whose simple request is to have what everyone else wants—a home of his or her own. This transition as yet is hardly achieved and will reveal a new set of challenges to be confronted in assuring full citizenship to people with disabilities. Nonetheless, this is happening. The final point of this chapter for the reader to consider is the role you have to play in this larger transition as you assist in its occurrence in the life of individual students and in your home communities.

Critical Point In the final analysis, the ultimate measure of educational effectiveness is the extent to which the school system contributes to the quality of life of its graduates.

Study Questions

1. Why have schools often failed to adequately prepare students for transition to independent adult life?
2. During the last 25 years, what factors have moved the field of mental retardation from one dominated by institutional care to the emergence of supported living?
3. How are both supported living and personal assistance services (PAS) radical departures from the traditional models of services for people with disabilities?
4. What factors currently limit access to supported living and PAS?
5. What agencies and organizations should be involved in planning for transition to adult living for people with developmental disabilities?
6. Explain the linkage between the independent living movement, the disability rights movements, and PAS.
7. What is person-centered planning? How does it contribute to effective transition planning?
8. What four factors are critical in planning for successful transition to adult living?

Websites

American Disabled for Attendant Programs Today (ADAPT)
http://www.adapt.org/

"There's no place like home, and we mean real homes, not nursing homes. We are fighting so people with disabilities can live in the community with real supports instead of being locked away in nursing homes and other institutions."

Center for Community Change Through Housing and Support
http://www.communitychange.org/index2.htm

The Center for Community Change, with over a decade of experience working with systems and agencies around the world, combines values of empowerment, community integration, and recovery with planning, program development, and training skills to help design consumer-directed, family-supporting, outcome-focused and cost-effective systems of care.

Center on Human Policy
http://soeweb.syr.edu/thechp/

A Syracuse University-based policy, research, and advocacy organization involved in the national movement to ensure the rights of people with disabilities. Since its founding, the Center has been involved in the study and promotion of open settings (inclusive community opportunities) for people with disabilities. Through the National Resource Center on Supported Living and Choice and other funded projects, the center distributes bulletins, research reports, articles, information packages, and other materials on a broad range of topics related to integration or inclusion for people with disabilities (*http://soeweb.syr.edu/thechp/tchppub.htm*).

These materials include detailed resources on housing, supported living, and community support.

Freedom Clearinghouse
http://www.freedomclearinghouse.org/

"How would you like to spend the rest of your life in a nursing home or other institution? Neither would we. Let's do something about it NOW. Activate your license to change the system! Sign up to be part of our team of advocates across the nation. Or browse this site to learn more about how people can stay in their own homes and out of nursing homes and other institutions. Become part of our network of friends who support our work."

ILRU (Independent Living Research Utilization)
http://www.bcm.tmc.edu/ilru/

This program is a national center for information, training, research, and technical assistance in independent living. Its goal is to expand the body of knowledge in independent living and to improve utilization of results of research programs and demonstration projects in this field. It is a program of TIRR (The Institute for Rehabilitation and Research), a nationally recognized medical rehabilitation facility for persons with disabilities.

ILRU-DIMENET Independent Living Library
http://www.dimenet.com

Presents an on-line library of independent living-related resource materials that have been developed by staff at independent living centers and other organizations involved in the independent living and disability rights movements over the years. This on-line library is developed in response to numerous requests for resource materials on such subjects as board and staff training curricula and manuals, policies and procedures, bylaws, job descriptions, independent living history and philosophy, key state and federal statutes and regulations, for-profit initiatives, and so on. The library is intended to be super user-friendly, and this includes being searchable by subject and author.

Independent Living Resource Centre
http://www.ilrc.nf.ca/

Located in St. John's, Newfoundland, Canada, the Independent Living Resource Centre is a consumer-controlled organization committed to providing supports, resources, and opportunities for empowerment, which enable persons with disabilities to make informed choices about their lives.

Institute on Community Integration
http://ici.umn.edu

Believes that persons with developmental disabilities should live as valued members of our communities, receiving the services and supports they need to fully develop their potential. Research and Training Center on Community Living (http://ici2.umn.edu) is part of the institute and focuses on community supports for persons with developmental disabilities and their families; providing research, evaluation, training, and technical assistance activities in these areas: national data collection and analysis, personnel research and training, self-determination and self-advocacy, integrated recreation and leisure, quality assurance and quality enhancement, and positive behavior management and communication.

Institute on Disability
http://iod.unh.edu/

The institute is a University Affiliated Program (UAP) located at the University of New Hampshire that promotes full inclusion of people with disabilities in their communities.

National Clearinghouse on Managed Care and Long-Term Supports and Services for People with Developmental Disabilities and Their Families
http://www.mcare.net/

The primary objective of the clearinghouse is to meet the informational needs of individuals with disabilities, their families, policy makers, service providers, advocates, and others in the area of managed care and long-term supports and services.

National Home of Your Own Alliance
http://alliance.unh.edu/

The National Home of Your Own Alliance is a partnership between the federal government and nationally recognized advocates and leaders whose goal is to create housing and support opportunities that people choose and control.

Oaks Group
http://oaksgroup.org/

The Oaks Group is a value-based stakeholder organization whose members believe persons with developmental disabilities should be fully included in the mainstream of community life, that children should have the opportunity to grow up in families, and adults should receive the help needed to live as close as possible to the way people without developmental disabilities live.

Opening Doors: A Housing Initiative for the Disability Community
http://www.c-c-d.org

Opening Doors is a housing initiative designed to provide information and technical assistance on affordable housing issues to people with disabilities, their families, advocates, and service providers across the United States.

Options in Community Living
http://www.optionsmadison.com/

Options' mission is to provide support and coordinate services to enable adults with developmental disabilities to live in their own homes. The agency assists people to make informed choices and reach their own goals, with support available to the extent and for as long as it is needed. Options strives to help people with disabilities, their families, and the larger community learn from one another, in order to promote mutual understanding, personal satisfaction, and fulfillment of the potential of each individual.

Research Information on Independent Living (RIIL)
http://www.lsi.ku.edu/lsi/

This database contains reviews of research materials concerning independent living issues. RIIL is a joint effort of the Research & Training Center on Independent Living (RTC/IL) at the University of Kansas and the Independent Living Research Utilization (ILRU) program of TIRR.

State of the States in Developmental Disabilities
http://www.cusys.edu/ColemanInstitute/stateofthestates/home.htm

Established in 1982 to investigate the determinants of public spending for mental retardation/developmental disabilities (MR/DD) services, this project maintains a 20-year longitudinal record of revenue, spending, and programmatic trends in the 50 states and the District of Columbia. Analysis of the rich detail of the database reveals the impact over time of federal and state fiscal policy, and illustrates important service delivery trends in the states in community living, public and private residential institutions, family support, supported employment, supported living, Medicaid Waivers, demographics, and related areas.

Supported Life Institute
http://www.supportedlife.org/

"A supported life is a life that is rich in qualities a person most desires, and one which shows how connected we all are to each other. It is a life which: grows from a person's own choices, desires and dreams; it is not controlled by what kind of services are currently available; goes beyond just meeting a person's basic needs, to reaching a rich quality of life; includes all areas of a person's life; is always changing throughout a person's life; is the kind of life we all want and is not unique to people who happen to have disabilities."

TASH (formerly The Association for Persons with Severe Handicaps)
http://www.tash.org/

An international advocacy association of people with disabilities, their family members, other advocates, and people who work in the disability field. TASH believes that no one with a disability should be forced to live, work, or learn in a segregated setting; that all individuals deserve the right to direct their own lives. TASH's mission is to eliminate physical and social obstacles that prevent equity, diversity, and quality of life.

World Institute on Disability (WID)
http://www.wid.org/

An international public policy center dedicated to carrying out cutting-edge research on disability issues and overcoming obstacles to independent living. The Research and Training Center on Personal Assistance Services is one of the institute's valuable projects.

16

Recreation and Leisure in the Community

Joyce Strand

Janice Kreiner

LEARNING OBJECTIVES

The objectives of this chapter are:

1. Discuss the purposes and advantages of leisure activities for individuals with disabilities.
2. Discuss the purpose and desired outcomes of community-based leisure activities for individuals with disabilities.
3. Characterize the four principles of IDEA in terms of the implications for leisure activities for individuals with disabilities.
4. Describe the procedures for the individualization of leisure activities.
5. Describe various perspectives of community-based leisure programming.
6. Identify and exemplify the benefits of community-based leisure programming.
7. Understand and characterize implementation of the four principles of IDEA in terms of leisure activities.

8. Describe and give examples of appropriate leisure activities for transition-age students.
9. Analyze the integrative framework of community-based leisure programming.
10. Implement assessment strategies used to aid student choices in leisure programming.
11. Implement techniques to facilitate participation in leisure activities for individuals with disabilities.

Introduction

The previous chapter provided a description of the issues and strategies regarding accessing and planning a successful transition to living in the community. In this chapter, issues related to recreation and leisure are discussed. The importance of recreation and leisure pursuits cannot be overly emphasized. As one can see in reviewing Halpern's (1985) model, recreation and leisure activities are separate factors as they are related to employment and independent living. However, recreation and leisure experiences are intricately linked to overall success and satisfaction of the individual with a disability. To accomplish independence, planning and programmatic efforts for students with disabilities should include a significant emphasis on recreation and leisure pursuits.

Of critical importance to the discussion of recreation and leisure and transition services is the inclusion of the way in which the four major elements of transition interweave into the recreation and leisure planning outcomes. In general, the emphasis of this chapter involves discussing recreation and leisure skills and training as they relate to the student's needs and preferences, the outcome-oriented process, interagency linkages, and movement activities from school to postschool environments. Other issues that are considered include implementation issues, leisure options, transportation, roles and responsibilities, community supports, safety, and various assessment methods and models.

What did you do last night? If you would ask this question to your friends and acquaintances in your community, you would probably have a variety of responses. These responses may include activities such as played softball, went bowling, went to a movie, went to a civic meeting, chauffeured kids, watched TV, worked in the garden, went biking, and so on. If you asked individuals with disabilities in your community, the responses would probably be quite different. For example, individuals with disabilities may go home from work, fix dinners with or without assistance from paid staff or family members, and then listen to radio or watch TV. If their residence is a group home, dinner may be made without their assistance or input, and the "group" may have a planned activity in the community. If the individual with a disability lives at home with older parents, it is common to go home and straight to his or her room, eat alone, talk on the phone or watch TV, again in his or her room, and then go to bed.

Critical Point There is no pleasure in having nothing to do; the fun is having lots to do and not doing it (Mary Wilson Little).

The purpose of this chapter is to provide an understanding of leisure programming in community-based settings. Leisure skills are a critical component of the transition process because they provide many connections and relationships for common participation. A key to enhancing the leisure component of the transition process is to provide administrators, parents, teachers, and individuals with disabilities resources and strategies to incorporate leisure in the transition plan.

Community Participation, Recreation, and Leisure

Transition Needs

The inclusion of a chapter on leisure and recreation in the community for persons with disabilities is easily justified because of its importance. For example, individuals with disabilities can learn work skills and obtain and hold jobs (McDonnell, Wilcox, & Hardman, 1991; Rusch & Chadsey, 1998; Wehman, 1992). An individual with a disability can reside in an apartment, cook the dinner, shop, and perform most if not all the chores associated with living independently. However, individuals with disabilities have few, if any, friends, other than family, paid support staff, or other people with disabilities (Condeluci, 1995). The individual with a disability goes to work and then home. The importance of learning leisure skills should be a focus, especially in the transitional years of adolescence.

Critical Point All people need to be involved in recreation and leisure.

> We have only begun to sense the tragic wounds some mentally retarded persons may feel when it dawns on them that the only people relating with them—outside of relatives—are paid to do so. If you or I came to such a sad realization about ourselves, it would rip at our souls to even talk about it. Chances are some of us would cover it up with one noisy, awkward bluff after another and chances are, some professionals seeing us act this way, would say we had "maladaptive" behavior. Think about what it would feel like to have even one person come to us and without pay, develop a reliable, long-term relationship with us because he or she wanted to literally accept us as we are. Then, think of the unspeakable feelings we might possess if—when others were "talking down" to us and "putting us in our place"—that kind person could be counted on to defend us and stick up for us as well. Most of us do have persons like that in our lives. But will the day ever come when retarded citizens will have them too? (Bob Perske, from *Listen People*.)

In his book, *Interdependence: The Route to Community* (1995), Condeluci refers to four basic themes that, in his experience, are the main thrust of rehabilitation and are vital to every person. In fact, these rehabilitation goals are the same as the major goals of most people. These goals are (1) a safe place to live, (2) meaningful things to do, (3) intimacy, and (4) rejuvenation. Although it is the intent of transition services to focus upon all these areas, the focus of this chapter is to look at the goal of rejuvenation. This is the time and opportunity to "refresh and recollect ourselves," something that is necessary for all individuals. Condeluci provided details on these issues:

> In 1980, a survey was administered to persons with disabilities in Pittsburgh regarding the areas of service or programs that were essential to them. The typical list of vital services was listed on the poll. They included housing, transportation, jobs, accessibility issues, attitudes, and the like. Prior to this survey, some of us surmised which areas would be tops. We were certain that housing, jobs, or transportation would be first on the list. Top on the list, however, was recreation. Certainly, the others were important, but recreation far outpolled its closest competitor, housing.
>
> Without question, recreation is a vital need of all people. Our 1980 survey was testimony to two important facts: (1) recreation was most important and (2) there were precious few recreational opportunities for people with disabilities. Today, we are seeing more recreational opportunities, but these efforts often are segregated, isolated, or terribly childlike (Condeluci, 1995, pp. 9–10).

What Condeluci (1995) was talking about is evident across the country. For example, while arenas and stadiums are beginning to think about people with disabilities and to make their facilities accessible, they often assume, incorrectly, that all people with disabilities want to sit together. This is without consideration that the designated sections are separate from their partners or family members without disabilities, in specialized handicapped sections. There are special "handicapped days" at attractions like Sea World, zoos, amusement parks, and county fairs. YMCAs as well as other local pools have set up special "handicapped swim nights." Service providers continue to fill the big yellow school buses with individuals who have disabilities to take them on outings en masse. Many programs such as city recreation programs, libraries, bowling lanes, shopping, and so on, only seem to address the issue of serving individuals with disabilities on an as-needed basis, if at all.

One might argue that participating in recreational activities with others that have commonalties is not such a "bad" thing. For example, it is quite common for senior citizens to travel together on organized bus tours. The difference is that they do this by choice, but they have other options from which to choose when they want to interact or socialize with diverse groups from their community. This often is *not* the case for people with disabilities. It is not that these segregated trips for individuals with disabilities are bad in themselves. What is "bad" is that, for individuals with disabilities, these segregated opportunities are all that they have available to them: They often have no other choices.

Opportunities for recreation are increasing for individuals with disabilities, but they may not always be appropriate. If the experiences do not afford the opportunity to meet new people and to develop relationships with others who do not have disabilities, then a vital link to rejuvenating interdependently in integrated community environments is missing.

Critical Point Few recreation and leisure alternatives are available to individual with disabilities in either integrated or nonintegrated settings.

Health and Wellness

A report from the Surgeon General in 1996 emphasized that:

> Regular physical activity can help people with chronic, disabling conditions improve their stamina and muscle strength and can improve psychological well-being and quality of life by increasing the ability to perform activities of daily life.
>
> . . . People with disabilities are less likely to engage in regular moderate physical activity than people without disabilities, yet they have similar needs to promote their health and prevent unnecessary disease. Social support from family and friends has been consistently and positively related to regular physical activity.

The recommendations of this report included (1) community-based programs, (2) environments and facilities that are accessible and safe, (3) persons with disabilities who are involved in planning physical activity programs, (4) provision of quality daily physical education for youth with disabilities, and (5) discussions with parents to make sure physical activity is included in their son's or daughter's life.

The rationale for any physical activity and health and wellness program is readily available. Individuals with disabilities have lower fitness than the general population as well as more health problems. These health problems could be reduced and fitness levels improved with a moderate increase in physical activity. The report recommended community-based programming. What better support is there for a community-based leisure activity program that focuses upon moderate exercise for students with disabilities than the Surgeon General's report from the U.S. government? With improvement in cardiovascular endurance, muscle strength, and flexibility, persons with disabilities would be better able to complete daily living activities, remain in more demanding employment positions, and recreate with a wider variety of options in their leisure activities.

Critical Point Recreation and leisure are crucial in promoting health and wellness.

Community-Based Programs

Historically, individuals with disabilities have relied upon legislative mandate to secure their rights to education. However, the enactment of the Americans with Disabilities Act (ADA) signified more than the mere expansion of previous legislation for persons with disabilities. ADA spearheaded a major shift in the attitude toward individuals with disabilities. The physical and procedural alterations of the community environment to allow persons with disabilities access to community life equivalent to that of their peers who are not disabled was indicative of this major shift of attitude (Daniels, 1990). The special education initiative, particularly at the secondary level, mirrors this conceptual shift—also from focusing upon the inadequacies of the person with a disability to removing environmental barriers and providing experiences tied as closely as possible to those of their peers without disabilities (McDonnell, Wilcox, & Hardman, 1992).

In this same vein, and providing a philosophical foundation for the ADA provisions, the principle of normalization requires education approaches dictated by age-appropriate environments in contrast to traditional education, which alters the setting to fit the didactic techniques (Wolfensberger, 1972). McCord (1983) asserted that students learn appropriate skills most efficiently in settings that demand knowledge of those skills. An appropriate environment not only reinforces age-appropriate skills and social behavior, but it also provides a basis for relevant goals and objectives for instructional planning. In addition, research indicates that persons without disabilities perceive persons with disabilities as more competent when interaction occurs in an integrated community setting (Voeltz, 1984). Studies investigating interaction between students with disabilities and their peers without disabilities document positive personal outcomes for persons without disabilities, such as enhanced self-esteem, social confidence, and acceptance of diversity (Peck, Donaldson, & Pezzoli, 1990).

One basic premise of the community-based program is that when individuals have positive experiences with a group or an individual from a specific group, their attitude can change. Since many attitudes are based on hearsay and not on direct experience (Ajzen & Fishbein, 1982), providing direct experiences that are positive (Allport, 1954, 1960) for community members may be the best strategy a teacher can implement for a successful transition program. If a teacher can change the attitudes of community members, the consequences of the attitude change may be far reaching. An individual with a disability can learn leisure skills, but there must be an attitude of welcome from the community. Even more than in vocational and residential settings, the community has to provide an attitude that all members of society have the right to participate. For in leisure, if this attitude is not present, individuals with disabilities are, indeed, excluded and segregated.

Critical Point Inclusive community activities must be planned with appropriate supports in order to support leisure and recreation lifelong experiences.

Recognizing the implications of community inclusion, leaders in special education advocate for community-based curricula for secondary programs for persons with disabilities (Wehman, Moon, Everson, Wood, & Barcus, 1988). The ultimate goals for special education are adult interdependence and participation in community life, which can only be achieved by lifelong, true-to-life experiences. The current failure of special education graduates to achieve adult

Leisure and recreation skills are often neglected.

interdependence, especially in leisure and social settings, emphasizes the need for functional community-based programs. The education transition planning for adolescent students must establish linkages that will continue throughout a student's lifetime in order for a person with a disability to become a successful community member.

Essential Elements of Transition

Halpern's (1985) model of transition identified the secondary curriculum as the foundation for the three pillars of adult community adjustment: residential, employment, and social interpersonal. In practice, the bulk of transition services have focused almost exclusively upon employment experiences in the community. Transitional work experiences in the community, following employment guidelines, provide on-the-job training and continued support on an individual basis to allow secondary students with disabilities to explore employment options and to develop marketable skills prior to graduation. At the same time, however, secondary special education curriculum must retain an academic focus fostered by characteristics of the high school setting (McDonnell et al., 1991). The resulting lack of coordination between school curriculum and transitional programs hampers job placements and restricts social interaction as well as residential options. By their nature and physical location, secondary schools do not bridge the gap to adult living and working or leisure activities. When the secondary school is located in rural or small towns, the options are even more restricted. For this reason it is imperative that community-based leisure programming begin in high school transition programs.

Critical Point Individuals with disabilities typically have had little input into decisions affecting their lives.

Individuals with disabilities generally have had little input into decisions affecting their lives. Current service delivery models, federal and state legislation, and individual programming have dramatically impacted the lives of individuals with disabilities by initiating a person-centered approach. Systems influence and maintain one another. For example, legislation is built upon the current best practices of service delivery; then, programming often is mandated and supervised. IDEA (Individuals with Disabilities Education Act) emphasizes four underlying essentials for transition planning that translate readily into a real person-centered approach to service delivery. The four underlying essentials will be examined in relation to leisure/recreational activities for adolescents with disabilities in the following sections of this chapter.

Students' Needs, Interests, and Preferences

What Does IDEA Say?

The language of IDEA states, "The coordinated set of activities must: (a) be based on individual student's needs; and (b) take into account student's preferences and interests." The intent of this section of IDEA is to reinforce the fact that students with disabilities and their families are to be afforded the right (and responsibility) to become actively involved in the planning, objective development, decision-making process, and service coordination for their future. Prior to this provision of the law, teachers and other professionals commonly made prescriptive choices for the student, often out of their own convenience (Martin, Marshall, & Maxon, 1993; Wehmeyer & Ward, 1995).

Why Is It Important?

The right to freely make choices and decisions regarding one's own life is something that most Americans take for granted. Making decisions regarding ordinary life choices, unfortunately, has not been afforded to individuals with disabilities. Too often, the need to "habilitate" overrides the provision of decision-making opportunities in the lives of individuals with disabilities. When choices are provided for individuals with disabilities, the choices are often ones that have no significant impact or control over an individual's daily routine.

Critical Point Making decisions regarding ordinary life choices, unfortunately, has not been afforded to individuals with disabilities.

However, a review of the pertinent literature indicates several important factors:

1. Individuals with disabilities indeed have a preference for tasks or activities (Bambara, Ager, & Koger, 1994; Bambara, Koger, Katzer, & Davenport, 1995; Parsons, Reid, Reynolds, & Bumgarner, 1990).
2. Individuals with severe disabilities will attend to a task twice as much when they have chosen that task (Parsons, Reid, Reynolds, & Bumgarner, 1990).
3. Positive effects of choice making on increasing participation in activities were demonstrated (Bambara, Koger, Katzer, & Davenport, 1995; Dunlap, DePerczel, Clarke, Wilson, Wright, White, & Gomez, 1994).
4. Individuals provided with choices increased performance in activities and prevented or reduced problem behaviors (Bambara, Ager, & Koger, 1994; Bambara, Koger, Katzer, & Davenport, 1995; Dyer, Dunlap, & Winterling, 1993; Parsons, Reid, Reynolds, & Bumgarner, 1990).
5. Preferences for a task may be an important determinant in the effectiveness of choice making in influencing task performance (Bambara, Ager, & Koger, 1994; Parsons, Reid, Reynolds, & Bumgarner, 1990).
6. The act of choosing may be preferred over being assigned, even when assigned a preferred task (Bambara, Ager, & Koger, 1994).

"One of the simplest but frequently overlooked techniques of managing problem behavior is giving people choices . . . individuals in all kinds of social situations are likely to behave more constructively when they perceive that they have the power to make choices that are important to them. Conversely, people often behave badly when they feel "boxed in," perceiving [that] they have no choices" (Kaufman, Hallahan, Mostert, Trent, & Nuttycombe, 1993, pp. 44–45).

These studies were conducted in a variety of settings, including work, residential, and classrooms. Regardless of the setting, it remains that individual students and their families have the right to be actively involved in the planning, the decision-making process, and in everyday choices that are afforded to individuals without disabilities. Educators are well practiced in determining employment needs, preferences, and desires. Ultimately, if educators desire that their students gain a level of interdependence in the area of leisure and recreation, these same skills and knowledge need to be applied to the world of leisure.

How Do We Do It?

First, students need to have exposure to many diverse leisure experiences. How can you ask any person to choose a leisure activity if the activity is not known or not available to him or her? Individuals need to be provided real-life, age-appropriate options, with many opportunities to experience the activities. Otherwise, informed choice is just an abstract concept. Students need to experience many activities, to try them out, and to evaluate what they like or dislike. They need to begin making decisions and choices early in life. Their opinions and choices should be respected so that they learn that it is important to express their opinions and choices. Individuals with disabilities have the right to learn that consequences occur from all choices. If they make a poor choice, they are not "bad" or "dumb" because all persons make poor choices or decisions at some time or another. However, in order to learn from the real-life experiences of making decisions, individuals with disabilities need to relish or suffer the consequences of their decisions. In a school environment, supports can be provided to help students learn to make informed choices. These supports also can be a protective mechanism to ensure that students, while learning to make decisions, are still safe. As an educator, safety of your students should be a primary consideration; but it should be assured that the educator's concern for safety is reasonable and prudent and not restrictive or handicapping.

Critical Point Individuals need to be provided real-life, age-appropriate options, with many opportunities to experience the activities.

Although providing for individual choices is a must, and a best practice, we should not forget about the reasonableness of these choices. For example, depending on the part of the country you are from, surfing, downhill skiing, rock climbing, or beachcombing are viable options for leisure activities. However, would you provide a choice of beachcombing to one who is living in Kansas?

Another, yet often forgotten, factor when working with students with disabilities is that the students have the right to change their mind. Who among us does not have a tennis racquet, roller blades, or stationary bike in our basement collecting dust? After all, who has not changed his or her mind about participating or attending some leisure activity? Changing one's mind is a typical human behavior that all persons have the right to choose actively.

Critical Point Students have the right to change their mind.

Choice is also closely aligned with freedom—for choice, surely, is the essence of freedom (Warner, 1992, p. 58).

A leisure assessment should be conducted to find out interests and needs. Typically, the types of leisure assessments utilized by schools and agencies are (1) checklists of leisure activities and/or (2) pictorial representations of leisure activities. Another way to ascertain needs, interests, and preferences is to expose individuals with disabilities to a variety of leisure and recreational activities. Leisure assessment instruments will be discussed later in the chapter. However, the critical component of any assessment instrument is that it works for your students and your community. The important question that a teacher needs to ask is, "Does the information that one gets from this assessment help to provide activities for the students?"

Outcome-Oriented Process

What Does IDEA Say?

Transition services must be "designed within an outcome-oriented process." The intent of this statement within the legislation is to get teachers, parents, and other professionals to start planning for what the student, parent, and professionals want for this student over the long term. Instead of planning annual goals and short-term objectives, as educators are accustomed to doing with the Individualized Education Program (IEP), educators are required to develop plans for longer periods (one to seven years). The student's desired outcome is supposed to be at the forefront of the process in the transition planning. This long-term planning, with the student's life after high school the focus, in turn should then drive the IEP.

Why Is It Important?

Students in high school make plans on what they are going to do when they graduate. Sometimes these plans include college, technical school, getting a job, moving from the family home, or getting married. During the 1980s, professionals, families, and adults with disabilities began to realize that the current academic-based curriculum for students with disabilities was not adequate or appropriate for preparation for adulthood. Unemployment rates were extremely high, students with disabilities were dropping out of high school at higher numbers than their peers without disabilities, and students and parents were not equipped to navigate the multiple adult service agencies and did not understand the entitlement versus eligibility issue. Consequently, a change in focus from the academically based goals of the past to a functional long-term approach was propitious. With the student's long-term functional goals in mind, the academic program takes on a different perspective. To ensure successful integration into the community after graduation, the process of integration needs to occur while the student is still in high school.

Critical Point During the 1980s, professionals, families, and adults with disabilities began to realize that the current academic-based curriculum for students with disabilities was not adequate or appropriate for preparation for adulthood.

Ideally, integration into the community happens naturally throughout the childhood of the individual with a disability. Often due to family concerns, medical restrictions, societal barriers or other life factors, individuals with disabilities have little "normal" life experience. Therefore, educators have to assume that part of their role in the educational process of students with disabilities includes integration strategies and social skill development. Educators should be focusing upon building a support system, making community connections to assure that the process works. This is extremely important in community leisure and recreational programs. When dealing with residential and employment issues, one assumes that individuals have certain rights that go along with living and working in the community. However, this frequently is not extended to include recreational programs or leisure time activities. (I may work with you and even live in the same building as you, but I do not have to "play" with you.)

It is important to start making connections to the community while the student is still in secondary school. Ideally, of course, this should be a moot point. Students should have these connections to their community beginning in infancy. However, since educators are not dealing with the ideal situation, reality makes it critical that we start the process of connecting to community leisure activities and recreation programs while the student is still in school. This would provide the student with a support system in terms of school personnel and structure. The school personnel can assist the individual in learning how to make choices and to become self-confident in these choices. The school can provide the learning environment that is necessary for learning the social, psychomotor, and cognitive skills needed for learning the leisure activity. The student has the opportunity to practice appropriate social skills and to learn the nuances of social situations in leisure and recreational environments.

Critical Point It is important to start making connections to the community while the student is still in school.

How Do We Do It?

The first issue is whether the student is prepared to make decisions and choices. Does the student realize his or her options for leisure activities? Has the student tried out these options? Does the student know what he or she likes and dislikes in leisure activities? Think of the fishing tackle that is sitting in garages because people thought they would like to fish. At what level does the student want to participate? Does he or she want to be competitive? Is this a recreational pursuit or an ongoing hobby? Only after some of these questions have been explored can outcome-based objectives be written.

Critical Point Students must be provided training in choice making to be able to contribute in determining their needs and preferences.

After the students have an idea of what recreational and leisure activities they would like to pursue after graduation, then the educators should provide the skills for students and their families to initiate contacts within the community. It is important that the families and the students have these skills prior to graduation. They will be responsible for the continuation of the activities.

Another method in which the school can assist the student in connecting with the community is through instruction and advocating with community services. Community integration is not a one-way process. Educators have the responsibility of providing accurate information to the community regarding disability awareness issues. Community integration is no longer "getting the person ready" to meet the expectations of society; rather, it is a collaborative effort between the community and the students, where the community will accept the diversity of its citizens.

Critical Point Educators have the responsibility of providing accurate information to the community regarding disability awareness issues.

In order for the outcome-oriented process to be successful, it is important that teachers know the students' community, the leisure and recreational options for their students, and how to access these options. Teachers need to know their local parks and recreation administrators, YMCA, YWCA, fitness centers, sport organizations, church groups, youth leagues, and other recreational organizations. If a university, college, or community college is located in their community, the university facilities may be available for usage by community members. Community and school resources and the teacher's imagination are the only limitations to opportunities for transition teachers to implement creative and unique lessons. Special education teachers should remember that the underlying philosophy of special education is determining the students' needs and providing a program that appropriately meets those needs. Although this is a philosophy for all special education students, it is extremely important to follow through with these actions in the transition years.

Critical Point Teachers need to know and communicate with the recreation and leisure settings in their community to assure that students are provided a broad array of experiences.

Interagency Responsibility or Linkages

What Does IDEA *Say?*

Section 614(d)(1)(vii)(II) of IDEA requires that the transition statement "include, when appropriate, a statement of the interagency responsibilities or any needed linkages." The intent is to get teachers, students, and parents thinking about what kind of support services might be needed once the student leaves high school, as well as providing adult service agencies information so that they can best serve the student's needs. In addition, the intent is to begin the eligibility process for a smooth transition from high school services into adult services.

Why Is It Important?

With the narrow focus on the goals of secondary education, it was recognized that the academic-based curriculum was not preparing students with disabilities for the adult world. This was especially true for families and students who had to navigate the adult service systems. The families may be surprised to learn that the adult service systems operate much differently from the school systems. The families in many cases have spent the last 12 to 15 years in learning about the school system in order to get what their son or daughter needs in an entitlement system. They will be leaving a system with which they possibly have become comfortable, and then suddenly they are thrust into systems that are based on eligibility and availability. There are many rules, procedures, and different agencies for families to learn about within the adult service systems. If not handled appropriately, this transition can lead to loss of valuable services and training time for the students. For example, a simple process of being put on a waiting list while the student is still in high school can facilitate movement up the list while the student is still in school rather than being placed on the bottom of the list upon graduation.

Critical Point Academic-based curriculum, generally, does not prepare students with disabilities for the adult world.

Although these are important issues that families and students face, leisure and recreational pursuits are not always a priority for individuals with disabilities in adult service programs (Chadsey & Sheldon, 1998). In the individual planning process (e.g., IP, IHP, ISP, IPE, etc.),[1] leisure programming usually takes a back seat to issues of housing and employment. However, without leisure and appropriate social skills, individuals with disabilities lead a lonely, isolated, mundane life. If the educators complete their recreational assessments, provide opportunities for leisure activities, and have a community base of support, then the transition to adult life is much easier. If a transition teacher has provided an appropriate leisure skills program, then the individual will choose to participate in leisure activities. Adult service agencies will have to respond to knowledgeable and skilled individuals with disabilities in the leisure domain.

Another important aspect to the development and planning of leisure activities collaboratively with adult service agencies is interagency linkage. By planning prior to graduation, these community and adult service agency linkages can lead to a more rewarding lifestyle for the individuals receiving services. When these linkages or connections are established, information regarding housing and employment needs can be shared to provide more opportunities for those who need it the most.

Critical Point Prior to graduation, planning should focus upon developing these community and adult service agency linkages in order to facilitate a more rewarding lifestyle for the individuals who will be receiving services.

[1]Individual plan (IP); individual habilitation plan (IHP); individual service plan (ISP); individual plan for employment (IPE)

How Do We Do It?
What are the steps in setting up linkages with adult service systems? In terms of recreation and leisure, the student's needs, interests, and preferences should be shared with the adult agency. Educators need to find out what types of leisure activities are provided through the agency. Which types of leisure services are not provided? Who is the contact person (i.e., therapeutic recreation specialist)? Are there established procedures for participating in recreational programs or leisure activities? A good way to begin this process is to develop a database listing the adult service agencies, what services they provide, eligibility requirements, and specific contact information. The database can be as simple or as complex as desired. However, a simple card index with this information is all that is needed. It is important to keep the information updated, as contact personnel change. It requires educators to teach students and their families about the systems and how to make contacts independently.

Critical Point Develop a database listing the adult service agencies, what services they provide, eligibility requirements, and specific contact information.

Educators can match agencies and services to fit the leisure needs of their students. A list of contact persons given to a student can mean the difference between success and failure in connecting and becoming actively involved with the recreational community. Since the transition planning meeting can include all persons that seem to be important in developing the transition plan, educators need to invite recreation representatives to the IEP meeting. When this occurs, there is a better understanding on both sides about individual needs and services to meet recreational needs.

Movement from School to Postschool Activities

What Does IDEA Say?
IDEA requires that the transition plan focus upon movement from school to postschool activities. This means that not only do educators need to help students and families identify the adult service agencies that they may need upon graduation but that the transition process must start prior to graduation. The students should be using these services before leaving school. This will assist with the intent of a smooth transition from school activities to adult activities.

Why Is It Important?
By having school personnel available while they are trying out various community-based leisure activities, and learning to navigate the adult service systems, the students have the support of the school as a safety net to regroup and try again, in the event of a failed attempt at a community activity. It is important that the students have people around them with whom they are familiar as well. Remember, the more learning opportunities that can be provided for the students in the actual environment in which it is expected they will be performing, the more likely the students will make the transition to adult activities successfully. A smooth movement to postschool environments is facilitated by providing the student with practice in community-based leisure activities.

Critical Point One of the most important factors that educators must consider when planning or developing leisure programming for individuals with disabilities is the students' developing interests and choices.

Another reason that it is important to focus upon movement from school to postschool activities in a community-based setting is the increase in the number of contacts that the student can make while participating in the community. These contacts can increase a student's potential for success. First, community-based leisure experiences can positively impact the community's attitudes toward individuals with disabilities. This will increase the potential for successful integration as well as the potential for natural supports. Second, the more students with disabilities get out in the community and make known their abilities, skills, interests, and goals, the more potential they have for making contacts that may later lead to a job or residential opportunity. Third, community members will discover that individuals with disabilities are more like them than different from them.

Critical Point Community leisure skill practice and regular contacts with the community foster successful outcomes for students with disabilities.

How Do We Do It?

What does a teacher or administrator do to facilitate the movement from school to postschool activities? This is where the teaching strategy of community-based activities takes on a greater meaning. Not only does community-based training work for residential and vocational training, it also is imperative for postschool successful leisure activities. The more opportunities the student gets out of the school environment and practice using the available community resources, the smoother the transition will be. Leisure and recreational activities lend themselves well to community-based programming.

Another factor to be considered, particularly for students with disabilities ages 18 to 22, is that juniors and seniors without disabilities are no longer considered "peers." Most high school activities are no longer the most appropriate kinds of activities for students nearing their twenties. While integrating transition-age students into regular extracurricular school activities is a great situation for practicing social skills related to leisure, it becomes less appropriate once the students' age-peers have graduated. It is more appropriate after the age of 18 to focus upon activities in the community with individuals of similar ages and interests. For example, older transition students may have access to university facilities where their age-peers also are recreating. So, would it not be more appropriate to practice their leisure skills in that setting?

Critical Point Most high school activities are no longer the most appropriate kinds of activities for students nearing their twenties.

The four IDEA essentials in relation to leisure/recreation—(1) student's needs, interests, and preferences; (2) outcome-oriented process; (3) interagency responsibility or linkages; and (4) movement from school to postschool activities—can be implemented by special education teachers who know their school and community resources, develop innovative opportunities for their students, and believe that their students can be successful in their community. Successful transition programs are not necessarily the programs with the greatest financial resources. Successful transition programs are those that have teachers who work hard and have administrative support and collaborate with community leaders. The four essential elements of IDEA, if followed, can be the guiding light to a transition leisure program that will impact your student's adult life.

Leisure Program Options

Numerous programs and agencies provide services to individuals with disabilities. Many of these agencies provide regular or therapeutic recreational programs for individuals with disabilities who are receiving services within their agencies. However, these programs may be segregated programs held at convenient times for staff. The following sections describe the types of programs and how, because of collaborative efforts, recreational opportunities should be available for individuals with disabilities.

Independent Living Programs

Independent living programs are designed to have persons with disabilities live outside their family home but in a less restrictive environment than that of a group home or other communal setting for persons with disabilities. The setting may be an apartment or house, with or without supervision from paid staff, and located in any type of community (see Chapter 15). Often there will be two individuals living in the same apartment or house. Options for leisure activities vary greatly from program to program. Some independent living programs provide many opportunities for recreation, whereas others provide only a minimal offering. Examples of leisure activities include parks and recreation regular programming, parks and recreation therapeutic programming, special "Boy or Girl" Scout troops, fitness centers, and other club organizations in the community. Communities sometimes provide individuals with disabilities free admission to high school or university sporting events on a regular basis. Transportation is a major obstacle for individuals living in a community with limited supervision. Other alternatives include utilizing family members, paid staff, or public transportation to address commuting. Moving within a reasonable walking distance also may increase the likelihood of the individual gaining access to clubs and other organizations.

Critical Point Transportation is a major obstacle for individuals living in a community with limited supervision.

Developmental Disability Programs

Developmental Disability (DD) programs are usually a single point of entry for individuals with mental retardation and developmental disabilities. These DD programs can be inclusive from birth to death. When leisure programs are offered for individuals receiving services from the DD programs, frequently they are self-contained or segregated—even when in a community setting. The DD programs often hire therapeutic recreation specialists to run their leisure programs. The programs consist of a variety of activities, including Special Olympic training, dances, ceramics, open gym nights, fitness activities, aquatics, and numerous others. Many times these programs could not be implemented without paid staff and/or volunteers. If the DD program is unable to fund the staff, then these programs are discontinued.

Critical Point DD programs offer a wide variety of services that meet the needs of youth and adults with disabilities.

Mental Health Programs

Mental health programs also vary in their approach to leisure activities and recreational programs. Many of these programs are emotionally therapeutic in nature. In other words, they focus upon cognitive and behavioral learning to deal with fears, anxieties, and phobias surrounding community interactions. The therapeutic approach is generally classroom-type counseling with "mock" interactions and practice, with a gradual reentry into community activities. Often leisure opportunities are limited for individuals with mental health problems because recreational activities are segregated: (1) by the agency and (2) by the community. Historically, individuals with mental health issues have had a more difficult time integrating into the community due to society's fear of "mental patients."

Parks and Recreation

City or county parks and recreation departments offer therapeutic recreation programs for individuals with disabilities as well. Depending on the park and recreation budgetary constraints, the programs offered can be extensive. However, unless a parent or individual with a disability enrolls specifically in regular recreational programs, the person will be steered to the therapeutic recreation programs, which are typically segregated. In one parks and recreation exemplary program, a parent wanted the five-year-old daughter to be in the regular dance class offered for children ages 4 to 5. The parks and recreation department was aware of its obligation under the law, so the student enrolled in the dance class. The psychomotor and behavioral skills of the student with a disability were assessed as below age level.

The student's attendance in the program was impacting the dance class negatively in terms of behavior and teacher attention to the rest of the students. Rather than asking the student with a disability to withdraw from the dance class, the parks and recreation department hired an assistant for the dance instructor. This was a successful accommodation for a student and one that impacted all the students in the class. The student with a disability was impacted well into her transition years because she had the opportunity to participate with her peers in a regular community-based setting. The other nondisabled peers also benefited by having access to a wide range of associates with whom to interact.

Other

Other recreation program alternatives can be found in local resource guides, such as the yellow pages in phone books, which list youth organizations and centers, fitness centers, scouting organizations, church groups, park and recreation departments, and social service agencies. Depending on the organization, the mechanism for running these programs varies slightly. These programs are planned for the general populace and add or design specialized programs to fit the needs of individuals with disabilities. Sometimes the organization will permit staff from a school or agency that provides services for individuals with disabilities to use their facilities for free or for a nominal fee.

Each type of organization has its own staffing and funding systems in place. The staff education requirements vary within recreational programs. A few require a therapeutic recreation specialist degree from an accredited university. Many will accept any related degree that could include physical education, special education, or even social services. Other recreation programs will hire anyone who applies and is willing to work. Funding is a big issue for most cities, states, agencies, and schools. However, with the support from federal legislation, specifically the ADA, individuals with disabilities have the right to access and participate in leisure activities. Programs that are involved in leisure activities are typically aware of their obligation to provide access and services to individuals with disabilities. However, some of these programs still must be prodded into provision of those services.

Implementation of Leisure Programs

Community Awareness and Models of Service Delivery

In conjunction with determining and developing the leisure options for individuals with disabilities, community awareness has to be provided. The transition teacher requires a working knowledge not only of work and residential options, but also of the leisure activities and recreation programs that are available in their community. The program choices that are available may not be the problem; the problem may be societal acceptance. Emphasis on community awareness is extremely important. Your community may have a mayor's council for disability awareness or other similar programs. This is an appropriate avenue to get the school, community, and service organizations involved in disability awareness programs.

Teachers need to concentrate on the principles of generalization and durability (i.e., students learn best when they actually must use their skills) in least restrictive, most normal settings. Leisure skills and recreational programming can easily occur in the most normal setting when the foundations of community awareness have been established. Administrators in the public schools need to understand the transition provisions in IDEA, which require community instruction, the environment that is most normal and easily argued as the least restrictive.

Critical Point Teachers need to concentrate on the principles of generalization and durability in the least restrictive, most normal settings.

There are three models of service delivery for leisure programs (Schleien, Green, & Heyne, 1993). The first is called *reverse mainstreaming*. The program is structured to meet the needs of individuals with disabilities. Individuals without disabilities are usually asked to participate. Reverse mainstreaming does provide opportunities for interactions with persons without disabilities but usually does not promote long-term types of interactions. One benefit of this type of program is the availability of professional staff to assist with programming. The second model for leisure programming is called *integrated generic mainstreaming*. This model is founded on the premise that the regular leisure program is provided for all individuals, with accommodations only being made for those who require some assistance. These programs have a larger menu with respect to all programs that are available to all community members. However, the cost of a single accommodation may limit the resources of the entire recreational program. Typically, staff trained in therapeutic recreation or adapted physical education are not available for these types of programs. The third model for leisure programming is called *zero exclusion programs*.

Ideally, these programs are based on a collaborative effort between professionals in the regular recreation and therapeutic recreation departments. The focus is on an integrated, normalized setting with natural supports and accommodations as required. Again, there is little evidence of long-term alliances being forged between individuals with disabilities and individuals without disabilities. It would be wonderful to think that students with disabilities have a right to participate in all leisure activities in all possible situations; however, with rights there is responsibility.

Critical Point The three models of service delivery for recreation and leisure are reverse mainstreaming, integrated generic mainstreaming, and zero exclusion programs.

CASE STUDY A

An example of a viable and inexpensive approach to providing students with opportunities to experience a variety of leisure activities that are typically not available was developed through a collaborative effort between a university and an agency. The agency had a therapeutic recreation program and the university had preservice university students and facilities. The problem for the therapeutic recreation program in their annual assessment of students and adults with disabilities was the limited knowledge and exposure to different types of leisure activities. Their primary exposure was through Special Olympics. It was decided that individuals with disabilities who were interested in participating would be provided an opportunity to experience three different leisure activities each week. The adapted physical education class was to develop three lesson plans each week to provide minimal instruction and opportunity for the individuals with disabilities to participate actively. The criteria were established that the activities had to be age-appropriate and could not be repeated within the semester time frame. Some activities that the adapted physical education students provided were boccie, walleyball, racquetball, Ping Pong, line dancing, miniature golf, flying disc golf, and more traditional activities of basketball, softball, and weight training. Overall, 30 activities were used to provide the individuals with disabilities a foundation upon which to base preferences and choices. The collaborative effort also provided opportunities for the university students to work with individuals with disabilities in order to find the commonalties rather than the differences. This approach was extremely effective during discussions with the individuals with disabilities in the determination of leisure activities within the therapeutic recreation department. The knowledge base of the individuals with disabilities had been increased. They could make an informed choice about what they did and did not want to do with their leisure time based on actual experiences in a fun and successful environment.

Roles and Responsibilities

School Responsibilities

Administrators of special education programs are usually anxious about increased liability for leisure programs, especially when they involve community-based training. The community-based programming must be part of the student's IEP. The individualized community-based leisure program should be clear and concise regarding who, what, when, and where services are delivered. If students have recreation and leisure activities incorporated into their IEP, insurance will cover community-based training (McDonnell et al., 1991).

Special education transition teachers should receive ongoing training in the provision of community-based leisure programming. Training must include methods to increase student safety. For example, having a formal procedure in place so that all students riding in a car or van to a community outing must have their seat belt buckled before starting the vehicle is a smart practice. In most physical activities, there is an inherent risk of injury that is not commonly associated with classroom tasks. Teachers need to be aware about the added risk of movement activities in terms of student accidents. Teacher training in procedures that must be followed in regard to any emergency should be documented and reviewed annually. Teachers should have a method to document student progress in the community-based leisure setting. Often, because it is a leisure activity, progress is not documented like other academically oriented tasks.

Critical Point The school's insurance needs to cover any community-based instruction, especially if the activity is included in the IEP.

An extremely important component to community-based leisure training is transportation. How will the student get to the location? Will the teacher be required to drive? What vehicle is to be utilized? In many cases, the answer is simple. Educationally, the best mode of transportation would be one that the student can access and participate in learning how to use. Having the student use a municipality-run bus or train system might be a preferred educational alternative. This could be accomplished by targeting utilization of the mass transit as a training program or an IEP objective to facilitate independence. Although this method of transportation might be one that allows for more potential problems, independence is more readily fostered when the student has learned to perform the activity on his or her own.

In another instance, the school may need to provide the transportation. In some school districts, teachers can drive (check with your school district policy) if they are properly licensed and in good standing. On the other hand, some school districts will let only their bus drivers transport students. This increases the cost of community-based programming dramatically.

Sometimes a big yellow bus arrives with four students and one teacher. However, teachers are under the constraints of their school policy. The vehicle that is to be used can vary with each school. We believe that it is prudent not to use a privately owned vehicle. Depending on the insurance company, liability and coverage can be rendered void in some instances if a teacher transports students in his or her car. The bus, van, or car needs to have documented history of maintenance (usually a state requirement). Procedures for transporting any school-age students must be rigorously followed. This is a protection for the student, teacher, administrator, and school district.

Generally, teachers are protected when they drive students to community-based sites: If the teacher obeys the rules of the road and makes decisions based on what others would do in the same circumstance, then liability insurance will cover the teacher. However, if the teachers are negligent in their duties (i.e., running a stop sign or not having students buckled into their seats), then liability insurance will not provide the necessary protection. The bottom line for administrators is to make sure that (1) liability insurance coverage is adequate and current, (2) school personnel have the proper credentials and in-service training, and (3) transportation is appropriate and properly maintained.

Critical Point Various methods can be utilized in gaining transportation access to recreation and leisure activities. The preferred method should be one that the student can perform independently.

Teacher Responsibilities

The teacher who is providing a program in the community for the first time may be scared or inadequately prepared. The teacher may not want to take students with disabilities into the community nor to deal with community attitudes toward individuals with disabilities. It is uncomfortable for everyone when a manager, store owner, or agency asks you to leave a location. Sometimes this happens because a student is exhibiting inappropriate behavior, or other patrons feel uncomfortable, or because of society's ignorance of the law and/or disabilities. Like most new situations, the teacher will overcome this anxiety quickly. The teacher's responsibilities in leisure community-based training include teaching students appropriate leisure skills, expecting students to act and interact appropriately, supervising student safety, making sure the student wants to do the activity, monitoring student progress, acting in a prudent manner in all situations, and ensuring positive interactions with the community members in order to change attitudes positively toward individuals with disabilities. A teacher needs to remember that a student should never be forced to participate in a leisure activity; encouraged, yes, but forced, no.

Critical Point Teachers are the primary conduit for achieving recreational and leisure goals and they should be well-versed in operating community-based activities.

Student Responsibilities

The student with disabilities has a responsibility to learn the leisure skills, to participate, and to interact appropriately. In a community-based setting, it is important that the student wants to be there and to participate. The student also has the responsibility for saying "No" when he or she does not want to take part in the activity. For example, "Today, I do not want to go swimming." The student should be informed and understand the consequences of his or her choices.

Supposing you have tried and failed again and again. You may have a fresh start any moment you choose, for this thing that we call "failure" is not the falling down, but the staying down (Mary Pickford, cited in Warner, 1992).

Individualized Leisure Planning and Supports

Generally, students with disabilities will be engaged enthusiastically in leisure activities when the student has had a choice in the activity. An important consideration for students with disabilities when making their choices is to remember whether that activity is a viable option for the student. For example, golf may be the activity of choice, but if greens fees are beyond the means of the student and his or her family, is it worth the time or is it fair to the student and the teacher? However, this does not mean that you cannot experiment with activities in which your students are not normally engaged. Teachers should be aware of family resources, long-term participation opportunities, and availability of needed supports.

Planning

Preparation for recreation and leisure pursuits for everyone needs to start early in the student's life. This is a developed attitude toward attaining and maintaining a level of physical and psychological wellness. However, this is a difficult task for transition-age students with disabilities, who, due to numerous factors, have not been actively involved with leisure activities or recreational programming. Collaboration with families, friends, and community agencies is critical to developing a positive attitude toward leisure and recreational pursuits for this age group.

CASE STUDY B

One parent of an adult child with a severe disability was frustrated that her son only participated in leisure activities if she initiated the activity and participated with him. She realized that this was not "normal" for a 20-year-old young man. Plus, their interests did not always match—she was not much interested in attending drag races and monster truck rallies, and he was not amused by window shopping. So, as difficult as it was for her initially, she paid a male acquaintance, who was a college student around the same age as her son, to take him places. They went fishing and to gun shows, to movies, out to eat, and so on. Not only did this give her some respite from the caregiver role, but also her son was extremely pleased to participate in activities of his liking. The college student was happy to have some extra spending money. Much to everyone's pleasant surprise, the "paid friend" relationship developed into a true friendship. They now continue their relationship, doing things and going places together, and the "paid friend" even attends family functions such as Christmas and birthdays.

Prior to the individual planning meeting, assessments and conversations with the student and parent should focus on leisure activities. The student, through the combined efforts of the school and parents, should be exposed to a variety of age-appropriate community-based leisure activities. Exposure and opportunities to experience leisure activities give the student a knowledge base on which to determine preferences and choices. This is vital for attaining accurate and reliable information from the student. Many activities sound good or look good on paper, but being involved as an active participant can help to determine whether an activity is liked or disliked.

Taking a systematic approach best completes the development of leisure activities and recreational programs. The teacher and parents can survey the community to determine community-based options. This can begin by asking friends and relatives, looking in the yellow pages of the phone book, visiting the local parks and recreation department, YMCAs, YWCAs, and other social service agencies that focus upon leisure activities and recreational programming.

Community Leisure Supports

We believe that the principal reason that individuals with disabilities fail in the process of community integration is the lack of natural community supports. Teachers are primed to provide support systems in vocational placements. This typically does not carry over into residential placements or leisure activities. The lack of natural supports does not prevent residential placements because supports and linkages are discussed in the planning process. Parents often play an integral part in residential "supervision" or adult service agencies will pay staff to provide assistance. These essential individuals will assure that the student with a disability has his or her laundry done, groceries bought, and meals prepared. The same does not apply for recreational programming.

Memberships may be purchased to local health or fitness centers. A paid staff or family member may accompany the student for the first few times. Then, they expect the training or orientation to carry over because the student is independent in the setting. The student can perform all the needed skills to be successful in that setting. However, the student may refuse to go and the parents and the professionals feel defeated. The failure is not due to the training, the parents, or even the professionals. The failure occurs when the natural support network is not established for the individual with a disability. A collaborative effort of family, friends, and teachers needs to be established to support that individual in the community leisure setting. For the leisure program to be successful, the student should have fun and friends to accompany him or her in the leisure activity. The challenge for professionals is to develop a network that will sustain itself for the individual with a disability.

CASE STUDY C

A new high school special education teacher entered her classroom of profoundly retarded teenagers and was frustrated that her students did not know what to do with themselves during free time. They did not know how to initiate activities nor how to choose a desired activity when presented with choices. To make matters worse, there was very little in the way of things to choose from, and the school was on an extremely limited budget (and so was she!). But she wanted to teach the students that when they finished their work, they could be rewarded with free time, and she wanted to teach them how to fill their free time. So, she started by purchasing a deck of cards and a basketball. When the students finished their task, they were allowed to choose between playing cards or playing ball and were expected to follow through with their choice. The teacher gradually added equipment, materials, and supplies to the repertoire over the course of 2 years. They have options of playing cards, ball, board games, looking at photo albums, making crafts, writing, flying kites, going for walks outside, and so on. She made a wallet-sized notebook of pictures of each of the activity options. And now, after introducing activities one at a time in conjunction with the picture representation, the students not only can choose between two activities, but they can choose an activity from the laundry list of activities in the notebook. They are developing preferences for activities and are now learning to initiate filling their free time.

Assessment

Assessment is a critical component to the special education process. Teachers need assessment information for individual education/transition planning. Assessment is a critical component to the leisure or recreational area of transition of youth with disabilities. The problem, as outlined in the following paragraphs, is how to conduct the assessment with virtually little in the way of instrumentation and a lack of real-life experiences of individuals with disabilities. Other than limited, adapted physical education classes, where the focus is on motor skill development or team sports, individuals with disabilities do not know how to spend their leisure time.

Information that is important when trying to ascertain leisure skills and interests include leisure interests, leisure participation history, current activity patterns, family and friend involvement in leisure pursuits, medical considerations (i.e., limitations and precautions), and strengths and weaknesses in leisure and social skills.

Leisure assessment instruments are either checklists, pictorial representations of checklists, and an observation or verbal report. The checklists can be lists of any known activity. The evaluator will sit with a student and quiz him or her on what he or she would like to do. For example, "Do you like to play basketball?" "Do you like to fish?" "Do you like to play badminton?" The student responds accordingly (usually with a "yes") and often does not have any idea what the activity actually entails. After responding "yes" to many of the items, the student realizes that he or she should say "no" to some; so, the student responds according to expectations with a few "nos." The diligent teacher will ask each student every item on the pages of the activities listed, whether or not it is appropriate. Another often used approach is termed the "menu approach." The school has only four leisure options available for students with disabilities. These are bowling, basketball, track and field, and aquatics. The students get to make a choice and the majority wins. However, typically, the school will only offer one option per semester.

Critical Point Leisure assessment instruments consist of checklists, pictorial representations of checklists, and an observation or verbal report.

In another local situation, a high school special education teacher uses home-school "journaling" to communicate to parents the progress that is being made at school, as well as relating daily activities for those students who are nonverbal. The teacher also can communicate when more medication, or a change of clothes is needed at school, as well as to find out about things that are happening at home that might be affecting the student's behavior. While this teacher provides spiral steno notebooks for each student, one parent has purchased a diary-type journal to use so that they can save the memories.

Another method for assessment in the leisure area is asking parents what their child likes to do in his or her free time. Parents often are surprised about this question being asked. Teachers frequently are surprised by the activities that their students are involved in at home. For example, a 17-year-old female student colors in a coloring book and listens to records all evening. If the teacher probes, the parents might indicate that their daughter chooses to do this every evening. The next logical question to the parents should be "What are the other options from which she can choose?"

A method used frequently by teachers is direct observation. Through observation of students over a period of time, the watchful teacher can tell you what each student prefers to do in his or her leisure time (at school). Of course, this requires that the teacher allow free time and provide plenty of options from which the students can choose during this free time. It may even require that the teacher teach the student how to make a decision regarding the choices.

Of course, this seems to be the best-guess method of assessing the leisure area. For the question to professionals is, "How can a student make a choice or respond to interest inventories with limited leisure experiences on which to base the choices?" If you remember the typical response from a student with a developmental disability to the question, "Where do you want to work?" The typical response is "McDonalds." Do all students with developmental disabilities want to work at McDonalds? Probably not, but based on their experiences of seeing an individual with a disability work at the local McDonalds; commercials on television suggesting individuals with disabilities can work there; questions from professionals asking if they want to work at a place like McDonalds; and the place where they probably eat the most often—their choice, based on their life experiences, is McDonalds. The authors believe (based on our experience) that limited exposure is the cause of many individuals with developmental disabilities selecting bowling as their preferred leisure activity. This lack of experience may be the reason that many leisure assessments, without some prior groundwork, are not valid. It may be reliable, though, because you may get the same response year after year.

To provide a more valid method of assessing leisure activity for your students and assessing their actual skill ability, select a variety of leisure activities for your students to try. Make each activity fun. After utilizing this leisure sampling technique, ask the student questions about preferences from the assortment of checklists and pictorial questionnaires.

Critical Point Teachers need to assure that students learn skills that are functional and beneficial in their own community and that the students do not exhibit behavior that would draw undue attention to themselves.

Conclusion

Meaningful leisure activities are a vital component in the balance of anyone's life. We know this not only because of the importance of leisure in our own personal lives, but also because IDEA has mandated that we consider this aspect in the lives of our students. When teachers seriously take their commitment to helping students reach their potential, in all areas of their lives, students with disabilities can only benefit. Since people with disabilities typically have more leisure time, it becomes even more important to consider the leisure aspect of the student's life. Teachers need to assess student's leisure interests and skills, teach appropriate leisure and social skills, and link students up with appropriate community activities and organizations. Remember, not only is it okay to have fun; it's necessary!

Study Questions

1. Why is it important to implement and/or access leisure activities for individuals with disabilities?
2. Why is it imperative that leisure activities for students with disabilities are implemented in the community?
3. What are the four principles of IDEA? What are the implications of these principles for leisure activities for individuals with disabilities?
4. What are the procedures for individualizing leisure activities for individuals with disabilities?
5. What are the various perspectives of community-based leisure programming? What are the implications of these perspectives?

Websites and Addresses

Check out the following web sites and addresses for a listing of leisure and therapeutic recreation assessments with individuals to contact for further information.

Therapeutic Recreation
www.recreationtherapy.com/trnet/trnassess.htm

American Association Health, Physical Education, Recreation, and Dance
www.aahperd.org

One-Handed Keyboard
www.infogrip.com

Lifting Aids
www.blvd.com/blf

AbleInform Newsletter
www.sasquatch.com/ableinfo

Recreation Therapy
http://www.recreationtherapy.com

Canine Companions
http://caninecompanions.org/

Watchminder
www.watchminder.com/index.htm

Brain Injury Links
www.biawa.org/tbi.html

Communication Aids
http://peabody.vanderbilt.edu/projects/proposed/asttech/commaid/comaid.htm

Fishing Program
www.castforkids.org

Adaptive Equipment
www.achievableconcepts.com.au

Leisure Activity Profile:
Total Leisure Counseling, Inc.
2730 Wilshire Boulevard, Suite 350
Santa Monica, CA 90403

Leisure Diagnostic Battery:
Division of Recreation and Leisure Studies
Box 13875, NT Station
Denton, TX 76203

Leisurescope:
Leisure Dynamics
1425 Timber Valley Road
Colorado Springs, CO 80919

Appendixes

Appendix

A

Life-Centered Career Education

Transition Model and Competencies

FIGURE A–1
Curriculum/LCCE Transition Model

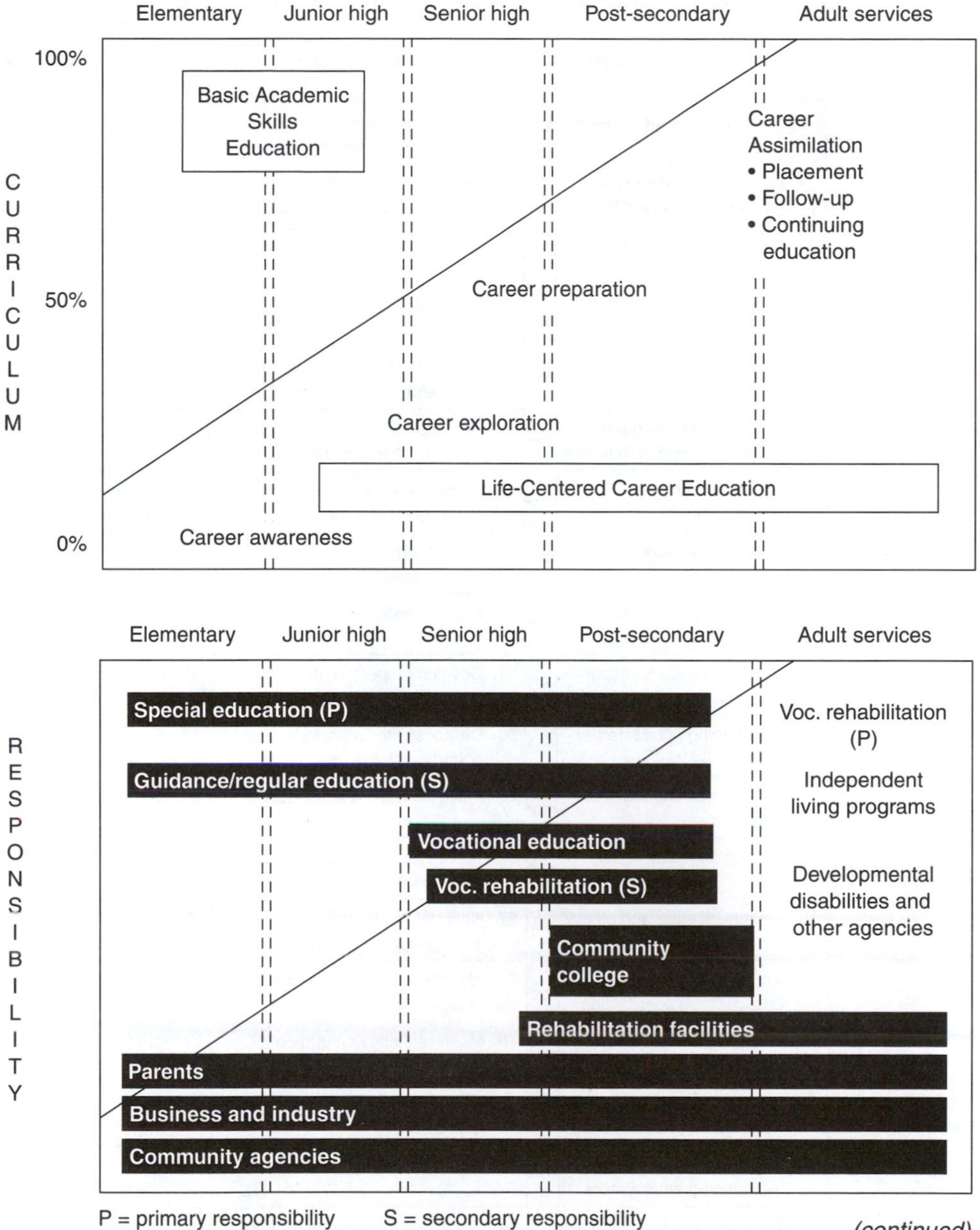

(continued)

Source: From *Life-centered career education: professional development activity book* (p. 43) by the Council for Exceptional Children, 1993. Reston, VA: The Council for Exceptional Children. Copyright 1993 by the Council for Exceptional Children. Reprinted by permission.

FIGURE A–2 *(continued)*
Life-centered Career Education Competencies

Curriculum area	Competency	Subcompetency: The student will be able to:	
Daily Living Skills	1. Managing personal finances	1. Count money and make correct change	2. Make responsible expenditures
	2. Selecting and managing a household	7. Maintain home exterior/interior	8. Use basic appliances and tools
	3. Caring for personal needs	12. Demonstrate knowledge of physical fitness, nutrition and weight	13. Exhibit proper grooming and hygiene
	4. Raising children and meeting marriage responsibilities	17. Demonstrate physical care for raising children	18. Know psychological aspects of raising children
	5. Buying, preparing, and consuming food	20. Purchase food	21. Clean food and preparation areas
	6. Buying and caring for clothing	26. Wash/clean clothing	27. Purchase clothing
	7. Exhibiting responsible citizenship	29. Demonstrate knowledge of civil rights and responsibilities	30. Know nature of local, state, and federal governments
	8. Utilizing recreational facilities and engaging in leisure	33. Demonstrate knowledge of available community resources	34. Choose and plan activities
	9. Getting around the community	38. Demonstrate knowledge of traffic rules and safety	39. Demonstrate knowledge and use of various means of transportation
Personal-Social Skills	10. Achieving self-awareness	42. Identify physical and psychological needs	43. Identify interests and abilities
	11. Acquiring self-confidence	46. Express feelings of self-worth	47. Describe others' perception of self
	12. Achieving socially responsible behavior—community	51. Develop respect for the rights and properties of others	52. Recognize authority and follow instructions
	13. Maintaining good interpersonal skills	56. Demonstrate listening and responding skills	57. Establish and maintain close relationships
	14. Achieving independence	59. Strive toward self-actualization	60. Demonstrate self-organization
	15. Making adequate decisions	62. Locate and utilize sources of assistance	63. Anticipate consequences
	16. Communicating with others	67. Recognize and respond to emergency situations	68. Communicate with understanding
Occupational Guidance and Preparation	17. Knowing and exploring occupational possibilities	70. Identify remunerative aspects of work	71. Locate sources of occupational and training information
	18. Selecting and planning occupational choices	76. Make realistic occupational choices	77. Identify requirements of appropriate and available jobs
	19. Exhibiting appropriate work habits and behaviors	81. Follow directions and observe regulations	82. Recognize importance of attendance and punctuality
	20. Seeking, securing, and maintaining employment	88. Search for a job	89. Apply for a job
	21. Exhibiting sufficient physical-manual skills	94. Demonstrate stamina and endurance	95. Demonstrate satisfactory balance and coordination
	22. Obtaining specific occupational skills		

3. Keep basic financial records	4. Calculate and pay taxes	5. Use credit responsibly	6. Use banking services	
9. Select adequate housing	10. Set up household	11. Maintain home grounds		
14. Dress appropriately	15. Demonstrate knowledge of common illness, prevention and treatment	16. Practice personal safety		
19. Demonstrate marriage responsibilities				
22. Store food	23. Prepare meals	24. Demonstrate appropriate eating habits	25. Plan/eat balanced meals	
28. Iron, mend, and store clothing				
31. Demonstrate knowledge of the law and ability to follow the law	32. Demonstrate knowledge of citizen rights and responsibilities			
35. Demonstrate knowledge of the value of recreation	36. Engage in group and individual activities	37. Plan vacation time		
40. Find way around the community	41. Drive a car			
44. Identify emotions	45. Demonstrate knowledge of physical self			
48. Accept and give praise	49. Accept and give criticism	50. Develop confidence in oneself		
53. Demonstrate appropriate behavior in public places	54. Know important character traits	55. Recognize personal roles		
58. Make and maintain friendships				
61. Demonstrate awareness of how one's behavior affects others				
64. Develop and evaluate alternatives	65. Recognize nature of a problem	66. Develop goal-seeking behavior		
69. Know subtleties of communication				
72. Identify personal values met through work	73. Identify societal values met through work	74. Classify jobs into occupational categories	75. Investigate local occupational and training opportunities	
78. Identify occupational aptitudes	79. Identify major occupational interests	80. Identify major occupational needs		
83. Recognize importance of supervision	84. Demonstrate knowledge of occupational safety	85. Work with others	86. Meet demands for quality work	87. Work at a satisfactory rate
90. Interview for a job	91. Know how to maintain postschool occupational adjustment	92. Demonstrate knowledge of competitive standards	93. Know how to adjust to changes in employment	
96. Demonstrate manual dexterity	97. Demonstrate sensory discrimination			
There are no specific subcompetencies as they depend on skill being taught				

Source: From *Life-centered career education: A competency-based approach* (4th ed., pp. 12–13) by D. E. Brolin, 1993. Reston, VA: The Council for Exceptional Children. Copyright 1993 by The Council for Exceptional Children. Reprinted by permission.

Appendix B

Glossary of Terms Commonly Used in Transition Planning

Accommodation Refers to any alteration of existing facilities or procedures to make them readily accessible to persons with disabilities.

Adult Services Refers to the many agencies and programs that are provided to adults with specific needs such as disability, health, and income.

Advocacy Speaking on behalf of another person or group of persons.

Age of Majority The age that the state has determined persons able to make decisions on their own (usually age 18) unless determined incompetent to do so by a court of law.

Agency Fairs A panel and/or exhibits designed to acquaint participants with the services, eligibility requirements, and referral procedures of adult service agencies.

Aptitudes The particular strengths, knowledge, or skills that a person has, generally related to an occupation or career.

Apprenticeships Periods of part-time work experience that may extend to a year or more, usually associated with a specific occupation.

Audiologist A person who is qualified to assess a person's hearing and provide interventions to improve it.

Backward Planning A step-wise planning process that starts with desired goals and plans backward to the current level of functioning and support.

Bureau of Employment Services A program that helps individuals find jobs through job listings, computer services, and counseling.

Career Development Index *See* Career Maturity Index.

Career Fairs Panels and/or exhibits designed to provide information on a range of careers.

Career Maturity Index This assessment, along with the Career Development Inventory (1990), can direct counseling (or the use of a computerized DISCOVER program) to address competencies in the areas of student, leisurite, citizen, worker, and homemaker.

Career Planning Refers to the general planning process related to helping the individual develop and achieve meaningful adult roles. Transition planning is a specific form of career planning.

Career Portfolios Organized samples (often a notebook) of student work—and classroom activities that include writing samples, photographs, videos, and other demonstrations of student performance.

Career Portfolio Assessment A standardized method of assessing the student's career portfolio activities by measuring mastery (e.g., novice, apprentice, expert) or level of independence.

Case Manager A person from an agency who is responsible for seeing that services are obtained and coordinated for an individual.

A transition coordinator is a form of case manager.

ChoiceMaker A self-determination approach that focuses on: (a) choosing goals, (b) expressing goals, and (c) taking action.

COACH A form of person-centered planning that stands for Choosing Options and Accommodations for Children. Includes the family's values and dreams in IEP planning.

Career and Technical Education The educational system that used to be known as vocational education, which includes high school vocational programs, 2+2 programs, and some postsecondary career education programs.

Community College A postsecondary education program (generally 2-year) that leads to an occupation or entrance into a university.

Course of Study Refers to the type of educational program that a student is enrolled in including vocational education, college preparation, and apprenticeships.

Ecological Models A model that focuses on individuals and stresses working with all of the environments that affect their lives.

Education of All Handicapped Children Act Landmark 1975 legislation that required education for all students with disabilities and introduced the terms IEP, Least Restrictive Environment, Free Appropriate Public Education, and the Multi-factored Evaluation to Education.

Eligibility A set of rules that determine whether students or families are qualified to receive services based on the nature and severity of the disability, income, or other characteristics.

Employability Life Skills Assessment This criterion-referenced checklist may be used yearly to assess a student's level of performance in 24 critical employability skills areas in the domains of personal, social, and daily living habits.

Employment Specialist In supported employment, a person who provides job placement, training, and sometimes follow-along services to a worker with a disability. Sometimes used interchangeably with job coach.

Empowerment Education and practices aimed at transferring power to or strengthening individuals and groups.

Enclave A form of supported employment where a group of no more than eight persons with disabilities work in an integrated employment setting often with professional supervision.

Entitlements Programs that must be provided to all eligible persons upon demand. Special education and Social Security are entitlements; many adult services are not.

Follow-Along Services In supported employment this term refers to services and supports provided to a worker with a disability after job training is completed.

DD *See* Developmental Disability.

Developmental Disability A disability that is acquired during the period the person is developing, generally before age 21 or at birth, and that significantly impacts several life activity areas such as self-care, self-direction, learning, mobility, speech, and independent living.

FAPE *See* Free Appropriate Public Education.

Free Appropriate Public Education The requirement, introduced by the EHA of 1975, that requires schools to provide an education relevant to the needs of students with disabilities. The courts have generally stated that appropriateness does not mean optimal, only that the student is progressing at a reasonable rate.

Functional Vocational Evaluation Evaluation that focuses on identifying skills demonstrated by the student in actual vocational and life activities. Situational and work assessments are functional. IQ tests and tests of standardized reading levels are not.

Goals 2000: Educate America Act of 1993 Legislation that established eight educational goals that state and local education agencies were to achieve by the year 2000.

Group Action Planning A self-determination approach that helps students take charge of personal futures planning.

Guardian A person or agency that assumes limited or unlimited authority to make decisions for a minor or an adult who has been determined to be incompetent in a court of law. Includes medical guardianships, guardianship of the person, and guardian of the estate.

Guidance Counselor A person who is qualified to assess an individual's career interests and provide counseling and support in making career decisions.

HUD *See* Housing and Urban Development.

Housing and Urban Development A federal program that provides or funds subsidized housing for low-income persons.

IDEA *See* Individuals with Disabilities Education Act.

IEP *See* Individualized Education Program.

IEP/Transition Meeting The meeting in which transition is discussed. This meeting should occur *no later than age* 14 to discuss the student's course of study, and *no later than age* 16 to discuss services and supports needed to achieve the student's desired postschool outcomes.

IEP/Transition Plan *See* Transition Plan.

ILC *See* Independent Living Center.

Impairment Related Work Expense Certain expenses for things a person with a disability needs because of his/her impairment in order to work may be deducted when determining eligibility for SSDI or SSI.

Inclusion The process of including students with disabilities in the environments, activities, and curriculum of typical students and persons. Inclusion may mean different things to different people. Sometimes used interchangeably with the term "integration."

Independent Living Centers Established by the Rehabilitation Act in response to consumer and People First Movements. ILCs are run predominately by consumers and can fund or support accommodations in vehicles and housing to make persons with disabilities more independent.

Individuals with Disabilities Education Act An updated version of the Education of All Handicapped Children's Act (EHA) that required the statement of needed transition services as part of the IEP in 1990.

Individualized Education Program A statement of the programs and services that will be provided to a student with a disability that is eligible under the IDEA.

Individualized Service Plans Plans developed for specific individuals that describe services provided by an agency to help an individual achieve desired goals. These include Individual Habilitation Plans (MR/DD), Individual Work Related Plans (VR), Individual Plans for Employment (VR).

Informational Interviews Interviews with employers to find out about their organization, jobs, and the types of people they employ.

Integration In the disability context, the process of including persons with disabilities in the environments, activities, and social networks of typical persons. Sometimes used interchangeably with the term "inclusion."

Internship *See* Apprenticeships.

IPLAN A form of person-centered planning that stands for Inventory, Plan, Listen, Ask, and Name your goals.

IRWE *See* Impairment Related Work Expense.

Job Analysis The process of analyzing a job in terms of essential elements, skills needed, and characteristics to aid in job matching and training.

Job Carving A technique used in advanced supported employment programs where a job is divided into components that can be done by a person with a severe disability.

Job Coach *See* Job Trainer.

Job Placement The process of helping an individual find a job.

Job Trainer In supported employment, generally a paraprofessional who provides on-site job training and supports to a worker with a disability. Sometimes used interchangeably with "employment specialist" or "job coach."

Job Shadowing The practice of allowing a student to observe a real work setting to determine their interest and to acquaint them with the requirements of the job.

Job Sharing The practice of having two or more persons share a job to provide accommodations in work scheduling or job duties.

Language Specialist *See* Speech Pathologist.

Least-Restrictive Environment A concept introduced to education by the EHA in 1975 that required a continuum of services for students with disabilities so that they could be educated in as integrated an environment as possible while still providing FAPE.

Life-Centered Career Education This career development approach delineates 22 major competencies that can be infused into primary, middle, and secondary curricula to address the major life domains of work, home, and academics.

Life Style Planning A form of person-centered planning that describes future goals and defines the steps needed to reach them.

LRE *See* least-restrictive environment.

Mainstreaming A term that was used widely in the 1970s to refer to the practice of placing students with disabilities in the regular education curriculum. This term lost favor when it was found that many students were being placed in regular classes without needed supports.

Making Action Plans (or formerly McGill Action Planning System—MAPS) A person-centered planning approach that focuses on seven areas: (a) nonnegotiables, (b) strong preferences, (c) highly desirables, (d) personal characteristics, (e) personal concerns, (f) needed supports, and (g) action steps.

Medicaid A health care program serving eligible low-income persons with disabilities whose income and assets are below specific levels. Generally, available to persons receiving SSI or SSI work incentives.

Medicare An insurance program serving persons 65 and older and individuals with disabilities regardless of income if they are eligible for SSDI.

Mental Health Services Services provided to persons with significant behavioral or mood disorders that are not related to mental retardation or developmental disabilities.

Myers-Briggs This assessment identifies four personality temperaments that can be used to develop self- and career awareness (e.g., extroverted, intuitive, feeling, perceptive—ENFP).

MFE *See* Multifactored Evaluation.

MH *See* Mental Health Services

MH/MR In some states mental health and mental retardation and developmental disability services are combined and referred to as MH/MR.

Mental Retardation and Development Disability Services Services that are provided to persons with disabilities that were identified at birth or before age 21. In some states referred to as Developmental Disability Services.

Mobile Work Crew A supported employment placement where a group of no more than eight persons provide contract services to businesses (e.g., janitorial, landscaping), usually under the supervision of a professional.

MR/DD *See* Mental Retardation and Development Disability Services.

Multifactored Evaluation Introduced by the EHA of 1975. An evaluation by a variety of professionals to determine whether a student is in need of special education services. Originally, required before entering special education and every 3 years thereafter. With the

IDEA of 1997, the MFE was changed to include assessment by nonprofessionals and parents.

Natural Supports Refers to the use of persons, practices, and things that naturally occur in the environment to meet the support needs of an individual.

Next S.T.E.P. A field-tested student-directed transition approach that consists of 16 lessons that address: (a) getting started, (b) self-exploration and evaluation, (c) developing goals and activities, and (d) putting a plan into place.

Occupational Work Adjustment A program that places a person in jobs or environments in order to develop appropriate work and social behaviors.

Occupational Work Experience Refers to programs that allow a person to try one or more jobs for periods of a year or less in order to explore interests and develop job skills.

Occupational Therapist A person qualified to develop and implement programs, develop fine motor skills and skills and accommodations related to work and daily living.

PASS *See* Plan for Achieving Self-Support.

People First A movement of persons with disabilities that started in the late 1970s to take greater control of programs affecting them. Originated the concept of person-first language.

Person-Centered Planning Refers to a number of planning approaches that tailor services and supports to meet the needs of the individual, as opposed to programs that try to fit individuals into available services.

Person-First Language The practice of referring to persons with disabilities with the term denoting disability following and not supplanting terms referring to them as an individual (e.g., a person with a visual impairment, a person who uses a wheelchair). Person-first avoids impersonal, negative, and medical terminology (e.g., the disabled, cripples, retardates).

Personal Futures Planning A type of person-centered planning that involves dreaming, describing, and doing with the family and their support system.

Physical Therapist A person qualified to develop and implement programs to develop fine and gross motor skills and rehabilitation services to persons with physical disabilities.

Plan for Achieving Self-Support A savings account that can be excluded from income and assets of persons with disabilities to allow them to save up for something that would make them self-sufficient (e.g., college fund).

Postsecondary Education Educational programs that follow high school, including colleges, universities, technical and vocational schools, and community colleges.

Postsecondary Programs Programs that occur after high school (secondary education).

Proficiency Tests Tests that are designed to determine if students are measuring up to educational standards set by the state and/or district.

Psychologist A person who is qualified to assess an individual's emotional, intellectual, and coping skills and provide counseling or interventions to improve them.

Psychiatrist A medical doctor who can assess an individual's emotional, intellectual, and coping skills and typically provides medical interventions or medications to improve them.

Referral The process of notifying an agency to request services. A referral is often followed by an eligibility determination.

Rehabilitation Services Commission A name for the agency that oversees the provision of vocational rehabilitation services in Ohio.

Rehabilitation Technologist A person qualified to apply technology to meet the needs of persons with disabilities.

Related Services Services that are not necessarily educational in nature, but that are provided as part of an educational program. Speech, language, hearing, social work, and psychology services are examples of related services.

SCANS Report *See* Secretary's Commission on Achieving Necessary Skills.

School-to-Work Programs Refers to general education secondary programs developed under the School-to-Work Opportunity Act that include career education, work-based instruction experiences, and efforts to connect students with vocational and postschool programs.

Secretary's Commission on Achieving Necessary Skills Report Competencies identified by employers that will be needed by workers of the future.

Section 8 Housing Refers to housing subsidized by Housing and Urban Development (HUD).

Self-Advocacy The ability and opportunity to speak on behalf of oneself.

Self-Determination Refers to the ability and the opportunity for students to make decisions for themselves.

The Self-Directed Search This instrument identifies six personality types and matches them with six matching categories of jobs to help students make a career choice related to their needs and preferences.

SGA *See* Substantial Gainful Employment.

Social Security Administration The agency that oversees the provision of Social Security Disability and Supplemental Security income and related work incentives.

Social Security Disability Insurance In this context, a monthly check provided to children of parents who have retired or become disabled and have paid into Social Security. Only paid to individuals whose income falls below SGA after accounting for work incentives.

Social Worker A person employed by a school or agency to help individuals, families, or groups in coping with their environments and obtaining needed services.

Speech Pathologist A person who is qualified to assess a person's speech and provide interventions to improve it. Sometimes referred to as a language specialist.

SSA *See* Social Security Administration. Sometimes used to refer to SSDI payments.

SSI *See* Supplemental Security Income.

SSDI *See* Social Security Disability Insurance.

Subsidized Housing Generally HUD housing where a person pays rent based on income (e.g., 33% of income).

Substantial Gainful Employment The amount of income a person can make after a trial work period and still receive SSDI payments.

Summer Youth Employment Programs Subsidized summer employment for low-income youth, and sometimes youth with disabilities, through the Work Incentive Act.

Supplemental Security Income An income support payment administered by the Social Security Administration that is provided to children with disabilities and adults who are disabled and whose income and assets fall below a prescribed level after accounting for Social Security work incentives.

Supported Employment A form of employment where training is done at the job site and ongoing supports are provided to maintain employment. Supported employment is meant for persons with the most severe disabilities. Supported employment jobs are in integrated settings and may consist of individual placements, mobile work crews, or enclaves.

Supports Refers to accommodations, persons in the environment, or practices that help an individual in conducting life activities, including employment.

Standards-Based Reform Refers to school accountability efforts to assure that all students attain a common standards and a level of proficiency defined by the state or district.

Statement of Needed Transition Services *See* Transition Plan.

Student Earned Income Exclusion Income that can be excluded for a student under age 22 in calculating SSI benefits.

STW *See* School-to-Work.

Take Charge A student-directed collaborative approach that pairs youth with adults of the same gender with similar challenges, and uses four primary strategies: (a) skill facilitation, (b) mentoring, (c) peer support, and (d) parent support to develop student skills in achievement, partnership, and coping.

Tech-Prep A coordinated curriculum in the final 2 years of high school with a planned transition to a postsecondary institution, usually for an additional 2 years in a technical or health field.

Technical Schools Refers to educational programs that lead to certification in a highly specialized vocation such as electrical engineer.

Technology Refers to machines, services, and adaptations that allow the individual to better control their environment.

Transition The process of moving from adolescence to adult roles where the child reconciles their needs, interests, and preferences with adult norms and roles.

Transition Coordinator A person or agency responsible for assuring that planned services are provided in a timely manner and in a way that complements other services provided to a student.

Transition Plan Also known as the Statement of Needed Transition Services or Individual Transition Plan (ITP). The IEP/transition plan states in the IEP what services, supports, and activities will be provided to students to help them reach their career goals.

Transition Planning The process of helping students and their families plan services to help them reach career goals and adult living objectives related to their needs, interests, and preferences. The IDEA requires transition-planning activities documented in the IEP for students aged 14 and older.

Transition Planning Inventory An inventory approach that focuses on student skill and support needs in the areas of: (a) employment, (b) further education, (c) daily living, (d) leisure activities, (e) community participation, (f) health, (g) self-determination, (h) communication, and (i) interpersonal relationships.

Trial Work Period The amount of time that an individual receiving SSDI can exceed SGA without losing benefits (currently up to 9 nonconsecutive months in a 60-month period).

Vocational Education Refers to secondary and postsecondary programs that teach skills related to specific occupations. Also referred to as "career and technical education."

Vocational Rehabilitation Services A federal and state program that provides a range of services to persons with disabilities, typically to achieve a particular career goal.

VR *See* Vocational Rehabilitation Services

Waiting List A list of persons who have been determined eligible for services that are in short supply and cannot be provided until openings arise or services are expanded.

What Color Is Your Parachute This publication provides an overview of career development and some useful exercises and examples related to identifying interests, researching jobs, developing resumes, and conducting interviews.

Whose Future Is It Anyway? A self-determination curriculum designed for persons with cognitive disabilities that consists of 36 lessons that address: (a) self-awareness, (b) making decisions, (c) obtaining supports and transition services, (d) writing and evaluating transition objectives, and (e) leadership skills.

Work Adjustment *See* Occupational Work Adjustment.

Work Experience *See* Occupational Work Experience.

Work Incentives A number of Social Security work incentives that allow a person to exclude part of his or her income to maintain eligibility for SSI or SSDI. Includes PASS, IRWEs, Student Earned Income Exclusion, and extended eligibility for Medicaid.

Work Study Jobs developed by the high school where the student receives credit toward graduation.

Workforce Investment Act A 1998 Act of Congress that brought a number of job service programs together as part of "One Stop Shops." Covers the old Job Training Partnership, Rehabilitation Services (that still maintains separate offices), and the Bureau of Employment Services.

Appendix

C

Sample Blanket Release of Information and Member Agreement

SUMMIT COUNTY LOCAL INTERAGENCY TRANSITION TEAM
CONSENT FOR RELEASE OF INFORMATION

______________________ Youth - Full Name

______________________ Date of Birth

______________________ Social Security Number (Optional)

______________________ Student/Case Number

The following agencies have my permission to share information for the purpose of helping the student/youth move from school to adult services and to reduce paperwork:
(Please check or cross out any agencies you do ***not*** *want to share information)*

- ☐ Akron Child Guidance Center
- ☐ The Summit County Health Department
- ☐ The Summit County Health Department
- ☐ County of Summit Board of Mental Retardation and Developmental Disabilities
- ☐ Summit County Children Services
- ☐ The Summit County Department of Human Services
- ☐ The Private Industry Council
- ☐ Rehabilitation Services Commission
- ☐ The Department of Youth Services
- ☐ Public School Systems (specify): ______________________

I authorize sharing of the following information: (circle yes or no and initial)

yes	no	______	Identifying Information: name, birth date, sex, race, address, telephone number, social security number, disability, type of services being received and name of agency providing services to me or the individual named above.
yes	no	______	Case Information: the above Identifying Information, plus medical and social history, treatment/service history, psychological evaluations, Individualized Education Plans (IEPs), transition plans, vocational assessments, grades and attendance, and other personal information regarding me or the individual named above. Information regarding the following shall not be released unless initialed below: ______ HIV and AIDS related diagnosis and treatment ______ Substance abuse diagnosis and treatment

I understand that the Consent for Release of Information expires 180 days from the date it is signed (*). I also understand that I may cancel this Consent for Release of Information at any time by stating so in writing with the date and my signature. This does not include any information which has been shared between the time that I gave permission to share information and the time that it was canceled.

This consent expires on,______________ 20 ___

______________________ Signature of person authorized to consent

______________________ Relationship to Youth

______________________ Signature of Individual

______________________ Date

______________________ Witness/Agency Representative

______________________ Date

* This release of information will expire in 90 days for information concerning substance and alcohol abuse diagnosis and treatment.

CONSENT FOR RELEASE OF INFORMATION

I understand that my signing or refusing to sign this consent will not affect public benefits or services that I am otherwise entitled to.

CASE INFORMATION:

If the release authorized the disclosure of **Case Information**, consent to such disclosure may include the following types of information, if they are in the files of the agency releasing the information.

1. **Educational records**, including but not limited to the results of diagnostic evaluations, teacher observations, vocational assessments, grades, attendance, individualized education programs (IEPs) and transition plans.
2. **Medical records**, including but not limited to the results of physical and mental examinations, diagnoses of physical and mental disorders, medication history, physical and mental health status and history, summary of treatment or services received, and summary of treatment plans and treatment needs.
3. **Psychological and medical testing**, including but not limited to any IQ tests or other tests, of cognitive or emotional or mental status, and any reports of physical tests such as x-rays, CT scans, diagnostic blood testing, or other results.
4. **HIV, AIDS, and AIDS related diagnoses and test results**, including information about treatment planned and received. (This information will be disclosed only if page 1 is initialed to permit it.)
5. **Drug and alcohol abuse diagnoses and treatment**, including but not limited to results of evaluations, diagnoses, treatment and services received, treatment plans and treatment needs. (This information will be disclosed only if page 1 is initialed to permit it.)
6. All records of services provided by Summit County Children Services except child abuse investigation reports.
7. **Second-hand information** may require an additional release of information from the original source.

TO ALL AGENCIES RECEIVING INFORMATION DISCLOSED AS A RESULT OF THIS SIGNED CONSENT:

1. If the records released include information of any diagnosis or treatment of drug or alcohol abuse, the following statement applies:

   Information disclosed pursuant to this consent has been disclosed to you from records whose confidentiality is protected by Federal law.

   Federal regulations (42 CFR Part 2) prohibit you from making any further disclosure of it without the specific written consent of the person to whom it pertains, or as otherwise permitted by such regulations. A general authorization for the release of medical or other information is NOT sufficient for this purpose.

2. If the records released include information of an HIV-related diagnosis or test result, the following Statement applies:

   > This information has been disclosed to you from confidential records protected from disclosure by state law. You shall make no further disclosure of this information without the specific, written, and informed release of the individual to whom it pertains, or as otherwise permitted by state law. A general authorization for the release of medical or other information is NOT sufficient for the purpose of the release of HIV test results or diagnoses.

Agencies and/or individuals added to the release will be apprised of the Summit County LITT "Member Agreement for Information Sharing"

SUMMIT COUNTY INTERAGENCY TRANSITION TEAM
Member Agreement for Information Sharing

Member Agencies:

Alcohol, Drug Addiction, Mental Health Service Board (ADAMH)
Summit County Health Department
Akron Public Schools
Stow City Schools
Hudson Local Schools
Nordonia Local Schools
County of Summit Board of Mental Retardation and Developmental Disabilities
Summit County of Children Services
Department of Youth Services
Department of Human Services
Private Industry Council
Rehabilitation Services Commission

This agreement is by and among the member agencies comprising the Summit Local Interagency Transition Team.

This agreement is entered into for the benefit of those who seek to share information without risk of liability from unauthorized release, and for the benefit of students and their families who wish to receive, without unreasonable diminution of their rights of privacy and avoidance of self-incrimination, the improved services which information sharing may produce. The Summit LITT agencies agree to:

1. Share information regarding students in compliance with the "Summit County Local Interagency Transition Team Consent for Release of Information" (here in after "Consent") signed by each student and by his/her parent or guardian if under the age of 18, **unless greater release of information is otherwise required or authorized by law.**
2. Use information only for the purpose of improving the quality, efficiency or coordination of the delivery of transition services to the youth and his/her family. **No information first obtained from the consent may be used or transmitted by a member agency for the purpose of criminal investigation, prosecution, or sentencing, except as required by law or judicial order.**
3. Establish internal management systems to help assure that information-sharing activities will be limited to the terms of this agreement and of the student's Consent and will promptly cease upon expiration or revocation of the Consent.
4. Forward a copy of the signed Consent to all member agencies identified on the Consent.
5. Forward immediately to all member agencies any written notice of revocation of a student's Consent which it may receive.
6. Execute this agreement with all above-named member agencies. Member's information-sharing privileges under this agreement shall extend only to sharing agencies identified in the Consent.

This Agreement shall continue in force and effect for a period of one year, automatically renewed unless earlier terminated. This agreement may be terminated by any member agency, upon written notice. Any amendment to this agreement shall be executed in writing by all member agencies.

AGREED:

____
____
____
____
____
____
____
____

Member Agency — Date

Appendix D

Self-Survey of Transition Practices

SURVEY OF TRANSITION PRACTICES

Purpose. The goal of this survey is to obtain information on transition practices relating to the Individuals with Disabilities Education Act (IDEA) Amendments of 1997.

Demographic Information-Students and parents-fill out letters A-D and G-K. Educators and adult service providers-fill out letters A-K.

A: The person(s) completing this survey (CHECK ALL THAT APPLY):

- ❑ administrator
- ❑ special education coordinator
- ❑ VOSE coordinator
- ❑ option IV coordinator
- ❑ work study coordinator
- ❑ special education teacher
- ❑ vocational education teacher
- ❑ regular education teacher
- ❑ school psychologist
- ❑ parent/guardian
- ❑ student
- ❑ other: ____________________

B: My school setting is: (CHECK ONE THAT BEST APPLIES):

❑ rural ❑ suburb of city of 100,000 or more ❑ small city up to 100,000 ❑ large city more than 100,000

C: My school/district is: (OPTIONAL): ______________________________

D: The county(s) I work with is (are): (LIST ALL IN THE SPACE PROVIDED BELOW):

____

E: What is the number of students <u>you</u> serve and their age breakdown? (GIVE BEST ESTIMATE FOR EACH CATEGORY):

- ❑ total served by you each year= ______
- ❑ 19-22 years (_____%)
- ❑ 17-18 years (_____%)
- ❑ 15-16 years (_____%)
- ❑ 13-14 years (_____%)
- ❑ less than 13 years (_____%)

F: What is the breakdown of disability categories for students you serve? (GIVE BEST ESTIMATES):

- ❑ specific learning disabilities-LD (____%)
- ❑ developmental disabilities-DH (____%)
- ❑ multiple disabilities-MH(_____%)
- ❑ orthopedic disabilities-OH(_____%)
- ❑ severe behavior disabilities-SBH (____%)
- ❑ hearing impairments (_____%)
- ❑ visual impairments (_____%)
- ❑ traumatic brain injury (_____%)
- ❑ autism (_____%)
- ❑ other health impaired (_____%)
- ❑ other ______________ (_____%)

G: The ethnic breakdown of students you serve (GIVE BEST ESTIMATES):

- ❑ White (_____%)
- ❑ Hispanic (_____%)
- ❑ African-American (_____%)
- ❑ NativeAmerican (_____%)
- ❑ Asian (_____%)
- ❑ Other (_____%)

H: How many hours of transition training have you had to date (CHECK BEST ESTIMATE):

- ❑ zero hours
- ❑ 1-2 hours
- ❑ 3-5 hours
- ❑ 6-8 hours
- ❑ 9-15 hours
- ❑ more than 15 hours

I: In the past 3 years, what kinds of transition training have you had? (CHECK ALL THAT APPLY):

- ❑ in-house training
- ❑ in-service training (e.g., SERRC, Project LIFE)
- ❑ transition college coursework
- ❑ other ____________________

J: What role do you have in transition planning? (CHECK ALL THAT APPLY):

- ❑ no role in transition planning
- ❑ provide transition services
- ❑ attend IEP/transition meetings
- ❑ coordinate IEP/transition meetings
- ❑ supervise transition staff/planning
- ❑ other ____________________

K: Does your school/district have an interagency transition team?

❑ Yes ❑ No ❑ Don't Know

Directions. This survey is divided into five transition planning and service sections: (A) parent notification, (B) participation in meetings, (C) IEP content, (D) agency responsibility, and (E) other transition practices. For each section, a range of strategies (e.g., 1a - 1e) are described that school districts might use to implement the transition component of IDEA. The response options, defined below, are based on the assumption that some strategies are used more often and others only in special circumstances.

1 = Almost Never **2 = Sometimes** **3 = Frequently** **4 = Almost Always**

Circle the number (e.g., 1 - Almost Never, 4 - Almost Always) for each activity listed under each question.

A: PARENT NOTIFICATION:

1. Parents are notified of the IEP meeting in which transition is discussed using the following strategies:

(a) mailing a standard form letter or memo.	1 2 3 4
(b) mailing a personalized letter.	1 2 3 4
(c) contacting the parent at home or work over the telephone.	1 2 3 4
(d) asking the student to remind their parent of the upcoming transition IEP meeting.	1 2 3 4
(e) sending a notice of the meeting home with the student.	1 2 3 4
(f) other (specify):______________________________.	1 2 3 4

2. If communication is not established through the first parent notice, alternative steps are taken to inform parents of the upcoming meeting:

(a) mailing the notice to a different address.	1 2 3 4
(b) calling at varying times - weekdays, evening, or weekends.	1 2 3 4
(c) making a home visit.	1 2 3 4
(d) contacting a parent through a relative.	1 2 3 4
(e) contacting the parent through a community service agency provider.	1 2 3 4
(f) other (specify): ______________________________.	1 2 3 4

3. A mutually agreed upon time and location for the IEP meeting in which transition is discussed is determined by:

(a) contacting the parent prior to sending out the parent notice.	1 2 3 4
(b) sending out a notice that offers the parent a choice of times.	1 2 3 4
(c) sending out a notice that offers the parent a choice of locations.	1 2 3 4
(d) records are kept of attempts to arrange a mutually agreed upon time and place by attaching personal notes, logs or standardized forms to the IEP or records folder.	1 2 3 4
(e) other (specify): ______________________________.	1 2 3 4

Parent Notification (continued)

1 = Almost Never *2 = Sometimes* *3 = Frequently* *4 = Almost Always*

4. If no parent can attend the IEP meeting in which transition is discussed, the methods used to involve parents in planning include:

(a) holding an individual meeting with the parent.	1 2 3 4
(b) a telephone conference call.	1 2 3 4
(c) an invitation to parents to submit their input in writing.	1 2 3 4
(d) mailing a draft of student transition goals and objectives to the parent for review and feedback.	1 2 3 4
(e) encouraging the parent to have a family friend or some other advocate attend in their absence.	1 2 3 4
(f) other (specify): ______.	1 2 3 4

5. The district assures that parents understand the proceedings of the IEP meeting in which transition is discussed using the following strategies:

(a) notifying parents prior to the meeting by telephone or mail.	1 2 3 4
(b) disseminating information to parents on the transition planning process.	1 2 3 4
(c) providing formal workshops for parents of transition-age youth.	1 2 3 4
(d) providing informal consultation to parents upon request individually or in small groups.	1 2 3 4
(e) explaining the pamphlet "Whose IDEA Is It?" to the student/parent.	1 2 3 4
(f) other (specify): ______.	1 2 3 4

Parent Notification Comments: ______

______

______

______

B: PARTICIPATION IN MEETINGS - student/agency participation

1 = Almost Never *2 = Sometimes* *3 = Frequently* *4 = Almost Always*

6. Students are invited to participate in their IEP meetings in which transition is discussed using the following practices:

(a) a verbal invitation from a staff member.	1 2 3 4
(b) a formal notice (e.g., memo or letter) sent directly to the student.	1 2 3 4
(c) other (specify): ______.	1 2 3 4

1 = Almost Never *2 = Sometimes* *3 = Frequently* *4 = Almost Always*

7. Do the following school representatives attend the IEP meeting in which transition is discussed?

(a) regular education teacher (if student is or might be in regular education classes).	1 2 3 4
(b) at least one special education teacher.	1 2 3 4
(c) a representative from the local educational agency who is qualified and knowledgeable about the general curriculum and special education resources.	1 2 3 4
(d) an individual who can interpret evaluation.	1 2 3 4
(e) other (specify): ______.	1 2 3 4

8. By no later than age 16, agencies (e.g., vocational rehabilitation, social security, mental retardation/developmental disabilities, mental health) are encouraged to participate in student IEP meetings in which transition is discussed using the following strategies:

(a) parent or student request for agency representative to participate in IEP meeting in which transition is discussed.	1 2 3 4
(b) standard form letter or memo of invitation.	1 2 3 4
(c) unstandardized letter or memo drafted individually by a staff member.	1 2 3 4
(d) verbal invitation over the telephone or in person.	1 2 3 4
(e) maintaining regular contact with the service agencies over time.	1 2 3 4
(f) other (specify): ______.	1 2 3 4

9. If an agency invited to send a representative does not do so, the following steps are taken to obtain their participation in the planning of transition services:

(a) a copy of the IEP/transition plan is forwarded to the agency.	1 2 3 4
(b) a subsequent meeting is arranged with the agency to discuss students' transition needs.	1 2 3 4
(c) the agency is contacted via telephone or mail to find out their agreement to provide services.	1 2 3 4
(d) other (specify): ______.	1 2 3 4

10. Preferences, and interests of students are incorporated into the IEP using the following strategies:

(a) verifying with the student verbally that their preferences are incorporated in each transition goal.	1 2 3 4
(b) reviewing student survey results regarding their preferences as each goal is being drafted.	1 2 3 4
(c) obtaining feedback regarding IEP content from adults who are knowledgeable about the youths preferences, needs, and interests.	1 2 3 4
(d) student led IEP meeting where students describe and discuss their goals.	1 2 3 4
(e) formal surveys, interviews, or having someone represent the student if they cannot be at their meeting.	1 2 3 4
(f) other (specify): ______.	1 2 3 4

Participation in Meetings Comments: ____
____
____
____

C: CONTENT OF IEP:

11. By age 14, or earlier if determined appropriate by the IEP team, the IEP/transition plan specifies services needed (e.g., readers, instructional adaptations, more time to take tests) that focus on the general course of study for individual students (e.g., such as participation in advanced-placement courses or a vocational education program)?	1 2 3 4

12. Starting at the age of 16, or earlier if determined by the IEP team, students have a statement of needed transition services that includes:	
(a) instruction.	1 2 3 4
(b) related services.	1 2 3 4
(c) community experiences.	1 2 3 4
(d) development of employment or postsecondary education objectives.	1 2 3 4
(e) development of other postschool adult living objectives (e.g., community participation, residential).	1 2 3 4
(f) other (specify): ________________________________.	1 2 3 4

13. Starting at the age of 16, if appropriate, do students have a statement of needed transition services that includes:	
(a) acquisition of daily living skills.	1 2 3 4
(b) functional vocational evaluation.	1 2 3 4
(c) a statement of interagency responsibilities or any needed linkages.	1 2 3 4
(d) other (specify): ________________________________.	1 2 3 4

14. By the age of 17, the IEP includes a statement that the students and their parents have been notified in writing of the transfer of rights to students at the age of 18 in the areas of:	
(a) due process.	1 2 3 4
(b) IEP requirements.	1 2 3 4
(c) placement.	1 2 3 4
(d) eligibility.	1 2 3 4
(e) other (specify): ________________________________.	1 2 3 4

1 = Almost Never *2 = Sometimes* *3 = Frequently* *4 = Almost Always*

15. Do students with disabilities participate in general State and district-wide assessment programs (9th and 12th grade) with:	
(a) no special training or accommodation.	1 2 3 4
(b) with tutoring to prepare for test.	1 2 3 4
(c) with additional time.	1 2 3 4
(d) with a reader.	1 2 3 4
(e) with use of technology.	1 2 3 4
(f) other (specify): ______.	1 2 3 4

Content of IEP Comments: ______

______

______

D: AGENCY RESPONSIBILITY:

16. If a participation agency fails to provide agreed-upon transition services contained in the IEP:

(a) the local education agency reconvenes the IEP team for the purpose of identifying alternative strategies to meet the transition objectives and, if necessary, revise the student's IEP.	1 2 3 4
(b) a different agency or agency representative is asked to deliver the services in question.	1 2 3 4
(c) an alternative plan for meeting the identified needs is developed with the same agency representative.	1 2 3 4
(d) the IEP goal or objective in question is modified or removed because no other agency is available to deliver the service.	1 2 3 4
(e) other (specify): ______.	1 2 3 4

Agency Responsibility Comments: ______

______

______

E: OTHER TRANSITION PRACTICES:

17. Students are provided opportunities to participate in activities designed to enhance their decision-making skills and involvement in the transition process using the following strategies:

(a) offering classes specifically designed to enhance decision-making skills.	1 2 3 4
(b) interviewing or talking with students about their goals for the future.	1 2 3 4
(c) promoting self-determination and goal setting throughout the curriculum and instructional approaches.	1 2 3 4
(d) engaging students in the dialogue during their IEP meetings.	1 2 3 4
(e) sending information home to assist parents in preparing their child for participation.	1 2 3 4
(f) using person-centered planning strategies (e.g., personal futures planning, self-determination curricula.)	1 2 3 4
(g) other (specify): ______.	1 2 3 4

1 = Almost Never	*2 = Sometimes*	*3 = Frequently*	*4 = Almost Always*

18. Programs or strategies used to involve and empower families in transition planning include:

(a) offering trainings/workshops on transition planning and related areas (e.g., residential living options, work incentives).	1 2 3 4
(b) coordinating agency fairs where families can ask questions and gather information on transition services.	1 2 3 4
(c) use of parent mentors/volunteers to provide families assistance throughout the transition process (e.g., Connecting Advisory Program).	1 2 3 4
(d) developing transition newsletters to provide current information on transition resources and services available.	1 2 3 4
(e) developing transition resource kits to provide current information on transition resources and services available.	1 2 3 4
(f) other (specify): ______________________________.	1 2 3 4

19. Do you participate on an interagency transition team in your school or district? ❑ Yes. ❑ No.

If yes, does your interagency transition team include representatives from the following areas?

(a) special education.	1 2 3 4
(b) general education.	1 2 3 4
(c) vocational education.	1 2 3 4
(d) special education administration.	1 2 3 4
(e) special education related services (e.g., occupational therapy, physical therapy, speech therapy).	1 2 3 4
(f) parents.	1 2 3 4
(g) students/consumers.	1 2 3 4
(h) adult service programs.	1 2 3 4
(i) school to work.	1 2 3 4
(j) employers.	1 2 3 4
(k) other (specify): ______________________________.	1 2 3 4

20. How much does your school/district participate in the following activities?

(a) information sharing (e.g., regularly scheduled meetings).	1 2 3 4
(b) cross-agency training (e.g., inservices).	1 2 3 4
(c) agency fairs.	1 2 3 4
(d) single referral documents.	1 2 3 4
(e) pooled funding to develop a program or hire a staff person.	1 2 3 4
(f) other (specify): ______________________________.	1 2 3 4

1 = Almost Never *2 = Sometimes* *3 = Frequently* *4 = Almost Always*

21. How does your agency conduct follow-up studies of students who have exited school?	
(a) talk to students informally.	1 2 3 4
(b) survey students 1 year after graduation.	1 2 3 4
(c) survey students 3 years after graduation.	1 2 3 4
(d) survey students 5 years after graduation.	1 2 3 4
(e) use surveys to continuously improve services.	1 2 3 4
(f) other (specify): ________________.	1 2 3 4

22. When invited, how often do the following individuals attend the IEP meeting in which transition is discussed?	
(a) students.	1 2 3 4
(b) parents/guardians.	1 2 3 4
(c) vocational education teachers.	1 2 3 4
(d) vocational rehabilitation personnel.	1 2 3 4
(e) mental retardation/developmental disabilities personnel.	1 2 3 4
(f) mental health professionals.	1 2 3 4
(g) other (specify): ________________.	1 2 3 4

Other Transition Practice Comments: ________________

THANK YOU FOR YOUR TIME!!!!

Return completed surveys to: Rachel McMahan, Transition Center, 300 White Hall, Kent State University, Kent, OH 44242

Confidentiality. Answers to these questions are for research purposes. Your identity and that of the school district and community will be kept confidential.

* This survey (1998/2001) has been adapted from the Report on the National Survey of the Implementation of the IDEA Transition Requirements by David R. Johnson, Michael Sharpe, and Mary Fox Sinclair - University of Minnesota, National Transition Network, Institute on Community Integration. Ohio's Cross-Training Committee of Project LIFE and Kent State University's Transition Center developed the 1998 version. The 2001 version was adapted by the Kent State Transition Center. Copy by permission - Transition Center, 300 White Hall, Kent State University, Kent, Ohio 44242 - (330) 672-3833.

Appendix E

Postschool Participant Phone Survey

Post School Participant Phone Survey

MARKING INSTRUCTIONS

- Use a No. 2 pencil or a blue or black ink pen only.
- Do not use pens with ink that soaks through the paper.
- Make solid marks that fill the response completely.
- Make no stray marks on this form.

CORRECT: ● INCORRECT: ✓ ☒ ◒ ◔

Interviewer: ______________________

School: ______________________

Time Spent Doing Survey: ______________

This survey was developed by the Miami Valley Transition Team and Kent State University. Copy by permission-call (330)672-0722

Fill out the following before the interview. This data can be retrieved from EMIS.

1. Year Graduated

YEAR			
0	0	0	0
1	1	1	1
2	2	2	2
3	3	3	3
4	4	4	4
5	5	5	5
6	6	6	6
7	7	7	7
8	8	8	8
9	9	9	9

2. What is the up to six digit survey code number assigned by the teacher?

This code should not be identifiable to anyone but the teacher.

0	0	0	0	0	0
1	1	1	1	1	1
2	2	2	2	2	2
3	3	3	3	3	3
4	4	4	4	4	4
5	5	5	5	5	5
6	6	6	6	6	6
7	7	7	7	7	7
8	8	8	8	8	8
9	9	9	9	9	9

3. Gender
   - ○ Male
   - ○ Female

4. Ethnicity
   - ○ Native American
   - ○ Hispanic
   - ○ African-American
   - ○ Caucasian
   - ○ Other ______________

5. How old was the student when he or she received the diploma?

0	0
1	1
2	2
3	3
4	4
5	5
6	6
7	7
8	8
9	9

6. In what type of school setting was the student educated?
   - ○ Urban
   - ○ Suburban
   - ○ Rural

7. What type of school?
   - ○ Joint Vocational School
   - ○ High School
   - ○ Other ______________

8. Disability Type (Please mark identified disability from EMIS record. Do not ask on telephone interview.)
   - ○ Autism
   - ○ Deaf-blindness
   - ○ Deafness and hearing impairment
   - ○ Mental retardation (DH, CD)
   - ○ Multiple disabilities (MH, MD)
   - ○ Orthopedic impairment (OI)
   - ○ Serious emotional disturbance (SBH, ED)
   - ○ Specific learning disability
   - ○ Speech and language impairment
   - ○ Traumatic brain injury
   - ○ Visual impairment
   - ○ Other health impaired (OHI)

9. In what types of classes did the student participate in regular classrooms 9-12th grade? *(Bubble all that apply)*
   - ○ Academics
   - ○ Vocational Classes
   - ○ Only Specials or Electives (e.g. PhysEd, Music Art)
   - ○ None. Self-contained

10. Was the student in work-study?
    - ○ Yes
    - ○ No

11. Was the student in vocational education?
    - ○ Yes
    - ○ No

    If yes, what program? ______________________

12. Was the student in Option 4 (Job Training Coordinator Services)?
    - ○ Yes
    - ○ No

IDEAs that Work

Phone Interview: (*You may paraphrase questions, if necessary*)

Hello, my name is ________ and I am a teacher at _______. We are conducting a survey to identify programs that helped our students obtain jobs or postsecondary education. Will you answer a few questions about what you (or your son or daughter) is doing now? All of your responses will be strictly confidential and no identifiable information will be on this survey.

- *If "yes" proceed with the questions.*
- *If "no" then say "Thank you for your time."*

Informant was:
- ○ Graduate
- ○ Parent/Guardian
- ○ Other: ____________

If informant was not the graduate, why?
____
____

1. When you were *in high school* did you participate in: (Bubble all that apply)

- IEP meetings ○
- School supervised paid work in the community ○
- School supervised volunteer work ○
- In-school job ○
- Job shadowing ○
- Paid work on your own ○
- Classes at a community college ○
- Extracurricular activities ○
- Vocational rehabilitation (BVR, BSVI) services ○
- MR/DD services ○
- Other school-to-career activities ○
- Specify: ____________________

2. Did the school prepare you to get a job? ○ **Yes** ○ **No**
Specify if possible: ____________________
____

3. Did you have a paying job at the time you left high school? ○ **Yes** ○ **No**
Specify if possible: ____________________
____

4. Since you *left high school* have you: (Bubble all that apply)

- Worked full-time (30 hours or more) ○
- Worked part-time (29 hours or less) ○
- Attended a 2 year college ○
- Attended a 4 year college ○
- Attended a technical school ○
- Enlisted in the military ○
- Received vocational rehabilitation (BVR/BSVI) services ○
- Received other training or services ○
- Specify: ____________________

5. Are you *currently* doing any of the following: (Bubble all that apply)

- Working full-time (30 hours or more) ○
- Working part-time (29 hours or less) ○
- Attending a 2 year college ○
- Attending a 4 year college ○
- Attending a technical (vocational) school ○
- Working in the military ○
- Receiving vocational rehabilitation (BVR, BSVI) services ○
- Receiving MR/DD services ○
- Receiving other training or services ○
- Specify: ____________________

6. If you are *currently* working, what kind of job do you have? (Bubble ONE)

- Food service ○
- Auto mechanics ○
- Computers/technology ○
- Construction ○
- Industry/factory work ○
- Marketing/sales ○
- Secretarial/clerical ○
- Janitorial/custodial ○
- Agriculture/farming ○
- Child care ○
- Cosmetology/barbering ○
- Health care ○
- Human services (counseling, teaching) ○
- Other: ____________________ ○

Continue Survey on Next Page

7. What are your *current* living arrangements? (Bubble all that apply)

- Living with parents or relative ○
- Living with no one ○
- Living with friends ○
- Living with a husband or wife ○
- Living with children ○
- Living with a foster family ○
- Living in a group home ○
- On a waiting list for residential services ○
- Other: ____________ ○

8. How do you spend your free time? (Bubble all that apply)

- Working ○
- Studying ○
- Hanging out with friends ○
- Watching TV ○
- Listening to music ○
- Playing sports ○
- Doing hobbies ○
- Going to church or religious activities ○
- Going to the mall or movies ○
- Doing outdoor activities ○
- Other: ____________ ○

9. Do you currently have: (Bubble all that apply)

- Registration to vote ○
- Medical Benefits ○
- A driver's license ○
- A car ○
- A bus pass ○
- Someone who provides transportation ○
- A computer at work/school ○
- Assistive technology (e.g.communication device) ○
- Other: ____________ ○

10. How do you pay for the things you need? (Bubble all that apply)

- Competitive Work ○
- Sheltered Work ○
- Medicaid for health expenses ○
- Family members help ○
- Disability benefits (such as SSI) ○
- Food stamps ○
- Aid to dependent children ○
- Aid in paying rent ○
- Scholarships ○
- Other: ____________ ○

11. Please rate how helpful the following school activities were to you.

	Very Helpful	Helpful	Somewhat Helpful	Not Helpful at All	No Opinion
General education academic classes	○	○	○	○	○
Special education academic classes	○	○	○	○	○
Career/technical (vocational classes)	○	○	○	○	○
Help in finding a job	○	○	○	○	○
Help in getting into college	○	○	○	○	○
Community work experiences	○	○	○	○	○
Extra curricular activities	○	○	○	○	○

Comments:

____

____

____

____

12. Please rate how satisfied you are with the following:

	Very Satisfied	Somewhat Satisfied	Dissatisfied	Very Dissatisfied	No Opinion
Your current job	○	○	○	○	○
Your current residence	○	○	○	○	○
Your current contact with friends	○	○	○	○	○
Your current transportation arrangements	○	○	○	○	○
Adult services (BVR, MR/DD)	○	○	○	○	○

Comments:

____

____

____

____

____

Sampling Procedures – General

1. Identify the population that graduated from Special Education in the years you are studying (e.g., 2002 and 2000). Do not include students who have speech only as a special education service.

2. Divide the population for each year (e.g., 2002 and 2000) by the number of students you want to try to interview for that year. (For example, to randomly select 25 students out of 200, divide 200 by 25 = 8. Choose every 8th student on 2000 list.) Repeat for the other years you are sampling.

3. For the students you have selected, complete page one of the survey from the student records and/or Ohio's Educational Management Information System (EMIS). Write down phone numbers for selected students on a separate piece of paper to ensure confidentiality of the surveys.

4. Set up a comfortable area to conduct your phone interviews. If you fail to reach a selected student, do one of the following: (a) leave a message that you will call on a given day or time, (b) try to obtain an alternative phone number for the selected student, or (c) if the selected student cannot be reached or cannot respond to the survey, ask a parent or relative whether they can provide the survey information.

5. It will be necessary for you to interview 30 of your selected students for Kent State to identify simple correlations between your school's programs and student outcomes. To develop more sophisticated analyses yielding odds ratios, you will need to interview about 100-120 selected students. If you run out of students from your first random sample, go back to the population and repeat steps 1-4 until you reach at least 15 students for each year studied.

6. Send *all* (surveys with EMIS only data *and* surveys that have been fully completed) to: Robert Baer, 300 White Hall, Kent State University, Kent, Ohio 44242-0001. On a separate sheet of paper include how many *total* students graduated from Special Education for the years you studied. Descriptive and correlational information should be returned to you in about two weeks. (Be sure to give your mailing address, fax, phone, and E-mail.)

7. If you have particular questions you want to find from the data (e.g., what were the characteristics of students with mental retardation who went on to full-time employment), E-mail or call (330) 672-0722. These consults will be provided based on available time of research staff but generally should be no problem.

Advanced Study 1 - Comparison with regular education students

1. One of the best ways of evaluating special education services is to compare outcomes with typical students who are in the general curriculum. To do so, repeat steps 1-7, drawing from the list of regular education graduates.

Advanced Study 2 – Focus on special populations

1. Because certain types of disabilities are relatively rare, you may want to conduct a focused study that selects these students. To do so, repeat steps 1-7 drawing from a list of students with the characteristic (e.g., multiple disabilities) that you would like to focus on.

Robert Baer (2003)

Robert Baer

300 White Hall
Kent State University
Kent, Ohio 44242-0001
330-672-0722

IDEAs that Work

References

Adams, G., & Englemann, S. (1996). *Research on direct instruction: 20 years beyond* DISTAR. Seattle, WA: Educational Achievement Systems.

ADAPT (Americans Disabled for Attendant Programs Today). (1999a). *Senators Harkin and Specter introduce landmark legislation, S-1935 supports real choice in the new millennium.* Denver, CO: Author.

ADAPT (Americans Disabled for Attendant Programs Today). (1999b). *Summary of Olmstead Decision.* Denver, CO: Author.

Agran, M., Snow, K., & Swaner, I. (1999). Teacher perceptions of self-determination: Benefits, characteristics, strategies. *Education and Training in Mental Retardation and Developmental Disabilities,* 34, 293–301.

Airasian, P. W. (1994). *Classroom assessment.* New York: McGraw-Hill.

Ajzen, I., & Fishbein, M. (1982). Attitude-behavior relations: A theoretical analysis and review of empirical research. *Psychological Bulletin,* 84, 888–918.

Alberto, P. A., & Troutman, A. C. (1995). *Applied behavior analysis for teachers* (4th ed.). Upper Saddle River, NJ: Merrill/Prentice Hall.

Albin, R. W., Lucyshyn, J. M., Horner, R. H., & Flannery, K. B. (1996). Contextual fit for behavioral support plans: A model for "goodness of fit." In L. K. Koegel, R. L. Koegel, & G. Dunlap (Eds.). *Positive behavioral support: Including people with difficult behavior in the community* (pp. 81–98). Baltimore: Paul H. Brookes.

Albright, L., & Cobb, R. B. (1988). Curriculum based vocational assessment. *Journal for Vocational Special Needs Education,* 10(2), 13–16.

Al-Darmarki, F., & Kivlighan, D. M. (1993). Congruence in client-counselor expectations and the working alliance, *Journal of Counseling Psychology,* 40(4), 379–384.

Allen, S. K., Smith, A. C., Test, D. W., Flowers, C., & Wood, W. M. (2001). The Effects of *self-directed* IEP on Student Participation in IEP meetings. *Career Development for Exceptional Individuals,* 24(2), 107–120.

Allport, G. W. (1954). *The nature of prejudice.* Boston: Addison-Wesley.

Allport, G. W. (1960). *Personality and social encounter.* Boston: Beacon Press.

Althen, G. (1988). *American ways: A guide for foreigners in the United States.* Yarmouth, MD: Intercultural Press.

American Council on Education. (1996). *Higher education and national affairs.* April 8, pp. 4, 6.

American Vocational Association. (1990). *The AVA guide to the Carl D. Perkins Vocational and Applied Technology Education Act of 1990.* Alexandria, VA: Author.

American Youth Policy Forum/Center on Education Policy (2002). *Twenty-five years of educating children with disabilities: The good news and the work ahead.* Washington, DC: Author.

Americans with Disabilities Act of 1990, 42 U.S.C.A. § 12101 *et seq.*

Ammons, R. B., Butler, M. N., & Herzog, S. A. (1950). A projective test for vocational research and guidance at the college level. *Journal of Applied Psychology,* 34, 198–205.

Anderson, R. J., & Strathe, M. I. (1987). Career education for special needs youth. In G. D. Meers (Ed.). *Handbook of vocational special needs education* (2nd ed., pp. 259–274). Rockville, MD: Aspen.

Anderson, W., Beckett, C., Chitwood, S., & Hayden, D. (1984). *Next S.T.E.P.: Planning for employment.* Alexandria, VA: Parent Educational Advocacy Training Center.

Armstrong, D. G. (1990). *Developing and documenting the curriculum.* Boston: Allyn & Bacon.

Arnold, L., & Martin, J. E. (2003). *Teaching IEP participation skills to students with learning disabilities and mental retardation.* Manuscript submitted for publication.

Aslanian, C. B. (1996). *Adult learning in America: Why and how adults go back to school.* Washington, DC: Office of Adult Learning Services, the College Board.

Asselin, S. B., Hanley-Maxwell, C., & Syzmanski, E. (1992). Transdisciplinary personnel preparation. In F. R. Rusch, L. DeStefano, J. Chadsey-Rusch, L. A. Phelps, & E. Syzmanski (Eds.). *Transition from school to adult life* (pp. 265–284). Sycamore, IL: Sycamore Publishing.

Asselin, S. B., Todd-Allan, M, & deFur, S. (1998). Transition coordinators: Define yourselves. *Teaching Exceptional Children,* 30, 11–15.

Association on Higher Education and Disability (AHEAD). (1987). *Unlocking the doors: Making the transition from secondary to postsecondary education.* Columbus, OH: Author.

Association on Higher Education and Disability (AHEAD). (1998). *Expanding postsecondary options for minority students with disabilities.* Columbus, OH: Author.

Astin, A. (1993). *What matters in college: Four critical years revisited.* San Francisco: Jossey-Bass.

Aune, E. (1991). A transition model for postsecondary-bound students with learning disabilities. *Learning Disabilities Research & Practice*, 6, 177–187.

Azrin, N. H., & Besalel, V. B. (1979). A *behavioral approach to vocational counseling*. Baltimore: University Park Press.

Azrin, N. H., & Phillips, R. A. (1979). The job club method for handicapped: A comprehensive outcome model. *Rehabilitation Counseling Bulletin*, 23, 144–155.

Baer, R. (1996). *The Summit County* L.I.F.E. *Project: Linkages for individual and family empowerment* (Report) Kent, OH: Kent State University, Center for Innovation in Transition and Employment.

Baer, R., Flexer, R., Beck, S., Amstutz, N., Hoffman, L., Brothers, J., Steltzer, D., & Zechman, D. (2003). A collaborative followup study on transition. *Career Development for Exceptional Individuals*, 26(1), 7–25.

Baer, R., Goebel, G., & Flexer, R. W. (1993). An interdisciplinary team approach to rehabilitation. In R. W. Flexer & P. L. Solomon (Eds.), *Psychiatric rehabilitation in practice*. Boston: Andover Publishers.

Baer, R., Martonyi, E., Simmons, T., Flexer, R., & Goebel, G. (1994). Employer collaboration: A tri-lateral group process model. *Journal of Rehabilitation Administration*, 18(3), 151–163.

Baer, R., McMahan, R., & Flexer, R. (1999). *Effective transition planning: A guide for parents a guide for parents and professionals*. Manual published by Kent State University.

Baer, R., Simmons, T., & Flexer, R. (1996). Transition practice and policy compliance in Ohio: A survey of secondary special educators. *Career Development for Exceptional Individuals*, 19(1), 61–72.

Baer R., Simmons, T., Flexer, R., & Smith, C. (1994). A study of the costs and benefits of supported employment for persons with severe physical and multiple disabilities. *Journal of Rehabilitation Administration*, 17(2), 122–131.

Baker, E. T., Wang, M. C., & Walberg, H. J. (1995). The effects of inclusion on learning. *Education Leadership*, 52(4), 33–35.

Ball-Brown, B., & Frank, Z. L. (1993). Disabled students of color. *New Directions for Student Services*, 64, 79–88.

Bambara, L. M., Ager, C., & Koger, F. (1994). The effects of choice and task preference on the work performance of adults with severe disabilities. *Journal of Applied Behavior Analysis*, 27, 555–556.

Bambara, L. M., Koger, F., Katzer, T., & Davenport, T. A. (1995). Embedding choice in the context of daily routines: An experimental case study. *Journal of the Association for Persons with Severe Handicaps*, 20, 185–195.

Barrera, I., & Kramer, L. (1997). From monologues to skilled dialogues—Teaching the process of crafting culturally competent early childhood environments. In P. J. Winton, J. A. McCullum, & C. Catlett (Eds.), *Reforming personnel preparation in early intervention* (pp. 217–251). Baltimore: Paul H. Brookes.

Bartholomew, K. (1985, November). Options for individuals. *Institutions, Etc.*, pp. 2–3.

Bates, P. (1990). *Best practices in transition planning: Quality indicators*. Carbondale, IL: Illinois Transition Project.

Bauder, D. K. Lewis, P., Gobert, C., & Bearden, C. (1997). *Assistive technology guidelines for Kentucky schools*. Frankfort, KY: Kentucky Department of Education.

Bauder, D. K., Lewis, P., & Whitlock, B. (1996). *Project future: Training personnel for the education of individuals with disabilities; Special projects* (CFDA 84.029K). Louisville, KY: enTECH.

Becker, C. W., & Carnine, D. W. (1982). Direct instruction: A behavior theory model for comprehensive educational intervention with the disadvantaged. In S. W. Bijou & R. Ruiz (Eds.), *Behavior modification: Contributions to education* (pp. 145–210). Hillsdale, NJ: Erlbaum.

Bedore-Bideaux, K. A. (1998). *Engaging self-determination in the* IEP *through student participation*. Unpublished master's thesis. Ogden, UT: Weber State University.

Behrmann, M. (Ed.). (1984). *Handbook of microcomputers in special education*. San Diego: College-Hill Press.

Behrmann, M. (1995). Assistive technology training. In K. F. Flippo, K. J. Inge, & J. M. Barcus (Eds.), *Assistive technology: A resource for school, work, and community* (pp. 211–222). Baltimore: Paul H. Brookes.

Behrmann, M., McCallen, M. H., & Morrissette, S. K. (1993). *Assistive technology issues for Virginia schools: Final report*. Submitted to the Virginia State Special Education Advisory Committee, Fairfax, VA: Virginia State Dept. of Education.

Behrmann, M. M. (1994). Assistive technology for students with mild disabilities. *Intervention in School and Clinic*, 30(2), 70–83.

Behrmann, M. M., & Schepis, M. (1994). Assistive technology assessment: A multiple case study review of three approaches with students with physical disabilities during the transition from school to work. *Journal of Vocational Rehabilitation*, 4(3), 202–210.

Beirne-Smith, M., Ittenbach, R. F., & Patton, J. R. (1998). *Mental retardation*. Upper Saddle River, NJ: Merrill/Prentice Hall.

Bellamy, T. G., Rhodes, L. E., Bourbeau, P. E., & Mank, D. M. (1986). Mental retardation services in sheltered workshops and day activity programs. In F. R. Rusch (Ed.), *Competitive employment: Issues and strategies* (pp. 257–271). Baltimore: Paul H. Brookes.

Bellini, J. (2002). Correlates of multicultural counseling competencies of vocational rehabilitation counselors. *Rehabilitation Counseling Bulletin*, 45, 66–75.

Bender, M., Richmond, L., & Pinson-Millburn, N. (1985). *Careers, computers, and the handicapped*. Austin, TX: PRO-ED.

Benz, M. R., & Halpern, A. S. (1986). Vocational preparation for high school students with mild disabilities: A statewide study of administrator, teacher, and parent perceptions. *Career Development for Exceptional Individuals*, 9(1), 3–33.

Benz, M. R., & Halpern, A. S. (1987). Transition services for secondary students with mild disabilities: A statewide perspective. *Exceptional Children*, 53(6), 507–514.

Benz, M. R., & Halpern, A. S. (1993). Vocational and transitional services needed and received by students with disabilities during their last year of high school. *Career Development for Exceptional Individuals*, 16(2), 197–212.

Benz, M. R., Johnson, D. K., Mikkelsen, K. S., & Lindstrom, L. E. (1995). Improving collaboration between school and vocational rehabilitation: Stakeholder-identified barriers and strategies. *Career Development for Exceptional Individuals*, 18, 133–144.

Benz, M. R., & Kochhar, C. A. (1996). School-to-work opportunities for all students: A position statement of the division on career development and transition. *Career Development for Exceptional Individuals*, 19(1), 31–48.

Benz, M. R., Yavonoff, P., & Doren, B. (1997). School-to-work components that predict postschool success for students with and without disabilities. *Exceptional Children*, 63(2), 151–166.

Berliss, J. R., Vanderheiden, G. C., & Borden, P. A. (1989). Campus/library information systems accessibility manual. *Journal of Rehabilitation Research & Development*, 26(suppl.), 170–171.

Berman, L. M., & Roderick, J. A. (1977). *Curriculum: Teaching what, how, and why of living*. Columbus, OH: Merrill.

Beveridge, S., Craddock, S. H., Liesener, J., Stapleton, M., & Hershenson, D. (2002). INCOME: A framework for conceptualizing the career development of persons with disabilities. *Rehabilitation Counseling Bulletin*, 45, 195–206.

Bickel, W. E., & Bickel, D. D. (1986). Effective schools, classrooms, and instruction: Implications for special education. *Exceptional Children*, 52, 489–500.

Biddle, B. J. (1979). *Role theory*. New York: Academic Press.

Biklen, D., & Knoll, J. (1987a). The disabled minority. In S. J. Taylor, D. Biklen, & J. A. Knoll (Eds.), *Community integration for people with severe disabilities* (pp. 3–24). New York: Teachers' College Press.

Biklen, D., & Knoll, J. (1987b). The community imperative revisited. In J. A. Mulick & R. F. Antonak (Eds.), *Transitions in mental retardation* (Vol. 3, pp. 1–27), Norwood, NJ: Ablex.

Bisconer, S. W, Stodden, R. A., & Porter, M. (1993). A psychometric evaluation of curriculum-based vocational assessment rating instruments used with students in mainstream vocational courses. *Career Development for Exceptional Individuals*, 16, 19–26.

Blackhurst, A. E. (1997). Perspectives on technology in special education. *Teaching Exceptional Children*, 29(5), 41–48.

Blackhurst, A. E. (1998). *Technology self-assessment for special education teachers*. Lexington, KY: Department of Special Education and Rehabilitation Counseling, University of Kentucky.

Blackhurst, A. E., Bausch, M. E., Bell, J. K., Burleson, R. B., Cooper, J. T., Cassaway, L. J., McCrary, N. E., & Zabala, J. S. (1999). *Assistive technology consideration form: The university of Kentucky assistive technology toolkit*. Lexington, KY: Department of Special Education and Rehabilitation Counseling, University of Kentucky.

Blackhurst, A. E., & Cross, D. P. (1993). Technology in special education. In A. E. Blackhurst & W. H. Berdine (Eds.), *An introduction to special education* (3rd ed., pp. 77–103). New York: HarperCollins.

Blackhurst, A. E., & Hofmeister, A. M. (1980). Technology in special education. In L. Mann & D. Sabatino (Eds.), *Fourth review of special education* (pp. 199–228). New York: Grune and Stratton.

Blackhurst, A. E., & Morse, T. E. (1996). Using anchored instruction to teach about assistive technology. *Focus on Autism and Other Developmental Disabilities*, 11(3), 131–141.

Blackhurst, A. E., & Shuping, M. B. (1990). A philosophy for the use of technology in special education. *Technology and media back-to-school guide*. Reston, VA: Council for Exceptional Children.

Blackorby, J., & Wagner, M. (1996). Longitudinal postschool outcomes of youth with disabilities: Findings from the National Longitudinal Transition Study. *Exceptional Children*, 62(5), 399–414.

Blackstone, S. (1992). For consumers: Rethinking the basics. *Augmentative Communication News*, 5, 1–3.

Blackwell, T. L., Conrad, D. A., & Weed, R. O. (1992). *Job analysis and the ADA: A step by step guide*. Athens, GA: Elliot & Fitzpatrick.

Blatt, B. (1966). *Christmas in purgatory*. Boston: Allyn & Bacon.

Blick, D. W., & Test, D. W. (1987). Effects of self-recording on high-school students on-task behavior. *Learning Disability Quarterly*, 10, 203–213.

Blocher, D. (1974). *Developmental counseling* (2nd ed.). New York: Ronald Press.

Blustein, D. (1987). Integrating career counseling and psychotherapy: A comprehensive treatment strategy. *Psychotherapy*, 24, 794–799.

Blustein, D. L., & Spengler, P. M. (1995). Personal adjustment: Career counseling and psychotherapy. In W. B. Walsh & S. H. Osipow (Eds.), *Handbook of vocational psychology* (2nd ed., pp. 295–329). Hillsdale, NJ: Erlbaum.

Board of Trustees of the Council for Learning Disabilities. (1986). Measurement and training of perceptual and perceptual-motor functioning. *Learning Disabilities Quarterly*, 9, 247.

Boesel, D., & McFarland, L. (1994). *National assessment of vocational education final report to Congress. Volume 1: Summary and recommendations*. Washington, DC: U.S. Department of Education, Office of Educational Research and Improvement.

Bolles, R. N. (1995). *What color is my parachute? A practical manual for job hunters and career changers*. Berkeley, CA: Ten Speed Press.

Bolles, R. N. (1999). *What color is your parachute?* Berkeley, CA: Ten Speed Press.

Bond, G. R. (1991). Vocational rehabilitation for persons with severe mental illness: Past, present, and future. In R. Lieberman (Ed.), *Rehabilitation of the psychiatrically disabled*. New York: Pergamon.

Bond, G. R., & Boyer, S. L. (1988). Rehabilitation programs and outcomes. In J. A. Ciardiello & M. D. Bell (Eds.), *Vocational rehabilitation of persons with prolonged mental illness*. (pp. 231–263). Baltimore: Johns Hopkins University Press.

Bond, G. R., Dietzen, L. L., McGrew, J. H., & Miller, L. D. (1995). Accelerating entry into supported employment for persons with severe psychiatric disabilities. *Rehabilitation Psychology*, 40(2), 91–111.

Bose, J. (1996). *Characteristics of the 100 largest public elementary and secondary school districts in the United States: 1993–94: Statistical analysis report*. Washington, DC: National Center for Educational Statistics.

Bowe, F. G. (1992). Employment: Dependence vs. independence. OSERS *News in Print*, 5(2), 4–7.

Bowser, G., & Reed, P. (1995). Educational TECH points for assistive technology planning. *Journal of Special Education Technology*, 7(4), 325–338.

Boyer, E. (1987). *College: The undergraduate experience in America*. New York: Harper & Row.

Braddock, D. (1987). *Federal policy toward mental retardation and developmental disabilities*. Baltimore: Paul H. Brookes.

Bradley, V. J., Ashbaugh, J. W., & Blaney, B. C. (1994). *Creating individual supports for people with developmental disabilities: A mandate for change at many levels*. Baltimore: Paul H. Brookes.

Brame, K. (1995). Strategies for recruiting family members from diverse backgrounds for roles in policy and program development. *Early Childhood Bulletin*, 5, 1–5. (ERIC Document Reproduction Service No. ED 398 721)

Brinckerhoff, L. C., McGuire, J. M., & Shaw. S. F. (2002). *Postsecondary education and transition for students with learning disabilties*. Austin, TX: PRO-ED.

Brinckerhoff, L. C., Shaw, S. F., & McGuire, J. M. (1992). Promoting access, accommodations, and independence for college students with learning disabilities. *Journal of Learning Disabilities*, 25, 417–429.

Brinckerhoff, L. C., Shaw, S. F., & McGuire, J. M. (1993). *Promoting postsecondary education for students with learning disabilities*. Austin, TX: PRO-ED.

Brislin, R. (1993). *Understanding culture's influence on behavior*. Fort Worth, TX: Harcourt Brace.

Brolin, D. E. (1976). *Vocational preparation of retarded citizens*. Columbus, OH: Merrill.

Brolin, D. E. (1989). *Life centered career education: A competency-based approach*. Reston, VA: The Council for Exceptional Children.

Brolin, D. E. (1992a). *Competency assessment knowledge batteries: Life-centered career education*, Reston, VA: The Council for Exceptional Children.

Brolin, D. E. (1992b). *Competency assessment performance batteries: Life-centered career education*, Reston, VA: The Council for Exceptional Children.

Brolin, D. E. (1992c). *Life-centered career education: Competency units for occupational guidance and preparation*. Reston, VA: The Council for Exceptional Children.

Brolin, D. E. (1992d). *Life-centered career education: Competency units for personal-social skills*. Reston, VA: The Council for Exceptional Children.

Brolin, D. E. (1993). *Life-centered career education* [videorecording]. Reston, VA: The Council for Exceptional Children.

Brolin, D. E. (Ed.). (1995). *Career education: A functional life skills approach* (3rd. ed.). Upper Saddle River, NJ: Prentice Hall.

Brolin, D. E. (1996). Reflections on the beginning . . . and the future directions! *Career Development for Exceptional Individuals*, 19(2), 93–100. Upper Saddle River, NJ: Merrill/Prentice Hall.

Brolin, D. E. (1997). *Life-centered career education: A competency-based approach*. Reston, VA: The Council for Exceptional Children.

Brolin, D. E., & Gysbers, N. C. (1979). Career education for persons with handicaps. *The Personnel and Guidance Journal*, 58, 258–262.

Brolin, D. E., & Schatzman, B. (1989). Lifelong career development. In D. E. Berkell & J. M. Brown (Eds.), *Transition from school to work for persons with disabilities*. New York: Longman.

Brookhiser, R. (1991). *The way of the wasp*. New York: Free Press.

Brophy, J. (1980). *Recent research on teaching*. East Lansing, MI: Institute for Research on Teaching, Michigan State University.

Brophy, J., & Good, T. L. (1986). Teacher behavior and student achievement. In M. C. Wittrock (Ed.), *Handbook of research on teaching* (3rd ed., pp. 328–375). New York: Macmillan.

Brotherson, M. J., Berdine, W. H., & Sartini, V. (1993). Transition to adult services: Support for ongoing parent participation. *Remedial and Special Education*, 14(4), 44–51.

Brown, C. (1992). Assistive technology, computers, and persons with disabilities. *Communications of the ACM*, 35(5), 36–45.

Brown, C., McDaniel, R., Couch, R., & McClanahan, M. (1994). *Vocational evaluation and software: A consumer's guide*. (Available from Materials Development Center, Stout Vocational Rehabilitation Institute, University of Wisconsin—Stout, Menomonie, WI 54751.)

Brown, D. (1990). Trait and factor theory. In D. Brown, L. Brooks, & Associates (Eds.), *Career choice and development:*

Applying contemporary theories to practice (2nd ed., pp. 13–36). San Francisco: Jossey-Bass.

Brown, D. (1996). Status of career development theories. In D. Brown, L. Brooks, & Associates (Eds.), *Career choice and development: Applying contemporary theories to practice* (3rd ed., pp. 513–526). San Francisco: Jossey-Bass.

Brown, D., & Brooks, L. (1984). Preface. In D. Brown, L. Brooks, & Associates (Eds.), *Career choice and development: Applying contemporary theories to practice* (pp. ix–xii). San Francisco: Jossey-Bass.

Brown, D., & Brooks, L. (1990). Introduction to theories of career development: Origins, evolution, and current efforts. In D. Brown, L. Brooks, & Associates (Eds.), *Career choice and development: Applying contemporary theories to practice* (2nd ed., pp. 1–12). San Francisco: Jossey-Bass.

Brown, D., & Brooks, L. (1991). *Techniques of career counseling*. Boston: Allyn & Bacon.

Brown, D., & Brooks, L. (1996). Introduction to theories of career development and choice: Origins, evolution, and current efforts. In D. Brown, L. Brooks, & Associates (Eds.), *Career choice and development* (3rd ed., pp. 1–30). San Francisco: Jossey-Bass.

Brown, L., Branston, M. B., Hamre-Nietupski, S., Pumpian, I., Certo, N., & Gruenewald, L. (1979). A strategy for developing chronological age appropriate and functional curricular content for severely handicapped adolescents and young adults. *Journal of Special Education*, 13, 81–90.

Brown, L., Long, E., Udvari-Solner, A., Davis, L., VanDeventer, P., Ahlgren, C., Johnson, F., Gruenewald, L., & Jorgesen, J. (1989). The home school: Why students with severe intellectual disabilities must attend the schools of their brothers, sisters, friends, and neighbors. *Journal of the Association for Persons with Severe Handicaps*, 16, 39–47.

Brown, L., Nietupski, J,. & Hamre-Nietupski, S. (1976). The criterion of ultimate functioning and public school service for severely handicapped students. In M. A. Thomas (Ed.), *Please don't forget about me! Education's investment in the severely, profoundly, and multiple handicapped child*. (pp. 2–15). Reston, VA: The Council for Exceptional Children.

Brown, P. M., & Foster, S. B. (1991). Integrating hearing and deaf students on a college campus. *American Annals of the Deaf*, 136, 21–27.

Browning. P. L. (1997). *Transition in action for youth and young adults with disabilities*. Montgomery, AL: Auburn University, Wells Printing.

Bucher, D. E., & Brolin, D. E. (1987). The life-centered career education (LCCE) inventory: A curriculum-based, criterion-related assessment instrument. *Diagnostique*, 12, 131–141.

Buckley, J., & Bellamy, G. T. (1985). *National survey of day and vocational programs for adults with severe disabilities: A 1984 profile*. Unpublished manuscript. Johns Hopkins University: Baltimore.

Bull, B. L., Fruehling, R. T., & Chattergy, V. (1992). *The ethics of multicultural and bilingual education*. New York: Teachers College Press.

Bullis, M. D., Kosko, K., Waintrup, M., Kelley, P., & Issacson, A. (1994). Functional assessment services for transition, education, and rehabilitation: Project FASTER. *American Rehabilitation*, 20(2), 9.

Bureau of Labor Statistics. (1992). *Employee tenure and occupational mobility in the early 1990s*. Washington, DC: U.S. Department of Labor.

Bureau of Labor Statistics, U.S. Department of Labor. (2001). Monthly Labor Review, Winter 2001–02. *Occupational Outlook Quarterly*.

Burkhead, E. J., Sampson, J. P., & McMahon, B. T. (1986). The liberation of disabled persons in a technological society: Access to computer technology. *Rehabilitation Literature*, 47(7–8), 162–168.

Burnette, J. (1998). *Reducing the disproportionate representation of minority students in special education*. Reston, VA: ERIC Clearinghouse on Disabilities and Gifted Education, ERIC/OSEP Digest #E566.

Buschner, P. C., Watts, M. B., Siders, J. A., & Leonard, R. L. (1989). Career interest inventories: A need for analysis. *Career Development for Exceptional Individuals*, 12(2), 117–123.

Carden, A. (1990). Narrative as a paradigm for career research. In R. A. Young & W. A. Borgen (Eds.), *Methodological approaches to the study of career* (pp. 71–86). New York: Praeger.

Carey, L. M. (1994). *Measuring and evaluating school learning*. Boston: Allyn & Bacon.

Carl D. Perkins Vocational and Applied Technology Education Act. (1990). Pub. L. No. 101-392, 104, Stat. 756.

Carl D. Perkins Vocational Education Act. (1984). Pub. L. No. 98-524, 98, Stat. 2435.

Carney, I. H., & Orelove, F. P. (1988). Implementing transition programs for community participation. In B. L. Ludlow, A. P. Turnbull, & R. Luckasson (Eds.), *Transitions to adult life for persons with mental retardation: Principles and practices*. Baltimore: Paul H. Brookes.

Carnine, D. W. (1992). Expanding the notion of teachers' rights: Access to tools that work. *Journal of Applied Behavior Analysis*, 25, 13–19.

Cartledge, G., & Milburn, J. A. (1986). *Teaching social skills to children: Innovative approaches* (2nd ed.). Boston: Allyn & Bacon.

Cavalier, A. R., & Brown, C. C. (1998). From passivity to participation: The transformational possibilities of speech-recognition technology. *Teaching Exceptional Children*, 30(6), 60–65.

Center for Applied Special Technology. (1998–1999). *The National Center on Accessing the General Curriculum* [On-line]. Available: *http://www.cast.org/initiatives/nationalcenter.html*.

Chadsey, J., & Sheldon, D. (1998). Moving toward social inclusion in employment and postsecondary school settings. In F. R. Rusch & J. G. Chadsey (Eds.), *Beyond high school: Transition from school to work* (pp. 383–405). Belmont, CA: Wadsworth.

Chadsey-Rusch, J., & Heal, L. (1995). Building consensus from transition experts on social integration outcomes and interventions. *Exceptional Children*, 165–187.

Chadsey-Rusch, J., Rusch, F. R., & O'Reilly, M. F. (1991). Transition from school to integrated communities. *Remedial and Special Education*, 12(6), 23–33.

Chambers, A. C. (1997). *Has technology been considered? A guide for IEP teams*. Albuquerque, NM: Council of Administrators in Special Education.

Chan, F., Reid, C., Kaskel, L., Roldan, G., Rahami, M., & Mpofu, E. (1997). Vocational assessment and evaluation of people with disabilities. *Physical Medicine and Rehabilitation Clinics of North America*, 8, 311–325.

Chan, S. (1998a). Families with Asian roots. In E. W. Lynch & M. H. Hanson (Eds.), *Developing cross-cultural competence: A guide for working with children and their families* (2nd ed., pp. 251–354). Baltimore: Paul H. Brookes.

Chan, S. (1998b). Families with Filipino roots. In E. W. Lynch & M. H. Hanson (Eds.), *Developing cross-cultural competence: A guide for working with children and their families* (2nd ed., pp. 355–408). Baltimore: Paul H. Brookes.

Clark, G. M. (1979). *Career education for the handicapped child in the elementary school*. Denver, CO: Love.

Clark, G. M. (1992, April). Providing transition services through a functional curriculum and functional instruction. Paper presented at The Council for Exceptional Children annual conference, Baltimore.

Clark, G. M. (1994). Is a functional curriculum approach compatible with an inclusive education model? *Teaching Exception Children*, 26(2), 36–39.

Clark, G. M. (1996). Transition planning assessment for secondary-level students with learning disabilities. *Journal of Learning Disabilities*, 29(1), 79–92.

Clark, G. M., & Kolstoe, O. P. (1995). *Career development and transition education for adolescents with disabilities* (2nd ed.). Needham, MA: Allyn & Bacon.

Clark, G. M., Carlson, B. C., Fisher, S., Cook, I. D., & D'Alonzo, B. J. (1991). Career development for students with disabilities in elementary schools: A position statement of the Division on Career Development. *Career Development for Exceptional Individuals*, 14(2), 109–120.

Clark, G. M., & Patton, J. R. (1997). *Transition planning inventory: Administration and resource guide*. Austin, TX: PRO-ED.

Clary, G. (1998, January). *Institutional and community resources for student support services and programs*. Paper presented at the Southeastern Association of Educational Opportunity Program Personnel Training Center Workshop. Memphis, TN.

Clary, G. K. (2001). *Barriers to postsecondary education for rural students with disabilities: A delphi investigation*. Unpublished doctoral dissertation, Kent State University.

Cobb, H. C. (1972). *The forecast of fulfillment*. New York: Teachers College Press.

Cobb, R. B., & Neubert, D. A. (1992). Vocational education models. In F. R. Rusch, L. Destefano, J. Chadsey-Rusch, L. A. Phelps, & E. Syzmanski (Eds.) *Transition from school to adult life*: Models, linkages, and policies. (pp. 93–113) Sycamore IL: Sycamore.

Cobb, R. B., & Neubert, D. A. (1998). Vocational education: Emerging vocationalism. In F. R. Rusch & J. G. Chadsey (Eds.), *Beyond high school: Transition from school to work* (pp. 101–126). Belmont, CA: Wadsworth Publishing.

Cohen, S., Agosta, J., Cohen, J., & Warren, R. (1989). Supporting families of children with severe disabilities. *Journal of the Association for Persons with Severe Handicaps*, 14(2), 155–162.

Cole, M., & Cole, S. (1993). *The development of children* (2nd ed.). New York: Scientific American Books.

Collignon, F. C., Noble, J. H., & Toms-Barker, L. (1987). Early lessons form the Marin County demonstration integrating vocational and mental health services. *Psychosocial Rehabilitation Journal*, 11(2), 76–85.

Colorado Department of Education. (1998). *Teach access skills*. Denver, CO: Author.

Condeluci, A. (1995). *Interdependence: The route to community*. Winter Park, FL: GR Press.

Cone, J. D., Delawyer, D. D., & Wolfe, V. V. (1985). Assessing parent participation: The parent/family involvement index. *Exceptional Children*, 51(5), 417–424.

Conley, D. T. (2002, April). Preparing students for life after high school. *Educational Leadership*, 60–66.

Consortium of Citizens with Disabilities (1991). *Recommended federal policy directions for personal assistance services for Americans with disabilities*. Washington, DC: Personal Assistance Task Force, Consortium of Citizens with Disabilities, p. 3.

Conte, L. E. (1983). Vocational development theories and the disabled person: Oversight or deliberate omission? *Rehabilitation Counseling Bulletin*, 27, 316–328.

Conyers, L., Koch, L., & Szymanski, E. (1998). Lifespan perspectives on disability and work: A qualitative study. *Rehabilitation Counseling Bulletin*, 42, 51–75.

Cook, A. M., & Hussey, S. M. (1995). *Assistive technologies: Principles and practice*. St. Louis: Mosby Publishing.

Cook, J. A., & Hoffschmidt, S. J. (1995). Comprehensive models of psychosocial rehabilitation. In R. W. Flexer and P. L. Solomon (Eds.), *Psychiatric rehabilitation in practice*. (pp. 81–98) Boston: Andover Publishers.

Cooper, J. O., Heron, T. E., & Heward, W. L. (1987). *Applied behavior analysis*. Upper Saddle River, NJ: Merrill/Prentice Hall.

Cooter, R. B., Jr., & Flynt, E. S. (1996). *Teaching reading in the content areas: Developing content literacy for all students*. Upper Saddle River, NJ: Merrill/Prentice Hall.

Cordiero, P. A., Reagan, T. G., & Martinez, L. P. (1994). *Multiculturalism and TQE: Addressing cultural diversity in schools.* Thousand Oaks, CA: Corwin.

Correa, V. I. (1989). Involving culturally diverse families in the educational process. In S. H. Fradd & M. H. Weismantel (Eds.), *Meeting the needs of culturally and linguistically different students: A handbook for educators* (pp. 130–144). Austin, TX: PRO-ED.

Coupe-O'Kane, J., Porter, J., & Taylor, A. (1994). Meaningful content and contexts for learning. In J. Coupe-O'Kane & B. Smith (Eds.), *Taking control* (pp. 14–30), London: David Fulton Publishers.

Cowen, S. (1993). Transition planning for LD college-bound students. In S. Vogel & P. Adelman (Eds.), *Success for college students with learning disabilities* (pp. 39–56). New York: Springer.

Crites, J. (1978). *The career maturity inventory.* Monterey, CA: CTB/McGraw-Hill.

Crites, J. (1978). *Theory and research handbook for the career maturity inventory.* Monterey, CA: McGraw-Hill.

Crites, J. O. (1981). Integrative test interpretation. In D. H. Montross & D. J. Shinkman (Eds.), *Career development in the 1980s: Theory and practice* (pp. 161–168). Springfield, IL: Charles C. Thomas.

Cronin, M., & Patton, J. R. (1993). *Life skills across the curriculum for youths with special needs.* Austin, TX: PRO-ED.

Cronin, M., & Patton, J. R. (1993). *Life skills instruction for all students: A practical guide for integrating real-life content into the curriculum.* Austin, TX: PRO-ED.

Cross, D., Collins, B. C., & Boam-Wood, D. (1996). *Interdisciplinary preparation for physical disabilities: Education and related services.* Lexington, KY: Department of Special Education and Rehabilitation Counseling, University of Kentucky.

Cross, T., Cooke, N. L., Wood, W. M., & Test, D. W. (1999). Comparison of the Effects of MAPS and ChoiceMaker on Student Self-Determination Skills. *Education and Training in Mental Retardation and Developmental Disablilities,* 34(4), 499–510.

Cummins, J. (1986). Psychological assessment of minority students: Out of context, out of focus, out of control? In A. C. Willing & H. F. Greenberg (Eds.), *Bilingualism and learning disabilities: Policy and practice for teachers and administrators* (pp. 3–11). New York: American Library Publishing.

Curnow, T. C. (1989). Vocational development of persons with disabilities. *Career Development Quarterly,* 37, 269–278.

Curran, B. (1999). *Focusing on results: Toward an education accountability system.* Washington, DC: National Governors' Association.

Dalke, C. (1993). Making a successful transition from high school to college: A model program. In S. A. Vogel & P. B. Adelman (Eds.), *Success for college students with disabilities* (pp. 57–80). New York: Springer Verlag.

Dalke, C., & Schmitt, S. (1987). Meeting the transition needs of college-bound students with learning disabilities. *Journal of Learning Disabilities,* 20(3), 176–180.

D'Alonzo, B. J., & Owen, S. D. (1985). *Transition services for the disabled: A national survey.* Paper presented at the 63rd Annual Council for Exceptional Children Conference, Anaheim, CA.

Daniels, S. (1990). Disability in America: An evolving concept, a new paradigm. George Washington University. *Policy Network Newsletter,* 3(1), 1–3.

Dattilo, J. (1987). Recreation and leisure literature for individuals with mental retardation: Implications for outdoor recreation. *Therapeutic Recreation Journal,* 21(1), 9–17.

Dautel, P. J., & Frieden, L. (1999). *Consumer choice and control: Personal attendant services and supports in America, Report of the National Blue Ribbon Panel on Personal Assistance Services.* Houston, TX: Independent Living Research Utilization.

Dawis, R. V. (1996). The theory of work adjustment and person-environment-correspondence counseling. In D. Brown, L. Brooks, & Associates (Eds.), *Career choice and development* (3rd ed., pp. 75–120). San Francisco: Jossey-Bass.

Dawis, R. V., & Lofquist, L. H. (1984). A *psychological theory of work adjustment: An individual-differences model and its applications.* Minneapolis, MN: University of Minnesota Press.

Day, R. M., Powell, T. H., & Stowitschek, J. J. (1980). SCIPPY: *Social competence intervention package for preschool youngsters.* Nashville, TN: Vanderbilt University.

Deci, E. L., & Chandler, C. L. (1986). The importance of motivation for the future of the LD field. *Journal of Learning Disabilities,* 19, 587–594.

Deci, E. L., & Ryan, R. M. (1985). *Intrinsic motivation and self-determination in human behavior.* New York: Plenum.

Deci, E. L., & Ryan, R. M. (1994). Promoting self-determined education. *Scandinavian Journal of Educational Research* (38), 3–14.

deFur, S. H. (2002). Education reform, high-stakes assessment, and students with disabilities: One state's approach. *Remedial and Special Education,* 23(4), 203–211.

deFur, S. H., & Patton, J. R. (1999). *Transition and school-based services: Interdisciplinary perspectives for enhancing the transition process.* Austin: PRO-ED.

deFur, S. H., & Taymans, J. M. (1995). Competencies needed for transition specialists in vocational rehabilitation, vocational education, and special education. *Career Development for Exceptional Individuals,* 62(1), 38–51.

deFur, S. H., Getzel, E. E., & Kregel, J. (1994). Individual transition plans: A work in progress. *Journal of Vocational Rehabilitation,* 4(2), 139–145.

deFur, S. H., Getzel, E. E., & Trossi, K. (1996). Making the postsecondary education match: A role for transition planning. *Journal of Vocational Rehabilitation,* 6, 231–240.

DeJong, G. (1979) Independent living: From social movement to analytic paradigm. *Archives of Physical Medicine and Rehabilitation,* 60, 435–446.

DeJong, G. (1984). Independent living: From social movement to analytic paradigm. In P. Marinelli & A. Dell Orto (Eds.), *The psychological and social impact of physical disability* (pp. 39–64). New York: Springer.

DeLoach, C. P. (1992). Career outcomes for college graduates with severe disabilities and sensory disabilities. *Journal of Rehabilitation*, 58(1), 57–63.

Dennis, R. E., & Giangreco, M. F. (1996). Creating conversation: Reflections on cultural sensitivity in family interviewing. *Exceptional Children*, 63, 103–116.

Deno, S. L. (1985). Curriculum-based measurement: The emerging alternative. *Exceptional Children*, 52, 219–232.

Dentzer, S. (1992). How to train workers for the 21st century. *U.S. News & World Report*, 21 September, pp. 72–78.

Derer, K., Polsgrove, L., & Rieth, H. (1996). A survey of assistive technology applications in schools and recommendations for practice. *Journal of Special Education Technology*, 13(2), 62–80.

Deshler, D., Ellis, E. S., & Lenz, R. K. (1996). *Teaching adolescents with learning disabilities* (2nd ed.). Denver: Love Publishing.

DeStefano, L. (1989). Facilitating the transition from school to adult life for youth with disabilities. In W. E. Kiernan & R. L. Schalock (Eds.), *Economics, industry, and disability: A look ahead* (pp. 169–177). Baltimore: Paul H. Brookes.

DeStefano, L., & Snauwaert, D. (1989). *A value-critical approach to transition policy analysis* [Monograph]. Special Education Programs: Washington, DC.

DeStefano, L., & Wagner, M., (1992). Outcome assessment in special education: Implication for decision-making and long-term planning in vocational rehabilitation. *Career Development for Exceptional Individuals*, 16(2), 147–158.

DeStefano, L., & Wermuth, T.R. (1993). IDEA (P.L. 101–476): Defining a second generation of transition services. In F. R. Rusch, L. DeStefano, J. Chadsey-Rusch, L. A. Phelps, & E. Szymanski (Eds.), *Transition from school to adult life: Models, linkages, and policy* (pp. 537–549). Sycamore, IL: Sycamore.

Dever, R. (1988). *Community living skills: A taxonomy* (Monograph of the American Association on Mental Retardation). Washington, DC: American Association on Mental Retardation.

DeVillar, R. A. (1994). The rhetoric and practice of cultural diversity in U.S. schools: Socialization, resocialization, and quality schooling. In R. A. DeVillar, D. J. Faltis, & J. P. Cummins (Eds.), *Cultural diversity in schools: From rhetoric to practice* (pp. 25–56). Albany, NY: State University of New York.

DeVries, D. L., & Slavin, R. E. (1978). Teams-games-tournament (TGT): Review of ten classroom experiments. *Journal of Research and Development in Education*, 12, 28–38.

DiGangi, S. A., Maag, J. W., & Rutherford, R. B., Jr. (1991). Self-graphing of on-task behavior: Enhancing the reactive effects of self-monitoring of on-task behavior and academic productivity. *Learning Disability Quarterly*, 14, 221–230.

Dinerstein, R. D., Herr, S. S., & O'Sullivan, J. L. (1999). *A guide to consent*. Washington, DC: American Association on Mental Retardation.

Dinnebell, L. A., & Rule, S. (1994). Congruence between parents' and professionals' judgment about the development of young children with disabilities: A review of the literature. *Topics in Early Childhood Education*, 14, 1–26.

Division of Career Development and Transition. (2000). *Transition specialist competencies*. Reston, VA: Council for Exceptional Children.

Dix, J. E., & Savickas, M. L. (1995). Establishing a career: Developmental tasks and coping responses. *Journal of Vocational Behavior*, 47, 93–107.

Dohm, A., & Wyatt, I. (2002). College at work: Outlook and earnings for college graduates, 2000–10. *Occupational Outlook Quarterly*, fall 2002. Retrieved Feb 20, 2003, from Proquest, *http://proquest.umi.com/pdqweb?*Did = 000000217986161

Doll, R. C. (1964). *Curriculum improvement: Decision-making and process*. Boston: Allyn & Bacon.

Donnellan, A., & Mirenda, P. (1984). Issues related to professional involvement with families of individuals with autism and other severe handicaps. *Journal of the Association for Persons with Severe Handicaps*, 9, 16–25.

Donovan, M. S., Bransford, J. D., & Pellegrino, J. W. (1999). *How people learn: Bridging research and practice*. Washington, DC: National Academies Press. [On-line]. Available: *http://books,nap.edu/html/howpeople2/ch2.html.*

Donovan, M. S., & Cross, C. T. (eds.) (2002). *Minority students in special and gifted education*. Washington, DC: National Academy Press, National Research Council Committee on Minority Representation in Special Education.

Dowdy, C., & Smith, T. E. (1991). Future-based assessment and intervention. *Intervention in School and Clinic*, 27, 101–106.

Doyel, A. W. (2001). *No More Job Interviews: Self-employment Strategies for People with Disabilities*. St. Augustine, FL: Training Resource Network.

Doyle, W. (1984). How order is achieved in classrooms: An interim report. *Journal of Curriculum Studies*, 16, 259–277.

Doyle, W. (1986). Classroom organization and management. In M. C. Wittrock (Ed.), *Handbook of research on teaching* (3rd ed., pp. 392–431). New York: Macmillan.

Droege, R. C. (1987). The USES testing program. In B. Bolton (Ed.), *Handbook of measurement and evaluation in rehabilitation*. (pp. 169–182). Baltimore: Paul H. Brookes.

DuBow, S., Geer, S., & Strauss, K. P. (1992). *Legal rights: The guide for deaf and hard of hearing people*. Washington, DC: Gallaudet University Press.

Ducharme, G., Beeman, P., DeMarasse, R., & Ludlum, C. (1994). Building community one person at a time: One candle power. In V. J. Bradley, J. W. Ashbaugh, & B. C. Blaney (Eds.), *Creating individual supports for people with developmental disabilities: A mandate for change at many levels* (pp. 347–360). Baltimore: Paul H. Brookes.

Duffey, J., Clark, D., Deitmen, K., Dellegrotto, J., Di Lullo, K., Di Martino, C., Laird, S., Oakes, K., & Rider, D. (1996). *Preparation for adult life: Adult life roles, post secondary education and training*. Harrisburg, PA: Pennsylvania Department of Education.

Dunham, M., Koller, J. R., & McIntosh, D. (1996). A preliminary comparison of successful and non-successful closure types among adults with specific learning disabilities in the vocational rehabilitation system. *The Journal of Rehabilitation*, 62(1), 42–47.

Dunlap, G., DePerczel, M., Clarke, S., Wilson, D., Wright, S., White, R., & Gomez, A. (1994). Choice-making to promote adaptive behavior for students with emotional and behavioral challenges. *Journal of Applied Behavior Analysis*, 27, 505–518.

Dunn, B. (1995). *The wild dream team*. University Park, PA: Pennsylvania State University, WPSX.

Dunn, R., & Griggs, S. A. (1995). *Multiculturalism and learning style: Teaching and counseling adolescents*. Westport, CN: Praeger.

Dunst, C., Trivette, C., & Deal, A. (1988). *Enabling and empowering families: Principles and guidelines for practice*. Cambridge, MA: Brookline Books.

Durlak, C. M., Rose, E., & Bursuck, W. D. (1994). Preparing high school students with learning disabilities for the transition to postsecondary education: Teaching the skills of self-determination. *Journal of Learning Disabilities*, 27(1), 51–59.

Dybwad, G. (1989). Self-determination: Influencing public policy. In R. Perske (Ed.), *National conference on self-determination*. Washington, DC: U.S. Department of Education, Office of Special Education and Rehabilitative Services.

Dyer, K., Dunlap, G., & Winterling, V. (1993). Effects of choice making in the serious problem behavior of students with severe handicaps. *Journal of Applied Behavior Analysis*, 23, 515–524.

Eber, L., Nelson, C. M., & Miles, P. (1997). School-based wraparound for students with emotional and behavior challenges. *Exceptional Children*, 63(4), 539–556.

Edelman, A., Schuyler, V., & White, P. (1998). *Maximizing success for young adults with chronic-related illnesses: Transition planning for education after high school*. Washington, DC: Heath.

Edgar, E. (1987). Secondary programs in special education: Are many of them justifiable? *Exceptional Parent*, 53(6), 555–561.

Edgar, E., & Levine, P. (1986). *Washington state follow-up studies of postsecondary special education students in transition*. Seattle, WA: University of Washington, Networking and Evaluation Team.

Edgar, E., Levin, P., Levine, R., & Dubey, M. (1988). *Washington state follow-along studies 1983–1987: Students in transition final report*. Seattle, WA: University of Washington.

Edgar, E., & Polloway, E. A. (1994). Education for adolescents with disabilities: Curriculum and placement issues. *The Journal of Special Education*, 27(4), 438–452.

Education Amendments of 1972, 20 U.S.C. § 1681 *et seq*.

Education Amendments of 1974, Pub. L. No. 93-380, 88 Stat. 580.

Education for All Handicapped Children Act of 1975, 20 U.S.C. § 1401 *et seq*.

Education for All Handicapped Children Act, Pub. L. No. 94-142, 20 U.S.C. 1412 (1975).

Education of the Handicapped Act of 1970, Pub. L. No. 91-230, § 601–662, 84 Stat. 175.

Education of the Handicapped Amendments of 1986, 20 U.S.C. § 1401 *et seq*.

Edwards, J. P., Kinneldorf, M., & Bradley, C. (1988). *Final report of the Portland State University secondary school-to-work transition projects emphasizing transition to work and leisure roles*. Portland, OR: Portland State University.

Elbaum, B., Vaughn, S., Hughes, M., & Moody, S. W. (1999). Grouping practices and reading outcomes for students with disabilities. *Exceptional Children*, 65, 399–415.

Elder, J. (1988). Transition from school to work: Changing attitudes and opportunities. *Exceptional Parent*, 18(1), 27–29.

Elementary and Secondary Education Act of 1965, Pub. L. No. 89-10, 79 Stat. 27.

Elementary and Secondary Education Act of 1965 (20 U.S.C. 6301 *et seq.*).

Elementary and Secondary Education Act, amended by Pub. L. No. 89-750. § 161 [Title VI], 80 Stat. 1204 (1966).

Ellis, A. K., & Fouts, J. T. (1997). *Research on educational innovations* (2nd ed.). Larchmont, NY: Eye on Education.

Ellis, E. S. (1997). Watering up the curriculum for adolescents with learning disabilities: Goals of the knowledge dimension. *Remedial & Special Education*, 18(6), 326–346.

Elrod, G. F., Sorgenfrei, T. B., & Gibson, A. P. (1989). The degree of agreement between the expressed and scale-determined career interests of adolescents with mild handicaps. *Career Development for Exceptional Individuals*, 12(2), 107–116.

Emmer, E., Evertson, C., & Anderson, L. (1980). Effective classroom management at the beginning of the school year. *Elementary School Journal*, 80, 219–231.

Engleman, S., Becker, W. C., Carnine, D., & Gersten, R. (1988). The direct instruction follow through model: Design and outcomes. *Education and Treatment of Children*, 11(4), 303–317.

Englert, C. S. (1983). Measuring special education teacher effectiveness. *Exceptional Children*, 50, 247–254.

Englert, C. S., Mariage, T. V., & Tarrant, K. L. (1992). Defining and redefining instructional practice in special education: Perspectives on good teaching. *Teacher Education and Special Education*, 15, 62–86.

Erikson, E. (1963). *Childhood and society* (2nd ed.). New York: W. W. Norton.

Erikson, E. (1968). *Identity, youth, and crisis*. Toronto: W. W. Norton.

Esposito, L., & Campbell, P. H. (1993). Computers and severely and physically handicapped individuals. In J. D. Lindsey (Ed.), *Computers and exceptional individuals* (2nd ed., pp. 159–171). Austin, TX: PRO-ED.

Eubanks, S. C. (1996). *The urban teacher challenge: A report on teacher recruitment and demand in selected great city schools*. Belmont, MA: Recruiting New Teachers.

Eudaly, J. (2002). A rising tide: Students with psychiatric disabilities seek services in record numbers. *Information from* HEATH, September, 2002. Retrieved May 12, 2003, from HEATH Resource Center, *http://www.heath.gwu.edu/Templates/Newsletter/issue3/issue4/i4%20Psychiatric%20Disability.dwt*

Everson, J. M. (1990). A local team approach. *Teaching Exceptional Children*, 23(1), 44–46.

Everson, J. M., & Guillory, J. D. (1998). Building statewide transition services through collaborative interagency teamwork. In F. Rusch & J. Chadsey (Eds.), *Beyond high school: Transition from school to work* (pp. 299–317). Belmont, CA: Wadsworth.

Everson, J. M., & McNulty, K. (1992). Interagency teams: Building local transition programs through parental and professional partnerships. In F. R. Rusch, L. DeStefano, J. Chadsey-Rusch, L. A. Phelps, & E. Szymanski (Eds.), *Transition from school to adult life: Models, linkages, and policy* (pp. 341–352). Sycamore, IL: Sycamore.

Everson, J. M., & Moon, M. S. (1987). Transition services for young adults with severe disabilities: Defining professional and parental roles and responsibilities. *Journal of the Association for Persons with Severe Handicaps*, 12(2), 87–95.

Everson, J. M., Barcus, M., Moon, M. S., & Morton, M. V. (1987). *Achieving outcomes: A guide to interagency training in transition and supported employment*. Richmond, VA: Virginia Commonwealth University, Project Transition into Employment.

Everson, J. M., & Rachal, P. (1996). *What are we learning about state and local interagency partnerships? An analysis of state and interagency activities for students who are deaf-blind in seventeen states*. Sands Point, NY: Helen Keller National Center—Technical Assistance Center.

Evertson, C. (1982). Differences in instructional activities in higher and lower achieving junior high English and mathematics classrooms. *Elementary School Journal*, 82, 329–351.

Evertson, C., Anderson, C., Anderson, L., & Brophy, J. (1980). Relationship between classroom behavior and student outcomes in junior high math and English classes. *American Elementary Research Journal*, 17, 43–60.

Evertson, C., & Emmer, E. (1982). Effective management at the beginning of the year in junior high classes. *Journal of Educational Psychology*, 74, 485–498.

Evertson, C., Emmer, E., Clements, B., Sanford, J., Worsham, M., & Williams, E. (1980). Predictors of effective teaching in junior high mathematics classrooms. *Journal of Research in Mathematics Education*, 11, 167–178.

Experience-based career education: Basic procedures manual. (1976). Fort Dodge, IA: Iowa Central Community College.

Fabian, E., Lent, R., & Willis, S. (1998). Predicting work transition outcomes for students with disabilities: Implications for counselors. *Journal of Counseling and Development*, 76, 311–316.

Fairweather, J. S., & Shaver, D. M. (1991). Making the transition to postsecondary education and training. *Exceptional Children*, 57(3), 264–270.

Falvey, M. (1989). *Community-based curriculum: Instructional strategies for students with severe handicaps*. Baltimore: Paul H. Brookes.

Falvey, M., Brown, L., Lyon, S., Baumgart, D., & Schroeder, J. (1980). Strategies for using cues and correction procedures. In W. Sailor, B. Wilcox, & L. Brown (Eds.), *Methods of instruction for severely handicapped students* (pp. 109–133). Baltimore: Paul H. Brookes.

Falvey, M. A. (1989). *Community-based curriculum: Instructional strategies for students with severe disabilities* (2nd ed). Baltimore: Paul H. Brookes.

Farren, C., Gray, J. D., & Kaye, B. (1984). Mentoring: A boon to career development. *Personnel*, 61, 20–24.

Federal Register. (1981, January 19). Washington, DC: U.S. Government Printing Office.

Ferguson, D., Droege, C., Lester, J., Meyer, G., Ralph, G, Sampson, N., & Williams, J. (2001). *Designing personalized learning for every student*. The Association for Supervision and Curriculum Development (ASCD).

Ferguson, G. (2001, Summer). The use of ritual in rites of passage. *The Voice for Adventure Edcuation*, 43, 14–19.

Ferguson, P. M., & Ferguson, D. L. (2000). The promise of adulthood. In M. E. Snell & F. Brown, *Instruction of students with severe disabilities* (5th ed., pp. 629–656). Upper Saddle River, NJ: Merill/Prentice Hall.

Ferguson, P. M., & Olsen, D. (Eds.). (1989). *Supported community life: Connecting policy to practice in disability research*. Eugene, OR: Specialized Training Program.

Fichten, C. S., & Ansel, R. (1988). Thoughts concerning interactions between college students who have a physical disability and their nondisabled peers. *Rehabilitation Counseling Bulletin*, 32, 23–40.

Fichten, C. S., Robillard, K., Tagalakis, V., & Ansel, R. (1991). Casual interaction between college students with various disabilities and their nondisabled peers: The internal dialogue. *Rehabilitation Psychology*, 36(1), 3–20.

Field, S., & Hoffman, A. (1994). Development of a model for self-determination. *Career Development for Exceptional Individuals*, 17(2), 159–169.

Field, S., & Hoffman, A. (1995). *Steps to self-determination*. Austin, TX: PRO-ED.

Field, S., Martin, J, Miller, R., Ward, M., & Wehmeyer, M. (1998). *A practical guide for teaching self-determination*. Reston, VA: The Council for Exceptional Children.

Field, S., Martin, J. E., Miller, R., Ward, M., & Wehmeyer, M. (1998). Self-determination for persons with disabilities: A position paper of the Division on Career Development and Transition. *Career Development for Exceptional Individuals*, 21(2), 113–128.

Fielder, I. (1996). Assistive devices: Empowerment issues. *American Rehabilitation*, 22(4), 26–29.

Finch, C. R., & Crunkilton. S. R. (1993). *Curriculum development in vocational and technical education* (4th ed.). Boston: Allyn & Bacon.

Fisher, S. K., & Gardner, J. E. (1999). Introduction to technology in transition. *Career Development for Exceptional Individuals*, 22(2), 131–152.

Fitcher, J. M. (1991). *Endangered spaces, enduring places: Change, identity, and survival in rural America*. Boulder, CO: Westview.

Flexer, R. (1996). Federal laws and program accessibility. In C. Flexer, D. Wray, R. Leavitt, & R. Flexer (Eds.), *How the student with hearing loss can succeed in college: A handbook for students, families, and professional* (2nd ed., pp. 13–27). Washington, DC: Alexander Graham Bell Association for the Deaf.

Flexer, R., Simmons, T., & Tankersley, M. (1997). Graduate interdisciplinary training at Kent State University. *Journal of Vocational Rehabilitation*, 8, 183–195.

Flexer, R. W., Goebel, G. W., Simmons, T. J., Baer, R., Shell, D., Steele, R., & Sabousky, R. (1994). Participant, employer, and rehabilitation resources in supported employment: A collaborative approach. *Journal of Applied Rehabilitation Counseling*, 25(4), 9–15.

Foley, R. M., & Munschenck, N. A. (1997). Collaboration activities and competencies of secondary school special educators: A national survey. *Teacher Education and Special Education*, 20, 47–60.

Ford, A., Schnorr, R., Meyer, L., Davern, L., Black, J., & Dempsey, P. (1989). *The Syracuse community-referenced curriculum guide for students with moderate and severe disabilities*. Baltimore: Paul H. Brookes.

Ford, B. A. (1992). Multicultural education training for special educators working with African-American youth. *Exceptional Children*, 59, 107–114.

Ford, L. (2001). Supported employment for people with psychiatric disabilities. In P. Wehman (Ed.), *Supported Employment in Business: Expanding the Capacity of Workers with Disabilities* (pp. 133–152). St. Augustine, FL: Training Resource Network.

Forest, M., & Lusthaus, E. (1989). Promoting educational equality for all students: Circles and MAPS. In S. Stainback, W. Stainback, & M. Forest (Eds.), *Educating all students in the mainstream of regular education* (pp. 43–57). Baltimore: Paul H. Brookes.

Forest, M., Pearpoint, J., & Snow, J. (1993). Natural support systems: Families, friends, and circles. In J. Pearpoint, M. Forest, & J. Snow (Eds.), *The inclusion papers: Strategies to make inclusion work* (pp. 116–132). Toronto: Inclusion Press.

Forness, S. R., Kavale, K. A., Blum, I. M., & Lloyd, J. W. (1997). Mega-analysis of meta-analyses: What works in special education and related services. *Teaching Exceptional Children*, 29(6), 4–9.

Foss, G., Bullis, M. D., & Vilhauer, D. A. (1984). Assessment and training of job-related social competence for mentally retarded adolescents and adults. In A. S. Halpern & M. J. Fuhrer (Eds.), *Functional assessment in rehabilitation* (pp. 145–157). Baltimore: Paul H. Brookes.

Foss, G., Cheney, D., & Bullis, M. D. (1986). TICE: *Test of interpersonal competence for employment*. Santa Monica, CA: James Stanfield.

Foss, G., & Vilhauer, D. A. (1986). *Working II: Interpersonal skills assessment and training for employment: Teachers guide*. Santa Monica, CA: James Stanfield.

Foss, P. D. (1990). *Transition from school to community: What works for students with disabilities?* Unpublished master's thesis, University of Central Florida.

Fox, L., Zakely, J., Morris, R., & Jundt, M. (1993). Orientation as a catalyst: Effective retention through academic and social integration. In M. L. Upcraft, R. H. Mullendore, B. O. Barefoot, & D. S. Fidler (Eds.), *Designing successful transitions: A guide for orienting students to college* [Monograph Series No. 13] 49–59. Columbia, SC: University of South Carolina.

Fradd, S. H., & Weismantel, M. J. (1989). Developing and evaluating goals. In S. H. Fradd & M. H. Weismantel (Eds.), *Meeting the needs of culturally and linguistically different students: A handbook for educators* (pp. 34–62). Austin, TX: PRO-ED.

Franca, V. M., Kerr, M. M., Reitz, A. L., & Lambert, D. (1990). Peer tutoring among behaviorally disordered students: Academic and social benefits to tutor and tutee. *Educational Treatment of Children*, 13, 109–128.

Francese, P. (2002). The college-cash connection. *American Demographics*, 24(3), 42–43.

Frank, K., & Wade, P. (1993). Disabled student services in postsecondary education: Who's responsible for what? *Journal of College Student Development*, 34, 26–30.

Frey, R. M., & Kolstoe, O. P. (1965). *A high school work-study program for mentally subnormal students*. Carbondale, IL: Southern Illinois University Press.

Friend, M., & Bursuck, W. D. (2002). *Including students with special needs: A practical guide for classroom teachers* (3rd ed.). Boston: Allyn & Bacon.

Friend, M., & Cook, L. (1990). Collaboration as a predictor for success in school reform. *Journal of Educational and Psychological Consultation*, 1, 69–86.

Fuchs, D., & Fuchs, L. S. (1995). Sometimes separate is better. *Education Leadership*, 52(4), 22–26.

Fuchs, L. S. (1993). Enhancing instructional programming and student achievement with curriculum-based measurement. In J. J. Kramer (Ed.), *Curriculum-based assessment: Examining old problems, evaluating new solutions* (pp. 65–103). Lincoln, NE: Buros Institute of Mental Measurements.

Fujiura, G. T., & Yamaki, K. (1997). Analysis of ethnic variations in developmental disability prevalence and household economic status. *Mental Retardation*, 35, 286–294.

Funk, D. (1992). *Transitional services for handicapped youth: Follow-up and follow along*. Final report submitted to the U.S. Department of Education, Office of Special Education and Rehabilitation Services. (ID# 15R80062-91), Washington, DC.

Gajar, A. (1998). Post-secondary education. In F. R. Rusch & J. G. Chadsey (Eds.), *Beyond high school: Transition from school to work* (pp. 383–405). Belmont, CA: Wadsworth.

Gajar, A., Goodman, L., & McAfee, J. (1993). *Secondary schools and beyond: Transition of individuals with mild disabilities*. Upper Saddle River, NJ: Merrill/Prentice Hall.

Gajar, A. H. (1998). Postsecondary education. In F. R. Rusch & J. G. Chadsey (Eds.), *Beyond high school: Transition from school to work* (pp. 383–405). Belmont, CA: Wadsworth.

Gallivan-Fenlon, A. (1994). "Their senior year": Family and service provider perspectives on the transition from school to adult life for young adults with disabilities. *Journal of the Association for Persons with Severe Handicaps*, 19(1), 11–23.

Garcia, E. (2002). *Student cultural diversity: Understanding and meeting the challenge* (3rd ed.). Boston: Houghton Mifflin.

Garcia, S. B., & Yates, J. R. (1986). Policy issues associated with serving bilingual exceptional children. In A. C. Willing & H. F. Greenberg (Eds.), *Bilingualism and learning disabilities: Policy and practice for teachers and administrators* (pp. 113–134). New York: American Library Publishing.

Gardner, J. A. (1987). *Transition from high school to postsecondary education: Analytical studies*. Washington, DC: Center for Educational Statistics (ERIC Reproduction Service No. ED280 370).

Gartin, B. C., Rumrill, P., & Serebreni, R. (1996). The higher education transition model: Guidelines for facilitating college transition among college-bound students with disabilities. *Teaching Exceptional Children*, 29(1), 30–33.

Gartner, A., & Lipsky, D. K. (1987). Beyond special education: Toward a quality system for all students. *Harvard Educational Review*, 57, 367–395.

Gault, A. (1989). *Mexican immigrant parents and the education of their handicapped children: Factors that influence parent involvement*. Unpublished doctoral dissertation, University of Illinois at Urbana-Champaign, Urbana, IL.

Gaylord-Ross, R., & Browder, D. (1991). Functional assessment: Dynamic and domain properties. In L. Meyer, C. Peck, & L. Brown (Eds.), *Critical issues in the lives of people with severe disabilities* (pp. 45–66). Baltimore: Paul H. Brookes.

Geraghty, M. (1996, July 19). More students quitting college before sophomore year, data show. *The Chronicle of Higher Education*, pp. A35–A36.

Gerber, P. J., Banbury, M. M., Miller, J. H., Griffin, H. D. (1986). Special educators' perceptions of parental participation in the individual education plan process. *Psychology in the Schools*, 23, 158–163.

Gerber, P. J., Ginsberg, R., & Reiff, H. B. (1992). Identifying alterable patterns in employment success for highly successful adults with learning disabilities. *Journal of Learning Disabilities*, 25, 475–487.

Gerber, P. J., Reiff, H. B., & Ginsberg, R. (1994). Critical incidents of highly successful adults with learning disabilities. *The Journal of Vocational Rehabilitation*, 4(2), 105–112.

German, S., Martin, J. E., Huber Marshall, L., & Sale, R. P. (2000). Promoting self-determination: Teaching goal attainment with the *Take Action* process. *Career Development for Exceptional Individuals*, 23, 27–38.

Gersten, R. Carnine, D., & White, W. A. T. (1984). The pursuit of clarity: Direct instruction and applied behavior analysis. In W. L. Heward, T. E. Heron, D. S. Hill, & J. Trapp-Porter (Eds.), *Focus on behavior analysis in education* (pp. 38–57). Columbus, OH: Merrill.

Gersten, R., Carnine, D., & Woodward, J. (1987). Direct instruction research: The third decade. *Remedial and Special Education*, 8(6), 48–56.

Gersten, R., Woodward, J., & Darch, C. (1986). Direct instruction: A research-based approach to curriculum design and teaching. *Exceptional Children*, 53, 17–31.

Gervey, R., & Shafer, M. (1995). Introduction to psychiatric impairment issue. *Journal of Vocational Rehabilitation*, 5, 73–74.

Getzel, E., Emanuel, E. J., Fesko, S., & Parent, W. (2000). *Factors that inhibit and facilitate transition-age youth in accessing and using SSI work incentives: Implications for policy, research, and practice*. Paper presented at Annual Project Directors' Meeting, National Transition Alliance for Youth with Disabilities, Washington, DC.

Getzel, E., Stodden, R., & Briel, L. (2000). Pursuing postsecondary educational opportunities for individuals with disabilities. In Wehman, P. (Ed.), *Life beyond the classroom: Transition strategies for young people with disabilities* (3rd ed., pp. 247–259). Baltimore: Paul H. Brookes.

Getzel, E. E., & Kregel, J. (1996). Transitioning from the academic to the employment setting: The employment connection program. *Journal of Vocational Rehabilitation*, 6, 273–287.

Giangreco, M.F., Cloninger, CJ., & Iverson, VS. (1993). *Choosing options and accommodations for children: A guide to planning inclusive education*. Baltimore: Paul H. Brookes.

Gill, D., & Edgar, E. (1990). Outcomes of vocational programs designed for students with mild disabilities: The Pierce County Vocational Special Education Cooperative. *Journal for Vocational Special Needs Education*, 12(3), 17–22.

Gillingham, M. G., & Topper, A. (1999). Technology in teacher preparation: Preparing teachers for the future. *Journal of Technology and Teacher Education*, 7, 303–321.

Gilliam, J. E., & Coleman, M. C. (1981). Who influences IEP committee decisions? *Exceptional Children*, 47(8), 642–644.

Gilmore, D., & Butterworth, J. (1996). *Work status trends for people with mental retardation*. Boston: Institute for Community Inclusion.

Gilmore, G. (1974). School psychologist-parent contact: An alternative model. *Psychology in the Schools*, 11, 170–173.

Gliedman, J., & Roth, W. (1980). *The unexpected minority: Handicapped children in America*. New York: Carnegie Council on Children.

Goals 2000: Educate America Act of 1994, 20 U.S.C.S. § 5801 *et seq*.

Goldman, Esq., C. D. (1991). *Disability Rights Guide* (2nd ed.). Lincoln, NE: Media Publishing.

Goldman, H. H., & Mandershied, R. W. (1987). The epidemiology of psychiatric disabilities. In A. T. Meyerson & T. Fine (Eds.), *Psychiatric disability: Clinical, legal, and administrative dimensions* (pp. 13–21). Washington, DC: American Psychiatric Association Press.

Goldstein, A. P., Sprafkin, R. P., Gershaw, N. J., & Klein, P. (1980). *Skillstreaming the adolescent*. Champaign, IL: Research Press.

Goldstein, S., Strickland, B., Turnbull, A. P., & Curry, L. (1980). An observational analysis of the IEP conference. *Exceptional Children*, 46(4), 278–286.

Goldstein, S., & Turnbull, A. P. (1982). Strategies to increase parent participation in IEP conferences. *Exceptional Children*, 48(4), 360–361.

Goodall, P., & Bruder, M. B. (1986, April). Parents and the transition process. *The Exceptional Parent*, 22–28.

Goode, D. (1990). Thinking about and discussing quality of life. In R. Schalock & M. Begab (Eds.), *Quality of life: Perspectives and issues* (pp. 41–58). Washington, DC: American Association on Mental Retardation.

Granger, M. (1996, March 22). Accommodating employees with disabilities: A matter of attitude. *Journal of Managerial Issues*, 8(14), 78.

Gray, A. (1997). Modeling transcultural leadership for transformational change. *The Journal for Vocational Special Needs Education*, 19, 78–84.

Gray, K. (1996). The baccalaureate game: Is it right for all teens? *Phi Delta Kappan*, 77(8), 528–534.

Gray, K. (2002). *The role of career and technical education in the American high school: A student centered analysis*. Washington, DC: U.S. Department of Education.

Grayson T. E. (1998). *Dropout prevention and special services*. In F. R. Rusch & J. G. Chadsey (Eds.), *Beyond high school: Transition from school to work* (pp. 77–98). New York: Wadsworth.

Green, J. W. (1999). *Cultural awareness in the human services: A multi-ethnic approach*. Boston: Allyn & Bacon.

Greenberg, H. F. (1986). Preface. In A. C. Willing & H. F. Greenberg (Eds.), *Bilingualism and learning disabilities: Policy and practice for teachers and administrators* (pp. xv–xvi). New York: American Library.

Greeenberger, E. & Steinberg, L. (1986). *When teenagers work: The psychological and social costs of adolescent employment*. New York: Basic Books.

Greene, G. (1996). Empowering culturally and linguistically diverse families in the transition planning process. *The Journal for Vocational Special Needs Education*, 19, 26–30.

Greene, G. (2003). Transition pathways. In G. Greene & C. A. Kochhar-Bryant (Eds.) *Pathways to successful transition for youth with disabilities*. (pp. 199–229). Columbus, Ohio: Merrill Prentice-Hall.

Greene, G., & Kochhar-Bryant, C. A. (2003). *Pathways to successful transition for youth with disabilities*. Columbus, OH: Merrill.

Greenfield, P. M. (1994). Independence and interdependence as developmental scripts: Implications for theory, research, and practice. In P. M. Greenfield & R. R. Cocking (Eds.), *Cross-cultural roots of minority child development* (pp. 1–37). Hillsdale, NJ: Erlbaum.

Greenwood, C. R. (1991). Longitudinal analysis of time, engagement, and achievement in at-risk versus nonrisk students. *Exceptional Children*, 57, 521–534.

Gresham, F. M. (1986). Conceptual issues in the assessment of social competence in children. In P. S. Strain, M. J. Guralnick, & H. M. Walker (Eds.), *Children's social behavior: Development assessment and modification* (pp. 143–179). New York: Academic Press.

Gresham, F. M., & Nagle, R. J. (1980). Social skills training with children: Responsiveness to modeling and coaching as a function of peer orientation. *Journal of Consulting and Clinical Psychology*, 48, 718–729.

Griffin, C., & Hammis, D. (2001). Self-employment as the logical descendant of supported employment. In P. Wehman (Ed.), *Supported employment in business: Expanding the capacity of workers with disabilities* (pp. 251–268). St. Augustine, Fl: Training Resource Network.

Grigal, M., Test, D. W., Beattie, J., & Wood, W. M. (1997). An evaluation of transition components of individualized education programs. *Exceptional Children*, 63(3), 357–372.

Gunning, T. G. (2003). *Creating literacy instruction for all children* (4th ed.). Boston: Allyn and Bacon.

Hagen, J. L. (1998). Jobs and case management development in 10 states. *Social Work*, 39, 197–204.

Hagner, D., & Dileo, D. (1993). *Working together: Workplace culture, supported employment, and persons with disabilities*. Cambridge, MA: Brookline Books.

Hagner, D., & Vander-Sande, J. (1998). School sponsored work experience and vocational instruction. In F. R. Rusch & J. G. Chadsey (Eds.), *Beyond high school: Transition from school to work* (pp. 340–366). Belmont, CA: Wadsworth.

Hagner, D., Fesko, S., Cadigan, M., Kiernan, W., & Butterworth, J. (1996). Securing employment: Job search and employer negotiation strategies in rehabilitation. In E. M. Szymanski & R. M. Parker (Eds.), *Work and disability: Issues and strategies in career development and job placement* (pp. 309–340). Austin, TX: PRO-ED.

Hagner, D., Helm, D., & Butterworth, J. (1996). "This is your meeting": A qualitative study of person-centered planning. *Mental Retardation*, 34, 159–171.

Hagner, D., Rogan, P., & Murphy, S. (1992). Facilitating natural supports in the workplace: Strategies for support consultants. *Journal of Rehabilitation*, 58, 29–34.

Hall, D. T. (Ed.). (1987). *Career development in organizations*. San Francisco: Jossey-Bass.

Hall, M., Kleinert, H., & Kearns, J. F. (2000). Going to college: Post-secondary programs for students with moderate and severe disabilities. *Teaching Exceptional Children*, 32(3), 58–65.

Hall, M., & Walker, P. (Eds.). (1998). *Annotated bibliography on community integration* (3rd ed.). Syracuse, NY: Syracuse University, Center on Human Policy.

Hallahan, D. P., Lloyd, J. W., Kosiewicz, M. M., Kauffman, J. M., & Graves, A. W. (1979). Self-monitoring of attention as a treatment for a learning disabled boy's off-task behavior. *Learning Disability Quarterly*, 2, 24–32.

Hallenbeck, B. A., & Kauffman, J. M. (1995). How does observational learning affect the behavior of students with emotional or behavioral disorders? A review of research. *Journal of Special Education*, 29, 45–71.

Halloran, W. D. (1993). Transition services requirement: Issues, implications, challenge. In R. C. Eaves & P. J. McLaughlin (Eds.), *Recent advances in special education and rehabilitation* (pp. 210–224). Boston: Andover Medical Publishers.

Halpern, A. S. (1985). Transition: A look at the foundations. *Exceptional Children*, 51, 479–502.

Halpern, A. S. (1990). A methodological review of follow-up and follow-along studies tracking post-school leavers of special education. *Career Development for Exceptional Individuals*, 13, 13–27.

Halpern, A. S. (1992). Transition: Old wine in new bottles. *Exceptional Children*, 58(3), 202–211.

Halpern, A. S. (1993). Quality of Life as a framework for evaluating transition outcomes. *Exceptional Children*, 59.

Halpern, A. S. (1994). The transition of youth with disabilities to adult life: A position statement of the Division on Career Development and Transition, The Council for Exceptional Children. *Career Development of Exceptional Individuals*, 17(2), 115–124.

Halpern, A. S. (1996). *Transition skills inventory*. Eugene, OR: Secondary Transition Program College of Education, University of Oregon.

Halpern, A. S., & Benz, M. R. (1987). A statewide examination of secondary special education for students with mild disabilities: Implications for the high school curriculum. *Exceptional Children*, 54(2), 122–129.

Halpern, A. S., Benz, M. R., & Lindstrom, L. E. (1992). A systems change approach to improving secondary special education and transition programs at the community level. *Career Development for Exceptional Individuals*, 15(1), 109–120.

Halpern, A. S., Doren, B., & Benz, M. R. (1993). Job experiences of students with disabilities during their last two years in school. *Career Development for Exceptional Individuals*, 16(1), 63–73.

Halpern, A. S., & Fuhrer, M. J. (Eds.). (1984). *Functional assessment in rehabilitation*. Baltimore: Paul H. Brookes.

Halpern, A. S., Herr, C. M., Wolf, N. K., Lawson, J. D., Doren, B., & Johnson, M. D. (1997). *Next S.T.E.P.: Student transition and education*. Austin, TX: PRO-ED.

Halpern, A. S., & Irvin, L. (1986). *Social and prevocational information battery-revised*. Monterey, CA: CTB McGraw-Hill.

Halpern, A. S., Irvin, L., & Landman, J. (n.d.). *Tests for everyday living*. Monterey, CA: CTB/McGraw-Hill.

Halpern, A.S., Lehmann, J., Irvin, L., & Heiry, T. (1982). *Contemporary assessment for mentally retarded adolescents and adults*. Baltimore: University Park.

Halpern, A. S., Yavonoff, P., Doren, B., & Benz, M. R. (1995). Predicting participation in postsecondary education for school leavers with disabilities. *Career Development for Exceptional Individuals*, 62(2), 151–164.

Hamburg, D. (1993). The opportunities of early adolescence. *Teachers College Record*, 94, 468.

Hammond, J., & Morrison, J. (1996). *The stuff Americans are made of*. New York: Macmillan.

Hamre-Nietupski, S., Krajewski, L., Nietupski, J., Ostercamp, D., Sensor, K., & Opheim, B. (1988). Parent/professional partnerships in advocacy: Developing integrated options within resistive systems. *Journal of the Association for Persons with Severe Handicaps*, 13(4), 251–259.

Hanley-Maxwell, C., & Collet-Klingenberg, L. (1994). *Synthesis in design of effective curricular practices in transition from school to the community*. Available: *http://darkwing.uoregan.edu/_ncite/otherRsc/research.html*

Hanley-Maxwell, C., & Szymanski, E. M. (1992). School-to-work transition and supported employment. In R. M. Parker & E. M. Szymanski (Eds.), *Rehabilitation counseling: Basics and beyond* (pp. 135–164). Austin, TX: PRO-ED.

Hanley-Maxwell, C. Pogoloff, S. M. & Whitney-Thomas J. (1998). Families: The heart of transition. In F. R. Rusch &

J. G. Chadsey (Eds.), *Beyond high school: Transition from school to work* (pp. 234–264). New York: Wadsworth.

Hanley-Maxwell, C., Szymanski, E., & Owens-Johnson, L. (1998). School-to-adult life transition and supported employment. In E. M. Szymanski & R. M. Parker (Eds.), *Rehabilitation counseling: Basics and beyond* (3rd ed., pp. 143–179). Austin, TX: PRO-ED.

Hanson, M. J. (1998a). Ethnic, cultural, and language diversity in intervention settings. In E. W. Lynch & M. H. Hanson (Eds.), *Developing cross-cultural competence: A guide for working with children and their families* (2nd ed., pp. 3–22). Baltimore: Paul H. Brookes.

Hanson, M. J. (1998b). Families with Native American roots. In E. W. Lynch & M. H. Hanson (Eds.), *Developing cross-cultural competence: A guide for working with children and their families* (2nd ed., pp. 93–126). Baltimore: Paul H. Brookes.

Hanson, M. J., & Carta, J. J. (1996). Addressing the challenges of families with multiple risks. *Exceptional Children, 62*, 201–212.

Hardman, M., & McDonnell, J. (1987). Implementing federal transition initiatives for youths with severe handicaps: The Utah community-based transition project. *Exceptional Children, 53*, 493–498.

Haring, K. A., Lovett, D. L., & Smith, D. D. (1990). A follow-up study of recent special education graduates of learning disabilities programs. *Journal of Learning Disabilities, 23*(2), 108–113.

Haring, N.G., McCormick, L., & Haring, T. G. (1994). *Exceptional children and youth: An introduction to special education*. New York: Macmillan.

Haring, T. G., & Breen, C. (1989). Units of analysis of social interaction outcomes in supported education. *The Journal of the Association for Persons with Severe Handicaps, 14*, 255–262.

Harmon, L. W., Hansen, J. C., Borgen, F. H., & Hammer, A. L. (1994). *Applications and technical guide for the Strong Interest Inventory*. Palo Alto, CA: Consulting Psychologists Press.

Harper, D. (1996). Emerging needs of adults with developmental disabilities. *The Journal of Rehabilitation, 62*(1), 7–10.

Harris, L., & Associates, Inc. (1986). *The ICD survey of disabled Americans: Bringing disabled Americans into the mainstream*. New York: Author.

Harris, L. & Associates, Inc. (1994). N.O.D./*Harris survey of Americans with disabilities* (Study No. 942003). New York: Author.

Harris, L., & Associates, Inc. (2001). N.O.D./*Harris survey of Americans with disabilities*. New York: Author.

Harry, B. (1992a). *Cultural diversity, families, and the special education system: Communication and empowerment*. New York: Teachers College Press.

Harry, B. (1992b). Making sense of disability: Low-income, Puerto Rican parents' theories of the problem. *Exceptional Children, 59*, 27–40.

Harry, B. (1992c). Restructuring the participation of African-American parents in special education. *Exceptional Children, 59*, 123–131.

Hasazi, S. B., Furney, K. S., & DeStefano, L. (1999). Implementing the IDEA transition mandates. *Exceptional Children, 65*(4), 555–566.

Hasazi, S. B., Gordon, L. R., & Roe, C. A. (1985). Factors associated with the employment status of handicapped youth exiting high school from 1979 to 1983. *Exceptional Children, 51*, 455–469.

Haskew, P., & Donnellan, A. M. (1992). *Emotional maturity and well-being: Psychological lessons of facilitated communion*. Danbury, CT: DRT Press.

Hayden, M. F., & Goldman, J. (1996). Families of adults with mental retardation: Stress levels and need for services. *Social Work, 41*(6), 657–667.

Haynes, J., & Justice, T. (1988). *Organizational barriers to transition: Summary*. Sacramento, CA: California Department of Education, Special Education Division.

Hazel, J. S., Schumaker, J. B., Sherman, J. A., & Sheldon-Wildgen, J. (1982). *Asset: A social skills program for adolescents*. Champaign, IL: Research Press.

Heal, L. W., Copher, J. I., Destefano, L. D., & Rusch, F.R. (1989). A comparison of successful and unsuccessful placements of secondary students with mental handicaps into competitive employment, *Career Development for Exceptional Individuals, 12*(2), 167–177.

Heal, L. W., Copher, J. I., & Rusch, F.R. (1990). Interagency agreements (IAA's) among agencies responsible for the transition education of students with handicaps from secondary schools to post-school setting. *Career Development for Exceptional Children, 13*(2), 121–127.

Heal, L. W., Gonzalez, P., Rusch, F. R., Copher, J. I., & DeStefano, L. (1990). A comparison of successful and unsuccessful placements of youths with mental handicaps into competitive employment. *Exceptionality, 1*(3), 181–196.

HEATH Resource Center. (1995). *Getting ready for college: Advising high school students with learning disabilities*. Washington, DC: American Council on Education, U.S. Department of Education.

HEATH Resource Center. (1996). Vast spaces and stone walls: Overcoming barriers to postsecondary education for rural students with disabilities. *Information from HEATH, 15*(2–3), 1–4.

HEATH Resource Center. (1997). *How to choose a college: Guide for the student with a disability*. Washington, DC: American Council on Education, U.S. Department of Education.

HEATH Resource Center. (2003, May). *Summer pre-college programs for students with disabilities 2003*. Retrieved May 22, 2003, from *http://www.heath.gwu.edu/SummerPreCollege.htm*

Heaven, P. C. L. (2001). *The social psychology of adolescence*. (2nd ed.). New York: Palgrave.

Hebbeler, K. (1993). Overview of the high school experience of students with disabilities. In M. Wagner (Ed.), *The secondary programs of students with disabilities*. Menlo Park, CA: SRI International.

Hecklinger, F., & Black, B. (1991). *Training for life: A practical guide for career and life planning.* Dubuque, IA: Kendall Hunt Publishing.

Heins, E. D., Lloyd, J. W., & Hallahan, D. P. (1986). Cued and noncued self-recording of attention to task. *Behavior Modification*, 10, 235–254.

Helge, D. I. (1984a). The state of the art of rural special education. *Exceptional Children*, 50, 294–305.

Helge, D. I. (1984b). Models for serving rural students with low-incidence handicapping conditions. *Exceptional Children*, 50, 313–324.

Henderson, C. (1992). *College freshman with disabilities: A statistical profile.* Washington, DC: HEATH Resource Center, American Council on Education, U. S. Department of Education.

Henderson, C. (1995). *College freshman with disabilities: A statistical profile.* Washington, DC: HEATH Resource Center, American Council on Education, U. S. Department of Education.

Henderson, C. (2001). *College freshman with disabilities: A biennial statistical profile.* Washington, DC: Heath Resource Center, American Council on Education.

Hendricks, D. J., & Hirsh, A. E. (1991). The Job accommodation network: A vital resource for the 90's. *Rehabilitation Education*, 5, 261–264.

Herr, E. L., & Cramer, S. H. (1992). *Career guidance and counseling through the lifespan: Systematic approaches* (4th ed.). New York: HarperCollins.

Herr, E. L., Rayman, J. R., & Garis, J. W. (1993). *Handbook for the college and university career center.* Westport, CT: Greenwood Press.

Hershenson, D. B., & Szymanski, E. M. (1992). Career development of people with disabilities. In R. M. Parker & E. M. Szymanski (Eds.), *Rehabilitation counseling: Basics and beyond* (2nd ed., pp. 273–303). Austin, TX: PRO-ED.

Heyward, S. M. (1996). *Frequently asked questions: Postsecondary education and disability.* Cambridge, MA: Heyward, Lawton & Associates.

Hilton, A., & Henderson, C. J. (1993, September). Parent involvement: A best practice or forgotten practice? *Education and Training in Mental Retardation*, 199–211.

Hitchcock, C. (2001). *Balanced instructional support and challenge in universally designed learning environments.* OSEP Futures Paper, Project Director's Meeting, Washington, D.C.

Hitchcock, C., Meyer, A., Rose, D., & Jackson, R. (2002). Providing new access to the general curriculum: Universal design for learning. *Teaching Exceptional Children*, 35(2) 8–17.

Hobbs, N. (1975). *The futures of children: Categories, labels, and their consequences: Report of the project on classification of exceptional children.* San Francisco: Jossey-Bass.

Hodge, M. & Draine, J. (1993). Case management. In R. W. Flexer and P. Soloman, (Eds.) *Psychiatric rehabilitation in practice.* Boston: Andover medical.

Hoffman, A., Field, S., & Sawilowsky, S. (1996). *Self-determination knowledge scale.* Austin, TX: PRO-ED.

Hoffman, R. C. (1988). Transition. In G. A. Robinson (Ed.), *Best practices in mental disabilities* (Vol. 2, pp. 114–126). (ERIC Document Reproduction Service No. ED 304 834)

Holburn, S., & Vietze, P. (1998). Has person-centered planning become the alchemy of developmental disabilities? *Mental Retardation*, 36(6), 485–488.

Holburn, S., & Vietze, P. M. (2002). *Person-centered planning: Research, practice, and future directions.* Baltimore: Paul H. Brookes.

Holder-Brown, L., & Parette, H. P. (1992). Children with disabilities who use assistive technology: Ethical considerations. *Young Children* 47(6), 73–77.

Holland, J. L. (1985a). *Making vocational choices: A theory of vocational personalities and work environments.* Upper Saddle River, NJ: Prentice Hall.

Holland, J. L. (1985b). *Manual for vocational preference inventory.* Odessa, FL: Psychological Assessment Resources.

Holland, J. L. (1992). *Making vocational choices: A theory of vocational personalities and work environments* (3rd ed.). Odessa, FL: Psychological Assessment Resources.

Holland, J. L., Fritzche, B. A., & Powell, A. B. (1994). *Self-directed search technical manual.* Odessa, FL: Psychological Assessment Resources.

Holtzman, W. H., Jr. (1986). Issues in the implementation of master's level training programs for bilingual special education. In AC. Willing & HF. Greenberg (Eds.), *Bilingualism and learning disabilities: Policy and practice for teachers and administrators* (pp. 137–146). New York: American Library Publishing.

Home of Your Own Project. (1995). *Extending the American dream: Home ownership through creative financing.* Durham, NH: University of New Hampshire, Institute on Disability.

Homstem, B. (1997). How the religious community can support the transition to adulthood: A parent's perspective. *Mental Retardation*, 35, 485–487

Hops, H., Fleishman, D. H., Guild, J., Paine, S., Street A., Walker, H. M., & Greenwood, C. R. (1978). *Program for establishing effective relationship skills* (PEERS). Eugene, OR: University of Oregon, Center at Oregon for Research in the Behavioral Education of the Handicapped.

Hops, H., & Walker, H. M. (1988). CLASS: *Contingency for learning academic and social skills.* Delray Beach, FL: Educational Achievement Systems.

Horne, M. D. (1985). *Attitudes towards handicapped students.* Hillsdale, NJ: Erlbaum.

Hoye, J. D. (1998, July). *Integrating school-to-work into preservice teacher education.* Paper presented at Conference for Professors of Education in Ohio, Kent, OH.

Hoyt, K. B. (1975). *Career education: Contributions to an evolving concept.* Salt Lake City, UT: Olympus.

Hoyt, K. B. (1977). *A primer for career education.* Washington, DC: U.S. Government Printing Office.

HSRI (Human Services Research Institute). (1991). *New models for the provision of personal assistance services: Final report.* Bethesda, MD: Human Services Research Institute.

Huber Marshall, L. H., Martin, J. E., Hughes, C., Jerman, P., & Maxson, L. (1997). *Choosing personal goals*. Longmont, CO: Sopris West.

Huber Marshall, L. H., Martin, J. E., Maxson, L., Hughes, W., Miller, T. L., McGill, T., & Jerman, P. (1996). *Take action: Making goals happen*. Longmont, CO: Sopris West.

Huber Marshall, L. H., Martin, J. E., Maxson, L., & Jerman, P. (1997). *Choosing employment goals*. Longmont, CO: Sopris West.

Hudson, P. J., Schwartz, S. E., Sealander, K. A., Campbell, P., & Hensel, J. W. (1988). Successfully employed adults with handicaps: Characteristics and transition strategies. *Career Development for Exceptional Individuals*, 11(1), 7–14.

Hughes, C., & Kim, J. (1998). Supporting the transition from school to adult life. In F. Rusch & J. Chadsey, *Beyond high school: Transition from school to work* (pp. 367–380). Belmont, CA: Wadsworth.

Hulgin, K., Shoultz, B., Walker, P., & Drake, S. (1996). *Innovative practices in supported living: An overview of organizations, issues, and resource materials*. Syracuse, NY: Syracuse University, Center on Human Policy.

Hulgin, K., Walker, P., Fisher, E., Handley, M., & Shoultz, B. (1995). *Housing for people with severe disabilities: A collection of resource materials*. Syracuse, NY: Syracuse University, Center on Human Policy.

Humes, C. W., & Brammer, G. (1985). LD career success after high school. *Academic Therapy*, 21(2), 171–177.

Individuals with Disabilities Education Act Amendments of 1997, 20 U.S.C. §1400 *et seq*.

Individuals with Disabilities Education Act Amendments of 1997, Pub. L. No. 105-17, 105th Cong., 1st sess.

Individuals with Disabilities Education Act of 1990, 20 U.S.C. §1400 et seq.

Individuals with Disabilities Education Act Regulations, 34 C.F.R. § 300.533 *et seq*. (1997).

Inge, K. J., & Shepherd, J. (1995). Assistive technology applications and strategies for school system personnel. In K.F. Flippo, K.J. Inge, & J.M. Barcus (Eds.), *Assistive technology: A resource for school, work, and community* (pp. 133–166). Baltimore, MD: Paul H. Brookes.

Intagliata, J. & Baker, F. (1983). Factors affecting case management for the chronically mentally ill. *Administration in Mental Health*, 11, 73–91.

International Survey of Faculty Attitudes. (1994, June 9). *The Chronicle of Higher Education*, pp. A35–A38.

Iowa Department of Education. (1998). *School to adult life: Working together towards successful transition*. Des Moines, IA: Author.

Iowa Department of Education, Division of Early Childhood, Elementary, and Secondary Education. (1998). *Working together towards successful transition: School to adult life*. Des Moines, IA: Author.

Ippoliti, C., Peppey, B., & Depoy, E. (1994). Promoting self-determination for persons with developmental disabilities. *Disability & Society* (9), 453–460.

Ivey, A. (1986). *Developmental therapy: Theory into practice*. San Francisco: Jossey-Bass.

Izzo, M. V., Cartledge, G., Miller, L., Growick, B., & Rutkowski, S. (2000). Increasing employment earnings: Extended transition services that make a difference. *Career Development for Exceptional Children*, 23(2), 139–156.

Jackson, N. F., Jackson, D. A., & Morroe, C. (1983). *Getting along with others: Teaching social effectiveness to children*. Champaign, IL: Research Press.

James, S. D., & Egel, A. L. (1986). A direct prompting strategy for increasing reciprocal interactions between handicapped and nonhandicapped siblings. *Journal of Applied Behavior Analysis*, 19, 173–186.

Janesick, V. J. (1995). Our multicultural society. In E. L. Meyen & T. M. Skrtic (Eds.), *Special education and student disability, an introduction: Traditional, emerging, and alternative perspectives* (4th ed., pp. 713–728). Denver, CO: Love.

Jansma, P. & French, R. (1994). *Special physical education: Physical activity sports & recreation*. Englewood Cliffs, NJ: Prentice-Hall.

Jarrow, J. (1992). *Title by title: The ADA's impact on postsecondary education*. Columbus, OH: Association on Higher Education and Disability (AHEAD).

Job Accommodation Network. (1987). *The president's committee on employment of people with disabilities' job accommodation network evaluation report*. West Virginia University, Morgantown, WV: Author.

Job Accommodation Network. (1995). *Accommodation benefit/cost data summary*. West Virginia University, Morgantown, WV: Author.

Joe, J. R., & Malach, R. S. (1998). Families with Native American roots. In E. W. Lynch & M. H. Hanson (Eds.), *Developing cross-cultural competence: A guide for working with children and their families* (2nd ed., pp. 127–164). Baltimore: Paul H. Brookes.

Johnson, D., Bruininks, R., & Thurlow, M. (1987). Meeting the challenge of transition service planning through improved interagency cooperation. *Exceptional Children*, 53 (6), 522–530.

Johnson, D., & Guy, B. (1997). Implications of lessons learned from a state systems change initiative on transition for youth with disabilities. *Career Development for Exceptional Individuals*, 20(2), 191–200.

Johnson, D. R., McGrew, K. S., Bloomberg, L., Bruininks, R. H., & Lin, H. C. (1997). Results of a national follow-up study of young adults with severe disabilities. *Journal of Vocational Rehabilitation*, 8, 119–133.

Johnson, D. R., Sharpe, M., & Sinclair, M. F. (1998). *Report on the national survey of the implementation of the IDEA transition re-*

quirements. Minneapolis: National Transition Network, Institute on Community Integration, University of Minnesota.

Johnson, D. R., Stodden, R. A., Emanuel, E. J., Luecking, R., & Mack, M. (2002). Current challenges facing secondary education and transition services: What research tells us. *Exceptional Children*, 68(4), 519–531.

Johnson, D. W., & Johnson, R. T. (1986). Mainstreaming and cooperative learning strategies. *Exceptional Children*, 52, 553–561.

Johnson, D. W., Maruyama, G., Johnson, R. T., Nelson, D., & Skon, L. (1981). The effects of cooperative, competitive, and individualistic goal structures on achievement: A meta-analysis. *Psychological Bulletin*, 89, 47–62.

Johnson, J. & Rusch, F. (1993). Secondary special education and transition services: Identification and recommendations for future research and demonstration. *Career Development for Exceptional Individuals*, 16(1), 1–18.

Johnson, T. Z. (1985). *Belonging to the community*. Madison, WI: Options in Community Living.

Johnson, D. R., Stodden, R. A., Emanuel, E. A., Luecking, R., & Mack, M. (2002). Current challenges facing the future of secondary education and transition services. What the research tells us. *Exceptional Children*, 68(4), 519–531.

Jones, R. T., Kazdin, A. E., & Haney, J. I. (1981). Social validation and training of emergency fire safety skills for potential injury prevention and life saving. *Journal of Applied Behavior Analysis*, 14, 249–260.

Jorgensen, C. M. (1998). Restructuring high school for all students: Taking inclusion to the next level. Baltimore: Paul H. Brookes.

June, J., & Kelley, Y. (1998). *Quality indicators handbook* [Monograph]. Louisville, KY: Jefferson County Public Schools.

Katz, M. R. (1993). *Computer-assisted career decision making: The guide in the machine*. Hillsdale, NJ: Erlbaum.

Kauffman, J. M. (1987). Research in special education: A commentary. *Remedial and Special Education*, 8(6), 57–62.

Kauffman, J. M. (1997). *Characteristics of emotional and behavioral disorders of children and youth* (6th ed.). Upper Saddle River, NJ: Merrill/Prentice Hall.

Kauffman, J. M. (1998). Are we all postmodernists now? *Behavioral Disorders*, 23, 149–152.

Kauffman, J. M. (1999). The role of science in behavioral disorders. *Behavioral Disorders*, 24, 265–272.

Kauffman, J. M., Hallahan, D. P., Mostert, M. P., Trent, S. C., & Nuttycombe, D. G. (1993). *Managing classroom behavior: A reflective case-based approach*. Boston: Allyn & Bacon.

Kazdin, A. E. (1989). *Behavior modification in applied settings* (4th ed.). Pacific Grove, CA: Brooks/Cole Publishing.

Kearns, J. & Dryer, L. (1997). *Teaching all students in Kentucky schools* (TASKS). Lexington, KY: University of Kentucky, Human Development Institute.

Keitel, M. A., Kopala, M., & Adamson, W. S. (1996). Ethical issues in multicultural assessment. In L. A. Suzuki, P. J. Meller, & J. G. Ponterotto (Eds.), *Handbook of multicultural assessment* (pp. 29–48). San Francisco: Jossey-Bass.

Kelly, W. J., Salzberg, C. L., Levy, S. M., Warrenfeltz, R. B., Adams, T. W., Crouse, T. R., & Beegle, G. P. (1983). The effects of role-playing and self-monitoring on the generalization of vocational skills by behaviorally disordered adolescents. *Behavioral Disorders*, 9, 27–35.

Kentucky Council on Postsecondary Education. (1998). *Futures: Your guide to life after high school*. Frankfort, KY: The Kentucky Council on Postsecondary Education.

Kern, L., Childs, K. E., Dunlap, G., Clarke, S., & Falk, G. D. (1994). Using assessment-based curricular intervention to improve the classroom behavior of a student with emotional and behavioral challenges. *Journal of Applied Behavior Analysis*, 27, 7–19.

Kerr, M. M., & Nelson, C. M. (1998). *Strategies for managing behavior in the classroom* (3rd ed.). Upper Saddle, NJ: Merrill/Prentice Hall.

Kezar, A. (1997a). At the fork in the path: Some guidance from the research. *The ERIC review: The path to college*, 5(3), 26–29.

Kezar, A. (1997b). How colleges are changing. *The ERIC review: The path to college*, 5(3), 29–32.

Khattri, N., Riley, K., & Kane, M. (1997). Students at risk in poor, rural areas: A review of the research. *Journal of Research in Rural Education*, 13(2), 79–100.

Kiburz, C. S., Miller, S. R., & Morrow, L. W. (1985). Structured learning using self-monitoring to promote maintenance and generalization of social skills across settings for a behaviorally disordered adolescent. *Behavior Disorders*, 11, 47–55.

Kim, V., & Choi, S. H. (1994). Individualism, collectivism, and child development. In P. M. Greenfield & R. R. Cocking (Eds.), *Cross-cultural roots of minority child development* (pp. 226–257). Hillsdale, NJ: Erlbaum.

King-Sears, M. E. (1997). Best academic practices for inclusive classrooms. *Focus on Exceptional Children*, 29, 1–22.

King-Sears, M. E. (2001). Three steps for gaining access to the general education curriculum for learners with disabilities. *Intervention in School and Clinic*, 37(2) 67–76.

Kinnison, L. R., Jr. (1987). Do parents know best? *The Journal for Vocational Special Needs Education*, 10 (1), 13–16.

Klein, J. (1992). Get me the hell out of here: Supporting people with disabilities to live in their own homes. In J. Nisbet (Ed.), *Natural supports in school, at work, and in the community for people with severe disabilities* (pp. 277–339). Baltimore: Paul H. Brookes.

Kleinert, H. L., Kearns, F. K., & Kennedy, S. (1997). Accountability for all students: Kentucky's alternate portfolio assessment for students with moderate and severe cognitive disabilities. *Journal of Association for Persons with Severe Disabilities*, 22(2), 88–101.

Knoll, J. (1992). Being a family: The experience of raising a child with a disability or chronic illness. In V. J. Bradley, J. Knoll, & J. M. Agosta (Eds.), *Emerging issues in family supports* (American Association on Mental Retardation Monograph Series No 18, pp. 9–56). Washington, DC: American Association on Mental Retardation.

Knoll, J. & Ford, A. (1987). Beyond caregiving: A reconceptualization of the role of the residential service provider. In S. J. Taylor, D. Biklen, & J. A. Knoll (Eds.), *Community integration for people with severe disabilities* (pp. 129–146). New York: Teachers' College Press.

Knopp, L., & Otuya, E. (1995). Who is teaching America's school children? *Research Briefs*, 6, 1–13.

Knowlton, E. (1998). Considerations in the design of personalized curricular supports for students with developmental disabilities. *Education and Training in Mental Retardation and Developmental Disabilities*, 33, 95–107.

Knowlton, H., Turnbull, D. R., Backus, L., & Turnbull, H. R. (1988). Letting go: Consent and the yes but . . . "problem in transition." In B. L. Ludlow, A. P. Turnbull, & R. Luckasson (Eds.), *Transitions to adult life for people with mental retardation* (pp. 45–66). Baltimore: Paul H. Brookes.

Knox, W., Lindsay, P., & Kolb, N. (1993). *Does college make a difference? Long-term changes in activities and attitudes*. Westport, CT: Greenwood Press.

Koch, L., & Johnston-Rodriguez, S. (1997). The career portfolio: A vocational rehabilitation tool for assessment, planning, and placement. *Journal of Job Placement*, 13(1), 19–22.

Koch, L. C., & Rumrill, P. D. (1998a). Interpersonal communication skills for case managers. *Healthcare and rehabilitation managers' desk reference*. Lake Zurich, IL: Vocational Consultants Press.

Koch, L. C., & Rumrill, P. D. (1998b). The working alliance: An interdisciplinary case management strategy for health professionals. *Work*, 10, 55–62.

Kochany, L., & Keller, J. (1981). An analysis and evaluation of the failures of severely disabled individuals in competitive employment. In P. Wehman (Ed.), *Competitive employment: New horizons for severely disabled individuals* (pp. 181–198). Baltimore: Paul H. Brookes.

Kochhar–Bryant, C. A., & Deschamps, A. B. (1992). Policy crossroads in preserving the right of passage to independence for learners with special needs: Implications of current change in national vocational and special education policies. *Journal for Vocational Special Needs Education*, 14(2–3), 9–19.

Kochhar–Bryant, C. A., & West, L. L. (1995). Future directions for federal legislation affecting transition services for individuals with special needs. *Journal for Vocational Special Needs Education*, 17(3), 85–93.

Kohler, P. D. (1993). Best practices in transition: Substantiated or implied? *Career Development for Exceptional Individuals*, 16, 107–121.

Kohler, P. D. (1996). Preparing youths with disabilities for future challenges: A taxonomy for transition planning. In P. D. Kohler (Ed.), *Taxonomy for transition planning: Linking research and practice* (pp. 1–62). Champaign, IL: Transition Research Institute at Illinois, University of Illinois at Urbana-Champaign [Monograph].

Kohler, P. D. (1998). Implementing a transition perspective of education: A comprehensive approach to planning and delivering secondary education and transition services. In F. R. Rusch & J. G. Chadsey (Eds.), *Beyond high school: Transition from school to work* (pp.179–205). New York: Wadsworth.

Kohler, P. D., DeStefano, L., Wermuth, T., Grayson, T., & McGinty, S. (1994). An analysis of exemplary transition programs: How and why are they selected? *Career Development for Exceptional Individuals*, 17(2), 187–202.

Kokaska, C., & Brolin, D. E. (1985). *Career education for handicapped individuals* (2nd ed.). Columbus, OH: Merrill.

Kolstoe, O. P., & Frey, R. M. (1965). *A high school work study program for mentally subnormal students*. Carbondale, IL: Southern Illinois University Press.

Kortering, L. J., & Edgar, E. B. (1988). Vocational rehabilitation and special education: A need for cooperation. *Rehabilitation Counseling Bulletin*, 3(3), 178–184.

Kounin, J. S. (1970). *Discipline and group management in classrooms*. New York: Holt, Rinehart and Winston.

Kounin, J. S. (1983). *Classrooms: Individuals or behavior settings?* [Monographs] in Teaching and Learning. (ERIC Document # ED 240 070).

Kozol, J. (1996). Amazing grace: The lives of children and the conscience of a nation. New York: Harper Perennial.

Kranstover, L. L., Thurlow, M. L., & Bruininks, R. H. (1989). Special education graduates versus non-graduates: A longitudinal study of outcomes. *Career Development for Exceptional Individuals*, 12, 153–166.

Kravets, M., & Wax, I. F. (Eds.). (1999). *The K & W guide to colleges for the learning disabled* (3rd ed.). Cambridge, MA: Educators Publishing Service.

Kregel, J., & Unger, D. (1993). Employer perceptions of the work potential of individuals with disabilities: An illustration from supported employment. *Journal of Vocational Rehabilitation*. 3(4). 17–25.

Kregel, J., Wehman, P., & Banks, P. D. (1989). The effects of consumer characteristics and type of employment model on individual outcomes in supported employment. *Journal of Applied Behavior Analysis*, 22, 407–415.

Kregel, J., Wehman, P., Seyfarth, J., & Marshall, K. (1986). Community integration of young adults with mental retardation: Transition from school to adulthood. *Education and Training of the Mentally Retarded*, 21, 35–42.

Kreutzer, J. S., Wehman, P., Morton, M. V., & Stonnington, H. H. (1988). Supported employment and compensatory strategies for enhancing compensatory strategies for enhancing vocational outcomes following traumatic brain injury. *Brain Injury*, 2, 205–223.

Krom, D. M. & Prater, M. A. (1993). IEP goals for intermediate-aged students with mild mental retardation. *Career Development for Exceptional Individuals*, 16(1), 87–95.

Krouse, J., Gerber, M. M., & Kauffman. J. M. (1981). Peer tutoring: Procedures, promises, and unresolved issues. *Exceptional Education Quarterly*, 1(4), 107–115.

Krouse, J. & Sabousky, R. (2001). Curriculum development and transition. In Robert W. Flexer, Thomas J. Simmons, Pamela Luft, & Robert M. Baer, *Transition planning for secondary students with disabilities* (pp. 227–246). Columbus, OH: Merrill.

Krumboltz, J. (1988). *The Career Beliefs Inventory*. Palo Alto, CA: Consulting Psychologists Press.

LaGreca, A. M., & Santogrossi, A. A. (1980). Social skills training with elementary school students. *Journal of Consulting and Clinical Psychology*, 48, 220–227.

LaGreca, A. M., Stone, W. L., & Bell, C. R. (1982a). *Vocational problem behavior inventory*. Miami, FL: Department of Psychology, University of Miami, Coral Gables.

LaGreca, A. M., Stone, W. L., & Bell, C. R. (1982b). Assessing the problematic interpersonal skills of mentally retarded workers in a vocational setting. *Applied Research in Mental Retardation*, 3, 37–53.

Lahm, E., & Morrissette, S. (1994). *Zap'em with assistive technology*. Paper presented at the annual meeting of the Council for Exceptional Children, April, 1994, Denver, CO.

Lahm, E. A. (Ed.). (1989). *Technology with low incidence populations: Promoting access to education and learning*. Reston, VA: Council for Exceptional Children.

Lakin, C., & Burwell, B. (1995) Medicaid community supported living arrangements: Five-year "pilot projects" with lasting effects. IMPACT 8(4), 4–5, 27.

Lakin, K., Hill, B., White, C., & Write, E. (1988). *Longitudinal change and interstate variability in the size of residential facilities for persons with mental retardation*. Minneapolis, MN: Center on Residential and Community Services, University of Minnesota.

Langone, J. (2000). Technology for individuals with severe and physical disabilities. In J.D. Lindsey (Ed.), *Technology and exceptional individuals* (3rd ed.) (pp. 327–350). Austin TX: PRO-ED.

LaPlante, M.P., Kennedy, J., Kaye, S.H., & Wenger, B.L. (1997). Disability and employment. *Disability statistics abstract*, 11, San Francisco: Disability Statistics Rehabilitation Research and Training Center, University of California.

Lareau, A. (1989). *Home advantage: Social class and parental intervention in elementary education*. London: Falmer Press.

Larrivee, B. (1986). Effective teaching for mainstreamed students is effective teaching for all students. *Teacher Education and Special Education*, 9, 173–179.

Larson, C. (1981). *State of Iowa dissemination model for* MD *and* LD *students*. Fort Dodge: IA: Iowa Central Community College.

Lawn, B., & Meyerson, A. T. (1995). A modern perspective on psychiatry in rehabilitation. In R. W. Flexer & P. L. Solomon (Eds.), *Psychiatric rehabilitation in practice*. (pp. 31–44). Boston, MA: Andover Publishers.

Lazzaro, J. J. (1996). Toward software both seen and heard. *Technology Review*, 99(7), 66–67.

Leake, D., & Stodden, B. (1994). Getting to the core of transition: A re-assessment of old wine in new bottles. *Career Development for Exceptional Individuals*, 17(1), 65–76.

LeConte, P. (1986). Vocational assessment of special needs learners: A vocational education perspective. Paper presented at Annual meeting of American Vocational Association in Atlanta, GA.

LeConte, P. J., & Kochhar, C. A. (1983). Agents for success in job training partnerships. *Journal for Vocational Special Needs Education*, 6(1), 24–28.

LeConte, P. J., & Neubert, D. (1987). Vocational education for special needs students: Linking vocational assessment and support. *Diagnostique*, 12, 156–167.

Lee, J. (1995). *A survey of regional special education assistive technology practices in North Dakota*. Cavalier, ND: Interagency Project for Assistive Technology.

Lehmann, J. P., Bassett, D. S., & Sands, D. J. (1999). Students' participation in transition-related actions: A qualitative study. *Remedial and Special Education*, 20, 160–169.

Lehmann, J. P., Deniston, T., & Grebenc, R. (1989). Counseling parents to facilitate transition: The difference parents make. *The Journal for Vocational Special Needs Education*, 11(3), 15–18.

Leventhal, J. D. (1996). Assistive devices for people who are blind or have visual impairments. In J. C. Galvin & M. J. Scherer (Eds.), *Evaluating, selecting, and using appropriate assistive technology* (pp. 125–143). Gaithersburg, MD: Aspen Publishers, Inc.

Levesque, K., Lauen, D., Teitelbaum, P., Martha, A., & Librera, S. (2000). Vocational Education in the United States: Toward the Year 2000, National Center for Education Statistics. U.S. Department of Education, Office of Educational Research and Improvement NCES 2000–02.

Lewis, R. D. (1997). *When cultures collide: Managing successfully across cultures*. London: Nicholas Brealey.

Lewis, W. C. (1972). *Why people change*. New York: Holt, Rinehart and Winston.

Lichstenstein, S. (1998). Characteristics of youth and young adults. In F. R. Rusch & J. G. Chadsey (Eds), *Beyond high school: Transition from school to work* (pp. 3–35). New York: Wadsworth.

Lindstrom, L., Benz, M., & Johnson, M. (1996). Developing job clubs for students in transition. *Teaching Exceptional Children*, 29(2), 18–21.

Lindstrom, L. E., & Benz, M. R. (2002). Phases of career development: Case studies of young women with learning disabilities. *Exceptional Children*, 69(1). 67–83.

Linn, R., & DeStefano, L. (1986). *Review of student assessment instruments and practices in use in the secondary/transition project*. Champaign, IL: Secondary Transition Intervention Effectiveness Institute, University of Illinois at Urbana-Champaign. (ERIC Document Reproduction Service No. ED 279 123)

Lippert, T. (1987). *The case management team: Building community connections*. St. Paul, MN: Metropolitan Council.

Litvak, S., Zukas, H., & Heumann, J. (1987). *Attending to America: Personal assistance for independent living*. Berkeley, CA: World Institute on Disability.

Lloyd, J. W., & Landrum, T. J. (1990). Self-recording of attending to task: Treatment components and generalization of effects. In T. E. Scruggs & B. Y. Wong (Eds.), *Intervention research in learning disabilities* (pp. 235–262). New York: Springer-Verlag.

Lloyd, J. W., Landrum, T. J., & Hallahan, D. P. (1991). Self-monitoring applications for classroom intervention. In G. Stoner, M. R. Shinn, & H. M. Walker (Eds.), *Interventions for achievement and behavior problems*. Harrisonburg, VA: NASP.

Loewen, G., & Iaquinto, M. (1990). Rebuilding a career plan: Issues for head injured students. In J. J. Vander Putten (Ed.), *Reaching new heights: Proceedings of the 1989 AHSSPPE Conference*. Columbus, OH: Association on Handicapped Student Service Programs in Postsecondary Education.

Lofquist, L., & Dawis, R. (1991). *Essentials of person-environment correspondence counseling*. Minneapolis, MN: University of Minnesota Press.

Lofquist, L. H., & Dawis, R. V. (1969). *Adjustment to work: A psychological view of man's problems in a work-oriented society*. New York: Appleton-Century-Crofts, Education Division, Meredith Corporation.

Lombard, R. C., Hazelkorn, M. N., & Miller, R. J. (1995). Special populations and tech prep. A national study of state policy and practice. *Career Development for Exceptional Individuals*, 18(2), 145–156.

Lombard, R. C., Hazelkorn, M. N., & Neubert, D. A. (1992). A survey of accessibility to secondary vocational education programs and transition services for students with disabilities in Wisconsin. *Career Development for Exceptional Individuals*, 15(2), 179–188.

Lovejoy, M. C., & Routh, D. K. (1988). Behavior disordered children's social skills: Increased by training, but not sustained or reciprocated. *Child and Family Behavior Therapy*, 10, 15–27.

Lovitt, T. C., Cushing, S. S., & Stump, C. S. (1994). High school students rate their IEPs: Low opinions and lack of ownership. *Intervention in School and Clinic*, 30, 34–37.

Lubin, R., Jacobson, J. W., & Kiely, M. (1982). Projected impact of the functional definition of developmental disabilities: The categorically disabled population and service eligibility. *American Journal of Mental Deficiency*, 87, 73–79.

Luckasson, R., Coulter, D., Pollaway, E., Reiss, S., Schalock, R., Snell, M., Spitalnik, D., & Stark, J. (1992). *Mental retardation: Definition, classification, and systems of supports* (9th ed.), Washington, DC: American Association on Mental Retardation.

Luckasson, R., & Spitalnik, D. (1994). Political and programmatic shifts of the 1992 AAMR definition of mental retardation. In V. J. Bradley, J. W. Ashbaugh, & B. C. Blaney (Eds.), *Creating individual supports for people with developmental disabilities: A mandate for change at many levels*. (pp. 81–95). Baltimore: Paul H. Brookes.

Luecking, R. G., & Fabian, R. G. (2000). Paid internships and employment success for youth in transition. *Career Development for Exceptional Individuals*, 23(2), 205–221.

Luft, P. (1995, April). *Addressing minority overrepresentation in special education: Cultural barriers to effective collaboration*. Presentation at the annual convention of the Council for Exceptional Children, Indianapolis, IN.

Luft, P. (1999). Assessment and collaboration: Key elements in comprehensive and cohesive transition planning. *Work*, 13, 31–41.

Luft, P., & Koch, L. (1998). Transition of adolescents with chronic illness: Overlooked needs and rehabilitation considerations. *Journal of Vocational Rehabilitation*, 10, 205–217.

Luft, P., & Koch, L. C. (2001). Career development: Theories for transition planning. In Robert W. Flexer, Thomas J. Simmons, Pamela Luft, and Robert M. Baer. *Transition planning for secondary students with disabilities* (pp. 69–94). Columbus, OH: Merrill.

Luft, P., Koch, L. C., Headmen, D., & O'Connor, P. (2001). Career and vocational education. In Robert W. Flexer, Thomas J. Simmons, Pamela Luft, & Robert M. Baer, *Transition planning for secondary students with disabilities* (pp. 162–196). Columbus, OH: Merrill.

Luft, P., Rumrill, P., & Snyder-Marks, J. L. (in press). Transition strategies for youths with sensory impairments. *Journal of Job Placement*.

Lusthaus, C. S., Lusthaus, E. W., & Gibbs, H. (1981). Parents' role in the decision process. *Exceptional Children*, 48(3), 256–257.

Lynch, E. C., & Beare, P. L. (1990). The quality of IEP objectives and their relevance to instruction for students with mental retardation and behavioral disorders. *Remedial and Special Education*, 11(2), 48–55.

Lynch, E. W. (1998a). Conceptual framework: From culture shock to cultural learning. In E. W. Lynch & M. H. Hanson

(Eds.), *Developing cross-cultural competence: A guide for working with children and their families* (2nd ed., pp. 23–46). Baltimore: Paul H. Brookes.

Lynch, E. W. (1998b). Developing cross-cultural competence. In E. W. Lynch & M. H. Hanson (Eds.), *Developing cross-cultural competence: A guide for working with children and their families* (2nd ed., pp. 47–90). Baltimore: Paul H. Brookes.

Lynch, E. W., & Stein, R. C. (1982). Perspectives on parent participation in special education. *Exceptional Education Quarterly, 3,* 56–63.

Lynch, E. W., & Stein, R. C. (1987). Parent participation by ethnicity: A comparison of Hispanic, Black, and Anglo families. *Exceptional Children, 54,* 105–111.

Lynch, R. T., & Gussel, L. (1996). Disclosure and self-advocacy regarding disability-related needs: Strategies to maximize integration in postsecondary education. *Journal of Counseling & Development, 74,* 352–357.

Maag, J. W. (1989). Assessment in social skills training: Methodological and conceptual issues for research and practice. *Remedial and Special Education,* 10(4), 6–17.

Maag, J. W., Reid, R., & DiGangi, S. A. (1993). Differential effects of self-monitoring attention, accuracy, and productivity. *Journal of Applied Behavior Analysis, 26,* 329–344.

MacDonald-Wilson, K. L., Revell, Jr., W. G., Nguyen, N. H., & Peterson, M. (1991). Supported employment outcomes for people with psychiatric disability: A comparative analysis. *Journal of Vocational Rehabilitation,* 1(3), 30–44.

Mackelsprang, R. W., & Salsgiver, R. O. (1996). People with disabilities and social work: Historical and contemporary issues. *Social Work,* 41(1), 7–14.

Maddy-Bernstein, C. (1997). Vocational preparation for students with disabilities. In H. M. Wallace, R. F. Bieh, J. C. MacQueen, & J. A. Blackman (Eds.), *Mosby's resource guide to children with disabilities and chronic illness* (pp. 381–392). St. Louis, MO: Mosby-Year Book.

Mahoney, J. & Cairns, R. (1997). Do extracurricular activities protect against early school dropout? *Developmental Psychology,* 33(2), 241–253.

Malian, I. M., & Love, L. L. (1998). Leaving high school: An ongoing transition study. *Teaching Exceptional Children,* 30 (1), 4–10.

Malone, B. L. (1995). Job clubs: Providing an empathetic ear, moral support, and a built-in EEO procedure. *Equal Employment Opportunity Career Journal,* 31 October, Vol. 30 (pp. 20–32).

Mangrum, C. T., & Strichart, S. S. (Eds.). (1997). *Peterson's colleges with programs for students with learning disabilities or attention deficit disorders* (5th ed.). Princeton, NJ: Peterson's Guides.

Mank, D., Cioffi, A. & Yovanoff, P. (1997). An analysis of the typicalness of supported employment jobs, natural supports, and wage and integration outcomes. *Mental Retardation,* 35(3), 185–197.

Mank, D., Oorthuys, J., Rhodes, L., Sandow, D., & Weyer, T. (1992). Accommodating workers with mental disabilities. *Training and Development Journal, 46,* 49–52.

Marder, C. (1992). *How well are youth with disabilities really doing? A comparison of youth with disabilities and youth in general.* Menlo Park, CA: SRI International.

Markel, G., & Greenbaum, J. (1981). Assertiveness training for parents of disabled children. *The Exceptional Parent,* 11(4), 17–22.

Markowitz, J. (1996, May). *Strategies that address the disproportionate number of students from racial/ethnic minority groups receiving special education services: Case studies of selected states and school districts, final report.* Paper presented at the National Association of State Directors of Special Education, Alexandria, VA.

Martin, J. E., & Huber Marshall, L. H. (1995). ChoiceMaker: A comprehensive self-determination transition program. *Intervention in School and Clinic,* 30(3), 147–156.

Martin, J. E., & Huber Marshall, L. H. (1996a). ChoiceMaker: Infusing self-determination instruction into the IEP and transition process. In D.J. Sands & M.L. Wehmeyer (Eds.), *Self-determination across the life span* (pp. 215–236). Baltimore: Paul H. Brookes.

Martin, J. E., & Huber Marshall, L. H. (1996b). *ChoiceMaker self-determination transition assessment.* Longmont, CO: Sopris West, Inc.

Martin, J. E., Huber-Marshall, L., Maxson, L. L., & Jerman, P. (1996). *Self-directed.* IEP. Longmont, CO: Sopris West.

Martin, J. E., Huber Marshall, L., & Sale, R. P. (1999). IEP *Team Tells All!* Manuscript submitted for publication.

Martin, J. E., Huber Marshall, L., & Sale, R. P. (in press). Student participation in their own IEP meetings: A three-year study. *Exceptional Children.*

Martin, J. E., Huber Marshall, L., Wray, D., O'Brien, J., & Snyder, L. (1999). *Choose and take action.* Software and lesson package submitted for publication.

Martin, J. E., Huber Marshall, L., Wray, D., Wells, L., O'Brien, J., Olvey, G., & Johnson, Z. (2004). *Choose and take action: Finding the right job for you.* Longmont, CO: Sopris West.

Martin, J. E., Hughes, W., Huber Marshall, L. H., Jerman, P., & Maxson, L. (1999). *Choosing education goals.* Longmont, CO: Sopris West.

Martin, J. E., Marshall, L. H., & Maxson, L. L. (1993). Transition policy: Infusing self-determination and self-advocacy into transition programs. *Career Development for Exceptional Individuals,* 16(1), 53–61.

Martin, J. E., Mithaug, D. E., Cox, P., Peterson, L. Y., Van Dycke, J. L., & Cash, M. E. (2003). Increasing self-determination: Teaching students to plan, work, evaluate, and adjust. *Exceptional Children,* 69(4), 431–447.

Martin, J. E., Mithaug, D. E., Oliphint, J., & Husch, J. V. (2002). *ChoiceMaker employment: A self-determination transition and supported employment handbook*. Baltimore: Paul H. Brookes.

Martin, J. E., Mithaug, D. E., Oliphint, J. H., Husch, J. V., & Frazier, E. S. (2002). *Self-directed employment: A handbook for transition teachers and employment specialists*. Baltimore: Paul H. Brookes.

Marzano, R. (2001). Classroom instruction that works: Research-based strategies for increasing student achievement. Alexandria, VA. ASCD.

Masino, L. L., & Hodapp, R. M. (1996). Parental educational expectations for adolescents with disabilities. *Exceptional Children*, 62(6), 515–524.

Maslow, A. H. (1970). *Motivation and personality* (2nd ed.). New York: Harper & Row.

Massenzio, S. (1983). Legal resource networks for parents of individuals with special needs. *Exceptional Children*, 50(3), 273–275.

Mastropieri, M. A., & Scruggs, T. E. (1987). *Effective instruction for special education*. Boston: Little, Brown.

Mastropieri, M. A., & Scruggs, T. E. (1994). *Effective instruction for special education* (2nd ed.). Austin, TX: PRO-ED.

Mastropieri, M. A., & Scruggs, T. E. (1994). Text-based vs. activities-oriented science curriculum: Implications for students with disabilities. *Remedial and Special Education*, 15, 72–85.

Mastropieri, M. A., & Scruggs, T. E. (2000). *The inclusive classroom: Strategies for effective instruction*. Upper Saddle River, NJ: Merrill/Prentice Hall.

Mastropieri, M. A., & Scruggs, T. E. (2002). *Effective instruction for special education* (3rd ed.). Upper Saddle River, NJ: Merrill/Prentice Hall.

Mattessich, B. W., & Monsey, B. R. (1992). *Collaboration: What makes it work*. St. Paul, MN: Amherst H. Wilder Foundation Publishing Center.

McCarthy, D., Thompson, T., & Olson, S. (1998). Planning a statewide project to convert day treatment to supported employment. *Psychiatric Rehabilitation Journal*, 22(1), 30–33.

McCaughrin, W., Ellis, W., Rusch, F., & Heal, L. (1993). Cost-effectiveness of supported employment. *Mental Retardation*, 31(1), 41–48.

McCord, W. (1983). The outcomes of normalization: strengthened bonds between handicapped persons and their communities. *Education and Training of the Mentally Retarded*, 18(3), 153–157.

McDonald, G., & Oxford, M. (n.d.). *History of independent living*. Dayton, OH: Access Center for Independent Living.

McDonnell, J., Ferguson, B., & Mathot-Buckner, C. (1992). Transition from school to work for students with severe disabilities: The Utah community employment placement project. In F. R. Rusch, L. DeStefano, J. Chadsey-Rusch, L. A. Phelps, & E. Szymanski (Eds.), *Transition from school to adult life: Models, linkages, and policy* (pp. 33–50). Sycamore, IL: Sycamore.

McDonnell, J., Hardman, M. L., & Hightower, J. (1989). Employment preparation for high school students with severe handicaps. *Mental Retardation*, 27(6), 396–405.

McDonnell, J., Wilcox, B., & Boles, S. M. (1986). Do we know enough to plan for transition? A national survey of state agencies responsible for services to persons with severe handicaps. *Journal of The Association for Persons with Severe Handicaps*, 11(1), 53–60.

McDonnell, J. J., Wilcox, B., Boles, S. M., & Bellamy, G. T. (1985). Issues in transition from school to adult services: A survey of parents of secondary students with severe handicaps. *The Journal of the Association for Persons with Severe Handicaps*, 10(1), 61–65.

McDonnell, J., Wilcox, B., & Hardman, M. L. (1992). *Secondary programs for students with developmental disabilities*. Boston: Allyn & Bacon.

McFall, R. (1982). A review and reformulation of the concept of social skills. *Behavioral Assessment*, 4, 1–33.

McGahee-Kovac, M. (1995). *A student's guide to the* IEP. Washington, DC: National Information Center for Children and Youth with Disabilities

McGaughey, M., Kiernan, W., McNally, L., Gilmore, D., & Keith, G. (1994). *Beyond the Workshop: National perspectives on integrated employment*. Boston: Institute for Community Inclusion.

McGinnis, E., Goldstein, A. P., Sprafkin, R. P., & Gershaw, N. J. (1984). *Skillstreaming the elementary school child*. Champaign, IL: Research Press.

McKnight, J. (1987). Regenerating community. *Social Policy*, Winter, 54–58.

McLaughlin, T. F. (1983). Effects of self-recording for on-task and academic responding: A long term analysis. *Journal of Special Education Technology*, 6(3), 5–12.

McMahan, R. K., & Baer, R. (2001). *Survey on transition policy compliance and best practices: Final report*. Kent, OH: Transition Center, Kent State University.

McNair, J., & Rusch, F. R. (1987). Parent survey: Identification and validation of transition issues. *Interchange*, 7(4), Urbana-Champaign, IL: University of Illinois, Transition Institute.

McNair, J., & Rusch, F. R. (1991). Parent involvement in transition programs. *Mental Retardation*, 29(2), 93–101.

McPhatter, A. R. (1997). Cultural competence in child welfare: What is it? How do we achieve it? What happens without it? *Child Welfare*, 50, 85–106.

McPherson, A., & Brackett, J. D. (1994). Postsecondary school transition issues affecting the vocational rehabilitation of young adults with LD. *The Journal of Vocational Rehabilitation*, 4(2), 131–138.

Meara, N. M., & Patton, M. J. (1994). Contribution of the working alliance in the practice of career counseling. *Career Development Quarterly*, 43, 161–178.

Meers, G. C. (1987). An introduction to vocational special needs education. In G. D. Meers (Ed.), *Handbook of vocational special needs education* (2nd ed., pp. 3–28). Rockville, MD: Aspen Publishers.

Meers, G. D. (1992). Getting ready for the next century: vocational preparation of students with disabilities. *Teaching Exceptional Children*, 24, 36–39.

Mehan, J., Hertweck, A., & Meihls, J. L. (1986). *Handicapping the handicapped: Decision-making in students' educational careers*. Palo Alto, CA: Stanford University.

Menchetti, B. M., & Piland, V. C. (1998). A person-centered approach to vocational evaluation and career planning. In F. R. Rusch & J. Chadsey (Eds.), *Beyond high school: Transition from school to work*. New York: Wadsworth.

Menchetti, B. M., Rusch, F. R., & Owens, D. M. (1983). Vocational training. In J. Matson & S. Breuing (Eds.), *Assessing the mentally retarded* (pp. 247–285). New York: Grune & Stratton.

Mercer, C. D., & Mercer, A. R. (2000). *Teaching students with learning problems* (6th ed.). Upper Saddle River, NJ: Merrill/ Prentice Hall.

Merrill, K. W. (1994). *Assessment of behavioral, social, and emotional problems*. New York: Longman.

Mertz, M. K. (1997). After inclusion: Next S.T.E.P.s for high-school graduates. *Exceptional Parent*, 27(9), 44–49.

Middleton, R. A., Rollins, C. W., Sanderson, P. L., Leung, P., Harley, D. A., Ebener, D., & Leal-Idrogo, A. (2000). Endorsement of professional multicultural rehabilitation competencies and standards: A call to action. *Rehabilitation Counseling Bulletin*, 43, 219–240.

Miller, S. M., & Roby, P. (1970). Poverty: Changing social stratification. In P. Townsend (Ed.), *The concept of poverty: Working papers on methods of investigation and life-styles of the poor in different countries* (pp. 124–145). New York: American Elsevier Publishing.

Miller, T. (Ed.). (1997). *The book of professional standards for higher education*. Washington, DC: Council for the Advancement of Standards in Higher Education (CAS).

Minnesota Governor's Planning Council on Developmental Disabilities. (1987). *A new way of thinking*. St. Paul, MN: Author.

Mitchell, K. (1997). Making the grade: Help and hope for the first-generation college student. *The ERIC Review: The Path to College*, 5(3), 13–15.

Mitchell, L. K., & Krumboltz, J. D. (1996). Krumboltz's learning theory of career choice and counseling. In D. Brown, L. Brooks, & Associates (Eds.), *Career choice and development* (3rd ed., pp. 233–280). San Francisco: Jossey-Bass.

Mithaug, D. E. (1993). *Self-regulation theory: How optimal adjustment maximizes gain*. Westport, CT: Praeger.

Mithaug, D. E., Horiuchi, C. N., & Fanning, P. N. (1985). A report on the Colorado statewide follow-up survey of special education students. *Exceptional Children*, 51, 397–404.

Mithaug, D. E., & Mar, D. K. (1980). The relation between choosing and working prevocational tasks in two severely retarded young adults. *Journal of Applied Behavior Analysis* (13), 177–182.

Mithaug, D. E., Mithaug, D. K., Agran, M., Martin, J. E., & Wehmeyer, M. L. (2003). *Self-determined learning theory*. Mahwah, NJ: Lawrence Erlbaum.

Mithaug, D. E., Wehmeyer, M. L., Agran, M., Martin, J. E., & Palmer, S. (1998). The self-determined learning model of instruction. In M. L. Wehmeyer & D. J. Sands (Eds.), *Making it happen: Student involvement in education planning, decision making, and instruction* (pp. 299–328). Baltimore: Paul H. Brookes.

Mokuau, N., & Tauili'ili, P. (1998). Families with native Hawaiian and Samoan roots. In E. W. Lynch & M. H. Hanson (Eds.), *Developing cross-cultural competence: A guide for working with children and their families* (2nd ed., pp. 409–440). Baltimore: Paul H. Brookes.

Monette, G. C. (1997). Tribal colleges: Tradition, heritage, and community. *The ERIC Review: The Path to College*, 5(3), 24–25.

Moon, M. S., Hart, D., Komissar, C., & Friedlander, R. (1995). Making sports and recreation activities accessible. In K. F. Flippo, K. J. Inge, & J. M. Barcus (Eds.), *Assistive technology: A resource for school, work, and community* (pp. 187–197). Baltimore, MD: Paul H. Brookes.

Moores, D. (1996). *Educating the deaf: Psychology, principles, and practices* (4th ed.). Boston: Houghton Mifflin.

Morgan, D. P., & Jemson, W. R. (1988). *Teaching behaviorally disordered students: Preferred practices*. Columbus, OH: Merrill.

Morgan, R. L., Moore, S. C., McSweyn, C. A., & Salzberg, C. L. (1992). Transition from school to work: Views of secondary special educators. *Education and Training in Mental Retardation*, 27(4), 315–323.

Morningstar, M. (1997). Critical issues in career development and employment preparation for adolescents with disabilities. *Remedial and Special Education*, 18, 307–320.

Morningstar, M. E., Turnbull, A. P., & Turnbull, H. R. III. (1995). What do students with disabilities tell us about the importance of family involvement in the transition from school to adult life? *Exceptional Children*, 62, 249–260.

Morningstar, M.E., Turnbull, A.P., & Turnbull, H.R. (1996). What do students with disabilities tell us about the importance of family involvement in the transition from school to adult life? *Exceptional Children*, 62, 249–260.

Morse, T. E. (2001). Designing appropriate curriculum for special education students in urban schools. *Education and Urban Society*, 34(1), 4–17.

Mosston, M. (1972). *Teaching: From command to discovery*. Belmont, CA: Wadsworth.

Mosston, M., & Ashworth, S. (1990). *The spectrum of teaching styles: From command to discovery*.

Mount, B. (1989). *Making futures happen: A manual for facilitators of personal futures planning*. St. Paul, MN: Governor's Council on Developmental Disabilities.

Mount, B. (1992). *Personal futures planning: Promises and precautions*. New York, NY: Graphic Futures.

Mount, B. (1994). Benefits and limitations of personal futures planning. In J. Bradlley, J. W. Ashbaugh, & B. C. Blaney (Eds.), *Creating individual supports for people with developmental disabilities* (pp. 97–98). Baltimore: Paul H. Brookes.

Mount, B., Beeman, P., & Ducharme, G. (1988). What are we learning about circles of support? Manchester, CT: Communitas.

Mount, B., & Zwernick. (1988). *It's never too early, it's never too late: A booklet about personal futures planning*. St. Paul, MN: Governor's Planning Council on Developmental Disabilities. Publication No. 421, 88–109.

Munk, D. D., & Repp, A. C. (1994). The relationship between instructional variables and problem behavior: A review. *Exceptional Children*, 60, 390–401.

Myers, L. B., & McCauley M. H. (1985). *Manual: A guide to the development and use of the Myers-Briggs type indicator.* Palo Alto, CA: Consulting Psychologists Press.

National Academics Press. How people learn: Bridging research and practice. [Online]. Available: *http://books, nap.edu/html/howpeople2/ch2.html*

National Association of Private Residential Resources (NAPRR). (1991). *Supported living*. Annandale, VA: Author.

National Association of Private Residential Resources (NAPRR), (1992) *Supported living*, Vol. II. Annandale, VA: Author.

National Association of Protection and Advocacy Systems. (1999, October). *Questions and answers about the Olmstead v. L. C. and E. W. decision*. Washington, DC: Author.

National Center for Educational Statistics (NCES). (1993). *Baccalaureate and beyond: Longitudinal study. 1st and 2nd follow-up*. Washington, DC: U.S. Government Printing Office.

National Center for Education Statistics. (1993). *Education of the Handicapped Act Amendment of 1990 (PL 101-476): Summary of major changes in parts A through H of the Act.* Washington, DC: U.S. Department of Education.

National Center for Education Statistics. (1999a). *Students with disabilities in postsecondary education: A profile of preparation, participation, and outcomes*. NCES 1999–187. Washington, DC: U.S. Department of Education.

National Center for Education Statistics. (1999b). *An institutional perspective on students with disabilities in postsecondary education*. NCES 1999-046. Washington, DC: U.S. Department of Education.

National Council on Disability. (2000). *Back to school on civil rights*. Washington, DC: Author.

National Information Center for Children and Youth with Disabilities. (1993). *Transition services in the IEP: Transition summary*, 3(1), Washington, DC: Office of Special Education Programs of the U.S. Department of Education.

National Institute of Disability and Rehabilitation Research/Social Security Administration (1999). *The summary of data on young people with disabilities*. Washington DC: Author.

Neel, R. S., & Billingsley, F. F. (1989). *Impact: A functional curriculum handbook for students with moderate to severe disabilities.* Baltimore: Paul H. Brookes.

Neubert, D. (1985). Use of vocational evaluation recommendations in selected public school settings. *Career Development for Exceptional Individuals*, 9, 98–105.

Neubert, D. A. (1997). Time to grow: The history and future of preparing youth for adult roles in society. *Teaching Exceptional Children*, 29(5), 5–17.

Neubert, D. A., & Repetto, J. B. (1992). Serving individuals with special needs through professional development: Meeting the intent of the Act. *Journal for Vocational Special Needs Education*, 2–3(14), 37–41.

Newman, L. (1991). Social activities. In M. Wagner, L. Newman, R. D'Amico, E. Jay, P. Butler-Nalin, C. Marder, & R. Cox (Eds.), *Youth with disabilities: How are they doing? The first comprehensive report from the National Longitudinal Transition Study of Special Education Students* (pp. 6–1 to 6–50). Menlo Park, CA: SRI International.

Newman, L., & Cameto, R. (1993). *What makes a difference? Factors related to postsecondary school attendance for young people with disabilities*. Paper presented at the Division J: Postsecondary Education of the American Educational Research Association annual meeting, Atlanta, GA.

NICHCY *News Digest*. (1993). 2(2) , 1–7. Washington, DC: The National Information Center for Children and Youth with Disabilities: Author.

NICHCY *Transition Summary*. (1990, December). *Vocational assessment: A guide for parents and professionals*. Washington DC: The National Information Center for Children and Youth with Disabilities: Author.

NICHCY. (1988). *Individualized education programs*. (2–17), Washington DC: The National Information Center for Children and Youth with Disabilities: Author.

NICHCY. (1993, March). *Transition services defined by IDEA*. 3(1), 2–19. Washington DC: The National Information Center for Children and Youth with Disabilities: Author.

Nieto, S. (2000). *Affirming diversity: The sociopolitical context of multicultural education* (3rd ed.). New York: Longman.

Ninness, H. A. C., Fuerst, J., Rutherford, R. D., & Glenn, S. S. (1991). Effects of self-management training and reinforcement on the transfer of improved conduct in the absence of supervision. *Journal of Applied Behavior Analysis*, 24, 499–508.

Nirje, B. (1972). The right to self-determination. In W. Wolfensberger (Ed.). *The principle of normalization in human services* (pp. 176–193). Toronto: National Institute on Mental Retardation.

Nisbet, J., Covert, S., & Schuh, M. (1992). Family involvement in the transition from school to adult life. In F. R. Rusch, L. DeStefano, J. Chadsey-Rusch, L. A. Phelps, & E. Szymanski (Eds.), *Transition from school to adult life: Models, linkages, and policy* (pp. 407–424). Sycamore, IL: Sycamore.

Nisbet, J., & Hagner, D. (1988). Natural supports in the workplace: A reexamination of supported employment. *Journal of the Association for Persons with Severe Handicaps*, 13, 260–267.

Nolet, V., & McLaughlin, M. J. (2000). *Accessing the general curriculum*. Thousand Oaks, CA: Corwin.

Norman, M. E., & Bourexis, P. S. (1995). *Including students with disabilities in school-to-work opportunities*. Washington, DC: Council of Chief State School Officers.

Nosek, M. A. (1990). Personal assistance: Key to employability of persons with physical disabilities. *Journal of Applied Rehabilitation Counseling*, 21(4), 3–8.

Obiakor, F. E., & Utley, C. A. (1996). *Rethinking preservice and inservice training programs for teachers in the learning disabilities field: Workable multicultural models*. (ERIC Document Reproduction Service No. ED 397 594)

O'Brien, C., & O'Brien, J. (1992a). *Checklist for evaluating personal assistance services (PAS) policies and programs*. Livonia, GA: Responsive Systems Associates.

O'Brien, J. (1987). A guide to life-style planning: Using the activities catalogue to integrate services and natural support system. In G. T. Bellamy & B. Wilcox (Eds.), *A comprehensive guide to the activities catalogue: An alternative curriculum for youth and adults with severe disabilities* (pp. 175–190). Baltimore: Paul H. Brookes.

O'Brien, J. (1993). *Supported living: What's the difference?* Livonia, GA: Responsive Systems Associates.

O'Brien, J., & Lovett, H. (1992). *Finding a way toward everyday lives: The contribution of person-centered planning*. Harrisburg, PA: Pennsylvania Office of Mental Retardation.

O'Brien, J., & O'Brien, C. (1991). *More than just a new address: Images of organizations for supported living agencies* Syracuse, NY: Center on Human Policy, Syracuse University.

O'Brien, J., & O'Brien, C. (1992b). *Remembering the soul of our work: Stories by staff of Options in Community Living, Madison, Wisconsin*. Madison, WI: Options in Community Living.

O'Brien, J., O'Brien, L., & Mount, B. (1997). Person-centered planning has arrived . . . or has it? *Mental Retardation*, 35 (6), 480–484.

O'Connell, M. (1988). *Community building in Logan Square: How a community grew stronger with the contribution of people with disabilities*. Evanston, IL: Center for Urban Affairs and Policy Research, Northwestern University.

Odens, S., & Asher, S. R. (1977). Coaching children in social skills for friendship making. *Child Development*, 48, 495–506.

Office of Special Education Programs, (1997). *The Individuals with Disabilities Education Act Amendments of 1997: Curriculum*. Washington, DC. U. S. Department of Education.

Ogusthorpe, M. R. (1978). *The career conversation: Training parents to help their children make career decisions*. (ERIC Document Reproduction Service No. ED 159 584)

Ohio Department of Education, Division of Special Education. (1999). *District self-study for the 1999–2000 school improvement review*. Worthington, OH: Author.

Ohio Department of Education. (1990). *Ohio speaks*. Columbus, OH: Author.

Ohio Rehabilitation Services Commission (1997). *Transition guidelines and best practices*. Columbus, OH: RSC Office of Public Information.

Olson, W. (1999). Under the ADA, we may all be disabled. *The Wall Street Journal*, May 17, A27.

O'Neill, R. E., Horner, R. H., Albin, R. W., Sprague, J. R., Storey, K., & Newton, J. S. (1997). *Functional assessment and program development for problem behavior: A practical handbook* (2nd ed.). Pacific Grove, CA: Brooks/Cole Publishing.

Orkwis, R., & McLane, K. (1998). A curriculum every student can use: Design principles for student access. Reston, VA: ERIC Clearinghouse on Disabilities and Gifted Education. Retrieved Jan. 2003 from *http://www.cec.sped.org/ericec.htm*

Orkwis, R. (December, 1999). Curriculum access and universal design for learning. ERIC/OSEP Digest #E586. (ERIC Document Reproduction Service No. ED437767)

Orkwis, R., & McLane, K. (1998). *A curriculum every student can use: Design principles for student access*. ERIC/OSEP Topical Brief, Fall 1998. Reston, VA: Council for Exceptional Childern.

Osborne, A. G. (1996). Legal issues in special education, Boston: Allyn and Bacon.

PACER Center. (2002). *Technology*. *http://www.pacer.org/*

Page, B., & Chadsey-Rusch, J. (1995). The community college experience for students with and without disabilities: A viable transition outcome? *Career Development for Exceptional Individuals*, 18(2), 85–96.

Pallas, A. (1993, Winter). Schooling in the course of human lives: The social context of education and the transition to adulthood in industrial society. *Review of Education Research*, 63, 409–447.

Pancsofar, E. L. (1986). Assessing work behavior. In F. R. Rusch (Ed.), *Competitive employment issues and strategies* (pp. 93–102). Baltimore: Paul H. Brookes.

Pancsofar, E. L., & Steere, D. E. (1997). The C.A.P.A.B.L.E. process: Critical dimensions of community-based assessment. *Journal of Vocational Rehabilitation*, 8, 99–108.

Parent, W. (1996). Consumer choice and satisfaction in supported employment. Paper presented at International Symposium on Supported Employment, Norfolk Virginia, *The Journal of Vocational Rehabilitation*, 6(1), 15–22.

Parent, W. Sherron, P., Stallard, D., & Booth, M. (1993). Job development and placement: Strategies for success. *Journal of Vocational Rehabilitation*, 3(3), 17–26.

Parent, W., Unger, D., Gibson, K., & Clements, C. (1994). The role of the job coach: Orchestrating community and natural supports. *American Rehabilitation*, 20(3), 2–11.

Parette, H. P. (1999). Transition and assistive technology planning with families across cultures. *Career Development for Exceptional Individuals*, 22(2), 213–231.

Parette, H. P., Brotherson, M. J., Hourcade, J. J., & Bradley, R. H. (1996). Family-centered assistive technology assessment. *Intervention in School and Clinic*, 32(2), 104–112.

Parette, H. P., & Hourcade, J. J. (1997). Family issues and assistive technology needs: A sampling of state practices. *Journal of Special Education Technology*, 13, 27–43.

Parette, H. P., Jr., Hourcade, J. J., & VanBiervliet, A. (1993). Selection of appropriate technology for children with disabilities. *Teaching Exceptional Children*, 25(3), 18–22.

Parette, H. P., Jr., Hourcade, J. J., & VanBiervliet, A. (1996). Family-centered assistive technology assessment. *Intervention in School and Clinic*, 32(2), 104–112.

Parette, H. P., & VanBiervliet, A. (1990). A prospective inquiry into technology needs and practices of school-age children with disabilities. *Journal of Special Education Technology*, 10, 198–206.

Parette, H. P., & VanBiervliet, A. (1991). School-age children with disabilities: Technology implications for counselors. *Elementary School Guidance & Counseling*, 25, 182–194.

Parker, R. M., & Schaller, J. L. (1996). Issues in vocational assessment and disability. In E. M. Szymanski & R. M. Parker (Eds.), *Work and disability: Issues and strategies in career development and job placement* (pp. 127–164). Austin, TX: PRO-ED.

Parsons, M. B., Reid, D. H., Reynolds, J., & Bumgarner, M. (1990). Effects of chosen versus assigned jobs on the work performance of persons with severe handicaps. *Journal of Applied Behavior Analysis*, 23, 253–258.

Pascarella, E., & Terenzini, P. (1991). *How college affects students: Findings and insights from twenty years of research*. San Francisco: Jossey-Bass.

PA-TASH. (1994). PA-TASH supports the right to communicate. PA-TASH *Newsletter*, 4(2), 1–4.

Pati, G., & Morrison, G. (1982). Enabling the disabled. *Harvard Business Review*, 60, 152–168.

Patterson, J. (1996). Occupational and labor market information and analysis. In E. M. Szymanski & R. M. Parker (Eds.), *Work and disability: Issues and strategies in career development and job placement* (pp. 209–254). Austin, TX: PRO-ED.

Patton, J. R., Cronin, M. E., Bassett, D. S., & Koppel, A. E. (1997). A life skills approach to mathematics instruction: Preparing students with learning disabilities for the real-life math demands of adulthood. *Journal of Learning Disabilities*, 30(2), 178–187.

Patton, J. R., & Polloway, E. A. (1990). Mild mental retardation. In N. G. Haring, L. McCormick, & T. G. Haring (Eds.), *Exceptional children and youth* (6th ed., pp. 212–256). Upper Saddle River, NJ: Merrill/Prentice Hall.

Patton, J. R., Smith, T. E. C., Clark, G. M., Polloway, E. A., Edgar, E., & Lee, S. (1996). Individuals with mild mental retardation: Postsecondary outcomes and implications for educational policy. *Education and Training in Mental Retardation and Developmental Disabilities*, 31(2), 75–85.

Paulson, R. I. (1993). Interagency collaboration among rehabilitation, mental health, and other systems. In R. W. Flexer and P. Solomon (Eds.) *Psychiatric rehabilitation in practice*. Boston: Andover Medical.

Pearlman, B. (2002, April). Reinventing the high school experience. *Educational Leadership*, 72–79.

Pearpoint, J. (1990). *From behind the piano: The building of Judith Snow's unique circle of friends*. Toronto, CA: Inclusion Press.

Pearpoint, J. (1993). Kick 'em out or keep 'em in: Exclusion or inclusion. In J. Pearpoint, M. Forest, & J. Snow (Eds.), *The inclusion papers: Strategies to make inclusion work* (pp. 80–88). Toronto: Inclusion Press.

Pearpoint, J., O'Brien, J., & Forest, M. (1993). PATH: A *workbook for planning positive possible futures*. Toronto Inclusion Press.

Peck, C., Donaldson, J., & Pezzoli, M. (1990). Some benefits some nonhandicapped adolescents perceive for themselves from their social relationships with peers who have severe handicaps. *The Journal of the Association for Persons with Severe Handicaps*, 15(4), 241–149.

Pennsylvania Association of Retarded Citizens v. Commonwealth of Pennsylvania, 343 F. Suppl. 279 (E.D. Pa. 1972).

Perske, R. (1973). *New hope for the families*. Nashville, TN: Abingdon.

Perske, R. (1988). Circles of friends: People with disabilities and their friends enrich the lives of one another. Nashville, TN: Abingdon Press.

Petric, J. (2002, May). *Labor laws and their effect on training programs*. Paper presented at 2002 Ohio Topical Conference, Columbus, OH.

Peterson, L. Y., Van Dycke, J. L., Crownover, C. A., Roberson, R. L., Borland, B. J., & Martin, J. E. (2004). Teaching students with high incidence disabilities to complete IEP plans of study. Manuscript submitted for publication.

Phelps, L. A., & Hanley-Maxwell, C. (1997). School-to-work transitions for youth with disabilities: A review of outcomes and practices. *Review of Educational Research*, 67(2), 197–226.

Phelps, L. A., & Maddy-Bernstein, C. (1992). Developing effective partnerships for special populations: The challenge of partnerships and alliances. *The Journal for Vocational Special Needs Education*, 14(2–3), 33–36.

Phillips, B. (1991). *Technology abandonment: From the consumer point of view*. Washington, DC: Request Publication.

Phillips, B. (1992). *Perspectives on assistive technology services in vocational rehabilitation: Client and counselors*. Washington, DC: National Rehabilitation Hospital, Assistive Technology/Rehabilitation Engineering Program.

Phillips, J. F., Reid, D. H., Korabek, C. A., & Hursh, D. E. (1988). Community-based instruction with profoundly mentally retarded persons: Client and public responsiveness. *Research in Developmental Disabilities*, 9, 3–21.

Phillips, S., & Sandstrom, K. (1990). Parental attitudes toward youth work. *Youth and Society*, 22,160–183.

Pierce, K., & Scheibman, L. (1995). Increasing complex social behaviors in children with autism: Effects of peer-implemented pivotal response training. *Journal of Applied Behavior Analysis*, 28, 285–295.

Pinderhughes, E. (1995). Empowering diverse populations: Family practice in the 21st century. *Families in Society*, 76, 131–140.

Pitman, J. A., & Slate, J. R. (1994). Students' familiarity with and attitudes toward the rights of students who are disabled. *Journal of Applied Rehabilitation Counseling*, 25(2), 38–40.

Plank, S. (2001). *Career and technical education in the balance: An analysis of high school persistence, academic achievement, and post-secondary destinations*. Columbus, OH: Ohio State University, National Center for Dissemination.

Polirstok, S. R. (1986). Training problematic adolescents as peer tutors: Benefits for the tutor and the school at large. *Techniques: A Journal for Remedial Education and Counseling*, 2, 204–210.

Pollitzer, W. S. (1994). Ethnicity and human biology. *American Journal of Human Biology*, 6, 3–11.

Pomplun, M. (1997). When students with disabilities participate in cooperative groups. *Exceptional Children*, 64, 49–58.

Powell, T., Pancsofar, E. L., Steere, D., Butterworth, J., Itzkowitz, J., & Rainforth, B. (1991). *Supported employment: Providing integrated employment opportunities for person with disabilities*. New York: Longman.

Power, P. (1991). A *guide to vocational assessment* (2nd ed.). Austin, TX: PRO-ED.

Powers, L. E. (1997). *Self-determination research results*. Colorado Springs, CO: Presentation at University of Colorado Self-Determination Meeting.

Powers, L. E., Sowers, J., Turner, A., Nesbitt, M., Knowles, E., & Ellison, R. (1996). TAKE CHARGE: A model for promoting self-determination among adolescents with challenges. In L. E. Powers, G. H. S. Singer, & J. Sowers (Eds.), *On the road to autonomy: Promoting self-competence for children and youth with disabilities* (pp. 291–322). Baltimore: Paul H. Brookes.

Presidents Panel on Mental Retardation. (1962). A *proposed program for national action to combat mental retardation*. Washington, DC: U.S. Government Printing Office.

Pruitt, P., & Wandry, D. (1998). Listen to us! Parents speak out about their interactions with special educators. *Preventing School Failure*, 42, 161–167.

Pugach, M. C., & Warger, C. L. (2001). Curriculum matters: Raising expectations for students with disabilities. *Remedial and Special Education*, 22(4) 194–196.

Pumpian, I., Campbell, C., & Hesche, S. (1992). Making person-centered dreams come true. *Resources*, 4(4), 1–6.

Pumpian, I., & Fisher, D. (1993). *Job placement: The final frontier?* Washington, DC: National Institute on Disabilities and Rehabilitation Research [NIDRR].

Pumpian, I., Fisher, D., Certo, N. J., & Smalley, K. A. (1997). Changing jobs: An essential part of career development. *Career Development for Exceptional Individuals*, 35, 39–48.

Putnam, J. W. (Ed.). (1998). *Cooperative learning and strategies for inclusion: Celebrating diversity in the classroom*. Baltimore: Paul H. Brookes.

Qin, Z., Johnson, D. W., & Johnson, R. T. (1995). Cooperative versus competitive efforts and problem solving. *Review of Educational Research*, 65(2), 129–143.

Quinn, M. M., Gable, R. A., Rutherford, Jr., R. B., Nelson, C. M., Howell, K. W. (1998) Functional Behavioral Assessment. Center for Effective Collaboration and Practice. Retrieved July 9, 2003, from *http://www.air.org/cecp/fba/default.htm*.

Racino, J. A. (1990). Preparing personnel to work in community support services. In A. P. Kaiser & C. M. McWhorter (Eds.), *Preparing personnel to work with persons with severe disabilities* (203–226). Baltimore: Paul H. Brookes.

Racino, J. A. (1999). *Policy, program evaluation, and research in disability: Community support for all*. Binghamton, NY: Haworth Press.

Racino, J. A., & Litvak, S. (1999). Moving toward universal access to support—policy is personal: Introduction. In J. A. Racino (Ed.), *Policy, program evaluation, and research in disability: Community support for all*. Binghamton, NY: Haworth Press.

Racino, J. A., O'Connor, S., & Walker, P. (1992). Conclusion. In J. A. Racino, P. Walker, S. O'Connor, & S. J. Taylor (Eds.), *Housing, support, and community: Choices and strategies for adults with disabilities*. Baltimore: Paul H. Brookes.

Racino, J. A., Walker, P., O'Connor S., & Taylor, S. J. (Eds.). (1992). *Housing, support, and community: Choices and strategies for adults with disabilities*. Baltimore: Paul H. Brookes.

Rae, S., Martin, G., & Smyk, B. (1990). A self-management package versus a group exercise contingency for increasing on-task behavior of developmentally handicapped workers. *Canadian Journal of Behavioral Science*, 22, 45–58.

Ragland, E. U., Kerr, M. M., & Strain, P. S. (1978). Effects of social initiations on the behavior of withdrawn autistic children. *Topics in Early Childhood Special Education*, 13, 565–578.

Rainforth, B., York, J., & MacDonald, C. (1992). *Collaborative teams for students with severe disabilities*. Baltimore: Paul H. Brookes.

Raskind, M. H. (1997/1998). A guide to assistive technology. *Their World*, 72–74.

Reed, C., & Rumrill, P. (1997). Supported employment: Principles and practices for interdisciplinary collaboration. *Work: A Journal of Prevention, Assessment, and Rehabilitation*, 9, 237–244.

Reed, P. (1997). *Assessing students' need for assistive technology.* Oshkosh, WI: Wisconsin Assistive Technology Initiative.

Rehabilitation Act Amendments of 1992, 29 U.S C. § 794 *et seq.*

Rehabilitation Act of 1973, Section 504, 29 U.S.C. § 794.

Rehabilitation, Comprehensive Services, and Developmental Disabilities Act of 1978, Pub. L. No. 95-062.

Rehabilitation Services Administration, Office of Special Education and Rehabilitation Services, U.S. Department of Education. (1999). Rehabilitation Services Administration (RSA) Programs: Centers for Independent Living. Retrieved January 15, 2000 from the World Wide Web: *http://www.ed.gov/offices/OSERS/RSA/rsa.html*

Repetto, J. B., & Correa, V. I. (1996). Expanding views on transition. *Exceptional Children* 62(6), 551–563.

Repetto, J. B., White, W. J., & Snauwaert, D. T. (1990). Individualized transition plans (ITP): A national perspective. *Career Development for Exceptional Individuals*, 13(2), 109–119.

Reschly, D. J. (1997). *Disproportionate minority representation in general and special education: Patterns, issues, and alternatives.* Washington, DC: Office of Special Education and Rehabilitative Services, and Mountain Plains Regional Resource Center.

Research and Training Center on Residential Services and Community Living. (1994). *Housing policy and persons with mental retardation.* Minneapolis, MN: Institute on Community Integration.

Reutzel, D. R., & Cooter, R. B. Jr. (1999). *Balanced reading strategies and practices: Assessing and assisting readers with special needs.* Upper Saddle River, NJ: Merrill/Prentice Hall.

Rhodes, L., Sandow, D., Mank, D., Buckley, J., & Albin, J. (1991). Expanding the role of employers in supported employment. *The Journal of the Association for Persons with Severe Handicaps*, 16(4), 213–217.

Richmond, G., Beatty, P., Tepper, S., & DeJong, G. (1997). The effect of consumer-directed personal assistance services on the productivity outcomes of people with disabilities. *Journal of Rehabilitation Outcomes Measurement*, 1(4), 48–51.

Richmond, W. V. (1934). *An introduction to sex education.* New York: New Home Library.

Rimmerman, A., Levy, J. M., & Botuck, S. (1995). Predicting the likelihood of job placement: A short-term perspective. *The Journal of Rehabilitation*, 61(1) 50–54, 50.

Rivera, D. P., & Smith, D. D. (1997). *Teaching students with learning and behavior problems* (3rd ed.). Boston: Allyn & Bacon.

Robinson, G. K. (1991). Choices in case management. *Community Support Network News*, 7, 11–12.

Rodriquez, R. F. (1994). Administrators' perceptions of teaching competencies for rural minority group children with exceptionalities. *Rural Special Education Quarterly*, 13, 40–44.

Roessler, R., & Bolton, B. (1985). Employment patterns of former vocational rehabilitation clients and implications for rehabilitation practice. *Rehabilitation Counseling Bulletin*, 28(3), 179–187.

Roessler, R., & Rumrill, P. (1995). Promoting reasonable accommodations: An essential postemployment service. *Journal of Applied Rehabilitation Counseling*, 26(4), 3–7.

Rogan, P., Grossi, T., Mank, D., Haynes, D., Thomas, F., & Majad, C. (2002). What happens when people leave the workshop? Outcomes of workshop participants now in SE. *Supported Employment Infolines*, 13(4), 1,3.

Rojewski, J. W. (1993). Theoretical structure of career maturity for rural adolescents with learning disabilities. *Career Development for Exceptional Individuals*, 16(1), 39–52.

Rojewski, J. W. (1996). Educational and occupational aspirations of high school seniors with learning difficulties. *Exceptional Children*, 62(5), 463–476.

Rojewski, J. W. (1999). Career-related predictors of work-bound and college-bound status of adolescents in rural and nonrural areas. *Journal of Research in Rural Education*, 15(3), 141–156.

Rokeach, M. (1975). *Beliefs, attitudes, and values: A theory of organization and change.* San Francisco: Jossey-Bass.

Rose, S. M. (1972). *The betrayal of the poor: The transformation of community action.* Cambridge, MA: Schenkman Publishing.

Rosenberg, M. S., Wilson, R., Maheady, L., & Sindelar, P. T. (1997). *Educating students with behavior disorders* (2nd ed.). Needham Heights, MA: Allyn & Bacon.

Rosenshine, B. V. (1986). Synthesis of research on explicit teaching. *Educational Leadership*, 43(7), 60–69.

Rosenshine, B. V., & Stevens, R. (1986). Teaching functions. In M. C. Wittrock (Ed.), *Handbook of research on teaching* (3rd ed., pp. 376–391). New York: Macmillan.

Rothschild, I., & Bianchi, J. (1986). Parent/educator meetings can work for your child. *Annual Education Issue of the Exceptional Parent*, 16(5) 23–28.

Ruben, B. D. (1976). Assessing communication competency for intercultural adaptation. *Group and Organizational Studies*, 1, 334–354.

Rudrud, E. H., Ziarnik, J. P., Berstein, G. S., & Ferrara, J. M. (1984). *Proactive vocational habilitation.* Baltimore: Paul H. Brookes.

Rumrill, P., & Koch, L. (1998). The career maintenance specialist: Broadening the scope of successful rehabilitation. *Journal of Rehabilitation Administration*, 22(2), 111–121.

Rumrill, P. D. (1994). The "win-win" approach to Title I of the Americans with Disabilities Act: Preparing college students with disabilities for career-entry placements after graduation. *Journal of Postsecondary Education and Disability*, 11(1), 15–19.

Rusch, F. R. (1979). Toward the validation of social/vocational survival skills. *Mental Retardation*, 17, 143–145.

Rusch, F. R. (1986). *Competitive employment: Issues, theories, and models.* Baltimore: Paul H. Brookes.

Rusch, F. R. (1990). *Supported employment: Models, methods and issues.* Sycamore, IL: Sycamore.

Rusch, F. R., & Chadsey, J. G. (1998). *Beyond high school: Transition from school to work*. The Wadsworth Special Education Series. Belmont, CA: Wadsworth.

Rusch, F. R., & DeStefano, L. (1989). Transition from school to work: Strategies for young adults with disabilities. *Interchange*, 9(3), 1–2. Urbana-Champaign, IL: University of Illinois, Secondary Transition Intervention Effectiveness Institute.

Rusch, F. R., DeStefano, L., Chadsey-Rusch, J., Phelps, L. A., & Szymanski, E. (1992). *Transition from school to adult life: Models, linkages, and policy*. Sycamore, IL: Sycamore.

Rusch, F. R., McKee, M., Chadsey-Rusch, J., & Renzaglia, A. (1988). Teaching a student with severe handicaps to self-instruct: A brief report. *Education and Training in Mental Retardation*, 23, 51–58.

Rusch, F. R., & Millar, D. M. (1998). Emerging transition best practices. In F. R. Rusch & J. G. Chadsey (Eds.), *Beyond high school: Transition from school to work* (pp. 36–60). New York: Wadsworth.

Rusch, F. R., Mithaug, D. E., & Flexer, R. W. (1986). Obstacles to competitive employment and traditional program options for overcoming them. In F. R. Rusch (Ed.), *Competitive employment: Issues and strategies* (pp. 7–21). Baltimore: Paul H. Brookes.

Rusch, F. R., Morgan, T. K., Martin, J. E., Riva, M., & Agran, M. (1985). Competitive employment: Teaching mentally retarded employees self-instructional strategies. *Applied Research in Mental Retardation*, 6, 389–407.

Rusch, F. R., Schultz, R. P., Mithaug, D. E., Stewart, J. E., & Mar, D. E. (1982). *Vocational assessment and curriculum guide*. Seattle, WA: Exceptional Education.

Rusch, F. R., Szymanski, E. M., & Chadsey-Rusch, J. (1992). The emerging field of transition services. In F. R. Rusch, L. Destefano, J. Chadsey-Rusch, L. A. Phelps, & E. Szymanski (Eds.), *Transition from school to adult life: Models, linkages, and policy*. Sycamore, IL: Sycamore.

Russo, C. J., & Talbert-Johnson, C. (1997). The overrepresentation of African American children in special education: The resegregation of educational programming? *Education and Urban Society*, 29, 136–148.

Ryan, C. (1995). Work isn't what it used to be: Implications, recommendations, and strategies for vocational rehabilitation. *Journal of Rehabilitation*, 61(4), 7–15.

Ryan, R. B., Connell, J. P., & Plant, R. W. (1990). Emotions in non-directed test learning. *Learning and Individual Differences*, 2, 736B–750.

Rylance, B. J. (1997). Predictors of high school graduation or dropping out for youth with severe emotional disturbances. *Behavior Disorders*, 23(1), 5–17.

Ryndak, D. L., & Alper, S. (1996). *Curriculum content for students with moderate and severe disabilities in inclusive settings*. Boston: Allyn & Bacon.

Sale, P., & Martin, J. E. (1997). Self-determination. In P. Wehman & J. Kregel (Eds.), *Functional curriculum for elementary, middle, and secondary age students with special needs* (pp. 43–67). Austin, TX: PRO-ED.

Sale, R. P., & Martin, J. E. (in press). Self-determination instruction. In P. Wehman & J. Kregel (Eds.), *Community-based instruction* (2nd edition). Austin, TX: PRO-ED.

Salembier, G., & Furney, K. S. (1997). Facilitating participation: Parents' perceptions of their involvement in the IEP/transition planning process. *Career Development for Exceptional Children*, 20, 29–42.

Salend, S. J. (1994). *Effective mainstreaming: Creating inclusive classrooms* (2nd ed.). Upper Saddle River, NJ: Merrill/ Prentice Hall.

Salend, S. J. (1998). *Effective mainstreaming: Creating inclusive classrooms* (3rd ed., pp. 244–252). Upper Saddle River, NJ: Merrill.

Salend. S. J. (2001). *Creating inclusive classrooms: Effective and reflective practices* (4th ed., pp. 244–252). Upper Saddle River, NJ: Merrill.

Salend, S. T., & Taylor, L. (1993). Working with families: A cross-cultural perspective. *Remedial and Special Education*, 14(5), 25–32.

Salzberg, C. L., & Morgan, J. (1995). Preparing teachers to work with paraeducators. *Teacher Education and Special Education*, 18(1), 49–55.

Sands, D. S., Adams, L., & Stout, D. M. (1995). A statewide exploration of the nature and use of curriculum in special education. *Exceptional Children*, 62(1), 68–83.

Sarason, S. B., & Doris, J. (1979). *Educational handicap, public policy, and social history: A broadened perspective on mental retardation*. New York: Free Press.

Sarkees, M. D., & Scott, J. L. (1985). *Vocational special needs* (2nd ed.). Home wood, IL: American Technical Publishers.

Sarkees-Wincenski, M., & Scott, J. L. (1995). *Vocational special needs* (3rd ed.). Homewood, IL: American Technical Publishers.

Sarkees-Wircenski, M., & Wircenski, J. (1994). Transition planning: Developing a career portfolio for students with disabilities. *Career Development for Exceptional Individuals*, 17, 203–214.

Savickas, M. L. (1989). Career-style assessment and counseling. In T. Sweeney (Ed.), *Adlerian counseling: A practical approach for a new decade* (3rd ed., pp. 289–320). Muncie, IN: Accelerated Development Press.

Savickas, M. L. (1996). A framework for linking career theory and practice. In M. L. Savickas & W. B. Walsh (Eds.), *Handbook of career counseling theory and practice* (pp. 191–208). Palo Alto, CA: Davies-Black.

Sax, C., Pumpian, I., & Fisher, D. (March, 1997). Assistive technology and inclusion. CISP *Issue Briefs*, 1–5.

SCANS (Secretary's Commission on Achieveing Necessary Skills). (1991). *What work requires of schools: A SCANS report for America* 2000. Washington DC: U.S. Department of Labor.

SCANS: Secretary's Commission on Achieving Necessary Skills (1992, June). SCANS *in the schools.* Washington, DC: SCANS, U.S. Dept. of Labor, Pelavin Assoc.

Schalock, R., Stark, J., Snell, M., Coulter, D., Pollaway, E., Luckasson, R., Reiss, S., & Spitalnik, D. (1994). The changing conception of mental retardation: Implications for the field. *Mental Retardation,* 32(3), 181–193.

Schalock, R. L., Wolzen, B., Ross, I., Elliott, B., Werbel, G., & Peterson, K. (1986). Post-secondary community placement of handicapped students: A five-year follow-up. *Learning Disability Quarterly,* 9(4), 295–303.

Scheerenberger, R. C. (1983). *A history of mental retardation.* Baltimore, Paul H. Brookes.

Scherer, M. (1991). Assistive technology use, avoidance and abandonment: What we know so far. In *Proceedings of the 6th annual technology and persons with disabilities conference* (pp. 815–826). Washington, DC: Rehabilitation Engineering Center, National Rehabilitation Hospital.

Scherer, M. J. (1997). Assessing individuals' predispositions to the use, avoidance, or abandonment of assistive technologies. *Journal of Rehabilitation Research & Development,* 31, 135–136.

Scherer, M. J., & Galvin, J.C. (1996). An outcomes perspective of quality pathways to the most appropriate technology. In J. C. Galvin & M. J. Scherer (Eds.), *Evaluating, selecting, and using appropriate assistive technology.* Gaithersburg, MD: Aspen Publishers, Inc.

Scherer, M. J. & Galvin, J. C. (1996). *Evaluating selecting, and using appropriate assistive technology.* Gaithersburg, MD: Aspen Publications.

Schirmer, B. R. (2000). *Language and literacy development in children who are deaf* (2nd ed.). New York: Macmillan.

Schleien, S. J., Green, F. P., & Heyne, L. A. (1993). Integrated community recreation. In M. E. Snell (Ed.), *Instruction of students with severe disabilities,* (4th ed., p. 530). Upper Saddle River, NJ: Merrill/Prentice Hall.

Schloss, P. J., & Smith, M. A. (1998). *Applied behavior analysis in the classroom* (2nd ed.). Boston: Allyn & Bacon.

Schloss, P. J., Smith, M. A., & Schloss, C. N. (1995). *Instructional methods for adolescents with learning and behavior problems* (2nd ed.). Boston: Allyn & Bacon.

Schniedewind, N., & Salend, S. J. (1987). Cooperative learning works. *Teaching Exceptional Children,* 19, 22–25.

School to Work Opportunity Act of 1994, Pub. L. No. 103–239, 20 U.S.C. § 6101 *et seq.*

Scott, S. B. (1997). Comparison of service delivery models influencing teacher's use of assistive technology for students with severe disabilities. *Occupational Therapy in Health Care,* 11(11), 61–70.

Scott, S. S. (1996). Understanding colleges: An overview of college support services and programs available to clients from transition planning through graduation. *Journal of Vocational Rehabilitation,* 6, 217–230.

Scruggs, T. E., Mastropieri, M. A., & Richter, L. (1985). Peer tutoring among behaviorally disordered students: Social and academic benefits. *Behavioral Disorders,* 11, 283–294.

Scruggs, T. E., Mastropieri, M., Veit, D. T., & Osguthorpe, R. T. (1986). Behaviorally disorders students as tutors: Effects on social behavior. *Behavioral Disorders,* 12(1), 36–44.

Scuccimarra, D., & Speece, D. (1990). Employment outcomes and social integration of students with mild handicaps: The quality of life two years after high school. *Journal of Learning Disabilities,* 23(4), 213–219.

Secretary's Commission on Achieving Necessary Skills. (1991). *What work requires of schools:* A SCANs *report for America* 2000. Washington D.C: U.S. Department of Labor.

Section 504 of the Rehabilitation Act of 1973, 29 U.S.C. § 794 *et seq.*

Senge, P. M. (1990). *The fifth discipline: The art and practice of learning organization.* New York: Doubleday/Currency—Dell Publishing Group.

Serebreni, R., Rumrill, P. D., Mullins, J. A., & Gordon, S. E., (1993). Project Excel: A demonstration of the higher education transition model for high-achieving students with disabilities. *Journal of Postsecondary Education and Disability,* 10, 15–23.

Sexton, D., Lobman, M., Constans, T., Snyder, P., & Ernest, J. (1997). Early interventionists' perspectives of multicultural practices with African-American families. *Exceptional Children,* 63, 313–328.

Shapiro, E. S., McGonigle, J. J., & Ollendick, T. H. (1980). An analysis of self-assessment and self-reinforcement in a self-managed token economy with mentally retarded children. *Applied Research in Mental Retardation,* 1, 227–240.

Shapiro, J. P. (1993). *No Pity.* New York: Times Books.

Sharifzadeh, V. S. (1998). Families with Middle Eastern roots. In E. W. Lynch & M. H. Hanson (Eds.), *Developing cross-cultural competence: A guide for working with children and their families* (2nd ed., pp. 441–482). Baltimore: Paul H. Brookes.

Sharon, S. (1980). Cooperative learning in small groups: Recent methods and effects on achievement, attitudes and ethnic relations. *Review of Educational Research,* 50, 241–249.

Shaw, S., Brinckerhoff, L. C., Kistler, J. K., & McGuire, J. M. (1991). Preparing students with learning disabilities for postsecondary education: Issues and future needs. *Learning Disabilities: A Multidisciplinary Journal,* 2(1), 21–26.

Sherif, C. W., Sherif, M., & Nebergall, R. E. (1965). *Attitude and attitude change.* Philadelphia: W. B. Saunders.

Shingleton, J. D., & Fitzpatrick, E. B. (1985). *Dynamics of placement: How to develop a successful career planning and placement program.* Bethlehem, PA: College Placement Council Foundation.

Siegel, S. (1998). Foundations for a school-to-work system that serves all students. In F. R. Rusch & J. G. Chadsey (Eds.), *Beyond high school: Transition from school to work* (pp. 146–178). New York: Wadsworth.

Siegel, S., Robert, M., Greener, K., Meyer, G., Halloran, W., & Gaylord-Ross, R. (1993). *Career ladders for challenged youths in transition from school to adult life.* Austin, TX: PRO-ED.

Siegel, S., & Sleeter, C. S. (1991). Transforming transition: Next stages for the school-to-work transition movement. *Career Development for Exceptional Individuals*, 14(2), 27–41.

Silbert, J., Carnine, D., & Stein, M. (1990). *Direct instruction mathematics* (2nd ed.). Columbus, OH: Merrill.

Simich-Dudgeon, C. (1986). A multidisciplinary model to educate minority language students with handicapping conditions. In A. C. Willing & H. F. Greenberg (Eds.), *Bilingualism and learning disabilities: Policy and practice for teachers and administrators* (pp. 95–110). New York: American Library Publishing.

Simmons, D. C., & Kame'enui, E. J. (1996). A focus on curriculum design. When children fail. *Focus on Exceptional Children*, 28(7) 1–16.

Simmons, T., & Baer, R. (1996). What I want to be when I grow up: Career planning. In C. Flexer, D. Wray, R. Leavitt & R. Flexer (Eds.), *How the student with hearing loss can succeed in college: A handbook for students, families, and professionals* (2nd ed., pp. 117–130). Washington, DC: Alexander Graham Bell Association for the Deaf.

Simmons, T. J. (1996). *Postsecondary higher educational settings: Model environment for the delivery of secondary special education services.* Model demonstration Grant funded by the Office of Special Education. Washington, DC: S. Department of Education.

Simmons, T. J., & Flexer, R. W. (1992). Community based job training for persons with mental retardation: An acquisition and performance replication. *Education and Training in Mental Retardation*, 15, 261–272.

Simmons, T. J., Selleck, V., Steele, R. B., & Sepetauc, F. (1993). Supports and rehabilitation for employment. In R. W. Flexer and P. L. Solomon (Eds.), *Psychiatric rehabilitation in practice,* (pp. 119–136), Boston: Andover Medical Publishers.

Simmons, T. J., & Whaley B. (2001). Transition to employment. In R. W. Flexer, Simmons, T. J. Luft, P. & Bion, R. (Eds.) *Transition planning for students with disabilities.* Columbus, OH: Merrill.

Simon, M., Cobb, B., Halloran, W., Norman, M., & Bourexis. (1994). *Meeting the needs of youth with disabilities: Handbook for implementing community-based vocational education programs according to the Fair Labor Standards Act.* Minneapolis: National Transition Network.

Simpson, G. W. (1997). To grow a teacher. *American School Board Journal*, 184, 42–43.

Simpson, R. L. (1982). *Conferencing parents of exceptional children.* Rockville, MD: Aspen.

Sindelar, P. T., Smith, M. A., Harriman, N. E., Hale, R. L., & Wilson, R. J. (1986). Teacher effectiveness in special education programs. *The Journal of Special Education*, 20, 195–207.

Siperstein, G. N. (1988). Students with learning disabilities in college: The need for a programmatic approach to critical transitions. *Journal of Learning Disabilities*, 21, 431–436.

Sitlington, P. L. (1996a). Transition assessment: Where have we been and where should we be going? *Career Development for Exceptional Individuals*, 19, 159–168.

Sitlington, P. L. (1996b). Transition assessment—Where have we been and where should we be going? *Career Development for Exceptional Children*, 19, 159–168.

Sitlington, P. L. (1996c). Transition to living: The neglected component of transition programming for individuals with learning disabilities. *Journal of Learning Disabilities*, 29(1), 31–41.

Sitlington, P. L., Clark, G. M., Kolstoe, O. P. (Eds.). (2000) *Transition education and services for adolescents with disabilities* (3rd ed.). Boston: Allyn & Bacon.

Sitlington, P. L., & Frank, A. R. (1990). Are adolescents with learning disabilities successfully crossing the bridge into adult life? *Learning Disabilities Quarterly*, 13(2), 97–111.

Sitlington, P. L., Neubert, D., Begun, W., Le Conte, W., & Lombard, R. (1996). *Assess for success: Handbook for transition assessment.* Reston, VA: The Council for Exceptional Children.

Sitlington, P. L., Neubert, D. A., & LeConte, P. J. (1997). Transition assessment: The position of the Division on Career Development and Transition. *Career Development for Exceptional Individuals*, 20(1), 69–79.

Siu-Runyan, Y., and Faircloth, C. V. (1995). *Beyond separate subjects: Integrative learning at the middle level.* Norwood, MA: Christopher Gordon Pub.

Skinner, D., Bailey, D. B., Jr., Correa, V., & Rodriguez, P. (1999). Narrating self and disability: Latino mothers' construction of identities vis-à-vis their child with special needs. *Exceptional Children*, 65, 481–495.

Slaney, R. B., & McKinnon-Slaney, F. (1990). The use of vocational card sorts in career counseling. In C. E. Watkins, Jr., & V. L. Campbell (Eds.), *Testing in counseling practice* (pp. 317–371). Hillsdale, NJ: Erlbaum.

Slavin, R. E. (1978). Student teams and achievement divisions. *Journal of Research and Development in Education*, 12, 39–49.

Slavin, R. E. (1991). Synthesis of research on cooperative learning. *Educational Leadership*, 48(5), 71–82.

Slavin, R. E., Madden, N. A., & Stevens, R. J. (1990). Cooperative learning models for the 3 R's. *Educational Leadership*, 47(4), 22–28.

Slavin, R. E., Stevens, R. J., & Madden, N. A. (1988). Accommodating student diversity in reading and writing instruction: A cooperative learning approach. *Remedial and Special Education*, 9(1), 60–66.

Smith, B. (1994). Handing over control to people with learning difficulties. In J. Coupe-O'Kane & B. Smith (Eds.), *Taking Control* (pp. 4–13). London: David Fulton.

Smith, F., Lombard, R., Neubert, D., Le Conte, P., Rothenbacher, C., & Sitlington, P. (1996). The position statement of the interdisciplinary council on vocational evaluation and assessment. *Career Development for Exceptional Individuals*, 19, 73–76.

Smith, G. (1990). *Supported living: New directions in services for people with developmental disabilities*. Alexandria, VA: National Association of State Mental Retardation Program Directors.

Smith, M. D., Belcher, R. G., & Juhrs, P. D. (1995). *A guide to successful employment for individuals with autism*. Baltimore: Paul H. Brookes.

Smith, M. D., Belcher, R. G., Juhrs, P. D., & Nabors, K. (1994). Where people with autism work. *Journal of Vocational Rehabilitation*, 4(1), 10–17.

Smith, S. W. (1990). Individualized education programs (IEPs) in special education: From intent to acquiescence. *Exceptional Children*, 57(1), 6–14.

Smith, T. E. C., Polloway, E. A., Patton, J. R., & Dowdy, C. A. (2001). *Teaching students with special needs in inclusive settings* (3rd ed.). Boston: Allyn & Bacon.

Smull, M., & Bellamy, T. (1990). Community services for adults with disabilities: Policy challenges in the emerging support paradigm. In L. H. Meyer, C. A. Peck, & L. Brown (Eds.), *Critical issues in the lives of people with severe disabilities* (pp. 527–536). Baltimore: Paul H. Brookes.

Smull, M., & Burke-Harrison, S. (1992). Supporting people with severe reputations in the community. Alexandria, VA: National Association of State Mental Retardation Program Directors.

Smull, M. W., Sanderson, H., & Harrison, S. B. (1996). *Reviewing essential lifestyle plans: Criteria for best plans*. Kensington, MD: Support Development Associates.

Snell, M. E. (1981). Daily living skills. In J. M. Kauffman & D. P. Hallahan (Eds.), *Handbook of special education* (pp. 530–551). Upper Saddle River, NJ: Prentice Hall.

Snell, M. E. (1983). Developing the IEP: Selecting and assessing skills. In M. E. Snell (Ed.), *Systematic instruction of the moderately and severely handicapped* (2nd ed., pp. 76–112). Upper Saddle River, NJ: Merrill/Prentice Hall.

Snell, M. E. (1987). *Systematic instruction of the moderately to severely handicapped* (3rd ed.). Columbus, OH: Merrill.

Snell, M. E. (1993). *Instruction of students with severe disabilities* (4th ed.). New York: Merrill.

Snell, M. E., & Browder, D. M. (1986). Community-referenced instruction: Research and issues. *Journal of the Association for Persons with Severe handicaps*, 11, 1–11.

Snyder, E.P. (2002). Teaching students with combined behavioral disorders and mental retardation to lead their own IEP meetings. *Behavioral Disorders*, 27(4), 340–357.

Snyder, E. P., & Shapiro, E. D. (1997). Teaching students with emotional/behavioral disorders the skills to participate in the development of their own IEPs. *Behavioral Disorders*, 22, 246B–259.

Social Security Administration. (2003). *Fast Facts and Figures about Social Security*, 2003 [data file]. Available from Social Security online website, *http://www.ssa.gov*

Sowers, J. (1991). Employment for persons with physical disabilities and related technology, *Journal of Vocational Rehabilitation*, 1(2) 55–64.

Sowers, J. (1995). Adaptive environments in the workplace. In K. F. Flippo, K. J. Inge, & J. M. Barcus (Eds.), *Assistive technology: A resource for school, work, and community* (pp. 167–185). Baltimore: Paul H. Brookes.

Sowers, J. & Powers, L. (1991). *Vocational preparation and employment of students with physical and multiple disabilities*. Baltimore: Paul H. Brookes.

Sowers, J., & Powers, L. (1995). Enhancing the participation and independence of students with severe physical and multiple disabilities in performing community activities. *Mental Retardation*, 33(4), 209–220.

Speigel-McGill, P., Bambara, L. M., Shores, R. E., & Fox, J. J. (1984). The effects of proximity on socially oriented behaviors of severely multiple handicapped children. *Education and Treatment of Children*, 7, 365–378.

Spokane, A. R. (1996). Holland's theory. In D. Brown, L. Brooks, & Associates (Eds.), *Career choice and development* (3rd ed., pp. 33–74). San Francisco: Jossey-Bass.

Staab, M. J. (1996). *The role of the school psychologist in transition planning* (Doctoral dissertation, University of Kansas, Lawrence, 1996). Dissertation Abstracts International, 58, 281.

Stageberg, D., Fischer, J., & Barbut, A. (1996). University students' knowledge of civil rights laws pertaining to people with disabilities. *Journal of Applied Rehabilitation Counseling*, 27(4), 25–29.

Stainback, W., Stainback, S., Nietupski, J., & Hamre-Neitupski, S. (1986). Establishing effective community work stations. In F. R. Rusch (Ed.),*Competitive employment: Issues and strategies* (pp. 93–102). Baltimore: Paul H. Brookes.

Stanford Research Institute (SRI) International. (1990). *National longitudinal transition study of special education students*. Washington, DC: The Office of Special Education Programs.

Stanford Research Institute (SRI) International. (1992). *What happens next? Trends in postschool outcomes of youth with disabilities*. Washington, DC: The Office of Special Education Programs.

State Agency Exchange. (1969). *The rehabilitation agency focus*. Washington, DC: U.S. Government Printing Office.

Steele, L. (1991). Early work experience among white and non-white youths: Implications for subsequent enrollment and employment. *Youth and Society*, 22, 419–447.

Steere, D. E., & Cavaiuolo, D. (2002). Connecting outcomes, goals, and objectives in transition planning. *Teaching Exceptional Children*, 34(6), 54–59.

Steere, D. E., Panscofar, E., Wood, R., & Hecimovic, A. (1990). Principals of shared responsibility. *Career Development for Exceptional Individuals*, 13(2), 143–153.

Steere, D. E., Wood, R., Panscofar, E. L., & Butterworth, J. (1990). Outcome-based school-to-work transition planning for students with severe disabilities. *Career Development for Exceptional Individuals*, 13(1), 57–70.

Stern, D., McMillion, M., Hopkins, C., & Stone, J. (1990). Work experience for students in high school and college. *Youth and Society*, 21, 355–389.

Stevens, N. B. (1973). Job-seeking behavior: A segment of vocational development. *Journal of Vocational Behavior*, 3, 209–219.

Stevens, R. J., & Slavin, R. (1995). The cooperative elementary school: Effects on students' achievement, attitudes, and social relations. *American Educational Research Journal*, 32, 321–351.

Stevens, R. J., & Slavin, R. E. (1995). Effects of a cooperative learning approach in reading and writing on academically handicapped and nonhandicapped students. *Elementary School Journal*, 95, 241–262.

Stewart, E. D., Danielian, J., & Festes, R. J. (1969). *Simulating intercultural communication through role playing*. Alexandria, VA: Human Resources Research Organization.

Stodden, R. A. (1986). Vocational assessment: An introduction [Special issue]. *Career Development for Exceptional Individuals*, 9, 67–68.

Stodden, R. A. (1998). School-to-work transition: Overview of disability legislation. In F. R. Rusch & J. G. Chadsey (Eds.), *Beyond high school: Transition from school to work* (pp. 60–76). Belmont, CA: Wadsworth.

Stodden, R. A., Ianacone, R. N., Boone, R., & Bisconer, S. W. (1987). *Curriculum-based vocational assessment: A guide for addressing youth with special needs*. Honolulu, HI: Center Publications, International Education.

Stodden, R. A., & Leake, D. W. (1994). Getting to the core of transition: A re-assessment of old wine in new bottles. *Career Development for Exceptional Individuals*, 17(1), 65–76.

Storey, K., & Mank, D. (1989). Vocational education of students with moderate and severe disabilities: Implications for service delivery and teacher preparation. *Career Development for Exceptional Individuals*, 12(1), 11–24.

Storms, J., O'Leary, E., & Williams, J. (2000). IDEA 1997 *transition requirements: A guide for states, districts, schools, universities, and families*. (Available from Publications Office, Institute on Community Integration, University of Minnesota, 109 Pattee Hall, 150 Pillsbury Drive, SE, Minneapolis, MN 55455).

Stowell, M. A. (1978). *Handicapped learner participation in vocational education: A report on student, parent, and teacher interviews*. (ERIC Document Reproduction Service No. ED 162 479)

Stowitschek, J. J., & Kelso, C. A. (1989). Are we in danger of making the same mistakes with ITPs as were made with IEPs? *Career Development for Exceptional Individuals*, 12(2), 139–151.

Strain, P. S., Kerr, M. M., & Ragland, E. U. (1979). Effects of peer-mediated social initiations and prompt reinforcement procedures on the social behavior of autistic children. *Journal of Autism and Developmental Disorders*, 9, 41–54.

Strain, P. S., Odom, S. L., & McConnell, S. (1984). Promoting social reciprocity of exceptional children: Identification, target behavior selection, and intervention. *Remedial and Special Education*, 5(1), 21–28.

Strain, P. S., Shores, R. E., & Timm, M. A. (1977). Effects of peer initiations on the social behavior of withdrawn preschool children. *Journal of Applied Behavior Analysis*, 10, 289–298.

Strong, S. R., & Claiborn, C. D. (1982). *Change through interaction*. New York: John Wiley.

Stroul, B. A. (1989). Rehabilitation in community support systems. In R. W. Flexer and P. L. Solomon (Eds.), *Psychiatric rehabilitation in practice*. (pp. 45–61). Boston: Andover Publishers.

Strully, J., & Strully, C. (1985). Friendship and our children. *Journal of the Association for Persons with Severe Handicaps*, 10, 224–227.

Subich, L. (Ed.). (1993). How personal is career counseling? *Career Development Quarterly*, 42, 129–191.

Sue, D. W. (1996, Fall). ACES endorsement of multicultural counseling competencies: Do we have the courage? *ACES Spectrum Newsletter*, 9–10.

Suelzle, M., & Keenan, V. (1981). Changes in family support networks over the life cycle of mentally retarded persons. *American Journal of Mental Deficiency*, 86(3), 267–274.

Sugai, G., & Rowe, P. (1984). The effect of self-recording on out-of-seat behavior of an EMR student. *Education and Treatment of the Mentally Retarded*, 19, 23–34.

Summers, J. A. (1981). The definition of developmental disabilities: A concept in transition. *Mental Retardation*, 19, 259–265.

Sumner, S., & Fritts, M. (1997). *The IEP planner [computer file]:* LCCE *transition skills program*. Highland Park, IL: Rodan Associates.

Super, D. (1957). *The psychology of careers: An introduction to vocational development*. New York: Harper & Brothers.

Super, D. E. (1954). Career patterns as a basis for vocational counseling. *Journal of Counseling Psychology*, 1, 12–20.

Super, D. E. (Ed.). (1974). *Measuring vocational maturity for counseling and evaluation*. Washington, DC: National Career Development Association.

Super, D. E. (1975). *The psychology of careers*. New York: Harper & Row.

Super, D. E. (1984). Career and life development. In D. Brown, L. Brooks, & Associates (Eds.), *Career choice and development: Applying contemporary theories to practice* (pp. 192–234). San Francisco: Jossey-Bass.

Super, D. E. (1990). A life-span, life-space approach to career development. In D. Brown, L. Brooks, & Associates (Eds.), *Career choice and development: Applying contemporary theories to practice* (2nd ed., pp. 197–261). San Francisco: Jossey-Bass.

Super, D. E., Savickas, M. L., & Super, C. M. (1996). The life-span, life-space approach to careers. In D. Brown, L. Brooks, & Associates (Eds.), *Career choice and development* (3rd ed., pp. 121–178). San Francisco: Jossey-Bass.

Super, D. E., Thompson, A. S., Lindeman, R. H., Jordaan, J. P., & Myers, R. A. (1981). *Career development inventory*. Palo Alto, CA: Consulting Psychologists Press.

Sweeney, M. (1996). *The effects of self-determination training on student involvement in the IEP process*. Unpublished doctoral dissertation., Tallahassee, FL: Florida State University.

Sylvester, L., Martin, J. E., Woods, L., & Chistianson, R. (2003). *Comparison between caregiver and student vocational preferences*. Manuscript submitted for publication.

Szymanski, E., Fernandez, D., Koch, L., & Merz, M. (1996). *Career development: Planning for placement*. Madison, WI: University of Wisconsin, Rehabilitation Research and Training Center on Career Development and Advancement.

Szymanski, E. M. (1994). Transition: life-span, life-space considerations for empowerment. *Exceptional Children*, 60, 402–410.

Szymanski, E. M. (1998). Career development, school to work transition, and diversity: An ecological approach. In F. R. Rusch & J. G. Chadsey (Eds.), *Beyond high school: Transition from school to work* (pp. 127–145). New York: Wadsworth.

Szymanski, E. M., & Hanley-Maxwell, C. (1997). Career development of people with developmental disabilities: An ecological model. *The Journal of Rehabilitation*, 62(1), 48–55.

Szymanski, E. M., Hanley-Maxwell, C., & Asselin, S. (1990). Rehabilitation counseling, special education, and vocational special needs education: Three transitional disciplines. *Career Development for Exceptional Individuals*, 13(1), 29–38.

Szymanski, E. M., Hanley-Maxwell, C., & Asselin, S. B. (1992). Systems interface: Vocational rehabilitation, special education, and vocational education. In F. R. Rusch, L. Destefano, J. Chadsey-Rusch, L. A. Phelps, & E. Szymanski (Eds.), *Transition from school to adult life: Models, linkages, and policy*. (pp. 153–172). Sycamore, IL: Sycamore.

Szymanski, E., & Hershenson, D. (1998). Career development of people with disabilities: An ecological model. In E. M. Szymanski & R. M. Parker (Eds.), *Rehabilitation counseling: Basics and beyond* (3rd ed., pp. 327–378). Austin, TX: PRO-ED.

Szymanski, E. M., Hershenson, D. B., Enright, M. S., & Ettinger, J. M. (1996). Career development theories, constructs, and research: Implications for people with disabilities. In E. M. Szymanski & R. M. Parker (Eds.), *Work and disability: Issues and strategies in career development and job development* (pp. 79–126). Austin, TX: PRO-ED.

Szymanski, E. M. & Parker, R. M. (1996). Work and disability: Introduction. In E. M. Szymanski & R. M. Parker (Eds.). *Work and disability: Issues and strategies in carrer development and job placement* (pp. 1–7). Austin. TX: PRO-ED.

Szymanski, E. M., Turner, K. D., & Herschenson, D. B. (1992). Career development and work adjustment of persons with disabilities: Theoretical perspectives and implications for transition. In F. R. Rusch, L. Destefano, J. Chadsey-Rusch, L. A. Phelps, & E. Szymanski (Eds.), *Transition from school to adult life: Models, linkages, and policy* (pp. 391–406). Sycamore, IL: Sycamore.

Talbert-Johnson, C. (1998). Why [are] so many African-American children in special ed? *School Business Affairs*, 64, 30–35.

Taylor, R. (1997). *Assessment of exceptional students: Educational and psychological procedures* (4th ed.). Boston: Allyn & Bacon.

Taylor, S., & Bogden, R. (1990). Quality of life and the individual perspective. In R. L. Schalock & M. Bogale (Eds.), *Quality of life: Perspectives and issues* (pp. 27–40). Washington, DC: American Association of Mental Retardation.

Taylor, S. J. (1988). Caught in the continuum: A critical analysis of the principle of the least restrictive environment. *Journal of the Association for Persons with Severe Handicaps*, 13, 41–53.

Taylor, S. J., Biklen, D., & Knoll, J. A. (Eds.). (1987). *Community integration for people with severe disabilities*. New York: Teachers' College Press.

Taylor, S. J., Bogdan, R., & Racino, J. A. (Eds.). (1991). *Life in the community: Case studies of organizations supporting people with disabilities*. Baltimore: Paul H. Brookes.

Taylor, S. J., Racino, J., Knoll, J., & Lutfiyya, Z. (1987). *The nonrestrictive environment: A resource manual on community integration for people with the most severe disabilities*. Syracuse, NY: Human Policy Press.

Technology-Related Assistance for Individuals with Disabilities Act of 1988, 29 U.S.C § 2201 *et seq*.

Test, D., Hinson, K., Solow, J., & Kuel, P. (1993). Job satisfaction of persons in supported employment. *Education and Training in Mental Retardation*, 28(1), 38–46.

Thomas, A. & Grimes, J. (1995). Best practices in school psychology III. Washington, DC: NASP.

Thompson, L., Powers, G., & Houchard, B. (1992). The wage effects of supported employment. *Journal of the Association for Persons with Severe Handicaps*, 17, 87–94.

Thorkildsen, R. (1994). *Research synthesis on quality and availability of assistive technology devices. Executive summary.* Technical report No. 8. (ERIC Document Reproduction Service No. ED 386 856)

Thurlow, M. (2002). Positive educational results for all students. The promise of standards-based reform. *Remedial and Special Education*, 23(4) 195–202.

Thurlow, M., & Elliott, J. (1998). Student assessment and evaluation. In J. R. Rusch & J. G. Chadsey (Eds.), *Beyond high school: Transition from school to work* (pp. 265–296). New York: Wadsworth Publishing Company.

Tileston, D. W. (2000). *Ten best teaching practices: How brain research, learning styles, and standards define teaching competencies.* Thousand Oaks, CA: Corwin.

Tilson, G. P., Lueking, R. G., & Donavan, M. R. (1994). Involving employers in transition: The BRIDGES from school to work model. *Career Development for Exceptional Individuals*, 17(1), 77–89.

Tilson, G. P., Jr., & Neubert, D. A. (1988). School-to-work transition of mildly disabled young adults: Parental perceptions of vocational needs. *The Journal for Vocational Special Needs Education*, 11(1), 33–37.

Tinto, V. (1993). *Leaving college: Rethinking the causes and cures of student attrition* (2nd ed.). Chicago: University of Chicago Press.

Todis, B. (1996). Tools for the task? Perspectives on assistive technology in educational settings. *Journal of Special Education Technology*, 13, 49–61.

Todis, B., & Walker, H. (1993). User perspective on assistive technology in educational settings. *Focus on Exceptional Children*, 26, 1–16.

Tower, K. D. (1994). Consumer-centered social work practice: Restoring client self-determination. *Social Work*, 39(2), 191–196.

Trace Center. (1996). CO-Net, HyperAbleDATA [CD-Rom program]. Madison: University of Wisconsin, Author.

Trivette, C. M., Dunst, C. J., Boyd, K., & Hamby, D. W. (1996). Family-orientated program models, helping practices and parental control appraisals. *Exceptional Children*, 62(3), 237–248.

Tucker, J. A. (1985). Curriculum-based assessment: An introduction. *Exceptional Children*, 52, 199–204.

Tuckman, B. W., & Jensen, M. A. C. (1977). States in small group development revisited. *Group and Organizational Studies*, 2, 419–442.

Turnbull, A. P., Barber, P., Kerns, G. M., & Behr, S. K. (1995). The family of children and youth with exceptionalities. In E. L. Meyen & T. M. Skrtic (Eds.), *Special education and student disability, an introduction: Traditional, emerging, and alternative perspectives* (4th ed., pp. 141–170). Denver, CO: Love.

Turnbull, A. P., & Morningstar, M. E. (1993). Family and professional interaction. In M. E. Snell (Ed.), *Instruction of students with severe disabilities* (4th ed., pp. 31–60). Upper Saddle River, NJ: Merrill/Prentice Hall.

Turnbull, A. P., Summers, J. A., & Brotherson, M. J. (1984). *Working with families with disabled members: A family systems approach.* Lawrence, KS: University of Kansas, Kansas University Afffiliated Facility.

Turnbull, A. P., Summers, J. A., & Brotherson, M. J. (1986). Family life cycle. In J. J. Gallagher & P. M. Vietz (Eds.), *Families of handicapped persons* (pp. 45–65). Baltimore: Paul H. Brookes.

Turnbull, A. P., & Turnbull, H. R. (1985). Developing independence. *Journal of Adolescent Health Care*, 6(2), 108–119.

Turnbull, A. P., & Turnbull, H. R. (1988). Toward great expectations for vocational opportunities: Family-professional partnerships. *Mental Retardation*, 26(6), 337–342.

Turnbull, A. P., & Turnbull, H. R. (1990). *Families, professionals, and exceptionality: A special partnership* (2nd ed.). Upper Saddle River, NJ: Merrill/Prentice Hall.

Turnbull, A. P., & Turnbull, H. R. (1993). Empowerment and decision-making through Group Action Planning. In *Lifelong transitions: Proceedings of the third annual parent/family conference.* Washington, DC: U.S. Department of Education.

Turnbull, H. Rutherford, III. (1993). *Free appropriate public education: The law and children with disabilities* (4th ed.). Denver, CO: Love.

Turnbull, H. R., Turnbull, A. P., Bronicki, G. J., Summers, J. A., & Roeder-Gordon, C. (1989). *Disability and the family: A guide to decisions for adulthood.* Baltimore: Paul H. Brookes.

Turnbull, H. R., Turnbull, A. P., Wehmeyer, M. L., & Park, J. (2003). A quality of life framework for special education outcomes. *Remedial and Special Education*, 24(2), 67–74.

Turner, L. (1996). Selecting a college option: Determining the best fit. In C. Flexer, D. Wray, R. Leavitt, & R. Flexer (Eds.), *How the student with hearing loss can succeed in college: A handbook for students, families, and professionals* (pp. 142–164). Washington, DC: Alexander Graham Bell Association for the Deaf.

Turner, L. P. (1996). *Parent involvement in transition planning.* Unpublished doctoral dissertation, Kent State University, Kent, OH.

Turner, L. P., & Simmons, T. J. (1996). Getting ready for transition to college. In C. Flexer, D. Wray, R. Leavitt, & R. Flexer (Eds.), *How the student with hearing loss can succeed in college: A handbook for students, families, and professionals* (2nd ed., pp. 131–145). Washington, DC: Alexander Graham Bell Association for the Deaf.

U. S. Census Bureau. (2001, March). *Overview of race and Hispanic origin: Census 2000 brief.* Washington, DC: U.S. Department of Commerce, U.S. Census Bureau. Available online: *www.census.gov/prod/2002pubs/censr.4.pdf*

U.S. Census Bureau. (2001, April). Washington, DC: U.S. Department of Commerce, U.S. Census Bureau. Available online: *www.census.gov/prod/2002pubs/censr.4.pdf*

U.S. Census Bureau. (2002, November). *Demographic trends in the 20th century: Census 2000 special reports.* Washington, DC:

U.S. Department of Commerce, U.S. Census Bureau. Available online: *www.census.gov/prod/2002pubs/censr.4.pdf*

U.S. Census Bureau. (2003, August). *School enrollment 2000: Census 2000 brief.* Washington, DC: U.S. Department of Commerce, U.S. Census Bureau. Available online: *www.census.gov/prod/2002pubs/censr.4.pdf*

U.S. Census Bureau. (2003, May). *Poverty: 1999: Census 2000 brief.* Washington, DC: U.S. Department of Commerce, U.S. Census Bureau. Available online: *www.census.gov/prod/2002pubs/censr.4.pdf*

United States Department of Commerce. (2000). *United States census* 2000 [datafile]. Available from U.S. Census Bureau Website, *http://www.census.gov*

U.S. Department of Education. (1995). *Seventeenth annual report to Congress on the implementation of the Individuals with Disabilities Education Act.* Washington, DC: Author.

U.S. Department of Education. (1996). *Eighteenth annual report to Congress on the implementation of the Individuals with Disabilities Education Act.* Washington, DC: Author.

U.S. Department of Education. (1997). *Nineteenth annual report to Congress on the implementation of the Individuals with Disabilities Education Act.* Washington DC: Author.

U.S. Department of Education. (1997). *The implementation of the Individuals with Disabilities Education Act: Section 618. Nineteenth Annual Report to Congress.* Washington, DC: Author.

U.S. Department of Education, Office for Civil Rights. (1987). *1986 elementary and secondary school civil rights survey: National summaries.* Arlington, VA: DBS Corporation, subcontract from Opportunity Systems, Inc.

U.S. Department of Education, Office for Civil Rights. (1994). *1992 elementary and secondary school civil rights compliance report (draft).* Washington, DC: Author.

U.S. Department of Education, Office of Special Education Programs. (2001). Students with disabilities' secondary education, transition, and employment (Expert Strategy Panel Report). Available: *http://www.ed.gov/offices/osers/osep.* Washington, DC: Author.

U.S. Department of Labor. (1991). *The revised handbook for analyzing jobs.* Washington, DC: Employment and Training Administration.

U.S. Department of Labor. (1993). Learning a living: A blueprint for high performance (SCANS report). Washington, DC: U.S. Government Printing Office.

Vallentutti, P. S., Bender, M., & Sims-Tucker, B. (1996). *A functional curriculum for teaching students with disabilities: Functional academics* (2nd ed.). Austin, TX: PRO-ED.

van Keulen, J. E., Weddington, G. T., & DeBose, C. E. (1998). *Speech, language, learning, and the African American child.* Boston: Allyn & Bacon.

Van Reusen, A. K., & Bos, C. S. (1990). I Plan: Helping students communicate in planning conferences. *Teaching Exceptional Children* 22(4), 30–32.

Van Reusen, A. K., & Bos, C. (1994). Facilitating student participation in individual educational programs through motivation strategy instruction. *Exceptional Children*, 60(5), 466–475.

Van Reusen, A. K., Bos, C. S., Schumaker, J. B., & Deshler, D. D. (1994). *Self-advocacy strategy for education and transition planning.* Lawrence, KS: Edge Enterprises.

Vandercook, T., York, J., & Forest, M. (1989). The McGill action planning system (MAPS): A strategy for building the vision. *Journal of the Association for Persons with Severe Handicaps*, 14(3), 205–215.

Varney, G. H. (1989). *Building productive teams: An action guide and resource book.* San Francisco: Jossey-Bass.

Vasa, S. F., & Steckelberg, A. L. (1980). Parent programs in career education for the handicapped. *Career Development for Exceptional Individuals*, 3, 74–82.

Vaughn, S., Bos, C. S., Harrell, J. E., & Lasky, B. A. (1988). Parent participation in the initial placement/IEP conference: Ten years after mandated involvement. *Journal of Learning Disabilities*, 21, 82–89.

Vaughn, S., Bos, C. S., & Schumm, J. S (2000). *Teaching exceptional, diverse, and at-risk students in the general education curriculum* (2nd ed.). Boston: Allyn & Bacon.

VEWAA glossary. (1988). (Available from Materials Development Center, Stout Vocational Rehabilitation Institute, University of Wisconsin–Stout, Menomonie, WI 54751). Author.

Vincent, L., Salisbury, C., Walter, G., Brown, P., Gruenwald, L., & Powers, M. (1980). Criteria of the next environment. In W. Sailor, B. Wilcox, & L. Brown (Eds.), *Methods of instruction for severely handicapped students* (pp. 303–328). Baltimore: Paul H. Brookes.

Voeltz, L. (1984). Program and curriculum innovations to prepare children for integration. In N. Certo, N. Haring, & R. York (Eds.) *Public school integration of severely handicapped students: Rational issues and progressive alternatives.* (pp. 155–181). Baltimore: Paul H. Brookes.

Vogel, S. A., & Adelman, P. B. (1992). The success of college students with learning disabilities: Factors related to educational attainment. *Journal of Learning Disabilities*, 25(7), 430–441.

Vogel, S. A., & Forness, S. R. (1992). Social functioning in adults with learning disabilities. *School Psychology Review*, 21(3), 375–386.

Wagner, M. (1989). *Youth with disabilities during transition: An overview of descriptive findings from the national longitudinal transition study.* Menlo Park, CA: SRI International.

Wagner, M. (1991). *Dropouts with disabilities: What do we know? What can we do?* (A report from the National Longitudinal Transition Study of Special Education Students). Menlo Park, CA: SRI International.

Wagner, M., & Blackorby, J. (1996). Transition from high school to work or college: How special education students fare.

The Future of Children: Special Education for Students with Disabilities, 6(1), 103–110.

Wagner, M., Blackorby, J., Cameto, R., & Newman, L. (1993). *What makes a difference? Influence on post-school outcomes of youth with disabilities: The third comprehensive report from the National Longitudinal Transition Study of Special Education Students*. Menlo Park, CA: SRI International.

Wagner, M., Cameto, R., & Newman, L. (2003). *Youth with disabilities: A changing population. A report of findings from the National Longitudinal Transition Study (NLTS) and the National Longitudinal Transition Study-2 (NLTS2)*. [Executive Summary]. Menlo Park, CA: SRI International.

Wagner, M., D'Amico, R., Marder, C., Newman, I., & Blackorby, J. (1992). *What happens next? Trends in postschool outcomes of youth with disabilities*. Menlo Park, CA: SRI International.

Wagner, M., Newman, L., & Shaver, D. M. (1989). The *National Longitudinal Transition Study of Special Education Students: Report on procedures for the first wave of data collection (1987)*. Menlo Park, CA: SRI International.

Wald, J. L. (1996). *Culturally and linguistically diverse professionals in special education: A demographic analysis*. Reston, VA: National Clearinghouse for Professions in Special Education and OSERS.

Walden, R. J. (2002). *Teaching a goal attainment process to university students with learning disabilities*. Unpublished doctoral dissertation University of Oklahoma, Norman.

Walker, H. M., Colvin, G., & Ramsey, E. (1995). *Antisocial behavior in schools: Strategies and best practices*. Pacific Grove, CA: Brooks/Cole Publishing.

Walker, H. M., Hops, H., & Greenwood, C. (1993). RECESS: A *program for reducing negative-aggressive behavior*. Seattle, WA: Educational Achievement Systems.

Walker, H. M., Hops, H., Greenwood, C. R., & Todd, N. (1979). Differential effects of reinforcing topographic components of free play and social interaction: Analysis and direct replication. *Behavior Modification*, 3, 291–320.

Walker, H. M., McConnell, S. R., Holmes, D., Todis, B., Walker, J., & Golden N. (1983). ACCEPTS: A *children's curriculum for effective peer and teacher skills*. Austin, TX: PRO-ED.

Walls, R. T., & Tseng, M. S. (1987). Measurement of client outcomes in rehabilitation. In B. Bolton (Ed.), *Handbook of measurement and evaluation in rehabilitation* (pp. 183–201). Baltimore: Paul H. Brookes.

Ward, M. J. (1988). The many facets of self-determination. *National Information Center for Children and Youth with Handicaps: Transition Summary*, 5, 2–3. Washington, DC: Office of Special Education Programs of the U.S. Department of Education.

Ward, M. J. (1994, Winter). Self-determination: A means to an end. *Impact*, 6, 8.

Ward, M. J. (1996). Coming of age in the age of self-determination: An historical and personal perspective. In D. J. Sands & M. L. Wehmeyer (Eds.), *Self-determination across the life span* (pp. 1–14). Baltimore: Paul H. Brookes.

Ward, M. J., & Halloran, W. J. (1989). Transition to uncertainty: Status of many school leavers with severe disabilities. *Career Development for Exceptional Individuals*, 12(2), 71–78.

Ward, M. J., & Halloran, W. (1993, Fall). Transition issues for the 1990s. OSERS *News in Print*, 6(1) 4–5. (ERIC Document Reproduction Service No. ED 364035)

Warner, C. (1992). *Treasury of women's quotations*. Upper Saddle River, NJ: Prentice-Hall.

Warrenfeltz, R. B., Kelly, W. J., Salzberb, C. L., Beegle, C. P., Levy, S. M., Adams, T. A., & Crouse, T. R. (1981). Social skills training of behavior disordered adolescents with self-monitoring to promote generalization to a vocational setting. *Behavioral Disorders*, 7, 18–27.

Weaver, R., & DeLuca, J. R. (1987). *Employability life skills assessment: Ages 14–21*. Dayton, OH: Miami Valley Special Education Center.

Webb, N. (1985). Student interaction and learning in small groups: A research summary. In R. Slavin, S. Sharon, R. Hertz-Lazarowitz, C. Webb, & R. Schmuck (Eds.), *Learning to cooperate, cooperating to learn*. New York: Plenum.

Weber, D., & Demchak, M. A. (1996). Using assistive technology with individuals with severe disabilities. *Computers in the Schools*, 12(3), 43–57.

Weber, J. (1988). Dropout rates for students in different high school curricula: another look. *Journal of Vocational Education Research*, 13(1), 35–39.

Webster, D. D. (1999, July). *Developing the leadership potential of postsecondary students with disabilities*. Paper presented at AHEAD Conference, Atlanta, GA.

Webster, D. D. (2001). *Giving voice to students with disabilities who have transitioned to college: Or how LL Slim became "the best darn gimp on the planet"* (Doctoral dissertation, Kent State University, 2001). Dissertation Abstracts International, 62/05, 1796.

Wehman, P. (1990). School-to-work: Elements of successful programs. *Teaching Exceptional Children*, 23(1), 40–43.

Wehman, P. (1992). Transition for young people with disabilities: Challenges for the 1990's. *Education and Training in Mental Retardation*; 27, 112–118.

Wehman, P. (1996). *Life beyond the classroom: Transition strategies for young people with disabilities* (2nd ed.). Baltimore: Paul H. Brookes.

Wehman, P. (1997a). Editorial. *Journal of Vocational Rehabilitation*, 8(1), 1–3.

Wehman, P. (1997b). *Exceptional individuals in school, community, and work*. Austin Texas: PRO-ED.

Wehman, P. (Ed.). (2001). *Life beyond the classroom: Transition strategies for young people with disabilities* (3rd ed.). Baltimore: Paul H. Brookes.

Wehman, P. (2001b). *Supported employment in business: Expanding the capacity of workers with disabilities*. St. Augustine, FL: Training Resource Network

Wehman, P., & Bricout, J. (2001). Supported Employment: New directions for a new millenium. In P. Wehman (Ed.) *Supported employment in business: Expanding the capacity of workers with disabilities*. (pp. 3–22). St. Augustine, Fl: Training Resource Network.

Wehman, P., & Hill, J. (1985). *Competitive employment for persons with mental retardation* (Vol. 1). Richmond, VA: Rehabilitation Research and Training Center, Virginia Commonwealth University.

Wehman, P., Hill, M., Hill, J., Brooke, V., Pendleton, P., & Britt, C. (1985). Competitive employment for persons with mental retardation: A follow-up after six years. *Mental Retardation*, 23, 274–281.

Wehman, P., & Kregel, J. (1985). A supported work approach to competitive employment of individuals with moderate and severe handicaps. *Journal of the Association for Persons with Severe Handicaps*, 10, 3–11.

Wehman, P., Kregel, J., & Barcus, J. M. (1985). From school to work: A vocational transition model for handicapped students. *Exceptional Children*, 52(1), 25–37.

Wehman, P., Kregel, J., & Seyfarth, J. (1985a). Transition from school to work for individuals with severe handicaps: A follow-up study. *Journal of the Association for Persons with Severe Handicaps*, 10(3), 132–136.

Wehman, P., Kregel, J., & Seyfarth, J. (1985b). Employment outlook for young adults with mental retardation. *Rehabilitation Counseling Bulletin*, 29, 90–99.

Wehman, P., Kregel, J., Sherron, P., Nguyen, S., Kreutzer, J., Fry, R., & Zasler, N. (1993). Critical factors associated with the successful supported employment of patients with severe traumatic brain injury. *Brain Injury*, 7(1), 31–44.

Wehman, P., Moon, M. S., Everson, J. M., Wood, W., & Barcus, J. M. (1988). *Transition from school to work: New challenges for youth with severe disabilities*. Baltimore: Paul H. Brookes.

Wehman, P., Revell, G., & Kregel, J. (1998). Expanding supported employment opportunities for persons with severe disabilities. TASH *Newsletter*, 22(6), 24–25.

Wehman, P., Revell, W. G., & Kregel, J. (1998b). Supported employment: A decade of rapid growth and impact. *American Rehabiliation*, 24(1), 31–43.

Wehman, P., Wood, W., Everson, J. M., Goodwyn, R., Conley, S. (1988). *Vocational education for multihandicapped youth with cerebral palsy*. Baltimore: Paul H. Brookes.

Wehmeyer, M. (2002). Transition principles and access to the general education curriculum. In C. A. Kochar-Bryant & D. Bassett (Eds.). *Aligning transition and standards-based education: Issues and strategies*. Arlington, VA: Council for Exceptional Children.

Wehmeyer, M., & Lawrence, M. (1996). Whose future is it anyway? Promoting student involvement in transition planning. *Career Development for Exceptional Individuals*, 18(2), 69–84.

Wehmeyer, M., & Schwartz, M. (1997). Self-determination and positive adult outcomes: A follow-up of youth with mental retardation or learning disabilities. *Exceptional Children*, 63(2), 245–255.

Wehmeyer, M. L. (1992). Self-determination: Critical skills for outcome-oriented transition services. *The Journal for Vocational Special Needs Education*, 15, 3–9.

Wehmeyer, M. L. (1993). Perceptual and psychological factors in career decision-making of adolescents with and without cognitive disabilities. *Career Development for Exceptional Individuals*, 16(2), 135–146.

Wehmeyer, M. L. (1994). Perceptions of self-determination and psychological empowerment of adolescents with mental retardation. *Education and Training in Mental Retardation and Developmental Disabilities*, 29, 9–21.

Wehmeyer, M. L. (1995). *The ARC's self-determination scale: Procedural guidelines*. (Available from The ARC of the United States, 500 E. Border Street, Suite 300, Arlington, TX 76010.)

Wehmeyer, M. L. (1996). Self determination as an educational outcome. In D. J. Sands & M. L. Wehmeyer (Eds.), *Self-determination across the life span: Independence and choice for people with disabilities* (pp. 17–36). Baltimore: Paul H. Brookes.

Wehmeyer, M. L. (1997). Student-directed learning and self-determination. In M. Agran (Ed.), *Student directed learning: Teaching self-determination skills* (pp. 28–59). Pacific Grove, CA: Brooks/Cole Publishers.

Wehmeyer, M. L. (1998). National survey of the use of assistive technology by adults with mental retardation. *Mental Retardation*, 36, 44–51.

Wehmeyer, M. L. (1998). Student involvement in transition-planning and transition-program implementation. In F. R. Rusch & J. G. Chadsey (Eds.), *Beyond high school: Transition from school to work*. (pp. 206–233). Belmont CA: Wadsworth.

Wehmeyer, M. L. (1999). Assistive technology and students with mental retardation: Utilization and barriers. *Journal of Special Education Technology*, 14, 48–58.

Wehmeyer, M. L., Agran, M., & Hughes, C. (1998). *Teaching self-determination to students with disabilities: Basic skills for successful transition*. Baltimore: Paul H. Brookes.

Wehmeyer, M. L., Agran, M., & Lattin, D. (2001). Achieving access to the general curriculum for students with mental retardation: A curriculum decision-making model *Education and Training in Mental Retardation and Developmental Disabilities*, 36(4), 327–342.

Wehmeyer, M. L., & Kelchner, K. (1995a). *The ARC's self-determination scale*. Arlington, TX: ARC.

Wehmeyer, M. L., & Kelchner, K. (1995b). *Whose future is it anyway?* Arlington, TX: ARC.

Wehmeyer, M. L., & Palmer, S. B. (2003). Adult outcomes for students with cognitive disabilities three-years after high school: The impact of self-determination. *Education and Training in Developmental Disabilities*, 38(2), 131–144.

Wehmeyer, M. L., Palmer, S. B., Agran, M., Mithaug, D. E., & Martin, J. E. (2000). Promoting casual agency: The self-determined learning model of instruction. *Exceptional Children*, 66(4), 439–453.

Wehmeyer, M. L., Lattin, D., & Agran, M. (2001). Achieving access to the general curriculum for students with mental retardation: A curriculum decision-making model. *Education and Training in Mental Retardation and Development Disabilities*, 36, 327–342.

Wehmeyer, M. L., & Ward, M. J. (1995). The spirit of IDEA mandate: Student involvement in transition planning. *Journal of the Association for Vocational Special Needs Education*, 17, 108–111.

Welsh Office, Department of Education. (1994). *Code of practice on the identification and assessment of special education needs*. Cardiff, Wales, UK: Author.

Wermuth, T. (1991). Impact of educational legislation on transition and supported employment programs. *The Advance*, 3, 3–4. Richmond, VA: Association for Persons in Supported Employment [APSE].

West, J. (1991). *The Americans with Disabilities Act: From policy to practice*. New York: Milbank Fund.

Westling, D. L., & Fox, L. (2000). *Teaching students with severe disabilities* (2nd ed.). Upper Saddle River, NJ: Merrill/Prentice Hall.

White, W. A. T. (1988). A meta-analysis of effects of direct instruction in special education. *Education and Treatment of Children*, 11, 364–374.

Whitehead, C. W. (1977). *Sheltered workshop study: A nationwide report on sheltered workshops and their employment of handicapped individuals* (Workshop Survey, Vol. I, U.S. Department of Labor Services Publications). Washington, DC: U.S. Government Printing Office.

Whitney-Thomas, J., & Hanley-Maxwell, C. (1996). Packing the parachute: Parents experiences as their children prepare to leave high school. *Exceptional Children*, 63(1), 75–88.

Whitney-Thomas, J., Shaw, D., Honey, K., & Butterworth, J. (1998). Building a future: A study of student participation in person-centered planning, *The Journal of the Association for Persons with Severe Handicaps*, (23)2, 119–133.

Wiggins, G., & McTighe, J. (1998). *Understanding by design*. Alexandria, VA: Association for Supervision and Curriculum Development.

Wilcox, B., & Bellamy, G. T. (1987). *The activities catalog: An alternative curriculum for youth and adults with severe disabilities*. Baltimore: Paul H. Brookes.

Will, M. (1983). OSERS *programming for the transition of youth with disabilities: Bridges from school to working life*. Washington, DC: U.S. Department of Education, Office of Special Education and Rehabilitative Services. (ERIC Document Reproduction Service No. ED 256 132)

Will, M. (1984). Supported employment for adults with severe disabilities: An OSERS program initiative. Washington, DC.

Williams, B. (1991). Assistive technology in the eye of the beholder. *Journal of Vocational Rehabilitation*, 1(2)9–12.

Williams, J. M., & O'Leary, E. (2001). What we've learned and where we go from here. *Career Development for Exceptional Individuals*, 24(1), 51–71.

Willig, A. C. (1986). Special education and the culturally and linguistically different child: An overview of issues and challenges. In A. C. Willing & H. F. Greenberg (Eds.), *Bilingualism and learning disabilities: Policy and practice for teachers and administrators* (pp. 191–209). New York: American Library Publishing.

Willis, W. (1998). Families with African American roots. In E. W. Lynch & M. H. Hanson (Eds.), *Developing cross-cultural competence: A guide for working with children and their families* (2nd ed., pp. 165–208). Baltimore: Paul H. Brookes.

Wilson, K., & Getzel, E. (2001). Creating a supportive campus: The VCU professional development academy. *The Journal for Vocational Special Needs Education*, 23(2), 12–18.

Winterbottom, C., Liska, D. W., & Obermaier, K. M. (1995). *State-level databook on health care access and financing*. Washington, DC: The Urban Institute.

Winup, K. (1994). The role of a student committee in promotion of independence among school leavers. In J. Coupe-O'Kane & B. Smith (Eds.), *Taking control* (pp. 103–116). London: David Fulton Publishers.

Wise, W. E., & Matthews, C. L. (1987). *A study of the relationship of education and transition factors to the job status of mildly and moderately handicapped students*. (Rep. No. 95-01/87/06/04). Dover, DE: Delaware State Department of Public Instruction.

Wisniewski, L., & Sedlak, R. (1992). Assistive devices for students with disabilities: Integrating learners with disabilities in regular education programs. *Elementary School Journal*, 92, 297–314.

Wolfe, P. S., Boone, R. S., and Barrera, M. (1997). Developing culturally sensitive transition plans: A reflective process. *The Journal for Vocational Special Needs Education*, 20, 30–33.

Wolfe, V. V., Boyd, L. A., & Wolfe, D. A. (1983). Teaching cooperative play to behavior-problem preschool children. *Education and Treatment of Children*, 6, 1–9.

Wolfensberger, W. (1972). *The principal normalization in human services*. Toronto: National Institute on Mental Retardation.

Wolfensberger, W. (1991). *A brief introduction to SRV as a high-order concept for structuring human services*. Syracuse, NY: Training Institute for Human Service Planning, Leadership and Change Agency.

Wolffe, K. (1997). *Career counseling for people with disabilities: A practical guide to finding employment*. Austin, TX: PRO-ED.

Wolman, J. M., Campeau, P. L., DuBois, P. A., Mithaug, D. E., & Stolarski, V. S. (1994). AIR *self-determination scale and user guide*. Palo Alto, CA: American Institutes for Research.

Wood, J. W. (1998). *Adapting instruction to accommodate students in inclusive settings* (3rd ed.) Upper Saddle River, NJ: Merrill/Prentice Hall.

Woolcock, W. W., Stodden, R. A., & Bisconer, S. W. (1992). Process and outcome-focused decision making. In F. R. Rusch, L. DeStefano, J. Chadsey-Rusch, L. A. Phelps & E. Szymanski (Eds.), *Transition from school to adult life: Models, linkages, and policy* (pp. 219–244). Sycamore, IL: Sycamore.

Workman, E. A., Helton, G. B., & Watson, P. J. (1982). Self-monitoring effects in a four-year-old child: An ecological behavior analysis. *Journal of School Psychology*, 20, 57–64.

World Institute on Disability. (1991). *Personal assistance services: A new millennium. Resolution on personal assistance services passed by participants of the international personal assistance services symposium*. Oakland, CA: World Institute on Disability.

Yoshida, R. K., Fenton, K. S., Maxwell, J. P., & Kaufman, N. J. (1978). Ripple effect: Communication of planning team decisions to program implementation. *Journal of School Psychology*, 16, 178–183.

Young, C. C., & Kerr, M. M. (1979). The effects of a retarded child's social initiations on the behavior of severely retarded school-aged peers. *Education and Training of the Mentally Retarded*, 14, 185–190.

Ysseldyke, J. E., & Algozzine, B. (1995). *Special education: A practical approach for teachers* (3rd ed.). Boston: Houghton Mifflin.

Ysseldyke, J. E., Algozzine, B., & Thurlow, M. L. (1992). *Critical issues in special education* (2nd ed.). Boston: Houghton Mifflin.

Ysseldyke, J. E., & Thurlow, M. L. (1994). *Educational outcomes for students with disabilities*. New York: Haworth Press.

Zabala, J. (1994). *The SETT framework: Critical questions to ask when making informed assistive technology decisions*. Paper presented at Closing the Gap Conference, Oct, 1994, Minneapolis, MN.

Zigmond, N., & Miller, S. E. (1992). Improving high school programs for students with learning disabilities: A matter of substance as well as form. In F. R. Rusch, L. Destefano, J. Chadsey-Rusch, L. A. Phelps, & E. Symanski (Eds.), *Transition from school to adult life: Models, linkages, and policy* (pp. 17–31). Sycamore, IL: Sycamore.

Zuniga, M. E. (1998). Families with Latino roots. In E. W. Lynch & M. H. Hanson (Eds.), *Developing cross-cultural competence: A guide for working with children and their families* (2nd ed., pp. 209–250). Baltimore: Paul H. Brookes.

Name Index

Subject Index